THE BIG BOOK OF
ITALIAN
COOKING

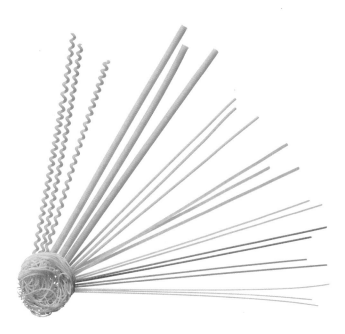

THE BIG BOOK OF ITALIAN COOKING was conceived, edited, and designed
by McRae Books, Florence, Italy
Borgo Santa Croce, 8 - 50122 Florence (Italy)
Publishers: Anne McRae and Marco Nardi
info@mcraebooks.com

Project editors: Anne McRae, Laura Ottina
Text: Maria Paola Dèttore, Rosalba Gioffrè, Sara Vignozzi, Leonardo Castellucci,
Carla Bardi, Elisabetta Lotti
Editing: Loredana Agosta, Holly Willis, Alison Leach, Susan Kelly
Photography: Marco Lanza
Set Design: Cinzia Calamai, Elisabetta Lotti, Sara Vignozzi, Rosalba Gioffrè
Graphic Design: Marco Nardi
Layout and cutouts: Ornella Fassio, Adriano Nardi, Giovani Mattioli, Laura Ottina

The publishers would like to thank Mastrociliegia (Fiesole),
Eugenio Taccini (Montelupo Fiorentino), Maioliche Otello Dolfi (Camaioni
Montelupo), Forno Frosecchi (Florence) and Alessandro Frassinelli and Walter
Mericchi for their assistance during the production of this book.
Color separations: Fotolito Toscana, Florence (Italy) and Litocolor, Florence (Italy)

ISBN 88-89272-52-X

Printed and bound in China

THE BIG BOOK OF
ITALIAN
COOKING

Photographs by Marco Lanza

McRae Books

Contents

Introduction

Italian cooking combines simplicity with the use of fresh, natural ingredients to create a mouth-watering array of tasty, easy-to-prepare dishes. Drawing on the many regional traditions that make up modern Italian cuisine, The Big Book of Italian Cooking *brings you more than 700 classic recipes. From the hot, sun-baked south and the islands of Sicily and Sardinia, come suggestions for fish, and spicy or sweet and sour dishes. From central Italian areas, such as Rome, Tuscany, and Bologna, come recipes for fresh pasta, lamb, and traditional desserts and cookies. From the more temperate north we have included wonderful recipes for steaming risottos, polenta, and hearty meat dishes. Many recipes are introduced by snippets of Italian folklore or helpful hints, while others finish with variations. Most recipes include a wine recommendation, to complement the special flavors of the dish. To complete our panorama of Italian cooking, the opening pages introduce ingredients and basic recipes, while others show how to prepare fresh pasta and pizza and bread dough. Here you have everything you will ever need to create authentic Italian food in your own home. As we say in Italy,* Buon appetito!

Barley soup, p. 255

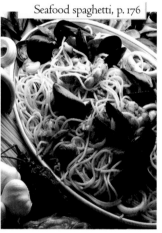

Seafood spaghetti, p. 176

Chicken with olives, p. 458

Plum pie, p. 714

Herbs and Spices

These are precious ingredients. Many dishes owe their special character to a particular herb or spice (or a combination of two or more). Most herbs can now be obtained fresh throughout the year in markets and fresh vegetable stores. The few seasonal varieties can be used in dry form. None of the spices here are rare or hard to find.

JUNIPER BERRIES
Usually used in dry form to flavor food, juniper berries have a fragrant, spicy aroma and a slightly bittersweet flavor.

NUTMEG
Always buy nutmegs whole, together with a nutmeg grater, and grate as needed. Powdered nutmeg loses its flavor very quickly. Store the whole nutmegs in an airtight jar.

THYME
Fresh or dried, thyme is used to flavor a wide variety of foods, including meats, sauces, cheese and vegetables. When fresh, the small grayish-green leaves have a pungent, slightly lemony flavor and warm fragrance.

BAY LEAVES
Fresh bay leaves have a very intense flavor and should be used sparingly. The dried variety also produce excellent results.

SAGE
Sage is used as leaves or twigs either whole or chopped. Fresh sage has a very strong and intense flavor. In its dried form it is blander and sweeter, but still good.

CHILLIES
The many different types vary greatly in shape, size, and spiciness. They can be used crushed, chopped, or whole. Small red hot chillies are the most common type in Italy and they are usually crumbled directly into dishes during cooking. If preferred, use crushed dried chillies as a substitute.

SAFFRON
Saffron is usually sold in powdered form. It is also available as threads which should be soaked in a little cold water for 30 minutes before use. It is a fairly expensive spice, although it is normally used in very small quantities.

GARLIC
Garlic can be used in a variety of ways, depending on how much of its distinctive flavor you want to include in a dish. It can be added whole, chopped, crushed, or lightly bruised. Stored in a dry, well-aired place, it will keep for months.

MINT
There are many varieties of mint, but the ones most commonly used in cookery are peppermint and spearmint. Best fresh, mint can be used in dry form, but never powdered.

BLACK AND WHITE PEPPERCORNS
Black pepper is the whole seed of the pepper tree; the white variety is the same without its outer covering. Black pepper has a full, rounded flavor. White pepper is spicier and more pungent. Both should be ground just before use.

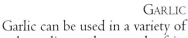

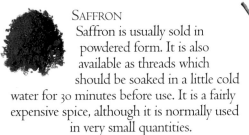

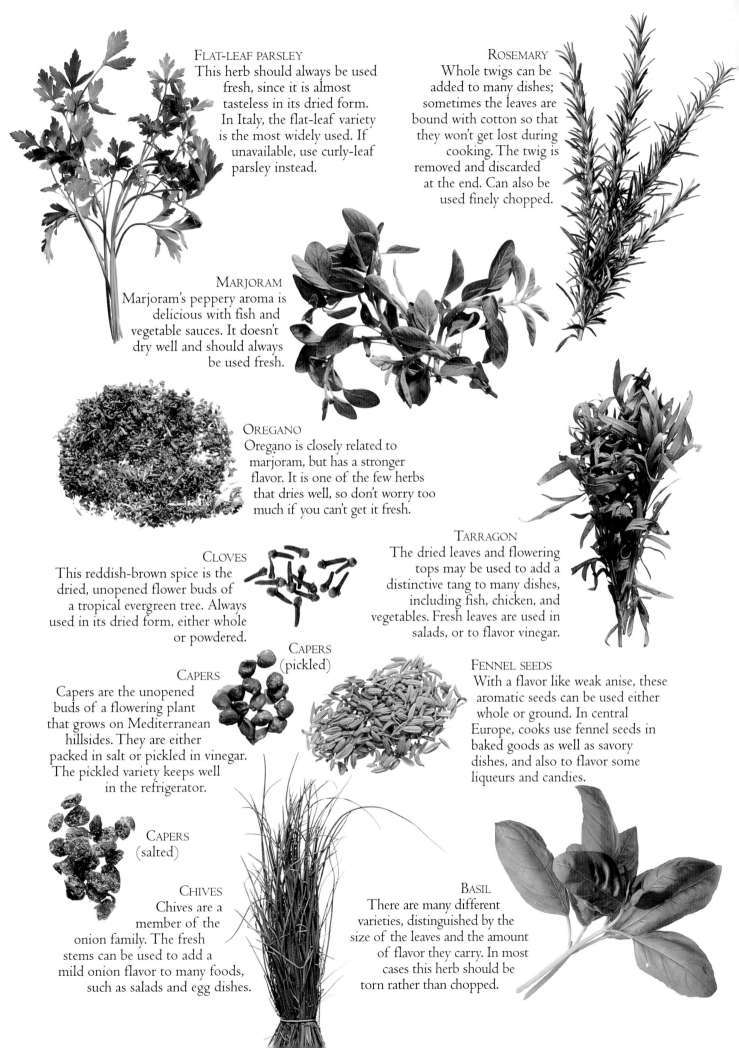

FLAT-LEAF PARSLEY
This herb should always be used fresh, since it is almost tasteless in its dried form. In Italy, the flat-leaf variety is the most widely used. If unavailable, use curly-leaf parsley instead.

ROSEMARY
Whole twigs can be added to many dishes; sometimes the leaves are bound with cotton so that they won't get lost during cooking. The twig is removed and discarded at the end. Can also be used finely chopped.

MARJORAM
Marjoram's peppery aroma is delicious with fish and vegetable sauces. It doesn't dry well and should always be used fresh.

OREGANO
Oregano is closely related to marjoram, but has a stronger flavor. It is one of the few herbs that dries well, so don't worry too much if you can't get it fresh.

CLOVES
This reddish-brown spice is the dried, unopened flower buds of a tropical evergreen tree. Always used in its dried form, either whole or powdered.

TARRAGON
The dried leaves and flowering tops may be used to add a distinctive tang to many dishes, including fish, chicken, and vegetables. Fresh leaves are used in salads, or to flavor vinegar.

CAPERS
(pickled)

CAPERS
Capers are the unopened buds of a flowering plant that grows on Mediterranean hillsides. They are either packed in salt or pickled in vinegar. The pickled variety keeps well in the refrigerator.

FENNEL SEEDS
With a flavor like weak anise, these aromatic seeds can be used either whole or ground. In central Europe, cooks use fennel seeds in baked goods as well as savory dishes, and also to flavor some liqueurs and candies.

CAPERS
(salted)

CHIVES
Chives are a member of the onion family. The fresh stems can be used to add a mild onion flavor to many foods, such as salads and egg dishes.

BASIL
There are many different varieties, distinguished by the size of the leaves and the amount of flavor they carry. In most cases this herb should be torn rather than chopped.

Vegetables

For those of us without green fingers or a garden, the vegetables we eat will be bought at a supermarket or market. If you have the choice, buy at a market where the vegetables will be fresher. When buying vegetables, quality and freshness are of utmost importance. Generally speaking, products should be firm to touch, with good color, and no withered or yellowing leaves. Another important rule is that all vegetables need to be very thoroughly washed in abundant cold running water before you begin preparing them.

ARTICHOKES

Choose artichokes with plump heads and tightly folded leaves. Young artichokes can be eaten raw; the maturer ones are better cooked. Only the inner leaves and heart are edible. To clean an artichoke, remove all but the pale inner leaves by pulling the outer ones down and snapping them off. Cut off the stem at the base of the head and the top third of the leaves. Cut the artichokes in half lengthwise and scrape any fuzzy choke away with a knife. Soak them in a bowl of cold water with the juice of 1 lemon for 10 minutes to stop them turning black.

ASPARAGUS

The asparagus season is mid-spring to early summer, although nowadays specialty markets keep imported asparagus all year round. Often expensive, it pays to choose these vegetables with care. They should be firm, with well-formed, compact stalks. Asparagus should be cooked and eaten as soon as possible. Trim the tough parts off the stems, wash well, and cook in (or steam over) a pot of salted, boiling water until tender.

CARDOONS

Cardoons taste like artichokes, although they look more like a head of celery to buy. Choose crisp, unwilted heads. Trim the tops, strip off the outer, bitter-tasting leaves and serve raw or cooked.

FAVA BEANS (BROAD BEANS)

Fava beans are in season from early spring to midsummer. Buy them when their pods are bright green and crisp. In Italy, very young fava beans are eaten raw with a little salt, pecorino cheese, or salami. The maturer beans can be cooked in many different ways. They are also available in frozen and dried forms.

GREEN BEANS

Also known as French beans, they are best in spring and summer. They should be bright green with no blemishes or spots. Snap the end off one between your thumb and forefinger; if fresh, the bean will break easily. To prepare, trim the ends and wash well.

PEAS

Fresh green peas appear in the markets in spring and summer. The younger they are, the sweeter they will be. Choose those with plump, bright green pods. They should be eaten as soon as possible. During the rest of the year frozen peas are an acceptable substitute and widely available.

CAULIFLOWER

Traditionally a winter vegetable, it is now available throughout the year. The white head should show no blemishing or discoloring and the leaves should be fresh and unwilted. Remove the leaves to cook and divide the head into florets. The stalk is also tasty but takes longer to cook than the florets. Peel it, dice it up, and add to the pot 5 minutes before the florets.

BROCCOLI

Broccoli is best in fall and winter. Choose deep-green broccoli with tightly closed florets. Broccoli stem is also tasty; peel and dice it.

CABBAGE

There are many different varieties of cabbage, including Savoy, red, or the common pale green type. Normally a winter vegetable, some varieties also grow during spring and summer. Most cabbages have tightly packed leaves and will keep in the refrigerator for 4–5 days. Remove the tough stem and wilted outer leaves and cut or chop the vegetable as required.

CELERY

Choose fresh, crisp heads of celery with bright white stalks and unwilted green leaves. Use only the inner stalks and hearts in salads. To cook, remove the strings from the larger, outer stalks before chopping.

ONIONS

There are many types of onions available throughout the year. The large white and yellow varieties are used to flavor many cooked dishes, while the large red variety is sweet enough to be served (thinly sliced) in salads. Squeeze onions before you buy them to make sure they are not rotting beneath their skins.

ZUCCHINI (COURGETTES)

Their natural season is spring to fall, although they are now available all year round. Zucchini should be firm to touch, with glossy, blemish-free skins. They are at their peak in early summer and can be eaten raw then. In Italy, zucchini blossoms are considered a delicacy. Use the male flowers that grow on a stem, not the female ones attached to the zucchini.

SPRING ONIONS

Available from early spring to fall. Trim the tops and bottoms, peel off the outer layers of white skin, and chop into salads.

LEEKS

A member of the onion family. Trim off the green tops and roots, and peel the outer layers of the white stalk. Although sometimes served in salads, their strong flavor makes them more suitable for cooking. Buy them with their green tops, which should be fresh-looking and unwilted.

CUCUMBER

Now available throughout the year, they are much tastier in their natural season, from late spring to fall. Buy them firm, with bright green skins.

BABY ONIONS

White, baby onions can be pickled, grilled, or served in sweet and sour sauces.

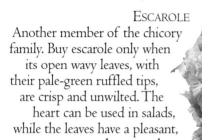

SPINACH
Available from fall to spring.
Choose young, tender spinach with
crisp, deep-green leaves. Separate
the leaves and wash very
thoroughly. Frozen spinach is
an acceptable substitute
in summer.

ARUGULA (ROCKET)
This Mediterranean herb has
been naturalized in many parts
of North America. With
its pungent, peppery
flavor, it is widely used
in salads and to flavor
dishes. Choose crisp,
dark-green arugula,
with unblemished
leaves. It will keep a
day or two in the
refrigerator.

ESCAROLE
Another member of the chicory
family. Buy escarole only when
its open wavy leaves, with
their pale-green ruffled tips,
are crisp and unwilted. The
heart can be used in salads,
while the leaves have a pleasant,
earthy taste when
cooked.

RADICCHIO
There are several
types of round or
long red radicchio available in Italy
throughout the year. They are all
more or less bitter in taste and can
be served either raw in salads, or
baked or grilled. There are also
many varieties of small green
radicchio (both wild and cultivated).
They are usually served in salads.

BELGIAN ENDIVE
Also known as French
endive. Another
member of the chicory
family. Choose white,
well-closed heads and
store them in the dark –
the light will turn the leaves
green. Clean by removing the
outer leaves and chopping
the tough part off the bottom.
Serve in salads or cooked.

CATALONIA
Part of the chicory family, this is
a bitter cooking green with long,
tapering leaves, white at the
bottom and dark green toward the
tops. Choose compact, unwilted
heads. If you enjoy bracing bitter
flavors, serve it boiled or steamed,
dressed with a little olive oil and
lemon juice.

LETTUCE
There are many different types of
lettuce available throughout the year.
Common cutting lettuce is usually
round, with pale green and white
leaves folded over each other. The
central white heart is the best part.
Romaine lettuce
has elongated
dark green
leaves.
Choose
lettuces
with crisp
well-colored
leaves. Trim the
bottoms, detach the
leaves, and wash accurately.

SWISS CHARD (SILVER BEET)
The dwarf varieties are
sweeter and lack the large
white stalk of the
larger ones. They
can be served raw
in salads or cooked.
The large stalks are
nearly always cooked.
Choose fresh, bright green
heads with crisp leaves.

FENNEL

With its mild taste of aniseed, fennel is a refreshing salad vegetable. It can also be braised, sautéed, baked, or fried. Only the bulb is used; the stalks and leaves are usually discarded. Available year round, its natural season is winter and spring. Generally speaking, the plump bulbs are best in salads, while the longer, flatter ones are better cooked.

PORCINI MUSHROOMS

Porcini mushrooms grow wild in the woods in Italy after heavy rainfall from spring to fall. They grow large enough to be grilled and served as a main course. Fresh porcini lose their flavor quickly, so even if you do find them in specialty markets, make sure the caps are firm and the stalks are not withered or woody. Dried porcini are now widely available, and by mixing a small amount (soaked in a bowl of cold water) with cultivated mushrooms, much of their special flavor is imparted to sauces and soups.

RADISHES

Available throughout the year. Try to buy them with their tops attached, since these will show how fresh they are. Cut off the roots and tops, wash well, and serve the tiny red bulbs in salads, or by themselves (with a dish of salt).

EGGPLANTS (AUBERGINES)

There are many varieties of eggplant, including the long thin ones, and the round or pear-shaped varieties. Now available throughout the year, their natural season is summer and they are best then. They should be firm to touch, with glossy, smooth, dark-purple skins. Most recipes require you to purge them of their bitter liquid before use. This is done by trimming the ends, slicing, and sprinkling with salt. Place the slices on a large flat plate and cover with another plate with a heavy weight on top. Leave for 2–3 hours. Rinse well to remove excess salt before cooking.

TOMATOES

The tomato is ubiquitous in Italian cuisine. Fresh tomatoes are now available year round, although the outdoor, summer varieties have an unbeatable flavor. Canned tomatoes are an acceptable substitute for fresh ones in sauces and soups during the winter months.

BELL PEPPERS (CAPSICUMS)

Green, yellow, and red bell peppers are in season throughout the summer months. Choose well-shaped peppers and check for soft spots in the flesh, which mean they are going off. To remove the skins, put the peppers in a hot oven, under a broiler, or in a grill pan until the skins turn black. The skins are easy to remove by hand when burned.

CHERRY TOMATOES

In season, tiny cherry tomatoes are packed with flavor.

CARROTS

Carrots are available throughout the year. Baby carrots are often sold with their tops; if the leaves are bright green and unwilted the carrots will be fresh. Choose older carrots carefully; they should be bright orange in color, well-shaped, and firm. Scrub well or peel before use.

Dried Pasta

At first glance, the variety of pasta shapes available may seem bewildering. New ones are being invented all the time and many of the traditional ones go by different names depending on the region or manufacturer. However, it is not as confusing as it seems and by keeping just a few general guidelines in mind you will be able to match sauce and shape perfectly. The long and short pasta shapes on this page are store-bought and made from dried hard-wheat flour and water, while the smaller soup pasta shapes may also be made from egg and soft-wheat flour.

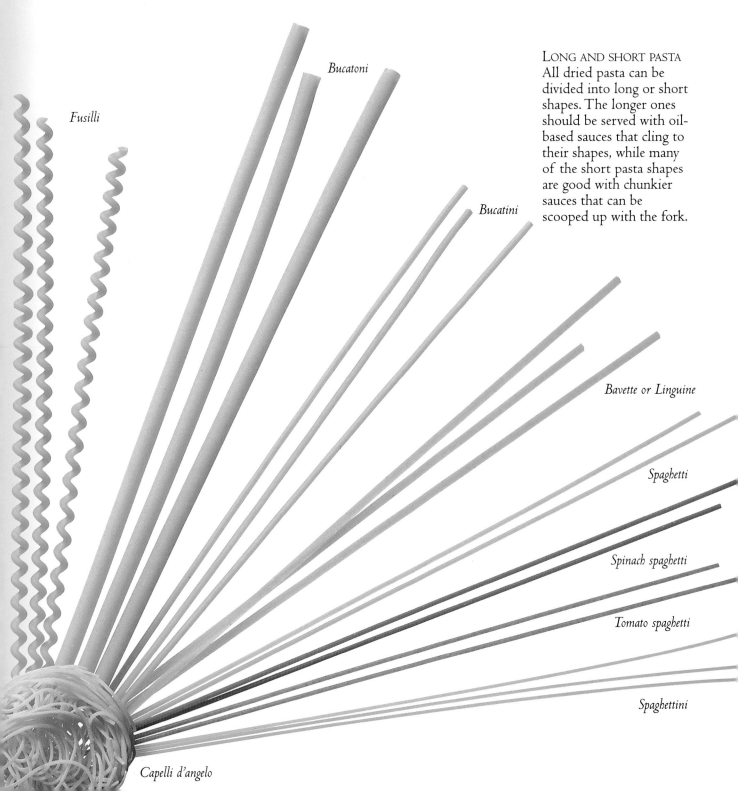

LONG AND SHORT PASTA
All dried pasta can be divided into long or short shapes. The longer ones should be served with oil-based sauces that cling to their shapes, while many of the short pasta shapes are good with chunkier sauces that can be scooped up with the fork.

Fusilli

Bucatoni

Bucatini

Bavette or Linguine

Spaghetti

Spinach spaghetti

Tomato spaghetti

Spaghettini

Capelli d'angelo

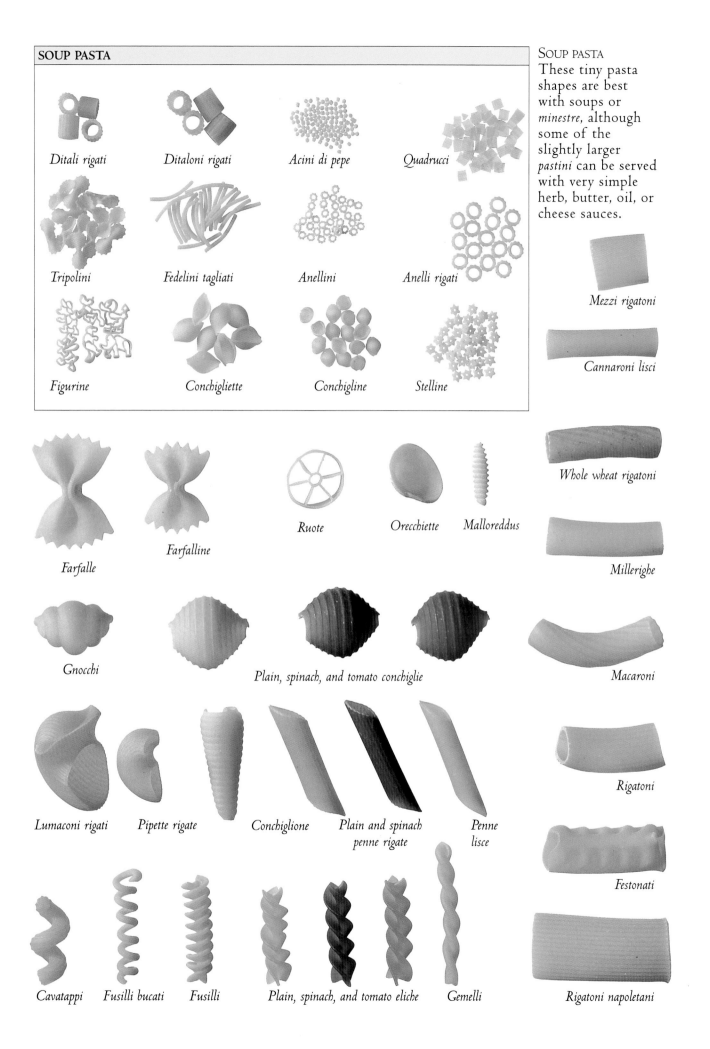

SOUP PASTA

Ditali rigati

Ditaloni rigati

Acini di pepe

Quadrucci

Tripolini

Fedelini tagliati

Anellini

Anelli rigati

Figurine

Conchigliette

Conchigline

Stelline

SOUP PASTA
These tiny pasta shapes are best with soups or *minestre*, although some of the slightly larger *pastini* can be served with very simple herb, butter, oil, or cheese sauces.

Mezzi rigatoni

Cannaroni lisci

Whole wheat rigatoni

Millerighe

Farfalle

Farfalline

Ruote

Orecchiette

Malloreddus

Macaroni

Gnocchi

Plain, spinach, and tomato conchiglie

Rigatoni

Lumaconi rigati

Pipette rigate

Conchiglione

Plain and spinach penne rigate

Penne lisce

Festonati

Cavatappi

Fusilli bucati

Fusilli

Plain, spinach, and tomato eliche

Gemelli

Rigatoni napoletani

Fresh and Filled Pasta and Gnocchi

Fresh pasta is made from egg and soft-wheat flour, although the term "fresh" is somewhat misleading, since egg pasta can also be dried. In fact you will find that commercially-made dried tagliatelle, fettuccine, pappardelle, and others, are often a better (and certainly more economical) alternative to the refrigerated "fresh" pasta available in supermarkets and specialty stores. However, the best fresh pasta you can get is the homemade variety. If you have the time, and a little patience, the results will be better than anything you can buy. See instructions on pages 198–201. As with dried, store-bought pasta, the names and shapes of fresh and filled pasta types vary from region to region in Italy. This is a selection of the most common types, in their most usual shapes, and with their most common names.

Spinach ravioli

Agnolotti

Cappelletti

Tortelli

FILLED PASTA
Fresh pasta can be filled with a variety of different stuffings, including meat, cheese and spinach, potatoes, and other vegetables. Depending on the shape, the pasta is called tortellini, tortelli, ravioli, or agnolotti, to name just a few.

Tortellini

Tortelloni

Potato gnocchi

Spinach and ricotta gnocchi

Gnocchi alla romana

Spinach and potato gnocchi

GNOCCHI
The most common type of gnocchi, often called *topini* ("little mice"), is made of a mixture of cooked potatoes and flour, with the addition of an egg in some regions. Green gnocchi can be made of spinach and potato or spinach and ricotta. The spinach and ricotta gnocchi are called *malfatti* ("badly made") because they are made with the ingredients for stuffing ravioli but lack the pasta casing. *Gnocchi alla romana* are made with semolina and baked in the oven.

Pappardelle

Tagliolini

Fettuccine

Paglia e fieno

Tagliatelle

Maltagliati

Lasagne

Serving suggestions
High quality fresh and filled pasta are good with simple butter, cream, or butter and herb sauces, well sprinkled with freshly grated Parmesan cheese. These simple sauces should highlight the delicate taste of the pasta without overpowering it. Mushroom, truffle, asparagus, and walnut sauces are also good. Some traditional recipes include sauces based on game — such as duck, wild boar, or rabbit — as well as tasty, well-cooked lamb and veal.

Cheese

More than 400 different types of cheese are produced in Italy. Cheese is widely used in cooking. These are a selection of the cheeses included in the recipes in this book. Don't be alarmed if you can't find the exact cheese in your local supermarket or specialty store, use a similar local product in its place.

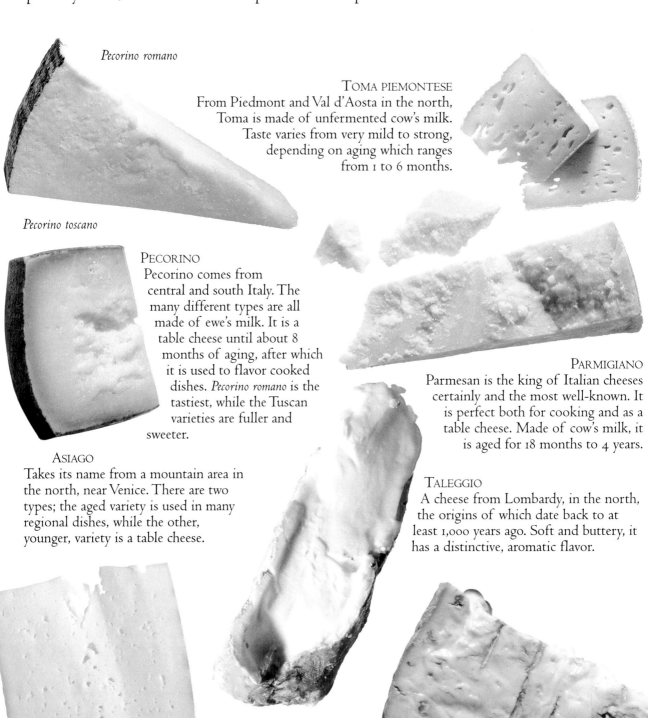

Pecorino romano

TOMA PIEMONTESE
From Piedmont and Val d'Aosta in the north, Toma is made of unfermented cow's milk. Taste varies from very mild to strong, depending on aging which ranges from 1 to 6 months.

Pecorino toscano

PECORINO
Pecorino comes from central and south Italy. The many different types are all made of ewe's milk. It is a table cheese until about 8 months of aging, after which it is used to flavor cooked dishes. *Pecorino romano* is the tastiest, while the Tuscan varieties are fuller and sweeter.

PARMIGIANO
Parmesan is the king of Italian cheeses certainly and the most well-known. It is perfect both for cooking and as a table cheese. Made of cow's milk, it is aged for 18 months to 4 years.

ASIAGO
Takes its name from a mountain area in the north, near Venice. There are two types; the aged variety is used in many regional dishes, while the other, younger, variety is a table cheese.

TALEGGIO
A cheese from Lombardy, in the north, the origins of which date back to at least 1,000 years ago. Soft and buttery, it has a distinctive, aromatic flavor.

GORGONZOLA
A creamy northern cheese, made in two versions – sweet and spicy. Made of cow's milk, it is characterized by blue-green veins and blobs of tasty mold.

GRUYÈRE AND EMMENTAL
From Switzerland, France, and Holland, these cheeses are widely used in Italian cooking.

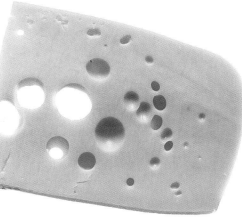

FONTINA
This well-known cheese, from the alpine Val d'Aosta, has an intense almost sweet flavor. Many similar cheeses are produced across northern Italy; they are usually called Fontal.

PROVOLONE
Originally a southern cheese from Campania, the area around Naples. It is now produced in many regions, each one giving it a special shape. Aging determines taste; the younger varieties are mild and the older ones tasty.

MOZZARELLA
From Campania, it was originally made of water buffalo milk. Nowadays it is made throughout the peninsula, usually of cow's milk. It is widely used in cooking and also as a table cheese.

SCAMORZA
From Abruzzo and Molise in southern Italy, it is similar to Mozzarella but harder and drier. It is recognizable by the shape it gets from being hung. The smoked variety has a much darker skin. Both a table and a cooking cheese.

Smoked scamorza

CACIOCAVALLO
A tasty, southern Italian table or cooking cheese. When aged it can also be grated.

CAPRINO
A delicate, slightly tart fresh cheese made of goat's milk, or a mixture of goat's and cow's milk.

ROBIOLA
A fresh, creamy cheese, with a slightly sharp taste.

RICOTTA
Fresh Ricotta has a deliciously light and delicate flavor. It is widely used in Italian cooking. Buy it in a good deli or specialty cheese store. Try to avoid Ricotta sold in plastic containers, which bears very little resemblance to the real thing.

MASCARPONE
Made from cow's cream, Mascarpone is a fresh cheese that will only keep a day or two in the refrigerator. It is widely used for cakes and desserts.

Pork Products

In traditional Italian cuisine, little or nothing of the pig is wasted. The various parts are preserved and cured in a variety of ways and used to flavor many different dishes. Although these are typically Italian products, most are now readily available in supermarkets and specialty stores. However, if you can't find prosciutto, pancetta, or any of the others, don't be afraid to substitute them with similar local products.

PANCETTA
Pancetta is made by curing pork slowly in a mixture of salt, pepper, and spices. Usually unsmoked, some smoked varieties are available. When smoked it is very similar to bacon.

SPECK
This is a specialty of Alto Adige, in northeastern Italy. It is made by curing pork in various spices and salt, then leaving it to age for 3 weeks. It is then smoked. If you can't get speck, use bacon in its place.

SMOKED PANCETTA

PROSCIUTTO
Produced throughout Italy, prosciutto is made by curing ham. The techniques are similar throughout the country, but the results vary greatly depending on the ability of the producers and also the climate and environmental conditions. Parma ham is generally considered the best, but there are some other excellent varieties available.

HAM
Italian ham is prepared in a similar way to American ham; it is flavored with various spices, then slowly cooked in vapor. Be sure to trim off and discard excess fat.

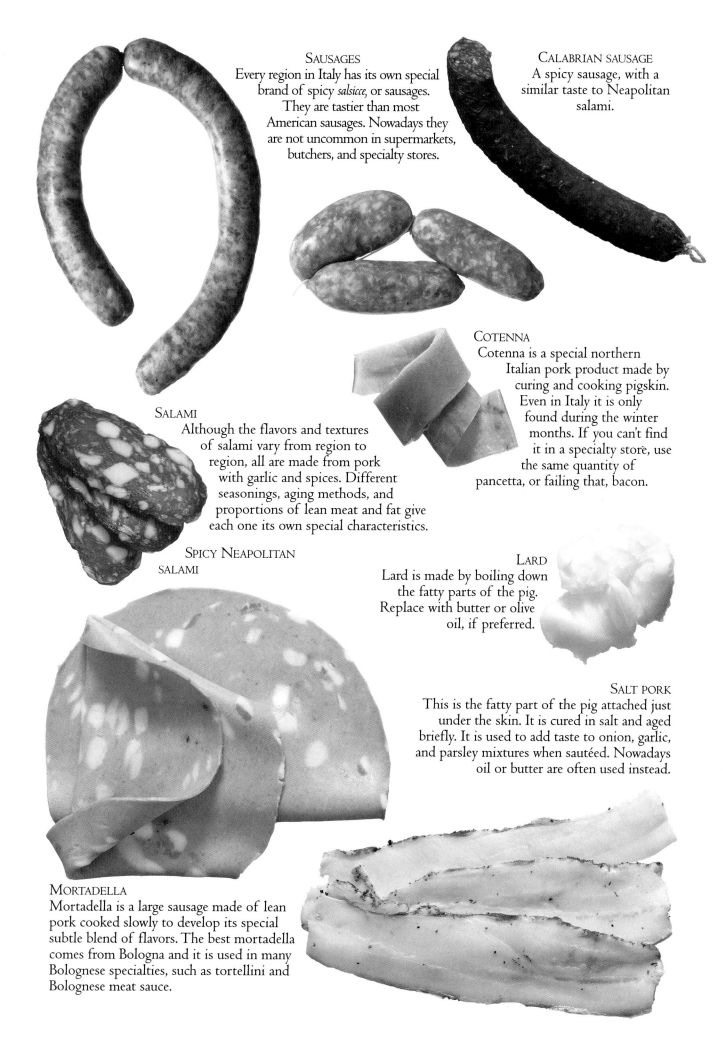

SAUSAGES

Every region in Italy has its own special brand of spicy *salsicce*, or sausages. They are tastier than most American sausages. Nowadays they are not uncommon in supermarkets, butchers, and specialty stores.

CALABRIAN SAUSAGE

A spicy sausage, with a similar taste to Neapolitan salami.

COTENNA

Cotenna is a special northern Italian pork product made by curing and cooking pigskin. Even in Italy it is only found during the winter months. If you can't find it in a specialty store, use the same quantity of pancetta, or failing that, bacon.

SALAMI

Although the flavors and textures of salami vary from region to region, all are made from pork with garlic and spices. Different seasonings, aging methods, and proportions of lean meat and fat give each one its own special characteristics.

SPICY NEAPOLITAN SALAMI

LARD

Lard is made by boiling down the fatty parts of the pig. Replace with butter or olive oil, if preferred.

SALT PORK

This is the fatty part of the pig attached just under the skin. It is cured in salt and aged briefly. It is used to add taste to onion, garlic, and parsley mixtures when sautéed. Nowadays oil or butter are often used instead.

MORTADELLA

Mortadella is a large sausage made of lean pork cooked slowly to develop its special subtle blend of flavors. The best mortadella comes from Bologna and it is used in many Bolognese specialties, such as tortellini and Bolognese meat sauce.

INGREDIENTS

Fish and Seafood

Delicious fish and seafood are an important part of the healthy Mediterranean diet. Many contain vitamins and oils that are thought to lower cholesterol and protect against heart disease. When buying unfrozen fish always follow your nose – very fresh fish will have almost no odor. If you don't live on the coast or close to a good fresh fish supplier, frozen fish are a reliable alternative.

SEA BASS
This is one of the best small fish for serving whole, as it has firm flesh and is easy to bone. When buying sea bass, make sure that the gills are bright red, and the upper fin has been removed.

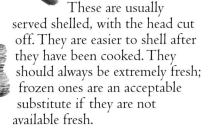

WHITEBAIT
These have silvery bodies and a rich, oily flavor.

SHRIMP AND PRAWN
These are usually served shelled, with the head cut off. They are easier to shell after they have been cooked. They should always be extremely fresh; frozen ones are an acceptable substitute if they are not available fresh.

SCORPION FISH
Found widely throughout tropical and temperate waters, they are also known as rockfish or stonefish.

TROUT
Members of the salmon family, trout usually have firm, flaky flesh colored orange, white, or pink. Wild trout is delicious, with its rich, creamy, pink flesh, but very difficult to find.

SQUID
An Italian favorite, squid is also becoming popular in other parts of the world. Frozen squid is readily available, but it can be found fresh in season. In Italy, the black ink is often used to flavor and color pasta and risotto dishes.

CUTTLEFISH
Known in Italy as *seppia*, cuttlefish are used to flavor many dishes, and are often served as part of seafood salads.

MONKFISH
Also known as the "poor man's lobster," monkfish is known by many other names. It is found in the Mediterranean Sea and the Atlantic Ocean. The lean, firm tail flesh is the only edible part – it is sweet, pearl-colored, and rich in flavor.

SARDINES
Sardines are also known as pilchards, or sprats. They are usually bought cured, pickled, smoked, or packed in sauce or oil. Fresh sardines are especially good for broiling, and are best in the spring.

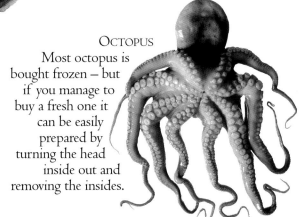

OCTOPUS
Most octopus is bought frozen – but if you manage to buy a fresh one it can be easily prepared by turning the head inside out and removing the insides.

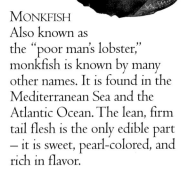

PORGY

This fish is low in fat, with white, tender flesh and a mild, sweet flavor. Its many small bones make it difficult to fillet, so ask your fishmonger to do this for you.

RED MULLET

With rose-colored skin, the flavor of this lean, firm fish is almost like prawn. The liver is not removed during cooking, because it is regarded as a delicacy.

CLAMS

With a flavor that ranges from mild to sweet, clams are found in coastal waters around the world. Whole clams must be sold alive – their shells will be shut tight – and are often served steamed. Giant sea clams are often canned or frozen.

HAKE

The several varieties of hake are lean with white flesh. Commonly sold as whole fish, as well as fillets and steaks.

SOLE

This fish has eyes on top of its head, and swims on its side. The finely-textured, sweet flesh is usually sliced into delicate fillets, which can be cooked very quickly. When buying whole fish, make sure it is fresh by checking that the gills are red.

SCALLOP

Their ability to swim makes scallops an unusual type of bivalve. Many mollusk-lovers believe that scallops have the most tender, creamy flesh and the sweetest flavor of all. They range in color from red, purple, yellow, or orange, through to white.

SALMON

There are many different species of salmon. Generally, the flesh ranges in color from pale pink to orange or red. The distinctive rich flavor of salmon means it can not be easily substituted with another type of fish.

FRESH SALMON

MACKEREL

Versatile, moist, and sweet, mackerel is also relatively cheap to buy. It has tasty skin, no scales, and is easy to fillet. It must be eaten while very fresh, as the color and quality deteriorate quickly.

SMOKED SALMON

SALTED ANCHOVIES

FRESH ANCHOVIES

ANCHOVIES

Anchovies are often marinated, canned in olive oil or cured in salt. A small quantity of crumbled anchovy fillets make a delicious addition to many dishes.

TUNA

Some tuna are very large – the bluefin can weigh up to 1,800 lb (900 kg). In Italy, canned tuna is very popular. There are many different ways of serving this fish fresh, and it also freezes very well.

MUSSELS

Mussels should be bought clean and used very fresh – they can be steamed open and served with sauce, or baked in their half shells with tasty toppings.

ANCHOVY FILLETS IN OLIVE OIL

Other Ingredients

Most ingredients used in Italian kitchens are common throughout the world and need little introduction. Others, some of which are shown below, are more specific to the Italian pantry and may require some explanation.

ITALIAN BREAD

Italian bread differs from region to region – in Tuscany the bread is traditionally made without salt, while in the south it often includes olive oil. Nearly all have solid, chewy crusts and firm textures, which means that they can be served with olive oil or with moist toppings without becoming soggy or unpalatable.

UNSALTED TUSCAN BREAD

BALSAMIC VINEGAR

The best Italian vinegar is sweet and mellow in flavor – it is made from concentrated grape juice that has been aged in a series of barrels. The production of genuine balsamic vinegar is controlled by strict Italian laws – it must be aged for no less than 12 years. When aged for 20 years or more, the vinegar is called "stravecchio."

ANCHOVY PASTE

Usually sold in a tube, anchovy paste is made from anchovies that have been pounded, then mixed with spices and vinegar.

DRIED FAVA BEANS (BROAD BEANS)

TRUFFLE

Truffles are a kind of subterranean fungus that grow in woodlands around the roots of trees. They are very rare and expensive, as they cannot be cultivated commercially. Their season is from October to December. They can be eaten raw or cooked, and are used to flavor oil.

OLIVE OIL

Every cuisine is associated with a range of recurrent tastes and flavors. Olive oil plays a predominant role in Italian cooking. Don't economize on olive oil or use other vegetable oils in its place, even for cooking. The quality of the oil can make or break a dish and ruin or exalt all your efforts. For this reason always buy Italian-made olive oil which is clearly labeled *"extra-vergine."* Make sure too that it is fresh; top quality new oil is a limpid green color, not murky yellow.

EXTRA-VIRGIN OLIVE OIL

BEANS

Beans hold an important place in northern and central Italian cooking. Common varieties include fava beans (broad beans) and cannellini beans, and pulses such as lentils and chickpeas. Some are only available fresh briefly, and only in Italy. If you cannot get fresh beans, dried beans should be used as a substitute rather than tinned, which do not have such good flavor and texture.

PINE NUTS

Pine nuts are actually pine kernels, and are used in a wide range of both sweet and savory Italian recipes, including cakes, pesto, and meat dishes. They are usually lightly toasted until golden brown, but they can be eaten raw.

TOSCANELLI BEANS (similar to white beans)

CANNELLINI BEANS (also available as a red bean, they are similar to kidney beans)

RICE

It is very important to choose the correct type and quality of rice for the different dishes. Choose a plump, short-grain Italian rice for risotti—*arborio* is the best choice, while *vialone nano*, whose kernel offers some resistance to the bite, is ideal for rice salads. Brown rice is also very tasty in salads. Smaller, short-grain rices are generally used in soups.

RICE FOR SOUPS

ARBORIO RICE

SPELT

Known in Tuscany as *farro*, this ancient type of wheat has been grown in Italy for thousands of years. A very hard grain, spelt must be boiled for up to three hours before eating. It is used mainly as an ingredient for soups.

GAETA OLIVES

BLACK OLIVES

OVEN-BAKED OLIVES

BREAD CRUMBS

The bread crumbs used in Italian cooking are simply stale, finely-ground, good quality bread. They have no flavoring added and you must ensure that they are very dry.

OLIVES

Olives are grown throughout the Mediterranean — most are used to produce oil, although some are served as table olives or used in cooking. Processed in salt, they are widely used to flavor salads and other dishes. Both green (unripened) and black (mature) olives have an unpleasantly bitter flavor when in their natural state — before eating they must be washed, soaked, and pickled.

STUFFED GREEN OLIVES

GARBANZO BEAN (CHICKPEA) FLOUR

Used to make *farinata*, a type of flatbread from the northwest coastal region of Italy.

CHESTNUT FLOUR

Used to make regional flatbreads, chestnut flour is also a vital ingredient in *castagnaccio* (chestnut cake), which is a traditional Tuscan cake.

YEAST

Fresh yeast produces the best bread and pizza. Be sure to check its expiry date when buying. If you can't get compressed yeast, use active dry yeast in its place. Remember that dry yeast is about twice as potent as the compressed variety; use about half the quantities given in the recipes in this book for the same results. The high-speed yeasts now available work very quickly, but the results are decidedly inferior.

FRESH YEAST

COARSE-GRAIN CORNMEAL

Cornmeal is basically dried, ground corn kernels. Coarse-grain cornmeal (different from fine-grain or medium-grain) is cooked to form polenta, which has been a staple in northern Italy for hundreds of years.

ACTIVE DRY YEAST

Utensils

Most well-stocked kitchens will already have the following equipment. If you need extra pieces they will be easy to find in kitchen-supply stores. If you can, always choose good quality equipment. It will last longer and the results will be better.

POT
Large capacity pot with a close-fitting lid, especially useful for cooking pasta.

PASTA MACHINE
This is a basic hand-cranked pasta machine. Electric versions are also available.

SKILLET
Heavy, shallow-sided pan in aluminum, stainless steel, or cast iron.

SLOTTED SPOON
Used for removing gnocchi from the pan and for skimming broth.

SAUTÉ PAN
Deep-sided pan, large enough to hold sauce and whatever it is intended to coat (such as pasta, vegetables, etc).

WHEEL CUTTER
To give fluted edges when cutting fresh pasta.

ROLLING PIN
A pasta rolling pin is longer and thinner than the normal one.

COLANDER
Large metal colander for draining liquids from solids.

METAL TONGS
For picking up or serving spaghetti. Tongs are also useful for picking up and turning things while frying.

EARTHENWARE POT
Earthenware pots will give your dishes a special earthy flavor.

WOODEN SPOON AND FORK
For stirring pasta and sauces.

BAKING DISH
Large, rectangular, ovenproof baking dish with lid.

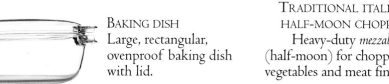

TRADITIONAL ITALIAN HALF-MOON CHOPPER
Heavy-duty *mezzaluna* (half-moon) for chopping vegetables and meat finely.

CHEESE GRATER
Rounded or flat graters with small to medium holes are perfect for grating Parmesan and other cheeses.

FOOD MILL
A hand-cranked mill for puréeing ingredients for soups, sauces, and fillings.

FOOD PROCESSOR
For chopping, shredding, and puréeing ingredients for sauces and soups.

ICE CREAM MAKER
To chill and churn the ice cream mixture.

CANNOLI CYLINDERS
Used to shape cannoli–pieces of the dough are wrapped around the cylinders before being fried.

RHUM BABA MOLDS
These individual baking molds give traditional rhum babas their mushroom shape.

PEPPER GRINDER
Always use freshly ground pepper.

POLENTA CAULDRON
If you are planning to make a lot of polenta, be sure to invest in a large cauldron or pot for cooking it in and a hefty, long-handled wooden spoon for stirring.

ELECTRIC POLENTA CAULDRON
If you are put off by the amount of hard work involved in cooking polenta, you can buy an electric polenta cauldron.

WHEEL FOR CUTTING PIZZA
A heavy, finely-honed wheel for cutting pizza with ease.

OLIVE PITTER
Essential for pitting olives.

BAKING STONE
Pizza, bread, and focacce are best when baked on baking stones, which distribute the very high heat evenly and absorb the moisture of the dough, creating crisper crusts.

PIZZA PANS
Pizzas and focacce can also be baked on ordinary baking pans (be sure to oil or flour them, or cover with parchment paper before use so that the dough doesn't stick).

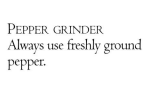

Cooking Pasta

TIMING: One of the most difficult things for the novice pasta cook is knowing when the pasta is cooked. It should be boiled until the outer layers are soft enough to absorb the delicious sauce you have prepared, while the inside is firm enough to pose some resistance to the bite. This is called *al dente*.

WATER: Pasta needs lots of water to cook properly. Allow about 4 quarts (8 pints/4 liters) for each pound (500 g) of pasta. Never cook even a small amount of pasta in less than 3 quarts (6 pints/3 liters).

SALT: Allow at least 1 heaped tablespoon of salt for each pound (500 g) of pasta. Add the salt once the water is boiling, just before adding the pasta.

QUANTITY: As a general guideline, allow about 4 oz (125 g) per head. If the pasta is a first course between an appetizer and the main course, you may need less. If you are just serving pasta with a salad, you may need more.

COOKING: When the water is boiling, add all the pasta at once.

Stir with a wooden spoon so it doesn't stick together. Cover the pot with a lid and bring it back to a boil as soon as possible. When the water is boiling again, leave to cook uncovered, stirring frequently.

DRAINING: Drain the pasta in a colander as soon as it is cooked. Don't leave it sitting in the water or it will become overcooked.

SERVING: Pasta should be served immediately. If it is left sitting, it will turn into a sticky lump.

Preparing Seafood and Fish

CLEANING SHELLFISH: rinse under cold running water then place in a large bowl of cold water for 1 hour. This will purge them of sand. Since it can be especially difficult to remove every trace of sand from clams, give the bowl or pan containing the clams a good shake every 20 minutes or so and then change the water. Mussels need to be scraped with a knife or scrubbed with a wire brush to clean and remove their "beards."

OPENING SHELLFISH: since the best scallops are almost always shucked immediately and then frozen, you will probably never have to do this. In Italy, scallops in shell are available and they are shucked using a sharp knife, without applying heat. Clams and mussels are opened by placing them in a large skillet over high heat (by themselves or with oil or wine) and cooking for about 10 minutes. Any shells that do not open should be discarded. Don't try to open them with a knife.

CLEANING CRUSTACEANS: shrimp, prawns, scampi, crabs, crayfish, lobsters, etc., are all cleaned by rinsing under cold running water, and then using sharp kitchen scissors to remove their tough outer shells and claws. Shrimp are sometimes shelled before cooking and sometimes not. Follow the suggestions in the recipes. High quality, fresh shrimp will not require deveining.

CLEANING CEPHALOPODS: squid and cuttlefish are cleaned by grasping the tentacles and pulling them away from the sac. The pulpy insides will come away with them. Cut off the tentacles just above the eyes and discard. Squeeze off the small, bony beak at the base of the tentacles. Rinse under cold running water, rubbing off as much of the skin as possible. Most of the octopus available now is already cleaned. If you do buy one that requires cleaning, just turn the head inside out, like a sock, and remove the insides. The rest is all edible.

CLEANING FISH: increasingly, fish are available already scaled and gutted, if not as fillets. If you do acquire a whole fish, proceed as follows: scale it by running the back of a knife from tail to head all over. The scales will come off easily, although they do tend to fly all over the place. You may like to do this job outside. To gut, use a sharp, small knife, and cut a slit from the fish's anal opening to the gills. Pull the guts out with your fingers, then scrape out the kidneys that remain attached to the backbone. Use a spoon to scrape out any remaining gut. If serving a fish whole, or using it to make stock, remove the gills, which are bitter tasting, by lifting the gill covers and cutting them out with a sharp pair of kitchen scissors. You can also remove fins with kitchen scissors. Rinse the cleaned fish under cold running water and dry well before cooking.

Preparing and Cooking Meat

BRAISING: braised meat is usually marinated before cooking. Braising calls for long, slow cooking over low heat. The cooking juices are normally served with the meat.

CARPACCIO: carpaccio is very thinly sliced top quality beef, usually fillet. Because it is eaten raw, the meat must be very good and very fresh.

BOILING: boiled meats are cooked in tall, narrow pans. The meat is generally immersed in cold water with vegetables, herbs, salt and black pepper. Boiled meats can be served either hot or cold.

FRYING: slice the meat thinly or chop in small pieces, dip it into beaten egg and then dredge in bread crumbs or flour. Fry in very hot (but not smoking) olive oil until crisp and golden brown. Drain well on paper towels and serve very hot.

STEWING: when stewing meats, add all the ingredients to a heavy-bottomed pan at the same time. Cook slowly over low heat.

SCALOPPINE: scaloppine are thin slices of veal cut from a single, solid piece of top round (topside). The veal should be sliced across the grain of the meat, so it doesn't become tough during cooking. The meat should be cut in slices about ¼ in (6 mm) thick and lightly pounded before cooking.

GRILLING, BARBECUING, and BROILING: barbecued or grilled meat can be marinated for an hour or two before cooking. To barbeque, place the meat over glowing coals or embers; flames will burn the outside and leave the inside raw. If grilling, the grill pan should be very hot when the meat is added; when the meat has formed a thin crust, lower the heat to medium and cook until tender. Prepared meat can also be broiled under an electric or gas coil.

ROASTING: to oven-roast, sprinkle meat with a little salt and pepper (and sometimes aromatic herbs) before placing it in a preheated oven. To pan-roast, the prepared meat should be placed in a heavy-bottomed pan over an element at medium heat. The secret lies in leaving the pan partially covered and keeping just enough liquid in the bottom so the roast doesn't stick.

Grilling and Frying food

Grilling is a traditional Italian cooking method. There are just two basic rules: choose only the freshest and best foods for grilling, and heat the grill pan to very hot before beginning. This stops pieces from sticking, and cooks them quickly (so they won't dry out). To obtain perfect results when frying foods you will need a deep-sided skillet (frying pan), a slotted spoon, tongs (or two forks), and abundant olive oil. Fried dishes should be eaten hot; serve them as you cook or as soon afterward as possible.

TEMPERATURE: Don't begin frying before the oil is hot enough.

Ideal cooking temperatures are:

Medium (275–300°F/130–150°C): ideal for pieces of raw food that need time to cook inside;

Hot (300–325°F/150–160°C): ideal for precooked foods, croquettes, and to seal fillings in;

Very hot (325–350°F/160–180°C): ideal for vegetables in julienne strips, leaves, or tiny pieces of food which require instant frying.

Initially, you may prefer to use a thermometer to gauge heat. Otherwise, check temperature by putting a small piece of the food you wish to cook in the oil to see how it reacts and adjust temperature accordingly.

Temperature should never exceed 350°F/180°C. Don't wait until the oil is smoking; this is dangerous as it may catch fire (if it does, don't use water to extinguish it, just turn off the gas or electricity and cover the pan with a lid).

Always use plenty of oil. The food should float. When you add it to the pan the whole surface should seal immediately against the oil. The less oil that enters the surface, the lighter and healthier the fried dish will be.

Never use the same oil more than once. During cooking, keep the oil clean; if you leave tiny pieces of batter or food in the pan, they will burn and their acrid flavor will contaminate the taste of what you fry next. Keep the oil topped up to the same level during cooking.

The food you want to fry should be at room temperature. If it is too cold, it will take longer to cook and absorb more oil.

Don't put too many pieces in the pan at once. This will lower the temperature of the oil, increasing cooking time and causing food to absorb more oil. The pieces may also stick together in a single unappetizing lump.

If using a wire basket, heat it in the oil first to prevent the food from sticking to it.

BASIC RECIPES

Simple tomato sauce
Salsa al pomodoro

Oil-based tomato sauce goes well with all dried, hard-wheat pasta, such as spaghetti, spaghettini, penne, bucatini, and fusilli. It is also good with spinach and whole wheat pasta.

Serves: 6; Preparation: 15 minutes; Cooking: 20 minutes; Level of difficulty: Simple

Put the garlic and oil in a large skillet (frying pan) and sauté over medium heat until the garlic is pale gold. § Add the basil and tomatoes. Season with salt and pepper, and simmer for about 15–20 minutes, or until the oil begins to separate from the tomato.

VARIATIONS
– Sauté 1 small onion, 1 carrot, 1 stalk celery, and 1 tablespoon parsley, all finely chopped, with the garlic.
– Add ½ teaspoon crushed chillies.
– Crumble 2 anchovy fillets into the sauce with the tomatoes.
– Add 1 tablespoon small salted capers.

■ INGREDIENTS

• 3 cloves garlic, finely chopped
• 4 tablespoons extra-virgin olive oil
• 2 tablespoons fresh basil leaves, torn
• 1½ lb (750 g) tomatoes, fresh or canned, peeled and chopped
• salt and freshly ground black pepper

Fresh tomato sauce
Salsa di pomodoro fresco

A simple sauce to serve in summer when tomatoes are tasty and abundant. It goes well with spaghetti, penne, fusilli, and many other dried pastas.

Serves: 4; Preparation: 10 minutes; Level of difficulty: Simple

Combine the tomatoes, garlic, oil, and basil in a bowl and season with salt and pepper. Mix well. § Set aside for about 15 minutes before tossing with the cooked pasta.

■ INGREDIENTS

• 1 lb (500 g) firm, ripe tomatoes, diced
• 1 clove garlic, finely chopped
• 4 tablespoons extra-virgin olive oil
• 12 fresh basil leaves, torn
• salt and freshly ground black pepper

Tomato and butter sauce
Salsa di burro e pomodoro

This sauce is delicious with all types of fresh pasta and gnocchi.

Serves: 4; Preparation: 10 minutes; Cooking: 30 minutes; Level of difficulty: Simple

Combine the garlic and onion in a skillet (frying pan) with the butter and oil. Sauté over medium heat until the onion is transparent. § Add the tomatoes and season with salt and pepper. Simmer over medium-low heat for about 25 minutes. Add the basil just before removing from heat.

VARIATION
– Stir 1 cup (250 ml) light (single) cream into the sauce after removing from heat for a *rosé* or pink sauce.

■ INGREDIENTS

• 1 clove garlic, finely chopped
• 1 onion, finely chopped
• 4 tablespoons butter
• 1 tablespoon extra-virgin olive oil
• 12 oz (350 g) tomatoes, fresh or canned, peeled and chopped
• 6 fresh basil leaves, torn
• salt and freshly ground black pepper

Right: *Salsa al pomodoro*

Bolognese meat sauce
Ragù di carne alla bolognese

The secret of a successful ragù lies in the cooking; it should be simmered over low heat for at least 2½ hours. It can be made ahead of time and kept in the refrigerator for up to 3 days, or frozen. Ragù is very versatile and can be served with most dried pasta shapes, with fresh, long pasta, such as tagliatelle, with many filled pasta dishes, and with potato and spinach gnocchi.

Serves: 6; Preparation: 30 minutes; Cooking: 3 hours; Level of difficulty: Simple

Combine the pancetta, onion, celery, and carrot in a sauté pan with the butter and cook over medium heat until the onion is light gold in color. § Add the beef, pork, and sausage and cook until the mixture is all the same color. Add the clove, cinnamon, and pepper. Stir in the tomatoes and continue to cook over medium heat for 15 minutes. § Add the milk and season with salt. Turn the heat down to low and simmer for at least 2½ hours, stirring from time to time.

■ INGREDIENTS

- 2 oz (60 g) pancetta, diced
- 1 medium onion, 1 stalk celery, 1 small carrot, all finely chopped
- 4 tablespoons butter
- 8 oz (250 g) ground beef
- 2 oz (60 g) ground pork
- 2 oz (60 g) Italian pork sausage, crumbled
- 1 clove, ground
- dash of cinnamon
- ¼ teaspoon freshly ground black pepper
- 14 oz (450 g) tomatoes, canned, peeled and chopped
- 1 cup (250 ml) whole (full cream) milk
- dash of salt

Tomato meat sauce
Ragù al pomodoro

This tomato ragù goes very well with any pasta and it is also perfect for simple or baked polenta (prepared with alternating layers of béchamel and grated or flaked cheese).

Serves: 4; Preparation: 10 minutes; Cooking: 2 hours; Level of difficulty: Simple

Melt the butter in a heavy-bottomed saucepan until it bubbles. Add the pancetta, onion, carrot, and celery and sauté over low heat for 10 minutes, stirring often. § Add the pork and veal or beef and cook for 5 minutes more, mixing well. § Add half the wine and, when it has partially evaporated, add a third of the stock. § Simmer until the liquid has reduced, then add the tomato paste and a little more wine and stock. § After 10–15 minutes, add the tomatoes, salt and pepper. § Continue cooking over low heat, gradually stirring in the remaining wine and stock. When cooked, the sauce should be fairly thick. This will take about 2 hours in all.

■ INGREDIENTS

- 4 tablespoons butter
- 2 oz (60 g) pancetta, diced
- 1 small onion, 1 small carrot, 1 stalk celery, all finely chopped
- 8 oz (250 g) ground veal or beef
- 3½ oz (100 g) lean ground pork
- 1 cup (250 ml) dry red wine
- 1¼ cups (300 ml) *Beef stock* (see recipe p. 48)
- 1 tablespoon tomato paste
- 12 oz (350 g) tomatoes, fresh or canned, peeled and chopped
- salt and freshly ground black pepper

Right: *Polenta con Ragù al pomodoro*

Italian mushroom sauce
Intingolo di funghi porcini

Fresh porcini mushrooms are hard to find outside of Italy and France but are widely available in their dried form. If you can't get fresh porcini, combine a small amount of soaked, dried porcini with fresh white mushrooms. The dried porcini have such a strong musky taste they will flavor the dish almost as well as the fresh ones. Mushroom sauce is very good with fresh pasta and also with long, dried pasta shapes. Try replacing the meat sauce in Lasagne al forno (see recipe p. 228) with 1 quantity of this sauce.

Serves: 4; Preparation: 15 minutes + time to soak the mushrooms; Cooking: 30 minutes; Level of difficulty: Simple

If you are using dried porcini, soak them in 1 cup (8 fl oz/250 ml) of warm water for about 20 minutes. Drain and squeeze out the excess water. Chop coarsely. § Put the garlic and rosemary in a large skillet (frying pan) with the butter and oil and sauté over medium heat for 4–5 minutes. Add the mushrooms and season with salt and pepper. Cover and cook over medium-low heat for about 20–25 minutes, or until the mushrooms are very tender.

■ INGREDIENTS

- 14 oz (450 g) fresh porcini mushrooms, coarsely chopped, or 12 oz (350 g) fresh white mushrooms and 1 oz (30 g) dried porcini)
- 2 cloves garlic, finely chopped
- sprig of fresh rosemary, finely chopped
- 2 tablespoons butter
- 4 tablespoons extra-virgin olive oil
- salt and freshly ground black pepper

Quick meat sauce
Sugo di carne veloce

Serves: 4; Preparation: 20 minutes; Cooking: 25 minutes; Level of difficulty: Simple

Soak the mushrooms in a bowl of tepid water for 20 minutes. Rinse well and chop coarsely. § Put the onion, garlic, pancetta, and oil in a skillet (frying pan) and sauté over medium heat until the onion is transparent. Add the sausage and sauté for 5 more minutes. § Add the tomatoes and mushrooms, season with salt and pepper, and simmer over medium-low heat for about 20 minutes, stirring frequently.

■ INGREDIENTS

- 1 oz (30 g) dried porcini mushrooms
- 1 large onion, finely chopped
- 1 clove garlic, finely chopped
- 2 oz (60 g) pancetta, diced
- 2 tablespoons extra-virgin olive oil
- 8 oz (250 g) Italian pork sausage, peeled and crumbled
- 14 oz (450 g) tomatoes, canned, peeled and chopped
- salt and freshly ground black pepper

Walnut sauce
Intingolo di noci

Walnut sauce is good with fresh pasta and potato gnocchi.

Serves: 4; Preparation: 20 minutes; Cooking: 15 minutes; Level of difficulty: Simple

Roast the pine nuts in the oven at 350°F/180°C/gas 4 for 5–10 minutes, or until they are light golden brown. Take them out and leave to cool. § Shell the walnuts and combine in a food processor with the pine nuts, garlic, parsley, and oil. Chop finely. Season with salt.

■ INGREDIENTS

- 1 lb (500 g) walnuts, in shell
- ⅓ cup (45 g) pine nuts
- 2 cloves garlic
- 1 cup (30 g) parsley
- ½ cup (125 ml) extra-virgin olive oil
- dash of salt

Right: *Intingolo di funghi porcini*

Onion and tomato sauce
Sugo di cipolla

If you like onions, this sauce is for you. Serve with fresh and dried pasta or on bread or toast.

Serves: 4; Preparation: 5 minutes; Cooking: 1¼ hours; Level of difficulty: Simple

Sauté the onions in the oil in a heavy-bottomed pan for 6–7 minutes. Add the pancetta and sauté for 5 minutes more. § Add the tomatoes and then the wine. Season with salt and pepper. Cover and cook over medium-low heat for about 1 hour, stirring from time to time.

■ INGREDIENTS

- 1¼ lb (600 g) white onions, sliced
- 4 tablespoons extra-virgin olive oil
- 3 oz (90 g) pancetta, diced
- 2 large tomatoes, diced
- ½ cup (125 ml) dry red wine
- salt and freshly ground black pepper

False meat sauce
Sugo finto

This light sauce is just as versatile as any meat sauce. Serve it hot with all pasta shapes. For an entirely vegetarian sauce, omit the pancetta and add 1 oz (30 g) of dried porcini mushrooms.

Serves: 4; Preparation: 15 minutes; Cooking: 35 minutes; Level of difficulty: Simple

Put the pancetta, parsley, onion, carrots, celery, and garlic in a skillet (frying pan) with the oil and butter. Cook over medium-high heat for 5 minutes. § Add the tomatoes and season with salt and pepper. § Simmer over medium-low heat for about 25 minutes.

■ INGREDIENTS

- 3 oz (90 g) pancetta, diced
- 1 cup (30 g) parsley, finely chopped
- 1 large onion, 2 carrots, 2 stalks celery, 2 cloves garlic, all finely chopped
- 2 tablespoons extra-virgin olive oil
- 4 tablespoons butter
- 2 large tomatoes, peeled and chopped
- salt and freshly ground black pepper

Fish sauce
Ragù di pesce

Many different sorts of fish will work in this sauce. Ask your fish vendor for fish that are suitable for making soup. Long, dried shapes, like spaghetti and spaghettini, are the classic choice of pasta. Short, dried pasta shapes, such as penne and macaroni, are also a good match.

Serves: 4; Preparation: 15 minutes; Cooking: 50 minutes; Level of difficulty: Medium

Place the fish in a pot with abundant water and the rosemary and bring to a boil. Cook for 15 minutes over medium-low heat. Take the fish out, remove the skin and bones, and crumble the cooked meat. Strain the liquid and reserve. Discard the rosemary leaves. § Sauté the onion and garlic in a large skillet (frying pan) with the oil until light gold in color. Add the fish meat and 3 cups (750 ml) of the reserved stock. Season with salt and pepper and simmer over low heat for about 30–35 minutes.

■ INGREDIENTS

- 1½ lb (750 g) assorted fresh fish, such as hake, sea bass, sea bream, and red snapper, gutted
- 2 tablespoons fresh rosemary leaves
- 1 onion, finely chopped
- 1 clove garlic, finely chopped
- ½ cup (125 ml) extra-virgin olive oil
- salt and freshly ground black pepper

Right: *Maccheroni al ragù di pesce*

Genoese basil sauce
Pesto alla genovese

Pesto comes from the Liguria region in northern Italy and is named for its capital city, Genoa. Traditionally it is served with trenette, a local egg-based pasta similar to fettuccine. It is also good with dried pasta, particularly the long shapes (spaghetti, spaghettini, linguine), and is delicious with potato gnocchi or instead of meat sauce in lasagne.

Serves: 4; Preparation: 10 minutes; Level of difficulty: Simple

Combine the basil, pine nuts, garlic, oil, and salt in a food processor and chop until smooth. Place the mixture in a large serving bowl and stir in the cheeses. § Add the water and butter and stir well.

■ INGREDIENTS
- 2 cups (60 g) fresh basil leaves
- 2 tablespoons pine nuts
- 1 clove garlic
- ½ cup (125 ml) extra-virgin olive oil
- dash of salt
- 2 tablespoons Parmesan cheese, freshly grated
- 2 tablespoons Pecorino cheese, freshly grated
- 2 tablespoons water from the pasta pot
- 1 tablespoon of butter for serving

Tuscan-style pesto
Pesto toscano

This recipe is an updated version of a sauce said to have been developed by the chefs of the Medici family in Florence in the 16th century. It can be served with most long and short dried pasta shapes.

Serves: 4; Preparation: 10 minutes; Level of difficulty: Simple

Put the walnuts, basil, and garlic in a food processor and chop to a cream. Transfer to a mixing bowl. § Remove the crust from the bread roll and soak the inside in the stock. Squeeze well and add to the walnut mixture. Add salt to taste, lemon juice, and oil (you may need slightly more or slightly less oil depending on how much the walnuts absorb), and mix well.

■ INGREDIENTS
- 20 walnuts, shelled
- 1 cup (30 g) fresh basil leaves
- 1 clove garlic
- 1 medium bread roll
- 1 cup (250 ml) *Beef stock* (see recipe p. 48)
- dash of salt
- juice of 1 lemon
- 2 tablespoons extra-virgin olive oil

Chicken liver sauce
Intingolo di fegatini

This sauce is very good with polenta and with all egg-based, fresh pasta. It can also be served on simple boiled rice. It is particularly good with Risotto bianco al parmigiano (see recipe p. 301).

Serves: 4; Preparation: 15 minutes; Cooking: 30 minutes; Level of difficulty: Simple

Heat the oil in a small skillet (frying pan) and sauté the onion, carrot, and celery over medium-low heat for 6–7 minutes. § Add the chicken livers and cook for 2–3 minutes. Season with salt and pepper. § Pour in the wine and after another 2–3 minutes, add the tomato paste diluted in ⅔ cup (150 ml) of water. Mix well, and add the peas. § Cook for another 15–20 minutes.

■ INGREDIENTS
- ⅓ cup (100 ml) extra-virgin olive oil
- 1 large onion, 1 large carrot, 1 stalk celery, all finely chopped
- 8 chicken livers, cleaned and coarsely chopped
- 4 tablespoons dry red or white wine
- 1 tablespoon tomato paste
- 4 oz (125 g) peas, shelled
- salt and freshly ground white pepper

Right: *Linguine al pesto toscano*

Béchamel sauce
Salsa besciamella

Béchamel sauce is used in many recipes. It is quick and easy to prepare.

Serves: 4; Preparation: 5 minutes; Cooking: 7-8 minutes; Level of difficulty: Simple

Heat the milk in a saucepan until it is almost boiling. § In a heavy-bottomed saucepan, melt the butter with the flour over low heat, stirring rapidly with a wooden spoon. Cook for about 1 minute. § Remove from heat and add half the hot milk, stirring constantly. Return to low heat and stir until the sauce starts to thicken. § Add the rest of the milk gradually and continue stirring until it comes to a boil. § Season with salt to taste and continue stirring until the béchamel is the right thickness. § If any lumps form, beat the sauce rapidly with a fork or whisk until they dissolve.

■ INGREDIENTS

- 2 cups (500 ml) milk
- 4 tablespoons butter
- ½ cup (75 g) all-purpose (plain) flour
- dash of salt

Butter and parmesan pasta sauce
Salsa di burro e parmigiano

This simple sauce is perfect with all kinds of dried and fresh pasta.

Serves: 4; Preparation: 5 minutes; Cooking: 5 minutes; Level of difficulty: Simple

Cook the pasta, drain well and transfer to a heated serving dish. § Add half the Parmesan until it melts creamily over the pasta. § Add the remaining cheese and the butter and toss until the butter has melted. Serve hot.

■ INGREDIENTS

- 1½ cups (150 g) Parmesan cheese, freshly grated
- ⅔ cup (150 g) butter

Butter and sage sauce
Salsa di burro e salvia

The clean taste of fresh sage melted in the butter combines well with pasta and many baked vegetables.

Serves: 4; Preparation: 5 minutes; Cooking: 5 minutes; Level of difficulty: Simple

Cook the butter and sage in a heavy-bottomed pan over very low heat until the butter turns light gold.

■ INGREDIENTS

- ½ cup (4 oz/125 g) butter
- 10 fresh sage leaves, torn

Butter and rosemary sauce
Salsa al burro e rosmarino

This sauce is particularly good with fresh and filled pasta.

Serves: 4; Preparation: 2 minutes; Cooking: 3-4 minutes; Level of difficulty: Simple

Combine the garlic, butter, and rosemary in a skillet (frying pan) over medium heat and cook for 3–4 minutes.

■ INGREDIENTS

- 2 cloves garlic, finely chopped
- ½ cup (125 g) butter
- 4 tablespoons fresh rosemary leaves, finely chopped

Right: *Salsa besciamella*

Mixed herb sauce
Salsa alle erbe aromatiche

Serves: 4; Preparation: 12 minutes; Level of difficulty: Simple

Shell the egg and chop it very finely. Place in a mixing bowl and add the parsley, tarragon, thyme, calamint, and garlic. § Mix well, then stir in the oil and vinegar, whisking to form a paste. If the mixture is too stiff, add a little more oil. § Season with salt and pepper and mix again. This sauce goes very well with poached fish.

■ INGREDIENTS

- 1 hard-cooked (hard-boiled) egg
- 2 tablespoons parsley, chopped
- 1 teaspoon each tarragon, thyme, calamint, chopped
- 1 clove garlic, chopped
- ⅔ cup (150 ml) extra-virgin olive oil
- 4 tablespoons white wine vinegar
- salt and freshly ground black pepper

Hot tomato sauce
Salsa piccante al pomodoro

This versatile sauce is particularly good with mixed boiled, braised, or grilled meats.

Serves: 8-10; Preparation: 5 minutes; Cooking: 1 hour; Level of difficulty: Simple

Heat the oil in a heavy-bottomed pan over low heat. § Add the garlic and tomatoes. Sprinkle with salt, add the chillies and cook, partially covered, for at least 1 hour. § Serve hot or at room temperature.

■ INGREDIENTS

- ⅓ cup (100 ml) extra-virgin olive oil
- 10 whole cloves garlic
- 1 lb (500 g) tomatoes, fresh or canned, peeled and chopped
- dash of salt
- 2 small hot chillies, dried or fresh, crumbled or sliced

Yogurt and tuna sauce
Salsa allo yogurt e tonno

Serves: 4; Preparation: 10 minutes; Level of difficulty: Simple

Place the yogurt, capers, tuna, salt, and pepper in a blender and mix until smooth. This very delicate sauce is good with any kind of steamed or poached fish.

■ INGREDIENTS

- 1 cup plain yogurt
- 1 oz (30 g) capers
- 3 ½ oz (100 g) tuna packed in oil
- salt and freshly ground black pepper

Butter and anchovy sauce
Salsa acciugata

This sauce is particularly good with fried lamb chops. It also makes an excellent pasta sauce.

Serves: 6-8; Preparation: 10 minutes; Cooking: 5 minutes; Level of difficulty: Simple

Place the anchovies in a heavy-bottomed pan over medium-low heat. Mash well with a fork. Add the butter and cook, mixing frequently until creamy. § Serve hot.

■ INGREDIENTS

- 10 salted anchovy fillets, crumbled
- ⅔ cup (150 g) butter

Right: *Salsa piccante al pomodoro*

Mayonnaise
Salsa maionese

Serves: 4; Preparation: 15-20 minutes; Level of difficulty: Medium

BY HAND: use a fork or hand whisk to beat the egg yolk in a bowl with the salt. § Add the oil a drop at a time at first, then in a steady drizzle, stirring all the time in the same direction. § When the mayonnaise begins to thicken, add, very gradually, the lemon juice (or vinegar), pepper, and a few more drops of oil until it is the right density. § If the mayonnaise curdles, start over again with another egg yolk and use the curdled mayonnaise in place of the oil.

IN THE BLENDER: use the same ingredients as above, except for the egg, which should be whole. § Place the egg, salt, pepper, 1–2 tablespoons of oil, and the lemon juice (or vinegar) in the blender and blend for a few seconds at maximum speed. § When the ingredients are well mixed, pour the remaining oil into the mixture very gradually. Blend until the right density is reached.

■ INGREDIENTS

- 1 fresh egg yolk
- dash of salt
- ⅔ cup (150 g) extra-virgin olive oil
- freshly ground black pepper
- 1 tablespoon lemon juice (or white vinegar)

Garlic mayonnaise
Agliata

This tasty sauce is perfect with all boiled meats and with many roast or braised ones too.

Serves: 4; Preparation: 15-20 minutes; Level of difficulty: Medium

Prepare the mayonnaise. Be sure to use lemon juice instead of white vinegar because it goes better with the garlic. § When the mayonnaise is ready, stir in the garlic, oil, and pepper. Leave to stand for at least 1 hour before serving.

■ INGREDIENTS

- 1 quantity mayonnaise, made with lemon juice (see recipe above)
- 2 cloves garlic, very finely chopped
- 1 tablespoon extra-virgin olive oil
- freshly ground black pepper

Cocktail sauce
Salsa cocktail

Serves: 4; Preparation: 5 minutes; Level of difficulty: Simple

Put the mayonnaise, ketchup, and Tabasco in a bowl and mix thoroughly. § Serve with most steamed or poached fish. § A few drops of lemon juice can be added to the sauce, if liked.

■ INGREDIENTS

- 1 quantity mayonnaise (see recipe above)
- ½ cup (125 ml) tomato ketchup (catsup)
- 3 drops Tabasco

VARIATION
– The amount of mayonnaise and ketchup can be adjusted to taste, depending on whether you want a strong pink color, or a lighter-colored sauce.

Right:
Salsa maionese

Tartare sauce
Salsa tartara

Serves: 4; Preparation: 5 minutes; Level of difficulty: Simple

Place the mayonnaise, mustard, gherkins, and cocktail onions in a blender or food processor and blend until smooth. § Serve with steamed or poached fish.

■ INGREDIENTS

• 1 quantity *Mayonnaise* (see recipe p. 42)
• 1 teaspoon mustard
• 3 small pickled gherkins
• 4 cocktail onions

Black olive sauce
Salsa alle olive nere

Serves: 4; Preparation: 10 minutes; Level of difficulty: Simple

Shell the egg, cut it in half, and remove the yolk. Put the yolk in a small bowl. § In another small bowl, combine the olives, parsley, capers, and garlic and mix well. Add the egg yolk, vinegar, salt, and pepper and mix until creamy. § Serve with any kind of steamed or poached fish.

■ INGREDIENTS

• 1 hard-cooked (hard-boiled) egg yolk
• 6 black olives, pitted and chopped
• 3 tablespoons parsley, finely chopped
• 1 teaspoon capers, finely chopped
• 1 clove garlic, chopped
• ½ teaspoon vinegar
• salt and freshly ground black pepper

Anchovy sauce
Salsa all'acciuga

Serves: 4; Preparation: 10 minutes; Level of difficulty: Simple

Place the anchovies in a small bowl and mash with a fork. Add the capers and gherkin and mix well. § Stir in the stock. § Serve with poached fish.

■ INGREDIENTS

• 8 anchovy fillets
• 1 tablespoon capers, chopped
• 1 pickled gherkin, chopped
• 4 tablespoons vegetable stock, fresh or from a stock cube

Parsley sauce with capers, anchovies, garlic, and oil
Salsa verde

This sauce is traditionally served with boiled meats.
It is also very good with thinly-sliced, fried or braised meats.

Serves: 4; Preparation: 15 minutes; Level of difficulty: Simple

Place all the ingredients in a food processor and blend. Salt should not be necessary because of salt in the anchovies. § Serve at room temperature.

■ INGREDIENTS

• 1 cup (30 g) fresh parsley
• 2 tablespoons capers
• 2 anchovy fillets
• 1 clove garlic
• ½ cup (30 g) bread crumbs soaked in 2 tablespoons vinegar and squeezed thoroughly
• ½ cup (125 ml) extra-virgin olive oil

Right: Salsa verde

Mustard sauce
Salsa mostarda

This sauce is typical of many regions of northern Italy where it is served with mixed, boiled meats. It also goes well with roast meats. The most famous version comes from Cremona. Leftover mustard sauce can be stored in sealed jars.

Serves: 12 (or more); Preparation: 15 minutes; Cooking: 1 hour; Level of difficulty: Medium

Wash and peel the fruit. Cut into fairly large pieces, leaving the grapes and cherries whole. § Put the fruit in a heavy-bottomed saucepan and cover with water. Place over medium heat. § Peel the lemon. Chop the rind coarsely and squeeze the juice. Add to the pan with 2 tablespoons of honey. § In a separate saucepan, simmer the wine with the remaining honey over medium-low heat. § After 10 minutes add the mustard to the wine and honey. Stir thoroughly and cook until thick. § Pour the mustard and wine mixture over the fruit and mix carefully. § Serve at room temperature.

■ INGREDIENTS

- 2 lb (1 kg) mixed fruit (white grapes, apples, pears, apricots, cherries, etc.)
- 1 lemon, juice and peel
- ½ cup (125 ml) liquid honey
- 1⅓ cup (350 ml) dry white wine
- ⅓ cup (40 g) mustard powder

Vinaigrette (Salad dressing)
Salsa vinaigrette

Serves: 4; Preparation: 10 minutes; Level of difficulty: Simple

Put the vinegar in a bowl and dissolve the salt in it. § Add the oil and pepper and beat with a whisk or fork to emulsify.

■ INGREDIENTS

- 1 tablespoon vinegar
- dash of salt
- 3 tablespoons extra-virgin olive oil
- 3 dashes freshly ground black pepper

Onion sauce
Salsa alle cipolle

This sauce is very simple to prepare, but takes a long time to cook. Make a double quantity and freeze half. Onion sauce goes well with boiled and roast meats, and makes an excellent pasta sauce.

Serves: 4; Preparation: 15 minutes; Cooking: 3 hours; Level of difficulty: Simple

Place the onions in a heavy-bottomed pan with the oil over low heat. § Season with a little salt (use less than you normally would because the very slow cooking enhances the taste of the salt). Add a grinding of pepper and cover. § Cook gently over low heat for at least 3 hours. The onions must not burn, but should slowly melt. Stir frequently, adding stock, if necessary, to keep the sauce moist. § When cooked, the sauce should be creamy and golden.

■ INGREDIENTS

- 4 large white onions, very thinly sliced
- 5 tablespoons extra-virgin olive oil
- salt and freshly ground black pepper
- ¾ cup (200 ml) *Beef stock* (see recipe p. 48)

Right:
Salsa mostarda

Beef stock
Brodo di carne

Homemade beef stock is used as the basis for many soups, to serve filled pasta such as tortellini and agnolotti, and to flavor a wide range of other pasta and risotto dishes. It can be made ahead of time and kept in the refrigerator for up to 3 days or frozen.

Makes: about 2 quarts (2 liters); Preparation: 15 minutes; Cooking: 3 hours; Level of difficulty: Simple

Put the meat, vegetables, herbs, salt, and pepper in a large pot with the water. Cover and bring to a boil over medium heat. Simmer over low heat for 3 hours. Skim the foam off the top at intervals so that the stock will be light and fresh to taste. § Remove from heat and leave to cool. When the stock is cool, a layer of fat will form on the top. This should be skimmed off.

■ INGREDIENTS

- 2 lb (1 kg) beef
- 2 lb (1 kg) meat bones
- 1 carrot
- 1 onion
- 1 stalk celery
- 1 whole clove
- 1 bay leaf
- 1 clove garlic
- 5 sprigs parsley
- 1 leek
- 1 ripe tomato
- salt and freshly ground black pepper
- 2½ quarts (2.5 liters) water

Fish stock
Brodo di pesce

Fish stock makes a delicious change from beef stock as the basis for pasta soups.

Makes: about 1¼ quarts (1.2 liters); Preparation: 15 minutes; Cooking: 1¼ hours; Level of difficulty: Simple

Put the fish, vegetables, and herbs in a large pot with the water. Bring to a boil. § Cover and leave to simmer over low heat for 1 hour. Season with salt and simmer for 15 more minutes.

■ INGREDIENTS

- 1¼ lb (600 g) assorted fresh fish (such as hake, sea bass, sea bream, and red snapper), cleaned and gutted
- 2 stalks celery
- 1 carrot
- 1 medium onion
- 2 cloves garlic
- 2 ripe tomatoes
- 1 tablespoon parsley
- 1½ quarts (1.5 liters) water
- dash of salt

Vegetable stock
Brodo di verdure

Vegetable stock is an essential ingredient in many soups and risotti. Vegetarians can use it in recipes that call for chicken or beef stock. For a completely fat-free stock, omit the butter and put all the ingredients together in the lightly salted water, and simmer for about 1 hour.

Makes: 3½ quarts (3.5 liters); Preparation: 15 minutes; Cooking: 1¼ hours; Level of difficulty: Simple

Melt the butter in a fairly large pot and add the vegetables. Cover and simmer over low heat for 10 minutes, stirring occasionally. § Add the parsley, peppercorns, cloves, bay leaf, and season with salt. § Add the water and simmer for 1 hour over low heat, skimming off the foam occasionally. § Strain the stock, discarding the vegetables.

■ INGREDIENTS

- 4 tablespoons butter
- 2 onions, 2 carrots, 1 leek, 2 stalks celery with leaves, cut in 4 pieces
- 3 tomatoes, cut in half
- 6 sprigs parsley
- 8 black peppercorns
- 1 clove
- 1 bay leaf (optional)
- dash of salt
- 4 quarts (4 liters) cold water

Right:
Minestrina in brodo

Chicken stock
Brodo di pollo

The tastiest chicken stock is made with free-range chickens; unfortunately they are not easy to find nowadays. Soup chickens do still exist however, even if battery-raised. Once again, it pays to make a large amount of stock and freeze it in small quantities to be used as needed. The chicken can be served hot or cold with a favorite sauce, or in chicken aspic, or salad.

Makes: about 2½ quarts (2.5 liters); Preparation: 10 minutes; Cooking: 3 hours; Level of difficulty: Simple

Put the chicken, whole, in a very large pot. Add the celery, carrots, onion, salt and peppercorns. Cover with the cold water and simmer for 3 hours over medium-low heat. The water should barely move. § Strain the stock, discarding the vegetables. § To remove the fat, in part or completely, let the stock cool, then refrigerate for about 2 hours. The fat will solidify on the top and can easily be lifted off.

■ INGREDIENTS

- 1 chicken, cleaned, about 4 lb (2 kg)
- 2 stalks celery with leaves, washed and broken into 3 pieces
- 2 medium carrots, scraped and cut in half
- 1 large onion, stuck with 2 cloves (optional)
- dash of salt
- 4 black peppercorns
- 4 quarts (4 liters) cold water

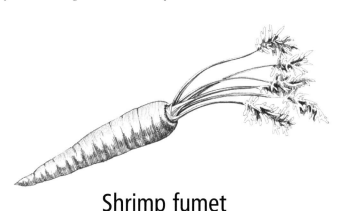

Shrimp fumet
Fumetto di crostacei

Makes: about 1 quart (2 pints/1 liter); Preparation: 15 minutes; Cooking: 50 minutes; Level of difficulty: Medium

Heat the oil in a large pan over medium heat and sauté the onion, carrot, and celery for 4 minutes. § Add the white wine and cook until it evaporates. § Add the shrimp trimmings, cook for 2 minutes then stir in the tomato purée and add the parsley, bay leaf, and peppercorns. § Pour in the water, partially cover, and bring to a boil. Lower the heat to medium and boil for 40 minutes. § Remove from heat and sieve the stock, pressing down on the shells.

■ INGREDIENTS

- 4 tablespoons extra-virgin olive oil
- 1 onion, coarsely chopped
- 1 carrot, coarsely chopped
- 1 stalk celery, coarsely chopped
- ½ cup (125 ml) dry white wine
- 8 oz (250 g) shrimp trimmings (shells and heads)
- 3 tablespoons tomato paste
- 1 bunch parsley
- 1 bay leaf
- 6 peppercorns
- 1½ quarts (1.5 liters) water
- handful of coarse sea salt

VARIATION
– To clarify the shellfish fumet, whisk in 3 egg whites to form a filter which will draw all the impurities, leaving the stock clear: the stock will taste even better the next day; it will keep, covered, in the refrigerator, for up to 2 days.

Right: *Brodo di pollo*

Basic polenta
Polenta

Serves: 4; Preparation: 5 minutes; Cooking: 50-60 minutes; Level of difficulty: Medium

Bring the salted water to a boil in a heavy-bottomed pot large enough to hold 4 quarts (4 liters). § Add the cornmeal gradually, stirring continuously and rapidly with a whisk so that no lumps form. § To cook, stir the polenta over high heat by moving a long, wooden spoon in a circular motion. At a certain point the polenta will begin to withdraw from the sides of the pot on which a thin crust is forming. § The polenta should be stirred almost continuously for the 50–60 minutes it takes to cook. § Quantities and method are the same when using an electric polenta cauldron. Stir the cornmeal into the boiling water gradually, then turn on the mixer. Leave for 50–60 minutes. § Serve hot or cold as suggested in the recipes.

■ INGREDIENTS

- 2½ quarts (2.5 liters) water
- 2 tablespoons coarse sea salt
- 3½ cups (450 g) coarse-grain yellow cornmeal

Fried polenta
Crostini di polenta

In Italy Crostini di polenta are usually made with polenta leftover from the day before. Prepare the polenta at least 12 hours before serving; it needs time to become firm before frying.

Serves: 8-12; Preparation 5 minutes + 12 hours to rest; Cooking: 50-60 minutes; Level of difficulty: Medium

Prepare the polenta. § Spread out on a cutting board to a thickness of about 2 in (5 cm), cover with a damp cloth, and let cool. § Cut into slices about ½-in (1-cm) thick. § Fry the polenta slices a few at a time in the hot oil for 6–8 minutes, or until golden brown on both sides. § Serve as is or spread with a topping.

■ INGREDIENTS

- 1 quantity basic polenta (see recipe above)
- 2 cups (500 ml) oil, for frying

White polenta
Polenta bianca

This polenta, typical of Veneto and Friuli in the northeast, is made with white cornmeal in exactly the same way as yellow cornmeal polenta.

Serves: 4; Preparation: 5 minutes; Cooking: 50-60 minutes; Level of difficulty: Medium

Prepare the polenta following the method for Basic polenta. § Spread out on a cutting board to a thickness of about 2 in (5 cm), cover with a damp cloth, and let cool. § Cut into slices about ½-in (1-cm) thick and roast on a charcoal grill or in a sizzling grill pan. § The slices can also be fried in oil or lard. § Serve hot or cold.

■ INGREDIENTS

- 2½ quarts (2.5 liters) water
- 2 tablespoons coarse sea salt
- 3 cups (350 g) white cornmeal

Right: *Polenta and crostini di polenta*

Toasted bread with garlic, salt, and oil
Bruschetta alla romana

■ INGREDIENTS

- 4 large, thick slices of white, unsalted bread
- 2 cloves garlic
- salt and freshly ground black pepper
- 4 tablespoons extra-virgin olive oil

Bruschetta is a classic Roman appetizer, although many regions of Italy have similar dishes. It is difficult to recreate the authentic taste abroad because Roman bread is white, very compact, and unsalted. Choose bread that is not too fresh; yesterday's leftover loaf is best. Toast in the oven or under the broiler (or over a barbecue or open fire), rather than in the toaster. This will dry it out to just the right point.

Serves: 4; Preparation: 5 minutes; Cooking: 10 minutes; Level of difficulty: Simple

Toast the bread until golden brown on both sides. § Rub each slice with the garlic, sprinkle with salt and pepper, and drizzle with oil. § Serve hot.

Batter
Pastella per friggere

■ INGREDIENTS

- 1 cup (150 g) all-purpose (plain) flour
- 1 egg, separated
- 1 tablespoon extra-virgin olive oil
- dash of salt
- cold water

Serves 4; Preparation: 45 minutes; Level of difficulty: Simple

Sift the flour into a bowl, make a hole at the center and add the egg yolk. § Add the oil and salt and stir in the water a little at a time to obtain a thick but fluid batter without lumps. Set aside for 30–40 minutes. § Just before frying, stir the batter well, beat the egg white until stiff and fold it gently into the batter.

Potato gnocchi
Gnocchi di patate

■ INGREDIENTS

- 1½ lb (750 g) boiling potatoes
- 2 eggs
- 2⅔ cups (250 g) all-purpose (plain) flour

Potato gnocchi are a simple mixture of boiled, mashed potatoes, eggs, and flour. The choice of potato is important. Don't use new potatoes or baking potatoes; the humble boiling potato is best. Potato gnocchi can be served with a wide variety of pasta sauces.

Serves: 6; Preparation: 20 minutes; Cooking: 35 minutes; Level of difficulty: Medium

Cook the potatoes in their skins in a pot of salted, boiling water until tender. Drain and peel while still hot. Mash until smooth. § Place in a bowl and add the eggs and most of the flour. Stir, adding more flour as required, until the mixture is soft and smooth, but just slightly sticky. The amount of flour will depend on how much the potatoes absorb, so don't add it all at once. § Dust a work surface with flour, take a piece of the dough and roll it into a long sausage about ¾ in (2 cm) in diameter. Cut into pieces about 1 in (2.5 cm) in length. Repeat until all the dough has been made into gnocchi. § Set a large pot of salted water to boil. The gnocchi should be cooked in batches. Lower the first batch (20–24 gnocchi) gently into the boiling water. After a few minutes they will rise to the top. Leave them to bob about for 1–2 minutes, then scoop them out with a slotted spoon. Place on a heated serving dish. Repeat until all the gnocchi are cooked.

Right:
A selection of common Italian breads, many of which can be used to make crostini or bruschetta. Note the bruschetta in the foreground with garlic cloves on top.

Boat-shaped pastries
Barchette

Barchette in Italian means "little boats" and refers to the shape of the molds traditionally used to prepare these little savory pastries. Freshly baked, they are delicious with all sorts of toppings and sauces. If you don't have boat-shaped molds on hand, use any small cake or other molds you have in the kitchen.

Serves: 4-6; Preparation: 15 minutes + 30 minutes to rest; Cooking: 15 minutes; Level of difficulty: Simple

Sift the flour onto a clean work surface, and work the butter into the flour with your fingertips until the mixture is the same texture as a coarse meal. § Make a well in the center and add the water and salt. Mix until you have a rather soft dough. § Form a ball, wrap in plastic wrap, and set aside in a cool place for 30 minutes. § Flour the work surface, then roll the dough out using a floured rolling pin to about ⅛ in (3 mm) thick. § Line the molds with the dough and prick the bottom with a fork. Cover with pieces of plastic wrap and fill with dried beans. § Bake the barchette in a preheated oven at 350°F/180°C/gas 4 for *12–15* minutes. § Invert the molds, remove the waxed paper and beans, and set the barchette aside to cool. Use as indicated in the recipes.

■ INGREDIENTS

• 2 cups (300 g) all-purpose (plain) flour
• ⅔ cup (150 g) butter
• 3 tablespoons cold water
• ½ teaspoon salt
• 1 lb (500 g) dried beans

Puff pastry
Pasta sfoglia

If this pastry is being used for a sweet dessert, dissolve a dash of sugar in the water.

Serves: 4-6; Preparation: 50 minutes + 30 minutes to rest; Level of difficulty: Complicated

Sift the flour and salt in a mound on a clean work surface, make a well in the center, and pour about half the water into it. Using your hands, mix until the dough is about the same consistency as the softened butter. Add flour or water to achieve the required consistency. § Roll the dough into a ball, wrap in plastic wrap and set aside for 30 minutes. § Use a rolling pin to roll the dough out on a floured work surface into a square shape until about ½ in (1 cm) thick. § Cut the softened butter in pieces and place them at the center of the square. Fold the 4 sides of the square so that the butter is completely sealed in, and roll the dough out in a rectangular shape about ½ in (1 cm) thick. § Fold the rectangle in 3, turn the folded dough, and roll it out again. Fold it again and let stand for about 10 minutes. § Repeat this operation 3 times, letting the dough rest each time for 10 minutes. § Roll out to ¼ in (1 cm) thickness and use as indicated.

■ INGREDIENTS

• 2 cups (300 g) all-purpose (plain) flour
• dash of salt
• about 1 cup (250 ml) water
• 1 cup (250 g) butter, softened
• dash of sugar (optional)

Right: *Barchette*

Plain pastry

Makes: pastry to line and cover a 10-in (25-cm) pan; Preparation: 10 minutes + 30 minutes to chill

Combine the flour in a large bowl with the salt. Make a hollow in the center and fill with the egg, butter, and water. Mix the ingredients with a fork, mashing the butter as you work. § After 2–3 minutes the dough will have absorbed almost all the flour. It should be quite crumbly. § Transfer to a lightly floured work surface and shape into a soft compact ball, kneading as little as possible. § Place in a springform pan or pie plate and flatten a little. Using the heels of your palms and your fingertips, spread the dough so that it covers the base of the pan and three-quarters of the sides evenly. Use a fork to shape the sides and bring to the same height. § Cover with plastic wrap and chill in the refrigerator for at least 30 minutes. § This pastry can be prepared a few hours ahead, or even the day before.

■ INGREDIENTS

- 2 cups (8 oz/300 g) all-purpose (plain) flour
- 2 teaspoons salt
- 1 egg yolk
- ½ cup (125 g) butter, at room temperature, thinly sliced
- 2 tablespoons water

Ricotta pastry

Makes: pastry to line and cover a 10-in (25-cm) pan; Preparation: 10 minutes + 30 minutes to chill

Proceed as explained for plain pastry (above). Add the Ricotta when the flour and butter are almost mixed.

■ INGREDIENTS

- 1½ cups (225 g) all-purpose (plain) flour
- 2 level teaspoons salt
- ½ cup (125 g) butter
- ⅓ cup (100 g) soft Ricotta cheese

Special pastry

Pasta matta

Makes: pastry to line and cover a 10-in (25-cm) pan; Preparation: 15 minutes + 30 minutes to chill

Combine the flour in a large bowl with the salt. Make a hollow in the center and fill with the butter and water. Mix the ingredients with a fork, mashing the butter as you work. § When the ingredients are roughly mixed, transfer to a lightly floured work surface and knead until the dough is soft, smooth, and elastic. § Flatten the dough with a rolling pin and shape it into a rectangle. Fold the shorter sides of the rectangle inward, one over the other. Roll the dough into another rectangle, working in the opposite direction to the folds. Fold the shorter sides of the rectangle inward again. Repeat the two steps once more. § Roll the dough into a rectangle or circle, depending on the pan or pie plate you are using. The dough should be about ¼ in (½ cm) thick. § Line the base and sides of the pan or pie plate, cover with plastic wrap and chill in the refrigerator for at least 30 minutes.

■ INGREDIENTS

- 2 cups (300 g) all-purpose (plain) flour
- 2 teaspoons salt
- 4 tablespoons butter, at room temperature, thinly sliced
- ⅓ cup (100 ml) cold water

Right: *Ricotta pastry*

Sweet plain pastry
Pasta frolla

This crumbly, melt-in-the-mouth pastry is used as a base for many pies. It is easy to make, but there are one or two things to bear in mind. Firstly, although the dough must be well-mixed, it should not be kneaded for too long or it will become tough. Work quickly when kneading. You may prefer to divide the mixture into half and knead separately. Remember, too, that this pastry improves with time, so it is best made a day ahead.

Makes: pastry to line and cover a 10-in (25-cm) pan; Preparation: 10 minutes + 30 minutes to chill; Cooking: 30 minutes; Level of difficulty: Simple

Combine the flour with the sugar and salt and add the lemon zest, if using. § Transfer to a floured work surface and shape into a mound. Make a well in the center and drop the butter into it. § Knead the mixture as quickly as possible with your fingertips to obtain a mixture resembling fine bread crumbs. § Shape the mixture into a mound, make a well in the center and drop the egg yolks into it. Knead until smooth, then shape into a ball. Wrap the dough with plastic wrap and chill in the refrigerator for at least 30 minutes. § Roll out the dough and place in a buttered and floured springform pan. Prick the base all over with a fork to prevent air bubbles forming. § At this point, depending on the recipe, the dough can either be covered with a filling and cooked or baked "blind." If baking blind, cover the dough with a sheet of nonstick baking paper and sprinkle with dry beans or peas to stop the pastry from rising during cooking. Bake in a preheated oven at 350°F/180°C/gas mark 4 for about 30 minutes.

■ INGREDIENTS

- 2 cups (300 g) all-purpose (plain) flour
- ½ cup (100 g) sugar
- dash of salt
- dash of grated lemon rind, yellow part only (optional)
- ½ cup (125 g) butter, chopped into small pieces
- 2 egg yolks

Short crust pastry
Pasta brisé

This pastry is similar to the one above, except that it contains no egg. It is mainly used without sugar for savories.

Makes: enough pastry to line and cover a 10-in (25-cm) pan; Preparation: 20 minutes + 30 minutes to chill; Cooking: 20 minutes; Level of difficulty: Simple

Pour the sifted flour, salt, and sugar onto a clean work surface. Make a well in center of the flour and fill with the butter. Work the mixture with rapid movements of the balls of the thumbs until it is the consistency of coarse sand. § Shape this mixture into a mound, make a well in the center, and fill with the water. Work the water into the butter and flour. Shape the dough into a ball, wrap in plastic wrap, and chill in the refrigerator. Use as directed in the recipes, or freeze for later use.

■ INGREDIENTS

- 2 cups (300 g) all-purpose (plain) flour
- dash of salt
- 1 tablespoon sugar (optional)
- ½ cup (125 g) butter, cut in small pieces
- about ½ cup (125 ml) warm water

Right: *Pasta frolla*

Crêpes
Crespelle

*Crêpes are small pancakes made with milk, egg, and flour. They are never eaten
on their own but are used as the basis for countless sweet and savory recipes.*

*Makes: 10-12 crêpes; Preparation: 10 minutes + 2 hours to rest; Cooking: 30 minutes; Level of difficulty:
Simple*

Beat the eggs, sugar, and salt with the sifted flour. § Pour in the milk
gradually, followed by the melted butter. Beat the batter until smooth
then set aside to rest for 2 hours. § Brush a small, heated skillet (frying
pan) with the remaining butter, and add a small ladleful of batter.
Spread evenly by tipping the pan, so that it forms a thin film. Cook the
crêpe on both sides, taking care not to let it color too much. When the
edges curl slightly, it is done. § If not using immediately, crêpes can be stored in
the refrigerator, piled one on top of the other in a covered container.

VARIATIONS
– Flavor the batter with two tablespoonfuls of rum or cognac.
– Other types of flour can also be used in the making of crêpes,
such as buckwheat or whole-meal.

■ INGREDIENTS

- 2 eggs
- 1 teaspoon sugar
- dash of salt
- 1 cup (150 g) all-purpose
  (plain) flour
- 1 cup (250 ml) milk
- 1½ tablespoons butter,
  melted, plus 1 teaspoon
  butter, at room
  temperature, to grease
  the pan

Italian sponge cake
Pan di spagna

*This recipe dates back to the 17th century. As the Italian name implies,
this sponge cake was introduced to Italy by the Spaniards. In addition to its use
in layer cakes and puddings, it can also be sliced and toasted for breakfast.*

Serves: 6; Preparation: 30 minutes; Cooking: 40 minutes; Level of difficulty: Medium

Place the eggs and sugar in the top part of a double boiler and whisk
until frothy. § Remove from heat and add the lemon zest (yellow part
only) and continue to whisk until cool. § Fold in the sifted flours and
salt gently, using slow movements and keeping the blade of the spatula
pointing downward. Pour the dough into a greased, floured 10-in (25-
cm) springform pan and bake in a preheated oven at 325°F/160°C/gas 3
oven for 40 minutes.

VARIATIONS
– Whisk the eggs in the top half of a double-boiler. The heat will
make them coagulate slightly, thus providing a better base for the
flour and making it easier for the dough to rise.
– Sponge cake can be flavored to taste with vanilla extract (essence).

■ INGREDIENTS

- 6 eggs
- ¾ cup (150 g) sugar
- 2 teaspoons grated lemon
  zest
- ¾ cup (100 g) all-purpose
  (plain) flour
- dash of salt
- ½ cup (75 g) potato
  starch (potato flour)

Right: *Preparing crêpes*

Sugar syrup
Caramello

Sugar syrup is not difficult to make, although it does require extreme care. To prepare the syrup, you will need a heavy-bottomed saucepan, preferably one made of thick-gauge copper, as this ensures even cooking. Do not use a tin-plated saucepan; sugar melts at a very high temperature and may cause the tin to melt. Professional confectioners measure the degree to which sugar is cooked by using a Baumé scale or a candy thermometer. We have suggested a series of "stages," to be used in home cooking.

Put three parts sugar and one of water in a heavy-bottomed pan and add a few drops of lemon juice to prevent crystallization. Place the saucepan over medium heat, and when the liquid starts to boil, use a moistened pastry brush to remove the froth that will form at the sides. Never stir the liquid, as the cold spoon would cause the sugar to crystallize. § As soon as a thick layer of bubbles starts to form, the sugar will pass through the following stages, from which it is possible to tell how far it is cooked: Glazing: this is the initial stage. At this point, if you dip a spatula into the liquid it will be coated with a thin film of syrup. Thin thread: if you take a little sugar between two fingers it forms a fine thread that breaks easily. Strong thread: as above but the thread is stronger. Feathery: if you remove a little of the sugar from the pan with a perforated spoon and blow through it, bubbles form. Soft ball: if you dip a little of the sugar in cold water and hold it between two fingers it forms a soft elastic ball. Firm ball: a firmer ball forms than at the previous stage. Soft crack: the ball will stick to your teeth if you bite it, but doesn't snap or break. Hard crack or caramel: a breakable ball forms, and the sugar is amber-colored.

Whipped cream
Panna montata

Whipped cream is easy to prepare. It is widely used in confectionery for cake decoration, filling for meringues and small items of confectionery, and as a garnish for fruit based preparations. It is also an ingredient in complicated jellycreams, or quite simply used to top a cup of hot chocolate.

Serves: 6; Preparation: 5-10 minutes; Level of difficulty: Simple

Place the cream in a mixing bowl. Both the cream and the bowl should be well-chilled. Use a large bowl, since cream doubles in bulk as it fills with air. § If using an electric whisk, add the sugar first, and begin beating slowly at first, increasing the speed after a few minutes, until the cream is stiff. If using a hand-whisk, carefully add the sugar at the end. § Do not overbeat because the cream will turn into butter. Whipped cream should always be used immediately, as it tends to collapse and separate very quickly.

■ INGREDIENTS

- 2 cups (500 ml) heavy (double) cream
- 4 tablespoons confectioners' (icing) sugar

Right:
Caramello

Meringue
Meringa

Meringue is made of egg whites whisked as stiffly as possible and mixed with confectioners' (icing) sugar. Meringue can be used to decorate cakes and pies, or cooked and served as individual meringues. A meringue is defined as light if the weight of the sugar is double that of the egg whites, or heavy if the weight of the sugar is three times that of the egg whites. It is very important to ensure that no trace of yolk remains in the egg whites. There are two basic methods of making meringues.

Makes: 12 meringues; Preparation: 20 minutes; Cooking: 50-60 minutes; Level of difficulty: Medium

RAW OR COLD METHOD. Add the salt to the egg whites and begin beating them with the electric whisk. §When they begin to stiffen, gradually stir in half the confectioners' sugar. Decrease the speed of the whisk, and gradually add the rest of the sugar. Continue whisking until the mixture is extremely stiff. § Place the mixture in a piping-bag with a plain or fluted nozzle. Line a baking sheet with parchment paper and squeeze out lumps of the mixture, leaving about 2 in (4 cm) between them. § Sprinkle with superfine sugar and bake in a preheated oven at 250°F/120°C/gas 1 for about 50 minutes. § Baking meringues is a delicate operation. They must dry out without turning brown, so it is a good idea to leave the oven door ajar while they are baking.

HOT MERINGUE MIXTURE. The ingredients and method are the same as for the above recipe, but the egg whites and sugar are combined in a double-boiler and whisked over warm water until very frothy.

■ INGREDIENTS

- dash of salt
- 3 egg whites
- 1½ cups (225 g) confectioners' (icing) sugar
- superfine (caster) sugar, for sprinkling on the meringue

Custard
Crema inglese

Egg custard is the simplest of the creamy, egg-based creams used in confectionery. The classic recipe consists of eggs, sugar, and milk. This recipe includes potato starch, which will prevent the custard from curdling. If preferred, use vanilla extract (essence) instead of the vanilla bean.

Makes about 2 cups (500 ml) custard; Preparation: 10 minutes; Cooking: 10 minutes; Level of difficulty: Simple

Boil the milk with the vanilla bean. § Leave to infuse then remove the bean. § Whisk the egg yolks and sugar until frothy. Stir in the potato starch, then gradually add the milk, stirring constantly. § Heat the mixture in the top of a double-boiler over very low heat until thick. Cool quickly in a small bowl over a larger bowl filled with ice and salt.

■ INGREDIENTS

- 2 cups (500 ml) milk
- 1 vanilla bean
- 5 egg yolks
- ⅓ cup (80 g) sugar
- 1 teaspoon potato starch (potato flour)

VARIATION
– The milk may be flavored with lemon rind instead of vanilla.

Right: *Meringa*

Vanilla pastry cream
Crema pasticcera

This is another basic recipe used in confectionery to make desserts and fillings. There are numerous variations of the main ingredients and a variety of liqueurs and other flavorings can be added.

Makes: approximately 2 cups (500 ml) custard; Preparation: 10 minutes; Cooking: 10 minutes; Level of difficulty: Simple

Whisk the egg yolks and sugar until very pale and creamy. Stir in the flour. § Bring the milk to the boil, then remove from heat. § Stir the egg and flour mixture into the milk, then cook over very low heat, stirring constantly to prevent the mixture from becoming lumpy. § When thick, add the vanilla extract, and pour into a bowl. Cover with a layer of plastic wrap so that it touches the surface, to prevent a skin from forming.

> VARIATIONS
> — To make chocolate pastry cream, melt 4 oz (100 g) of grated bittersweet (baking) chocolate in the milk and omit the salt.
> — To make lemon pastry cream, boil the rind of a lemon in the milk.
> — To make hazelnut or almond pastry cream, add 2 tablespoons of ground hazelnuts or almonds to the cream while still hot.
> — To make liqueur pastry cream, add one or two tablespoons of rum, cognac, or other liqueur to the cream while still hot.

■ INGREDIENTS

• 5 egg yolks
• ¾ cup (150 g) sugar
• ⅓ cup (50 g) all-purpose (plain) flour
• 2 cups (500 ml) milk
• dash of salt
• 2-3 drops vanilla extract (essence)

Zabaione
Zabaglione

Zabaglione is similar to custard, but the milk is replaced by a dry Marsala wine. The recipe is popular all over Italy. Zabaglione probably derives its name from San Pasquale Baylon, patron saint of the confectioners of Turin, who dedicated this exquisite preparation to him in the 18th century. However, it appears to have been known to the Court of the Gonzaga family of Mantua as long ago as the second half of the 17th century. Zabaglione can be eaten hot or cold, served in a bowl by itself or with fruit or cookies, or else used as a filling for cakes and fritters.

Serves: 4; Preparation: 15 minutes; Cooking: 10 minutes; Level of difficulty: Simple

Put the egg yolks and sugar in a heavy-bottomed saucepan and whisk until pale and creamy. § Add the Marsala gradually, still beating, then place the saucepan in a larger pan of hot water over very low heat (or use a double-boiler). Cook, beating all the time with the whisk, until the mixture thickens. Keep the heat very low and never let the zabaione boil or it will curdle. § If serving cold, cover with a layer of plastic wrap so that it touches the surface, to prevent a skin from forming as the mixture cools.

■ INGREDIENTS

• 4 egg yolks
• 4 tablespoons sugar
• ½ cup (125 ml) dry Marsala

Right: *Crema pasticcera*

Vegetable Appetizers

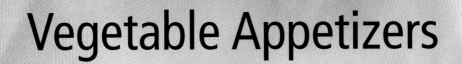

A salad or vegetable-based appetizer is a light and healthy way to begin a meal. A few of the recipes included in this chapter are fried or baked and thus heavier; in that case be sure to balance the meal by serving something light to follow.

Hot and spicy green olives
Olive condite

This tasty dish comes from Sicily. In some parts of the island the olives will sometimes appear on your table served in tiny, hollowed-out bread rolls. The bread helps offset some of the fire in the dressing. Use only the highest quality green olives packed in brine.

Serves: 4; Preparation: 10 minutes + 2 hours to marinate; Level of difficulty: Simple

Rinse the olives in cold water and pat dry with paper towels. § Lightly crush the olives with a meat-pounding mallet. § Use the same instrument to bruise the cloves of garlic. Place the olives and garlic in a serving dish. § Remove the rosemary leaves from the sprig and add to the olives, together with the mint, oregano, chilies, and oil. Mix well and cover. Set aside in a cool place (not the refrigerator) for at least 2 hours before serving. § Serve with fresh bread.

■ INGREDIENTS

• 1½ cups (300 g) green olives, pitted
• 4 cloves garlic, peeled
• 1 sprig fresh rosemary
• 1 tablespoon fresh mint, coarsely chopped
• ½ teaspoon oregano
• ½ teaspoon crushed chilies
• 2 tablespoons extra-virgin olive oil

Wine: a dry white (Etna Bianco)

VARIATION
– Add 2 tablespoons of finely chopped scallions (spring onions).

Bruschetta with fresh tomato topping
Bruschetta con pomodori freschi

If you want to prepare this dish ahead of time, keep the bruschetta and tomato mixture separate until just before serving, otherwise the dish will become soggy and unappetizing.

Serves: 4; Preparation: 10 minutes; Cooking: 10 minutes; Level of difficulty: Simple

Prepare the bruschetta. § Dice the tomatoes into bite-size chunks. Place them in a bowl and mix with the oil, basil, oregano, salt, and pepper. § Cover each bruschetta with a quarter of the tomato mixture. § Serve immediately.

■ INGREDIENTS

• 4 slices *Bruschetta* (see recipe p. 54)
• 2 large ripe tomatoes
• 4 tablespoons extra-virgin olive oil
• ½ fresh basil leaves, torn
• 1 teaspoon oregano
• salt and freshly ground black pepper

Wine: a dry white (Orvieto Classico)

VARIATIONS
– Add 3½ oz (100 g) diced Mozzarella cheese to the tomato mixture.
– Add ⅓ teaspoon crushed chilies or 1 chopped fresh chili to the tomato mixture.
– Add 1 tablespoon small capers to the tomato mixture.

Right: *Olive condite*

Bruschetta with white beans
Bruschetta con fagioli

- 4 slices *Bruschetta* (see recipe p. 54)
- 14 oz (450 g) white beans, canned
- salt and freshly ground black pepper
- 2 tablespoons extra-virgin olive oil

Wine: a young, dry red (Vino Novello)

Serves: 4; Preparation: 10 minutes; Cooking: 10 minutes; Level of difficulty: Simple

Prepare the bruschetta. § Heat the beans in a small saucepan. Taste for salt; season if necessary. § When hot, pour over the *bruschetta*. § Sprinkle with pepper and drizzle with oil. § Serve hot.

VARIATIONS
– Add 6 fresh sage leaves to the beans when heating.
– For homemade baked beans; cook 2 large diced tomatoes in the saucepan before adding the beans. Serve hot.

Carrot salad with garlic, oil, and lemon
Carote all'olio, aglio e limone

This light, refreshing, and vitamin-packed salad is a perfect appetizer for hot summer evenings.

Serves: 4; Preparation: 10 minutes + 30 minutes to marinate; Level of difficulty: Simple

Place the carrots, garlic, parsley, and mint in a small salad bowl. Add the lemon juice, oil, salt, and pepper to taste. Mix well. § Set aside for at least 30 minutes before serving.

■ INGREDIENTS

- 4 large carrots, coarsely grated
- 1 clove garlic, finely chopped
- 2 tablespoons finely chopped parsley
- 1 tablespoon finely chopped mint leaves
- juice of 1 lemon
- 3 tablespoons extra-virgin olive oil
- salt and freshly ground black pepper

Wine: a light, dry white (Soave)

Roasted bell peppers with anchovies
Peperoni arrostiti con acciughe

This dish is tastier if prepared the day before. Store in the refrigerator, but take out at least two hours before serving. If well covered with olive oil, roasted bell peppers with anchovies will keep for up to a week in the refrigerator.

Serves: 8; Preparation: 15 minutes + 2 hours to marinate; Cooking: 15-20 minutes; Level of difficulty: Simple

Cut the bell peppers in half lengthwise. Remove the seeds and pulpy core. Rinse under cold running water and pat dry with paper towels. Bake in a preheated oven at 400°F/200°C/gas 6 until the skins are wrinkled and black. Take the bell peppers out of the oven and leave to cool. Remove the charred skins with your fingers. § Cut the peeled bell peppers lengthwise into strips about 2 in (5 cm) wide. Choose a serving dish that will hold 4–5 layers of bell peppers, and line the bottom with one layer. § Crumble 4 of the anchovy fillets in a small mixing bowl and add the garlic, parsley, capers, oregano, and oil. § Place a layer of this mixture over the bell peppers. Cover with another layer of bell peppers and anchovy mixture. Repeat the procedure until all the ingredients have been used. § Garnish the top layer with the remaining anchovy fillets and the basil. Set the dish aside to marinate for at least 2 hours before serving.

■ INGREDIENTS

- 2 yellow, 2 green, and 2 red bell peppers (capsicums)
- 8 anchovy fillets
- 4 cloves garlic, finely chopped
- 2 tablespoons parsley, finely chopped
- 2 tablespoons capers
- ½ teaspoon oregano
- 4 tablespoons extra-virgin olive oil
- 8 fresh basil leaves, torn

Wine: a dry red (Chianti Classico)

Right:

Peperoni arrostiti con acciughe

Grilled zucchini with fresh mint and garlic
Zucchine grigliate con menta fresca e aglio

Serves: 4; Preparation: 20 minutes + 2 hours to cool; Cooking: 10 minutes; Level of difficulty: Simple

Wash and dry the zucchini, trim the ends, and cut lengthwise into ¼-in (6-mm) thick slices. § Heat the grill pan to very hot and cook the slices for 4–5 minutes on each side. Remove and set aside to cool. § Put the oil in a bowl with the salt, parsley, and mint, and beat with a fork or whisk until well mixed. § Arrange the zucchini slices in a small, fairly deep-sided serving dish. Sprinkle with the garlic and grind the mixed pepper over the top. § Pour the oil mixture over the zucchini (make sure that the zucchini are well-covered with oil) and refrigerate for at least 2 hours before serving.

| VARIATIONS
— Sprinkle 6 crumbled anchovy fillets over the zucchini together with the garlic.
— For a spicy dish, add ½ teaspoon crushed chilies to the oil and mix with the parsley, mint, and salt.

■ INGREDIENTS

• 8 zucchini (courgettes)
• ¾ cup (200 ml) extra-virgin olive oil
• dash of salt
• 2 tablespoons finely chopped parsley
• 1 tablespoon finely chopped fresh mint
• 1 teaspoon mixed red, black, green peppercorns
• 2 cloves garlic, finely chopped

Wine: a dry white (Trebbiano di Lugana)

Marinated zucchini with spicy mayonnaise
Zucchine crude con maionese piccante

Serves: 4; Preparation: 20 minutes + 2 hours to marinate; Level of difficulty: Simple

Wash and dry the zucchini, trim the ends, and slice thinly (skin and all). § Place in a bowl, add the vinegar, and sprinkle with salt. Mix well and leave to marinate for at least 2 hours. § Prepare the mayonnaise and stir in the mustard. § Drain the zucchini, and squeeze them gently in your hands to remove as much vinegar as possible. § Mix the zucchini with the spicy mayonnaise and transfer to a serving dish. § Garnish with the parsley and serve.

■ INGREDIENTS

• 4 large zucchini (courgettes)
• 4 tablespoons white wine vinegar
• salt and freshly ground black pepper
• 1 quantity *Mayonnaise* (see recipe p. 42)
• 2 teaspoons hot mustard
• 8 sprigs parsley

Wine: a dry white (Traminer Aromatico)

Right: *Zucchine grigliate con menta fresca e aglio*

Caesar's mushroom salad
Insalata di ovoli

This eyecatching salad calls for very fresh Caesar's (also known as royal agaric) mushrooms. For a perfect salad, choose the ones with the caps still closed around the stems and serve them the same day they are purchased. They must be absolutely fresh.

Serves: 4-6; Preparation: 10 minutes; Level of difficulty: Simple

Clean the mushrooms and rinse them carefully in cold water. Pat dry with paper towels. § Slice the mushrooms finely and arrange them on a serving dish. § Sprinkle with the walnuts and Parmesan flakes. § Mix the oil, salt, pepper, and lemon juice in a bowl and pour over the mushrooms. § Serve immediately, before the flavor begins to change.

■ INGREDIENTS

- 14 oz (450 g) Caesar's (royal agaric) mushrooms
- 1 cup (100 g) walnuts, shelled and chopped
- 3½ oz (100 g) Parmesan cheese, flaked
- ⅓ cup (90 ml) extra-virgin olive oil
- salt and freshly ground white pepper
- juice of 1 lemon

Wine: a dry, sparkling white (Asti Spumante Brut)

VARIATIONS
– Add a finely chopped clove of garlic to the olive oil dressing.
– Replace the Caesar's mushrooms with the same quantity of closed white button mushrooms. In this case, serve on a bed of fresh, crisp arugula (rocket).

Crostoni with eggs and mushrooms
Crostoni con uova e funghi

Serves: 4; Preparation: 10 minutes; Cooking: 15 minutes; Level of difficulty: Simple

Clean the mushrooms, wash them carefully, and pat dry with paper towels. § Slice the mushrooms and sauté in a skillet (frying pan) with half the butter and the thyme for about 10 minutes. § Add the ham and season with salt just before removing from heat. Mix well. § Toast the bread in the oven or under the broiler (grill) and set aside in a warm place. § Melt the remaining butter in a saucepan over medium-low heat, break in the eggs, and let them set slightly before breaking them up with a fork. Continue cooking and stirring until the eggs are cooked but still soft. Season with salt. § Arrange the toasted bread on a serving dish and cover each slice with a quarter of the egg mixture followed by a quarter of the mushroom mixture. § Sprinkle with the parsley and pepper and serve.

■ INGREDIENTS

- 4 oz (125 g) white mushrooms
- 3 tablespoons butter
- 1 teaspoon fresh thyme, finely chopped
- 2 oz (60 g) ham, chopped
- salt and freshly ground black pepper
- 4 large slices white or whole-wheat (wholemeal) bread
- 4 eggs
- 1 tablespoon finely chopped parsley

Wine: a dry red (Sangiovese di Romagna)

Right: *Insalata di ovoli*

INGREDIENTS

- 1¼ lb (600 g) white mushrooms
- 4 cloves garlic, minced
- ½ cup (4 fl oz/125 ml) extra-virgin olive oil
- 1 bay leaf, and 2 cloves
- 10 black peppercorns
- ⅓ cup (3½ fl oz/100 ml) dry white wine
- dash of salt
- juice of 1 lemon

Tasty braised mushrooms
Funghi insaporiti

Serves: 4; Preparation: 10 minutes; Cooking: 20 minutes; Level of difficulty: Simple

Clean the mushrooms. Wash and dry them carefully, then peel and slice. § Sauté the garlic in a skillet (frying pan) with the oil for 2–3 minutes, then add the mushrooms, bay leaf, cloves, and peppercorns. § Cook over high heat for a few minutes, then add the wine, lemon juice, and salt. § Cover the skillet and finish cooking over medium-low heat. § Transfer the mushrooms to a serving dish and serve either hot or at room temperature with fresh bread or toast.

Wine: a dry white (Orvieto)

Platter of stuffed vegetables
Teglia di verdure ripiene al forno

Serves: 6-8; Preparation: 15 minutes; Cooking: 40-50 minutes; Level of difficulty: Simple

Blanch the zucchini in salted water for 5 minutes, drain, and cool. Cut in half horizontally, scoop out the pulp, and set aside. § Peel the onions and blanch in salted water for 5 minutes, drain, and cool. § Cut the onions in half horizontally and hollow them out, leaving ½-in (1-cm) thick sides. Chop the pulp and set aside. § Wash the tomatoes and cut them in half. Scoop out the pulp, and set aside. Be careful not to pierce the skin. § Cut the bell peppers in half and remove the seeds and core. § Beat the eggs in a bowl and add the bread crumbs, parsley, garlic, most of the Parmesan, salt, and pepper. § Stir in about half the tomato, zucchini, and onion pulp, mixing well. § Fill the vegetables with the mixture and sprinkle with the remaining Parmesan. § Pour the oil into a large ovenproof dish and arrange the vegetables in it. § Cook in a preheated oven at 400°F/200°C/gas 6 for 30–40 minutes. § Serve piping hot.

■ INGREDIENTS

- 6 round zucchini (courgettes)
- 3 medium onions
- 3 medium tomatoes
- 1 red, 1 green, and 1 yellow bell pepper (capsicum)
- 3 eggs
- 2 cups (120 g) fine dry bread crumbs
- 3 tablespoons finely chopped parsley
- 3 cloves garlic, finely chopped
- ½ cup (60 g) freshly grated Parmesan cheese
- salt and freshly ground black pepper
- ⅓ cup (90 ml) extra-virgin olive oil

*Wine: a dry white
(Soave Classico)*

Tomato and basil salad
Insalata di pomodori e basilico

Tomato and basil salad is simple and typical of Italian summer cookery. It makes a tasty appetizer, a great side dish, or can be served between courses to revive the palate. Choose only the tastiest red tomatoes, and dress with the highest quality oil and the freshest of basil leaves.

Serves: 4; Preparation: 15 minutes; Level of difficulty: Simple

Peel the garlic and rub the insides of a salad bowl with the clove. § Wash, dry, and slice the tomatoes. Remove the seeds. § Sprinkle the slices with a little salt and place on a slightly inclined cutting board. Leave them for about 10 minutes so the water they produce can drain away. § Transfer the tomatoes to the salad bowl and sprinkle with the basil. § In a small bowl, beat the oregano, salt, pepper, and oil with a fork until well mixed. § Pour over the tomatoes and toss quickly. § Cover and set aside for about 15 minutes before serving.

■ INGREDIENTS

- 1 clove garlic
- 6 large tomatoes, firm and ripe
- salt and freshly ground black pepper
- 15 fresh basil leaves, torn
- dash of oregano
- ⅓ cup (90 ml) extra-virgin olive oil

Wine: a dry, lightly sparkling white (Verdicchio)

*Right:
Teglia di verdure ripiene al forno*

Fennel, celery, and carrots with apple and gorgonzola sauce
Insalata al Gorgonzola

■ INGREDIENTS

- 2 fennel bulbs
- 2 carrots
- 5 stalks celery
- 1 Granny Smith apple
- 1 clove garlic, finely chopped
- salt and freshly ground black pepper
- 3 tablespoons extra-virgin olive oil
- 5 oz (150 g) mild Gorgonzola cheese
- 1 tablespoon parsley, finely chopped

Wine: a dry white (Tocai di San Martino della Battaglia)

Serves: 6; Preparation: 15 minutes; Level of difficulty: Simple

Discard the outer leaves of the fennel and cut the bulbs in half. Wash and cut into ⅛-in (3-mm) thick slices. § Trim the carrots, scrape, and cut in julienne strips. § Trim the celery, removing any damaged or tough outer leaves, and cut the stalks in slices like the fennel. § Wash the apple and cut in thin wedges. § Put the garlic, apple, and vegetables in a salad bowl and season with salt, pepper, and 2 tablespoons of oil. § Dice the Gorgonzola and put it in a heavy-bottomed saucepan with 1 tablespoon of oil. Melt slowly over low heat, stirring continuously. § When it is barely lukewarm and has become creamy, pour it over the vegetables. § Sprinkle with the parsley and serve.

Celery filled with gorgonzola and ricotta cheese
Coste di sedano farcite

■ INGREDIENTS

- 5 oz (150 g) Gorgonzola cheese
- ¾ cup (200 g) Ricotta cheese
- 4 tablespoons whole (full cream) milk
- 1 onion, finely chopped
- dash of paprika
- 1 tablespoon extra-virgin olive oil
- 1 tablespoon celery, finely chopped
- salt and freshly ground black pepper
- 12 stalks celery
- 8 sprigs parsley

Wine: a young, dry white (Vermentino Ligure)

Left: Insalata al Gorgonzola

Serves: 4-6; Preparation: 15 minutes + 1 hour in the refrigerator; Level of difficulty: Simple

Melt the Gorgonzola in a heavy-bottomed saucepan over very low heat. § Remove from the heat when lukewarm and melted, and add the Ricotta and enough milk to obtain a creamy but dense mixture. § Add the onion, paprika, oil, celery, salt, and pepper. Mix well. § Cover and place in the refrigerator for about 1 hour. § Prepare the celery, removing the outer stalks and any stringy fibers. Rinse under cold running water, dry and slice into pieces about 2 in (5 cm) long. § Fill the celery stalks with the mixture and arrange on a serving dish. Garnish with the parsley and serve.

VARIATIONS
– Replace the onion with 1 tablespoon finely chopped mint, 1 tablespoon finely chopped parsley, and 1 finely chopped garlic clove.
– Slice a crisp, tangy eating apple into wedges and arrange on the serving dish with the celery.

Winter salad
Insalata invernale

This simple salad makes an excellent, light appetizer. For a richer dish, add a few sliced button mushrooms or diced Mozzarella cheese. For best results, season with the mayonnaise just before serving.

Serves: 4-6; Preparation: 30 minutes; Level of difficulty: Simple

Clean the artichokes by removing the stalks and tough outer leaves. Trim off and discard the tops. Cut in half lengthwise and remove the fuzzy inner choke with a sharp knife. Remove the tough outer leaves from the fennel bulb. § Wash and dry the artichoke and fennel hearts and cut in thin strips. § Peel the eggs and cut in thin slices. § Clean, wash, and slice the radishes. § Put all the vegetables in a bowl and season with the oil, salt, pepper, and vinegar. Toss well. § Prepare the mayonnaise. Using a hand whisk, mix the mayonnaise and cream. § Transfer the salad to a bowl, arrange the eggs on top, and dress with the mayonnaise. § Garnish with the parsley and serve.

■ INGREDIENTS

- 3 artichokes
- 1 fennel bulb
- 3 hard-cooked (hard boiled) eggs
- 10 radishes
- 2 tablespoons extra-virgin olive oil
- salt and freshly ground black pepper
- 1 tablespoon white wine vinegar
- 1 quantity *Mayonnaise* (see recipe p. 42)
- 3 tablespoons fresh cream
- 3 sprigs parsley, to garnish

Wine: a dry white (Orvieto Classico)

Crostoni with asparagus and orange sauce
Crostoni con asparagi

Serves: 6-8; Preparation: 30 minutes; Cooking: 30 minutes; Level of difficulty: Medium

Clean the asparagus, trim the stalks, and cook in a pot of salted, boiling water for 8–10 minutes. § Drain well and cut off all but the very tenderest part of the stalks and tips. § Squeeze the orange and set the juice aside. Cut half the rind into thin strips. § Blanch in a pot of boiling water for a few seconds. Drain and dry with paper towels. § Toast the bread and transfer to a serving dish. § Arrange the asparagus on the toast. § To prepare the sauce: place a large pan of water over medium heat. § Combine the egg yolks with a few pieces of butter, a dash of salt, and 1 tablespoon of water in a small pot. Beat well with a whisk. § Put the small pot in the larger one filled with water, keeping the heat low so the water doesn't boil. § As soon as the butter begins to melt, add the rest a little at a time, so that it is gradually absorbed, whisking all the time and taking care that the sauce never boils. § When the sauce is whipped and creamy, add another dash of salt and, very gradually, the orange juice, stirring carefully. § Remove from the heat and stir in the sliced orange rind. § Pour the orange sauce over the crostoni and serve.

■ INGREDIENTS

- 3 lb (1.5 kg) asparagus
- 1 orange
- 12 slices plain or whole wheat (wholemeal) bread
- 3 egg yolks
- ⅔ cup (150 g) butter, cut in small pieces
- 2 dashes of salt

Wine: a dry white (Albano di Romagna)

Right:
Insalata di cetrioli e cipolle

Cucumber and onion salad
Insalata di cetrioli e cipolle

This refreshing summer salad comes from Calabria, in the south of Italy.
It is really delicious when served with fresh Ricotta or Caprino cheese.

■ INGREDIENTS

• 5 medium sweet red onions
• salt and freshly ground
  black pepper
• 4 tablespoons extra-virgin
  olive oil
• 1 tablespoon white wine
  vinegar
• 2 medium cucumbers
• 1 tablespoon capers
• 6 leaves fresh basil, torn

*Wine: a dry white
(Cirò Bianco)*

Serves: 4-6; Preparation: 15 minutes + 30 minutes resting; Level of difficulty: Simple

Peel the onions and slice in thin wheels. § Put the onions in a salad bowl, sprinkle with the salt, pepper, oil, and vinegar. Toss well and set aside for 30 minutes. § Peel the cucumbers and slice very thinly. § Add the cucumbers and capers to the onions and toss well. § Garnish with the basil and serve.

Pear and bell pepper salad
Insalata di pere e peperoni

This salad can be made using bell peppers of one color, but it will be more attractive and appetizing if you use three different colors. Always choose fresh, fleshy bell peppers and firm, ripe pears. The salad must be served as soon as it is made, otherwise the pears will turn black.

Serves: 4-6; Preparation: 15 minutes; Level of difficulty: Simple

Clean the bell peppers by removing the top, seeds, and core. § Wash and cut in short, thin strips. § Peel and core the pears and cut into thin strips. § Combine the pear and bell pepper strips in a salad bowl, and add the garlic, salt, pepper, parsley, and oil. § Serve immediately.

■ INGREDIENTS

- 1 red, 1 yellow, 1 green bell pepper (capsicum)
- 2 firm ripe pears
- 1 clove garlic, finely chopped (optional)
- salt and freshly ground black pepper
- 1 tablespoon finely chopped parsley
- 4 tablespoons extra-virgin olive oil

Wine: a dry, sparkling white (Asti Spumante)

Vegetable omelet Emilia-Romagna style
Erbazzone emiliano

Serves: 4-6; Preparation: 15 minutes; Cooking: 30 minutes; Level of difficulty: Simple

Clean and wash the greens. Cook them in a pot of salted, boiling water for 8–10 minutes. § Drain well, squeeze out excess water, and chop finely. § Sauté the garlic, parsley, and onion in the lard (or butter) over medium heat until the onion is transparent. § Add the greens, season with salt and pepper, and cook for 5 minutes more. § In a bowl, beat the eggs until foamy, mix in the vegetables, and then add the Parmesan, flour, and bread crumbs. § Heat the oil in a large skillet (frying pan) and add the mixture, taking care to spread it evenly in the pan. § Cook until it begins to turn brown underneath, then carefully detach it from the sides of the skillet using a wooden spoon, and turn it over (with the help of a lid or plate). Brown on the other side. § Slide onto a serving dish and serve hot.

■ INGREDIENTS

- 1½ lb (750 g) mixed fresh spinach and Swiss chard (silver beet)
- 4 cloves garlic, finely chopped
- 1 cup (30 g) finely chopped parsley
- 1 small onion, finely chopped
- 4 tablespoons lard or butter
- salt and freshly ground black pepper
- 4 eggs
- 1 cup (125 g) freshly grated Parmesan cheese
- 2 tablespoons all-purpose (plain) flour
- 2 tablespoons bread crumbs
- 4 tablespoons extra-virgin olive oil

Wine: a young, dry red (Gutturnio dei Colli Piacentini)

Right:
Erbazzone emiliano

■ INGREDIENTS

- 7 oz (200 g) lollo rosso, or other leafy salad
- 7 oz (200 g) arugula (rocket)
- salt and freshly ground black pepper
- 2 oz (60 g) peas, canned, well-drained
- 5 oz (150 g) Emmenthal cheese, diced
- ½ cup (125 ml) extra-virgin olive oil
- 1 tablespoon mustard
- 1 tablespoon white wine vinegar
- 4 hard-cooked (hard-boiled) eggs, sliced
- 1 carrot, grated
- 8 radishes, finely sliced
- 1 white truffle (optional)

Wine: a light, dry, sparkling white (Prosecco di Conegliano)

■ INGREDIENTS

- 1 lb (500 g) dense grain, day-old bread
- 5 medium tomatoes
- 2 red onions
- 1 cucumber
- 12 leaves fresh basil, torn
- ⅓ cup (90 ml) extra-virgin olive oil
- salt and freshly ground black pepper
- 1 tablespoon red wine vinegar

Wine: a dry red (Chianti dei Colli Senesi)

Rainbow salad
Insalata arcobaleno

If you like truffles, slice a white one very thinly and add it to the mushrooms. The salad will be even more fragrant and tasty.

Serves: 4-6; Preparation: 20 minutes; Level of difficulty: Simple

Wash and dry the salad greens and chop coarsely. § Arrange in the bottom of a salad bowl and season with salt and pepper. § Sprinkle the peas over the top. § Clean, wash, peel, and thinly slice the mushrooms. Place them in a bowl with the cheese. § Prepare a dressing by beating the oil, mustard, salt, and vinegar together in a bowl. Pour half of it over the mushrooms and toss well. § Sprinkle the mushroom mixture over the salad and cover with the eggs, carrots, and radishes. § Just before serving, drizzle with the remaining dressing and toss again. § Serve immediately.

Tuscan bread salad
Panzanella

Panzanella is a typical Tuscan dish. The ingredients used vary according to which part of Tuscany it is made in. The addition of cucumber, for example, is shunned in the area around Siena, while it is always included in Florence. The salad can be enriched by adding diced carrots, fennel, celery, hard-cooked (hard-boiled) eggs, capers, or Pecorino cheese.

Serves: 4-6; Preparation: 15 minutes + 15 minutes to rest; Level of difficulty: Simple

Soak the bread in a bowl of cold water for at least 10 minutes. § Use your hands to squeeze out as much water as possible. Crumble the almost dry bread into a large salad bowl. § Slice the tomatoes and remove the seeds. Clean the onions and slice in thin wheels. Peel the cucumber and slice thinly. § Add the tomatoes, cucumber, basil, and onions to the bread. Season with salt, pepper, and 4 tablespoons of the oil and mix carefully. § Set aside in a cool place or the refrigerator for 15 minutes. § Add the vinegar and remaining oil just before serving.

Left: *Panzanella*

Porcini mushroom salad
Insalata di funghi porcini

This mouthwatering salad is often served in Italy during the early summer months when porcini mushrooms are readily available. If you can't get porcini, you may want to experiment with other types of wild or cultivated mushrooms.

Serves: 6; Preparation: 15 minutes; Level of difficulty: Simple

Clean the mushrooms, peel, rinse carefully under cold running water, and pat dry. § Without peeling, cut them in thin slices. § Wash the celery, remove any stringy fibers, and slice thinly. § Wash the lettuce hearts and slice thinly. § Place the lettuce in the bottom of a salad bowl and arrange the celery and mushrooms over the top. Cover with the Parmesan. § In a small bowl, beat the oil, lemon juice, salt, and pepper together with a fork. § Pour over the salad, toss carefully, and serve.

VARIATION
– Add 3½ oz (100 g) of diced prosciutto and toss well.

■ INGREDIENTS

- 1 lb (500 g) fresh porcini mushrooms
- 6 stalks celery
- 2 lettuce hearts
- 3½ oz (100 g) Parmesan cheese, flaked
- ½ cup (125 ml) extra-virgin olive oil
- juice of 1 lemon
- salt and freshly ground black pepper

Wine: a dry, young red (Vino Novello)

Mushrooms with bay leaf, cinnamon, and garlic
Funghi alle spezie

Serves: 4; Preparation: 25 minutes; Cooking: 20 minutes; Level of difficulty: Simple

Clean the mushrooms, peel, rinse under cold running water, and pat dry. § Put the bay leaf, cinnamon, and half the lemon juice in a pot full of water and bring to a boil. § Add the mushrooms and boil for 2–3 minutes. Drain well and cut the mushrooms in half. § Transfer to a skillet (frying pan) with the oil, the remaining lemon juice, salt, and peppercorns, and cook for 15 minutes. § Remove from heat, drain, and set aside to cool. § Sprinkle with the parsley and garlic, and serve.

■ INGREDIENTS

- 1 lb (500 g) button mushrooms
- 1 bay leaf
- 1 stick cinnamon
- juice of 1 lemon
- ⅓ cup (90 ml) extra-virgin olive oil
- dash of salt
- 10 black peppercorns, bruised
- 1 cup (30 g) finely chopped parsley
- 1 clove garlic, finely chopped

Wine: a dry, sparkling red (Lambrusco di Sorbara)

Right:
Insalata di funghi porcini

INGREDIENTS

- 12 slices Mozzarella cheese
- 12 slices firm red tomato
- 7 oz (200 g) mixed vegetables: onion, bell pepper (capsicum), celery, zucchini (courgette), carrots, all finely chopped
- 1 tablespoon capers
- salt and freshly ground black pepper
- 1 tablespoon extra-virgin olive oil
- 6 leaves fresh basil, torn

Mozzarella and tomato slices with fresh vegetables

Mozzarella e pomodoro con verdure fresche

These eyecatching Mozzarella and vegetable slices make a light and tasty start to any meal. If you like garlic, add a clove (very finely chopped) to the vegetable mixture.

Serves: 4-6; Preparation: 10 minutes; Level of difficulty: Simple

Arrange the slices of Mozzarella on a serving dish and cover each one with a slice of tomato. § Combine the chopped vegetables in a bowl with the capers, salt, pepper, and oil. § Spread the vegetable mixture over the tomatoes. § Garnish with the basil and serve.

Stuffed olives
Olive all'ascolana

This dish requires time and patience but these delicious little olives are so good that you will be tempted to make them again and again. The recipe comes from the Marches area in central Italy.

Serves: 4-6; Preparation: 30 minutes; Cooking: 40 minutes; Level of difficulty: Medium

Sauté the beef and pork in a skillet (frying pan) with the olive oil for 5 minutes. Add the tomato paste and continue cooking for 15 minutes. § Add the chicken livers and cook for 5 minutes more. § Remove from heat, chop the meat very finely, and return to the skillet. § Soak the bread roll in cold water, squeeze out excess moisture, and crumble. § Add the bread, one of the eggs, the Parmesan, salt, pepper, nutmeg, and cinnamon to the meat mixture. § Mix well with a fork and then stuff the pitted olives. § Arrange three bowls, the first with the flour, the second with 2 beaten eggs, and the third with the bread crumbs. § Dredge the olives in the flour, dip them in the egg, and then in the bread crumbs. Remove excess crumbs by rolling them in your hands. § Heat the oil in a deep-sided skillet (frying pan) until very hot and fry the olives in small batches. When a crisp, golden crust forms around each olive, remove from the pan with a slotted spoon. Place them on paper towels to drain excess oil. § Transfer to a serving dish, garnish with slices of lemon and parsley, and serve hot.

- ■ INGREDIENTS
- 5 oz (150 g) pork, coarsely chopped
- 5 oz (150 g) beef, coarsely chopped
- 4 tablespoons extra-virgin olive oil
- 2 tablespoons tomato paste
- 3½ oz (100 g) chicken livers, coarsely chopped
- 1 day-old bread roll
- 3 eggs
- 4 tablespoons Parmesan cheese, freshly grated
- salt and freshly ground black pepper
- dash each of nutmeg and cinnamon
- 1½ lb (750 g) giant green olives, pitted
- 1 cup (150 g) all-purpose (plain) flour
- 2½ cups (150 g) fine dry bread crumbs
- 2 cups (16 fl oz/500 ml) oil, for frying
- 1 lemon, sliced
- 8 sprigs parsley

Wine: a dry red (Rosso Conero)

Cherry tomatoes filled with soft fresh cheese
Pomodorini cremosi

Serves: 4-6; Preparation: 15 minutes + 20 minutes to chill; Level of difficulty: Simple

Wash the tomatoes and dry well. § Turn them upside down and slice off a "lid." Set aside. § Using a small teaspoon, carefully remove the pulp. § Leave the tomatoes hole-side-down to drain for 10 minutes. § In a bowl, mix the oil, olives, garlic, basil, salt, pepper, cheese, and enough of the tomato pulp to make a smooth cream. Don't add all the tomato at once as it may make the cream too liquid. § Stuff the tomatoes with the mixture. Place a "lid" on top of each and set aside in the refrigerator for 20 minutes before serving.

- ■ INGREDIENTS
- 12 cherry tomatoes
- ½ tablespoon extra-virgin olive oil
- 10 green olives, 1 clove garlic, finely chopped
- 6 fresh basil leaves, torn
- salt and freshly ground black pepper
- 1 cup (250 g) soft goat's or Ricotta cheese

Wine: a dry white (Verduzzo)

Right: *Olive all'ascolana*

Fried polenta with mushroom, peas, and cheese
Polenta fritta splendida

Serves: 4-6; Preparation: 15 minutes; Cooking: 30 minutes; Level of difficulty: Simple

Heat the oil in a skillet (frying pan) and add the mushrooms and peas. Mix well and cook over medium heat for 10 minutes. § Add the capers, salt and pepper. Cook for 5–10 minutes more, or until the vegetables are soft, stirring occasionally. § Lightly flour the polenta slices, dip them into the egg, and then into a bowl containing the bread crumbs. § Heat the frying oil in a deep-sided skillet (frying pan) until very hot and fry the slices of polenta in small batches until golden brown. § Drain on paper towels and arrange in a buttered baking dish. § Cover each slice with a spoonful of peas and mushrooms, and a slice of Mozzarella. § Bake in a preheated oven at 400°F/200°C/gas 6 for about 10 minutes, or until the Mozzarella is melted and golden. § Remove from the oven, sprinkle with the basil, and serve immediately.

■ INGREDIENTS

- 2 tablespoons extra-virgin olive oil
- 7 oz (200 g) white mushrooms, sliced
- 8 oz (250 g) fresh or frozen peas
- 1 tablespoon capers
- salt and freshly ground black pepper
- 4 tablespoons all-purpose (plain) flour
- 6 large slices cold *Basic polenta* (see recipe p. 52)
- 1 egg, beaten
- 1 cup (60 g) fine dry bread crumbs
- 2 cups (500 ml) oil, for frying
- 3½ oz (100 g) Mozzarella cheese
- 4 tablespoons finely chopped basil

Wine: a dry red (Chianti Classico)

Fried polenta pieces with porcini mushroom sauce
Polenta fritta con salsa di funghi porcini

If you can't get fresh porcini for this mushroom sauce, combine 1 oz (30 g) of soaked, dried porcini mushrooms with fresh white mushrooms.

Serves: 6; Preparation: 30 minutes; Cooking: 40 minutes; Level of difficulty: Medium

Clean the mushrooms, rinse carefully under cold running water, and pat dry with paper towels. § Detach the stalks from the heads. § Sauté the garlic with the olive oil in a skillet (frying pan) over medium heat until pale gold. § Coarsely chop the mushrooms. § Add the stalks to the skillet first (they need longer to cook than the caps), and after about 5 minutes, add the caps. Add the calamint (or thyme) and season with salt and pepper. § Stir carefully for 4–5 minutes more. The time the porcini take to cook will depend on how fresh they are. Don't let them become mushy. § Heat the frying oil in a large deep-sided skillet until very hot and fry the polenta slices until golden brown. § Spoon the mushroom sauce onto the polenta slices and serve hot.

■ INGREDIENTS

- 2 lb (1 kg) porcini mushrooms
- 2 cloves garlic, minced
- ⅓ cup (90 ml) extra-virgin olive oil
- 2 tablespoons finely chopped calamint or thyme
- salt and freshly ground black pepper
- 2 cups (500 ml) oil, for frying
- 6 large slices cold *Basic polenta* (see recipe p. 52)

Wine: a dry red (Nobile di Montepulciano)

Right: *Polenta fritta con salsa di funghi porcini*

Sicilian-style crostini
Crostini siciliani

■ INGREDIENTS

- 4-8 slices dense grain bread
- 1 cup (250 ml) oil, for frying
- 2 tablespoons vinegar
- 1 teaspoon sugar
- 1 teaspoon capers
- 1 teaspoon pine nuts
- 1 teaspoon raisins
- 1 teaspoon candied lemon peel, diced
- 2 ripe tomatoes, diced

Wine: a dry red (Valpolicella)

Serves: 4; Preparation: 10 minutes; Cooking: 10 minutes; Level of difficulty: Simple

Cut the slices of bread in half and remove the crusts. § Heat the oil in a large deep-sided skillet (frying pan) until very hot and fry the bread until golden brown on both sides. § Drain on paper towels. § Bring the vinegar, sugar, and 2 tablespoons of water to a boil, then add the capers, pine nuts, raisins, candied lemon peel, and tomatoes. § Cook for 5 minutes, stirring with care. § Spread the fried crostini with this mixture and serve hot.

Rice croquettes
Arancini di riso

Serves: 4-6; Preparation: 20 minutes; Cooking: 55 minutes; Level of difficulty: Medium

Cook the rice in as you would a risotto (see, for example, *Risotto with bay leaves*, p. 293), using half the oil, then gradually stirring in the boiling stock as needed. When the rice is cooked, all the liquid should have been absorbed. § Sauté the onion in a skillet (frying pan) over medium heat with the oil until pale gold. § Wash the chicken livers, chop coarsely, and add to the skillet. Add the veal, peas, and wine. § When the liquid has evaporated, add the tomato pulp and season with salt and pepper. § Continue cooking, stirring often, until the sauce is thick. § Combine the rice, Parmesan, and butter in a bowl. § Mix well and mold into balls. Hollow out the center of each ball and fill with meat sauce and a piece of hard-cooked egg. § Close the rice around the filling. § Beat the raw eggs with a fork in a shallow dish. Dip the balls into the egg and then roll in bread crumbs. § Heat the oil in a deep-sided skillet until very hot and fry the balls in small batches until golden brown. § Drain on paper towels and serve piping hot.

■ INGREDIENTS

- 2 cups (450 g) short-grain rice
- 4 tablespoons extra-virgin olive oil
- 2 cups (500 ml) *Beef stock* (see recipe p. 48)
- 1 small onion, chopped
- 4 oz (125 g) chicken livers
- 2 oz (60 g) ground veal
- 8 oz (250 g) peas
- 2 tablespoons white wine
- 2 tablespoons tomato pulp
- salt and freshly ground black pepper
- 2 tablespoons freshly grated Parmesan cheese
- 2 tablespoons butter
- 2 hard-cooked (hard-boiled) eggs
- 2 raw eggs
- 1½ cups (90 g) fine dry bread crumbs
- 2 cups (500 ml) oil, for frying

Wine: a dry red (Corvo Rosso)

Artichokes with mozzarella
Carciofi con la mozzarella

Serves: 4-6; Preparation: 20 minutes; Cooking: 40 minutes; Level of difficulty: Medium

Clean the artichokes by removing the stalks and tough outer leaves. Trim off and discard the tops. Place the hearts in a bowl of cold water with the lemon juice. § Mix the Mozzarella with the Parmesan, bread crumbs, and egg. Season with salt, pepper, and 1 tablespoon of oil. § Drain the artichokes, dry, open and use a sharp knife to remove the centers. § Put some of the Mozzarella mixture in each artichoke and set them upright, one next to the other, in an oiled braiser or ovenproof casserole. § Pour the remaining oil over the top, add 2 glasses of water, cover and bring to a boil. § Transfer to a preheated oven at 350°F/180°C/gas 4 and cook for 40 minutes, basting frequently with the liquid in the braiser.

■ INGREDIENTS

- 8 artichokes
- juice of 1 lemon
- 4 oz (125 g) Mozzarella cheese, finely chopped
- 2 tablespoons Parmesan cheese, freshly grated
- ¾ cup (45 g) fine dry bread crumbs
- 1 egg
- salt and freshly ground black pepper
- ½ cup (125 ml) extra-virgin olive oil

Wine: a dry white (Corvo di Salaparuta)

Right: *Arancini di riso*

Filled mushroom caps

Teste di funghi ripiene

Serves: 4-6; Preparation: 30 minutes; Cooking: 30 minutes; Level of difficulty: Medium

Clean the mushrooms and carefully wash them under cold running water. Pat dry with paper towels and separate the stems from the caps. § Chop the stems, garlic, crumbled bread, salt, and pepper together. § Transfer to a bowl and combine until the mixture has the consistency of thick cream (add milk if it is too dry). § Stir in the eggs, Parmesan, oregano, calamint (or thyme), and 1 tablespoon of oil. § Mix thoroughly and taste for salt. Fill the hollow of each mushroom cap with the mixture, and smooth the surface with a moistened knife blade. § Arrange the mushrooms in a lightly oiled ovenproof dish. § Drizzle with oil and bake in a preheated oven at 350°F/180°C/gas 4 for about 30 minutes. § Serve hot straight from the baking dish.

■ INGREDIENTS

- 12 Caesar's (royal agaric) mushrooms
- 1 clove garlic
- 2 slices bread, soaked in warm milk, squeezed, and crumbled
- salt and freshly ground black pepper
- 1 egg and 1 yolk
- 1 cup (125 g) freshly grated Parmesan cheese
- dash of oregano
- 3 sprigs calamint or thyme
- 4 tablespoons extra-virgin olive oil

Wine: a dry white (Albenga)

Mixed baked vegetables

Strisce colorate

Be sure to arrange the vegetables in strips—a strip of onions, followed by one of green bell peppers, then zucchini, tomatoes, eggplant, red bell peppers, and lastly, the yellow peppers. Not all the vegetable varieties are essential, but keep the idea of color in mind when choosing them and try to have at least two or three different colors.

Serves: 4-6; Preparation: 30 minutes; Cooking: 1 hour; Level of difficulty: Simple

Wash the bell peppers, remove the seeds and cores, and cut into narrow strips, keeping the colors separate. § Clean the onions and cut into thin rings. § Cut the eggplant and the zucchini into julienne strips. § Cut the tomatoes in half, remove the seeds, and squeeze out excess water. Cut into small wedges. § Arrange the vegetables in strips (not layers), alternating the colors, in an ovenproof dish. § Season with salt and pepper, and drizzle with the oil. § Cover with aluminum foil and seal well around the edges of the dish. § Bake in a preheated oven at 325°F/160°C/gas 3 for about 1 hour. § Check the vegetables after 30 minutes and increase the heat if there is too much liquid or add a drop if they are too dry. When cooked, all the liquid should have been absorbed but the vegetables should not be dried out. § Serve hot or cold.

■ INGREDIENTS

- 1 yellow, 1 green, and 1 red bell pepper (capsicum)
- 2 onions
- 1 large eggplant (aubergine)
- 2 large zucchini (courgettes)
- 6 plum tomatoes
- salt and freshly ground black pepper
- 3 tablespoons extra-virgin olive oil

Wine: a light, dry white (Soave Classico)

Right:
Strisce colorate

Green bean mold
Sformato di fagiolini

Serves: 4-6; Preparation: 20 minutes; Cooking: 1¼ hours; Level of difficulty: Medium

Clean and wash the beans and cook for 10 minutes in lightly salted, boiling water. Drain and pass under cold running water. § Drain again and transfer to a dry kitchen towel. § Put the oil and half the butter in a skillet (frying pan). Add the onion, celery, and parsley, and when the onion begins to change color, add the beans. § Sauté until the beans have absorbed the seasoning. § Dissolve the stock cube in the water and add. § Cover the pan and simmer for about 20 minutes. § Add the Parmesan and pepper to the béchamel sauce. § Drain the beans and transfer to a bowl. Add half the béchamel sauce and the eggs. Mix well. § Butter a mold and sprinkle with the bread crumbs. Fill with the beans and cover with the remaining béchamel sauce. § Place a large container of cold water in a preheated oven at 350°F/180°C/gas 4. Place the mold in the water-filled container and cook for 40 minutes. § Invert the mold onto a serving dish, slice and serve.

VARIATIONS
– Serve with 1 quantity of *Simple tomato sauce* (see recipe p. 28).
– Add 3 oz (90 g) diced ham to the skillet with the beans.

■ INGREDIENTS

- 14 oz (450 g) fresh green beans
- 2 tablespoons extra-virgin olive oil
- 4 tablespoons butter
- ½ onion, finely chopped
- 1 stalk celery, finely chopped
- 1 tablespoon parsley, finely chopped
- ½ stock cube
- ½ cup (125 ml) boiling water
- 4 tablespoons freshly grated Parmesan cheese
- salt and freshly ground black pepper
- ½ quantity *Béchamel sauce* (see recipe p. 38)
- 2 eggs, beaten
- 2 tablespoons fine dry bread crumbs

Wine: a dry white (Bianco di Custoza)

Spinach fritters
Beignets di spinaci

Serves: 4-6; Preparation: 15 minutes; Cooking: 30 minutes; Level of difficulty: Simple

Prepare the béchamel sauce. § Put the spinach in a pot to defrost over medium-low heat. § When the liquid has evaporated, squeeze dry and chop coarsely. § Return to the pot, add the butter and sauté for 5 minutes. § Remove from the heat and transfer to a bowl. § Add the béchamel sauce and mix well. Add the eggs, one at a time, and then the nutmeg, salt, and pepper. Mix again until smooth. § Heat the frying oil in a deep-sided skillet (frying pan) until hot. § Add a few spoonfuls of the spinach mixture to the oil. Keep them well-spaced. § Turn the fritters and brown them evenly as they cook. § Remove with a slotted spoon and place on paper towels to drain. § Repeat until all the fritters are cooked. § Sprinkle with salt and serve hot.

■ INGREDIENTS

- ½ quantity *Béchamel sauce* (see recipe p. 38)
- 1 lb (500 g) frozen spinach
- 2 tablespoons butter
- 2 egg yolks + 1 whole egg
- dash of nutmeg
- salt and freshly ground black pepper
- 2 cups (500 ml) oil, for frying

Wine: a dry red (Chianti Montalbano)

Right:
Sformato di fagiolini

■ INGREDIENTS

• 8 *Barchette* (see recipe p. 56)
• 1 quantity *Mayonnaise*
  (see recipe p. 42)
• 2 hard-cooked
  (hard-boiled) eggs
• 1 tablespoon each of
  finely chopped parsley
  and marjoram
• 1 small white truffle

Wine: a dry white
(Tocai di Lison)

Barchette with herb mayonnaise and truffles

Barchette con maionese agli aromi

Serves: 4; Preparation: 15 minutes + time to make mayonnaise and barchette; Level of difficulty: Simple

Prepare the *barchette* and set aside. § Prepare the mayonnaise. § Chop the eggs. § Transfer to a bowl and mix with the parsley, marjoram, and mayonnaise. § Fill the *barchette* with the sauce, arrange on a serving dish, and sprinkle with slivers of truffle. § Serve soon after filling so that the *barchette* are still crisp and fresh.

Baked Neapolitan-style tomatoes
Pomodori alla vesuviana

Serves: 4; Preparation: 20 minutes; Cooking: 30 minutes; Level of difficulty: Simple

Wash and dry the tomatoes and cut them in half horizontally. § Scoop out the seeds and part of the pulp and sprinkle the insides with a little salt and pepper. Turn them upside down and leave for 15 minutes to eliminate excess water. Pat dry with paper towels. § Combine the parsley, garlic, most of the bread crumbs, the capers, salt, pepper, and oregano in a bowl and mix well. § Fill the tomatoes with the mixture and arrange them in a well-oiled baking dish (use half the oil). § Drizzle with the remaining oil, sprinkle with the remaining bread crumbs, and bake in a preheated oven at 350°F/180°C/gas 4 for about 30 minutes. § Serve either hot or at room temperature.

■ INGREDIENTS

- 4 large round tomatoes, ripe but firm
- salt and freshly ground black pepper
- 4 tablespoons finely chopped parsley
- 2 cloves garlic, finely chopped
- 1 cup (60 g) fine dry bread crumbs
- 1 tablespoon capers
- dash of oregano
- 4 tablespoons extra-virgin olive oil

Wine: a dry white
(Greco di Tufo)

Stuffed onions
Cipolle ripiene dolci delicate

Serves: 4; Preparation: 15 minutes; Cooking: 1 hour; Level of difficulty: Simple

Peel and crumble the sausage and sauté in a skillet (frying pan) with half the butter. § Add the veal, stir well, and let brown slightly. Remove from heat. § Peel the onions and cook for 10 minutes in a small pan of salted, boiling water. Drain well and pat dry with paper towels. § Cut the onions in half horizontally and carefully scoop out the center with a spoon. Chop the pulp finely and add to the meat and sausage mixture. § Stir in 1 egg, salt, pepper, nutmeg, most of the Parmesan, the parsley, and the amaretti cookie, and mix well. § Fill the onions with the mixture and arrange in a buttered baking dish. § Drizzle with the grappa. § Beat the remaining egg to a foam and brush over the onions. Dust with the bread crumbs mixed with the remaining Parmesan. Dab each onion with the remaining butter. § Bake in a preheated oven at 350°F/180°C/gas 4 for 45 minutes, or until a golden crust has formed on the surface. § Serve hot.

■ INGREDIENTS

- 1 Italian pork sausage
- 2 tablespoons butter
- 5 oz (150 g) ground veal
- 4 large onions
- 2 eggs
- salt and freshly ground black pepper
- dash of nutmeg
- ⅓ cup (45 g) freshly grated Parmesan cheese
- 1 tablespoon finely chopped parsley
- 1 amaretti cookie (macaroon), crumbled
- 1 tablespoon grappa
- 2 tablespoons bread crumbs

Wine: a dry red
(Dolcetto d'Alba)

Left: *Cipolle ripiene dolce delicate*

Egg and Cheese Appetizers

An almost endless variety of appetizers can be made using eggs and cheese. The following recipes are a selection of some personal favorites.

Hard-cooked eggs with bell pepper sauce
Uova sode con salsa di peperoni

Serves: 4-6; Preparation: 15 minutes + 30 minutes to chill; Cooking: 25-30 minutes; Level of difficulty: Simple

Combine the bell peppers, onion, garlic, parsley, and basil in a skillet (frying pan) with a dash of salt and the oil and sauté over medium heat. § To peel the tomatoes, bring a large pot of water to a boil. Plunge the tomatoes into the boiling water for 30 seconds and then transfer to cold water. The skins will slip off easily in your hands. § Dice the tomatoes and add to the saucepan. Cook over medium-low heat until the sauce is thick and smooth. § Add the vinegar and sugar, and mix well. Season with salt and pepper. § Remove from heat and set aside to cool. § Peel the hard-cooked eggs and cut in half lengthwise. § Remove the yolks, mash them, and add to the tomato and bell pepper sauce. Mix well. § Fill the egg whites with the mixture and arrange them on a serving dish. Pour any extra sauce over the top (or serve on slices of toasted bread or bruschetta with the eggs). § Place the eggs in the refrigerator for at least 30 minutes before serving.

■ INGREDIENTS
- 1 yellow and 1 red bell pepper (capsicum), finely chopped
- 2 white onions, finely chopped
- 2 cloves garlic, finely chopped
- 1 tablespoon finely chopped parsley
- 6 leaves fresh basil, finely chopped
- salt and freshly ground black pepper
- 2 tablespoons extra-virgin olive oil
- 6 fresh tomatoes
- 1 tablespoon vinegar
- ½ tablespoon sugar
- 6 hard-cooked (hard-boiled) eggs

Wine: a dry white (Vernaccia di San Gimignano)

Crostini with four cheeses
Crostini ai quattro formaggi

The four cheeses given here are suggestions since all cheeses are delicious when toasted on bread. Replace them with your particular favorites or with what you have in the refrigerator. Cheese crostini also make a nourishing after-school or late night snack.

Serves: 4; Preparation: 10 minutes; Cooking: 15 minutes; Level of difficulty: Simple

Combine the cheeses in a bowl with the oil. Season with salt, oregano, and marjoram. § Mash the cheeses with a fork and mix well until you have a fairly smooth cream. If the mixture is too thick to spread, add more oil. § Spread on the bread and cut each slice in half to form a triangle. Grind a little black pepper over the top. Arrange the crostini on a baking sheet. § Bake in a preheated oven at 400°F/200°C/gas 6 for 10–15 minutes, or until the cheese is golden brown. § Serve hot.

■ INGREDIENTS
- ½ cup (125 g) Caprino cheese, plus 1 cup (125 g) freshly grated Parmesan cheese
- 3½ oz (100 g) Gorgonzola cheese, diced
- 3½ oz (100 g) Fontina cheese, freshly grated
- 2 tablespoons extra-virgin olive oil
- salt and freshly ground black pepper
- dash of oregano
- 8 slices plain or whole-wheat (wholemeal) bread

Wine: a dry, sparkling red (Lambrusco)

Right: *Uova sode con salsa di peperoni*

Mixed cheeses with cumin seeds
Formaggi misti al cumino

■ INGREDIENTS

- ½ cup (125 g) butter
- ⅔ cup (150 g) each of Ricotta, Mascarpone, and Gorgonzola cheese
- 1 clove garlic, finely chopped
- 1 tablespoon cumin seeds
- 1 tablespoon finely chopped parsley
- 2 tablespoons brandy
- salt and freshly ground black pepper

Serves: 4; Preparation: 10 minutes + 4 hours to chill; Level of difficulty: Simple

Soften the butter over very low heat. § Combine the butter, Ricotta, Gorgonzola, Mascarpone, garlic, cumin, parsley, and brandy in a bowl and mix well with a fork. Season with salt and pepper and continue mixing until smooth and creamy. § Place the mixture on a sheet of waxed paper and shape it into a log. § Wrap tightly in the paper and place in the refrigerator for at least 4 hours. § Unwrap and transfer to a serving dish. § Serve with fresh bread or toast.

Pears with gorgonzola cheese
Pere con gorgonzola dolce

■ INGREDIENTS

- 4 large eating pears
- juice of 2 lemons
- 5 oz (150 g) Gorgonzola cheese
- 2 tablespoons light (single) cream
- 4 tablespoons extra-virgin olive oil
- 1 tablespoon finely chopped mint, + sprigs for garnishing
- salt and freshly ground white pepper

Wine: a dry white (Pinot Grigio)

Serves: 4; Preparation: 25 minutes + 1 hour to chill; Level of difficulty: Simple

Wash the pears thoroughly, dry well, and remove the cores with a corer. § Brush the cavities with the juice of 1 lemon. § Combine the Gorgonzola and cream in a bowl and mix until smooth. § Stuff the pears with the mixture, pressing it down so that the cavities are completely filled. § Place in the cold part of the refrigerator for at least 1 hour. § Combine the oil, remaining lemon juice, chopped mint, salt, and pepper in a bowl and whisk until well mixed. § Use a sharp knife to cut the pears in thin round slices. § Arrange the rounds on individual serving dishes and spoon the sauce over the top. § Garnish with sprigs of mint and serve.

Cheese and walnut mousse
Mousse di formaggio e noci

■ INGREDIENTS

- 3 large eating pears
- ¾ cup (200 g) Ricotta
- 1 cup (250 g) each Mascarpone and Gorgonzola cheese
- 2 cups (250 g) walnuts, finely chopped
- freshly ground black pepper
- 2 tablespoons grappa
- 1 tablespoon butter
- 2 tablespoons finely chopped chives

Wine: a dry white (Soave)

Serves: 6; Preparation: 15 minutes + 1 hour to chill; Level of difficulty: Simple

Wash the pears, peel, core, and chop the pulp finely. § Combine the cheeses in a bowl, mix well, then add the walnuts, pepper, and grappa. § Stir the pear pulp into the cheese mixture. § Butter six small molds and fill with the mixture. Chill in the refrigerator for at least 1 hour. § Just before serving, invert the molds onto serving plates and garnish with the chives.

Baby zucchini with pecorino cheese
Insalata di zucchine tenere

■ INGREDIENTS

- 14 oz (450 g) baby zucchini (courgettes)
- 5 oz (150 g) Pecorino romano cheese, flaked
- 4 tablespoons extra-virgin olive oil
- salt and freshly ground black pepper

Wine: a dry white (Lugana)

Left: *Pere con gorgonzola dolce*

Serves: 4; Preparation: 30 minutes; Level of difficulty: Simple

Wash the zucchini, trim the ends, and slice them very thinly. § Transfer to a serving dish and sprinkle with the Pecorino. § Pour the oil over the top and sprinkle with salt and pepper. § Toss well and serve.

VARIATIONS
- Replace the Pecorino cheese with the same quantity of Parmesan.
- Add the juice of 1 lemon together with the oil.

Bell peppers filled with parmesan and ricotta
Peperoni ripieni di parmigiano e ricotta

Be sure to choose rounded bell peppers that will sit upright in the baking dish during cooking.

Serves: 4; Preparation: 15 minutes; Cooking: 35 minutes; Level of difficulty: Simple

Cut the tops off the bell peppers and discard the seeds and cores. § Wash them carefully under cold running water and pat dry with paper towels. § Combine the bread crumbs, parsley, mint, garlic, and Parmesan in a food processor and blend until smooth. § Transfer the mixture to a large bowl and stir in the eggs and Ricotta. Season with salt, pepper, and oil, and mix until smooth. § Fill the peppers with the mixture and arrange them in an ovenproof dish. § Sprinkle with the butter and cook in a preheated oven at 400°F/200°C/gas 6 for about 35 minutes, or until the bell peppers are cooked. § Serve hot or at room temperature.

VARIATION
– For a more substantial dish, add 5 oz (150 g) finely chopped ham to the bread and Parmesan mixture.

- INGREDIENTS
- 4 yellow bell peppers (capsicums)
- 1 cup (60 g) bread crumbs
- 1 tablespoon finely chopped parsley
- 4 finely chopped mint leaves
- 1 clove garlic, finely chopped
- 1 cup (125 g) freshly grated Parmesan cheese
- 2 eggs, beaten
- ¾ cup (200 g) Ricotta cheese
- salt and freshly ground black pepper
- 2 tablespoons extra-virgin olive oil
- 3 tablespoons butter, chopped

Wine: a dry red (Carmignano)

Gorgonzola and celery served "porcupine-style"
Ricci di gorgonzola e sedano

Serves: 4-6; Preparation: 20 minutes + 1 to chill; Level of difficulty: Simple

Melt the butter in a saucepan over low heat. § Combine the butter and Gorgonzola in a bowl and mix well. § Gradually add the oil, lemon juice, and pepper, and stir carefully with a wooden spoon until the mixture becomes a thick cream. § Divide the cheese mixture in two equal parts and shape into balls. Wrap each ball in aluminum foil and chill in the refrigerator for 1 hour. § Wash and dry the celery and chop into sticks about 3 in (8 cm) long and ¼ in (6 mm) wide. § Unwrap the cheese and arrange on a serving dish. Press pieces of celery into the cheese balls so that they stick out like a porcupine's quills. § Serve cold.

- INGREDIENTS
- 4 tablespoons butter
- 14 oz (450 g) Gorgonzola cheese
- 2 tablespoons extra-virgin olive oil
- juice of 1 lemon
- freshly ground white pepper
- 12 large stalks celery

Wine: a dry white (Fiano di Avellino)

Right:
Ricci di gorgonzola e sedano

■ INGREDIENTS

• 10 oz (300 g) spring carrots

• 1¼ cups (300 g)
  Mascarpone cheese

• salt and freshly ground
  black pepper

• 4 slices *Bruschetta*
  (see recipe p. 54)

• sprigs of parsley, to
  garnish

Wine: a dry white
(Pinot Bianco)

Bruschetta with spring carrots and mascarpone
Bruschetta di carotine al mascarpone

Use the small, sweet carrots that appear in the markets in spring.
The cheese and carrot mixture is also good as a snack spread on crackers, toast, or fresh bread.

Serves: 4; Preparation: 10 minutes; Level of difficulty: Simple

Wash the carrots thoroughly. § Grate them into a bowl and add the Mascarpone, salt, and pepper. Mix well. § Prepare the bruschetta and spread the mixture on the slices. § Garnish with the sprigs of parsley and serve.

■ INGREDIENTS

- ⅔ cup (150 g) soft Caprino cheese
- 4 tablespoons finely chopped fresh herbs (parsley, chives, mint, thyme, marjoram, tarragon, dill, basil)
- 1 small cantaloupe (rock melon), about 12 oz (350 g)
- 1 cucumber, peeled
- juice of 1 orange
- salt and freshly ground black pepper
- 12 cherry tomatoes
- 6 small radishes
- 4 tablespoons extra-virgin olive oil
- 5 oz (150 g) purple grapes
- fresh spinach or grape leaves for garnish

Wine: a semisweet sparkling white (Moscato d'Asti Spumante)

■ INGREDIENTS

- 8 oz (250 g) Pecorino romano cheese
- 2 large eating pears
- 1¼ cups (5 oz/150 g) walnuts
- 1 bunch watercress
- 15 fresh spinach leaves
- 3 tablespoons extra-virgin olive oil
- juice of 1 small lemon
- salt and freshly ground black pepper
- 1 clove garlic, bruised

Wine: a dry or medium, lightly sparkling red (Freisa)

Caprino cheese and fruit salad
Palline di caprino e frutta

Serves: 6; Preparation: 25 minutes; Level of difficulty: Simple

Shape the Caprino into marble-size balls. Roll them in a dish filled with the chopped herbs until they are well coated. Set aside. § Use a small melon baller to make small balls from the cantaloupe and cucumber. § Sprinkle the cantaloupe balls with 1 tablespoon of orange juice and dust with the black pepper. § Drizzle the cucumber balls with salt and 1 tablespoon of oil. § Wash, dry, and remove the stems from the tomatoes. § Wash, dry, and trim the radishes, cutting off roots and leaves. § Wash and dry the grapes (and peel them, if preferred). § Line a large serving bowl with grape leaves or fresh spinach leaves. § Arrange the cheese, vegetables, and fruit on top. § Drizzle with the remaining oil and orange juice just before serving.

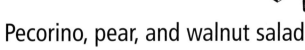

Pecorino, pear, and walnut salad
Insalata di pecorino pere e noci

Serves: 4-6; Preparation: 15 minutes; Level of difficulty: Simple

Chop the Pecorino into ½-in (1-cm) dice. § Wash, peel, and core the pears. Chop into ½-in (1-cm) dice. § Shell the walnuts and chop coarsely. § Wash and dry the watercress. § Arrange the spinach leaves in the bottom of a salad bowl and add the pears, cheese, watercress, and walnuts. § Put the oil, lemon juice, salt, pepper, and garlic in a small jar. Screw the top down and shake vigorously for 2–3 minutes. When the dressing is well mixed, remove the garlic and drizzle over the salad. § Toss carefully, without disturbing the spinach leaves, and serve.

VARIATION
– Sprinkle 2 oz (60 g) pitted and chopped black olives over the salad just before tossing.

Left: Palline di caprino e frutta

Eggs fairy-style
Uova delle fate

These colorful eggs are perfect for a children's party. Served with a cool dry white wine, they also make an eyecatching appetizer for an adult or family meal.

Serves: 3-6; Preparation: 20 minutes + 30 minutes to chill; Level of difficulty: Simple

Peel the hard-cooked eggs. Rinse under cold running water to remove any remaining pieces of shell and pat dry with paper towels. Cut a slice off the bottom of each egg so it will stand upright. § Prepare the mayonnaise and spread 1 quantity over the bottom of a serving dish. Set the eggs, upright, in the mayonnaise, not too close to each other. § Cut the plum tomatoes in half, remove the pulp and seeds, and use the halves to put a "hat" on each upright egg. § Dot the tomato caps with the remaining mayonnaise, to look like the spots on mushrooms. § Sprinkle the parsley over the mayonnaise so that it looks like grass. § Garnish with the pieces of bell pepper and gherkin to look like flowers. § Chill in the refrigerator for 30 minutes before serving.

■ INGREDIENTS

• 6 hard-cooked (hard-boiled) eggs
• 1½ quantities *Mayonnaise* (see recipe p. 42)
• 3 red plum tomatoes
• 4 tablespoons finely chopped parsley
• ¼ red and ¼ yellow bell pepper (capsicum), cut in tiny diamond shapes
• 6 pickled gherkins, sliced

Wine: a dry, lightly sparkling white (Galestro)

Ricotta with herbs
Ricotta alle erbe

This recipe comes from Trentino-Alto Adige in northeastern Italy. Its delicate flavor calls for the finest quality, freshest Ricotta available. When the cheese and herbs are well mixed, store in the refrigerator for about an hour before serving so that the flavor of the herbs will have time to penetrate.

Serves: 6; Preparation: 10 minutes + 1 hour to chill; Level of difficulty: Simple

Combine the Ricotta, basil, and parsley in a bowl and mix well. § Add the bay leaves, fennel, salt, and pepper, and mix again. § Place in the refrigerator to chill. § Remove the bay leaves and garnish with sprigs of parsley. § Serve cold.

VARIATION
– Replace the basil with the same amount of finely chopped fresh mint.

■ INGREDIENTS

• 1½ cups (14 oz/ 450 g) Ricotta cheese
• 2 tablespoons basil, finely chopped
• 2 tablespoons finely chopped parsley + sprigs to garnish
• 2 bay leaves
• 1 teaspoon fennel seeds
• salt and freshly ground black pepper

Wine: a dry white (Sauvignon)

Right:
Uova delle fate

Parmesan puffs
Bigné al parmigiano

Serves: 4; Preparation: 10 minutes; Cooking: 30 minutes; Level of difficulty: Medium

Put the water in a small saucepan with 2 tablespoons of softened butter over medium heat. § When the water starts to boil, remove the pan from heat and incorporate the sifted flour and salt, stirring constantly with a wooden spoon. § Return the saucepan to the heat and cook until the dough is thick, mixing all the time. § Remove from heat and stir in the Parmesan and paprika. Set aside to cool. § To blanch and peel the almonds, place them in a bowl and pour boiling water over the top so they are barely covered. Leave for 1 minute. Drain and rinse under cold water. Pat dry and slip off the skins. § Chop the almonds finely. § Add the eggs to the dough one at a time. Do not add the second until the first has been thoroughly incorporated. § Beat the dough vigorously. Transfer to a pastry bag with a smooth tube about ¼ in (6 mm) in diameter. § Butter a baking sheet and dust with flour. § Place marble-size balls of dough on the baking sheet and sprinkle with the almonds, making sure they stick to the puffs. § Bake in a preheated oven at 400°F/200°C/gas 6 for 15–20 minutes. The puffs will swell and dry as they bake. § Serve cool.

■ INGREDIENTS

- ⅔ cup (150 ml) cold water
- 3 tablespoons butter
- 1 cup (150 g) all-purpose (plain) flour, + 2 tablespoons
- dash of salt
- ½ cup (60 g) freshly grated Parmesan cheese
- dash of paprika
- 2 oz (60 g) sweet almonds
- 2 eggs

Wine: a dry sparkling white (Prosecco di Conegliano)

Little pizzas with tomato, onion, and mozzarella
Pizzette semplici

Serves: 4; Preparation: 10 minutes + 2 hours to rest; Cooking: 25-30 minutes; Level of difficulty: Simple

In a small bowl, gently stir the yeast into half the warm water. Set aside to rest for 10 minutes. § Sift a quarter of the flour into a large bowl and make a well in the center. Add the olive oil. § Gradually stir in the yeast mixture and the flour, adding as much of the remaining water as necessary to obtain a smooth, firm dough. § Add the salt. § Turn the dough out onto a clean, lightly floured counter. Form it into a ball and then knead and fold until a smooth, elastic dough has been obtained. § Sprinkle with flour and wrap the dough in a clean dishcloth. Place in a warm spot in the kitchen (or wrap in a woolen

■ INGREDIENTS

BASE
- 1 oz (30 g) fresh yeast, or 2 (¼ oz) packages active dry yeast
- 1 cup (250 ml) warm water
- 3⅓ cups (500 g) all-purpose (plain) flour
- 2 tablespoons extra-virgin olive oil
- 1 teaspoon salt

Right:

Pizzette semplici

TOPPING
- 14 oz (450 g) canned
  tomatoes chopped
- 1 tablespoon capers
- 1 clove garlic and 1 onion,
  finely chopped
- generous dash of oregano
- salt and freshly ground
  black pepper
- 5 oz (150 g) Mozarella
  cheese, diced

*Wine: a light, dry red
(Vino Novello)*

garment) and leave to rise until it has doubled in size. This will take about 1½–2 hours. § Mix the tomatoes, capers, garlic, onion, oregano, salt, and pepper together in a bowl. § Oil a baking sheet. § Break the dough into four pieces and press each one out to form a small round pizza. § Distribute the tomato mixture evenly over the top of each. § Bake in a preheated oven at 400°F/200°C/gas 6 for 20–25 minutes. § Remove from the oven and sprinkle with the Mozzarella. Return to the oven for about 5 minutes, or until the Mozzarella has melted and browned a little. § Take the pizzas out of the oven and serve hot or at room temperature.

Egg and bell pepper cream
Crema di uova e peperoni

Egg and bell pepper cream makes a refreshing and unusual antipasto for summer dinner parties, and bell peppers are now available in many colors. However, I strongly recommend that you try it out a few times before the invitations go out. A lot depends on the quantity of water the bell peppers produce during cooking and the size of the eggs.

Serves: 4-6; Preparation: 50 minutes + 2 hours to chill; Cooking: 30 minutes; Level of difficulty: Complicated

Wash the bell peppers, dry, and remove the seeds and cores. Cut into small pieces, keeping the colors separate. § Place 2 tablespoons of oil in three separate saucepans, divide the onion in three parts, and sauté a third in each. § When the onion is transparent, add salt, pepper, 2 tablespoons of water, and bell peppers, keeping the colors separate in each pan. § Cover each pan and cook over medium heat for about 30 minutes, or until the bell peppers are soft and well-cooked. § Remove the pans from heat and let the mixtures cool. § Purée the contents of each pan separately in a food processor. § Soften the gelatin in a little water. § Heat the milk in a pot, but don't let it boil. § Beat the egg yolks in a bowl and add the hot milk a little at a time, stirring continuously. Season with salt and pepper. § Transfer to a saucepan and heat to just below boiling point, stirring frequently. Add the gelatin. § Remove from heat and beat with a fork so that the gelatin dissolves. § Pour equal parts of the mixture into three different bowls and let cool. § Add one color of bell pepper purée to each and stir. § Whip the cream to stiff peaks and fold in equal parts to each of the three bowls. § Moisten a rectangular mold with water and pour in the yellow mixture. Place the mold in the refrigerator for 10 minutes. § Remove and pour in the red mixture. Return the mold to the refrigerator for 10 more minutes. § Remove again and add the green mixture. § Refrigerate for at least 2 hours. § Just before serving, dip the mold for a second in hot water and invert the cream on a serving dish.

■ INGREDIENTS

- 2 lb (1 kg) bell peppers (capsicums), in equal quantities of red, yellow, and green
- ⅓ cup (90 ml) extra-virgin olive oil
- 1 medium-large onion, finely chopped
- salt and freshly ground white pepper
- 1 oz (30 g) gelatin
- 3 cups (750 ml) milk
- 6 egg yolks
- 1¾ cups (450 ml) heavy (double) cream

Wine: a dry white (Cortese di Gavi)

Right:
Crema di uova e peperoni

Fried parmesan puffs
Bomboline di parmigiano

Serves: 6; Preparation: 20 minutes; Cooking: 20 minutes; Level of difficulty: Medium

Combine the water with the salt and butter in a saucepan and bring to a boil. § Add the sifted flour all at once, remove from heat, and stir vigorously with a wooden spoon. § When the mixture is smooth, return to heat and cook until the batter pulls away from the sides of the pan. Set aside to cool. § Add the eggs one at a time and mix each one in before adding the next. § Add the cheeses and nutmeg. § Mold the mixture into marble-size balls. § Heat the oil in a deep-sided skillet (frying pan) until very hot and fry the puffs in small batches until golden brown. § Place on paper towels to drain, sprinkle with salt, and serve hot.

■ INGREDIENTS

- ¾ cup (200 ml) water
- 1 teaspoon salt
- 3 tablespoons butter
- 1 cup (150 g) all-purpose (plain) flour
- 4 eggs
- 1 cup (125 g) freshly grated Parmesan cheese
- ½ cup (60 g) freshly grated Emmenthal cheese
- dash of nutmeg
- 2 cups (500 ml) oil, for frying

Wine: a dry red (Grignolino)

Crêpes with four-cheese filling
Crêpes ai quattro formaggi

Serves: 6; Preparation: 20 minutes + 1 hour for the crêpes; Cooking: 20 minutes; Level of difficulty: Medium

Prepare the crêpes and the béchamel sauce. § Add half the Parmesan, and all the Gruyère, Fontina, and Gorgonzola to the béchamel. Cook over low heat until the cheeses have melted into the sauce. § Spread 2–3 tablespoons of the cheese mixture on each crêpe. Roll the crêpes up and place them in a lightly buttered ovenproof dish. § Cover with the remaining cheese sauce and sprinkle with the remaining Parmesan. Grind a little black pepper over the top and dot with the remaining butter. § Bake in a preheated oven at 350°F/180°C/gas 4 for 15 minutes, or until the topping is golden brown. § Serve piping hot straight from the oven.

■ INGREDIENTS

- 1 quantity *Crespelle* (see recipe p. 62)
- 1 quantity *Béchamel* (see recipe p. 38)
- ¾ cup (90 g) freshly grated Parmesan cheese
- ½ cup (60 g) freshly grated Gruyère cheese
- 2 oz (60 g) Fontina cheese, diced
- 2 oz (60 g) Gorgonzola cheese, diced
- 6 tablespoons butter, to grease the crêpe pan
- freshly ground black pepper

Wine: a young, dry red (Roero)

Right: *Crêpes ai quattro formaggi*

Mozzarella crostini Puglia-style
Crostini pugliesi

■ INGREDIENTS

- 1 onion, finely chopped
- 4 tablespoons extra-virgin olive oil
- 14 oz (450 g) canned tomatoes chopped
- 6 leaves fresh basil, torn
- 1 teaspoon dried oregano
- dash of salt
- 4 slices plain or whole wheat (wholemeal) bread
- 5 oz (150 g) Mozzarella cheese, thinly sliced

Wine: a dry rosé (Lizzano)

Serves: 4; Preparation: 15 minutes; Cooking: 45 minutes; Level of difficulty: Simple

Sauté the onion in half the oil until transparent. § Add the tomatoes, basil, half the oregano, and salt, and simmer for 30 minutes. § Cut the slices of bread in half, cover with the Mozzarella, and place in an oiled baking dish. Sprinkle with the remaining oregano, drizzle with the rest of the oil, and bake in a preheated oven at 400°F/200°C/gas 6 until the bread is crisp and the Mozzarella has melted. § Remove from the oven and spread with the tomato sauce. § Serve hot.

Omelet roll

Rotolone d'uovo

Serves: 6; Preparation: 20 minutes + 4 hours to chill; Cooking: 20 minutes; Level of difficulty: Medium

In a bowl whisk the eggs with the flour, Parmesan, milk, and salt. § Melt the butter in a skillet (frying pan) and pour in the egg mixture. Cook until golden on one side, then flip and cook on the other. § Drain on paper towels and set aside to cool. § Prepare the mayonnaise and mix with the mustard and gherkins. § Arrange the ham on the omelet and spread with a layer of mayonnaise. Cover with the mortadella and roll the omelet up, being careful not to break it. § Wrap in aluminum foil and keep in the refrigerator for at least 4 hours. § Just before serving, cut the roll in slices and arrange on a serving dish. Garnish with radishes and cucumber.

■ INGREDIENTS

- 6 eggs
- 1 tablespoon all-purpose (plain) flour
- 1 tablespoon freshly grated Parmesan cheese
- 2 tablespoons milk
- dash of salt
- 2 tablespoons butter
- ½ quantity *Mayonnaise* (see recipe p. 42)
- 1 tablespoon mustard
- 6 pickled gherkins, finely chopped
- 3½ oz (100 g) ham, sliced
- 3 oz (90 g) mortadella, in a single thick slice
- 8 radishes, chopped
- 1 cucumber, thinly sliced

Wine: a dry red (Merlot dell'Isonzo)

Zucchini and parmesan pie

Parmigiana di zucchine

Serves: 6; Preparation: 20 minutes; Cooking: 35 minutes; Level of difficulty: Simple

Wash the zucchini and trim the ends. Slice lengthwise in ¼-in (6-mm) strips. § Heat the frying oil in a deep-sided skillet (frying pan) until very hot and fry the zucchini in small batches until golden brown. § Drain well on paper towels and set aside in the warming oven. § Sauté the garlic and onion over medium heat in a skillet with the olive oil. § Remove the garlic and add the tomatoes, basil, and salt. Cook for 10 minutes, stirring from time to time with a wooden spoon. § Grease an ovenproof dish with a little olive oil and cover the bottom with a layer of tomato sauce. Add a layer of zucchini slices, another of tomato sauce, sprinkle with Parmesan, and cover with a layer of Mozzarella slices. Repeat until all the ingredients are used up, leaving a little Mozzarella and Parmesan for the topping. § Dot with the butter and grind a little black pepper over the top. § Bake in a preheated oven at 350°F/180°C/gas 4 for 15 minutes, or until the topping is golden brown.

■ INGREDIENTS

- 1½ lb (750 g) zucchini (courgettes)
- 2 cups (500 ml) oil, for frying
- 2 cloves garlic
- 1 onion, finely chopped
- 1 tablespoon extra-virgin olive oil
- 14 oz (450 g) tomatoes, peeled and chopped
- 8 fresh basil leaves, torn
- salt and freshly ground black pepper
- ¾ cup (90 g) freshly grated Parmesan cheese
- 7 oz (200 g) Mozzarella cheese, in thin slices
- 1 tablespoon butter

Wine: a dry red (Elba rosso)

Right: *Parmigiana di zucchine*

Semolina molds
Sformatini di semolino

Serves: 4; Preparation: 15 minutes + time for the meat sauce; Cooking: 30 minutes; Level of difficulty: Simple

Prepare the meat sauce. § Place the milk in a large saucepan, add a dash of salt, and bring to a boil. § As the milk begins to boil, sift in the semolina, stirring constantly. Cook for about 10 minutes over low heat, stirring all the time. § Remove from heat and add the nutmeg, half the butter, the Parmesan, and 2 egg yolks. § Butter four pudding molds 4 in (10 cm) in diameter and sprinkle with bread crumbs. Line the sides and the bottom with the semolina mixture. § Put a piece of Fontina and 1 tablespoon of meat sauce in the center of each one, then fill completely with semolina. § Bake in a preheated oven at 400°F/200°C/ gas 6 for 15–20 minutes. § When cooked, remove from the oven and invert into a casserole. § Return to the oven for a few minutes to brown. § Serve hot with the remaining sauce.

■ INGREDIENTS

- 1 quantity *Bolognese* or *Quick meat sauce* (see recipes pp. 30, 32)
- salt and freshly ground black pepper
- 3 cups (750 ml) whole (full cream) milk
- 1 cup (150 g) semolina
- dash of nutmeg
- ⅓ cup (100 g) butter
- 4 tablespoons freshly grated Parmesan cheese
- 2 egg yolks
- 3½ oz (100 g) Fontina cheese, coarsely chopped
- 2 tablespoons fine dry bread crumbs

Wine: a dry, full-bodied red (Barolo)

Mint omelet
Frittata di menta

Serves: 6; Preparation: 10 minutes; Cooking: 10 minutes; Level of difficulty: Simple

Beat the eggs in a bowl until foamy, then add the bread crumbs, Pecorino, mint, parsley, and a dash of salt and pepper . § Heat the oil in a skillet (frying pan) until very hot. § Pour in the egg mixture. Spread it out over the bottom and cook over medium heat until the underside turns golden brown. § Flip the omelet with the help of a lid or plate. Don't let it cook too much; a good *frittata* is supposed to be fairly soft. § Serve hot.

■ INGREDIENTS

- 6 eggs
- ½ cup (30 g) bread crumbs
- 1 cup (125 g) freshly grated Pecorino cheese
- 12 mint leaves, finely chopped
- 2 tablespoons finely chopped parsley
- salt and freshly ground black pepper
- 4 tablespoons extra-virgin olive oil

Wine: a dry white (Bianco di Pitigliano)

VARIATION
— For a completely different but equally delicious dish, replace the mint with 10 oz (300 g) of fresh cauliflower florets. The cauliflower should be sautéed for 8–10 minutes in the oil before adding the egg mixture. Zucchini (courgettes are also good when prepared in this way).

Right:
Sformatini di semolino

INGREDIENTS

- 14 oz (450 g) aged Provolone cheese
- 4 tablespoons extra-virgin olive oil
- 1 clove garlic, cut in two
- 1 tablespoon white wine vinegar
- 1 teaspoon oregano
- 1 teaspoon sugar

Wine: a dry red (Cirò)

Sweet and sour fried cheese
Caciu all'argintera

This simple and tasty dish comes from Sicily, in the south.
Provolone is a hard cheese and will not melt during cooking.

Serves: 4; Preparation: 5 minutes; Cooking: 15 minutes; Level of difficulty: Simple

Cut the cheese in slices about ¼ in (6 mm) thick. § Heat the oil with the garlic in a skillet (frying pan). As soon as it is hot, add the slices of cheese and brown on both sides. § When they are browned, drizzle with the vinegar and dust with the oregano and sugar. § Serve immediately.

Saffron cheese pie
Crostata di formaggio allo zafferano

Serves: 6; Preparation: 20 minutes + 1 hour to chill; Cooking: 45 minutes; Level of difficulty: Simple

Prepare the dough: mix the flour with the butter (set aside 1 teaspoon), oil, salt, 1 whole egg, and 1 yolk. Do not overmix as the dough could become hard. § Wrap in a sheet of waxed paper and chill in the refrigerator for 1 hour. § For the filling: put the Ricotta in a bowl and mash with a fork. Add the Gruyère, softened butter, saffron and, one at a time, the egg yolks, mixing well. § Beat the egg whites until stiff and fold into the mixture. § Roll out the dough and line a buttered pie pan about 8 in (20 cm) in diameter. § Fill with the cheese mixture. § Bake in a preheated oven at 350°F/180°C/gas 4 for 45 minutes. § Serve hot or at room temperature.

■ INGREDIENTS

DOUGH
- 2⅓ cups (350 g) all-purpose (plain) flour
- 4 tablespoons butter, softened and chopped
- 2 tablespoons extra-virgin olive oil
- dash of salt
- 1 egg and 1 yolk

FILLING
- 1½ cups (450 g) Ricotta cheese
- 1½ cups (180 g) freshly grated Gruyère cheese
- ⅓ cup (90 g) butter
- generous dash of saffron
- 6 eggs, separated

Wine: a dry white (Frascati)

Cheese tortelli
Tortelli di formaggio

Serves: 6; Preparation: 20 minutes; Cooking: 20 minutes; Level of difficulty: Simple

Put the two cheeses, flour, parsley, fennel seeds, and nutmeg in a bowl. Add 3 of the eggs, and half the bread crumbs, and mix well. § Beat the remaining egg with a fork in a shallow dish. Season with salt and pepper. § Shape the cheese mixture into walnut-sized balls, dusting your hands with flour to stop the mixture sticking. § Dip the balls first in the beaten egg, and then in the remaining bread crumbs. § Melt the butter in a skillet (frying pan), add the tortelli balls, and fry until golden brown. Drain on paper towels. § Transfer to a serving dish, sprinkle with salt, and serve hot.

■ INGREDIENTS

- 2½ cups (300 g) Gruyère cheese, grated
- ¾ cup (90 g) freshly grated Parmesan cheese,
- 2 tablespoons all-purpose (plain) flour
- 1 tablespoon finely chopped parsley
- dash of fennel seeds
- dash of nutmeg
- 4 eggs
- 1½ cups (90 g) bread crumbs
- salt and freshly ground mixed pepper
- 2 tablespoons butter

Wine: a dry red (Dolcetto)

Right: *Crostata di formaggio allo zafferano*

Ham and cheese tidbits
Bocconcini di formaggio e prosciutto

Serves: 4-6; Preparation: 10 minutes + 30 minutes to rest; Cooking: 20 minutes; Level of difficulty: Simple

Mix the flour with the butter, 2 eggs, and salt. If necessary, add a little water and knead until the dough is smooth. § Wrap the dough in a cloth and set aside in a cool place for 30 minutes. § Roll out the dough in a thin sheet and cut into rectangles. § Cut the slices of ham and Fontina to the same size as the pieces of dough. § Place pieces of ham, Fontina, and anchovy on half the pieces of dough, cover with the remaining dough and press the edges together to seal. § Beat the remaining egg and brush the tops with it. § Place the tidbits on a buttered baking sheet and bake in a preheated oven at 350°F/180°C/gas 4 for 25 minutes, or until golden brown. § Serve hot.

■ INGREDIENTS

• 2⅓ cups (300 g) all-purpose (plain) flour
• ⅔ cup (150 g) butter, softened
• 3 eggs
• dash of salt
• 10 oz (300 g) ham, cut in thick slices
• 5 oz (150 g) Fontina cheese, sliced
• 8 anchovy fillets, crumbled

Wine: a dry, sparkling red (Lambrusco di Sorbara)

Egg, provolone, apple, and radicchio salad
Insalata di uovo, provolone, mele e radicchio rosso

Serves: 4-6; Preparation: 15 minutes + 1 hour for the radicchio rosso; Level of difficulty: Simple

To clean the radicchio rosso, discard the outer leaves, wash several times, dry well and place in the bottom of a salad bowl. § Season with the lemon juice and half the oil, toss well and set aside for about 1 hour. § Slice the eggs with an egg cutter. § Peel the apples and dice. § Dice the Provolone. § Add the eggs, apples, Provolone, and olives to the salad bowl. § Mix the mustard, vinegar, remaining oil, salt, and pepper together in a bowl. Beat vigorously with a fork and pour over the salad. § Toss well and serve.

VARIATIONS
– Add a few chopped walnuts to give extra flavor to the salad.
– Replace the radicchio rosso with the same quantity of fresh spinach.

■ INGREDIENTS

• 10 oz (300 g) radicchio rosso (red-leaf chicory)
• juice of 1 small lemon
• ⅓ cup (90 ml) extra-virgin olive oil
• 3 hard-cooked (hard-boiled) eggs
• 3 crisp eating apples
• 7 oz (200 g) Provolone cheese
• 16 large black olives, pitted and chopped
• 2 tablespoons hot mustard
• 1 tablespoon white wine vinegar
• salt and freshly ground black pepper

Wine: a dry white (Galestro)

Right: *Insalata di uovo, provolone, mele e radicchio rosso*

Cheese-filled barchette
Barchette di formaggio

A simple creamy cheese and béchamel filling highlights the delicate flavor of the pastry.
Experiment with mixes of your favorite cheeses.

Serves: 4-6; Preparation: 20 minutes + time to make the barchette; Cooking: 20 minutes; Level of difficulty: Simple

Prepare the *barchette*. § Make a thick béchamel sauce. § Cut the cheeses in pieces, add to the béchamel sauce, and stir well over very low heat until melted. § Fill the *barchette* with the sauce and cook in a preheated oven at 350°F/180°C/gas 4 for 5–10 minutes to brown. § Serve hot.

■ INGREDIENTS

• 12 Barchette
  (see recipe p. 56
• 1 quantity *Béchamel sauce*
  (see recipe p. 38)
• 3 oz (90 g) Emmental
  cheese
• 7 oz (200 g) Mozzarella
  cheese
• 3 oz (90 g) Fontina cheese

Wine: a dry white (Corvo)

■ INGREDIENTS

- 2⅓ cups (300 g) all-purpose (plain) flour
- 2 cups (300 g) buckwheat flour
- ½ cup (125 ml) milk
- 8 oz (250 g) Fontina cheese, diced
- ½ cup (125 g) butter
- dash of nutmeg
- salt and freshly ground black pepper
- 2 eggs (beaten) + 1 yolk
- 1¾ cups (100 g) bread crumbs
- 2 cups (500 ml) oil, for frying

*Wine: a dry red
(Chianti Classico)*

Fontina croquettes
Crocchete di fontina

This dish is a rather filling antipasto and should be followed by something light.

Serves: 6-8; Preparation: 15 minutes; Cooking: 15 minutes; Level of difficulty: Simple

Mix the two types of flour together in a saucepan. Stir in the milk, Fontina, butter, nutmeg, salt, and pepper. § Cook over low heat for about 20 minutes, stirring continuously until a fairly dense cream forms. § Remove from heat and add the egg yolk, continuing to stir with a wooden spoon. Pour the mixture into a buttered dish and let cool. § Mold the mixture into small oblong croquettes, dip them in the beaten egg, and roll in the bread crumbs. § Heat the oil in a deep-sided skillet (frying pan) until very hot and fry the croquettes in batches until golden brown. § Sprinkle with a little salt, and serve hot.

■ INGREDIENTS

- 8 oz (250 g) Mozzarella cheese
- ½ cup (75 g) all-purpose (plain) flour
- 2 eggs
- 1½ cups (90 g) bread crumbs
- 2 cups (500 ml) oil, for frying
- dash of salt

*Wine: a dry red
(San Severo Rosso)*

Fried mozzarella
Mozzarella fritta

Serves: 4; Preparation: 5 minutes; Cooking: 10 minutes; Level of difficulty: Simple

Cut the Mozzarella in rather thick slices and cover with flour. § Beat the eggs in a bowl and dip the slices in the egg and then in the bread crumbs. § Heat the oil in a deep-sided skillet (frying pan) until very hot and fry the Mozzarella in batches until golden brown on both sides. § Drain on paper towels, sprinkle with salt, and serve piping hot.

■ INGREDIENTS

- 12 slices tomato
- 12 slices Mozzarella
- 8 oz (250 g) mixed pickled vegetables

*Wine: a light, sparkling red
(Lambrusco)*

Mozzarella and mixed pickled vegetables
Mozzarella piccante

Serves: 4; Preparation: 10 minutes + 30 minutes to chill; Level of difficulty: Simple

Place a slice of mozzarella on each slice of tomato. § Purée the pickled vegetables together in a food processor. § Place a spoonful of vegetables on each slice of Mozzarella. § Keep in the refrigerator for 30 minutes before serving.

Left:
Barchette di formaggio

Meat and Fish Appetizers

When serving a meat-based dish as an appetizer remember that meat is filling. If you are planning to follow it with pasta and a main dish in the traditional Italian manner, keep the quantities to tempting tidbit-size or your guests will spoil their appetites and all your hard work and planning will be wasted.

Italian seafood cookery is simpler than in most other cuisines. But traditionally, it relies on the freshest, highest quality ingredients. With the exception of the smoked salmon, tuna fish, and salt cod, all the recipes in this section call for fresh fish. However, frozen fish is often just as good. Experiment with the recipes to discover which you prefer.

Stuffed baked mussels
Cozze ripiene al forno

Serves: 6; Preparation: 20 minutes + 1 hour to soak mussels; Cooking: 25 minutes; Level of difficulty: Simple

Soak the mussels in a large bowl of water for at least 1 hour to purge them of sand. Pull off their beards, scrub, and rinse well in abundant cold water. § Put the mussels in a large skillet (frying pan) over medium-high heat, sprinkle with the wine, and cover. § When all the shells are open (discard any that don't open), remove from the skillet. Discard all the empty half shells, keeping only those with the mussel inside. § Remove the crusts from the rolls and soak the insides in the milk for 10 minutes. Squeeze out excess moisture with your hands. § Combine most of the parsley and garlic in a bowl with the bread. Add 4 tablespoons of grated Parmesan, the oil, salt, and pepper. Mix well. § Fill the shells with the mixture, then arrange them in a large, greased baking dish. Dust with the remaining Parmesan and bake in a preheated oven at 400°F/200°C/gas 6 for about 15 minutes. § Sprinkle with the remaining garlic and parsley just before serving.

■ INGREDIENTS

- 1¾ lb (800 g) mussels, in shell
- ½ cup (125 ml) dry white wine
- 3 day-old bread rolls
- 1 cup (250 ml) milk
- 4 tablespoons finely chopped parsley
- 4 cloves garlic, finely chopped
- ⅓ cup (45 g) freshly grated Parmesan cheese
- 2 tablespoons extra-virgin olive oil
- salt and freshly ground black pepper

Wine: a dry white (Cinqueterre)

Mussels in pepper sauce
Impepata di cozze

This fiery dish makes a perfect appetizer when followed by oven-roasted fish. Vary the amount of pepper depending on your tastes.

Serves: 6; Preparation: 10 minutes + 1 hour to soak mussels; Cooking: 10 minutes; Level of difficulty: Simple

Soak the mussels in a large bowl of water for at least 1 hour to purge them of sand. Pull off their beards, scrub, and rinse well in abundant cold water. § Sauté the parsley and garlic in a skillet (frying pan) with the oil for 4–5 minutes. Season with salt. § Add the mussels and cook over medium heat until they are all open. Discard any that haven't opened. § Add the pepper and cook for 2 minutes more, stirring all the time. § Prepare the *bruschetta* and place a slice in each serving dish. Cover with mussels and spoon some of the sauce from the skillet over each portion. § Serve hot.

■ INGREDIENTS

- 1¾ lb (800 g) mussels, in shell
- 4 tablespoons finely chopped parsley
- 1 clove garlic, finely chopped
- 2 tablespoons extra-virgin olive oil
- dash of salt
- 2 teaspoons freshly ground black pepper
- 6 slices *Bruschetta* (see recipe p. 54)

Wine: a dry white (Corvo Bianco)

Right: Impepata di cozze

Clams in fresh cream sauce
Vongole in salsa di panna fresca

Serves: 6; Preparation: 30 minutes + 1 hour to soak clams; Cooking: 15 minutes; Level of difficulty: Simple
Soak the clams in a large bowl of water for at least 1 hour to purge them of sand. Rinse well in abundant cold water. § Put them in a skillet (frying pan) with the wine, cover, and cook over medium-high heat. Take the clams out as they open. Arrange them on a serving dish and keep them in a warm place. § Strain the liquid left in the skillet and set aside to cool. § In the same skillet, sauté the onion and garlic in the butter until they turn golden. Add the flour and mix rapidly. § Gradually add the strained clam liquid and mix well until you have a thick, creamy sauce. Season with salt and pepper. § Beat the cream, egg, parsley, and lemon juice together and add to the clam sauce. Mix rapidly and then pour over the clams. § Serve at once.

■ INGREDIENTS

- 4 lb (2 kg) clams, in shell
- 1 cup (250 ml) dry white wine
- 1 medium onion, finely chopped
- 2 cloves garlic, finely chopped
- 4 tablespoons butter
- 2 tablespoons all-purpose (plain) flour
- salt and freshly ground black pepper
- 1¼ cups (300 ml) light (single) cream
- 1 egg, beaten
- 1 tablespoon finely chopped parsley
- juice of ½ lemon

Wine: a dry white (Roero Arneis)

Baked mussels
Cozze gratinate al forno

Serves: 4; Preparation: 30 minutes + 1 hour to soak mussels; Cooking: 15 minutes; Level of difficulty: Simple
Soak the mussels in a large bowl of water for at least 1 hour to purge them of sand. Pull off their beards, scrub, and rinse well in abundant cold water. § Transfer to a skillet (frying pan), cover, and cook over medium-high heat until they are all open. Discard any that haven't opened. § Set the liquid they produce aside. § Mix the parsley and garlic together in a bowl with the bread crumbs, 1 tablespoon of oil, salt, and pepper. Strain the mussel liquid and add about 3 tablespoons to the bread mixture. Mix well. § Arrange the mussels in a buttered ovenproof dish. Fill each one with some of the mixture and drizzle with the remaining oil and lemon juice. § Bake in a preheated oven at 400°F/200°C/gas 6 for 15–20 minutes, or until the bread crumbs turn golden brown. § Serve hot.

■ INGREDIENTS

- 2 lb (1 kg) fresh mussels
- 2 tablespoons finely chopped parsley
- 2 cloves garlic, finely chopped
- 1¾ cups (100 g) bread crumbs
- 3 tablespoons extra-virgin olive oil
- salt and freshly ground black pepper
- 1 tablespoon butter
- juice of 1 small lemon

Wine: a dry white (Ischia Bianco)

Right: *Vongole in salsa di panna fresca*

Salt cod fritters
Frittelle di baccalà

When buying salt cod, always choose meaty, cream-colored fillets. Avoid the brown ones.

■ INGREDIENTS

• 14 oz (450 g) salt cod, skinned and boned

• 1 cup (150 g) all-purpose (plain) flour

• ½ cup (125 ml) warm water

• 1 tablespoon extra-virgin olive oil

• dash of salt

• 2 cups (500 ml) oil, for frying

Wine: a dry white (Colli di Luni Bianco)

Serves: 4; Preparation: 15 minutes + 24 hours to soak cod; Cooking: 20 minutes; Level of difficulty: Simple

Put the salt cod in a bowl of cold water to soak a day ahead. § In a separate bowl combine the flour and enough of the water to obtain a thick batter. Add the olive oil, season with salt, and stir continuously for 5 minutes. § Wash the salt cod in running water, dry, and cut in pieces. § Heat the oil in a deep-sided skillet (frying pan) until very hot. Dip the pieces of salt cod in the batter, then fry until golden brown. § Drain on paper towels, sprinkle with salt, and serve hot.

Filled sweet squid
Calamari dolci delicati

Serves: 4; Preparation: 20 minutes; Cooking: 30 minutes; Level of difficulty: Simple

Choose small squid that are all about the same size. § To clean the squid, separate the tentacles and head from the body by grasping the head and pulling it apart from the body. Remove the ink sac from the head. Peel off the skin. Remove the bony part and clean out the insides. Rinse well in cold running water. § Cut off the tentacles and blanch the bodies in boiling water for 2–3 minutes. Set aside to cool. § Chop the tentacles in small pieces and put them in a bowl with the onion, raisins, pine nuts, bread crumbs, and egg. Mix well and season with salt and pepper. § Fill the squid bodies with the mixture and close them with a toothpick so the filling won't come out during cooking. § Heat the oil in a heavy-bottomed saucepan, add the filled squid, and cook slowly over medium-low heat. Turn them often so they won't stick to the bottom. § After about 15 minutes, add the white wine and continue cooking until the liquid has evaporated. § Serve hot.

■ INGREDIENTS

- 2 lb (1 kg) small squid
- 1 small onion, finely chopped
- 1 cup (180 g) muscatel raisins (sultanas)
- ⅔ cup (75 g) pine nuts
- 1¾ cups (100 g) bread crumbs
- 2 eggs, beaten to a foam
- salt and freshly ground white pepper
- 2 tablespoons extra-virgin olive oil
- 1 cup (250 ml) white wine

Wine: a dry white (Verdicchio dei Castelli di Jesi)

Skewered grilled shrimp
Spiedini di scampi

This recipe calls for a grill pan to place over the element on a gas or electric stove to cook the shrimp. They are also very good if cooked over a barbecue, from which they will take a delicious smokey flavor.

Serves: 6; Preparation: 30 minutes; Cooking: 30 minutes; Level of difficulty: Simple

Shell the shrimp and remove the dark intestinal veins. Chop off the heads and rinse thoroughly in cold running water. § Thread the shrimp onto skewers and sprinkle with the flour. § Melt the butter in a saucepan and pour half of it over the shrimp. Sprinkle with salt and pepper. § Heat the grill pan to very hot and place the skewers in it. Let the shrimp cook on one side before turning to cook on the other. § Lay the skewers on a serving dish, garnish with lemon and parsley, and serve hot. The remaining melted butter can be served separately in a warmed dish.

■ INGREDIENTS

- 2 lb (1 kg) giant shrimp
- 4 tablespoons all-purpose (plain) flour
- ⅓ cup (100 g) butter
- salt and freshly ground black pepper
- 1 lemon, and sprigs of parsley, to garnish

Wine: a dry white (Sauvignon del Collio)

Right:
Calamari dolci delicati

Scallop shells with fish, potato, and mayonnaise
Conchiglie di pesce

This tasty fish appetizer is easy to make and can be prepared ahead of time. Ask your fish vendor for scallop shells or serve the fish mixture in the curved inner leaves of lettuce hearts.

Serves: 4; Preparation: 15 minutes; Cooking: 40 minutes; Level of difficulty: Simple

Prepare the mayonnaise. § Chop the boiled fish and mix with the diced potatoes. § Add the parsley, capers, mayonnaise, salt, and pepper. Mix carefully. § Spoon the mixture into the scallop shells and set aside in a cool place for 30 minutes before serving. Garnish with the lemon and parsley.

■ INGREDIENTS

- ½ quantity *Mayonnaise* (see recipe p. 42)
- 14 oz (450 g) boiled fish fillets (hake, sea bream, sea bass, or other)
- 3 boiled potatoes, peeled and diced
- 1 tablespoon finely chopped parsley
- 1 tablespoon capers
- salt and black pepper
- slices of lemon and sprigs of parsley, to garnish

Wine: a dry white (Verduzzo Friulano)

Seafood salad
Insalata di mare

Serves: 8; Preparation: 1 hour + 30 minutes to chill; Cooking: 30 minutes; Level of difficulty: Medium

Clean the squid and separate the tentacles and head from the body by grasping the head and pulling it apart from the body. Remove the ink sac from the head. Remove the bony part and clean out the insides. § To clean the cuttlefish, cut each one lengthwise and remove the internal bone and the stomach. Discard the internal ink sac. § Place the cuttlefish in a pot with 2.5 quarts (5 pints/2.5 liters) of cold water and 1 tablespoon of salt and bring to a boil over high heat. § When the cuttlefish have been simmering for 5 minutes, add the squid and cook for 15 minutes more. § Drain and set aside to cool. § Chop the tentacles in small pieces and slice the bodies in rings. Transfer to a salad bowl. § Bring 1½ quarts (3 pints/1.5 liters) of water and 1 tablespoon of salt to a boil. Rinse the shrimp thoroughly and add to the pot. Cook for 2 minutes. Drain and set aside to cool. § Shell the shrimp and add them to the salad bowl. § Soak the clams and mussels in a large bowl of water for at least 1 hour. Pull the beards off the mussels. Scrub well and rinse in abundant cold water. § Place the shellfish in a large skillet (frying pan) with 2 tablespoons of oil and cook over medium heat until they are all open. Discard any that have not opened. § Discard the shells and add the mussels and clams to the salad bowl. § Mix the parsley, garlic, chillies, lemon juice, remaining oil, salt, and pepper in a bowl. Pour over the salad and toss well. § Chill in the refrigerator for 30 minutes before serving.

■ INGREDIENTS

- 1 lb (500 g) squid
- 14 oz (450 g) cuttlefish
- 2 tablespoons salt
- 14 oz (450 g) shrimp
- 14 oz (450 g) clams, in shell
- 14 oz (450 g) mussels, in shell
- 2 tablespoons finely chopped parsley
- 2 cloves garlic, finely chopped
- 1 teaspoon crushed chillies (optional)
- juice of ½ lemon
- 4 tablespoons extra-virgin olive oil
- freshly ground black pepper

Wine: a dry white (Greco di Tufo)

Right: *Insalata di mare*

Tuna fish mousse
Mousse di tonno

Serves: 4; Preparation: 15 minutes + 6 hours to chill; Level of difficulty: Simple

Put the tuna fish, with a teaspoon of its oil, in a food processor and blend for 1–2 minutes. § Transfer to a bowl and add the Mascarpone. Mix well, then add the pickled onions and parsley. Season with salt and pepper. § Lightly butter a mold and line with aluminum foil. Fill with the tuna mixture and chill in the refrigerator for 6 hours. § Wash and dry the arugula and arrange on a serving dish. Invert the mousse onto the bed of arugula. § Garnish with the olives and serve.

■ INGREDIENTS

- 8 oz (250 g) tuna fish packed in oil, drained
- 1 cup (250 g) Mascarpone cheese
- 2 oz (60 g) pickled onions, drained and very finely chopped
- 1 tablespoon finely chopped parsley
- salt and freshly ground black pepper
- 1 tablespoon butter
- 1 oz (30 g) arugula (rocket)
- 8 black olives, pitted and chopped

Wine: a dry white (Locorotondo)

Mussel dumplings
Bignoline di cozze

Serves: 4-6; Preparation: 30 minutes + 1 hour to soak mussels; Cooking: 30 minutes; Level of difficulty: Medium

Soak the mussels in a large bowl of water for at least 1 hour to purge them of sand. Pull off their beards, scrub, and rinse well in abundant cold water. § Put the mussels in a large skillet (frying pan) over high heat, sprinkle with the wine, and cover. § When all the shells are open (discard any that don't open), remove from the skillet. Pick the mussels out of their shells one by one. § Bring the water, butter, and half the salt to a boil in a small pot, add the flour, and remove from heat. Beat with a wooden spoon until the mixture is thick and well blended. § Return to medium heat and stir until the mixture sticks to the sides and bottom of the pot. § Let cool. Transfer to a bowl, stir in the eggs one by one, and add the parsley, Parmesan, and mussels. § Heat the oil in a deep-sided skillet until very hot. Fry spoonfuls of the mussel mixture in batches until the dumplings swell and turn golden brown. § Drain on paper towels, sprinkle with the remaining salt, and serve hot.

■ INGREDIENTS

- 1½ lb (750 g) mussels, in shell
- ½ cup (125 ml) dry white wine
- ¾ cup (200 ml) cold water
- 2 tablespoons butter
- 1 teaspoon salt
- 1 cup (125 g) all-purpose (plain) flour
- 4 eggs
- 2 tablespoons finely chopped parsley
- 4 tablespoons freshly grated Parmesan cheese
- 2 cups (500 ml) oil, for frying

Wine: a dry rosé (Teroldego Rotaliano)

Right: *Mousse di tonno*

■ INGREDIENTS

- 12 scallops, in shell
- 2 tablespoons finely chopped parsley
- 1 clove garlic, finely chopped
- 3 tablespoons extra-virgin olive oil
- salt and freshly ground black pepper
- juice of 1 lemon

Wine: a dry rosé (Teroldego Rotaliano)

Scallops Venetian-style
Cape sante alla veneta

Serves: 4; Preparation: 10 minutes; Cooking: 10 minutes; Level of difficulty: Simple

Pry open the shells, take out the scallops, and rinse under cold running water. § Sauté the parsley and garlic with the scallops in the oil. Season with salt and pepper. § Cook for 4–5 minutes over high heat, stirring continuously. Remove from heat and add the lemon juice. § Arrange in four shells and serve.

Scallops with mushrooms and béchamel sauce
Cape sante con funghi e besciamella

Serves: 4; Preparation: 15 minutes; Cooking: 40 minutes; Level of difficulty: Medium

Wash the scallops well in cold running water. § Cook over high heat in a skillet (frying pan) until they open. § Remove the meat and simmer for 15–20 minutes in a pot of boiling water. § Boil the shells in a pot of water for a few minutes. Let cool and clean thoroughly. Set aside. § Trim the mushrooms, wash carefully, and pat dry with paper towels. Chop coarsely. § Sauté the onion and garlic in 4 tablespoons of the butter. Add the thyme, ham, and mushrooms. Season with salt and pepper and cook for 10 minutes. § Prepare the béchamel sauce. § Use the remaining butter to grease the shells. § Chop the scallop meat coarsely and fill the shells. § Stir the mushroom mixture into the béchamel sauce and spoon over the scallops. § Sprinkle with the Parmesan and place on a baking sheet (tray) in a preheated oven at 400°F/200°C/gas 6 for 10–15 minutes. § Serve hot.

■ INGREDIENTS

- 8 fresh scallops, in shell
- 10 oz (300 g) white mushrooms
- 1 small onion, finely chopped
- 1 clove garlic, finely chopped
- 5 tablespoons butter
- ½ tablespoon finely chopped fresh thyme
- 2 oz (60 g) ham, chopped
- salt and freshly ground black pepper
- 1 quantity *Béchamel sauce* (see recipe p. 38)
- 4 tablespoons freshly grated Parmesan cheese

Wine: a dry white (Tocai di Lison)

Shrimp pie
Torta di gamberi

Serves: 6; Preparation: 30 minutes; Cooking: 50 minutes; Level of difficulty: Simple

Prepare the pastry dough. § Shell the shrimp and remove the dark intestinal veins. Chop off the heads, and rinse well in cold running water. § Sauté over medium-high heat for 5 minutes in a skillet (frying pan) with the garlic and butter. § Pour in the brandy and cook for 2 minutes more, stirring all the time. Season with salt and pepper and remove from the heat. § Roll out the pastry dough very thinly and line an ovenproof pie dish (tin) 8 in (20 cm) in diameter. § In a bowl, combine the eggs, flour, salt, and pepper, and mix until smooth. § Add the parsley, cream, shrimp, and the liquid they produced while cooking. Pour into the pie dish and bake in a preheated oven at 400°F/200°C/gas 6 for 40 minutes. § Serve hot or at room temperature.

■ INGREDIENTS

- 1 quantity plain pastry (see recipe p. 58)
- 1½ lb (750 g) shrimp
- 2 cloves garlic, finely chopped
- 3 tablespoons butter
- 2 tablespoons brandy
- salt and freshly ground black pepper
- 3 eggs
- 2 tablespoons all-purpose (plain) flour
- 4 tablespoons finely chopped parsley
- ¾ cup (200 ml) fresh cream

Wine: a dry white (Traminer Aromatico)

Right:
Cape sante con funghi e besciamella

Marinated herrings
Aringhe fresche marinate

Serves: 6-8; Preparation: 30 minutes + 24 hours; Cooking: 40 minutes; Level of difficulty: Medium

Sauté half the carrots, thyme, bay leaves, and peppercorns in a skillet (frying pan) with the butter for 3–4 minutes. § Add the flour and cook for 2–3 minutes more. § Add the wine, vinegar, salt, sugar, parsley, cinnamon, cilantro, and cloves. Bring to a boil and cook over low heat for about 30 minutes, or until the liquid has reduced by about a third. § Remove from heat and add the marjoram. § Clean the herrings, cut off the heads, wash, and pat dry with paper towels. § Arrange the herrings in a single layer in a large pan and pour the hot marinade over the top. Cover and cook over low heat for 10–12 minutes. § When cool, transfer the herrings to a large flat dish and cover with the marinade. Chill in the refrigerator for at least 24 hours. § Remove from the marinade and arrange on a serving dish. Sprinkle with the remaining carrots, the onion, the lemon juice, and a tablespoon or two of marinade.

■ INGREDIENTS

• 3 carrots, very finely sliced
• dash each salt, thyme, cinnamon, marjoram
• 2 bay leaves
• 10 white peppercorns
• 2 tablespoons butter
• 1 tablespoon all-purpose (plain) flour
• 2 cups (500 ml) dry white wine
• 1 cup (250 ml) white wine vinegar
• 1 tablespoon sugar
• 1 tablespoon finely chopped parsley
• 1 teaspoon cilantro (coriander leaves)
• 4 cloves
• 12 fresh herrings
• 1 onion, finely chopped
• juice of 1 lemon

Wine: a dry rosé (Salice Salentino)

Grapefruit filled with shrimp
Pompelmi ripieni

Serves: 4; Preparation: 20 minutes + 30 minutes to cool; Cooking: 10 minutes; Level of difficulty: Simple

Cut the grapefruit in half and use a sharp knife to extract the pulp. Take care not to cut or spoil the grapefruit shells which are used to serve the shrimp. Remove the white membrane and dice the pulp (in a dish or plate so that the juice is conserved). § Put the onion, celery, bay leaves, and shrimp in a small pot of cold water and simmer over medium heat for about 10 minutes, or until the shrimp are cooked. § Prepare the mayonnaise and combine with the mustard. Mix well and stir in the lemon and grapefruit juice. § Remove the shells from the shrimps and cut off the heads. Chop coarsely and add to the mayonnaise sauce. Stir in the diced grapefruit and fill the grapefruit cups with the mixture. § Chill in the refrigerator for about 30 minutes before serving.

■ INGREDIENTS

• 2 grapefruit
• 1 small onion
• 1 stalk celery
• 2 bay leaves
• 1 lb (500 g) shrimp
• dash of salt
• 1 quantity *Mayonnaise* (see recipe p. 42)
• 2 teaspoons mild mustard
• juice of 1 lemon

Wine: a dry white (Torgiano Bianco)

VARIATIONS
– Sprinkle 2 tablespoons of *bottarga* (roe of tuna fish or gray mullet) over the grapefruit just before serving.
– Spread 2 tablespoons of caviar over the grapefruit just before serving.

Right:
Pompelmi ripieni

Tuna-fish lemon cups
Coppini di limoni al tonno

Serves: 4; Preparation: 20 minutes; Level of difficulty: Simple

Cut the lemons in half crosswise. § Using a sharp knife, scoop out the insides without piercing the rind so they can be used as cups. § Chop the tuna fish, capers, gherkins, and egg yolks in a food processor until smooth. § Transfer the mixture to a bowl and add the oil, mayonnaise, and lemon juice. Mix well and fill the lemons. § Arrange the lettuce leaves on a serving plate and place the filled lemons on top. Garnish with olives, gherkins, and bell peppers, and serve.

■ INGREDIENTS

- 4 lemons
- 7 oz (200 g) tuna fish packed in oil, drained
- 2 tablespoons capers
- 2 tablespoons pickled gherkins
- 2 hard-cooked (hard-boiled) egg yolks
- 2 tablespoons extra-virgin olive oil
- 1 quantity *Mayonnaise* (see recipe p. 42)
- dash of salt
- a few lettuce leaves, olives, slices of pickled gherkin and bell peppers (capsicums)

Wine: a dry white (Locorotondo)

Fried squid and shrimp
Fritto di calamari e scampi

There are one or two golden rules to remember when preparing fried dishes. First, make sure the oil is hot enough before adding the seafood. Check by adding a tiny piece of bread: if it turns golden brown immediately, the oil is ready. Second, don't fry too many squid rings or shrimp at once. If you completely fill the pan, the squid and shrimp will stick together in an unappetizing lump. You will also lower the temperature too much and the seafood will not seal immediately against the oil, and will take longer to cook. This means it will absorb more oil and the dish will be heavier.

Serves: 4-6; Preparation: 30 minutes; Cooking: 30 minutes; Level of difficulty: Simple

Clean the squid following the instructions on page 138. Cut in ¼-in (5-mm) rings. § Remove the shells and dark intestinal veins from the shrimp, chop off the heads, and rinse thoroughly in cold running water. § Heat the frying oil to very hot in a deep-sided skillet (frying pan). § Place the flour in a bowl and add the squid rings. Take them out a few at a time, shake off excess flour, and plunge them into the hot oil. Each panful will need about 8 minutes to cook. § Repeat the process with the shrimp, which will take about 5 minutes to cook. § Drain on paper towels to eliminate excess oil, sprinkle with salt, and garnish with slices of lemon and sprigs of parsley. § Serve immediately.

■ INGREDIENTS

- 1 lb (500 g) small squid
- 8 oz (250 g) giant shrimp
- 2 cups (500 ml) oil, for frying
- 1 cup (150 g) all-purpose (plain) flour
- dash of salt
- 1 lemon and 6–8 sprigs parsley, to garnish

Wine: a dry white (Bianco di Pitigliano)

Right:
Coppini di limoni al tonno

INGREDIENTS

- 1½ lb (750 g) shrimp
- 1¼ cups (300 ml) whole (full cream) milk
- 3 eggs
- 2 tablespoons chives, finely chopped
- salt and freshly ground black pepper
- 1 tablespoon butter

Wine: a dry white (Orvieto Classico)

Shrimp molds
Sformati di gamberi

Serves: 6; Preparation: 40 minutes; Cooking: 30 minutes; Level of difficulty: Medium

Shell the shrimp and remove the dark intestinal veins. Chop off the heads, and rinse thoroughly in cold running water. Dry well and chop into small pieces. § Combine the milk, eggs, chives, salt, and pepper in a bowl and beat with a fork until well mixed. § Add the shrimp and pour the mixture into six 4-in (10-cm) buttered molds. § Place a large container filled with water in a preheated oven at 350°F/180°C/gas 4. Place the mold pans in the water and cook for 30 minutes. § Serve at room temperature.

Tuna and pickled vegetable crostini
Crostini alla crema di tonno e sottacetti

This recipe is so easy it makes an excellent last-minute hors d'oeuvre,
and is also very appetizing!

Serves: 4; Preparation: 10 minutes: Level of difficulty: Simple

Place the tuna, cocktail onions, pickled vegetables, and mayonnaise in a blender or food processor. § Process finely until you have obtained a paste. § Spread the paste over the bread slices, transfer to a serving platter, and serve.

> VARIATION
> – The tuna and pickled vegetable paste can be prepared a few hours in advance and spread on the bread slices just before serving.

■ INGREDIENTS

• 250 g (8 oz) tuna fish, packed in oil, drained
• 2½ oz (70 g) cocktail onions
• 2½ oz (70 g) mixed pickled vegetables, drained
• 1 quantity *Mayonnaise* (see p. 42)
• 1 baguette, cut into ¼-in (6-mm) thick slices

Wine: a dry white
(Trebbiano di Aprilia)

Shrimp crostini
Crostini con gamberetti

Serves: 4; Preparation: 15 minutes; Cooking: 2 minutes to cook the shrimp + 2 minutes to toast the bread; Level of difficulty: Simple

Clean and peel the shrimp as described on page 138. § Pour plenty of water into a medium-sized pan and bring to a boil over medium heat. Plunge in the shrimp and cook for 2 minutes. Drain and chop in a food processor, reserving a few whole shrimp for garnish. § Put the shrimp mixture into a large bowl, add the chopped capers, butter, mustard, and puréed tomatoes. Season with salt and mix gently. § Lightly toast the bread in a preheated oven at 400°F/200°C/gas 6 or in the toaster. § Spread the shrimp mixture on the toasted bread and transfer to a serving platter. § Garnish with the reserved whole capers and shrimp.

■ INGREDIENTS

• 1¼ lb (600 g) shrimp
• 3 tablespoons capers, chopped, reserve a few whole capers for garnish
• 2 tablespoons butter, at room temperature
• 1 tablespoon mustard
• 3 tablespoons puréed tomatoes (passata)
• dash of salt
• 1 small baguette (French loaf), cut into ¼-in (6-mm) thick slices

Wine: a dry white
(Oltrepo Pavese Pinot Nero)

Right:
Tuna and pickled vegetable crostini

Seafood bruschetta
Bruschette di frutti di mare

These bruschetta are easy to make and delicious to eat. Be sure to spoon the seafood sauce over the bruschetta just before serving. To prepare ahead of time, proceed as far as the thickened sauce and set aside. After an hour or two, reheat the sauce, add the seafood, and finish cooking.

■ INGREDIENTS

- 8 oz (250 g) mussels, in shell
- 8 oz (250 g) clams, in shell
- 2 cloves garlic
- 2 tablespoons finely chopped parsley
- 2 tablespoons extra-virgin olive oil
- 1 cup (250 ml) dry white wine
- 7 oz (200 g) small squid
- 8 oz (250 g) shrimp
- 1 red bell pepper (capsicum)
- 1 scallion (shallot), finely chopped
- ½ tablespoon butter
- 1 teaspoon saffron, dissolved in ½ cup (125 ml) lukewarm milk
- salt and freshly ground black pepper
- 8 slices *Bruschetta* (see recipe p. 54)

Wine: a dry white (Nosiola)

Serves: 4; Preparation: 30 minutes + 1 hour to soak; Cooking: 20 minutes; Level of difficulty: Medium

Soak the mussels and clams in a large bowl of cold water for at least an hour to purge them of sand. § Pull the beards off the mussels and scrub both clams and mussels well. Rinse thoroughly under cold running water. Drain well. § Sauté 1 clove garlic, 1 tablespoon olive oil, and 1 tablespoon parsley in a large skillet (frying pan) for 2–3 minutes. § Add the mussels and clams and pour in half the wine. § Cover the pan and place over medium-high heat. Shake the pan often, until the shells are all open. § Drain the liquid they have produced into a bowl, strain and set aside. Discard any shells that haven't opened. § Detach the mussels and clams from their shells and set them aside. § To clean the squid, separate the tentacles and head from the body by grasping the head and pulling it apart from the body. Remove the ink sac from the head. Peel off the skin. Remove the bony part and clean out the insides. Rinse well in cold running water. § Shell the shrimp and remove the dark intestinal veins. Chop off the heads, and rinse thoroughly in cold running water. § Carefully wash the bell pepper, cut in half, remove the seeds and core, and dice. § Sauté the scallion in a skillet with the butter and the remaining oil. Add the diced bell pepper and sauté briefly, stirring continuously with a wooden spoon. § Add the remaining wine and continue cooking over high heat. § When the wine has evaporated, add the mussel liquid and the saffron dissolved in lukewarm milk. Season with salt and pepper. § Continue cooking over high heat for a few minutes until the sauce is thick. Add the mussels, clams, shrimp, and squid and cook for 3 minutes more, mixing often. § Sprinkle with the remaining parsley. § Prepare the bruschetta. § Spoon the seafood sauce over the bruschetta and serve hot.

Right:
Bruschette di frutti di mare

Smoked salmon cones with potato salad
Cornetti di salmone affumicato con insalata russa

Serves: 4; Preparation: 40 minutes; Cooking: 20 minutes; Level of difficulty: Simple

Wash, peel, and dice the potatoes. Scrape and dice the carrots. Snap ends off the green beans and cut in small pieces. § Put the vegetables in a pot of salted, boiling water and cook over medium heat for 15–20 minutes. § Drain the vegetables and set aside to cool. § Prepare the mayonnaise. § When cold, put the cooked vegetables in a pot with the peas, capers, gherkin, and pepper. Add the mayonnaise, reserving some for garnish, and mix well. § Arrange the slices of smoked salmon on a serving platter and put a spoonful of potato salad on the center of each slice. § Roll the salmon up around the salad into a cone. § Garnish the plate with the remaining mayonnaise, sliced hard-cooked eggs, and a few sprigs of parsley. § Serve cold.

> VARIATION
> – Cones of prosciutto, or ham, or raw beef (of the type used for *carpaccio*) can also be used instead of the salmon.

■ INGREDIENTS

- 7 oz (200 g) potatoes
- 2 oz (60 g) carrots
- 2 oz (60 g) green beans
- 2 oz (60 g) frozen peas
- 1 quantity *Mayonnaise* (see recipe p. 42)
- 2 tablespoons extra-virgin olive oil
- 2 tablespoons capers
- 2 tablespoons pickled gherkins, diced
- juice of 1 lemon
- salt and freshly ground black pepper
- 8 slices smoked salmon
- 2 hard-cooked (hard-boiled) eggs + sprigs of parsley, to garnish

Wine: a dry white (Riesling dell'Alto Adige)

Octopus salad
Insalata di polpo

Serves: 6-8; Preparation: 30 minutes + 2 hours to soften; Cooking: 1 hour; Level of difficulty: Medium

Clean the octopus by removing the sac and beak. § Place the octopus in a large pot of cold water with the vinegar, carrot, celery, onion, garlic, parsley, and salt. § Cover and bring to a boil over high heat. Lower the heat and simmer for 1 hour. § Remove from heat and leave to cool in the cooking water. This will take at least 2 hours. This cooling process is very important because it makes the octopus meat tender. § Skin the octopus (it will come away easily, together with the suckers—a few of the latter can be added to the salad). Cut the sac in rings and the tentacles in small pieces. § Transfer to a serving dish and season with oil, lemon juice, salt, pepper, and chillies. § Toss well and serve.

■ INGREDIENTS

- 2 lb (1 kg) octopus
- 1 cup (250 ml) white wine vinegar
- 1 carrot
- 1 stalk celery
- 1 small onion
- 1 clove garlic
- 5 sprigs parsley
- salt and freshly ground black pepper
- 4 tablespoons extra-virgin olive oil
- juice of 1 lemon
- ½ teaspoon dried chillies

Wine: a dry white (Cirò bianco)

Right: *Cornetti di salmone affumicato con insalata russa*

Mixed sausage, chicken, and vegetable skewers
Piccoli spiedini alla salsiccia

Serves: 4; Preparation: 20 minutes + 1 hour to marinate; Cooking: 15 minutes; Level of difficulty: Simple

Wash and dry the zucchini. Trim the ends and chop into ½-in (1-cm) thick wheels. § Wash and dry the bell pepper. Remove the seeds and core and chop in squares. § Wash the tomatoes and leave them whole. § Chop the sausages into 1-in (2.5-cm) thick slices. § Chop the chicken into squares of about the same size. § Combine all the ingredients in a bowl with the sage, rosemary, parsley, salt, pepper, and oil, and leave to marinate in the refrigerator for 1 hour. § Prepare the skewers, alternating pieces of chicken, sausage, and vegetables. § Heat the grill pan to very hot. Place the skewers in it and cook for 10–15 minutes. § Serve hot.

■ INGREDIENTS

- 1 large zucchini (courgette)
- 1 red or yellow bell pepper (capsicum)
- 12 cherry tomatoes
- 2 Italian pork sausages
- 1 large chicken breast
- 2 tablespoons finely chopped mixed sage, rosemary, and parsley
- salt and freshly ground black pepper
- 2 tablespoons extra-virgin olive oil

Wine: a dry red (Chianti Ruffino)

Salami with fresh figs
Salame e fichi freschi

Figs begin to appear in the markets in Italy in June, but it is not until August that local fig trees begin producing this delicious fruit, and the markets are flooded with them. At that point Salame e fichi freschi makes a regular appearance as an appetizer on many Italian tables. The mixture of the sweet flesh of the fruit with the strong salty taste of the salami is perfect at the end of a long summer day.

Serves: 4-6; Preparation: 5 minutes; Level of difficulty: Simple

Wash the figs thoroughly and pat dry with paper towels. § Remove the rind from the salami, and cut in thin slices. § Arrange the figs and salami on a serving dish. If fresh fig leaves are available, place a layer on the serving dish before adding the figs and salami.

■ INGREDIENTS

- 10 oz (300 g) fresh green or black figs
- 7 oz (200 g) salami, thinly sliced

Wine: a dry rosé (Salice Salentino - Five Roses)

Right: *Salame e fichi freschi*

Prosciutto rolls filled with porcini mushrooms and fontina cheese
Fagottini di prosciutto dolce ai funghi porcini

If you can't get fresh porcini mushrooms, use white mushrooms in their place. Serve the rolls straight away; they are particularly tasty while still warm.

Serves: 4; Preparation: 20 minutes; Cooking: 15 minutes; Level of difficulty: Simple

Wash the mushrooms carefully under cold running water and pat them dry with paper towels. § Separate the stems and caps and dice them into bite-size pieces. § Sauté the stems in the oil with the garlic, calamint (or thyme), and salt and pepper for about 8–10 minutes. Add a little stock to keep the mixture moist. § Add the caps and cook for 5 minutes more, or until the mushrooms are cooked. § Add the cheese, turn off the heat immediately, and mix well. § Distribute the mixture evenly among the slices of prosciutto, placing it in the middle of each. § Fold the ends of the prosciutto around the mixture and tuck them under to form a package. Tie each with a chive. § Serve immediately.

■ INGREDIENTS

- 7 oz (200 g) porcini mushrooms
- 2 tablespoons extra-virgin olive oil
- 1 clove garlic, finely chopped
- 1 tablespoon calamint, or thyme, finely chopped
- salt and freshly ground black pepper
- ½ cup (125 ml) *Beef stock* (see recipe p. 48)
- 3½ oz (100 g) Fontina cheese
- 8 oz (250 g) prosciutto
- 8 long chives

Wine: a dry red (Pinot Nero)

Bresaola rolls filled with robiola cheese
Involtini di bresaola

Bresaola is dried salted beef fillet that has been aged for 2 months. It can be replaced with prosciutto.

Serves: 6-8; Preparation: 20 minutes; Level of difficulty: Simple

Wash and dry the arugula and chop finely. § Combine in a bowl with the Robiola, salt and pepper, and mix well. § Arrange on the slices of bresaola and roll them up. § Drizzle with the oil, sprinkle with pepper and serve.

■ INGREDIENTS

- 1 oz (30 g) arugula (rocket)
- 7 oz (200 g) Robiola or other soft, creamy cheese
- salt and freshly ground black pepper
- 7 oz (200 g) bresaola, thinly sliced
- 2 tablespoons extra-virgin olive oil

Wine: a dry red (Carmignano)

Prosciutto and cantaloupe
Prosciutto e melone

Be sure to choose the highest quality Parma prosciutto and the sweetest cantaloupe. This dish is best in summer since its outcome depends on the cantaloupe being exquisitely fresh.

Serves: 4; Preparation: 5 minutes; Level of difficulty: Simple

Wash the cantaloupe thoroughly under cold running water and slice into pieces measuring 1-1½ in (3-4 cm) wide. § Arrange on a serving dish with the ham and serve.

■ INGREDIENTS

- 10 oz (300 g) prosciutto, thinly sliced
- 1 cantaloupe (rock melon), about 1 lb (500 g)

Wine: a dry rosé (Leverano)

Right: *Prosciutto e melone*

INGREDIENTS

- 7 oz (200 g) Gorgonzola cheese
- ⅔ cup (150 g) Mascarpone cheese
- 1¼ cups (150 g) finely chopped walnuts + some whole to garnish
- dash of salt
- 12 oz (350 g) ham, cut in 8 thick slices

Wine: a dry red (Gattinara)

Ham rolls filled with gorgonzola and walnuts
Cannoli di prosciutto cotto e gorgonzola

Serves: 4; Preparation: 15 minutes; Level of difficulty: Simple

Combine the Gorgonzola, Mascarpone, walnuts, and salt in a bowl and mix to a thick cream. § Spread the mixture on the slices of ham and roll them up. § Chop each roll in half. § Arrange on a serving dish. The rolls will look more attractive if served on a bed of fresh salad leaves (whatever you have on hand) and garnished with a few whole walnuts. § Serve cold.

Tuscan-style liver crostini
Crostini toscani

Serves: 4; Preparation: 15 minutes; Cooking: 50 minutes; Level of difficulty: Medium

Trim any connective tissue and discolored parts from the chicken livers. Chop coarsely. § Sauté the onion over medium heat with the oil. Add the bay leaf and chicken livers. § Brown the chicken livers for 5 minutes, then add the wine and Marsala. § Remove the skin from the spleen and chop coarsely. § As soon as the liquid has completely evaporated, add the spleen to a skillet (frying pan) together with the capers and anchovies. § Season with salt and pepper and cook for 40 minutes. Add a little hot stock whenever the mixture starts to dry out. § Remove from heat, discard the bay leaf, and blend the mixture in a food processor. § Place the mixture in a heavy-bottomed pan over low heat and stir in the cream and half the butter. Stir continuously until it begins to bubble, then remove from heat. § Cut the bread in slices or triangles and spread lightly with the remaining butter. Place on a baking sheet and toast lightly in the oven. § Spread with the liver mixture, arrange on a serving dish, and serve.

■ INGREDIENTS

- 3 chicken livers
- ½ onion, finely chopped
- 2 tablespoons extra-virgin olive oil
- 1 bay leaf
- 4 tablespoons dry white wine
- 4 tablespoons dry Marsala
- 5 oz (150 g) milt (veal spleen)
- 1 tablespoon capers
- 4 anchovy fillets
- salt and freshly ground black pepper
- ½ cup (125 ml) *Beef stock* (see recipe p. 48)
- ¾ cup (200 ml) light (single) cream
- ⅓ cup (90 g) butter
- 4–8 slices white, dense grain, home-style bread

Wine: a dry red (Rosso di Montalcino)

Country-style liver crostini
Crostini rustici

Serves: 4; Preparation: 15 minutes; Cooking: 30 minutes; Level of difficulty: Simple

Chop the celery, carrot, onion, and garlic together coarsely. § Add the parsley and sauté in a skillet (frying pan) with the oil over medium heat. § Trim any connective tissue and discolored parts from the chicken livers. Chop coarsely. § Add the chicken livers to the skillet and sauté for 4–5 minutes. § Add the wine and continue cooking over low heat for 20 minutes. If the mixture drys out too much during cooking add a little stock made with boiling water and bouillon (stock) cube. § Add the capers and cook for 2–3 minutes. § Add the anchovies and season with salt and pepper. Remove from heat. § Toast the bread. Spread with the liver mixture and serve.

■ INGREDIENTS

- 1 stalk celery, 1 carrot, 1 onion, 1 clove garlic
- 1 tablespoon finely chopped parsley
- 4 tablespoons extra-virgin olive oil
- 3 chicken livers
- ½ cup (125 ml) wine
- 3 tablespoons capers, coarsely chopped
- 2 anchovy fillets, chopped
- salt and freshly ground black pepper
- 4–8 slices white, dense grain, home-style bread

Wine: a dry red (Chianti)

Right: *Crostini toscani*

Chicken and almond salad
Insalata di pollo e mandorle

Serves: 4-6; Preparation: 20 minutes + 2 hours to chill; Level of difficulty: Simple

Remove the skin from the chicken and discard sinews and bones. § Cut the meat into small pieces. § Blanch the almonds for 2–3 minutes in boiling water and peel. § Peel the avocados. Chop into cubes and sprinkle with lemon juice so they won't turn black. § Line a salad bowl with the leaves from the heart of the lettuce. § Arrange the chicken in the center and cover with the avocado and almonds. Season with salt and pepper. § Chill in the refrigerator for at least 2 hours. § Prepare the mayonnaise. § Add the carrots, celery, and parsley to the mayonnaise. § Just before serving, pour half the mayonnaise over the chicken and mix carefully. Serve the rest of the mayonnaise separately at table.

■ INGREDIENTS

- 1 boiled chicken
- 1 cup (150 g) almonds, shelled
- 2 avocados
- juice of 1 lemon
- 1 lettuce heart
- salt and freshly ground black pepper
- 2 quantities *Mayonnaise* (see recipe p. 42)
- 2 carrots, finely chopped
- 1 celery heart, finely chopped
- 2 tablespoons finely chopped parsley

Wine: a dry white (Frascati)

Chicken and celery salad
Insalata di pollo e sedano

Serves: 4-6; Preparation: 15 minutes + 30 minutes to chill; Level of difficulty: Simple

Remove the skin from the chicken and discard sinews and bones. § Cut the meat into small pieces. § Wash the celery and chop coarsely. § Slice the gherkins and dice the Gruyère and ham. § Combine the ingredients in a deep salad bowl and season with lemon juice, salt, and pepper. § Prepare the mayonnaise and pour over the salad. Toss carefully. § Chill in the refrigerator for 30 minutes before serving.

■ INGREDIENTS

- 1 boiled chicken
- 1 celery heart
- 5 pickled gherkins
- 3½ oz (100 g) Gruyère cheese
- 3½ oz (100 g) ham, in one thick slice
- juice of 1 lemon
- salt and freshly ground black pepper
- 1 quantity *Mayonnaise* (see recipe p. 42)

Wine: a dry white (Pinot Grigio)

Left:

Insalata di pollo e mandorle

Lombard-style pâté
Pâté lombardo

Serves: 8; Preparation: 25 minutes; Cooking: 40 minutes; Level of difficulty: Medium

Trim any connective tissue and discolored parts from the chicken livers and chop coarsely. § In a large skillet (frying pan), sauté the chicken and calf's liver together in the butter with the garlic and parsley for 5 minutes. Season with salt and pepper. § When the liver starts to dry out, add the Marsala and continue cooking for 5–10 minutes, or until the liver is cooked. § Remove the liver and add the bread crumbs to the juices in the pan. Mix well and remove from heat. § Chop the liver and bread crumbs in a food processor until smooth. § Combine the eggs and yolks, liver, bread crumbs, and Parmesan in a bowl and stir to obtain a fairly stiff mixture. If it is too dry or firm, soften with a tablespoon or two of stock made with boiling water and a bouillon (stock) cube. § Butter a medium-sized mold, line with waxed paper, and fill with the mixture. Put the mold in a large pan of boiling water and leave it for at least 30 minutes, so that the pâté will finish cooking. § Garnish with sprigs of parsley and serve warm or cold with toasted bread and plenty of butter.

■ INGREDIENTS

• 5 chicken livers
• 1 lb (500 g) calf's liver, coarsely chopped
• 4 tablespoons butter
• 1 clove garlic, finely chopped
• 2 tablespoons finely chopped parsley + sprigs to garnish
• salt and freshly ground black pepper
• 1 cup (250 ml) Marsala
• 1½ cups (90 g) bread crumbs
• 2 eggs + 2 yolks
• 1 cup (125 g) freshly grated Parmesan cheese

Wine: a dry red (Oltrepò Pavese)

Liver pâté
Pâté di fegato

Serves: 6; Preparation: 30 minutes; Cooking: 50 minutes; Level of difficulty: Medium

Sauté the onion in 1 tablespoon of butter over medium heat. § When it begins to turn golden, turn off the heat and add the remaining butter so it will melt without bubbling. § Cut the liver and lard in small pieces. § Transfer to a large bowl and add the onion, parsley, and tarragon, and mix well. § Chop finely in a food processor. § Add the flour, eggs, nutmeg, salt, and pepper, and mix thoroughly. § Butter a medium-sized mold, line with waxed paper, and fill with the mixture. Shake the mold to fill up any air pockets. § Cover with a sheet of waxed paper. Fill a large container with boiling water, place the mold in it and cook in a preheated oven at 350°F/180°C/gas 4 for about 45 minutes. § Invert the pâté on a serving dish. § Serve cold.

■ INGREDIENTS

• 1 onion, finely chopped
• ⅓ cup (3½ oz/100 g) butter
• 10 oz (300 g) calf's liver
• 1 cup (250 g) lard
• 1 tablespoon each finely chopped parsley and tarragon
• ½ cup (75 g) all-purpose (plain) flour
• 2 eggs
• dash of nutmeg
• salt and freshly ground white pepper

Wine: a dry red (Barolo)

Right: *Pâté lombardo*

Dried Pasta

By dried pasta we mean store-bought pasta made from hard-wheat flour and water. This includes classics such as spaghetti, penne, fusilli, and macaroni.

Spaghettini with garlic, oil, and chilies
Spaghettini con aglio olio e peperoncino

The sauce is very quick to make and should be used immediately, so begin by cooking the spaghettini in a large pot of salted, boiling water.

Serves: 4; Preparation: 3 minutes; Cooking: 10 minutes; Level of difficulty: Simple

While the pasta is cooking, combine the oil, garlic, and chilies in a small skillet (frying pan) and sauté over low heat until the garlic begins to change color. Remove from heat at once, taking care not to burn the garlic because it will give the sauce a bitter flavor. Add the parsley, if using, and a dash of salt. § Drain the pasta when al dente and place in a heated serving dish. Pour the sauce over the pasta and toss vigorously. § Serve immediately.

■ INGREDIENTS

- ¾ cup (200 ml) extra-virgin olive oil
- 3 cloves garlic, finely chopped
- ½ teaspoon crushed chilies
- 2 tablespoons finely chopped parsley (optional)
- dash of salt
- 1 lb (500 g) spaghettini pasta

Wine: a dry white (Trebbiano)

Spaghetti with eggs and pancetta
Spaghetti alla carbonara

La carbonara is a classic Roman sauce. According to some, it was first made during the last days of World War II as American troops advanced up the Italian peninsula bringing supplies of eggs and bacon which they asked the Italians to make into a sauce. Try replacing the pancetta with bacon and decide for yourself about the historical value of this theory!

Serves: 4; Preparation: 5 minutes; Cooking: 15 minutes; Level of difficulty: Simple

Chop the cloves of garlic in half. Combine the oil, garlic, and pancetta in a skillet (frying pan) and sauté over medium heat until the pancetta is golden brown but not crisp. Remove the skillet from heat and take out the pieces of garlic. § In a mixing bowl, lightly beat the eggs, Parmesan, Pecorino, and salt until smooth. Set aside. § Cook the spaghetti in a large pot of salted, boiling water until *al dente*. Drain and place in a large, heated serving dish. Add the egg mixture and toss. § Return the skillet with the pancetta to high heat for 1 minute. Pour the hot oil and pancetta over the pasta and egg, and toss vigorously. Grind a generous amount of black pepper over the top and serve.

■ INGREDIENTS

- 3 whole cloves garlic
- 3 tablespoons extra-virgin olive oil
- 6 oz (180 g) unsmoked pancetta, diced
- 4 fresh eggs
- 3 tablespoons freshly grated Parmesan cheese
- 3 tablespoons freshly grated Pecorino cheese
- salt and freshly ground black pepper
- 1 lb (500 g) spaghetti

Wine: a light, young red (Vino Novello)

Right:
Spaghetti alla carbonara

Bucatini with capers and black olives
Bucatini con capperi e olive

Serves: 4; Preparation: 10 minutes; Cooking: 15 minutes; Level of difficulty: Simple

Combine the oil, garlic, and parsley in a large skillet (frying pan) and sauté over medium heat until the garlic starts to change color. § Stir the olives and capers into the sauce and cook over low heat for 2–3 minutes. § Cook the bucatini in a large pot of salted, boiling water until *al dente*. Drain and transfer to the skillet. § Toss with the capers and olives over medium heat for 2 minutes. § Place in a heated serving dish and sprinkle with Pecorino. § Serve hot.

■ INGREDIENTS

• 4 tablespoons extra-virgin olive oil
• 2 cloves garlic, finely chopped
• 3 tablespoons finely chopped parsley
• 1 cup (100 g) pitted and chopped black olives
• 3 tablespoons capers
• 1 lb (500 g) bucatini pasta
• ½ cup (60 g) freshly grated Pecorino cheese

Wine: a dry red (Nebbiolo)

Bucatini with pancetta and spicy tomato sauce
Bucatini all'amatriciana

Serves: 4; Preparation: 5 minutes; Cooking: 30 minutes; Level of difficulty: Simple

Sauté the pancetta in a skillet (frying pan) with the oil for 2–3 minutes. Add the onion and cook until soft. § Stir in the tomatoes and chilies. Season with salt and cook over medium-low heat for about 20 minutes, or until the tomatoes have separated from the oil. § Cook the bucatini in a large pot of salted, boiling water until *al dente*. Drain well and transfer to a heated serving bowl. § Toss with the sauce and Pecorino and serve.

■ INGREDIENTS

• 6 oz (180 g) pancetta, diced
• 2 tablespoons extra-virgin olive oil
• 1 onion, finely chopped
• 1½ lb (750 g) tomatoes, canned, and chopped
• ¾ teaspoon crushed chilies
• dash of salt
• 1 lb (500 g) bucatini pasta
• ½ cup (60 g) freshly grated Pecorino cheese

Wine: a dry red (Refosco)

Spaghettini with spicy tomato sauce
Spaghettini alla puttanesca

This sauce is a specialty of the island of Ischia, off the coast of Naples in southern Italy.

Serves: 4; Preparation: 10 minutes; Cooking: 25–30 minutes; Level of difficulty: Simple

Sauté the garlic and chilies in a skillet (frying pan) with the oil over medium heat until the garlic begins to change color. § Peel and chop the tomatoes. Add them to the skillet with the capers and olives, and cook for 5 minutes. § Stir the anchovy fillets into the sauce. Season with pepper and simmer over medium heat for 15–20 minutes. § Cook the spaghettini in a large pot of salted, boiling water until *al dente*. Drain and transfer to a heated serving dish. Pour the sauce over the pasta and toss vigorously. Serve hot.

■ INGREDIENTS

• 2 cloves garlic, minced
• ½ teaspoon crushed chilies
• 4 tablespoons extra-virgin olive oil
• 1 lb (500 g) tomatoes
• 2 tablespoons capers
• 1½ cups (150 g) pitted and chopped black olives
• 6 anchovy fillets, crumbled
• salt and freshly ground black pepper
• 1 lb (500 g) spaghettini pasta

Wine: a dry white (Vernaccia)

Right: *Bucatini all'amatriciana*

Spaghetti with tomato and black olive sauce
Spaghetti con olive

Serves: 4; Preparation: 10 minutes; Cooking: 20 minutes; Level of difficulty: Simple

Place the tomatoes in a heavy-bottomed saucepan. Add the garlic and simmer over low heat for 15 minutes. § Add the oil, olives, oregano, and chilies and cook for 2 minutes more. Season with salt. § Cook the spaghetti in a large pot of salted, boiling water until *al dente*. § Drain and add to the tomato mixture. Toss briefly and serve.

■ INGREDIENTS

- 1 lb (500 g) tomatoes, coarsely chopped
- 2 cloves garlic, finely chopped
- 4 tablespoons extra-virgin olive oil
- 1½ cups (150 g) pitted and chopped black olives
- 2 teaspoons oregano
- ½ teaspoon crushed chilies
- dash of salt
- 1 lb (500 g) spaghetti

Wine: a dry white (Marino)

Left: *Capelli d'angelo olio e limone*

■ INGREDIENTS

- 2 whole cloves garlic, slightly crushed
- ½ cup (125 ml) extra-virgin olive oil
- 10 anchovy fillets
- 1 tablespoon finely chopped parsley
- 1 lb (500 g) tomatoes, peeled and chopped
- dash of salt
- 4 tablespoons fine dry bread crumbs, toasted
- 1 lb (500 g) spaghetti

Wine: a dry white (Alcamo)

■ INGREDIENTS

- 1 onion, finely chopped
- ¾ cup (200 ml) extra-virgin olive oil
- 1 lb (500 g) angel hair pasta
- juice of 3 lemons
- salt and freshly ground black pepper
- ⅓ cup (45 g) freshly grated Parmesan cheese

Wine: a dry white (Frascati)

■ INGREDIENTS

- 10 large ripe tomatoes
- 2 cloves garlic, minced
- ⅓ cup (90 ml) extra-virgin olive oil
- juice of 1 lemon
- dash of salt
- 1 lb (500 g) penne pasta
- 5 oz (150 g) Mozzarella cheese, diced
- 8 fresh basil leaves, torn

Wine: a dry white (Pinot Grigio)

Spaghetti with toasted bread crumbs
Spaghetti con pangrattato

Serves: 4; Preparation: 10 minutes; Cooking: 15 minutes; Level of difficulty: Simple

Sauté the garlic in the oil in a large skillet (frying pan) until it starts to color, then remove and discard. § Add the anchovies, crushing them with a fork so that they dissolve in the flavored oil. § Add the parsley and tomatoes. Simmer over low heat for 15–20 minutes. § Cook the pasta in a large pot of salted, boiling water until *al dente*. Drain, add to the sauce and toss briefly. § Transfer to a heated serving dish. Sprinkle with the bread crumbs and serve.

Angel hair with oil and lemon sauce
Capelli d'angelo olio e limone

Serves: 4; Preparation: 3 minutes; Cooking: 5 minutes; Level of difficulty: Simple

Combine the onion and oil in a large skillet (frying pan). Sauté over medium heat until the onion turns golden in color. § Cook the capelli d'angelo in a large pot of salted, boiling water until *al dente*. Drain well and transfer to the pan with the onion. Toss the pasta briefly with the onion over medium heat and transfer to a large, heated serving dish. Add the lemon juice, salt, pepper, and Parmesan. Toss well and serve.

Penne with fresh tomatoes, garlic, and mozzarella cheese
Penne con salsa di pomodoro fresco

Serves: 4; Preparation: 5 minutes; Cooking: 10 minutes; Level of difficulty: Simple

Peel and coarsely chop the tomatoes. Drain off any extra liquid, and place them in a serving bowl. Add the garlic, half of the oil, and the lemon juice. Season with salt. § Cook the penne in a large pot of salted, boiling water until *al dente*. Drain well and toss with the remaining oil. § Toss the pasta with the tomato sauce. Sprinkle with the Mozzarella and basil and serve.

Fusilli with tuna and oregano
Fusilli tonno e origano

Serves: 4; Preparation: 15 minutes; Cooking: 15–20 minutes; Level of difficulty: Simple

Sauté the garlic in the oil for about 3 minutes. Add the oregano, stir, and after 3 minutes, add the tuna. § Season with salt and cook for about 5 minutes (the tuna does not need to cook, but just blend in with the other flavors). § Cook the fusilli in a large pot of salted, boiling water until al dente. Drain, toss with the sauce, and serve.

■ INGREDIENTS

- 2 cloves garlic, minced
- ½ cup (125 ml) extra-virgin olive oil
- 1 tablespoon oregano
- 8 oz (250 g) tuna packed in oil, drained
- dash of salt
- 1 lb (500 g) fusilli pasta

Wine: a dry white (Pinot Bianco)

Penne with "angry" tomato sauce
Penne all'arrabbiata

Serves: 4; Preparation: 15 minutes; Cooking: 30 minutes; Level of difficulty: Simple

Put the pancetta, garlic, celery, and onion in a large skillet (frying pan) with the oil and cook until lightly browned. § Add the tomatoes, basil, parsley, and chilies. Season with salt and pepper. § Simmer over medium-low heat for about 20 minutes or until the tomatoes and oil begin to separate. § Cook the penne in a large pot of salted, boiling water until *al dente*. Drain and toss with the sauce in the pan over high heat for 2–3 minutes. Transfer to a heated serving dish and serve.

■ INGREDIENTS

- 3 oz (90 g) pancetta, diced
- 4 cloves garlic, 1 celery stalk, 1 medium onion, all finely chopped
- ⅓ cup (90 ml) extra-virgin olive oil
- 1½ lb (750 g) tomatoes, peeled and chopped
- 6 fresh basil leaves, torn
- 3 tablespoons finely chopped parsley
- ½ teaspoon crushed chilies
- salt and freshly ground black pepper
- 1 lb (500 g) penne pasta

Wine: a dry red (Chianti)

Penne Florentine-style
Penne strascicate

Serves: 4; Preparation: 5 minutes + 2 hours for the sauce; Cooking: 15 minutes; Level of difficulty: Simple

Prepare the meat sauce. § Cook the pasta in a large pot of salted, boiling water until just *al dente* but still with plenty of "bite". § Keep the meat sauce warm over low heat, add the drained pasta, toss together and leave for 5 minutes so that the pasta is coated thoroughly with the sauce and has absorbed its flavors. § Turn off the heat, stir in the Parmesan and serve.

■ INGREDIENTS

- 1 quantity *Tomato meat sauce* (see recipe p. 30)
- dash of salt
- 1 cup (125 g) freshly grated Parmesan cheese
- 1 lb (500 g) penne pasta

Wine: a young, dry red (Chianti dei Colli Fiorentini)

Right:
Penne strascicate

■ INGREDIENTS

- ¾ cup (200 ml) whole (full cream) milk
- 1 cup (250 g) very fresh Ricotta cheese
- 1 tablespoon sugar
- 1 teaspoon cinnamon
- salt and freshly ground white pepper
- 1 lb (500 g) penne pasta

Wine: a dry white (Verdicchio)

Penne with ricotta cheese
Penne con ricotta

This classic southern Italian recipe is very simple and relies on the quality and freshness of the Ricotta. Buy it loose from a specialty store or a good Italian deli. It is also good with fresh pasta.

Serves: 4; Preparation: 5 minutes; Cooking: 10 minutes; Level of difficulty: Simple

Warm the milk and place in a bowl with the Ricotta, sugar, cinnamon, and a dash of salt and white pepper. Mix with a fork to form a smooth, creamy sauce. § Cook the penne in a large pot of salted, boiling water until *al dente*. Drain well and place in a heated serving bowl. Toss with the sauce and serve.

Spaghetti with seafood sauce
Spaghetti allo scoglio

Serves: 4; Preparation: 25 minutes + 1 hour to soak shellfish: Cooking: 25 minutes; Level of difficulty: Medium

Scrub the mussels and clams and soak them in cold water for 1 hour. § Chop the bodies of the shrimp and cuttlefish into rounds and the tentacles into short lengths. § Do not peel the shrimp tails. § Pour 3 tablespoons of the oil into a large skillet (frying pan), add the mussels and clams, and steam open over medium heat. This will take about 10 minutes. Discard any that have not opened. § Heat the remaining oil in a large skillet and sauté the garlic, parsley, and chilies for 2 minutes over medium heat, taking care not to brown. § Add the squid and cuttlefish. Season with salt and pepper, cook briefly, then moisten with the wine. § Cook for 12 minutes, then add the shrimp tails. § After 5 minutes add the clams and mussels (if preferred, extract the mollusks from their shells, leaving just a few in the shell to make the finished dish look more attractive). Mix well and cook for 2 minutes more. Turn off the heat, cover, and set aside. § Meanwhile, cook the spaghetti in a large pot of salted, boiling water until *al dente*. Drain, and add to the pan with the seafood sauce. Toss for 1–2 minutes over medium-high heat. § Transfer to a heated dish and serve.

■ INGREDIENTS

- 10 oz (300 g) each of clams and mussels, in shell
- 10 oz (300 g) squid, cleaned
- 10 oz (300 g) cuttlefish, cleaned
- 10 oz (300 g) shrimp, washed and dried
- ½ cup (125 ml) extra-virgin olive oil
- 2 cloves garlic, minced
- 3 tablespoons finely chopped parsley
- 1 teaspoon crushed chilies
- salt and freshly ground black pepper
- ½ cup (125 ml) dry white wine
- 1 lb (500 g) spaghetti

Wine: a dry white (San Severo Bianco)

Rigatoni with zucchini
Rigatoni con gli zucchini

Serves: 4; Preparation: 10 minutes; Cooking: 25 minutes; Level of difficulty: Simple

Heat the butter and oil together in a skillet (frying pan). Cut the clove of garlic in half, add to the skillet, and sauté until it starts to change color. Remove the garlic and add the zucchini. Sauté over high heat until the zucchini begin to turn golden brown. § Turn the heat down, cover the pan with a lid, and simmer until the zucchini are tender. Season with salt and pepper. § Cook the rigatoni in a large pot of salted, boiling water until *al dente*. Drain and transfer to a heated serving dish. Add the zucchini, parsley, and Parmesan, and toss well. Serve hot.

■ INGREDIENTS

- 3 tablespoons butter
- 3 tablespoons extra-virgin olive oil
- 2 cloves garlic
- 6 zucchini (courgettes), sliced in thin wheels
- salt and freshly ground black pepper
- 1 lb (500 g) rigatoni pasta
- 3 tablespoons finely chopped parsley
- ⅓ cup (45 g) freshly grated Parmesan cheese

Wine: a dry white (Orvieto Classico)

VARIATION
– Add ½ teaspoon crushed chilies for a spicy dish.

Right: *Spaghetti allo scoglio*

Linguine with fava beans and fresh rosemary
Linguine con le fave

If fresh fava beans are out of season, use 1 lb (500 g) of frozen ones. This sauce is also good with many short pastas, such as conchiglie, lumaconi, or rigatoni.

Serves: 4; Preparation: 15 minutes; Cooking: 30 minutes; Level of difficulty: Simple

Remove the fava beans from their pods and set aside in a bowl of cold water. § Cut the cloves of garlic in two and combine with the rosemary, half the butter, and the oil in a skillet (frying pan). Sauté over medium heat until the garlic begins to change color. § Remove the garlic and rosemary, making sure that none of the leaves remain in the sauce. Lower heat to medium, add the onion, and sauté until transparent. § Drain the fava beans and add with the stock to the skillet. Season with salt and pepper. § Continue to cook over medium-low heat for about 20 minutes or until the beans are tender, stirring from time to time. § Cook the linguine in a large pot of salted, boiling water until *al dente*. Drain and place in a heated serving dish. Pour the sauce over the pasta and toss with the Parmesan and remaining butter until well mixed. Serve hot.

■ INGREDIENTS

• 3 lb (1.5 kg) fava (broad) beans, in their pods
• 2 cloves garlic
• 3 sprigs fresh rosemary
• 4 tablespoons butter
• 4 tablespoons extra-virgin olive oil
• 1 large onion, finely chopped
• 1⅓ cups (350 ml) *Beef stock* (see recipe p. 48)
• salt and freshly ground black pepper
• ⅓ cup (45 g) freshly grated Parmesan cheese
• 1 lb (500 g) linguine pasta

Wine: a light, dry white (Verdicchio)

Spaghetti with clams
Spaghetti alle vongole

Serves: 4; Preparation: 10 minutes + 1 hour to soak clams; Cooking: 30 minutes; Level of difficulty: Simple

Soak the clams in cold water for 1 hour. § Put the clams, white wine, and 2 tablespoons of the oil in a large skillet (frying pan) and sauté until the clams are open. § Remove the clams, discarding any that have not opened, and set aside. Put the cooking liquid in a bowl and set aside. § Combine the remaining oil and garlic in the same skillet and cook until the garlic begins to change color. § Add the tomatoes and cook over medium heat for about 5 minutes. § Pour in the clam liquid. Season with salt and pepper. Cook for 15 more minutes, or until the sauce has reduced. § Add the clams and parsley, and continue cooking for 2–3 minutes. § Cook the spaghetti in a large pot of salted, boiling water until *al dente*. Drain and transfer to the skillet with the sauce. Toss for 1–2 minutes over medium-high heat, and serve.

■ INGREDIENTS

• 50 clams, in shell
• ⅓ cup (90 ml) dry white wine
• ⅓ cup (90 ml) extra-virgin olive oil
• 3 cloves garlic, finely chopped
• 6 ripe tomatoes, peeled and chopped
• salt and freshly ground black pepper
• 2 tablespoons finely chopped parsley
• 1 lb (500 g) spaghetti

Wine: a dry white (Tocai)

Right:
Linguine con le fave

Farfalle with smoked salmon and vodka sauce
Farfalle al salmone e vodka

■ INGREDIENTS

- ⅓ cup (90 g) butter
- ¾ cup (200 ml) vodka
- juice of 1½ lemons
- 3 oz (90 g) smoked salmon
- 3 teaspoons caviar (optional)
- 3 tablespoons light (single) cream
- salt and freshly ground black pepper
- 1 lb (500 g) farfalle pasta

Wine: a dry white (Soave)

Serves: 4; Preparation: 5 minutes; Cooking: 15 minutes; Level of difficulty: Simple

Cook the butter, vodka, and lemon juice in a skillet (frying pan) over low heat until the vodka has evaporated. § Crumble the smoked salmon with a fork. Add the salmon and caviar (if using) to the pan. Cook over medium-low heat for 2–3 minutes. Add the cream, and season with salt and pepper. Remove from heat. § Cook the farfalle in a large pot of salted, boiling water until *al dente*. Drain well and transfer to the skillet. Toss well over medium heat and serve.

Spaghetti with cuttlefish
Spaghetti con le seppie

Serves: 4; Preparation: 20 minutes; Cooking: about 1 hour; Level of difficulty: Medium

Rinse the cuttlefish thoroughly in cold water. To clean, cut each cuttlefish lengthwise and remove the internal bone and the stomach. Take care not to break the internal ink sac. These can be added later, if liked. Set aside. § Cut the cuttlefish crosswise into thin half circles. § Combine the onion and garlic in a large skillet (frying pan) with the oil and cook over medium heat until they begin to change color. Add the cuttlefish and tomatoes. Season with salt and pepper. Turn the heat down low, cover, and simmer for about 45 minutes, or until the cuttlefish are tender. § Add the ink, if using, and stir over medium heat for 2–3 minutes. § Cook the spaghetti in a large pot of salted, boiling water until *al dente*. Drain well and transfer to a heated serving dish. Toss vigorously with the sauce and serve.

■ INGREDIENTS

- 8 cuttlefish
- 2 onions, finely chopped
- 2 cloves garlic, finely chopped
- ½ cup (125 ml) extra-virgin olive oil
- 8 oz (250 g) tomatoes, canned, peeled, and chopped
- salt and freshly ground black pepper
- 1 lb (500 g) spaghetti

Wine: a dry white (Pinot Grigio)

Penne with crab meat
Penne alla polpa di granchio

Serves: 4; Preparation: about 25 minutes; Cooking: 15 minutes; Level of difficulty: Simple

Roughly chop the crab sticks. § Pour the oil into a large skillet (frying pan) and fry the garlic and parsley over medium-low heat for 1 minute. § Add the crab sticks and orange rind. Mix well and cook for 1 minute. Pour in the cognac and cook until it has evaporated. Add the orange juice. § Season with salt and a generous grinding of pepper. Cook until the liquid has evaporated. § After about 10 minutes add the cream. § Cook the pasta in a large pot of salted, boiling water until *al dente*. Drain, and transfer the penne to the skillet and toss with the sauce for 1 minute. § Serve immediately.

■ INGREDIENTS

- 12 crab sticks, fresh or frozen
- ½ cup (125 ml) extra-virgin olive oil
- 2 small garlic cloves, minced
- 2 tablespoons finely chopped parsley
- 1 tablespoon orange rind, cut in julienne strips
- ⅓ cup (90 ml) cognac
- ½ cup (125 ml) orange juice
- salt and freshly ground black pepper
- ½ cup (125 ml) light (single) cream
- 1 lb (500 g) penne pasta

Wine: a dry white (Colli di Conegliano Bianco)

Right:
Penne alla polpa di granchio

Penne with smoked salmon
Penne al salmone

This delicious dish is easy to prepare and convenient because it can be made in advance and eaten cold.

Serves: 4; Preparation: 10 minutes; Cooking: 10 minutes; Level of difficulty: Simple

Put the celery, tomatoes, vinegar, oil, salt, and smoked salmon in a large bowl. § Pierce the garlic cloves with the tines (prongs) of a fork and use it to stir the ingredients in the bowl. The garlic will flavor the mixture (take care that the cloves do not come off). § Cook the penne in a large pot of salted, boiling water until al dente. Drain and transfer to the bowl. Add the Parmesan and toss vigorously. § Serve hot or at room temperature.

■ INGREDIENTS

- 2 stalks celery, 2 tomatoes, finely sliced
- 4 tablespoons vinegar
- 1 cup (250 ml) extra-virgin olive oil
- dash of salt
- 3 oz (90 g) smoked salmon, thinly sliced
- 2 cloves garlic, whole
- 1 lb (500 g) penne pasta
- ⅓ cup (45 ml) freshly grated Parmesan cheese

Wine: a dry white (Amelia Trebbiano)

Macaroni with bell peppers
Maccheroni con i peperoni

Serves: 4; Preparation: 10 minutes; Cooking: 40 minutes; Level of difficulty: Simple

Cut the bell peppers in half lengthwise. Remove the seeds and cores, and cut crosswise into strips about ¼ in (6 mm) wide. § Combine the oil, bell peppers, onion, and garlic in a large skillet (frying pan) and sauté until the garlic turns pale gold. Add the tomatoes, basil, and boiling water. Season with salt and pepper. Simmer over medium heat for 20–25 minutes, or until the bell peppers are tender, stirring often. § Stir in the vinegar and anchovies, and cook over high heat for 2–3 minutes until the vinegar evaporates. Remove from heat. § Cook the macaroni in a large pot of salted, boiling water until *al dente*. Drain well and transfer to a heated serving dish. § Pour the sauce over the pasta and toss until well mixed. Serve hot.

■ INGREDIENTS

- 1 green, 1 yellow, and 1 red bell pepper (capsicum)
- ½ cup (125 ml) extra-virgin olive oil
- 1 large onion, finely chopped
- 2 cloves garlic, finely chopped
- 12 oz (350 g) ripe tomatoes, peeled and chopped
- 9 basil leaves, torn
- 3 tablespoons boiling water
- salt and freshly ground black pepper
- 3 tablespoons vinegar
- 6 anchovy fillets
- 1 lb (500 g) macaroni

Wine: a dry red (Chianti Classico)

VARIATION
– For a more filling dish, put the cooked pasta in an ovenproof dish, pour the sauce over the top and mix well. Spread 7 oz (200 g) of thinly sliced Mozzarella cheese on top and bake in a preheated oven at 350°F/180°C/gas 4 for 10 minutes or until the Mozzarella is browned.

Left:

Penne al salmone

Spaghetti with tuna and tomato sauce
Spaghetti al tonno

Serves: 4; Preparation: 10 minutes; Cooking: 15 minutes; Level of difficulty: Simple

Sauté the garlic and parsley in the oil over medium-low heat for 2 minutes. § Add the tomatoes, season with salt, and cook for 4–5 minutes. § Mix in the tuna, stir, and turn off the heat immediately. § Cook the spaghetti in a large pot of salted, boiling water until *al dente*. § Drain well and transfer to a heated serving dish. Toss vigorously with the sauce and serve hot.

■ INGREDIENTS
- ½ cup (125 ml) extra-virgin olive oil
- 2 cloves garlic, minced
- 3 tablespoons finely chopped parsleyf
- 6 small tomatoes, sliced
- 8 oz (250 g) tuna packed in oil, drained and flaked
- dash of salt
- 1 lb (500 g) spaghetti

Wine: a dry white (Pinot Bianco)

Bucatoni with onion sauce
Bucatoni con le cipolle

Serves: 4; Preparation: 5 minutes; Cooking: 45 minutes; Level of difficulty: Simple

Sauté the onions in a skillet (frying pan) with the butter and oil over medium heat until they begin to change color. Season with salt and pepper. § Turn the heat down to low, cover, and simmer for about 40 minutes, or until the onions are very soft. § Uncover and add the wine. Turn the heat up to medium and stir while the wine evaporates. Remove from heat. § Break the thick bucatoni noodles in half and cook in a large pot of salted, boiling water until *al dente*. Drain well and transfer to a heated serving dish. § Pour the onion sauce over the pasta. Add the parsley and Parmesan, and toss vigorously. Serve hot.

■ INGREDIENTS
- 5 large onions, thinly sliced
- 4 tablespoons butter
- 3 tablespoons extra-virgin olive oil
- salt and freshly ground black pepper
- ¾ cup (200 ml) dry white wine
- 1 lb (500 g) bucatoni pasta
- 3 tablespoons finely chopped parsley
- ½ cup (60 g) freshly grated Parmesan cheese

Wine: a dry white (Orvieto)

Spaghetti with shrimp
Spaghetti agli scampi

Serves: 4; Preparation: 20 minutes; Cooking: 15 minutes; Level of difficulty: Simple

Clean the shrimp, without removing the shells. Cut them in half lengthwise and set aside in a small bowl. § In a skillet (frying pan), sauté the garlic and parsley in the oil for 2–3 minutes over low heat. Increase the heat slightly and add the shrimp. Season with salt and mix well. § Add the wine, allow to evaporate, and cook for 8 minutes. Turn off the heat and cover the skillet. § Cook the spaghetti in a large pot of salted, boiling water until *al dente*. § Drain well and return to the skillet. Add the shrimp sauce and cook for 2 minutes over medium heat. § Transfer to a heated serving dish and serve.

■ INGREDIENTS
- 1 lb (500 g) giant shrimp, in shell
- 4 tablespoons extra-virgin olive oil
- 2 cloves garlic, minced
- 1 tablespoon chopped parsley
- dash of salt
- ½ cup (125 ml) dry white wine
- 1 lb (500 g) spaghetti

Wine: a dry white (Frascati)

Right: Spaghetti al tonno

Farfalle with peas and ham
Farfalle con piselli e prosciutto

Serves: 4; Preparation: 5 minutes; Cooking: 20 minutes; Level of difficulty: Simple

Boil the peas in salted water until half-cooked. § Combine the peas, butter, and ham in a large skillet (frying pan). Sauté over medium-low heat for 10 minutes. § Stir in half the cream and cook until the sauce thickens. § Add the parsley, and season with salt and pepper. § Cook the farfalle in a large pot of salted, boiling water until al dente. Drain well and transfer to the skillet with the sauce. Add the remaining cream and the Parmesan. Toss well and serve.

■ INGREDIENTS

- 1½ cups (180 g) peas, fresh or frozen
- 4 tablespoons butter
- 7 oz (200 g) prosciutto, diced
- 3 tablespoons light (single) cream
- 2 tablespoons finely chopped parsley
- salt and freshly ground black pepper
- 1 lb (500 g) farfalle pasta
- 4 tablespoons freshly grated Parmesan cheese

Lumaconi with vegetables
Lumaconi all'ortolana

Serves: 4; Preparation: 10 minutes; Cooking: 35 minutes; Level of difficulty: Simple

Chop the onion coarsely. Peel the eggplant and dice it and the zucchini into bite-sized pieces. Remove the seeds and cores from the bell peppers and chop into ½-in (1-cm) squares. § Put the onion in a large skillet (frying pan) with the oil and cook over medium heat until it becomes transparent. Add the eggplant, bell peppers, and zucchini. Sauté the vegetables for 7–8 minutes. § Add the tomatoes, crushed chilies, and salt to taste. Cook for 20 minutes. § Cook the lumaconi in a large pot of salted, boiling water until *al dente*. Drain and add to the skillet with the vegetables. Toss over high heat for 2–3 minutes until well mixed. Add the basil and Parmesan. § Transfer to a heated serving dish and serve hot.

■ INGREDIENTS

- 1 large onion
- 1 large eggplant (aubergine)
- 2 large zucchini (courgettes)
- 1 green, 1 yellow, and 1 red bell pepper (capsicum)
- 4 tablespoons extra-virgin olive oil
- 1½ lb (750 g) tomatoes, peeled and chopped
- ½ teaspoon crushed chilies
- dash of salt
- 8 basil leaves, torn
- 4 tablespoons freshly grated Parmesan cheese
- 1 lb (500 g) lumaconi pasta

Wine: a dry white (Bianco San Severo)

Bucatini with cauliflower and raisins
Bucatini al cavolfiore

Serves: 4; Preparation: 15 minutes; Cooking: 40 minutes; Level of difficulty: Simple

Boil the cauliflower in a large pot of salted water until it is just tender. Drain, reserving the water. § Divide the cauliflower into small florets. Bring the water back to a boil and add the pasta. § Meanwhile, sauté the onion for 1–2 minutes in the oil in a large skillet (frying pan). § Add the anchovies, raisins, pine nuts, and saffron. Stir for 2–3 minutes, then add the cauliflower and continue cooking over very low heat, stirring occasionally. § When the pasta is cooked *al dente*, drain and add to the cauliflower mixture. § Combine carefully, then transfer to a heated serving dish. Sprinkle with a generous grinding of pepper. § Serve hot.

■ INGREDIENTS

- 1 small cauliflower
- dash of salt
- 1 onion, thinly sliced
- ⅓ cup (90 ml) extra-virgin olive oil
- 4 anchovy fillets
- 3 tablespoons seedless white raisins (sultanas)
- 3 tablespoons pine nuts
- ¼ teaspoon saffron, dissolved in 3 tablespoons hot water
- 1 lb (500 g) bucatini pasta
- freshly ground black pepper

Wine: a dry white (Alcamo)

VARIATION
– For a hearty winter dish, transfer the pasta and cauliflower mixture to a heated ovenproof dish and sprinkle with ½ cup (2 oz/60 g) freshly grated Pecorino cheese. Place in a preheated oven at 400°F/200°C/gas 6 for 10 minutes, or until the cheese topping has turned golden brown.

Right: *Bucatini al cavolfiore*

Malloreddus with Italian sausages and pecorino
Malloreddus

Malloreddus ("little bulls"), or gnocchi sardi as they are also known, are a specialty of the island of Sardinia. They are unlike the other dried pasta in this section, being made of bran flour and saffron. Malloreddus can be made fresh at home, but it is a difficult and time-consuming task and good commercial varieties are now available in specialty stores.

Serves: 4; Preparation: 5 minutes; Cooking: 30 minutes; Level of difficulty: Simple

Combine the oil, sausages, onion, garlic, and basil in a skillet (frying pan) and sauté over medium heat until the onion turns pale gold. Add the tomatoes and salt and pepper to taste. Simmer for 15–20 minutes or until the sauce becomes thick. § Cook the malloreddus in a large pot of salted, boiling water until *al dente*. Drain well and transfer to a heated serving dish. Add the sauce and Pecorino and toss well. Serve hot.

■ INGREDIENTS

- 3 tablespoons extra-virgin olive oil
- 9 oz (275 g) Italian pork sausages, skinned and crumbled
- 1 large onion, and 3 cloves garlic, finely chopped
- 8 basil leaves, torn
- 1¾ lb (800 g) fresh tomatoes, peeled and chopped
- salt and freshly ground black pepper
- ⅓ cup (45 g) freshly grated Pecorino cheese
- 1 lb (500 g) malloreddus pasta

Wine: a dry red (Cannonau)

Spaghetti with fried eggplant
Spaghetti alla Norma

Spaghetti alla Norma is a classic Sicilian dish. Debate rages about the origins of the name. Some say that it is named after Bellini's famous opera. Others maintain that it simply means la norma, or something that happens often. It may also derive from the Catanese dialect, in which norma means "the very best."

Serves: 4; Preparation: 1½ hours; Cooking: 40 minutes; Level of difficulty: Simple

Cut the eggplants into ¼-in (6-mm) thick slices, sprinkle with salt, and place on a slanted cutting board, so that the bitter liquid they produce can run off. This will take about 1 hour. § Sauté the garlic and olive oil in a skillet (frying pan) over medium heat until the garlic is pale gold. Add the tomatoes, basil, salt, and pepper to taste. Cook over medium-low heat for about 20 minutes, or until the oil and tomatoes begin to separate. § Run the eggplant under cold water and pat dry with paper towels. Put the vegetable oil in a large skillet. When the oil is very hot, add as many slices of eggplant as will fit without overlapping. Fry to golden brown on both sides and drain on paper towels. When all the eggplant is fried, chop it into large squares. § Cook the spaghetti in a large pot of salted, boiling water until *al dente*. Drain well and transfer to a heated serving dish. § Toss with the tomato sauce and fried eggplant. Sprinkle with the Pecorino and serve.

■ INGREDIENTS

- 3 large eggplants (aubergines)
- salt and freshly ground black pepper
- 3 tablespoons extra-virgin olive oil
- 3 cloves garlic, finely chopped
- 1½ lb (750 g) tomatoes, peeled and chopped
- 2 sprigs basil, torn
- ½ cup (125 ml) vegetable oil for frying
- 1 lb (500 g) spaghetti
- ½ cup (60 g) freshly grated Pecorino cheese

Wine: a dry rosé (Cirò Superiore)

Right:
Spaghetti alla Norma

Bavette with green beans, potatoes, and pesto
Bavette con fagiolini e pesto

If you order pasta with pesto sauce in its hometown of Genoa, it will almost certainly be served with potatoes and green beans.

Serves: 4; Preparation: 15 minutes; Cooking: 25 minutes; Level of difficulty: Simple

Cook the vegetables in a large pot of salted, boiling water until tender. Take them out with a slotted spoon and use the same water to cook the pasta. § While the pasta is cooking, prepare the pesto. Add 2 tablespoons of boiling water from the pasta pot to make the pesto slightly more liquid. § When the pasta is cooked *al dente*, drain and transfer to a heated serving dish. Toss with the pesto, butter, and vegetables. Sprinkle with the cheeses and serve hot.

■ INGREDIENTS

- 1½ oz (750 g) green beans, cut into lengths
- 3 medium new potatoes, peeled and diced
- 1 lb (500 g) bavette pasta
- 1 quantity *Pesto* (see recipe p. 36)
- 4 tablespoons butter
- 4 tablespoons freshly grated Pecorino cheese
- 4 tablespoons freshly grated Parmesan cheese

Wine: a dry white (Vermentino)

Orecchiette with Swiss chard
Orecchiette con le bietole

For slightly different but equally delicious dishes, replace the Swiss chard with the same quantity of florets and diced stalks of green broccoli, cauliflower, or shredded Savoy cabbage.

Serves: 4; Preparation: 10 minutes; Cooking: 15 minutes; Level of difficulty: Simple

Cook the chard in a pot of salted, boiling water (3–4 minutes for frozen, 8–10 minutes for fresh). Drain well and squeeze out any extra moisture. Chop finely. § Combine the garlic and anchovies in a large skillet (frying pan) with the oil. Sauté until the garlic turns pale gold. Add the chard. Season with salt and pepper. § Cook the orecchiette in a large pot of salted, boiling water until *al dente*. Drain well and transfer to the skillet with the sauce. Toss for 1–2 minutes over medium-high heat. Sprinkle with the Pecorino and serve hot.

■ INGREDIENTS

- 1 lb (500 g) fresh, or 12 oz (350 g) frozen, Swiss chard (silver beet)
- 3 cloves garlic, minced
- ½ cup (125 ml) extra-virgin olive oil
- 2 anchovy fillets, crumbled
- 1 teaspoon crushed chilies
- salt and freshly ground black pepper
- 1 lb (500 g) orecchiette
- 4 tablespoons freshly grated Pecorino cheese

Wine: a dry red (Cirò)

Spicy spinach spaghetti
Spaghetti di spinaci piccanti

Serves: 4; Preparation: 15 minutes + 35 minutes for the sauce; Cooking: 12 minutes; Level of difficulty: Simple

Prepare the tomato sauce, stirring in the chilies just before it is ready. § Cook the spaghetti in a large pot of salted, boiling water until *al dente*. Drain well and transfer to the pan with the sauce. Toss for 1–2 minutes over medium-high heat. § Serve hot.

■ INGREDIENTS

- 1 quantity *Simple tomato sauce* (see recipe p. 28)
- 1 teapoon crushed chilies
- 1 lb (500 g) spinach spaghetti

Wine: a dry red (Chianti)

Right: *Orecchiette con le bietole*

■ INGREDIENTS

- 1½ lb (750 g) asparagus
- 4 tablespoons butter
- 8 oz (250 g) ham, cut
  into thin strips
- 1 cup (250 ml) light
  (single) cream
- ½ cup (60 g) freshly
  grated Parmesan cheese
- 1 lb (500 g) penne pasta
- salt and freshly ground
  black pepper

Wine: a dry white (Soave)

Penne with asparagus
Penne con gli asparagi

Serves: 4; Preparation: 10 minutes; Cooking: 15 minutes; Level of difficulty: Simple

Cook the asparagus in a large pot of salted, boiling water until the tips are tender. Drain and cut the tough parts off each stalk. § Melt the butter in a saucepan with the ham. Cook for 2–3 minutes. Add the asparagus tips and cream and stir gently over medium heat for 3–4 minutes, or until the cream thickens. Season with salt and pepper. § Cook the penne in a large pot of salted, boiling water until *al dente*. Drain and place in a heated serving dish. Add the sauce and toss well. Sprinkle with the Parmesan and serve hot.

■ INGREDIENTS

- 10 leeks
- 2 tablespoons butter
- ⅓ cup (90 ml) extra-virgin olive oil
- 1 onion, 2 cloves garlic, finely chopped
- 4 oz (125 g) pancetta, diced
- 1¼ cups (300 ml) boiling water
- salt and freshly ground black pepper
- 2 egg yolks
- dash of sugar
- 4 tablespoons freshly grated Pecorino cheese
- 1 lb (500 g) fusilli lunghi

Wine: a sparkling, dry red (Lambrusco)

■ INGREDIENTS

- 1 large onion, finely chopped
- 2 cloves garlic, finely chopped
- 2 tablespoons finely chopped parsley
- ⅓ cup (90 ml) extra-virgin olive oil
- 1 teaspoon oregano
- salt and freshly ground black pepper
- 3 tablespoons bread crumbs
- 1 lb (500 g) spaghetti

Wine: a dry white (Velletri)

Long fusilli with leeks
Fusilli lunghi ai porri

Serves: 4; Preparation: 10 minutes; Cooking: 40 minutes; Level of difficulty: Simple

Prepare the leeks by discarding two layers of outer leaves and cutting off almost all the green part. Slice in thin wheels. Set aside. § Combine the butter, oil, onion, and garlic in a skillet (frying pan) and sauté over medium heat until the onion turns pale gold. Add the pancetta and stir until it browns. § Add the leeks and boiling water and simmer over low heat until the leeks are very tender. Season with salt and pepper. § Add the egg yolks and sugar and stir vigorously. Remove from heat. § Cook the fusilli in a large pot of salted, boiling water until *al dente*. Drain well and transfer to a heated serving dish. Toss with the sauce and sprinkle with Pecorino. Serve hot.

Spaghetti with onion, garlic, and bread crumbs
Spaghetti alla carrettiera classica

This is a classic Roman recipe. It is said to have been the favorite dish of the carrettieri (cart-drivers) who transported the Castelli Romani wine from the Alban Hills into Rome. There are many variations on the basic recipe given here. We have suggested the common tomato one below.

Serves: 4; Preparation: 10 minutes; Cooking: 15 minutes; Level of difficulty: Simple

Sauté the onion, garlic, and parsley in a skillet (frying pan) with the oil, oregano, salt, and pepper over medium heat until the onion and garlic turn pale gold. Remove from heat. § Toast the bread crumbs in the oven and mix with a few drops of oil. § Cook the spaghetti in a large pot of salted, boiling water until *al dente*. Drain well and transfer to a heated serving dish. Toss with the sauce and bread crumbs. Serve hot.

Spaghetti with onion, garlic, tomato and bread crumbs
Spaghetti alla carrettiera rossa

Serves: 4; Preparation: 10 minutes; Cooking: 15 minutes; Level of difficulty: Simple

Follow the instructions above, but add 6 medium peeled tomatoes and ¾ teaspoon crushed chilies to the onion and garlic mixture after it has changed color. § Cook over medium heat for 10–15 minutes until the tomatoes have reduced. Proceed as explained above.

Left:
Fusilli lunghi ai porri

Ruote salad with vegetables

Insalata di ruote con le verdure

Serves: 4; Preparation: 15 minutes; Cooking: 15 minutes; Level of difficulty: Simple

Cook the ruote in a large pot of salted, boiling water until *al dente*. Drain thoroughly. Transfer to a large salad bowl and toss vigorously with half the oil. Set aside to cool. § Cut the stalk and hard base off the eggplant and peel. Cut crosswise into slices about ½ in (1 cm) thick. Place the slices under the broiler (grill) and cook for about 10 minutes, or until tender. Dice the cooked slices in ¾-in (2-cm) squares. § Quarter the bell peppers lengthwise and slice each quarter into thin strips. § Slice the white, bottom part of the scallions very finely. § When the pasta is completely cool, combine with the remaining oil, capers, oregano, parsley, eggplant, bell peppers, and Pecorino and toss well. Sprinkle with salt and pepper and serve.

■ INGREDIENTS

- 1 lb (500 g) plain, whole wheat, or colored ruote pasta
- ⅓ cup (90 ml) extra-virgin olive oil
- 1 large eggplant (aubergine)
- 1 yellow and 1 red bell pepper (capsicum)
- 2 scallions (shallots)
- 2½ tablespoons capers
- 1 teaspoon dried oregano
- 2 tablespoons finely chopped parsley
- 3 tablespoons freshly grated Pecorino cheese
- salt and freshly ground black pepper

Wine: a dry white (Frascati)

Fusilli salad with tomato, garlic, and mozzarella cheese

Insalata di fusilli con pomodori, aglio, e mozzarella

Serves: 4; Preparation: 10 minutes; Cooking: 10 minutes; Level of difficulty: Simple

Cook the fusilli in a large pot of salted, boiling water until *al dente*. Drain well. Transfer to a large salad bowl and toss vigorously with half the oil. Set aside to cool. § Add the tomatoes to the pasta. Combine the garlic and parsley with the remainder of the oil and salt, and add to the salad bowl. Leave to cool completely. § Just before serving, dice the Mozzarella into ½-in (1-cm) cubes on a cutting board. Slant the board slightly so that the extra liquid runs off. Sprinkle over the top of the salad with the torn basil leaves and freshly ground black pepper. Serve cool.

■ INGREDIENTS

- 1 lb (500 g) plain or whole wheat fusilli pasta
- salt and freshly ground black pepper
- 4 tablespoons extra-virgin olive oil
- 4 large ripe tomatoes, cut in bite-sized pieces
- 2 cloves garlic, finely chopped
- 2 tablespoons finely chopped parsley
- 12 oz (350 g) Mozzarella
- 6 fresh basil leaves

Wine: a dry white (Colonna)

Right: Insalata di ruote con le verdure ed

Insalata di fusilli con pomodori

VARIATION
– Add 1 tablespoon of mustard to the oil for a sharper flavor.

INGREDIENTS

- 1 lb (500 g) conchiglie pasta
- dash of salt
- 4 tablespoons extra-virgin olive oil
- 4 hard-cooked (hard-boiled) eggs
- 3 large ripe tomatoes, diced
- 7 oz (200 g) tuna, packed in oil, drained
- 2 scallions
- 4 tablespoons *Mayonnaise* (see recipe p. 42)
- 2 tablespoons finely chopped parsley

Conchiglie with eggs, tomato, tuna, and mayonnaise
Insalata di conchiglie splendida

Serves: 4; Preparation: 5 minutes; Cooking: 12 minutes; Level of difficulty: Simple

Cook the conchiglie in a large pot of salted, boiling water until *al dente*. Drain very thoroughly. Transfer to a large salad bowl and toss well with half the oil. Set aside to cool. § Peel the eggs and cut into quarters lengthwise. Break the tuna up by lightly pressing with a fork. Slice the white, bottom part of the scallion thinly. § When the pasta is cool, add the eggs, tomatoes, tuna, parsley, remaining oil, and mayonnaise. Sprinkle with salt, toss thoroughly, and serve.

Fresh and Filled Pasta

Fresh pasta is made of egg and soft-wheat flour,
and includes tagliatelle, fettuccine, and tagliolini.
Filled pasta is made by wrapping small quantities
of meat or vegetable stuffing in fresh pasta. For the
recipes in this chapter, either make your own (see
instructions p. 198–201) or buy it freshly made.

Making Fresh Pasta at Home

Fresh pasta can be made either by hand or by using a pasta machine. I strongly advise you not to use the pasta machines that mix the dough as well as cut the pasta, since the finished product will be heavy and very inferior to handmade pasta.

MIXING PLAIN PASTA DOUGH

For 4 generous servings you will need 3 cups (450 g) of all-purpose (plain) white flour and 3 eggs. Place the flour in a mound on a flat work surface and hollow out a well in the center. Break the eggs into the well one by one and beat lightly with a fork for 1–2 minutes. Pull some of the surrounding flour down over the egg mixture and gradually incorporate it. Continue until the mixture is no longer runny. Using your hands

now, combine all the flour with the eggs. Work the mixture with your hands until it is smooth and moist, but quite firm.

To test the mixture for the correct consistency, press a clean finger into the dough. If it comes out easily and without any dough sticking to it, it is ready for kneading. If it is too moist, add more flour. If it is too dry, incorporate a little milk. Roll the mixture into a ball shape.

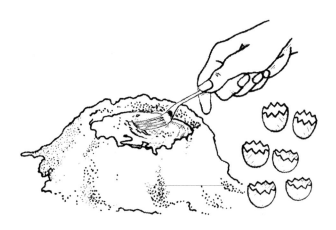
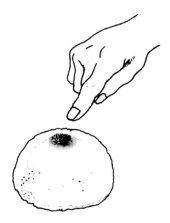

MIXING SPINACH PASTA DOUGH

For 4 generous servings you will need 2 cups (300 g) of all-purpose (plain) flour, 5 oz (150 g) of fresh spinach, or 3½ oz (100 g) thawed frozen spinach, and 2 eggs. Cook the spinach in a little

salted water until tender. Drain well and, when cool, squeeze out any excess moisture. Chop finely with a knife. Proceed as above for plain dough, working the spinach in together with the eggs.

KNEADING THE DOUGH

Clean any excess dough or flour off the work surface and lightly sprinkle with flour. Push down and forwards on the ball of pasta dough with the heel of your palm. Fold the slightly extended piece of dough in half, give it a quarter-turn, and repeat the process. Continue for about 10 minutes or until the dough is very smooth. Place the ball of pasta dough on a plate and cover with an upturned bowl. Leave to rest for at least 15–20 minutes.

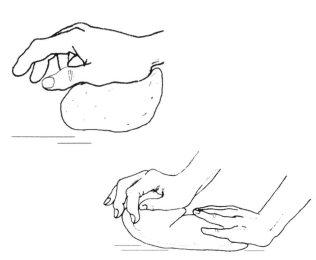

ROLLING THE DOUGH OUT BY HAND

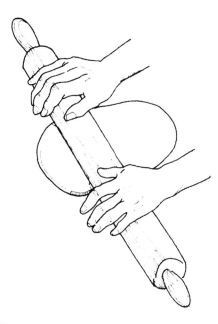

Place the ball of dough on a flat, clean work surface and flatten it a little with your hand. Place the rolling pin on the center of the flattened ball and, applying light but firm pressure, roll the dough away from you. Give the ball a quarter-turn and repeat. When the dough has become a large round disk about ¼ in (6 mm) thick, curl the far edge over the pin while holding the edge closest to you with your hand. Gently stretch the pasta as you roll it all onto the pin. Unroll, give the dough a quarter-turn, and repeat. Continue rolling and stretching the dough until it is transparent.

ROLLING THE DOUGH OUT USING THE PASTA MACHINE

Divide the dough into several pieces and flatten them slightly with your hand. Set the machine with its rollers at their widest, and run each piece through the machine. Reduce the rollers' width by one notch and repeat, reducing the rollers' width by one notch each time. Continue until all the pieces have gone through the machine at the thinnest roller-setting.

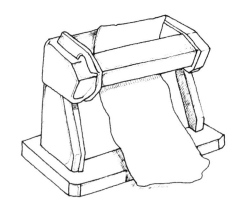

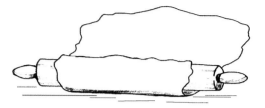

CUTTING THE PASTA BY HAND

For lasagna: cut the rolled-out pasta into oblong sheets about 3 x 12 in (8 x 30 cm).

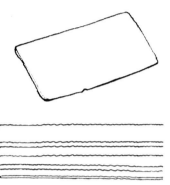

For tagliolini, fettuccine, tagliatelle, and pappardelle: fold the hand-rolled pasta into a loose, flat roll. Using a large sharp knife, cut the roll into ⅛-in (3-mm) slices (for tagliolini), ¼-in (6-mm) slices (for fettuccine), ⅓-in (8-mm) slices (for tagliatelle), or ¾-in (2-cm) slices (for pappardelle). Unravel the pasta and lay it out flat on a clean dishcloth. If you want fluted edges, use the wheel cutter on the pasta laid out flat. You will need a steady hand!

For maltagliati: fold the hand-rolled pasta into a loose, flat roll. Using a large sharp knife cut the pasta into diamond shapes. Separate the pieces and lay them out on a clean dishcloth.

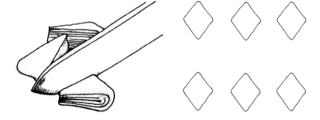

CUTTING THE PASTA BY MACHINE

Cut the pieces of pasta lengthwise so that they are about 12 in (30 cm) long. Attach the cutters to the pasta machine and set the machine at the widths given above for the various types of pasta. Lay the cut pasta out on clean dry dishcloths.

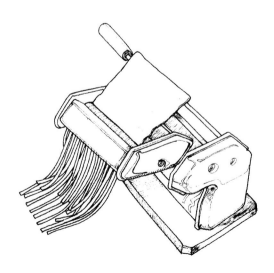

MAKING STUFFED PASTA

Pasta dough for stuffed pasta needs to be fairly moist, so try to work quickly and keep all the dough you are not using on a plate covered by an overturned plate.

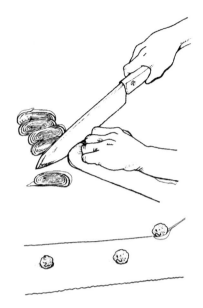

For agnolotti, tortelli, and square-shaped ravioli: these are the easiest filled pasta shapes to make. Using a large sharp knife, cut the rolled-out pasta into strips about 4 in (10 cm) wide. Place heaped teaspoonfuls of the mixture for the filling at intervals of about 2 in (5 cm) down the middle. Slightly moisten the edges of the pasta with your fingertips before folding them over and sealing them. Use a wheel cutter to cut between the stuffing. Run it along the sealed edges to give them a decorative, fluted edge.

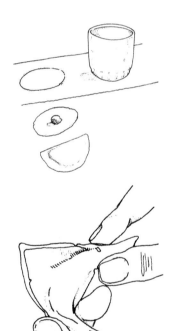

For half-moon shaped ravioli: use a glass or cookie cutter to cut the rolled-out pasta into circular shapes. Place a teaspoonful of the filling at the center, moisten the edges of the pasta with your fingertips and fold it over. Pinch the edges together with your fingers until they are well sealed. For fluted edges, run the pastry cutter around each shape.

For tortellini: use a glass or cookie cutter to cut the rolled-out pasta into circular shapes. Place ½ teaspoonful of the filling mixture in the middle of each circle. Moisten the edges of the pasta with your fingertips and fold the pasta over. Pick the tortellino up and twist it around your index finger until the edges meet. Pinch them together with your fingers and seal them.

For tortelloni: as above, but using a larger glass or a small bowl 3½ in (9 cm) in diameter and 1 teaspoonful of the filling mixture.

For cappelletti: using a large sharp knife, cut the rolled-out pasta into strips about 2 in (5 cm) wide. Cut each strip into 2-in (5-cm) squares. Place ½ teaspoonfuls of the filling mixture in the center of each. Fold the square diagonally in half to form a triangle. Moisten the edges slightly with your fingertips and seal them together. Pick up the triangle by one corner of its folded-over side. Take the other folded-over corner and wrap it around your index finger. Pinch the edges together to seal the pasta.

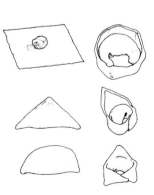

Tagliolini with artichoke and egg sauce
Tagliolini con carciofi

Serves: 4; Preparation: 5 minutes + time to make the pasta; Cooking: 5 minutes; Level of difficulty: Medium

Prepare the pasta. § Clean the artichokes as described on p. 84, slicing them thinly lengthwise. § Sauté the onion in the oil in a flameproof casserole until it is tender but not browned. § Add the artichokes and season with salt and pepper. Stir over medium heat for 2–3 minutes. § Pour in the water, cover and cook for about 20 minutes, or until very tender but not mushy. § Cook the tagliolini in a large pot of salted, boiling water until *al dente*. § Break the eggs into a deep, heated serving dish, beat with a fork, and add 5 tablespoons of the cheese. § Drain the pasta and mix with the egg mixture, then stir in the artichokes. § Sprinkle with the remaining cheese and serve hot.

■ INGREDIENTS

- 1 lb (500 g) tagliolini pasta (see recipe pp. 198–200)
- 8 baby artichokes
- 3 tablespoons onion, finely chopped
- 4 tablespoons extra-virgin olive oil
- salt and freshly ground black pepper
- ½ cup (125 ml) water
- 3 fresh eggs
- ½ cup (60 g) freshly grated Pecorino cheese

Wine: a dry white (Pinot Grigio)

Tagliolini with Mascarpone cheese sauce
Tagliolini al mascarpone

Serves: 4; Preparation: 5 minutes + time to make the pasta; Cooking: 5 minutes; Level of difficulty: Medium

Prepare the pasta. § Warm the Mascarpone in a saucepan. Remove from heat and stir in the egg yolks. Season with salt. § Cook the tagliolini in a large pot of salted, boiling water until al dente. Drain and toss with the sauce. Sprinkle with the Parmesan and freshly ground black pepper. Serve hot.

■ INGREDIENTS

- 1 lb (500 g) tagliolini pasta (see recipe pp. 198–200)
- 1 cup (250 g) Mascarpone cheese
- 2 egg yolks
- salt and black pepper
- ½ cup (60 g) freshly grated Parmesan cheese

Wine: a dry white (Verdicchio)

Tagliatelle with clams and cream
Tagliatelle alle vongole con panna

Serves: 4; Preparation: 10 minutes + time to make the pasta + 1 hour to soak clams; Cooking: 15 minutes; Level of difficulty: Medium

Prepare the pasta. § Soak the clams in cold water for 1 hour. § Put the clams in a large skillet (frying pan), cover, and place over high heat until they open. Discard any that do not open. Remove from the pan and set aside with their juice. § Sauté the garlic in the same pan over medium heat with the oil, chilies, and bay leaves. When the garlic begins to change color, add the clams and their cooking juices, cream, tomatoes, and salt. Simmer over medium heat for 5–10 minutes, or until the sauce has reduced. § Cook the tagliatelle in a large pot of salted, boiling water until *al dente*. Drain well and transfer to the skillet with the clams. Toss quickly over medium-high heat and serve.

■ INGREDIENTS

- 1 lb (500 g) tagliatelle pasta (see recipe pp. 198–200)
- 2 lb (1 kg) clams in shell
- 2 cloves garlic, minced
- 3 tablespoons extra-virgin olive oil
- ½ teaspoon crushed chilies
- 3 bay leaves
- ¾ cup (200 ml) light (single) cream
- 3 large tomatoes, chopped
- dash of salt

Wine: a dry white (Pinot Bianco)

Right: *Tagliolini con carciofi*

Pappardelle with wild hare sauce
Pappardelle sulla lepre

This is a classic Tuscan dish. Traditionally the recipe calls for wild hare,
but if this is hard to find use the same amount of rabbit in its place.

Serves: 4; Preparation: 20 minutes + time to make the pasta; Cooking: 2½ hours; Level of difficulty: Medium

Prepare the pasta. § Sauté the parsley, rosemary, onion, carrot, and celery with the oil in a heavy-bottomed pan over medium heat. When the onion and garlic begin to change color, add the hare meat and cook for 15–20 minutes or until the meat is well browned, stirring frequently. Add the wine and stir until it has evaporated. § Add the boiling water, milk, and tomato paste. Season with salt and pepper. Simmer over low heat for about 1½ hours. § Add the hare liver and, if necessary, more water. Cook for 30 minutes more, or until the hare is very tender. § Cook the pappardelle in a large pot of salted, boiling water until *al dente*. Drain well and place in a heated serving dish. Toss with the sauce and sprinkle with Parmesan. Serve hot.

■ INGREDIENTS

- 1 lb (500 g) pappardelle pasta (see recipe pp. 198–200)
- 3 tablespoons parsley, 1½ tablespoons fresh rosemary, 1 large onion, 1 large carrot, 1 stalk celery, all finely chopped
- ¾ cup (200 ml) extra-virgin olive oil
- 1¼ lb (600 g) boneless wild hare meat, with liver, coarsely chopped
- 3 cups (750 ml) red wine
- 4 cups (1 liter) water
- ½ cup (125 ml) milk
- 2 tablespoons tomato paste
- salt and freshly ground black pepper
- 4 tablespoons freshly grated Parmesan cheese

Wine: a dry red (Chianti)

Tagliatelle al prosciutto
Tagliatelle with prosciutto

Serves: 4; Preparation: 5 minutes + time to make the pasta; Cooking: 12 minutes; Level of difficulty: Medium

Prepare the pasta. § Sauté the onion and fat from the prosciutto with the butter in a skillet (frying pan) until the onion begins to change color. Add the prosciutto and sauté for 2–3 minutes. Add the wine and simmer until it evaporates. Season with salt and pepper. § Cook the tagliatelle in a large pot of salted, boiling water until *al dente*. Drain well and place in a heated serving dish. Pour the sauce over the pasta and toss vigorously. Sprinkle with Parmesan and serve hot.

■ INGREDIENTS

- 1 lb (500 g) tagliatelle pasta (see recipe pp. 198–200)
- 1 medium onion, finely chopped
- 8 oz (250 g) prosciutto, diced
- 4 tablespoons butter
- ¾ cup (200 ml) dry white wine
- salt and freshly ground black pepper
- 4 tablespoons freshly grated Parmesan cheese

Wine: a dry rosé (Rosato di Carmignano)

Right: *Pappardelle sulla lepre*

Tagliatelle with crispy-fried pancetta
Tagliatelle alla pancetta

Serves: 4; Preparation: 5 minutes + time to make the pasta; Cooking: 12 minutes; Level of difficulty: Medium

Prepare the pasta. § Sauté the pancetta, butter, and garlic over medium heat in a large skillet (frying pan) until the pancetta is crisp. § Cook the tagliatelle in a large pot of salted, boiling water until *al dente*. Drain well and transfer to the skillet with the pancetta. Toss quickly over medium heat. § Sprinkle with the Parmesan and season with pepper. Serve hot.

■ INGREDIENTS

- 1 lb (500 g) tagliatelle pasta (see recipe pp. 198–200)
- 6 oz (180 g) pancetta, diced
- 4 tablespoons butter
- 2 cloves garlic, finely chopped
- salt and freshly ground black pepper
- ½ cup (60 g) freshly grated Parmesan cheese

Paglia e fieno with cream and truffles
Paglia e fieno semplice

Two types of fettuccine, the plain yellow egg variety, and the green spinach variety, are often served together. This colorful mixture is called paglia e fieno, which means "straw and hay."

Serves: 4; Preparation: 5 minutes; Cooking: 10 minutes; Level of difficulty: Simple

Prepare the pasta. § Melt the butter in a heavy-bottomed pan and add the white truffle. Leave to cook for 1 minute over low heat, then add the cream. Season with salt and pepper. Simmer for 4–5 minutes or until the cream reduces. § Cook the paglia e fieno in a large pot of salted, boiling water until *al dente*. Drain well and add to the pan with the truffle sauce. § Sprinkle with the Parmesan and toss well over medium heat for 1–2 minutes. Serve hot.

■ INGREDIENTS

- 1 lb (500 g) paglia e fieno pasta (see recipe pp. 198–200)
- 4 tablespoons butter
- 1 white truffle, in shavings
- ¾ cup (200 ml) light (single) cream
- salt and freshly ground black pepper
- ⅓ cup (45 g) freshly grated Parmesan cheese

Wine: a dry white (Pinot Bianco)

Tuscan-style paglia e fieno
Paglia e fieno alla toscana

Serves: 4; Preparation: 30 minutes; Cooking: 45-50 minutes; Level of difficulty: Medium

Prepare the pasta. § Place the pancetta, prosciutto, onion, celery, and carrot in a skillet (frying pan) with half the butter and sauté over medium heat until the onion is soft. Add the tomatoes, mushrooms, nutmeg, salt, and pepper to taste. Cook over medium heat for 15 minutes. § Add the wine and, when it has all evaporated, the peas. Simmer over medium-low heat until the peas and mushrooms are tender, stirring in the meat stock as needed to keep the sauce liquid. § Cook the paglia e fieno together in a large pot of salted, boiling water until *al dente*. Drain well and transfer to a heated serving dish. Toss vigorously with the remaining butter. § Place the pasta, sauce, and Parmesan separately on the table so that everyone can help themselves to as much cheese and sauce as they like.

■ INGREDIENTS

- 1 lb (500 g) paglia e fieno pasta (see recipe pp. 198–200)
- 4 oz (125 g) pancetta, diced
- 2 oz (60 g) prosciutto, diced
- 1 large onion, 1 stalk celery, 1 large carrot, all finely chopped
- 4 tablespoons butter
- 1¼ lb (600 g) tomatoes, peeled and chopped
- 12 oz (350 g) mushrooms
- dash of nutmeg
- salt and freshly ground black pepper
- ¾ cup (200 ml) dry white wine
- 14 oz (450 g) peas, fresh or frozen
- ¾ cup (200 ml) *Beef stock* (see recipe p. 48)
- ¾ cup (90 g) freshly grated Parmesan cheese

Wine: a dry red (Chianti)

Right:
Paglia e fieno alla toscana

Tagliolini with curry sauce
Tagliolini al curry

■ INGREDIENTS

- 1 lb (500 g) tagliolini pasta
  (see recipe pp. 198–200)
- 1 quantity *Béchamel sauce*
  (see recipe p. 38)
- 1 cup (250 ml) heavy
  (double) cream
- 2 tablespoons curry powder
- salt and freshly ground
  black pepper
- 1 tablespoon butter
- ½ cup (60 g) freshly grated
  Parmesan cheese

Serves: 4; Preparation: 10 minutes + time to make the pasta; Cooking: 15 minutes; Level of difficulty: Simple

Prepare the pasta and the béchamel sauce. § Stir the cream and curry powder into the béchamel and cook for 2–3 more minutes. Season with salt and pepper. § Cook the tagliolini in a large pot of salted, boiling water until *al dente*. Drain well and transfer to a heated serving dish. § Toss with the butter and curry sauce. Sprinkle with Parmesan and serve immediately.

INGREDIENTS

- 1 lb (500 g) spinach tagliatelle pasta (see recipe pp. 198–200)
- 7 oz (200 g) peas, fresh or frozen
- 3 oz (90 g) Gorgonzola cheese
- 1¼ cups (300 ml) light (single) cream
- salt and freshly ground black pepper
- 2 tablespoons parsley, finely chopped
- ½ cup (60 g) freshly grated Parmesan cheese

Wine: a light, dry white (Soave)

Spinach tagliatelle with fresh cream, peas, and gorgonzola cheese
Tagliatelle verdi primaverili

Serves: 4; Preparation: 10 minutes + time to make the pasta; Cooking: 15 minutes; Level of difficulty: Medium

Prepare the pasta. § Cook the peas in a pot of salted, boiling water. Drain well and set aside. § Place the Gorgonzola, diced into ½-in (1-cm) squares, in a large heavy-bottomed pan over low heat. Stir the cheese until it melts. § Stir in the cream. Add the peas and salt and pepper to taste. § Cook the pasta in a large pot of salted, boiling water until *al dente*. Drain well and transfer to the pan containing the sauce. § Add the parsley and Parmesan. Toss well and serve.

INGREDIENTS

- 1 lb (500 g) maltagliati pasta (see recipe pp. 198–200)
- 4 cloves garlic, finely chopped
- ⅓ cup (90 ml) extra-virgin olive oil
- 1 lb (500 g) ground lamb
- 5 oz (150 g) lean ground pork
- 2 bay leaves
- 1½ lb (750 g) tomatoes, peeled and chopped
- 8 fresh basil leaves
- 1 teaspoon marjoram
- salt and freshly ground black pepper
- 1 cup (125 g) freshly grated Pecorino cheese

Wine: a dry red (Rosso di Montalcino)

Maltagliati with lamb sauce
Maltagliati al ragù di agnello

Maltagliati (literally "badly cut") are usually served in stock, with minestrone, or pasta soups, but they are sometimes prepared with sauces. In some Italian dialects this pasta is known as spruzzamusi, or bagnanasi, words which are difficult to translate but which mean that you are likely to get stock or sauce on your nose, cheeks, and chin.

Serves: 4; Preparation: 15 minutes + time to make the pasta; Cooking: 1¼ hours; Level of difficulty: Medium

Prepare the pasta. § Sauté the garlic with the oil in a heavy-bottomed pan over medium heat until the garlic turns light gold in color. Add the lamb, pork, and bay leaf and sauté for 8–10 minutes. § Add the tomatoes, basil, and marjoram. Season with salt and pepper, and simmer over low heat for 1 hour. § Cook the maltagliati in a large pot of salted, boiling water until *al dente*. Drain, transfer to a heated serving dish, and toss with the sauce and Pecorino. § Serve hot.

Left: *Tagliatelle verdi primaverili*

Tagliatelle with olives and mushrooms
Tagliatelle alla frantoiana

Serves: 4; Preparation: 10 minutes + time to make the pasta; Cooking: 25 minutes; Level of difficulty: Medium

Prepare the pasta. § Combine the garlic and parsley in a skillet (frying pan) with the oil and sauté until the garlic begins to change color. Add the mushrooms and cook until the water they produce has evaporated. § Add the olives, mint, salt, pepper, and boiling water. Simmer for 5 minutes. § Cook the tagliatelle in a large pot of salted, boiling water until *al dente*. Drain and transfer to a heated serving dish. Toss vigorously with the sauce and serve.

■ INGREDIENTS

- 1 lb (500 g) tagliatelle pasta (see recipe pp. 198–200)
- 2 cloves garlic, finely chopped
- 3 tablespoons parsley, finely chopped
- ½ cup (9125 ml) extra-virgin olive oil
- 12 oz (350 g) mushrooms, coarsely chopped
- 5 oz (150 g) black olives, coarsely chopped
- 8 mint leaves, torn
- salt and freshly ground black pepper
- ⅓ cup (90 ml) boiling water

Wine: a dry, sparkling red (Lambrusco)

Fettuccine alla romagnola
Fettuccine with simple butter and tomato sauce

Serves: 4; Preparation: 5 minutes + time to make the pasta; Cooking: 35 minutes; Level of difficulty: Medium

Prepare the pasta. § Sauté the garlic and parsley with the butter in a skillet (frying pan). When the garlic begins to change color, add the tomatoes and season with salt and pepper. Simmer over medium-low heat for about 30 minutes. § Cook the fettuccine in a large pot of salted, boiling water until *al dente*. Drain well and transfer to a heated serving dish. § Toss vigorously with the tomato sauce and basil. Serve hot.

■ INGREDIENTS

- 1 lb (500 g) fettuccine pasta (see recipe pp. 198–200)
- 3 cloves garlic, finely chopped
- 3 tablespoons parsley, finely chopped
- ½ cup (125 g) butter
- 2 lb (1 kg) tomatoes, chopped
- salt and freshly ground black pepper
- 8 fresh basil leaves, torn

Wine: a rosé (Castel del Monte)

Spinach tagliatelle with butter and fresh rosemary sauce
Tagliatelle verdi con burro e rosmarino

Serves: 4; Preparation: 5 minutes + time to make the pasta; Cooking: 10 minutes; Level of difficulty: Medium

Prepare the pasta and the sauce. § Cook the pasta in a large pot of salted, boiling water until *al dente*. Drain well and transfer to a heated serving dish. § Pour the sauce over the pasta, toss well, and serve.

■ INGREDIENTS

- 1 lb (500 g) spinach tagliatelle (see recipe pp. 198–200)
- 1 quantity *Butter and rosemary sauce* (see recipe p. 38)

Wine: a dry white (Verdicchio)

Right: *Fettuccine alla romagnola*

Tagliatelle with duck sauce
Tagliatelle al sugo d'anatra

Serves: 4; Preparation: 20 minutes + time to make the pasta; Cooking: 2½ hours; Level of difficulty: Medium

Prepare the pasta. § Wash the duck and pat dry with paper towels. Sprinkle with the oil, salt, pepper, rosemary, sage, and bay leaf, and roast in a preheated oven at 375°F/190°C/gas 5 for about 1 hour. Turn the duck and baste it with the white wine while it is cooking. Remove from the oven and set aside. § Sauté the garlic, onion, carrot, and celery in the gravy from the roast duck until the onion is translucent. Add the tomato paste and water. Season with salt and pepper. Simmer over medium-low heat for 15 minutes. § Bone the duck and chop the meat coarsely. Add to the pan with the vegetables and cook for 45 more minutes, adding water if necessary. § Cook the tagliatelle in a large pot of salted, boiling water until al dente. Drain well and transfer to a heated serving bowl. Pour the sauce over the pasta and sprinkle with the Parmesan. Toss well, and serve hot.

■ INGREDIENTS

- 1 lb (500 g) tagliatelle pasta (see recipe pp. 198–200)
- 1 duck, cleaned, about 2 lb (1 kg)
- 3 tablespoons extra-virgin olive oil
- salt and freshly ground black pepper
- 2 sprigs each of fresh rosemary and sage
- 1 bay leaf
- 1 cup (250 ml) dry white wine
- 2 cloves garlic, 1 medium onion, 1 carrot, 1 stalk celery, all finely chopped
- 4 tablespoons tomato paste, dissolved in 1 cup (250 ml) water
- ⅓ cup (45 g) freshly grated Parmesan cheese

Wine: a dry red (Sangiovese)

Tagliatelle in butter and rosemary sauce
Tagliatelle al rosmarino

This recipe comes from Piedmont in northern Italy. In another traditional Piedmontese recipe, the tagliatelle are served with the cooking juices left in the pan after roasting beef, pork, or poultry, and sprinkled with a little freshly grated Parmesan.

Serves: 4; Preparation: 30 minutes + time to make the pasta; Cooking: 3 minutes; Level of difficulty: Medium

Prepare the pasta. § Cook the tagliatelle in a large pot of salted, boiling water until al dente. § Drain well, transfer to a heated serving dish and sprinkle with the Parmesan. § Prepare the sauce. Drizzle over the tagliatelle and toss gently. § Top with slivers of fresh truffle, if using, and serve hot.

■ INGREDIENTS

- 1 lb (500 g) tagliatelle pasta (see recipe pp. 198–200)
- 3 tablespoons freshly grated Parmesan cheese
- 1 quantity *Butter and rosemary sauce* (see recipe p. 38)
- fresh white truffle, cut in wafer-thin slices (optional)

Wine: a young dry red (Roero)

Right: *Fettuccine all'Alfredo*

Fettuccine with butter and cream sauce
Fettuccine all'Alfredo

■ INGREDIENTS

- 1 lb (500 g) tagliatelle pasta (see recipe pp. 198–200)
- ⅓ cup (100 g) butter
- 1¼ cups (300 ml) heavy (double) cream
- ½ cup (60 g) freshly grated Parmesan cheese
- dash of nutmeg
- salt and freshly ground black pepper

Serves: 4; Preparation: 5 minutes + time to make the pasta; Cooking: 10 minutes; Level of difficulty: Medium

Prepare the pasta. § Place the butter and cream in a heavy-bottomed pan and cook over high heat for 2 minutes. Remove from heat. § Cook the fettuccine in a large pot of salted, boiling water until al dente. Drain well and transfer to the pan with the cream. Add the Parmesan, nutmeg, salt, and pepper to taste, and place over medium-low heat for 1 minute, tossing the pasta constantly. § Serve immediately.

Agnolotti with butter and sage sauce
Agnolotti con burro e salvia

Serves: 4; Preparation: 10 minutes + time to make and rest the pasta; Cooking: 15 minutes; Level of difficulty: Medium

Prepare the pasta dough. § Melt the butter for the filling in a saucepan and add the meat juices, cabbage, leek, and sausage meat. Cook for 5–6 minutes, stirring frequently and moistening, if necessary, with a little water. § Leave to cool before placing in a mixing bowl with the chopped roast meats, egg, Parmesan, nutmeg, salt, and pepper. Transfer to a food processor, blend thoroughly, then set aside. § Prepare the agnolotti as shown on page 201. § Spread the agnolotti out in a single layer on a lightly-floured clean cloth and leave to dry in a cool place for at least 2 hours. § Cook the agnolotti in a large pot of salted, boiling water until the pasta round the sealed edges is al dente. § Drain thoroughly and transfer to a heated serving dish. § Heat the butter and sage until golden brown and drizzle over the agnolotti. Sprinkle with the Parmesan and serve.

■ INGREDIENTS

PASTA: see recipe pp. 198–201
FILLING
- 2 tablespoons butter
- 3 tablespoons cooking juices from roast meat
- 3 oz (90 g) Savoy cabbage, finely chopped
- 1 small leek, white part only, finely chopped
- 2 oz (60 g) Italian sausage meat
- 6 oz (180 g) each of lean roast beef and pork, chopped
- 1 egg
- 2 tablespoons freshly grated Parmesan cheese
- dash of nutmeg
- salt and freshly ground white pepper

- 1 quantity *Butter and sage sauce* (see recipe p. 38)
- 4 tablespoons freshly grated Parmesan cheese

Wine: a light, dry red (Grignolino)

Agnolotti with meat sauce
Agnolotti con sugo di carne

Serves: 4; Preparation: 30 minutes + time to make the pasta and the meat sauce; Cooking: 15 minutes; Level of difficulty: Medium

Make the pasta dough. § Prepare the agnolotti filling as shown above. § Prepare the agnolotti as shown on page 201. § Prepare the meat sauce. § Cook the agnolotti in a large pot of salted, boiling water until the pasta round the sealed edges is *al dente*. Remove from the water using a slotted spoon and place on a heated serving dish. § Cover with the meat sauce. Sprinkle with the Parmesan and, if using, shavings of white truffle. Serve hot.

■ INGREDIENTS

PASTA: see recipe pp. 198–201
FILLING: see above
- 1 quantity *Bolognese* or *Quick meat sauce* (see recipes pp. 30, 32)
- 4 tablespoons freshly grated Parmesan cheese
- white truffle (optional)

Wine: a dry red (Dolcetto)

Right: *Agnolotti con burro e salvia*

Ravioli with Italian sausage filling in butter and sage sauce
Ravioli semplici al burro

Serves: 4; Preparation: 20 minutes + time to make the pasta; Cooking: 10 minutes; Level of difficulty: Medium

Make the pasta dough. § Cook the spinach and chard in a pot of salted, boiling water until tender (3–4 minutes if frozen, 8–10 minutes if fresh). Squeeze out excess moisture and chop finely. § Mix the sausages, Ricotta, eggs, half the Parmesan, and marjoram with the spinach and chard in a mixing bowl. Combine thoroughly and season with salt. § Prepare the ravioli as shown on page 201. § Cook in a large pot of salted, boiling water until the sealed edges of the ravioli are *al dente*. Drain and transfer to a heated serving dish. While the ravioli are cooking, prepare the sauce. § Pour the sauce over the ravioli and sprinkle with the remaining grated Parmesan.

VARIATION
– *Ravioli semplici* are also very good with meat sauces (see recipes pp. 30, 32) or *Tomato and butter sauce* (see recipe p. 28).

■ INGREDIENTS

PASTA: see recipe pp. 198–201
FILLING
• 8 oz (250 g) fresh or 5 oz (150 g) frozen spinach
• 1¼ lb (600 g) fresh or 12 oz (375 g) frozen Swiss chard (silver beet)
• 8 oz (250 g) Italian pork sausages, skinned and crumbled
• 1 cup (250 g) fresh Ricotta cheese
• 2 eggs
• 4 tablespoons freshly grated Parmesan cheese
• 1 teaspoon fresh marjoram
• dash of salt
• 1 quantity *Butter and sage sauce* (see recipe p. 38)

Wine: a dry red (Freisa)

Spinach ravioli with ricotta cheese filling in tomato sauce
Ravioli verdi al pomodoro

Serves: 4; Preparation: 30 minutes + time to make the pasta and the sauce; Cooking: 10 minutes; Level of difficulty: Medium

Make the spinach pasta dough. § Place the Ricotta in a mixing bowl. Add the parsley, basil, eggs, nutmeg, and salt. Combine the ingredients thoroughly and set aside. § Prepare the tomato and butter sauce. § Prepare the ravioli as shown on page 201. § Cook in a large pot of salted, boiling water until the sealed edges of the ravioli are *al dente*. Drain well and transfer to a heated serving dish. § Pour the hot tomato sauce over the ravioli and toss gently. Sprinkle with the Parmesan and serve hot.

■ INGREDIENTS

PASTA: see recipe pp. 198–201
FILLING
• 1 cup (250 g) fresh Ricotta cheese
• 4 cups (125 g) finely chopped parsley
• 5 cups (150 g) fresh basil, torn
• 2 eggs
• ¼ teaspoon nutmeg
• dash of salt
• 4 tablespoons freshly grated Parmesan cheese
• 1 quantity *Tomato and butter sauce* (see recipe p. 28)

Right: *Ravioli semplici al burro*

■ INGREDIENTS

PASTA: see recipe pp. 198–201

FILLING

- 1¾ cups (450 g) fresh
  Ricotta cheese
- 2 eggs
- ¼ teaspoon nutmeg
- 4 tablespoons freshly
  grated Parmesan cheese
- dash of salt
- 1 quantity *Butter and sage
  sauce* (see recipe p. 38)

Wine: a dry white (Frascati)

Ravioli with ricotta filling in butter and sage sauce

Ravioli di ricotta al burro e salvia

Serves: 4; Preparation: 10 minutes + time to make the pasta; Cooking: 10 minutes; Level of difficulty: Medium

Make the pasta dough. § Place the Ricotta in a mixing bowl and add eggs, nutmeg, Parmesan, and salt. Combine thoroughly. § Prepare the ravioli as shown on page 201. § Cook the ravioli in a large pot of salted, boiling water until the pasta around the sealed edges is al dente. Drain well and transfer to a heated serving dish. § Cover with the sage sauce and extra grated Parmesan. Toss gently and serve hot.

Tortellini in meat stock
Tortellini in brodo

■ INGREDIENTS

• ½ quantity *Beef stock*
  (see recipe p. 48)
PASTA: see recipe pp. 198–201
FILLING

• 4 tablespoons butter
• 4 oz (125 g) lean pork
  (tenderloin), chopped in
  small pieces
• 4 oz (125 g) mortadella
• 3 oz (90 g) prosciutto
• 1¾ cups (200 g) freshly
  grated Parmesan cheese
• 1 egg
• dash of nutmeg
• salt and freshly ground
  black pepper

*Wine: a dry, sparkling red
(Lambrusco di Sorbara)*

Serves: 4; Preparation: 1 hour + time to make the pasta and the stock; Cooking: 2–3 minutes; Level of difficulty: Medium

Prepare the stock. § Make the pasta dough. § Shape the dough into a ball and set aside to rest for about 1 hour, wrapped in plastic wrap (cling film). § Melt the butter in a skillet (frying pan) and gently fry the pork. § When cooked, grind it finely with the mortadella and prosciutto. § Transfer the meat mixture to a bowl and add the egg, Parmesan, nutmeg, salt, and pepper. Mix well. § Using this mixture, prepare the tortellini as shown on page 201. § Add the tortellini to the boiling stock and cook the tortellini in a large pot of salted, boiling water until the pasta round the sealed edges is *al dente*. Make sure that the stock is not boiling too fast, as the tortellini may come apart during cooking. § Serve in fairly deep soup dishes, allowing about 1 tablespoonful of stock for each tortellino.

Tortellini with woodmen-style sauce
Tortellini alla boscaiola

■ INGREDIENTS

PASTA: see recipe pp. 198–201
FILLING: see recipe above
SAUCE

• 10 oz (300 g) fresh or
  frozen peas
• 14 oz (450 g) mushrooms,
  coarsely chopped
• 2 cloves garlic, minced
• 3 tablespoons finely
  chopped parsley
• 4 tablespoons extra-virgin
  olive oil
• 1½ lb (750 g) tomatoes,
  canned, peeled, and
  chopped
• salt and freshly ground
  black pepper

Wine: a dry red (Sangiovese)

Serves: 4; Preparation: 25 minutes + time to make the pasta; Cooking: 35 minutes; Level of difficulty: Medium

Make the pasta dough. § Make the tortellini meat filling and set aside. § Cook the peas in boiling water. Drain and set aside. § Put the mushrooms, garlic, and parsley in a large skillet (frying pan) with the oil and cook for 5 minutes, or until the water the mushrooms produce has evaporated. Add the tomatoes and simmer for about 20 minutes. Add the cooked peas and salt and pepper to taste. Cook for 3–4 more minutes. § While the sauce is cooking, prepare the tortellini as shown on page 201. § Cook in a large pot of salted, boiling water until the sealed edges of pasta are *al dente*. Drain well and transfer to the sauté pan. Toss gently and serve.

Left: *Tortellini in brodo*

Ravioli with fish filling in vegetable sauce
Ravioli di pesce con salsa di verdure

Serves: 4; Preparation: 1 hour + time to make the pasta; Cooking: 15 minutes; Level of difficulty: Complicated

Make the pasta dough. § Melt the butter in a skillet (frying pan). Add the fish fillets and cook over medium heat for 5 minutes, or until tender. Chop the cooked fish very finely with a knife or in a food processor. § Cook the Swiss chard in a pot of salted water until tender (3–4 minutes if frozen, 8–10 minutes if fresh). Squeeze out excess moisture and chop finely. § Combine the fish and chard in a bowl with the Ricotta, eggs, Parmesan, and nutmeg. Season with salt and mix well. § Prepare the ravioli as shown on page 201. Set aside. § Put the mushrooms in a small bowl of warm water and leave for 10 minutes. § Remove from the water and chop finely. Combine the vegetables with the butter in the pan used to cook the fish, add the tomatoes and 1 cup of water, and cook over medium-low heat for 20 minutes. Add salt to taste. § Roast the pine nuts in the oven and chop finely in a food processor. Add to the tomato sauce. § Cook the ravioli in a large pot of salted, boiling water until the sealed edges of the pasta are al dente. Drain well and transfer to a heated serving dish. § Pour the sauce over the top, sprinkle with Parmesan, and serve.

■ INGREDIENTS

PASTA: see recipe pp. 198–201
FILLING
- 4 tablespoons butter
- 14 oz (450 g) sea bass fillets
- 12 oz (350 g) fresh or 7 oz (200 g) frozen Swiss chard (silver beet)
- 4 tablespoons Ricotta cheese
- 2 eggs
- ⅓ cup (60 g) freshly grated Parmesan cheese
- dash of nutmeg
- dash of salt

SAUCE
- 2½ tablespoons dried mushrooms
- 1 stalk celery, 1 medium onion, 1 tablespoon parsley, all finely chopped
- ½ cup (125 g) butter
- 4 ripe tomatoes, chopped
- dash of salt
- 3 tablespoons pine nuts
- ½ cup (60 g) freshly grated Parmesan cheese

Wine: a dry white (Cinqueterre)

Tortelli with swiss chard filling in butter and parmesan sauce
Tortelli con le biete

Serves: 4; Preparation: 45 minutes + time to make the pasta; Cooking: 10-15 minutes; Level of difficulty: Medium

Make the pasta dough. § Cook the chard in a pot of salted water until tender (3–4 minutes if frozen, 8–10 minutes if fresh). Drain well and squeeze out any extra moisture. Chop finely and place in a mixing bowl. Add the Ricotta, Mascarpone, Parmesan, eggs, and nutmeg. Mix well and add a dash of salt. § Prepare the tortelli as shown on page 201. § Cook the tortelli in a large pot of salted, boiling water until the sealed edges of the pasta are *al dente*. Drain well and transfer to a heated serving dish. Cover with the sauce, toss gently, and serve.

■ INGREDIENTS

PASTA: see recipe pp. 198–201
FILLING
- 1 lb (500 g) fresh or 12 oz (350 g) frozen Swiss chard (silver beet)
- 1 cup (250 g) Ricotta cheese
- ⅔ cup (150 g) Mascarpone cheese
- ⅓ cup (45 g) freshly grated Parmesan cheese
- 2 eggs
- ¼ teaspoon nutmeg
- dash of salt
- 1 quantity *Butter and Parmesan sauce* (see recipe p. 38)

Wine: a dry red (Brachetto d'Acqui)

Right: *Tortelli con le biete*

Ravioli with zucchini filling in butter and rosemary sauce

Ravioli alle zucchine

Serves: 4; Preparation: 30 minutes + time to make the pasta; Cooking: 10 minutes; Level of difficulty: Medium

Make the pasta dough. § Cook the zucchini in a pot of salted, boiling water until tender. Drain, transfer to a bowl, and mash finely with a fork. Add the amaretti cookies, Ricotta, three-quarters of the Parmesan, and nutmeg. Season with salt. Mix well to form a thick cream. If the filling is too liquid, add dry bread crumbs; if it is too thick add a little milk. § Prepare the ravioli as shown on page 201. § Cook the pasta in a large pot of salted, boiling water until the sealed edges of the pasta are *al dente*. Drain well and transfer to a heated serving dish. § While the pasta is cooking, prepare the sauce. Place the garlic in a small saucepan with the butter and rosemary and cook for 3–4 minutes over medium heat, stirring frequently. § Pour the sauce over the ravioli, sprinkle with the Parmesan, and serve.

- INGREDIENTS

PASTA: see recipe pp. 198–201
FILLING
- 2 medium zucchini (courgettes)
- ¾ cup (70 g) crushed amaretti cookies (macaroons)
- ⅔ cup (150 g) fresh Ricotta cheese
- 1 cup (125 g) freshly grated Parmesan cheese
- ¼ teaspoon nutmeg
- dash of salt
- 1 quantity *Butter and rosemary sauce* (see recipe p. 38)

Wine: a dry white (Pinot Bianco)

Stuffed pasta roll

Rotolo ripieno

Serves: 4; Preparation: 1 hour + time to make the pasta; Cooking: 1½ hours; Level of difficulty: Medium

Make the pasta dough. Roll it out to a thin, rectangular sheet measuring 12 x 16 in (30 x 40 cm). Cover with a clean cloth. § Wash the spinach leaves and cook until tender. Squeeze out excess moisture and chop coarsely. § Sauté the spinach in 2 tablespoons of butter and stir in 1 tablespoon of Parmesan. § Sauté the mushrooms in 2 tablespoons of butter for 4–5 minutes. § Poach the chicken livers in a little water, drain and chop finely. § Melt 1 tablespoon of butter in a saucepan and fry the sausage meat over a low heat with the chopped chicken livers and ground veal. Season with salt and cook for 10 minutes moistening with a little water if necessary. § Spread this mixture over the sheet of pasta dough, stopping just short of the edges. Cover with with an even layer of spinach. § Roll up lengthwise to form a long sausage. § Wrap tightly in a piece of cheesecloth (muslin) and tie the gathered ends of the cloth with string. § Place the roll in boiling water in an oval casserole dish and simmer for 50 minutes. § Remove from the water and set aside to cool a little, before untying and removing the cloth. § Slice and serve sprinkled with the remaining butter and Parmesan.

- INGREDIENTS

PASTA: see recipe pp. 198–201
FILLING
- 2 lb (1 kg) spinach leaves
- 7 oz (200 g) butter
- ¾ cup (90 g) freshly grated Parmesan cheese
- 7 oz (200 g) fresh mushrooms, thinly sliced
- 7 oz (200 g) trimmed chicken livers
- 3½ oz (100 g) fresh Italian sausage meat
- 7 oz (200 g) finely ground lean veal,
- dash of salt

Wine: a dry red (Sangiovese)

Right: *Rotolo ripieno*

Tortelli with potato filling in meat sauce
Tortelli di patate al ragù

■ INGREDIENTS

PASTA: see recipe pp. 198–201

- 1 quantity *Bolognese* or *Quick meat sauce* (see recipes p. 30, 32)

FILLING

- 1¼ lb (600 g) potatoes
- 1 medium onion
- 4 tablespoons butter
- ⅓ cup (45 g) freshly grated Parmesan cheese
- 3 eggs
- dash of nutmeg
- freshly ground black pepper

Serves: 4; Preparation: 40 minutes + time to make the pasta and the meat sauce; Cooking: 10-15 minutes; Level of difficulty: Medium

Make the pasta dough. § Prepare the meat sauce. § Use the ingredients listed to prepare the potato tortelli as explained on page 224. § Make the tortelli as shown on page 201. § Cook the tortelli in a large pot of salted, boiling water until the sealed edges of the pasta are *al dente*. Drain well and transfer to a heated serving dish. § Spoon the meat sauce over the tortelli. Sprinkle with Parmesan and serve.

Tortelli with potato filling in butter and sage sauce

Tortelli di patate al burro e salvia

Serves: 4; Preparation: 40 minutes + time to make the pasta; Cooking: 10-15 minutes; Level of difficulty: Medium

Make the pasta dough. § Peel the potatoes and cook them in salted, boiling water. § Put the onion and butter in a large skillet (frying pan) and cook until the onion is soft. § Mash the potatoes in a mixing bowl and add the onion, half the Parmesan, the eggs, nutmeg, and a dash of pepper. Mix thoroughly and set aside to cool. § Prepare the tortelli as shown on page 201. § Cook the tortelli in a large pot of salted, boiling water until the sealed edges of the pasta are *al dente*. Drain well and transfer to a heated serving dish. § Make the butter and sage sauce and pour over the tortelli. Sprinkle with Parmesan and serve.

■ INGREDIENTS

PASTA: see recipe pp. 198–201
FILLING
• 1¼ lb (625 g) potatoes
• 1 medium onion
• 4 tablespoons butter
• ⅓ cup (45 g) freshly grated Parmesan cheese
• 3 eggs
• ¼ teaspoon nutmeg
• freshly ground black pepper
• 1 quantity *Butter and sage sauce (see recipe p. 38)*

Wine: a light, dry white (Riesling dell'Oltrepò Pavese)

Tortelloni with veal, spinach, and rosemary filling in cheese sauce

Tortelloni valdostani

Tortelloni are the same shape as tortellini only larger.
This dish comes from the Val d'Aosta, near the French border in northern Italy.

Serves: 4; Preparation: 1½ hours + time to make the pasta; Cooking: 5-8 minutes; Level of difficulty: Medium

Make the pasta dough. § Place the rosemary in a sauté pan with the butter and sauté for 2–3 minutes. Add the veal and white wine, and simmer over medium-low heat. When the veal is tender, remove from the pan and chop finely with a knife or in a food processor. § Cook the spinach in a pot of salted, boiling water until tender (3–4 minutes if frozen, 8–10 minutes if fresh). Squeeze out excess moisture and chop finely. § Combine the veal and spinach in a bowl and add the eggs, Parmesan, and nutmeg. Season with salt and pepper. Mix well with a fork and set aside for 1 hour. § Prepare the tortelloni as shown on page 201. § Cook the tortelloni in a large pot of salted, boiling water until the sealed edges of the pasta are *al dente*. Drain well and transfer to a heated serving dish. § While the pasta is cooking, prepare the sauce. Combine the cheese, butter, and nutmeg in a small saucepan over very low heat until the cheese is melted. Pour over the tortelloni and serve hot.

■ INGREDIENTS

PASTA: see recipe pp. 198–201
FILLING
• 1 tablespoon finely chopped rosemary
• 4 tablespoons butter
• 10 oz (300 g) lean veal
• 2 tablespoons dry white wine
• 8 oz (250 g) fresh, or 5 oz (150 g) frozen spinach
• 1 egg and 1 egg yolk
• 4 tablespoons freshly grated Parmesan cheese
• dash of nutmeg
• salt and freshly ground black pepper
SAUCE
• 7 oz (200 g) Fontina cheese
• 4 tablespoons butter
• dash of nutmeg

Right: *Tortelloni valdostani*

Baked Pasta

Baked pasta dishes are hearty fare, well-suited to cold winter evenings. Lasagna is the classic baked pasta dish, but there are many others. Most baked dishes are based on precooked pasta combined with béchamel, tomato, or meat sauces, then sprinkled with tasty Parmesan cheese which forms a golden crust in the oven.

Rigatoni giganti filled with meat sauce
Rigatoni giganti farciti

Serves: 4; Preparation: 35 minutes + time to make the sauce; Cooking: 15 minutes; Level of difficulty: Medium

Prepare the meat sauce. § Cook the rigatoni in a large pot of salted, boiling water for half the cooking time indicated on the package. Drain well and place on dry dishcloths. § Sauté the mushrooms and half the butter over medium-low heat for 10 minutes, or until the mushrooms are tender. § Combine the mushrooms with the beef, half the meat sauce, the egg, flour, and wine in a heavy-bottomed pan. Mix well. Add all but 1 tablespoon of the tomato and water mixture. Season with salt and pepper. Cover, and cook over medium-low heat for about 15 minutes, stirring frequently. Remove from heat. § Fill a piping bag with the mixture and stuff the rigatoni. § Grease an ovenproof dish with butter and place the filled rigatoni in it. Combine the remaining tomato mixture and meat sauce together and pour over the top. Sprinkle with the Parmesan and dot with the remaining butter. § Bake in a preheated oven at 350°F/180°C/gas 4 for 15 minutes, or until a golden crust has formed on top.

■ INGREDIENTS

- 1 quantity *Bolognese* or *Quick meat sauce* (see recipes pp. 30, 32)
- 14 oz (450 g) rigatoni giganti pasta
- 3½ oz (100 g) mushrooms, chopped
- 4 tablespoons butter
- 10 oz (300 g) ground beef
- 1 egg
- ½ tablespoon all-purpose (plain) flour
- 4 tablespoons white wine
- 1 tablespoon tomato paste, dissolved in 1 cup (250 ml) hot water
- salt and freshly ground black pepper
- ½ cup (60 g) freshly grated Parmesan cheese

Wine: a dry red (Chianti)

Lasagne with Bolognese meat sauce
Lasagne al forno

Serves: 4; Preparation: 30 minutes + time to make the pasta and the sauce; Cooking: 20 minutes; Level of difficulty: Complicated

Prepare the meat sauce. § Make the pasta dough and prepare the lasagne. § Cook the lasagne 4–5 sheets at a time in a large pot of salted, boiling water for about 1½ minutes. Remove with a slotted spoon, plunge into a bowl of cold water to stop the cooking process. Remove quickly, and rinse gently under cold running water. Lay the sheets out separately on dry dishcloths and pat dry. § Prepare the béchamel and combine with the meat sauce. § Smear the bottom of a large oval baking dish with butter to stop the lasagne from sticking. Line with a single layer of cooked lasagne sheets. Cover with a thin layer of meat and béchamel sauce. Sprinkle with Parmesan, then add another layer of lasagne. Repeat until there are at least 6 layers. Leave enough sauce to spread a thin layer on top. Sprinkle with Parmesan and dot with butter. § Bake in a preheated oven at 400°F/200°C/gas 6 for 15–20 minutes, until a crust has formed on the top. Serve hot.

■ INGREDIENTS

- 1 quantity *Bolognese meat sauce* (see recipe p. 30)
- 1 lb (500 g) spinach lasagne (see recipe pp. 198–200)
- 1 quantity *Béchamel sauce* (see recipe p. 38)
- 3 tablespoons butter
- 1 cup (125 g) freshly grated Parmesan cheese

Wine: a dry red (Sangiovese)

Right: *Lasagne al forno*

Fusilli with tomatoes and mozzarella cheese
Fusilli con mozzarella e pomodoro

Serves: 4; Preparation: 30 minutes; Cooking: 30 minutes; Level of difficulty: Simple

Combine the garlic, parsley, and basil with the oil in a skillet (frying pan) and cook over medium heat until the garlic begins to change color. Add the tomatoes and chilies. Season with salt and pepper. Stir well and simmer over low heat for about 20 minutes, or until sauce has reduced. § Cook the fusilli in a large pot of salted, boiling water for half the time recommended on the package. Drain thoroughly and combine with the tomato sauce. Transfer the mixture to a greased baking dish and arrange the Mozzarella over the top. Sprinkle with the Pecorino. § Bake in a preheated oven at 350°F/180°C/gas 4 for about 30 minutes, or until the cheese is lightly browned.

■ INGREDIENTS

- 2 cloves garlic, minced
- 2 tablespoons finely chopped parsley
- 8 fresh basil leaves, torn
- ⅓ cup (90 ml) extra-virgin olive oil
- 1½ lb (750 g) tomatoes, canned, and chopped
- ½ teaspoon crushed chilies
- salt and freshly ground black pepper
- 14 oz (450 g) fusilli pasta
- 5 oz (150 g) Mozzarella cheese, thinly sliced
- ⅓ cup (45 g) freshly grated Pecorino cheese

Wine: a dry red (Oltrepò Pavese)

Cannelloni with ricotta and spinach filling in tomato and béchamel sauce
Cannelloni di ricotta e spinaci

Serves: 4; Preparation: 40 minutes; Cooking: 20 minutes; Level of difficulty: Medium

Prepare the tomato sauce. § Cook the spinach in a pot of salted water until tender (3–4 minutes if frozen, 8–10 minutes if fresh). Drain, squeeze out excess moisture and chop finely. § Put half the butter in a skillet (frying pan) with the spinach. Season with salt and pepper. Cook briefly over high heat until the spinach has absorbed the flavor of the butter. § Transfer to a bowl and mix well with the Ricotta, half the Parmesan, and the eggs. § Prepare the béchamel. § Cook the cannelloni in a large pot of salted, boiling water until half-cooked (about 5 minutes). Drain in a colander and pass under cold running water. Dry the cannelloni with paper towels and stuff with the Ricotta and spinach. § Line the bottom of an ovenproof dish with a layer of béchamel and place the cannelloni in a single layer on it. Cover with alternate spoonfuls of béchamel and tomato sauce. Sprinkle with the remaining Parmesan and dot with butter. § Cook at 400°F/200°C/gas 6 for about 20 minutes, or until a golden crust has formed on top. Serve hot.

■ INGREDIENTS

SAUCE
- ½ quantity *Tomato and butter sauce* (see recipe p. 28)
- 1 quantity *Béchamel sauce* (see recipe p. 38)

FILLING
- 1 lb (500 g) fresh or 10 oz (300 g) frozen spinach
- 4 tablespoons butter
- 1¼ cups (300 g) fresh Ricotta cheese
- ¾ cup (90 g) freshly grated Parmesan cheese
- 2 eggs
- salt and freshly ground black pepper
- 12 store-bought cannelloni, spinach or plain

Wine: a light, dry red (Vino Novello)

VARIATION
– Replace the tomato sauce with 1 quantity of *Bolognese* or *Quick meat sauce* (see recipes pp. 30, 32).

Left: *Cannelloni di Ricotta e spinaci*

INGREDIENTS

- 1 quantity *Genoese basil sauce:* (see recipe p. 36)
- 1 lb (500 g) spinach lasagne sheets (see recipe pp. 198–200)
- 3 tablespoons butter
- 1 cup (125 g) freshly grated Parmesan cheese
- 1 quantity *Béchamel sauce* (see recipe p. 38)

Wine: a dry red (Sangiovese)

Spinach lasagne with basil sauce
Lasagne verde al pesto

This is the perfect recipe for vegetarians who don't want to give up the pleasures of this delicious Bolognese dish. For a mushroom version, replace the basil sauce with mushroom sauce (see recipe p. 32) and proceed in the same way.

Serves: 4; Preparation: 30 minutes + time to make the pasta and the sauce; Cooking: 20 minutes; Level of difficulty: Complicated

Prepare the basil sauce. § Make the pasta dough and prepare the lasagne. § Continue in exactly the same way as for *Lasagne with Bolognese meat sauce* (see instructions page 228).

Baked penne rigate
Penne gratinate al forno

Serves: 4; Preparation: 30 minutes; Cooking: 30 minutes; Level of difficulty: Simple

Sauté the parsley, onion, and garlic with the oil in a skillet (frying pan) until lightly browned. Add the tomatoes and simmer over low heat for 25 minutes. § Cook the penne in a large pot of salted, boiling water for half the time shown on the package. Drain well. § Place a layer of pasta in a greased baking dish. Cover with a layer of pancetta, tomato mixture, and both cheeses. Repeat layers until the dish is full, reserving a little of both cheeses to sprinkle on top. They will turn golden brown in the oven. Bake in a preheated oven at 350°F/180°C/gas 4 for 30 minutes. Serve piping hot.

■ INGREDIENTS
- 4 tablespoons finely chopped parsley
- 1 large onion, 2 cloves garlic, finely chopped
- 4 tablespoons extra-virgin olive oil
- 1½ lb (750 g) fresh tomatoes, peeled, and chopped
- salt and freshly ground black pepper
- 14 oz (450 g) penne pasta
- 5 oz (150 g) pancetta, diced
- 8 oz (250 g) Mozzarella cheese, diced
- 1 cup (125 g) freshly grated Pecorino cheese

Macaroni baked with veal, salami, eggs, mozzarella cheese, and vegetables
Maccheroni incaciati

Serves: 4; Preparation: 1½ hours; Cooking 20 minutes; Level of difficulty: Simple

Cut the eggplants in ¼-in (6-mm) slices. To take away the harsh taste, sprinkle each slice with salt and place in a large bowl. Cover, and set aside for 1 hour. § Put the slices on a cutting board and remove the peel with a knife. Rinse under cold running water and pat dry with paper towels. § Dust the slices with flour. Heat the vegetable oil in a deep-sided skillet (frying pan) until very hot and fry the eggplant slices in batches until golden brown on both sides. Remove from the pan and place on a platter covered with paper towels. § Grease a deep-sided ovenproof dish with a little oil and line the bottom with slices of fried eggplant. § Cook the garlic in a large skillet with the olive oil until it begins to change color. Add the tomatoes, veal, salami, peas, and basil and simmer over medium-low heat for about 30 minutes, stirring occasionally with a wooden spoon. Add the chicken livers and cook for 5 more minutes. § Cook the macaroni in a large pot of salted, boiling water for half the cooking time indicated on the package. Drain well. § Mix with the sauce, eggs, and any remaining eggplant slices. Pour into the baking dish with the eggplant. Cover with the sliced Mozzarella and grated Pecorino. Bake in a preheated oven at 400°F/200°C/gas 6 for about 20 minutes, or until a golden crust has formed on top. Serve hot from the baking dish.

■ INGREDIENTS
- 2 eggplants (aubergines)
- salt and freshly ground black pepper
- 4 tablespoons all-purpose (plain) flour
- vegetable oil for frying
- 1 clove garlic, chopped
- 4 tablespoons extra-virgin olive oil
- 14 oz (450 g) tomatoes
- 3½ oz (100 g) veal, coarsely chopped
- 3 oz (90 g) salami, diced
- 3½ oz (100 g) peas
- 4 basil leaves, torn
- 3 ½ oz (100 g) chicken livers, coarsely chopped
- 14 oz (450 g) macaroni
- 2 hard-cooked (hard-boiled) eggs, cut in quarters
- 5 oz (150 g) Mozzarella cheese, sliced
- 4 tablespoons freshly grated Pecorino cheese

Right: *Penne gratinate al forno*

Macaroni with meat sauce, béchamel, and truffles, baked in a pastry casing
Timballo di maccheroni alla ferrarese

Serves: 4; Preparation: 30 minutes + time to make sauces; Cooking: 30 minutes; Level of difficulty: Complicated

Prepare the meat and béchamel sauces. § Prepare the pastry dough. § Cook the macaroni in a large pot of salted, boiling water for half the time indicated on the package. Drain well and mix with half the meat sauce. § Grease an ovenproof baking dish with butter and sprinkle with bread crumbs. Roll the dough out to about ⅛ in (3 mm) thick and line the baking dish. Cover with a layer of béchamel, then with pasta and meat sauce. Sprinkle with truffle. Repeat until all the ingredients are in the baking dish. The last layer should be of béchamel. Sprinkle with the Parmesan. § Bake in a preheated oven at 350°F/180°C/gas 4 for about 30 minutes. Serve hot.

■ INGREDIENTS

• 1 quantity *Bolognese meat sauce* (see recipes p. 30)
• 1 quantity *Béchamel sauce* (see recipe p. 38)
• 1 quantity *Plain pastry* (see recipe p. 58)
• 1 lb (500 g) macaroni
• 2 tablespoons butter
• 2 tablespoons fine dry bread crumbs
• 1 whole white truffle, in fine shavings
• 1 cup (125 g) freshly grated Parmesan cheese

Wine: a dry red (Barbaresco)

Baked spinach and ricotta roll
Strudel di spinaci al forno

Serves: 4; Preparation: 1 hour + time to make the pasta; Cooking: 45 minutes; Level of difficulty: Complicated

Make the pasta dough. § Cook the spinach in a pot of salted, boiling water until tender. Drain, squeeze out excess moisture, and chop finely. § Put the spinach in a bowl and add the Ricotta, Parmesan, and nutmeg. Combine thoroughly and season with salt. § Lightly flour a flat work surface and roll the pasta dough out until very thin. Cut the dough into a 12 x 16-in (30 x 40-cm) rectangle. § Spread the spinach and Ricotta mixture evenly over the top and roll it up. Seal the ends by squeezing the dough together. Wrap the roll tightly in cheesecloth (muslin), tying the ends with string. § Bring a large pot of salted water to a boil. The pot should be wide enough so that the roll can lie flat. Immerse the roll carefully in the boiling water and simmer for about 20 minutes. Remove from the pot and set aside. § While the roll is cooking, prepare the béchamel and tomato sauces. § Unwrap the spinach roll and cut into slices about ½ in (1 cm) thick. Cover the bottom of an ovenproof dish with a layer of béchamel and top with slices of spinach roll. Mix the remaining béchamel with the tomato sauce and cover the spinach slices. Sprinkle with extra Parmesan and bake in a preheated oven at 350°F/180°C/gas 4 for about 15 minutes, or until a golden crust forms on top. Serve hot.

■ INGREDIENTS

• 1 lb (500 g) pasta (see recipe pp. 198–200)

FILLING

• 1¾ lb (800 g) fresh, or 1 lb (500 g) frozen spinach
• 1 cup (250 g) fresh Ricotta cheese
• 3 tablespoons freshly grated Parmesan cheese
• ¼ teaspoon nutmeg
• dash of salt
• 1 quantity *Béchamel sauce* (see recipe p. 38)
• ½ quantity *Tomato and butter sauce*. (see recipe p. 28)

Wine: a dry red (Collio Merlot)

Right:
Strudel di spinaci al forno

Baked maltagliati with ham, cream, and eggs
Pasticcio di maltagliati al prosciutto

Serves: 4; Preparation: 15 minutes; Cooking: 1 hour; Level of difficulty: Medium

Prepare the pasta. § Melt the butter in a saucepan over low heat. Add the egg yolks, ham, and parsley, and stir with a wooden spoon for 2–3 minutes. Add the nutmeg and season with salt and pepper. Remove from heat. § Whip the cream until stiff. In a separate bowl, beat the egg whites until stiff. Gently stir the whipped cream into the egg whites and add to the butter mixture. § Cook the pasta in a large pot of salted, boiling water for half the time indicated on the package. Drain well and place on dry dishcloths. § Grease an ovenproof dish with butter and place the pasta in it. Cover with the egg, cream, and ham mixture. Sprinkle with the Parmesan cheese. Bake in a preheated oven at 350°F/180°C/gas 4 for about 50 minutes. Serve hot.

VARIATION
– Replace the cream and egg whites with 1 quantity of *Béchamel sauce* (see recipe p. 38).

Baked tomatoes with pasta filling
Pomodori ripieni di pasta

Choose firm, red tomatoes with their stalks still attached for this tasty, baked tomato dish. The tomatoes can be served hot straight from the oven or left to cool and served as a cold entrée.

Serves: 4; Preparation: 20 minutes; Cooking: 40 minutes; Level of difficulty: Simple

Rinse the tomatoes and dry well. Cut the top off each tomato (with its stalk) and set aside. Hollow out the insides of the tomatoes with a teaspoon. Put the pulp in a bowl. § Place a basil leaf in the bottom of each hollow shell. § Cook the pasta in a medium pot of salted, boiling water for half the time indicated on the package. Drain well. § Combine the pasta with the tomato mixture. Add the parsley and 2 tablespoons of the oil. Season with salt and pepper. § Stuff the hollow tomatoes with the mixture. § Grease an ovenproof dish with the remaining oil and carefully place the tomatoes on it. Cover with the tomato tops. § Bake for about 40 minutes in a preheated oven at 350°F/180°C/gas 4. Serve either hot or at room temperature.

Left:
Pomodori ripieni di pasta

Gnocchi

The most common type of gnocchi are the white
ones, made with mashed potatoes and flour.
But there are also spinach gnocchi, Ricotta gnocchi,
baked semolina gnocchi, and fried gnocchi.

Potato gnocchi with gorgonzola cheese sauce
Gnocchi di patate al gorgonzola

Serves: 6; Preparation: 10 minutes + time to make the gnocchi; Cooking: 10 minutes; Level of difficulty: Medium

Prepare the potato gnocchi. § Put the Gorgonzola and butter in a heavy-bottomed pan. Place over low heat and stir gently with a wooden spoon until the cheese and butter have melted. Add the cream and cook over low heat for 3–4 minutes, or until the cream has reduced and the sauce is thick and creamy. Season with salt and pepper. § Cook the gnocchi, following the instructions on page 54. Drain well and transfer to a heated serving dish. § Pour the Gorgonzola sauce over the gnocchi. Sprinkle with the Parmesan and serve immediately.

■ INGREDIENTS

• 1 quantity *Potato gnocchi*
  (see recipe p. 54)
SAUCE
• 7 oz (200 g) Gorgonzola
  cheese
• ⅓ cup (125 g) butter
• 1¼ cups (300 ml) light
  (single) cream
• salt and freshly ground
  black pepper
• ½ cup (60 g) freshly
  grated Parmesan cheese

*Wine: a dry white
(Corvo di Salaparuta)*

Potato and spinach gnocchi in sage sauce
Gnocchi di patate e spinaci al burro e salvia

Serves: 6; Preparation: 20 minutes; Cooking: 50 minutes; Level of difficulty: Medium

Cook the potatoes in their skins in a pot of salted, boiling water for 20 minutes, or until tender. Drain and peel while hot. § Cook the spinach in a pot of salted, boiling water until tender (3–4 minutes if frozen, 8–10 minutes if fresh). Drain and squeeze out excess moisture. § Purée the potatoes and spinach together in a food processor. Place the mixture on a flat work surface. Work the eggs and flour in gradually. Add the nutmeg. Season with salt and pepper. Knead the mixture until smooth. § To prepare and cook the gnocchi, follow the instructions for potato gnocchi on page 54. § When the gnocchi are cooked, quickly prepare the butter and sage sauce. Pour over the gnocchi and toss gently. Sprinkle with Parmesan and serve hot.

■ INGREDIENTS

• 1 lb (500 g) boiling potatoes
• 1 lb (500 g) fresh, or 10 oz
  (300 g) frozen spinach
• 2 eggs
• ½ cup (75 g) all-purpose
  (plain) flour
• ¼ cup (60 g) butter
• dash of nutmeg
• salt and freshly ground
  black pepper
• 2 tablespoons Parmesan
  cheese, freshly grated
• 1 quantity *Butter and sage
  sauce* (see recipe p. 38)

*Wine: a dry red
(Rosso di Montalcino)*

VARIATION
– These gnocchi make a delicious winter dish when baked. When they are cooked, drain well and place in an ovenproof baking dish. Pour the melted butter and sage sauce over the top (or replace with 1 quantity *Simple tomato sauce*–see recipe p. 28). Sprinkle with ½ cup (2 oz/60 g) freshly grated Parmesan and bake in a preheated oven at 350°F/180°C/gas 4 for about 15 minutes, or until the topping is golden brown.

Right:
Gnocchi di patate al gorgonzola

Potato gnocchi with four-cheese sauce
Gnocchi di patate ai quattro formaggi

Serves: 6; Preparation: 20 minutes + time to make the gnocchi; Cooking: 30 minutes; Level of difficulty: Medium

Prepare the potato gnocchi. § Prepare the béchamel sauce. Add the four cheeses and stir over low heat until they have melted and the sauce is smooth and creamy. Season with salt and pepper. § Cook the gnocchi in a large pot of salted, boiling water following the instructions on page 54. When all the gnocchi are cooked and laid out on a heated serving dish, pour the cheese sauce over the top and toss gently. Serve hot.

Parmesan and spinach gnocchi
Malfatti di parmigiano e spinaci

Malfatti in Italian means "badly made" and refers to the fact that these little dumplings are similar to the stuffing used for ravioli. They are badly made because they lack their pasta wrappings. In Tuscany they are sometimes called Strozzaprete, or "priest chokers," although the origin of this name remains obscure.

Serves: 6; Preparation: 20 minutes; Cooking: 20 minutes; Level of difficulty: Medium

Cook the spinach in a pot of salted, boiling water until tender (3–4 minutes if frozen, 8–10 minutes if fresh). Drain well and squeeze out excess moisture. Chop finely. § Mix the spinach with the Ricotta, eggs, Parmesan (reserving 2 tablespoons), and nutmeg. Season with salt and pepper. § Mold the mixture into walnut-sized balls. § Bring a large pot of salted water to a boil, add the dumplings, and cook until they rise to the surface. § Remove with a slotted spoon and place in a serving dish. § Prepare the sauce and pour over the dumplings. Sprinkle with the remaining Parmesan and serve hot.

■ INGREDIENTS

• 1½ lb (750 g) fresh, or 1 lb (500 g) frozen spinach
• ⅔ cup (150 g) Ricotta cheese
• 1 egg and 1 yolk
• 1 cup (125 g) freshly grated Parmesan cheese
• dash of nutmeg
• salt and freshly ground black pepper
• 1 quantity *Butter and sage sauce* or 1 quantity *Butter and Parmesan sauce* (see recipe p. 38)

Wine: a young, dry red (Vino Novello)

Spinach and ricotta gnocchi in tomato and butter sauce
Gnocchi di spinaci e ricotta al pomodoro

Serves: 6; Preparation: 45 minutes; Cooking: 25 minutes; Level of difficulty: Medium

Prepare the tomato and butter sauce. § Put the onion in a saucepan with the butter and sauté over medium heat until pale gold. Remove the onion with a fork, leaving as much butter as possible in the pan. § Cook the spinach in a pot of salted, boiling water until tender (3–4 minutes if frozen, 8–10 minutes if fresh). Drain and squeeze out excess moisture. Chop finely. § Add the spinach to the pan with the butter. Sauté over medium-low heat for 10 minutes. Remove from heat and set aside. § When the spinach is cool, put it in a bowl with the Ricotta, eggs, nutmeg, and all but 4 tablespoons of the Parmesan. Season with salt and pepper and mix well. Gradually stir in enough of the flour to obtain a firm dough. § Lightly dust your hands with flour and roll pieces of dough into walnut-size balls. Place the gnocchi on a lightly floured platter. § Cook the gnocchi following the instructions on page 54 for potato gnocchi. § Toss the gnocchi gently in the tomato sauce. Sprinkle with the remaining Parmesan and serve hot.

■ INGREDIENTS

• 1 quantity *Tomato and butter sauce* (see recipe p. 28)

GNOCCHI

• 1 small onion, sliced in thin rings
• 4 tablespoons butter
• 1½ lb (750 g) fresh, or 1 lb (500 g) frozen spinach
• ¾ cup (200 g) fresh Ricotta cheese
• 3 eggs
• dash of nutmeg
• 1½ cups (150 g) freshly grated Parmesan cheese
• salt and freshly ground black pepper
• 2 cups (300 g) all-purpose (plain) flour

Wine: a dry red (Lambrusco)

Right:
Malfatti di parmigiano e spinaci

Baked potato gnocchi in béchamel sauce
Timballo di gnocchi

Serves: 4-6; Preparation: 30 minutes + time to make the gnocchi; Cooking: 1 hour; Level of difficulty: Complicated

Sift the flour into a mixing bowl with the eggs, lemon rind, and salt. Add the butter (reserving 4 tablespoons) and mix well. When the dough is moist and firm but not sticky, roll it into a ball, cover with plastic wrap, and place in the refrigerator for 1 hour. § Roll the dough out until it is about ½ in (1 cm) thick. Grease the bottom and sides of a baking dish with butter and line with the dough. Prick well with a fork so that it doesn't swell while in the oven. § Bake in a preheated oven at 400°F/ 200°C/gas 6 for about 20 minutes, or until the pastry is golden brown. § Prepare and cook the potato gnocchi. § Prepare the béchamel sauce. § Put the cooked gnocchi in the béchamel and mix gently. Transfer to the baking dish with the pastry. Sprinkle with the Parmesan cheese. Return to the oven and bake for 10 minutes more. § Remove from the oven and slip the pastry casing containing the gnocchi out of the baking dish. Serve hot.

■ INGREDIENTS

PASTRY
- 1½ cups (225 g) all-purpose (plain) flour
- 2 egg yolks
- rind of 1 lemon, finely grated
- dash of salt
- 1 cup (250 g) butter

- 1 quantity *Potato gnocchi* (see recipe p. 54)
- 1 quantity *Béchamel sauce* (see recipe p. 38)
- ½ cup (60 g) freshly grated Parmesan cheese

Wine: a dry red (Chianti delle Colline Pisane)

Fried gnocchi
Gnocchi di latte

Serves: 4; Preparation: 20 minutes + 30 minutes to rest; Cooking: 40 minutes; Level of difficulty: Medium

Beat the egg yolks in a bowl with the sugar until smooth. § Place the potato flour in a heavy-bottomed pan. Stir the milk in gradually. Add the egg mixture, 2 tablespoons of the butter, the nutmeg, cinnamon, and salt. Mix well with a wooden spoon. § Place the pan over medium heat and, stirring continually, bring to a boil. Boil for 10 minutes, stirring all the time. Remove from heat. § Turn the gnocchi batter out onto a flat work surface. Using a spatula dipped in cold water, spread it out to a thickness of about ½ in (1 cm) and leave to cool for 30 minutes. § Cut the batter into ½-in (1-cm) cubes. Beat the remaining egg in a bowl with a fork. Dust the gnocchi with flour, drop them into the beaten egg, then roll them in bread crumbs. § Fry the gnocchi in the remaining butter until they are golden brown. Place on a heated serving dish. Sprinkle with Parmesan and serve immediately.

■ INGREDIENTS

- 1 egg and 5 egg yolks
- 1 tablespoon sugar
- ¾ cup (100 g) potato flour
- 2 cups (500 ml) milk
- ⅔ cup (150 g) butter
- ¼ teaspoon each of nutmeg and cinnamon
- dash of salt
- 4 tablespoons all-purpose (plain) flour
- ½ cup (30 g) bread crumbs
- ½ cup (60 g) freshly grated Parmesan cheese

Wine: a dry red (Collio Merlot)

Right: *Timballo di gnocchi and Gnocchi di latte*

Baked semolina gnocchi
Gnocchi alla romana

Serves: 6; Preparation: 25 minutes; Cooking: 45 minutes; Level of difficulty: Medium

Put the milk and 2 tablespoons of the butter in a heavy-bottomed pan and bring to a boil. Add the semolina very gradually just as the milk is beginning to boil. Stirring continually, cook over low heat for 15–20 minutes, or until the mixture is thick and no longer sticks to the sides of the pan. § Remove from heat and leave to cool for 2–3 minutes. Add the egg yolks, salt, 2 tablespoons of the Parmesan, and 2 tablespoons of the Gruyère and mix well. § Wet a flat work surface with cold water and turn the gnocchi batter out onto it. Using a spatula dipped in cold water, spread it out to a thickness of about ½ in (1 cm). Leave the batter to cool to room temperature. § Use a cookie cutter or small glass with a diameter of about 1½–2 in (4–5 cm) to cut the gnocchi into round disks. § Grease a baking dish with butter and place a row of gnocchi at one end. Lean the next row of gnocchi on the bottoms of the first, roof-tile fashion. Repeat until the baking dish is full. § Melt the remaining butter and pour over the gnocchi. Sprinkle with the remaining Parmesan and Gruyère. § Bake in a preheated oven at 400°F/200°C/gas 6 for about 20 minutes, or until a golden crust forms on top. Serve hot.

■ INGREDIENTS

- 4 cups (1 liter) whole (full cream) milk
- ½ cup (125 g) butter
- 1¾ cups (300 g) semolina
- 4 egg yolks
- 1 teaspoon salt
- ½ cup (60 g) freshly grated Parmesan cheese
- ½ cup (60 g) freshly grated Gruyère cheese

Wine: a medium red (Merlot di Aprilia)

Baked potato gnocchi
Gnocchi alla bava

Serves: 6; Preparation: 25 minutes + time to make the gnocchi; Cooking: 40 minutes; Level of difficulty: Medium

Prepare and cook the potato gnocchi. Place them in a greased baking dish and cover with the Fontina. Dot with butter and sprinkle with the Parmesan. § Bake in a preheated oven at 450°F/230°C/gas 7 for about 10 minutes, or until a golden crust has formed. Serve hot.

■ INGREDIENTS

- 1 quantity *Potato gnocchi* (see recipe p. 54)

SAUCE
- ½ cup (125 g) butter
- 8 oz (250 g) Fontina cheese, sliced thinly
- ½ cup (60 g) freshly grated Parmesan cheese

Wine: a dry red (Barbaresco)

VARIATIONS
– Melt half the butter with a clove of finely chopped garlic and pour over the gnocchi before adding the cheese.
– Spinach and Ricotta gnocchi can also be baked in the same way (see recipe p. 242).

Right:
Gnocchi alla romana

Soups

Soups are typical of the northern and central regions of Italy. They range from simple stocks and delicate creams, to rustic minestrone *and other hearty soups, often prepared with bread, rice, or pasta.*

Milanese-style minestrone
Minestrone alla milanese

Traditional Milanese minestrone contains cotenna and rice rather than pasta. If you can't find cotenna, double the quantity of pancetta. Traditionally, minestrone was simmered for 6 hours; there is a tendency to cut down on cooking time nowadays.

Serves: 4; Preparation: 30 minutes; Cooking: 2 hours; Level of difficulty: Simple

Scrape the cotenna and cut in ¼-in (6-mm) strips. Place in a large pot with the pancetta, garlic, onion, celery, parsley, rosemary, potatoes, carrots, zucchini, tomatoes, and beans. Add 3 quarts (3 liters) of boiling water, cover and simmer over low heat for at least 1¼ hours. § Chop the cabbage in ¾-in (2-cm) strips and add to the pot with the peas. Cook for another 25 minutes. § Season with salt and pepper and add the rice. § The minestrone will be cooked in about 20 minutes. § Serve with the Parmesan passed separately.

VARIATIONS
– Add 2 leaves of finely chopped sage.
– If you want a simple vegetable soup, omit the rice.

■ INGREDIENTS

• 5 oz (150 g) cotenna
• 3 oz (90 g) pancetta, diced
• 1 clove garlic, minced
• 1 onion, coarsely chopped
• 2 stalks celery, sliced
• 1 tablespoon coarsely chopped parsley
• 1 teaspoon fresh rosemary leaves, finely chopped
• 1 potato, 2 carrots,
• 2 zucchini (courgettes)
• 2 tomatoes, diced
• 5 oz (150 g) fresh red kidney beans
• ½ small Savoy cabbage
• 3 oz (90 g) peas, shelled
• salt and freshly ground black pepper
• ¾ cup (150 g) short-grain rice
• 4 tablespoons freshly grated Parmesan cheese

Wine: a light, dry red (Riviera del Garda Bresciano - Chiaretto)

Asti-style minestrone
Minestrone di Asti

Serves: 4; Preparation: 20 minutes; Cooking: 1¼ hours; Level of difficulty: Simple

Put the beans in a large pot, and cover with cold water to about 2 in (5 cm) above the top of the beans. § Cover and simmer over low heat for about 30 minutes. § Cut the cabbage in ¼-in (6-mm) thick strips, discarding the core. § Add the cabbage, potatoes, carrots, and celery to the pot, stir, and cook for 30 minutes more. § If needed, add a little boiling water, although the soup should be quite thick. § Add the rice and, after 15 minutes, the lard, garlic, and parsley. Stir well. § Season with salt and pepper. § Turn off the heat and let the minestrone stand for a few minutes while the rice finishes cooking. § Serve with the Parmesan passed separately.

■ INGREDIENTS

• 8 oz (250 g) fresh red kidney beans
• ½ small Savoy cabbage
• 2 medium potatoes, 2 small carrots, diced
• 2 celery stalks, sliced
• 1 cup (200 g) short-grain rice
• ½ cup (125 g) lard
• 1 clove garlic, minced
• 2 tablespoons finely chopped parsley
• salt and freshly ground black pepper
• 4 tablespoons Parmesan cheese, freshly grated

Right: Minestrone alla milanese

Pavia soup
Zuppa alla pavese

Serves: 4; Preparation: 10 minutes; Cooking: 5 minutes; Level of difficulty: Simple

Fry the bread in the butter until crisp and golden brown on both sides. § Place two slices in each preheated, individual soup bowl. § Break one or two eggs carefully over the slices, making sure the yolks remain whole. Sprinkle with cheese and dust with pepper. Pour the boiling stock into each plate, being careful not to pour it directly onto the eggs. § Leave to stand for 2–3 minutes before serving.

■ INGREDIENTS

- 8 thick slices dense grain, home-style bread
- ¼ cup (60 g) butter
- 4–8 fresh eggs
- 4 tablespoons freshly grated Parmesan cheese
- freshly ground black pepper
- 4 cups (1 liter) *Beef stock* (see recipe p. 48)

Wine: a dry white (Pinot Bianco)

Rice and parsley soup
Minestra di riso e prezzemolo

Serves: 4; Preparation: 5 minutes; Cooking: 20 minutes; Level of difficulty: Simple

Bring the stock to a boil and add the rice. § Simmer for about 15 minutes. § Just before removing from heat, add the parsley and butter. § Season with salt and serve immediately. Serve with the Parmesan passed separately.

■ INGREDIENTS

- 6 cups (1.5 liters) *Beef stock* (see recipe p. 48)
- 1 cup (200 g) short-grain rice
- 1 tablespoon finely chopped parsley
- 1 tablespoon butter
- dash of salt
- 4 tablespoons freshly grated Parmesan cheese

Cheese dumpling soup
Passatelli

Serves: 4; Preparation: 25 minutes + 30 minutes to rest dumplings; Cooking: 5 minutes; Level of difficulty: Simple

Mix the Parmesan with the bread crumbs and eggs in a mixing bowl. § Soften the butter in a small saucepan and combine with the bread crumbs. § Add the nutmeg, lemon rind, and salt and set aside for 30 minutes. § Blend the mixture in a food processor. Transfer to a piping bag with a nozzle about ½ in (1 cm) in diameter, and squeeze the bag to produce short, cylindrical dumplings, about 1½ in (4 cm) long. Cut them off with the tip of a sharp knife as they are squeezed out of the bag. § Let the little dumplings fall directly into a saucepan of boiling stock and simmer until they bob up to the surface. § Turn off heat. Leave to stand for a few minutes and then serve.

■ INGREDIENTS

- 1 cup (125 g) freshly grated Parmesan cheese
- 1¼ cups (150 g) very fine dry bread crumbs
- 3 eggs
- 1 tablespoon butter
- dash of nutmeg
- rind of 1 lemon, grated
- dash of salt
- 6 cups (1.5 liters) *Beef stock* (see recipe p. 48)

Wine: a dry white (Chardonnay)

Right: *Minestra di riso e prezzemolo*

■ INGREDIENTS

- 1 carrot, 1 medium turnip
  1 zucchini (courgette)
  1 large potato, diced
- 1 leek (white part only)
  2 small celery hearts,
  sliced
- 1 medium onion, 1 oz (30 g)
  spinach, coarsely chopped
- 1 tablespoon finely
  chopped parsley
- 3 oz (90 g) smoked
  pancetta, diced
- 2 quarts (2 liters) boiling
  Beef stock (see recipe p. 48)
- 1 cup (200 g) pearl barley
- salt and freshly ground
  black pepper
- 4 tablespoons extra-virgin
  olive oil

Wine: a dry rosè (Casteller)

Trento-style barley soup
Orzetto alla trentina

*Some versions of this delicious soup use pearl barley. I prefer to use unrefined brown barley,
which differs in flavor and consistency. If you are unable to find it,
use pearl barley. It will take about 30 minutes less to cook.*

Serves: 4; Preparation: 30 minutes; Cooking: 1½ hours; Level of difficulty: Simple

Put all the vegetables and the pancetta in a large pot. § Add the stock and when it begins to boil, add the barley (previously rinsed by putting it in a colander and passing it under a stream of cold water). Cover the pot, and simmer for 1½ hours, stirring occasionally. § Season with salt and pepper, stir in the oil, and serve.

■ INGREDIENTS

- ¼ cup (60 g) butter
- 1 medium potato, diced
- 2 small leeks (white part
  only), sliced
- 5 oz (150 g) fresh spinach,
  coarsely chopped
- 6 cups (1.5 liters) boiling
  Beef stock (see recipe p. 48)
- ¾ cup (150 g) short-grain
  rice
- dash of salt
- 4 tablespoons freshly
  grated Parmesan cheese

Wine: a dry white (Tocai di Lison)

Rice and vegetable soup
Minestra di riso e verdure

*There are many light and tasty soups in Milanese cuisine.
They are usually served for the evening meal.*

Serves: 4; Preparation: 20 minutes; Cooking: 30 minutes; Level of difficulty: Simple

Melt the butter in a saucepan over low heat and add the potato, leeks, and spinach. Sauté for a couple of minutes, stirring continuously. § Add the stock and simmer, covered, for 10 minutes or more. § Add the rice and stir. § The rice will be cooked in about 15 minutes. Season with salt and sprinkle with the Parmesan.

VARIATION
– Use the same quantity of Swiss chard (silver beet) instead of spinach.

Left: Orzetto alla Trentina

Rice and milk
Riso e latte

Serves: 4; Preparation: 5 minutes; Cooking: 35 minutes; Level of difficulty: Simple

Put the milk and water in a saucepan with ½ teaspoon salt and bring to a boil over high heat. § Add the rice and stir. Reduce the heat and cook for 25 minutes. The amount of cooking time depends on the quality of the rice, so taste it after about 20 minutes to see if it is ready. It should be *al dente* (slightly firm, but cooked). Add more salt if necessary. § Turn off the heat and add the butter. § Cover and let the soup stand for a few minutes before serving. Serve with the Parmesan passed separately.

■ INGREDIENTS

- 2 quarts (2 liters) whole (full cream) milk
- 1 cup (250 ml) water
- dash of salt
- 1½ cups (200 g) short-grain rice
- 1 tablespoon butter
- 1 cup (125 g) freshly grated Parmesan cheese

Wine: a dry white (Gambellara)

Cream of asparagus soup
Crema di asparagi

Serves: 4; Preparation: 10 minutes; Cooking: 20-25 minutes; Level of difficulty: Simple

Trim the tough white parts off the asparagus stalks and discard. § Melt half the butter in a heavy-bottomed pan and add the flour, stirring all the time. § Pour in the milk and then the stock. § Bring to a boil, add the asparagus, and season with salt and pepper. § Cook for about 15–20 minutes, or until the mixture is dense. § Press the mixture through a strainer and return to heat. § Mix the egg yolks, the remaining butter (softened), Parmesan, and cream together in a bowl. § Pour this mixture into the asparagus and stir until the cream is well mixed and dense. § Serve hot.

■ INGREDIENTS

- 2 lb (1 kg) asparagus
- ¼ cup (60 g) butter
- ½ cup (75 g) all-purpose (plain) flour
- 2 cups (500 ml) milk
- 2 cups (500 ml) *Beef stock (see recipe p. 48)*
- salt and white pepper
- 3 egg yolks
- ¾ cup (90 g) freshly grated Parmesan cheese
- ½ cup (125 ml) light (single) cream

Wine: a dry white (Breganze Vespaiolo)

Cream of pea soup
Crema di piselli

Serves: 4; Preparation: 10 minutes; Cooking: 20-25 minutes; Level of difficulty: Simple

Melt the butter in a saucepan over low heat. Add the onion and sauté until soft. § Stir in the peas and cook for 2 minutes. § Add two-thirds of the boiling stock and cook for about 20 minutes. § Make the béchamel and set aside. § When the peas are cooked, press them through a strainer, or use a food processor to chop into a smooth, fairly liquid purée. § Incorporate the béchamel sauce and mix thoroughly. If the soup seems too dense, add some of the remaining stock. Taste for salt. § Reheat for 2–3 minutes until the soup is hot enough to be served.

■ INGREDIENTS

- 2 tablespoons butter
- 1 onion, finely chopped
- 14 oz (450 g) shelled fresh peas
- 4 cups (1 liter) *Beef stock (see recipe p. 48)*
- dash of salt
- ½ quantity *Béchamel sauce (see recipe p. 38)*

Wine: a dry white (Pinot Grigio)

Right: *Crema di piselli*

Cream of celery soup
Crema di sedano

■ INGREDIENTS

- 6 stalks celery
- juice of 1 lemon
- salt and freshly ground black pepper
- 1 tablespoon butter
- 1 tablespoon white wine
- 1 tablespoon finely chopped parsley
- 1 clove garlic, finely chopped
- 1 cup (250 ml) *Vegetable stock* (see recipe p. 48)

Wine: a dry white (Frascati)

Serves: 4; Preparation: 15 minutes; Cooking: 20 minutes; Level of difficulty: Simple

Clean the celery and remove any tough outer stalks and stringy fibers. Chop coarsely and soak in a bowl of water with the lemon juice for 10 minutes. § Cook the celery in a pot of salted, boiling water for 5 minutes. Drain well. § Transfer to a heavy-bottomed pan and add the butter, wine, parsley, garlic, salt, and pepper. Cook until the wine evaporates. § Add the stock and simmer for 10–15 minutes more. § Purée in a food processor. Return to heat for 2–3 minutes before serving.

Lentil soup
Zuppa di lenticchie

*The amount of cooking time will vary depending on the age and quality of the lentils used.
If they are not soft after 50 minutes, add a little boiling water and continue cooking until they are.*

Serves: 4; Preparation: 10 minutes + 3 hours for soaking lentils; Cooking: 50 minutes; Level of difficulty: Simple

Put the lentils in a bowl and cover with cold water to about 1¼ in (3 cm) above the lentils. Let soak for 3 hours. § Drain the lentils and place in a saucepan with the onion, carrots, celery, bay leaf, and garlic. Add enough cold water to cover to about 2 in (5 cm) above the level of the lentils. § Cover and cook over low heat for about 45 minutes. § Discard the bay leaf, add the sage and rosemary, and continue cooking, still covered and over low heat, for another 5–10 minutes. § At this point the lentils should be very soft and will begin to disintegrate. Add salt and pepper to taste, drizzle with the oil, and serve.

VARIATION
– To make cream of lentil soup, press the cooked lentils through a strainer, or purée in a processor or with an electric hand mixer. Sprinkle with 1 tablespoon of finely chopped parsley just before serving.

■ INGREDIENTS

• 1½ cups (300 g) dry lentils
• 1 medium onion, finely chopped
• 2 small carrots, diced
• 2 stalks celery, thinly sliced
• 1 bay leaf
• 2 cloves garlic, whole or finely chopped (optional)
• 3 fresh sage leaves, finely chopped
• 2 tablespoons fresh rosemary, finely chopped
• salt and freshly ground white or black pepper
• 4 tablespoons extra-virgin olive oil

*Wine: a dry white
(Verdicchio dei Castelli di Jesi)*

Green Roman cauliflower soup
Zuppa di broccolo romanesco

This type of cauliflower is a beautiful emerald green and the florets are pointed rather than rounded as in white cauliflower. It is typical of Latium, the region around Rome. If you can't find it in your local market, use green sprouting broccoli in its place.

Serves: 4; Preparation: 10 minutes; Cooking: 10 minutes; Level of difficulty: Simple

Separate the florets from the core of the cauliflower, keeping the tender inner leaves. Rinse thoroughly and place in a pot of salted, boiling water. Cook for about 8–10 minutes. § In the meantime, toast the bread, rub the slices with the garlic, and place them in individual soup bowls. When the cauliflower is cooked, spoon several tablespoons of the cooking water over each slice. § Arrange the florets and leaves, well drained, on the toasted bread. Drizzle with the oil and lemon juice, and season with salt and pepper. Serve hot.

■ INGREDIENTS

• 1 green Roman cauliflower, about 2 lb (1 kg)
• 4 thick slices dense grain, home-style bread
• 1 large clove garlic
• ½ cup (125 ml) extra-virgin olive oil
• 1 tablespoon lemon juice
• salt and freshly ground white or black pepper

Wine: a dry white (Marino)

Right:
Zuppa di lenticchie

- 2 lb (1 kg) pumpkin, peeled and cut in pieces
- 10 oz (300 g) each carrots and leeks, diced
- 3 small stalks celery, from the heart, cut in pieces
- 4 cups (1 liter) *Beef stock* (see recipe p. 48)
- ½ cup (125 ml) light (single) cream
- salt and white pepper
- ⅓ cup (45 g) freshly grated Parmesan cheese

Wine: a dry red (Bardolino)

Cream of pumpkin
Crema di zucca

Serves: 4; Preparation: 30 minutes; Cooking: 30 minutes; Level of difficulty: Simple

Put all the vegetables in a pot and add the boiling stock, reserving a cup. Cover and simmer for 25 minutes, stirring occasionally. If necessary, add more stock. § Press through a strainer or use a food processor to obtain a smooth, not too liquid purée. § Set over medium heat for 1–2 minutes. § Stir in the cream and add salt and pepper. § Let stand for 1 minute, sprinkle with the Parmesan, and serve.

■ INGREDIENTS

- ½ cup (3 oz/90 g) coarse-grain semolina
- 6 cups (1.5 liters) *Beef stock* (see recipe p. 48)
- dash of salt
- 2 tablespoons butter
- freshly grated Parmesan cheese

Wine: a light white (Colli Euganei Bianco)

Semolina in beef stock
Semolino in brodo

Serves: 4; Preparation: 5 minutes; Cooking: 20 minutes; Level of difficulty: Simple

Sift the semolina slowly into the boiling stock, stirring with a wire whisk so no lumps will form. § Simmer for 20 minutes, stirring occasionally. § Season with salt. § One minute before serving, add the butter and stir one last time. § Serve with a bowl of freshly grated Parmesan passed separately.

■ INGREDIENTS

- 1 lb (500 g) fresh spinach
- 3 eggs
- salt and freshly ground black pepper
- dash of nutmeg
- ¾ cup (90 g) freshly grated Parmesan cheese
- 4 cups (1 liter) *Beef stock* (see recipe p. 48)

Spinach soup
Zuppa di spinaci

Serves: 4; Preparation: 15 minutes; Cooking: 20 minutes; Level of difficulty: Simple

Cook the spinach for 8–10 minutes in a little salted water. § Chop finely and combine with the eggs, salt, pepper, nutmeg, and Parmesan in a bowl. § Add to a saucepan with the boiling stock and cook, stirring all the time, for 1 minute. § Remove from heat, cover, and set aside for 4–5 minutes. The egg will form a thick layer on top. § Serve hot with croutons or bread lightly fried in butter and garlic.

Left: *Crema di zucca*

Spelt and vegetable soup
Zuppa di farro e verdure

Spelt has been grown in Italy for thousands of years. It has become popular again in recent years as healthier, wholefood eating habits have gained popularity. Look for it in specialty stores, or replace it with equal quantities of pearl barley.

Serves: 4; Preparation: 20 minutes + 4 hours to soak the spelt; Cooking: 1¾ hours; Level of difficulty: Simple

Put the spelt in a bowl, add enough cold water to cover by 2 in (5 cm) and leave to soak for 4 hours. Put the beans in a saucepan with the sage and enough cold water to cover by 2 in (5 cm). Cover, and simmer for 45 minutes. § Discard the sage. Press half the beans through a strainer (or use a food processor) with as much of the cooking water as needed to make a fairly dense cream. Then add the rest of the beans. § Combine the pancetta, leek, celery, carrot, Swiss chard, chilies, and garlic in a saucepan. § Add the stock, bring to a boil, and cook over medium heat for 15 minutes. § Add the spelt and half the oil and cook for 20 minutes. § Add the beans and cook for another 20 minutes. § Season with salt, pepper, and nutmeg. § Drizzle with the remaining oil just before serving.

■ INGREDIENTS

- ¾ cup (150 g) spelt
- 12 oz (350 g) dried red kidney, cranberry, or white beans, soaked
- 4 sage leaves
- 3 oz (90 g) pancetta, diced
- 1 small leek, 1 stalk celery, 1 carrot, sliced
- 7 oz (200 g) Swiss chard (silver beet) coarsely chopped
- ¼ teaspoon crushed chilies
- 1 clove garlic, crushed
- 6 cups (1.5 liters) boiling *Beef stock* (see recipe p. 48)
- ⅓ cup (90 ml) extra-virgin olive oil
- salt and freshly ground white or black pepper
- dash of nutmeg

Wine: a dry, aromatic red (Elba Rosso)

Right: *Zuppa di farro e verdure*

Rag soup
Stracciatella

The name comes from the fact that when the eggs are rapidly mixed into the stock they form strands or tatters, in other words, rags. Versions differ slightly from one region to the next. This Roman recipe is perhaps the most classic.

Serves: 4; Preparation: 2 minutes; Cooking: 1-2 minutes; Level of difficulty: Simple

Put the eggs, Parmesan, nutmeg, salt, and pepper in a bowl. § Whisk for a minute, until the mixture is well combined but not foamy. § Pour it into a pot containing the stock, place over medium heat, and mix rapidly with the whisk. As soon as the stock begins to boil again, the soup is ready and should be served immediately.

■ INGREDIENTS

- 4 eggs
- 4 tablespoons freshly grated Parmesan cheese
- dash of nutmeg
- salt and freshly ground white pepper
- 4 cups (1 liter) boiling *Beef* or *Chicken stock* (see recipes pp. 48, 50)

Wine: a lightly sweet white (Bianco Capena)

Cooked water
Acquacotta

This soup was originally prepared with water, a few herbs, oil, eggs, and stale bread. It was a staple in the diet of the butteri or cowboys of the Tuscan Maremma. It has become much richer over the years and there are many different versions.

Serves: 4; Preparation: 15 minutes; Cooking: 45 minutes; Level of difficulty: Medium

To peel the tomatoes, plunge them into a pot of boiling water for 30 seconds, then into cold. Slip off the skins, cut in half, and squeeze to remove the seeds. Cut the flesh in pieces. § Heat the oil in a large pot, add the onions and sauté over medium heat until they are soft. § Add the tomatoes, celery, and basil, and cook for 20 minutes; the sauce should be fairly thick. § Season with salt and pepper, add the stock and continue cooking for 20 minutes. § Reduce heat to very low. Break the eggs carefully into the soup, not too close together and taking care not to break the yolks. After 2–3 minutes the eggs will have set but still be soft. § Arrange the slices of bread in individual soup bowls and ladle out the soup with one or two eggs per serving. Sprinkle with Pecorino and serve.

■ INGREDIENTS

- 14 oz (450 g) ripe tomatoes
- 4 tablespoons extra-virgin olive oil
- 2 onions, sliced
- 2 stalks celery, cleaned and finely chopped
- 10 basil leaves
- salt and freshly ground black pepper
- 4 cups (1 liter) *Beef stock* (see recipe p. 48)
- 4–8 eggs
- 4–8 slices dense grain, home-style bread, toasted
- 4 tablespoons freshly grated Pecorino cheese

Wine: a dry white (Galestro)

Right:

Stracciatella

Sicilian Easter soup
Minestra pasquale

INGREDIENTS

- 8 oz (250 g) ground beef
- 3 eggs
- 3 tablespoons freshly grated Pecorino cheese
- ½ clove garlic, minced
- 1 tablespoon finely chopped parsley
- dash of nutmeg
- 2 dashes of salt
- 4 cups (1 liter) *Beef stock* (see recipe p. 48)
- 1 cup (250 g) fresh Ricotta cheese
- 3 tablespoons bread crumbs

Serves: 4; Preparation: 10 minutes; Cooking: 5 minutes; Level of difficulty: Simple

Combine the meat in a bowl with one egg, the Pecorino, garlic, parsley, nutmeg, and a dash of salt. § Mix well and shape heaped teaspoonfuls into little meatballs. § Bring the stock to a boil in a large saucepan. Drop in the meatballs and cook for 4–5 minutes. § Beat the remaining eggs and combine with the Ricotta, bread crumbs, and salt to make a smooth creamy mixture. § Pour the egg mixture into the stock and stir with a fork for about 1 minute, until the egg sets into tiny shreds. § Serve hot.

Rice and pea soup
Risi e bisi

Serves: 4; Preparation: 10 minutes; Cooking: 30 minutes; Level of difficulty: Simple

Melt half the butter in a pot with the oil. Add the onion and sauté until soft. § Add the garlic and parsley and sauté for 2–3 minutes. § Add the peas and a few tablespoons of the boiling stock, cover and cook over low heat for 8–10 minutes. § Stir in the remaining stock and the rice and cook for 13–14 minutes. § Taste to see if the rice is cooked. Season with salt. § Add the remaining butter and finish cooking. This will take another 2–3 minutes, depending on the rice. § Add the Parmesan, mix well, and serve.

■ INGREDIENTS

- ¼ cup (60 g) butter
- 3 tablespoons extra-virgin olive oil
- 1 onion, finely chopped
- ½ clove garlic, minced
- 1 tablespoon finely chopped parsley
- 12 oz (350 g) baby peas, shelled
- 4 cups (1 liter) *Beef stock* (see recipe p. 48)
- 1¼ cups (250 g) short-grain rice
- dash of salt
- 4 tablespoons freshly grated Parmesan cheese

Wine: a dry white (Soave)

Bread and garlic soup
Pancotto

This is a very old peasant recipe from Tuscany.

Serves: 4; Preparation: 8-10 hours to soak the fava beans; Cooking: 3 hours; Level of difficulty: Simple

Sauté the garlic in the oil for 2–3 minutes. § Pour in the stock, add the bread, and season with salt and pepper. Cook over medium-low heat for 15 minutes, stirring all the time. § Add the cheese, cover and set aside for 10 minutes before serving.

■ INGREDIENTS

- 4 cloves garlic, minced
- ⅓ cup (90 g) extra-virgin olive oil
- 4 cups (1 liter) boiling *Beef stock* (see recipe p. 48)
- 8 oz (250 g) day-old bread
- salt and freshly ground black pepper
- ⅓ cup (45 g) freshly grated Parmesan cheese

Fava bean soup
Minestra di fave

Serves: 4; Preparation: 8-10 hours to soak the fava beans; Cooking: 3 hours; Level of difficulty: Simple

Soak the fava beans in plenty of cold water for 8–10 hours. § Drain and transfer to a heavy-bottomed pan or earthenware pot. Add enough salted water to cover them by about 2 in (5 cm) above the level of the beans. § Cook over low heat for 3 hours, stirring frequently and mashing the fava beans with a fork. They should be completely disintegrated when cooked. § Add the oil, salt, and pepper and serve immediately.

■ INGREDIENTS

- 14 oz (450 g) dry fava (broad) beans
- ⅓ cup (90 ml) extra-virgin olive oil
- salt and freshly ground black pepper

Wine: a dry red (Cacc'e Mmitte di Lucera)

Right: *Risi e bisi*

Crushed fava beans
Macco di fave

The origins of this dish go back to Ancient Roman times when legumes or grains were an important part of the diet. The name comes from maccare or "to crush". It is common, with variations, throughout southern Italy. This recipe comes from Calabria.

Serves: 4; Preparation: 15 minutes + 10 hours to soak the fava beans; Cooking: 3 hours; Level of difficulty: Simple

Soak the fava beans in plenty of cold water for 10 hours. § Combine 2 tablespoons of oil, the drained fava beans, tomatoes, onion, and celery in a heavy-bottomed pan or earthenware pot. Add 2 quarts (4 pints/2 liters) of water. § Partially cover and cook over low heat for 3 hours, stirring frequently and mashing the fava beans with a fork. They should be a soft purée. § When cooked, add salt, pepper, and the remaining oil. § Serve the Pecorino passed separately.

■ INGREDIENTS

- 8 oz (250 g) dry fava (broad) beans
- 4 tablespoons extra-virgin olive oil
- 7 oz (200 g) canned tomatoes, peeled and chopped
- 1 large red onion, thinly sliced
- 3 stalks celery, chopped
- salt and freshly ground black pepper
- 3 tablespoons freshly grated aged Pecorino cheese (optional)

Wine: a dry red (San Severo Rosso)

Bread dumpling soup
Canederli

Serves: 4; Preparation: 45 minutes; Cooking: 15 minutes; Level of difficulty: Medium

Combine three-quarters of the milk with the bread in a large bowl and let stand for at least 30 minutes, mixing once or twice. The bread should become soft but not too wet. If necessary, add the remaining milk. § Squeeze out the excess milk by hand and put the bread back in the bowl, discarding the milk first. § Gradually add the eggs, sausage, pancetta, prosciutto, onion, half the parsley, and 3 tablespoons of flour, stirring continuously until the mixture is firm but elastic. If needed, add a little more flour. § In the meantime, bring 3 cups (750 ml) of water to a boil with 2 tablespoons salt in a fairly deep pot. § Make small balls about 2 in (5 cm) in diameter with the bread mixture and dust with flour. § When they are all ready, drop the dumplings into the boiling water. Turn the heat up to high until the water begins to boil, then lower heat slightly and cook for 15 minutes. § Remove from the water with a slotted spoon. Drain, transfer to a tureen, and ladle in the boiling stock. Garnish with the remaining parsley and serve.

■ INGREDIENTS

- 1¼ cups (300 ml) whole (full cream) milk
- 8 oz (250 g) dense grain, home-style, stale bread, cut in pieces
- 2 eggs
- 3 oz (90 g) fresh Italian pork sausage meat
- 3 oz (90 g) smoked pancetta, finely chopped
- 3 oz (90 g) prosciutto, finely chopped
- 1 tablespoon onion, finely chopped
- 2 tablespoons finely chopped parsley
- ½ cup (75 g) all-purpose (plain) flour
- 2 tablespoons salt
- 4 cups (1 liter) boiling *Beef stock* (see recipe p. 48)

White: a dry white (Terlano)

Omelet soup
Minestra di frittata

Serves: 4; Preparation: 45 minutes; Cooking: 15 minutes; Level of difficulty: Medium

Combine the eggs, flour, milk, parsley, salt, and pepper in a bowl. § Heat the butter in a skillet (frying pan) and add tablespoons of the egg and flour mixture to make little "omelets." When cooked on both sides set aside to cool. § Roll the omelets up and slice thinly (they should look like tagliolini when unrolled). § Transfer to a heated soup tureen and pour the boiling beef stock over the top. § Sprinkle with the finely chopped chives, salt, and pepper, and serve hot.

Above: *Canederli*

Crêpes in stock
Frittatine in brodo

Serves: 4; Preparation: 10 minutes; Cooking: 30 minutes; Level of difficulty: Medium

Beat the eggs in a bowl with 1 tablespoon of Pecorino, the parsley, salt, nutmeg, and one-third of the milk. § Gradually add the flour, alternating with the remaining milk. The batter should be fairly liquid. § Melt a quarter of the butter in a skillet (frying pan) about 6–7 in (15–18 cm) in diameter. When it is sizzling hot, pour in two spoonfuls of batter. § Tip and rotate the skillet, so that the batter spreads out to form a very thin crêpe. After less than a minute, turn it over with a spatula and cook for another minute or less on the other side. § Slide it onto a plate and repeat, adding a ½ teaspoon of butter to the skillet each time, until all the batter has been used. Stack the crêpes up in a pile. These quantities should make about 12 crêpes. § Dust each one with ½ tablespoon of Pecorino. Roll them up loosely and arrange in individual soup bowls, three per person. § Pour the boiling stock over the top and serve with the remaining cheese.

■ INGREDIENTS

- 3 eggs
- 1½ cups (150 g) freshly grated Pecorino cheese
- ½ tablespoon finely chopped parsley
- dash of salt
- dash of nutmeg
- ⅔ cup (150 ml) whole (full cream) milk
- 6–7 tablespoons all-purpose (plain) flour
- 3 tablespoons butter
- 4 cups (1 liter) boiling *Chicken stock* (see recipe p. 50)

Wine: a dry white (Trebbiano d'Abruzzo)

Bread soup with tomato
Pappa con il pomodoro

This Tuscan soup is a delicious way of using up leftover bread.

Serves: 4; Preparation: 15 minutes; Cooking: 20-25 minutes: Level of difficulty: Simple

Put the diced bread in a preheated oven at 325°F/160°C/gas 3 for 10 minutes to dry it out, but without toasting. § To peel the tomatoes, plunge them into a pot of boiling water for 30 seconds and then into cold. Slip off the skins, cut in half, and squeeze to remove the seeds. Chop the flesh into small pieces. § Pour 6 tablespoons of the oil into a heavy-bottomed pan or earthenware pot and add the garlic and bay leaves. § As soon as the oil is hot, add the diced bread and cook over medium-low heat for 3–4 minutes, stirring frequently. § Season with salt and pepper. § Stir in the tomatoes and, using a ladle, add about 2 cups (16 fl oz/500 ml) of water. § Cook for 15 minutes, stirring occasionally. If the soup becomes too thick, add a little more water (remember, however, that this soup should be very thick). § Drizzle the remaining oil over the top, and serve hot.

■ INGREDIENTS

- 8 oz (250 g) dense grain, home-style bread, cut in slices, and diced
- ½ cup (125 ml) extra-virgin olive oil
- 3 cloves garlic, crushed
- 2 bay leaves
- salt and freshly ground black pepper
- 14 oz (450 g) firm ripe tomatoes

Wine: a dry white (Bianco Vergine Val di Chiana)

Right:
Pappa con il pomodoro

Clam soup
Zuppa di vongole

■ INGREDIENTS

- 3½ lb (1.5 kg) clams, in shell
- 3 cloves garlic, crushed
- ½ cup (125 ml) extra-virgin olive oil
- 12 oz (350 g) tomatoes, coarsely chopped
- salt and freshly ground black pepper
- ½ cup (125 ml) dry white wine
- 3 tablespoons finely chopped parsley
- 5 thick slices dense grain, home-style bread, toasted

Serves: 4; Preparation: 30 minutes + 1 hour to soak the clams; Cooking: 25 minutes; Level of difficulty: Medium

Soak the clams in cold water to purge them of sand, then rinse in plenty of cold water, discarding any that are open. § Sauté the garlic in the oil in a large heavy-bottomed pan for 1–2 minutes. Add the tomatoes, season with salt and pepper, and simmer for 10 minutes. § Add the clams, cover and cook until they have all opened (discard any that do not open). § Add the wine and simmer for 10 minutes. § Arrange the toasted bread in individual soup bowls and ladle the clam soup over the top. Sprinkle with the parsley and serve.

Dice in stock
Dadolini in brodo

Serves: 4; Preparation: 10 minutes; Cooking: 1 hour; Level of difficulty: Simple

Combine the eggs, lukewarm melted butter, Parmesan, salt, and nutmeg in a bowl. Mix well with a fork, then slowly add the flour to the mixture, making sure that no lumps form. § Pour into a lightly buttered square or rectangular nonstick pan, large enough for the mixture to spread out to about ¾-in (2-cm) deep. § Bake in a preheated oven at 300°F/150°C/gas 2 for 1 hour. § Cut into squares when cool. Add to the tureen and pour the stock over the top. § Serve immediately.

■ INGREDIENTS

- 3 large eggs
- 2 tablespoons butter, melted
- ¾ cup (90 g) freshly gratedParmesan cheese
- dash of salt
- dash of nutmeg
- ¾ cup (90 g) all-purpose (plain) flour
- 6 cups (1.5 liters) *Beef* or *Chicken stock* (see recipes pp. 48, 50)

Wine: a dry white (Verduzzo)

Dumplings in meat or chicken stock
Zuppa Mariconda

Serves: 4; Preparation: 40 minutes + 1 hour to chill; Cooking: 5–7 minutes; Level of difficulty: Simple

Put the bread in a bowl with the milk to soften. After 15–20 minutes, drain and squeeze out some, but not all, of the milk. § Melt the butter in a skillet (frying pan). Add the bread and let it dry out over low heat, mixing well. This will take 2–3 minutes. The bread should stay soft because it will have absorbed the butter. § Transfer to a bowl and add the eggs, Parmesan, nutmeg, salt, and pepper. Mix well to obtain a smooth mixture. § Cover with a plate and place in the refrigerator for 1 hour. § Take teaspoonfuls of the mixture to make small dumplings, about the size of a large marble, and line them up on a clean work surface. § Bring the stock to a boil in a fairly deep pot and add the dumplings. § Lower the heat as soon as the stock begins to boil again. When the dumplings are cooked they will rise to the surface. § Serve hot.

■ INGREDIENTS

- 7 oz (200 g) day-old bread, without the crust, broken into pieces
- 1¼ cups (300 ml) whole (full cream) milk
- ¼ cup (60 g) butter
- 3 eggs
- 4 tablespoons freshly grated Parmesan cheese
- dash of nutmeg
- salt and freshly ground white pepper (optional)
- 6 cups (1.5 liters) *Beef* or *Chicken stock* (see recipes pp. 48, 50)

Wine: a light, dry white (Collio Goriziano)

Pasta and meat, chicken, fish, or vegetable stock
Minestrina in brodo

Serves: 4; Preparation: 5 minutes + time to make the stock; Cooking: 5–10 minutes; Level of difficulty: Simple

Prepare the stock. § Put the stock in a saucepan, add the pasta, and simmer until the pasta is *al dente*. § Sprinkle each portion with Parmesan and serve.

■ INGREDIENTS

- 4 cups (1 liter) *Stock* (see recipes pp. 48, 50)
- 8 oz (250 g) tiny pasta shapes
- 4 tablespoons freshly grated Parmesan cheese

Right: Dadolini in brodo

Pasta and bean soup
Minestra di pasta e fagioli

■ INGREDIENTS

- 1 lb (500 g) white or red kidney beans, canned or soaked and precooked
- 1 onion, finely chopped
- 1 tablespoon fresh rosemary, finely chopped
- 4 tablespoons extra-virgin olive oil
- 1 ripe tomato, chopped
- salt and freshly ground black pepper
- 7 oz (200 g) small, tubular pasta

Wine: a dry white (Tocai di Lison)

Serves: 4; Preparation: 5 minutes; Cooking 25 minutes + overnight soaking and cooking if using dried beans; Level of difficulty: Simple

Purée three-quarters of the beans in a food processor. § Combine the onion and rosemary in a heavy-bottomed pan with the oil and sauté briefly over high heat. Before the onion begins to change color, add the puréed beans, tomato, and, if necessary, one or two cups of water. Season with salt and pepper and simmer over medium-low heat for about 15 minutes. § Add the pasta and remaining whole beans, and cook for 6–7 minutes, or until the pasta is cooked *al dente*. Serve hot.

Garbanzo bean soup
Cacciucco di ceci

■ INGREDIENTS

- 10 oz (300 g) dry garbanzo beans (chick peas)
- 7 oz (200 g) young Swiss chard (silver beet)
- 4 tablespoons extra-virgin olive oil
- 1 onion, finely chopped
- 1–2 whole cloves garlic, lightly crushed
- 3–4 anchovy fillets in oil
- 3 plum tomatoes, peeled and chopped
- salt and freshly ground black pepper
- 4–8 slices dense grain, home-style bread, toasted
- 4 tablespoons freshly grated Pecorino cheese

Wine: a dry white (Montecarlo)

Serves: 4; Preparation: 30 minutes + 12 hours to soak the garbanzo beans; Cooking: 3½ hours; Level of difficulty: Medium

Place the garbanzo beans in a bowl and add enough cold water to cover them by at least 2 in (5 cm). Soak for 12 hours. § About 3½ hours before you intend to serve the soup, put the Swiss chard, well rinsed but not drained dry, in a pot and cook, covered, for 5 minutes over medium heat. Set aside. § Heat the oil in a large, heavy-bottomed pan or earthenware pot. Add the onion and garlic and sauté until the onion is soft. § Add the drained anchovy fillets, mashing them with a fork as you stir. § Drain the garbanzo beans and add to the pot, together with the chard, the liquid it was cooked in, and the tomatoes. Season with salt and pepper, stir, and add about 2¼ quarts (4½ pints/2.2 liters) of hot water. § Cover the pot and simmer over medium heat for at least 3 hours. The garbanzo beans should be very tender. § Arrange the toast in individual soup bowls and ladle the soup over the top. § Sprinkle with the Pecorino and serve.

Left: *Cacciucco di ceci*

Rice and potato soup
Minestra di riso e patate

Serves: 4; Preparation: 20 minutes; Cooking: 20-25 minutes; Level of difficulty: Simple

Put the pancetta, onion, and rosemary in a pot and sauté over low heat for 2–3 minutes, stirring frequently. § Add the potatoes and the boiling stock. As soon as it returns to the boil, add the rice, stir once or twice and cook for 15 minutes. § Taste for salt and to see if the rice is cooked. Add the parsley just before serving, and pass the cheese separately.

■ INGREDIENTS

• 2 oz (60 g) lean pancetta, finely chopped
• ½ onion, finely chopped
• 1 tablespoon rosemary leaves, finely chopped
• 2 medium potatoes, peeled and sliced
• 1 cup (200 g) short-grain rice
• 6 cups (1.5 liters) *Beef stock* (see recipe p. 48)
• dash of salt
• 1 tablespoon coarsely chopped parsley
• 4 tablespoons freshly grated Parmesan cheese

Wine: a dry white (Valdadige)

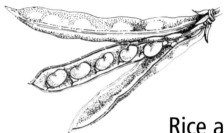

Rice and bean soup
Minestra di riso e fagioli

Cannellini or white beans are not available fresh throughout the year, and soaking and cooking dried beans requires time and forethought. This recipe for a typically Tuscan soup is based on canned beans.

Serves: 4; Preparation: 25 minutes; Cooking: 40-45 minutes; Level of difficulty: Medium

Put the oil, pancetta, onion, celery, garlic, parsley, basil, chilies, and sage in a pot, preferably earthenware. Cook over low heat for 7–8 minutes, stirring occasionally. § In the meantime plunge the tomatoes into boiling water for 10 seconds, then into cold. Peel and cut in half horizontally. Squeeze lightly to remove most of the seeds. Chop the flesh coarsely and stir into the pot. § Simmer for 15 minutes, covered, stirring occasionally. § Add the beans and boiling stock and cook for 5 more minutes. § Add the rice, which will take about 15 minutes to cook. If necessary, add a little more boiling stock or water (although bear in mind that the soup should be quite thick). Season with salt and serve hot.

■ INGREDIENTS

• 3 tablespoons extra-virgin olive oil
• 2 oz (60 g) lean pancetta, finely chopped
• 1 medium onion, 1 celery stalk, finely chopped
• 1 clove garlic, finely chopped
• ½ tablespoon finely chopped parsley
• 6 basil leaves, torn
• ¼ teaspoon crushed chilies
• 1 sage leaf, finely chopped
• 3 medium tomatoes
• 1½ lb (750 g) white beans, canned, and drained
• 4 cups (1 liter) *Beef stock* (see recipe p. 48)
• 1 cup (200 g) short-grain rice
• dash of salt

Wine: a dry red (Rosso delle Coline Lucchesi)

VARIATIONS
– Use 14 oz (450 g) canned tomatoes, well drained and chopped, in place of the fresh tomatoes.
– This soup can be served lukewarm or at room temperature particularly in summer.

Right: *Minestra di riso e patate*

Onion soup
Zuppa di cipolle

Serves 4; Preparation: 15 minutes; Cooking: 40 minutes; Level of difficulty: Simple

Combine the onions, oil, celery, and carrot in a deep, heavy-bottomed saucepan or earthenware pot. Cover and sauté over low heat, stirring frequently. § After 20 minutes season with salt and pepper. § Continue cooking, stirring and adding boiling stock as required, for another 20 minutes. § Dilute with the remaining stock. § Place the toast in a tureen or individual soup bowls and pour the soup over the top. Sprinkle with the Pecorino and serve.

■ INGREDIENTS

• 2 lb (1 kg) red onions, cut in thin slices
• ½ cup (125 ml) extra-virgin olive oil
• 1 small stalk celery, finely chopped
• 1 small carrot, finely chopped (optional)
• salt and freshly ground black pepper
• 4 cups (1 liter) *Beef stock* (see recipe p. 48)
• 4 slices dense grain, home-style bread, toasted
• 4 tablespoons freshly grated Pecorino cheese

Wine: a dry white (Bianco dei Colli Maceratesi)

Valpelline soup
Zuppa di Valpelline

This delicious soup comes from a village called Valpelline in the Valle d'Aosta, in the northwest.

Serves: 4; Preparation: 20 minutes; Cooking: 1 hour; Level of difficulty: Medium

Clean the cabbage and cut in quarters, discarding the core so that the leaves are no longer attached. § Melt the lard in a saucepan over low heat, add the cabbage leaves, cover and cook for 10–15 minutes, stirring occasionally. § Dry the bread out in a preheated oven at 300°F/150°C/gas 2 for 15 minutes. Make sure it doesn't get too dark. § Arrange a layer of toasted slices on the bottom of a large ovenproof baking dish and drizzle with 2 tablespoons of pan juices. Cover with one-third of the prosciutto and one-third of the cabbage. Season with a sprinkling of the spices and distribute one-third of the Fontina on top. Repeat the procedure twice. § Before adding the last layer of Fontina, pour on as much stock as needed to just cover the layers. § Arrange the remaining Fontina on the top and dot with dabs of butter. § Place the dish in a preheated oven at 300°F/150°C/gas 2 and gradually increase the temperature (in 15 minutes it should reach 400°F/200°C/gas 6). Cook for 30–40 minutes. § Serve hot straight from the oven.

■ INGREDIENTS

• 1 medium Savoy cabbage
• 2 tablespoons lard
• 8–10 slices dense grain, home-style bread, toasted
• ½ cup (125 ml) pan juices from a roast
• 5 oz (150 g) prosciutto, finely chopped
• dash of nutmeg
• dash of ground cloves
• dash of ground cinnamon
• 7 oz (200 g) Fontina cheese, cut in thin slivers
• 4 cups (1 liter) warm *Beef stock* (see recipe p. 48)
• 2 tablespoons butter

Wine: a dry, fruity white (Blanc de Morgex)

Right: *Zuppa di cipolle*

■ INGREDIENTS

• 2 lb (1 kg) turnips, cleaned and cut in half vertically, then sliced
• 5 oz (150 g) lean pancetta, diced
• ¼ cup (60 g) lard, finely chopped
• 1 clove garlic, finely chopped
• 2 quarts (2 liters) boiling Beef stock (see recipe p. 48)
• 4–8 slices toasted bread
• salt and freshly ground black pepper
• ¼ cup (45 g) freshly grated Parmesan cheese

Wine: a dry white
(Bianco di Custoza)

Turnip soup
Zuppa di rape

A rustic, winter soup from Piedmont, in the north.

Serves: 4; Preparation: 20 minutes; Cooking: 30 minutes: Level of difficulty: Simple

Put the turnips, pancetta, lard, and garlic in a heavy-bottomed saucepan. Add the stock, cover, and simmer over low heat for 30 minutes. § Season with salt and pepper. § Arrange the toast in individual soup bowls, sprinkle with half the cheese, and pour the soup over the top. § Serve the rest of the cheese passed separately.

VARIATIONS
– Sauté the pancetta, lard, and garlic for 4–5 minutes. Add the turnips, stir and sauté 2 more minutes before adding the stock.
– Serve the soup in a tureen, alternating a layer of toast sprinkled with cheese with 2 ladles of soup.

■ INGREDIENTS

• 1 oz (30 g) dried porcini mushrooms
• ½ tablespoon finely chopped calamint, or parsley
• 1 clove garlic, finely chopped
• 4 tablespoons extra-virgin olive oil
• 1¼ lb (600 g) porcini mushrooms, thinly sliced
• ½ cup (125 ml) dry white wine
• 4 cups (1 liter) boiling Vegetable stock (see recipe p. 48)
• 1 tablespoon flour
• salt and freshly ground black pepper
• 4 slices bread, toasted

Wine: a light, dry rosé
(Colli Altotiberini Rosato)

Mushroom soup
Zuppa di funghi

If you can't get fresh porcini, use the same quantity of white mushrooms. In this case, double the quantity of dried porcini.

Serves: 4; Preparation: 40 minutes; Cooking: 35-40 minutes; Level of difficulty: Medium

Soak the dried porcini mushrooms in 1 cup (8 fl oz/250 ml) of tepid water for 30 minutes, then drain and chop finely. § Strain the water in which they were soaked and set aside. § Sauté the calamint (or parsley) and garlic with 4 tablespoons of oil in a heavy-bottomed saucepan over medium heat for 30 seconds. § Add the dried mushrooms, and after a couple of minutes, the fresh mushrooms. Sauté for about 5 minutes. § Pour in the wine, and after a couple of minutes, begin gradually adding the stock and mushroom water. § Simmer for about 25 minutes. § Heat the remaining oil in a skillet (frying pan) over low heat. Add the flour and brown slightly, stirring carefully. § Remove the skillet from the heat and add 3–4 tablespoons of the mushroom liquid, mixing well so that no lumps form. § Pour this mixture into the soup. Cook for 2–3 minutes, stirring continuously. § Arrange the bread in individual soup bowls, or in a tureen, and pour the soup over the top.

Left: *Zuppa di funghi*

Fresh anchovy soup
Zuppa di acciughe

Serves: 4; Preparation: 30 minutes; Cooking: 25 minutes; Level of difficulty: Medium

Combine the oil, onion, celery, carrot, parsley, garlic, and chilies in a heavy-bottomed saucepan or earthenware pot and sauté over low heat for 6–7 minutes, or until the vegetables are soft. § Plunge the tomatoes into a pot of boiling water for 10 seconds and then into cold. Drain and peel. § Cut them in half horizontally, and squeeze to remove most of the seeds. Chop coarsely. § Add to the pan and continue cooking for about 10 minutes. § Add the anchovies, pour in the wine, and stir carefully. § Simmer for 5–8 minutes over low heat, adding the boiling water a little at a time. Don't stir during this stage, just shake the pan occasionally. § Pour the soup into individual soup bowls over the slices of toasted bread and serve.

■ INGREDIENTS

- 4 tablespoons extra-virgin olive oil
- ½ small onion, ½ stalk celery, ½ small carrot, all finely chopped
- ½ tablespoon finely chopped parsley
- 1 clove garlic, finely chopped
- ¼ teaspoon crushed chilies
- 2 medium-large tomatoes
- 2 lb (1 kg) fresh anchovies, without their heads, split, cleaned, and boned
- 1 cup (250 ml) white wine
- 2 cups (500 ml) salted, boiling water
- dash of salt
- 4–8 slices toasted bread

Wine: a dry white (Pigato di Albenga)

Octopus soup
Zuppa di moscardini

Moscardini are a kind of tiny octopus. If you can't get them fresh or frozen, use very small squid in their place. To clean them, turn the head inside out like a glove, remove the inner organs, and discard the eyes and the beak (the white ball in the middle of the base of the tentacles).

Serves: 4; Preparation: 20 minutes; Cooking: 40 minutes; Level of difficulty: Simple

Plunge the tomatoes into boiling water for 10 seconds, then into cold, slip off the skins, and cut into pieces. § Heat the oil with the parsley and garlic in a heavy-bottomed saucepan or an earthenware pot. § Add the moscardini and braise for 3 minutes over medium heat, stirring continuously. § Pour in the wine and when this has evaporated, add the tomatoes, chilies, and salt. § Stir one last time and cover the pot—the *moscardini* produce a good deal of liquid which, together with that of the tomatoes, has to be kept from evaporating. Cook for 30 minutes, shaking the pot frequently. § Taste for salt, then pour the soup over slices of toasted bread in a tureen and serve.

■ INGREDIENTS

- 4 medium tomatoes, ripe and firm
- 4 tablespoons extra-virgin olive oil
- 1 tablespoon finely chopped parsley
- 1 clove garlic, finely chopped
- 1½ lb (750 g) moscardini, cleaned, rinsed, and cut in pieces
- ½ cup (125 ml) dry white wine
- ¼ teaspoon crushed chilies
- dash of salt
- 4–8 slices toasted bread

Wine: a dry white (Vernaccia di San Gimignano)

VARIATIONS
– Add 1 teaspoon of fresh finely chopped rosemary with the tomatoes.
– For extra fragrance, add 2 tablespoons of olive oil just before serving.

Right: *Zuppa di moscardini*

Rice and Risotto

Remember that only short-grain rice is grown in Italy;
long-grain varieties are not suitable for these recipes.
Italian arborio rice is the best choice for making risotto.

Rainbow rice salad
Insalata di riso arcobaleno

Serves: 4; Preparation: 30 minutes; Cooking: 15 minutes; Level of difficulty: Simple

Bring 2½ quarts (2½ liters) of salted water to a boil. Add the rice, stir once or twice, and allow 13–15 minutes cooking time from when the water comes to a boil again. The rice should be *al dente* but not too firm. § Drain, pass under cold running water for 30 seconds to stop cooking. Drain again very thoroughly and transfer to a large salad bowl. § Season with oil, lemon juice, and pepper to taste. § Just before serving, add the remaining ingredients and toss well.

■ INGREDIENTS
- 1¼ cups (250 g) short-grain rice
- 4 tablespoons extra-virgin olive oil
- 2 tablespoons lemon juice
- salt and freshly ground white pepper
- 2 medium tomatoes, diced
- 6–8 red radishes, sliced
- 2 stalks celery, sliced
- 6 pickled gherkins, sliced
- 8 small white pickled onions, quartered
- 1 tablespoon capers
- 10 green olives in brine, drained, pitted and quartered
- 2 tablespoons golden raisins (sultanas), rinsed and drained
- 1 cup (125 g) flaked Parmesan cheese,

Wine: a dry white (Pinot Bianco)

Simple rice salad
Insalata di riso semplicissima

This is a basic Italian rice salad. The possible variations are almost infinite — from dressing the salad with mayonnaise or French mustard, to adding tuna fish, leftover roast chicken, hard-cooked (hard-boiled) eggs, artichoke hearts, or different kinds of cheese. Use your imagination and experiment to create your own favorite variations.

Serves: 4; Preparation: 30 minutes; Cooking: 15 minutes; Level of difficulty: Simple

Bring 2½ quarts (2½ liters) of salted water to a boil. Add the rice, stir once or twice, and allow 13–15 minutes cooking time from when the water comes to a boil again. The rice should be *al dente* but not too firm. § Drain, pass under cold running water for 30 seconds to stop cooking. Drain again very thoroughly and transfer to a large salad bowl. § Toss with the oil immediately. § Just before serving, add the remaining ingredients and mix well.

■ INGREDIENTS
- 1¼ cups (250 g) short-grain rice
- 4 tablespoons extra-virgin olive oil
- 2 medium firm tomatoes
- 1 medium cucumber, peeled and diced
- 1 tablespoon capers
- 10 green or black olives, pitted and chopped
- 4 oz (125 g) Emmenthal cheese, diced
- 6 leaves basil, torn

Wine: a dry white (Sauvignon)

Right: *Insalata di riso semplicissima*

Radicchio risotto
Risotto con radicchio

■ INGREDIENTS

• 1 onion, finely chopped
• 3 tablespoons extra-virgin
  olive oil
• 2 tablespoons butter
• 2 cups (450 g) arborio rice
• 4 cups (31 liter) *Beef stock*
  (see recipe p. 48)
• 3 heads of radicchio
  (red-leaf chicory), cut in
  short strips
• 1 teaspoon finely chopped
  mixed rosemary and parsley

Serves: 4; Preparation: 10 minutes; Cooking: 25 minutes; Level of difficulty: Simple

Sauté the onion in the oil and butter in a heavy-bottomed pan. § Add the rice and stir for 2 minutes. § Stir in a little stock followed by the radicchio. Gradually add the rest of the stock, stirring almost continuously. § Season with salt and freshly ground black pepper. § Stir in the rosemary and parsley just before serving. § Serve hot.

Rice salad with shrimp
Insalata di riso con gamberetti

■ INGREDIENTS

- 1¾ lb (800 g) raw shrimp, in shell
- juice of 1½ lemons
- ⅓ cup (3100 ml) extra-virgin olive oil
- 2 cups (450 g) short-grain rice
- 4 tablespoons arugula (rocket), coarsely chopped
- salt and freshly ground white pepper

Wine: a dry white (Pinot Bianco)

Serves: 4; Preparation: 30 minutes; Cooking: 15-20 minutes; Level of difficulty: Medium
Cook the shrimp in 2 quarts (2 liters) of salted, boiling water and the juice of 1 lemon for 5 minutes. § Drain, and let the shrimp cool. Shell the shrimp and remove the dark intestinal veins. Chop off the heads and rinse thoroughly in cold running water. Place in a bowl with almost all the oil. § Cook the rice in 2½ quarts (2.5 liters) of salted, boiling water, allowing 13–15 minutes cooking. § Drain the rice and pass under cold running water to stop cooking. Drain again, and transfer to the bowl with the shrimp. § Mix carefully, adding salt and pepper to taste. Add the remaining lemon juice and oil. § Just before serving, add the arugula and mix again.

Eggplant risotto
Risotto con melanzane

■ INGREDIENTS

- 2 eggplants (aubergines)
- 2 cloves garlic, minced
- 1 tablespoon finely chopped parsley
- ⅓ cup (100 ml) extra-virgin olive oil
- 2 cups (450 g) arborio rice
- 4 cups (1 liter) *Beef stock* (see recipe p. 48)

Serves: 4; Preparation: 10 minutes + 1 hour for the eggplants; Cooking: 15 minutes; Level of difficulty: Simple
Dice the eggplants, sprinkle with salt and place on a slanted cutting board so that the bitter liquid they produce can run off. § Sauté the the garlic and parsley in the oil in a heavy-bottomed pan. § Add the eggplant and cook over medium heat until soft. § Stir in the rice and cook for 2 minutes. § Gradually stir in the stock. The rice will be cooked in about 15–18 minutes. § Season with salt and pepper and serve hot.

Rice with chicken livers
Riso con fegatini

■ INGREDIENTS

- 2 cups (450 g) short-grain rice
- ¼ cup (60 g) butter
- 1 onion, finely chopped
- 2 tablespoons pine nuts
- 8 chicken livers, chopped
- salt and freshly ground white pepper
- 4 tablespoons dry Marsala
- 4 tablespoons dry white wine

Wine: a dry white (Müller Thurgau)

Serves: 4; Preparation: 10 minutes; Cooking: 15 minutes; Level of difficulty: Simple
Pour the rice into 2 quarts (2 liters) of salted, boiling water, stir well, and cook for 13–15 minutes. § Sauté the onion in the butter in a heavy-bottomed pan for 3 minutes. § Turn the heat up to medium-high, add the chicken livers, pine nuts, salt, and pepper. Stir for 1–2 minutes, then add half the Marsala and wine. Stir again before adding the rest. § Cook for 6–7 minutes, stirring occasionally. § When the rice is cooked, drain thoroughly and transfer to a serving dish. § Pour the chicken liver sauce over the top and serve hot.

Left: *Insalata di riso con gamberetti*

Rice with egg and cream
Riso all'uovo

Serves: 4; Preparation: 2 minutes; Cooking: 13-15 minutes; Level of difficulty: Simple

Cook the rice in 2 quarts (2 liters) of boiling, salted water for 13–15 minutes. § When the rice is almost ready, beat the egg yolks, cream, Parmesan, and pepper in a bowl. § Drain the rice thoroughly and transfer to a heated serving dish. § Season with the sauce and dot with butter. Stir quickly and serve immediately.

■ INGREDIENTS

- 2 cups (450 g) short-grain rice
- 3 fresh egg yolks
- ⅓ cup (90 ml) light (single) cream
- 4 tablespoons freshly grated Parmesan cheese
- dash of freshly ground white pepper
- 2 tablespoons butter

Wine: a dry white (Traminer)

Pear risotto
Risotto con le pere

Serves: 4; Preparation: 2 minutes; Cooking: 13-15 minutes; Level of difficulty: Simple

Peel, core, and dice the pears. § Sauté the onion in the butter in a heavy-bottomed pan until soft. § Stir in the rice and cook for 2 minutes, then add the wine. § When the wine has all been absorbed, add a ladleful of boiling stock and the pears. § Complete cooking, gradually adding the remaining stock. Season to taste. § Add the Taleggio and liqueur shortly before serving. § Stir well and serve hot.

■ INGREDIENTS

- 14 oz (450 g) pears
- 1 onion, finely chopped
- 2 tablespoons butter
- 2 cups (450 g) arborio rice
- 1 cup (250 ml) dry white wine
- 6 cups (1.5 liters) *Vegetable stock* (see recipe p. 48)
- 3 oz (90 g) creamy Taleggio cheese
- 2 tablespoons Williams pear liqueur

Brown rice with tomato sauce
Riso integrale con salsa di pomodoro

For winter meals, serve the brown rice hot with Simple tomato sauce. In summer, when fresh tomatoes are readily available and soaring temperatures make life in the kitchen unpleasant, serve with Fresh tomato sauce on hot or cold brown rice.

Serves: 4; Preparation: 25 minutes; Cooking: 45 minutes; Level of difficulty: Simple

Cook the rice in 2 quarts (2 liters) of salted, boiling water, stirring once or twice. It will be cooked in about 45 minutes. § Prepare the tomato sauce. § When the rice is done, drain thoroughly, and transfer to a large bowl. § Pour the remaining oil over the rice and toss vigorously. § Add the tomato sauce, toss carefully and serve.

■ INGREDIENTS

- 2 cups (450 g) brown rice
- 1 quantity *Fresh* or *Simple tomato sauce* (see recipes p. 28)

Wine: a light, dry rosé (Chiaretto del Garda)

Right: *Riso integrale con salsa di pomodoro crudo*

Asparagus risotto

Risotto con asparagi

The delicate flavors in this risotto call for high-quality, fresh asparagus.

Serves: 4; Preparation: 15 minutes; Cooking: 25 minutes; Level of difficulty: Medium

Rinse the asparagus and trim the stalks. Cut the green tips in two or three pieces. § Melt 3 tablespoons of butter in a deep, heavy-bottomed saucepan. Add the onion and sauté for 1 minute; then add the asparagus tips and sauté for 5 minutes. § Add the rice and pour in the wine. Stir well. § When the wine has been absorbed, begin adding the boiling stock, a little at a time, stirring frequently. § The risotto will be cooked in 15–18 minutes. § Add the remaining butter and the Parmesan. Mix well. § Check the seasoning and add salt and pepper if required.

■ INGREDIENTS

- 1¾ lb (800 g) asparagus
- 4 tablespoons butter
- ½ onion, finely chopped
- 2 cups (450 g) arborio rice
- ½ cup (125 ml) dry white wine
- 4 cups (1 liter) *Chicken* or *Beef stock* (see recipes pp. 48, 50)
- 4 tablespoons freshly grated Parmesan cheese
- salt and freshly ground white pepper

Chicken risotto

Risotto alla sbirraglia

Served with a green salad, this nourishing risotto is a meal in itself. It takes its name from the Austrian soldiers (sbirri) who occupied northern Italy in the 19th century. They were apparently very fond of it.

Serves 4; Preparation; 10 minutes: Cooking: 1 hour; Level of difficulty: Medium

Melt 3 tablespoons of butter with the oil in a deep, heavy-bottomed saucepan. Add the celery, onion, and carrot and sauté for 2 minutes over low heat. § Season the chicken with salt and pepper and place the pieces in the saucepan in a single layer. Increase the heat and brown, turning as required. § After 8–10 minutes begin sprinkling with wine. Cover and continue cooking, gradually adding the wine, for 25–30 minutes. § To test if the chicken is cooked, pierce with a fork or toothpick. The liquid that forms around the hole should be transparent rather than pink. § Remove the chicken and set aside in a warm oven. § Place the rice and chicken livers in the pan with the cooking juices and cook for 1 minute. § Gradually stir in the boiling stock. Continue cooking until the rice is tender, stirring frequently (it will take about 15–18 minutes). § Just before serving, add the remaining butter and Parmesan and mix well. § Transfer the risotto to a serving dish and arrange the pieces of chicken on top.

■ INGREDIENTS

- 4 tablespoons butter
- 3 tablespoons extra-virgin olive oil
- 1 celery stalk, 1 onion, 1 carrot, finely chopped
- 1 chicken, ready to cook, weighing about 2 lb (1 kg), cut in 8 pieces
- salt and freshly ground white pepper
- 1 cup (250 ml) dry white wine
- 2 cups (450 g) arborio rice
- 6 cups (1.5 liters) boiling *Beef stock* (see recipe p. 48)
- 1 chicken liver, cleaned and finely chopped
- 2 tablespoons freshly grated Parmesan cheese

Wine: a dry white (Galestro)

Right: *Risotto con asparagi*

Risotto with bay leaves
Risotto con alloro

To savor the full flavor of this fragrant risotto, serve without adding Parmesan cheese.

Serves: 4; Preparation: 5 minutes; Cooking: 20 minutes; Level of difficulty: Simple

Heat the oil in a large, heavy-bottomed saucepan and sauté the onion until it is soft. § Add the rice and bay leaves. Stir for 2 minutes and then begin adding the wine, a little at a time. § When the wine has been absorbed, add the nutmeg and continue cooking. Keep adding stock until the rice is cooked. It will take about 15–18 minutes. § Season with salt and serve.

Basil and parsley risotto
Risotto al prezzemolo e basilico

This traditional recipe contains all the fragrance of the Italian Riviera.

Serves: 4; Preparation: 10 minutes; Cooking: 25 minutes; Level of difficulty: Simple

Dissolve the marrow in a heavy-bottomed saucepan over low heat. § Add the butter, oil, and garlic, and sauté for 1 minute. § Add the rice and cook for 2 minutes, stirring continuously. § Begin adding the stock, a little at a time, stirring frequently. § The rice will take about 15–18 minutes to cook. § A few minutes before the rice is ready, add the basil and parsley. § Season with salt and pepper. § Add the Pecorino and serve hot.

■ INGREDIENTS

- 2 tablespoons ox-bone marrow, finely chopped
- 2 tablespoons butter
- 3 tablespoons extra-virgin olive oil
- 2 cloves garlic, minced
- 2 cups (450 g) arborio rice
- 6 cups (1.5 liters) *Vegetable stock (see recipe p. 48)*
- 1 tablespoon each finely chopped basil and parsley
- salt and freshly ground white pepper
- 3 tablespoons freshly grated Pecorino cheese

Wine: a dry white (Trebbiano)

Roasted rice
Riso arrosto

The original recipe for this Ligurian specialty calls for the juices produced by a roast. Nowadays butter or oil are generally used instead.

Serves: 4; Preparation: 35 minutes; Cooking: 45-50 minutes; Level of difficulty: Medium

Sauté the onion, sausage, mushrooms, artichokes, and peas in a large, heavy-bottomed pan in 3 tablespoons of oil. Season with salt and pepper. § Add the stock, cover, and continue cooking for about 10 minutes. § In the meantime, bring 4 cups (1 liter) of salted water to a boil, pour in the rice and cook for 7–8 minutes. § Drain partially (leave some moisture). Transfer to the pan with the sauce and stir. Add the cheese and mix well. Transfer to an ovenproof dish greased with the remaining butter or oil. § Bake in a preheated oven at 400°F/200°C/gas 6 for about 20 minutes. The rice will have a light golden crust when ready.

■ INGREDIENTS

- 4 tablespoons extra-virgin olive oil
- 1 onion, finely chopped
- 5 oz (150 g) Italian pork sausages, skinned and crumbled
- 7 oz (200 g) porcini mushrooms, sliced
- 2 artichokes, trimmed and thinly sliced
- 2 tablespoons peas
- salt and freshly ground black pepper
- 1 cup (250 ml) *Beef stock (see recipe p. 48)*
- 2 cups (450 g) short-grain rice
- 3 tablespoons freshly grated Pecorino cheese

Wine: a dry white (Vermentino)

VARIATION
– If fresh porcini mushrooms are unavailable, use 1 oz (30 g) dried porcini. Soak for 15 minutes in a cup of tepid water, then drain, chop coarsely, and combine with 4 oz (125 g) sliced white mushrooms.

Right: *Risotto al prezzemolo e basilico*

Artichoke risotto
Risotto ai carciofi

It is extremely important to clean the artichokes properly, discarding the tough tips, outer leaves and fuzzy choke. The inner hearts should be cut into slices less than ⅛ in (3 mm) thick.

Serves: 4; Preparation: 20 minutes; Cooking: 30 minutes; Level of difficulty: Medium

Clean the artichokes by removing the stalks and tough outer leaves. Trim off and discard the tops. Cut in half and remove the fuzzy inner choke with a sharp knife. Place in a bowl of cold water with the lemon juice. Soak for 10–15 minutes so they will not discolor. § Melt the butter in a large, heavy-bottomed saucepan. Add the onion and sauté for a few minutes. § Drain the artichoke slices and add to the onion; sauté for another 5 minutes. § Add the rice and stir for 2 minutes. Increase the heat slightly, and begin adding the stock, a little at a time, until the rice is cooked. It will take about 15–18 minutes. Season with salt and pepper. § Add the parsley and Pecorino at the last minute. Mix well to create a creamy risotto.

VARIATION
– For a slightly different flavor, replace half the butter with 3 tablespoons of extra-virgin olive oil.

■ INGREDIENTS

• 6–7 artichokes
• juice of 1 lemon
• 3 tablespoons butter
• ½ onion, finely chopped
• 2 cups (450 g) arborio rice
• 6 cups (1.5 liters) boiling water or *Vegetable stock* (see recipe p. 48)
• salt and freshly ground black pepper
• 1 tablespoon finely chopped parsley
• 4 tablespoons freshly grated Parmesan or Pecorino cheese

Wine: a dry white (Vernaccia di San Gimignano)

Rice with butter and cheese
Riso alla biellese

This dish comes from Piedmont and Valle d'Aosta, in northwestern Italy, where it was traditionally served at wedding banquets.

Serves: 4; Preparation: 5 minutes; Cooking: 13-15 minutes; Level of difficulty: Simple

Pour the rice into 2 quarts (2 liters) of salted, boiling water and stir once or twice. Allow 13–15 minutes cooking time from when the water comes to a boil again. § A couple of minutes before the rice is cooked, melt the butter in a saucepan until it turns golden brown. § Drain the rice over the serving bowl so it fills with the hot cooking water. Don't drain the rice too thoroughly. § Throw out the water in the bowl, which is now nicely warmed, and put in the rice, alternating it with spoonfuls of the cheese. Drizzle with hot butter, stir quickly, and serve, passing the pepper separately.

■ INGREDIENTS

• 2 cups (450 g) short-grain rice
• ⅓ cup (90 g) butter
• 5 oz (150 g) Fontina cheese, diced
• freshly ground white pepper (optional)

Wine: a dry red (Freisa)

Right: Risotto ai carciofi

Risotto with fennel
Risotto con finocchi

To make this simple and delicate risotto, it is essential to have truly tender fennel bulbs. Be sure to discard all the tough and stringy outer leaves.

Serves: 4; Preparation: 15 minutes; Cooking: 25 minutes; Level of difficulty: Simple

Cut the fennel bulbs vertically into slices about ⅛ in (3 mm) thick. § Melt half the butter in a large, heavy-bottomed saucepan with the oil. Add the onion, celery, and fennel and sauté for 5–7 minutes. § Add the rice and cook for 1 minute over medium heat; then begin adding the boiling stock, a little at a time, stirring frequently until the rice is cooked. It will take about 15–18 minutes. The risotto should be creamy but not too liquid. § Finally, add the remaining butter and the Parmesan and mix well. § Season with salt and pepper and serve hot.

■ INGREDIENTS

- 4–5 fennel bulbs, cleaned
- ¼ cup (60 g) butter
- 2–3 tablespoons extra-virgin olive oil
- 1 small onion, finely chopped
- 1 small stalk celery, finely chopped
- 2 cups (450 g) arborio rice
- 6 cups (1.5 liters) boiling *Beef stock* (see recipe p. 48)
- 4 tablespoons freshly grated Parmesan cheese
- salt and freshly ground white pepper

Wine: a dry white (Soave)

Risotto with quail
Risotto con le quaglie

In Lombardy quail are often served with Risotto alla milanese, a combination that works well. This one is more delicate and, I think, more harmonious.

Serves: 4; Preparation: 15 minutes; Cooking: 40 minutes; Level of difficulty: Medium

Season the quail inside and out with salt and pepper. Put the sage leaves inside. § Wrap the breasts with slices of pancetta secured with two or three twists of kitchen string. § In a large, heavy-bottomed saucepan, melt half the butter with the oil. Add the quail and brown well on all sides over medium heat. This will take about 6–7 minutes. § Sprinkle the quail with the brandy and when this has evaporated, lower the heat, partially cover and cook, adding a spoonful of stock occasionally. The quail will be cooked in about 15 minutes. § Remove the quail and set aside in a warm oven. § Add the rice to the juices left in the saucepan and stir well for 2 minutes. § Gradually stir in the remaining stock. The rice will be cooked in 15–18 minutes. § At the last moment, stir in the remaining butter and the cheese. § Serve the rice with the quail arranged on top. Remove the kitchen string but leave the pancetta in place.

■ INGREDIENTS

- 4 quail, cleaned
- salt and freshly ground white pepper
- 4 leaves sage
- 4 slices pancetta
- 3 tablespoons butter
- 2 tablespoons extra-virgin olive oil
- 3 tablespoons brandy
- 2 cups (450 g) arborio rice
- 6 cups (1.5 liters) boiling *Beef stock* (see recipe p. 48)
- 4 tablespoons freshly grated Parmesan cheese

Wine: a dry white (Cortese di Gavi)

Right:
Risotto con finocchi

Mushroom risotto Venetian-style
Risotto ai funghi

There are many different recipes for mushroom risotto. This one comes from the city of Venice.

Serves: 4; Preparation: 30 minutes; Cooking: 25-30 minutes; Level of difficulty: Medium

Soak the mushrooms for 15 minutes in 1 cup (250 ml) of tepid water. Drain, reserving the water, and chop coarsely. § Strain the water in which the mushrooms were soaked and set it aside. § Heat the oil in a large, heavy-bottomed saucepan. Add the onion and sauté over low heat until soft. § Add the mushrooms and sauté for 2–3 minutes. § Add the rice and stir for 2 minutes over medium heat. Add the wine gradually, and when it has been absorbed, stir in the mushroom water. § Begin adding the stock a little at a time, stirring often until the rice is cooked. It will take about 15–18 minutes. § Add the parsley just before the rice is cooked and mix. § Season with salt and serve hot.

VARIATION
– Add 4 tablespoons of freshly grated Parmesan at the end, or pass separately.

■ INGREDIENTS

• 1 oz (30 g) dried porcini mushrooms
• 4 tablespoons extra-virgin olive oil
• 1 small onion, finely chopped
• ½ cup (125 ml) dry white wine
• 4 cups (450 g) arborio rice
• 4 cups (1 liter) *Vegetable stock* (see recipe p. 48)
• 2 tablespoons finely chopped parsley
• dash of salt

Wine: a dry white (Pinot Grigio)

Simple risotto with parmesan cheese
Risotto bianco al parmigiano

Serves: 4; Preparation: 5 minutes; Cooking: 25 minutes; Level of difficulty: Medium

Melt half the butter in a large, heavy-bottomed saucepan. Add the onion and sauté over low heat until soft and translucent. § Add the rice, increase the heat, and stir for 2 minutes. § Pour in the wine, and when it has been completely absorbed, gradually stir in the boiling stock. Stir frequently, adding the nutmeg, if liked. § When the rice is almost cooked (it will take about 15–18 minutes), add a little over half the Parmesan. § Season with salt and pepper; and, finally, add the remaining butter, mixing well. § Serve with the remaining Parmesan passed separately.

VARIATION
– After the wine has evaporated, add 2 tablespoons of tomato paste. This will give you *Risotto rosso alla piemontese* or "Red risotto Piedmont-style." In this case, use a little less Parmesan.

■ INGREDIENTS

• 4 tablespoons butter
• 1 onion, finely chopped
• 2 cups (450 g) arborio rice
• ½ cup (125 ml) dry white wine
• 6 cups (1.5 liters) *Chicken* or *Beef stock* (see recipes pp. 48, 50)
• dash of nutmeg (optional)
• 4 tablespoons freshly grated Parmesan cheese
• salt and freshly ground white pepper

Wine: a light, dry red (Gutturnio)

Left:
Risotto ai funghi

Baked rice with cheese
Riso al formaggi

Many different combinations of cheeses can be used in this recipe. These four go particularly well together, but feel free to experiment with others.

Serves: 4; Preparation: 15 minutes; Cooking: 35 minutes; Level of difficulty: Simple

Put the rice into 2 quarts (2 liters) of salted, boiling water and stir once or twice. Cook for 13–15 minutes. § Butter an ovenproof baking dish. § Mix the bread crumbs with 1 tablespoon of the Parmesan. § Melt two-thirds of the remaining butter in a saucepan, and add the sage (or rosemary), nutmeg, and garlic, if using. Sauté until golden brown. § When the rice is cooked, drain well and transfer to a bowl. § Stir in the cheeses and sausage. § Remove the herbs from the butter and add to the rice. Stir rapidly. § Transfer the mixture to a baking dish. Smooth the surface, sprinkle with the mixed bread crumbs and Parmesan, and dot with the remaining butter. § Bake in a preheated oven at 400°F/200°C/gas 6 for 15 minutes, or until a golden crust has formed.

■ INGREDIENTS

- 2 cups (450 g) arborio rice
- 4 tablespoons butter
- 1 tablespoon bread crumbs
- ½ cup (60 g) freshly grated Parmesan cheese
- 5 leaves sage, fresh or dried, or 1 sprig rosemary
- dash of nutmeg (optional)
- 1 clove garlic (optional)
- 2 oz (60 g) each of Emmenthal, smoked Scamorza, and Fontina cheeses, all chopped
- 5 oz (150 g) Italian pork sausages, skinned and crumbled

Wine: a dry red (Cabernet)

Gorgonzola risotto
Risotto al gorgonzola

Rice and Gorgonzola cheese make a tasty partnership. Choose the best soft and creamy cheese.

Serves: 4; Preparation: 10 minutes; Cooking: 25 minutes; Level of difficulty: Simple

Melt the butter in a large, heavy-bottomed saucepan. § Add the onion and sauté over low heat until soft. § Add the rice and cook, stirring constantly, for 2 minutes. § Increase the heat slightly and pour in the wine. § When the wine has been absorbed, begin adding the boiling stock, a little at a time and stirring frequently. § The rice will take about 15–18 minutes to cook. § About 3–4 minutes before it is ready, add the Gorgonzola and mix well. Season with salt and pepper. § Add the Parmesan and serve.

■ INGREDIENTS

- 3 tablespoons butter
- ½ small onion, finely chopped
- 2 cups (450 g) arborio rice
- ⅔ cup (150 ml) dry white wine
- 6 cups (1.5 liters) *Beef stock* (see recipe p. 48)
- 8 oz (250 g) Gorgonzola cheese, chopped
- salt and freshly ground white pepper
- 4 tablespoons freshly grated Parmesan cheese

Wine: a dry red (Merlot)

VARIATIONS
– Replace the Gorgonzola with the same quantity of well-ripened Taleggio cheese; in this case add half a finely chopped garlic clove and a dash of nutmeg to the onion before adding the rice.
– Stir in 2–3 tablespoons of fresh cream just before serving.

Right:
Risotto al gorgonzola

Creamy lentil risotto
Risotto con lenticchie

Serves: 4; Preparation: 10 minutes; Cooking: 20-25 minutes; Level of difficulty: Simple

Heat the butter and oil in a large, heavy-bottomed saucepan. Add the onion and garlic and sauté for 5 minutes over low heat. § Increase the heat slightly and pour in the rice. Cook for 2 minutes, stirring continuously. § Add the boiling stock little by little, stirring frequently. After about 10 minutes, add the drained lentils and continue cooking. The rice will be ready in about 15–18 minutes. § Add half the cheese and season with salt and pepper. § Mix well and serve. The remaining cheese can be served separately.

VARIATION
– Add 1 tablespoon of tomato paste with the lentils.

■ INGREDIENTS

- 3 tablespoons butter
- 3 tablespoons extra-virgin olive oil
- 1 onion, finely chopped
- 1 clove garlic, minced
- 2 cups (450 g) arborio rice
- 6 cups (1.5 liters) *Beef stock* (see recipe p. 48)
- 14 oz (450 g) lentils, canned
- ¼ cup (45 g) freshly grated Pecorino or Parmesan cheese
- salt and freshly ground white or black pepper

Wine: a dry red (Rosso Conero)

Risotto with mussels
Risotto con i peoci

This recipe comes from Veneto, the region around the city of Venice. in local dialect mussels are called peoci.

Serves: 4; Preparation: 20 minutes + 1 hour to soak mussels; Cooking: 20 minutes; Level of difficulty: Medium

Soak the mussels in a large bowl of water for at least 1 hour to purge them of sand. Pull off their beards, scrub and rinse well in abundant cold water. § Combine the mussels and the whole clove of garlic in a large, shallow skillet (frying pan). Place over high heat and shake the skillet and stir with a wooden spoon until all the mussels are open. This will take 4–5 minutes. Discard any that have not opened. § Drain the mussels. Set aside a dozen of the largest, in their shells, to use as a garnish. § Take the remaining mussels out of their shells and put them in a bowl. § Strain the liquid left in the pan through a fine cloth or sieve and set it aside, discarding the garlic. § Sauté the oil, onion, and

■ INGREDIENTS

- 3½ lb (1.5 kg) mussels, in shell
- 2 cloves garlic, 1 of which finely chopped
- ⅓ cup (100 ml) extra-virgin olive oil
- ½ small onion, finely chopped
- 2 cups (450 g) arborio rice
- ⅓ cup (90 ml) dry white wine
- 3 cups (750 ml) boiling water
- 2 tablespoons finely chopped parsley
- salt and freshly ground black pepper

Wine: a dry white (Tocai Isonzo)

chopped garlic in the same skillet for a few minutes. § Add the rice and cook, stirring continuously, for 2 minutes. § Increase the heat slightly and pour in the wine. When all the wine has been absorbed, begin slowly adding the mussel liquid and then boiling water as required, stirring frequently, until the rice is cooked. This will take about 15–18 minutes. § Add the mussels and stir well. Sprinkle with the parsley and season with salt and pepper. § Transfer to a serving dish and garnish with the whole mussels. § Serve hot.

Above:
Risotto con lenticchie

VARIATION
— At the last minute add 2 tablespoons of butter and 4 tablespoons of freshly grated Parmesan cheese. Many consider this quite unorthodox, but the Venetians think otherwise.

Lemon risotto

Risotto al limone

The distinctive flavor of this risotto does not combine well with any wine.
Serve with cool, sparkling mineral water with slices of lemon.

Serves: 4; Preparation: 10 minutes; Cooking: 25 minutes; Level of difficulty: Simple

Sauté the onion in the oil for a few minutes over medium-low heat in a large, heavy-bottomed saucepan until it is soft. § Increase the heat slightly and add the rice; stir for 2 minutes. § Add the wine and, when it has been absorbed, gradually add the boiling stock as required. § After about 10 minutes, add the lemon zest, stirring well. § The rice will take about 15–18 minutes to cook. § Season with salt and pepper to taste. Add the lemon juice and parsley, stir well and serve.

■ INGREDIENTS

- ½ small onion, finely chopped
- 4 tablespoons extra-virgin olive oil
- 2 cups (450 g) arborio rice
- ⅓ cup (90 ml) dry, light white wine
- 6 cups (91.5 liters) *Beef stock* (see recipe p. 48)
- grated zest and juice of 1 large lemon
- salt and freshly ground white pepper
- 1 tablespoon finely chopped parsley

Milanese-style risotto

Risotto alla milanese

This is a traditional Milanese dish. Debate has always raged about whether wine should be added or not (and if so, whether it should it be red or white). Try it with both, and without, and decide for yourself.

Serves: 4; Preparation: 10 minutes; Cooking: 25 minutes; Level of difficulty: Medium

Melt half the butter in a large, heavy-bottomed saucepan. § Add the onion and sauté over low heat until soft. § Add the rice and cook over medium heat for 2–3 minutes, stirring continuously. § Pour in the wine, if using, and when it has been absorbed, add the stock, a little at a time, stirring continuously. If wine is not used, begin directly with the stock. Increase the heat slightly. § The rice will take about 15–18 minutes to cook. After 15 minutes, add half the Parmesan. § Add the saffron 1 minute before the rice is ready. Season with salt. § Stir in the remaining butter just before serving and mix well. The risotto should be very creamy, because of the slow and gradual release during cooking of the starch that binds the rice together. § Serve with the remaining Parmesan passed separately.

■ INGREDIENTS

- 4 tablespoons butter
- 1 small onion, finely chopped
- 2 cups (450 g) arborio rice
- ½ cup (125 ml) white or red wine (optional)
- 2 quarts (2 liters) boiling *Beef stock* (see recipe p. 48)
- ⅓ cup (45 g) freshly grated Parmesan cheese
- ½ teaspoon saffron
- dash of salt

Wine: a dry white
(Riesling dell'Oltrepò Pavese)

VARIATION
– Add shavings of white truffle to the risotto just before serving.

Right:
Risotto al limone

Risotto with pancetta and prosciutto
Risotto con pancetta e prosciutto

Serves: 4; Preparation: 15 minutes; Cooking: 25-30 minutes; Level of difficulty: Medium

Melt the butter in a large, heavy-bottomed saucepan, add the onion and, after 1 minute, the pancetta. Sauté over low heat, stirring occasionally, until the onion is soft. § Add the rice and cook for 2 minutes, stirring continuously. § Increase the heat slightly and pour in the wine. When it has been absorbed, gradually add the hot stock as required until the rice is cooked. This will take about 15–18 minutes. § Three minutes before the rice is cooked, add the nutmeg, pepper, ham, cream, and cheese, mixing carefully to combine the ingredients well. § Season with salt, and serve.

> VARIATIONS
> – Add 2 tablespoons of butter instead of the cream.
> – Emmenthal, or Scamorza cheese, in flakes or shavings, can be used instead of the Parmesan.

■ INGREDIENTS

- 3 tablespoons butter
- 1 onion, finely chopped
- 2 oz (60 g) lean pancetta, diced
- ⅓ cup (90 ml) dry white wine
- 2 cups (450 g) arborio rice
- 5 cups (1.2 liters) boiling *Beef stock* (see recipe p. 48)
- dash of nutmeg
- salt and freshly ground white pepper
- 4 oz (125 g) prosciutto, cut in thick slices and diced
- ⅓ cup (90 ml) light (single) cream
- 4 tablespoons freshly grated Parmesan cheese

Wine: a light, dry red (Lagrein Rosato)

Milanese-style risotto the day after
Risotto alla milanese 'al salto'

In Milan this was once the classic dish to order after an evening at the theater. It is prepared with leftover Risotto alla milanese, so make a double quantity and serve this one the day after. In the original recipe the portions are prepared individually, but since not everyone is able to juggle four skillets at once, I have simplified things a little.

Serves: 4; Preparation: 5 minutes; Cooking: 15 minutes; Level of difficulty: Simple

§ Melt a quarter of the butter in each of two skillets (frying pans) 12 in (30 cm) in diameter. § Divide the rice into two portions and flatten each out so as to have two round cakes about 1 in (2.5 cm) thick. § Cook them in the skillets over high heat for about 5 minutes, so that a crisp crust forms. § Turn them with the help of a plate and slip them back into the skillets in which you have melted the remaining butter. § When both sides are crisp and deep gold in color, sprinkle with the Parmesan and cut each one in half. § Serve immediately.

■ INGREDIENTS

- 1 quantity *Risotto alla milanese* (see recipe p. 306)
- 4 tablespoons butter
- 4 tablespoons freshly grated Parmesan cheese

Wine: a young, dry red (San Colombano)

Left:
Risotto con pancetta e prosciutto

Risotto with mozzarella cheese and cream
Risotto con mozzarella e panna

Because of its delicate flavor, this recipe requires very fresh Mozzarella if it is to be a success.

Serves: 4; Preparation: 5 minutes; Cooking: 20-25 minutes; Level of difficulty: Simple

Melt the butter in a large, heavy-bottomed saucepan. Add the onion and sauté over low heat for 2 minutes until soft. § Add the rice and cook for 2 minutes, stirring continuously. § Pour in the wine and when this has been absorbed, gradually add the stock, a little at a time, until two-thirds have been used. § After about 10 minutes add half the cream, stir well and then add the other half. § After 2–3 minutes add the Mozzarella. § Continue cooking until the rice is tender, stirring in the remaining stock as required. § Season with salt and pepper. Serve the risotto with the Parmesan passed separately.

■ INGREDIENTS

- 2 tablespoons butter
- ½ onion, finely chopped
- 2 cups (450 g) arborio rice
- ½ cup (125 ml) dry white wine
- 4 cups (1 liter) *Beef* or *Chicken stock* (see recipes pp. 48, 50)
- ⅔ cup (150 ml) light (single) cream
- 8 oz (250 g) Mozzarella cheese, diced
- salt and freshly ground white pepper
- 4 tablespoons freshly grated Parmesan cheese

Wine: a dry white (Ischia Bianco)

Piedmont-style risotto
Risotto alla piemontese

Thin shavings of white truffles sprinkled on the risotto just before serving are the perfect complement to this dish. Cooking time for the sauce is about 10 minutes, so it can be prepared when the risotto is well-advanced in its cooking and needs less attention.

Serves: 4; Preparation: 15 minutes + 3 hours to soak; Cooking: 25 minutes; Level of difficulty: Complicated

Put the Fontina in a bowl and cover it with the milk. Set aside for 3 hours. § When the Fontina has been soaking for 2½ hours, prepare the risotto following the instructions on page 301. § When the Fontina is ready, melt the butter (which must not bubble) in a double boiler or saucepan, and add the Fontina, and about half the milk in which it was soaked. Stir carefully with a wooden spoon over very low heat until the cheese melts and the mixture is creamy. § Add the first egg yolk and mix thoroughly before adding the second. Repeat this procedure before adding the third, mixing rather quickly to achieve a smooth, creamy sauce. § Season with salt and pepper (if serving with truffles, add less salt and pepper than you normally would). § Transfer the risotto to a serving dish and pour the sauce over the top. § Serve immediately.

■ INGREDIENTS

- 10 oz (300 g) Fontina cheese, cut in thin slices
- ¾ cup (200 ml) milk
- 1 quantity *Risotto bianco al parmigiano* (see recipe p. 301)
- 3 tablespoons butter
- 3 egg yolks, at room temperature
- salt and freshly ground white pepper

Wine: a dry red (Nebbiolo)

Right:
Risotto con mozzarella e panna

Risotto with tomato and mushrooms
Risotto all'onegliese

This dish, originally from the village of Oneglia, in Liguria, has spread all along the Italian Riviera.

Serves: 4; Preparation: 30 minutes; Cooking: 35 minutes; Level of difficulty: Medium

Soak the mushrooms in a bowl of warm water for about 15 minutes. Drain and chop coarsely. § If using fresh tomatoes, plunge them into a pot of boiling water for 30 seconds, and then into cold. Slip off the skins, cut in half, squeeze to remove some of the seeds, and then chop finely. § If using canned tomatoes, partially drain and chop finely. § In a heavy-bottomed saucepan, sauté the onion in the oil until soft. Add the mushrooms and, after another minute or so, the tomatoes. § Cook the sauce for 10 minutes, covered, then add the rice and stir well. § When part of the liquid has been absorbed, begin to add the boiling water, pouring it in a little at a time and stirring frequently. § Just before the rice is cooked, season with salt and pepper. § Serve the rice, passing the cheese separately.

■ INGREDIENTS

- ⅔ oz (20 g) dried mushrooms
- 14 oz (450 g) tomatoes, fresh or canned, peeled and chopped
- 1 small onion, finely chopped
- ⅓ cup (90 ml) extra-virgin olive oil
- 2 cups (450 g) arborio rice
- 4 cups (1 liter) boiling water
- salt and freshly ground black pepper
- 4 tablespoons freshly grated Pecorino or Parmesan cheese

Wine: a dry white (Pigato di Albenga)

Rice with butter
Ris in cagnon

A simple and pleasant dish from Lombardy, the region around Milan.

Serves: 4; Preparation: 5 minutes; Cooking: 15 minutes; Level of difficulty: Simple

Cook the rice in about 2 quarts (2 liters) of salted, boiling water, stirring a couple of times until it is cooked. It will take about 13–15 minutes. § Just before the rice is ready, slowly melt the butter in a saucepan with the sage leaves and garlic (remove garlic after 1 minute). The butter should turn dark golden brown. § Drain the rice thoroughly and transfer to a serving dish or individual plates. § Sprinkle with the Parmesan and drizzle with the hot butter, with or without the sage leaves.

■ INGREDIENTS

- 2 cups (450 g) arborio rice
- 4 tablespoons butter
- 6 sage leaves, fresh or dried, whole or crumbled
- 1 clove garlic, cut in half
- ⅓ cup (45 g) freshly grated Parmesan cheese

Wine: a dry white (Lugana)

Right:
Risotto all'onegliese

Risotto with wine
Risotto al vino

Try to find a Barolo or a Chianti wine for this dish. The wine can be added a third or a quarter of a cup at a time, or alternately with the stock.

Serves: 4; Preparation: 10 minutes; Cooking: 25 minutes; Level of difficulty: Simple

Melt 3 tablespoons of butter in a large, heavy-bottomed saucepan. Add the onion, celery, and carrot, and sauté over low heat for 5 minutes. § Increase the heat slightly, add the rice, and cook for 2 minutes, stirring continuously. § Gradually stir in the wine. § When this has been absorbed, begin adding the stock. § It will take about 15–18 minutes for the rice to cook. Season with salt and pepper. § Add the remaining butter just before serving. § Sprinkle with the Parmesan and serve.

> VARIATION
> – For *Risotto allo champagne* use the same quantity of high quality, dry sparkling wine or champagne in place of the red wine.

■ INGREDIENTS

- 4 tablespoons butter
- ½ onion, finely chopped
- 1 celery stalk, finely chopped
- 1 small carrot, scraped and finely chopped
- 2 cups (450 g) arborio rice
- 1¼ cups (300 ml) dry, full-bodied wine
- 4 cups (1 liter) boiling *Beef* or *Chicken stock* (see recipe pp. 48, 50)
- salt and freshly ground black pepper
- 4 tablespoons freshly grated Parmesan cheese

Wine: a light, dry red (Gutturnio)

Risotto with beans
Panissa

This is a hearty winter dish from the area around Vercelli, in the north. Traditionally, it is served with a generous sprinkling of pepper rather than with the usual grated cheese. If you can't get cotenna, just leave it out. The flavor will be a little different, but still very good.

Serves: 4; Preparation: 30 minutes; Cooking: 1¼ hours; Level of difficulty: Medium

Put the beans in a pot with the stock and cotenna. Cover and simmer over low heat for 50 minutes. § Take out the cotenna, dice, and return to the pot. § Place the pancetta in a heavy-bottomed saucepan over low heat. When the fat has melted a little, add the onion and sauté for 5 minutes, stirring frequently. § Pour in the rice and stir for 2 minutes. § Add the wine, half at a time. § When it has been absorbed, begin adding, one ladle at a time, the hot beans and their stock. § Stir continuously until the rice is cooked. It will take about 15–18 minutes. § Season with salt and pepper. The risotto should be creamy but not too liquid. § Serve hot.

> VARIATION
> – If using dry beans, soak in cold water for 10–12 hours, then cook slowly with the cotenna for a couple of hours. Continue as above.

■ INGREDIENTS

- 8 oz (250 g) fresh cranberry or red kidney beans, shelled
- 2 oz (60 g) fresh cotenna, scraped
- 4 cups (1 liter) *Vegetable stock* (see recipe p. 48)
- 3 oz (90 g) lean pancetta, finely chopped
- ½ onion, finely chopped
- 3 oz (90 g) lard, chopped
- 2 cups (450 g) arborio rice
- ¾ cup (200 ml) robust red wine
- salt and freshly ground white or black pepper

Wine: a dry red (Grignolino)

Right: *Panissa*

Black risotto with ink squid
Risotto nero con le seppie

For first-timers, the color of this extraordinary risotto may be a little surprising. If possible, get your fish vendor to clean the ink squid, making sure the internal ink sacs are set aside without being broken.

Serves: 4; Preparation: 25 minutes; Cooking: about 1¼ hours; Level of difficulty: Medium

To clean the ink squid, separate the tentacles and head from the body by grasping the head and pulling it apart from the body. The insides and two sacs will come out attached to the head. One of the sacs has the ink and the other is dark yellow. Some people also use the latter but the flavor is rather strong and it is better to discard it with the insides. Remove the ink sacs from the head and set them aside in a cup with 2–3 spoonfuls of cold water. Discard the eyes and the beaks at the base of the tentacles. Open the body at the side with kitchen scissors and extract the bone. Rinse the body and head well and cut into 1¼-in (3-cm) strips. § In a large, heavy-bottomed saucepan, heat the oil and add the onion, parsley, and ink squid. § Cover and cook for 15 minutes over low heat, stirring once or twice. § Add the tomato paste, wine, and ½ cup (125 ml) hot water, and continue cooking, covered and over low heat, for 20–40 minutes, stirring occasionally. Test the ink squid with a fork after 20 minutes; if they seem fairly tender, go on to the next stage (if cooked too long, ink squid become hard and rubbery). § In the meantime cut the ink sacs with scissors and collect the ink in a bowl, diluting with 2 cups (500 ml) of cold water. Throw the empty sacs away. § When the ink squid are tender, pour the black liquid into the saucepan, raise the heat slightly, and bring to a boil. § Cook for 5 minutes then add the rice. § Continue cooking, stirring frequently, and adding more boiling water if the mixture becomes too dry. § The rice will take about 15–18 minutes to cook. The risotto should be very creamy. § Season with salt and pepper and serve hot.

■ INGREDIENTS

- 2 fresh ink squid, about 1½ lb (750 g)
- ⅓ cup (90 ml) extra-virgin olive oil
- 1 small onion, finely chopped
- 1 clove garlic, finely chopped
- 1 tablespoon finely chopped parsley
- 1 tablespoon tomato paste
- ½ cup (125 ml) dry white wine
- 2 cups (450 g) arborio rice
- salt and freshly ground white pepper

Wine: a dry white (Locorotondo)

Right:
Risotto nero con le seppie

Milanese-style risotto with chicken liver sauce
Risotto alla milanese con salsa di fegatini

■ INGREDIENTS

- 1 quantity *Milanese-style risotto* (see recipe p. 306)
- 6 chicken livers
- 2 tablespoons butter
- ½ cup (125 ml) dry white wine
- 1 grated lemon rind
- salt and freshly ground black pepper
- 1 tablespoon finely chopped parsley

Wine: a dry red (Nebiolo)

Serves: 4; Preparation: 35 minutes; Cooking: 30 minutes; Level of difficulty: Medium

Prepare the *Milanese-style risotto*. § Wash the chicken livers thoroughly under cold running water. § Chop the livers coarsely and sauté in the butter for about 5 minutes over medium heat. § Add the wine and, when it evaporates, the lemon rind. Season with salt and pepper. § Place the risotto in a heated serving dish and spoon the liver sauce over the top. § Sprinkle with the parsley and serve.

INGREDIENTS

- 3 tablespoons butter
- ½ onion, finely chopped
- 1 celery stalk, chopped
- 1 leek, (white part only), sliced
- 8 oz (250 g) spinach, cooked, squeezed dry and finely chopped
- 2 cups (450 g) arborio rice
- 6 cups (1.5 liters) *Beef or Vegetable stock* (see recipes pp. 48, 50)
- salt and freshly ground white pepper
- dash of nutmeg (optional)
- 4 tablespoons freshly grated Parmesan cheese

Wine: a dry white (Valcalepio Bianco)

Spinach risotto
Risotto con spinaci

Serves: 4; Preparation: 20 minutes; Cooking: 25 minutes; Level of difficulty: Medium

Melt 2 tablespoons of butter in a large, heavy-bottomed saucepan, add the onion, celery, and leek and sauté for 3–4 minutes over low heat. § Add the spinach, stir well and sauté for 2 minutes. § Add the rice and after 1 minute begin adding the boiling stock, a little at a time, until the rice is cooked. It will take about 15–18 minutes. § Season with salt, pepper, and nutmeg (if liked). § Add the remaining butter and the Parmesan, mix carefully, and serve.

INGREDIENTS

- 10 oz (300 g) fresh cranberry or red kidney beans, shelled
- 1 small onion
- 4 sage leaves, or ½ bay leaf
- 4 oz (125 g) green beans
- 2 cups (450 g) short-grain rice
- 4 tablespoons extra-virgin olive oil
- salt and freshly ground black pepper

Wine: a dry white (Cortese di Gavi)

Rice and bean salad
Insalata di riso e fagioli

Serves: 4; Preparation: 10 minutes; Cooking: 40-50 minutes; Level of difficulty: Simple

Place the beans in a pot with the onion and sage (or bay leaf), and add enough cold water to cover them by about 2 in (5 cm). § Cover and cook over medium-low heat for about 40 minutes. Taste one to see if they are tender. § Season with salt just before removing from heat (if the salt is added earlier the skin of the beans will become tough). § Clean and rinse the green beans and cut each one in half. § About 20–25 minutes before the cranberry or kidney beans are ready, bring a saucepan containing 2 quarts (2 liters) of salted water to a boil and add the rice and green beans. Cook over medium heat, stirring occasionally. § Drain the rice and green beans and transfer to a salad bowl. § Drain the cranberry or kidney beans. Discard the onion and sage (or bay leaf), and add the beans to the rice, stirring rapidly. § Season with the oil and pepper. § This salad can be served hot or warm.

Left: *Risotto con spinaci*

Risotto with pumpkin
Risotto con zucca

*This exquisite dish of Venetian origin has almost been forgotten.
It is so delicious that it really deserves a revival.*

Serves: 4; Preparation: 15 minutes; Cooking: 30 minutes; Level of difficulty: Medium

Put the pumpkin in a large, heavy-bottomed saucepan with the garlic, oil, and half the butter. Sauté, stirring, over medium heat for 8–10 minutes. § Add the rice and cook for 2 minutes, stirring continuously. § Add the boiling stock gradually, stirring frequently. § The pumpkin will start to disintegrate, as it should. § The rice will cook in about 15–18 minutes. It should be quite creamy when ready. § Stir in the remaining butter, the parsley, Parmesan, salt, and pepper, and serve immediately. § Pass extra grated Parmesan separately.

■ INGREDIENTS

- 10 oz (300 g) pumpkin, cleaned and diced
- 1 large clove garlic, finely chopped
- 3 tablespoons extra-virgin olive oil
- 3 tablespoons butter
- 2 cups (450 g) arborio rice
- 4 cups (1 liter) *Beef stock* (see recipe p. 48)
- 1 tablespoon finely chopped parsley
- 4 tablespoons freshly grated Parmesan cheese
- salt and freshly ground white pepper

Wine: a light, dry red (Bardolino)

Rice in anchovy sauce
Riso in salsa di acciughe

*This dish combines the simple, summer flavors of the Italian Riviera with the
salty taste of the open sea. Use salt-preserved anchovies, instead of those kept
under oil, for a stronger flavor.*

Serves: 4; Preparation: 5-7 minutes; Cooking: 15 minutes; Level of difficulty: Simple

Bring 2 quarts (2 liters) of salted water to a boil. Add the rice, stir once or twice, and allow 13–15 minutes cooking time from when the water comes to a boil again. § Rinse the capers and chop finely with the anchovies. § Heat the oil in a small skillet (frying pan), add the capers and anchovies and cook over low heat for 2–3 minutes. § Add the lemon juice just before removing from heat. § Drain the rice well and transfer to a serving dish or individual plates. Pour the sauce over the top. § Garnish with the lemon slices and serve hot.

■ INGREDIENTS

- 2 cups (450 g) short-grain rice
- 8 anchovy fillets
- 1 tablespoon capers
- 4 tablespoons extra-virgin olive oil
- ½ tablespoon lemon juice
- thin slices of lemon to garnish

Wine: a dry white (Cinqueterre)

Right:
Risotto con zucca

Polenta

From its humble origins among the poorer peasants of northern Italy, polenta has gained an international reputation and a host of gourmet interpretations.

Polenta with traditional toppings
Polenta condita all'antica

These simple recipes give us a taste of how polenta was once served in peasant homes. A rather soft polenta is needed, so use slightly less yellow cornmeal than in the basic recipe.

■ INGREDIENTS

• 1 quantity *Basic polenta* (see recipe p. 52)
• 4 cups (1 liter) cold milk
• 4 tablespoons light (single) cream

Wine: a light, dry red (Lambrusco di Sorbara)

Polenta and milk
Polenta e latte

Serves: 4; Preparation: 5 minutes; Cooking: 50-60 minutes; Level of difficulty: Simple

Prepare the polenta. § Pour the milk and cream into a pitcher. § Pour the piping hot polenta into soup plates or, in the classic version, small bowls. § Serve the polenta and creamy milk separately, so that everyone can help themselves to as much as they like.

■ INGREDIENTS

• 1 quantity *Basic polenta* (see recipe p. 52)
• ⅓ cup (90 g) butter
• 4 tablespoons freshly grated Parmesan cheese

Wine: a dry red (Chianti Classico - Geografico)

Polenta with butter and cheese
Polenta con burro e formaggio

Serves: 4; Preparation: 5 minutes; Cooking: 50-60 minutes; Level of difficulty: Simple

Prepare the polenta. § Chop the butter in small pieces, dust with the Parmesan and place half in individual soup plates. § Pour the polenta into the plates, and sprinkle with the remaining butter and Parmesan. § This recipe is also good with the same quantity of Gorgonzola cheese instead of Parmesan.

■ INGREDIENTS

• 1 quantity *Basic polenta* (see recipe p. 52)
• 4 oz (125 g) lard
• 2 cloves garlic finely chopped
• 2 tablespoons finely chopped parsley

Wine: a dry, red (Grignolino)

Polenta and lard
Polenta e lardo

Serves: 4; Preparation: 5 minutes; Cooking: 50-60 minutes; Level of difficulty: Simple

Prepare the polenta. § Chop the lard and mash it with the garlic and parsley by holding the blade of a knife flat to achieve a smooth, almost creamy, mixture. § Place half the mixture in the bottom of individual soup plates. § Pour the hot polenta into the plates and cover with the remaining mixture. § Serve immediately.

Left: *Polenta e lardo*

Oropa-style polenta
Polenta d'Oropa

*Oropa is a tiny locality in Piedmont, in northern Italy. Apart from this dish,
it is also famous for its beautiful religious sanctuary.*

Serves: 4; Preparation: 10 minutes; Cooking: 50 minutes; Level of difficulty: Medium

Use the first four ingredients to prepare the polenta as explained on page 52.
These quantities will make a rather soft polenta. § After the polenta has been
cooking for about 30 minutes, add the Toma and continue cooking for
another 15 minutes, stirring energetically. § A few minutes before the polenta
is cooked, slowly melt the butter in a small saucepan until it starts to bubble.
§ Pour the polenta into a large serving dish, dust with pepper and sprinkle
with the Parmesan. Drizzle the hot butter over the top and serve.

VARIATION
– Toma cheese can be hard to find outside of northern Piedmont.
Use the same quantity of Fontina or Fontal in its place.

■ INGREDIENTS

- 4 cups (1 liter) boiling water
- 4 cups (1 liter) hot milk
- 1 tablespoon coarse sea salt
- 2¾ cups (300 g) coarse-grain cornmeal
- 14 oz (450 g) Toma cheese, cut in slivers
- ⅓ cup (90 g) butter
- freshly ground black pepper
- 4 tablespoons freshly grated Parmesan cheese

*Wine: a dry red
(Gamay della Valle d'Aosta)*

Potato polenta
Polenta di patate

*This delicious polenta comes from Trento in the northeast. It should be served with pickles,
particularly sweet-sour gherkins. For a complete meal, serve with grilled or baked pork ribs.*

Serves: 4; Preparation: 30 minutes; Cooking: 30-35 minutes; Level of difficulty: Medium

Mash the potatoes and transfer to the pot where the polenta is to be
cooked. § Add the cornmeal and buckwheat flour, mix well, and
continue to mix while adding the water. § Cook over medium-high heat,
stirring frequently and energetically. § Melt the butter and oil over
medium heat in a small saucepan. Add the onion and sauté until pale
gold. § Add the butter and oil to the polenta which will have been
cooking for about 10 minutes by this time. Stir continuously. § After 20
more minutes, add a little salt, a generous dash or two of pepper, and the
cheese, and continue stirring for 10 minutes. § Serve immediately. If there
is any left over, cut in slices when cold and serve broiled (grilled) or fried.

VARIATIONS
– Fine-grain yellow cornmeal can also be used.
– If you don't have buckwheat flour use a double quantity of cornmeal.

■ INGREDIENTS

- 2½ lb (1.2 kg) potatoes, boiled and peeled, still hot
- ½ cup (60 g) coarse-grain cornmeal
- ½ cup (60 g) buckwheat flour
- 1 cup (250 ml) boiling water
- 3 tablespoons butter
- 3 tablespoons extra-virgin olive oil
- 2 onions, thinly sliced
- salt and freshly ground black pepper
- 4 oz (125 g) fresh Asiago cheese, in slivers

*Wine: a hearty, dry red
(Breganze Rosso)*

Right:
Polenta d'Oropa

Polenta with taleggio cheese
Polenta al taleggio

Taleggio cheese comes from Lombardy. It should be creamy, fragrant, and well ripened.
If you can't get Taleggio, use the same quantity of Fontina cheese in its place.

Serves: 4; Preparation: 10 minutes; Cooking: 1 hour; Level of difficulty: Simple

Use the first four ingredients to prepare the polenta as explained on page 52. These quantities will make a rather soft polenta which will cook in about 45 minutes. § Lightly butter an ovenproof baking dish about 10 in (25 cm) in diameter and about 3 in (8 cm) deep. § When the polenta is ready, pour one-third into the dish, sprinkle with one-third of the Parmesan, one-third of the Taleggio, and one-third of the remaining butter. Repeat this procedure twice. § Bake in a preheated oven at 400°F/200°C/gas 6 for about 15 minutes, or until the surface turns golden brown. § Serve hot.

■ INGREDIENTS

- 6 cups (1.5 liters) boiling water
- 3 cups (750 ml) milk
- 1 tablespoon coarse sea salt
- 2¾ cups (300 g) coarse-grain cornmeal
- 2 tablespoons butter
- ½ cup (60 g) Parmesan cheese, flaked
- 10 oz (300 g) ripe Taleggio cheese, without its crust and cut in slices

Wine: a dry red
(Valcalepio Rosso)

Polenta with luganega sausage
Polenta con la luganega

Luganega is a type of fresh pork sausage found throughout northern Italy. If you can't find it,
replace it with another type of fresh Italian pork sausage and modify cooking method.

Serves: 4; Preparation: 5 minutes; Cooking: 50 minutes; Level of difficulty: Medium

Prepare the polenta. § About 20 minutes before the polenta is cooked, pierce holes about 1 in (2.5 cm) apart in the casing of the luganega with a toothpick, so that the fat will drain out during cooking and the heat will penetrate to the inside. Don't use a fork as the holes will be too close together and the casing will probably break. § Roll the luganega up in a flat spiral, piercing it horizontally with two long thin wooden or metal skewers, placed crosswise, so it will keep its shape. § Melt the butter in a skillet (frying pan). Add the oil and rosemary, and then carefully add the sausage. Brown for 3–4 minutes over medium heat, then turn so it will brown on the other side. § Increase the heat and pour the wine into the pan; as soon as it is hot, lower the heat and cover the pan. § Sauté for about 10 minutes, turning the luganega again after the first 5 minutes. § When it is cooked, remove the skewers and cut the sausage into pieces about 2 in (5 cm) long. § Transfer the polenta to a wide serving dish and arrange the sausage pieces on top. § Discard the rosemary from the pan and drizzle the juices over the polenta. § Serve hot.

■ INGREDIENTS

- 1 quantity *Basic polenta* (see recipe p. 52)
- 1 lb (500 g) luganega (or very fresh Italian pork sausage)
- 2 tablespoons butter
- 1 tablespoon extra-virgin olive oil
- 1 small sprig rosemary
- ⅔ cup (150 ml) dry white or red wine

Wine: a dry red
(Raboso del Piave)

Right:
Polenta con la luganega

Maremma-style polenta
Polenta alla maremmana

■ INGREDIENTS

- 2 quarts (2 liters) boiling water
- 1 tablespoon coarse sea salt
- 2¾ cups (300 g) coarse-grain cornmeal
- 1 lb (500 g) ripe tomatoes
- ½ onion, finely chopped
- 3 tablespoons extra-virgin olive oil
- ½ clove garlic, finely chopped
- 10 fresh basil leaves, torn
- 5 oz (150 g) lean pancetta, diced
- ¾ cup (90 g) freshly grated Pecorino cheese
- 3 tablespoons butter

Wine: a dry red
(Montescudaio Rosso)

Serves: 4; Preparation: 15 minutes; Cooking: 50 minutes; Level of difficulty: Simple

Use the first three ingredients to prepare the polenta as explained on page 52. These quantities will make a very soft polenta. § Meanwhile, prepare the sauce. To peel the tomatoes, plunge them into a pot of boiling water for 30 seconds and then into cold. Slip off the skins, cut in half, and squeeze to remove some of the seeds. Chop coarsely. § In a saucepan, over low heat, sauté the onion in the oil until soft. Add the garlic, tomatoes, and basil. § Turn up the heat a little and simmer the sauce for 15–20 minutes. § When the polenta is half cooked, add the pancetta, cheese, and pieces of butter; stir frequently. § When the polenta is ready, transfer to individual plates and spoon the tomato sauce over the top. § Serve hot.

Tuscan-Emilian-style polenta
Polenta alla tosco-emiliana

■ INGREDIENTS

- 2 quarts (2 liters) boiling water
- 1 tablespoon coarse sea salt
- 2¾ cups (300 g) coarse-grain cornmeal
- 1 tablespoon extra-virgin olive oil
- 10 oz (300 g) fresh Italian pork sausage, skinned and crumbled
- 3 oz (90 g) salt pork, finely chopped
- ½ tablespoon rosemary leaves, finely chopped
- 1 clove garlic, finely chopped
- 4 tablespoons freshly grated Parmesan cheese

Wine: a dry red
(Merlot Colli Bolognesi)

A hearty, winter dish. Followed by a salad and fruit, it is a complete meal.

Serves: 4; Preparation: 15 minutes; Cooking: 1 hour, 10 minutes; Level of difficulty: Medium

Use the first three ingredients to prepare the polenta as explained on page 52. These quantities will make a very soft polenta which will cook in about 45 minutes. § Oil an ovenproof baking dish large enough to contain the polenta in a 1-in (2.5-cm) layer. § Using a fork, carefully mix the sausage, salt pork, rosemary, and garlic together in a bowl. § When the polenta is cooked, pour it into the baking dish and smooth it out with a spatula. § Cover with the sausage mixture, gently pushing it into the polenta with your fingertips. § Bake in preheated oven at 400°F/200°C/gas 6 for 15 minutes. § Dust with the Parmesan just before serving.

VARIATION
– If salt pork is not liked, omit and add extra sausage.

Left: *Polenta alla Tosco-Emiliana*

Baked polenta, Milanese-style
Polenta pasticciata alla milanese

Serves: 4; Preparation: 1 hour; Cooking: 25-30 minutes; Level of difficulty: Medium

For the mushroom sauce: soak the mushrooms in 1 cup (250 ml) of tepid water for 15 minutes. Drain (reserving the liquid), squeeze out excess moisture, and chop coarsely. § Strain the water in which the mushrooms were soaked and set aside. § In a skillet (frying pan) melt 2 tablespoons of butter and sauté the onion for a few minutes over low heat; add the sausage, and the mushrooms and their water. § Cover and cook over medium heat for 30 minutes, stirring occasionally. Season with salt and pepper. (This sauce can be prepared ahead of time). § Prepare the béchamel sauce. § Butter an ovenproof baking dish about 8 in (20 cm) in diameter and 3 in (8 cm) deep. Cover the bottom with ¼-in (6-mm) thick slices of polenta. § Pour on one-third of the mushroom sauce, dust with one-third of the Parmesan, arrange one-third of the Gruyère on top and cover with one-third of the béchamel sauce. Repeat this procedure twice. § Bake in a preheated oven at 400°F/200°C/gas 6 for 25–30 minutes, or until the top is golden brown. § Serve hot.

■ INGREDIENTS

SAUCE:
- 1 oz (30 g) dried porcini mushrooms
- 3 tablespoons butter
- 1 small onion, finely chopped
- 4 oz (125 g) Italian pork sausage, skinned and crumbled
- salt and freshly ground black pepper

- 1 quantity *Béchamel sauce* (see recipe p. 38)
- 1 lb (500 g) cold *Basic polenta* (see recipe p. 52)
- ¾ cup (90 g) freshly grated Parmesan cheese
- 3½ oz (100 g) Gruyère cheese, cut in slivers

Wine: a dry red (Bonarda Oltrepò Pavese)

Baked polenta with cheese
Polenta pasticciata al formaggio

*Always make a generous quantity of polenta,
there are so many delicious ways of using up any that is leftover.*

Serves: 4; Preparation: 10 minutes; Cooking: 25-30 minutes; Level of difficulty: Simple

Cut the polenta into ¼-in (6-mm) thick slices, about 1¼ in (3 cm) long. § Butter an ovenproof baking dish deep enough for three layers of polenta. § Cover the bottom with slices of polenta, sprinkle with one-third of the Parmesan, one-third of the Gruyère, and dot with one-third of the butter. § Repeat this procedure twice. § Bake in a preheated oven at 400°F/200°C/gas 6 for 25–30 minutes, or until the top is golden brown. § Serve hot.

■ INGREDIENTS

- 1 lb (500 g) cold *Basic polenta* (see recipe p. 52)
- ⅓ cup (90 g) butter
- ⅓ cup (45 g) freshly grated Parmesan cheese
- 4 oz (125 g) Gruyère cheese, cut in slivers

Wine: a dry red (Donnaz)

Right:
Polenta pasticciata alla milanese

Baked polenta with tomato sauce
Polenta pasticciata con il pomodoro

Serves: 4; Preparation: 20 minutes; Cooking: 25-30 minutes; Level of difficulty: Simple

Prepare the tomato sauce. § Oil an ovenproof baking dish about 8 in (20 cm) in diameter and about 3 in (8 cm) deep. § Cover the bottom with ¼-in (6-mm) thick, short slices of the cold polenta, and scatter one-third of the diced Provolone evenly on top. § Dust with pepper and drizzle with one-third of the tomato sauce. § Repeat this procedure twice, finishing up with a layer of sauce. § Bake in a preheated oven at 400°F/200°C/gas 6 for 25–30 minutes. § Serve piping hot straight from the oven.

VARIATIONS
– Replace the tomato sauce with 1 quantity of either of the meat sauces on p. 30.

■ INGREDIENTS

• 1 quantity *Simple tomato sauce* (see recipe p. 28)
• 1 tablespoon extra-virgin olive oil
• 1 lb (500 g) cold *Basic polenta* (see recipe p. 52)
• 10 oz (300 g) mild Provolone cheese, diced
• freshly ground black pepper (optional)

Wine: a light, dry red (San Colombano)

Polenta with pizza sauce
Polenta alla pizzaiola

Children particularly love this delicious dish. It is also convenient because it can be prepared a few hours ahead, kept at room temperature, and then popped into the oven 20 minutes before serving.

Serves: 4; Preparation: 10 minutes; Cooking: 1¼ hours; Level of difficulty: Medium

Use the first three ingredients to prepare the polenta as explained on page 52. Cook for 50 minutes; it should be fairly solid but not too hard. § In the meantime prepare the sauce: cook the tomatoes in a small saucepan for 5 minutes over medium heat. § Add the garlic, oregano, and a little salt. Cover and cook over low heat for 15 minutes, stirring occasionally. § When the sauce is cooked, add 2 tablespoons of the oil. This sauce can also be prepared ahead of time. § Use 2 tablespoons of oil to grease an ovenproof

■ INGREDIENTS

• 2 quarts (2 liters) boiling water
• 1 tablespoon coarse sea salt
• 2¾ cups (350 g) coarse-grain cornmeal
• 4 tablespoons extra-virgin olive oil
• 8 oz (250 g) Scamorza cheese, diced
• 8 anchovy fillets, preserved in oil, crumbled

Right:
Polenta pasticciata con il pomodoro

SAUCE:

- 14 oz (450 g) tomatoes, canned, partially drained, and coarsely chopped
- 1 small clove garlic, finely chopped
- 1 teaspoon oregano
- dash of salt
- 2 tablespoons extra-virgin olive oil

Wine: a dry white (Greco di Tufo)

baking dish large enough for a layer of polenta about 1¼ in (3 cm) thick. § When the polenta is ready, transfer it to the dish and level with a spatula. § Cover the surface with the sauce. Distribute the Scamorza evenly on top, add the anchovies, and drizzle with the remaining oil. § Cook in a preheated oven at 400°F/200°C/gas 6 for about 15 minutes. § If the dish was prepared ahead of time and the polenta is no longer hot, preheat the oven to 350°F/180°C/gas 4 and cook at that temperature for the first 10–15 minutes, then increase to 400°F/200°C/gas 6 for the last 5–10 minutes, otherwise a tough, unpleasant crust will form on the Scamorza.

Baked polenta in cheese sauce
Polenta pasticciata in salsa di formaggio

Serves: 4; Preparation: 20 minutes; Cooking: 30 minutes; Level of difficulty: Simple

Melt the butter in a saucepan. When it stops foaming, add the flour and cook over low heat for a couple of minutes, stirring well. § Begin to add the milk, a little at a time, stirring continuously. The sauce should be a smooth and fluid béchamel. Season with a little nutmeg. § Turn up the heat and add the cheeses, a handful at a time. Keep stirring as they melt so the sauce will stay smooth. § Butter an ovenproof baking dish large enough to contain the polenta and sauce in a layer about 2 in (5 cm) thick. § Cut the polenta into ¾-in (2-cm) dice. § Cover the bottom of the dish with half the polenta and pour half the sauce over the top. Arrange the remaining polenta on top and cover with the remaining sauce. § Bake in a preheated oven at 400°F/200°C/gas 6 for 25–30 minutes, or until the top has a golden crust.

■ INGREDIENTS

SAUCE:
- 2 tablespoons butter
- 1 tablespoon all-purpose (plain) flour
- 1 cup (250 ml) milk
- dash of nutmeg
- 5 oz (150 ml) Gorgonzola cheese, cut in pieces
- 5 oz (150 g) Emmenthal, or Gruyère cheese, thinly sliced
- 4 tablespoons freshly grated Parmesan cheese

BASE:
- 1 tablespoon butter
- 1 lb (500 g) cold *Basic polenta* (see recipe p. 52)

Wine: a dry red (Barbacarlo Oltrepò Pavese)

Polenta with mushroom sauce
Polenta con i funghi

For a really tasty sauce, use highly prized wild mushrooms, such as porcini, shiitake, or chanterelle. If using cultivated varieties, combine with 1 oz (30 g) of dried porcini mushrooms. Soak the dried porcini in a bowl of warm water for 15 minutes, chop coarsely and mix with the fresh mushrooms. The distinctive musky flavor of the dried porcini will add that extra something to the sauce.

Serves: 4; Preparation: 20 minutes; Cooking: 50 minutes; Level of difficulty: Medium

Prepare the polenta. § To prepare the sauce: trim the stems of the mushrooms, rinse under cold running water and pat dry with paper towels. Slice thinly. § Heat the oil in a skillet (frying pan) over medium heat, add the garlic and sauté for 2–3 minutes, stirring often so that they don't burn. Discard. § Add the parsley (or calamint) and mushrooms and cook over high heat for 2–3 minutes. § Add the tomatoes and continue cooking over medium heat for 15–20 minutes, stirring frequently. § Transfer the polenta to a serving dish and pour the mushroom sauce over the top. § Serve hot.

■ INGREDIENTS

- 1 quantity *Basic polenta* (see recipe p. 52)

SAUCE:
- 14 oz (450 g) mushrooms
- 4 tablespoons extra-virgin olive oil
- 2 cloves garlic
- 1 tablespoon parsley or calamint, finely chopped
- 14 oz (450 g) tomatoes, fresh or canned, peeled and chopped
- salt and freshly ground white pepper

Wine: a light, dry red (Bardolino)

Right: Polenta con i funghi

Fried polenta with cheese topping
Crostoni di polenta al formaggio

Use your imagination in making these slices of fried polenta, depending on what kinds of cheese are available and how much you want to use. Some good cheeses are: Taleggio, Gorgonzola, Fontina, Asiago, Provolone, and Scamorza (smoked or plain).

Serves: 4; Preparation: 10 minutes; Cooking: 8 minutes; Level of difficulty: Simple

To prepare the cheese(s), remove the rind and chop into pieces if very soft, or in thin slices if harder. § Pour the oil into a skillet (frying pan) and when it is hot, but not smoking, add the slices of polenta together with the sage or rosemary. § Fry over high heat for about 3 minutes. Turn the slices over with a spatula and cover with the cheese, leaving a small border around the edges. § Cover the skillet (frying pan) and cook for another 3 minutes so that the slices of polenta get crisp on the underside and the cheese melts. § Serve immediately, with a sprinkling of pepper if liked.

■ INGREDIENTS

- choice of cheese (see introduction to recipe for some ideas)
- 1 quantity cold *Basic polenta* (see recipe p. 52), cut in slices ¾ in (2 cm) thick and about 4 in (10 cm) long
- ⅓ cup (90 ml) extra-virgin olive oil
- 4 sage leaves or 1 sprig rosemary
- freshly ground black pepper (optional)

Wine: a dry red (Franciacorta Rosso)

Polenta and beans
Polenta e fagioli

This recipe comes from Veneto, the region around Venice, and ideally the marbled pink and white Lamon beans (a type of red kidney bean) should be used, but they are not easy to find. Use cranberry or red kidney beans in their place. If using dried beans, soak for 12 hours first and extend the cooking time to 1 hour.

Serves: 4; Preparation: 5 minutes; Cooking: 1¼ hours; Level of difficulty: Medium

Put the beans in a pot that can hold about 4 quarts (4 liters). Add the onion, pancetta, and bay leaf with enough cold water to cover the beans by at least 2 in (5 cm). § Cover and cook over low heat for about 30 minutes. § Sift the cornmeal into the pot very slowly, stirring with a whisk so that no lumps form. When all the cornmeal has been added, continue stirring with a long wooden spoon. § It will take about 40 minutes for the polenta to cook. It should be very soft; if it is too hard, add a little more boiling water. § Season with salt when almost cooked. § Shortly before the polenta is cooked, melt the butter in a small saucepan to a golden color. § Serve the polenta in individual plates, sprinkle with Parmesan and drizzle with the hot butter.

■ INGREDIENTS

- 7 oz (200 g) fresh Lamon, cranberry, or red kidney beans, shelled
- ½ small onion, finely chopped
- 1 oz (30 g) pancetta, finely chopped
- 1 bay leaf
- 2¾ cups (300 g) fine-grain cornmeal
- dash of salt
- ¼ cup (60 g) butter
- ½ cup (60 g) freshly grated Parmesan cheese

Wine: a dry, fragrant red (Gutturnio)

Right:
Crostoni di polenta al formaggio

Polenta with leek sauce
Polenta con salsa di porri

■ INGREDIENTS

• 1 quantity *Basic polenta*
  (see recipe p. 52)
• 12 oz (350 g) leeks, (white
  part only)
• 3 tablespoons butter
• 1¼ cups (300 ml) light
  (single) cream
• 4 tablespoons milk
• salt and freshly ground
  white pepper

Wine: a dry, lightly sparkling red
(Barbera del Monferrato Vivace)

Serves: 4; Preparation: 15 minutes; Cooking: 50 minutes; Level of difficulty: Simple

Prepare the polenta. § Cut the leeks into ⅛ in (3 mm) thick slices. § Melt the butter in a heavy-bottomed saucepan over medium heat, add the leeks, cover and cook for 5 minutes, or until the leeks have wilted. § Season with salt and pepper. Add the cream and milk and cook for 20–25 minutes. § When the polenta is done (it should be very thick, almost stiff), turn it out onto a heated serving platter. § Serve hot with the leek sauce handed round separately in another heated serving dish.

Pizza

Invented in the backstreets of Naples, the pizza has conquered the world. These are the classic recipes of the truly Italian pizza.

Preparing the yeast and dough

The dough for pizza, calzoni, bread, focacce, and filled breads can be prepared in exactly the same way. The ingredients in the recipes may vary slightly; milk may be used instead of water, for example. Some recipes include additional ingredients, such as olive oil or lard. These should be added as indicated in the recipe while following the method given here.

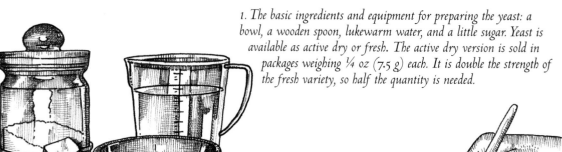

1. The basic ingredients and equipment for preparing the yeast: a bowl, a wooden spoon, lukewarm water, and a little sugar. Yeast is available as active dry or fresh. The active dry version is sold in packages weighing ¼ oz (7.5 g) each. It is double the strength of the fresh variety, so half the quantity is needed.

1.

1. PREPARING THE YEAST
Place the yeast in a small bowl. Add the sugar and half the lukewarm water and stir carefully until the yeast has dissolved. Set the bowl aside for 10–15 minutes. A foam will form on the surface. Stir the yeast again before proceeding to make the dough.

1.

2. The basic ingredients and equipment for mixing the dough: a large bowl, the flour, salt, yeast mixture, a wooden spoon, and the remaining water.

2. MIXING THE DOUGH
Place the flour in a large bowl and sprinkle with the salt. Make a hollow in the flour and pour in the yeast mixture, the remaining water, and any other ingredients listed in the recipe. Use a wooden spoon to stir the mixture. Stir well until the flour has almost all been absorbed.

2.

HELPFUL HINT
Don't add all the flour at once. Reserve a little to add at the end, and mix it in only if necessary. Some flours absorb a lot of water, others require less.

2.

3. PREPARING THE WORK SURFACE AND TRANSFERRING THE DOUGH
Sprinkle a work surface, preferably made of wood, with a little flour.
Note that the flour used to prepare the work surface is not included
in the quantities given for the doughs. You will need about ½ cup
(2 oz/60 g) extra for this. Use a spatula (or your hands) to transfer
the dough to the work surface. Curl your fingers around the dough
and press it together to form a compact ball.

4.

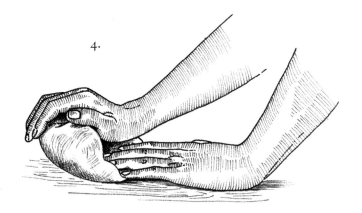

HELPFUL HINT
Try not to mix in a lot of extra flour as
you knead. Too much flour absorbed
during kneading will spoil the texture of
the bread or pizza.

4. – 5. KNEADING THE DOUGH
Press the dough down to spread it a little. Take the far end of the
dough, fold it a short distance toward you, then
push it away again with the heel of your palm.
Flexing your wrist, fold it toward you again, give
it a quarter turn, then push it away. Repeat these
motions gently, and with the lightest possible touch,
for about 7–8 minutes. When the dough is firm and
no longer sticks to your hands or the work surface,
lift it up and bang it down hard against the work
surface a couple of times. This will develop the gluten.
When ready, the dough should be smooth and elastic. It
should show definite air bubbles beneath the surface and should
spring back if you flatten it with your palm.

5.

6.

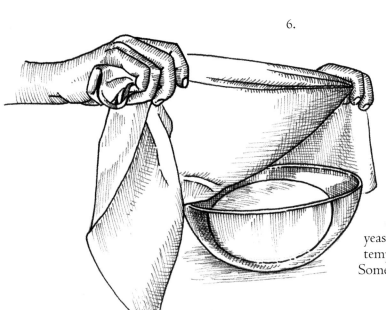

6. RISING
When the dough is fully kneaded, place it
in a large clean bowl and cover with a
cloth. Most of the breads in this book
have two rising times, while the pizzas are
left to rise just once. The dough should
double in volume during rising. To test
whether it has risen sufficiently, poke your
finger gently into the dough and see if the
impression remains; if it does, then the
dough is ready. The rising times given in
each recipe are approximate; remember that
yeast is a living ingredient and is affected by air
temperature and humidity, among other things.
Some days it will take longer to rise than others.

Making pizza and calzoni

■ INGREDIENTS

- ½ oz (15 g) fresh yeast or 1 package active dry yeast
- ⅔ cup (150 ml) lukewarm water
- 2–2½ cups (300–375 g) unbleached flour
- 1 teaspoon salt

The ingredients given here will make about 12 oz (350 g) of pizza dough. This is enough to make one round pizza, sufficient for one or two people.

Makes: 1 pizza, about 12 in (30 cm) in diameter; Preparation: 30 minutes; Rising time: about 1 hour; Cooking: 15–20 minutes; Level of difficulty: Medium

Prepare the yeast and dough as explained on pages 342–343. § When the rising time has elapsed, knead the dough for 1 minute on a lightly floured work surface. § If you are making more than one pizza, divide the dough into the number of pizzas you wish to make. Roll each piece of dough into a ball and flatten a little with your hands. § Use your hands or a rolling pin to shape the pizza. To shape by hand, push the dough outward with the palms of your hands and fingertips, opening it out into a circular shape. Press the dough out, stretching it as you go, until it is the required thickness. The thickness depends on personal preference; some people like thick, doughy pizza crusts while others like them thin and crispy. Experienced pizzamakers spread the dough by hand until it is about ½ in (1 cm) thick, then they pick it up and place it over their fists. By slowly moving their fists away from each other, they gently stretch the dough. They also bounce it in the air and twirl it on their fingertips. By all means, try one of these *virtuoso* performances when you feel confident enough, or simply shape with a rolling pin. § To finish, use your fingertips to make a rim around the edge of the pizza so that the topping won't drip off during cooking. § Transfer the dough to an oiled baking sheet. §

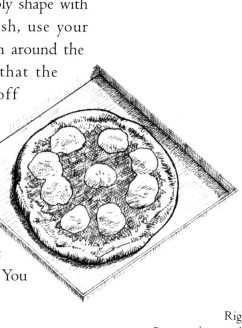

There are two schools of thought about when the topping should be added. Some say it should go on straight away and the pizza go directly into the oven; others believe that the shaped pizza dough should sit for 10 minutes. I prefer to put the topping on straight away. You may choose whichever method you prefer.

Right:

Pizza con olive, pomodoro, mozzarella e caperi

Neapolitan pizza
Pizza napoletana

Makes: 1 pizza, about 12 in (30 cm) in diameter; Preparation: 30 minutes; Rising time: about 1 hour; Cooking: 15-20 minutes; Level of difficulty: Medium

Prepare the dough as shown on pages 342–343. § When the rising time has elapsed, knead the dough for 1 minute on a lightly floured work surface. § Shape the pizza as explained on page 344 and transfer to an oiled baking sheet. § Spread the tomatoes evenly over the top, then add the Mozzarella, anchovies, and capers. Drizzle with 1 tablespoon of oil. § Bake in a preheated oven at 500°F/250°C/gas 8 for about 12 minutes. § Take the pizza out of the oven and sprinkle with the oregano. Return to the oven to finish cooking. § When cooked, drizzle with the remaining oil and serve hot.

■ INGREDIENTS

BASE
• 1 quantity pizza dough (see recipe p. 344)

TOPPING
• 8 oz (250 g) tomatoes, canned, drained and chopped
• 7 oz (200 g) Mozzarella cheese, thinly sliced
• 6 anchovy fillets,
• 1 tablespoon capers
• 3 tablespoons extra-virgin olive oil
• 1 heaped teaspoon oregano

Wine: a dry red (Rosso Vesuvio)

Pizza with tomatoes and garlic
Pizza marinara

Marinara means sailor-style. The topping is made with tomatoes, olive oil, and garlic. No cheese is added because it doesn't go well with the most readily available food at sea — fish. This is one of the most traditional pizza toppings.

Makes: 1 pizza, about 12 in (30 cm) in diameter; Preparation: 30 minutes; Rising time: about 1 hour; Cooking: 15-20 minutes; Level of difficulty: Medium

Prepare the dough as shown on pages 342–343. § To peel the tomatoes, plunge them into a pot of boiling water for 30 seconds and then into cold. Slip off the skins, cut in half, and squeeze to remove some of the seeds. Place in a colander to drain for 10 minutes. § When the rising time has elapsed, knead the dough for 1 minute on a lightly floured work surface. § Shape the pizza as explained on page 344 and transfer to an oiled baking sheet. § Spread the tomatoes and garlic evenly over the top. Sprinkle with the oregano and salt and drizzle with 1 tablespoon of oil. § Bake in a preheated oven at 500°F/250°C/gas 8 for about 12 minutes. § Take the pizza out of the oven and sprinkle with the basil leaves. Return to the oven to finish cooking. § When cooked, drizzle with the remaining oil and serve hot.

■ INGREDIENTS

BASE
• 1 quantity pizza dough (see recipe p. 344)

TOPPING
• 12 oz (350 g) ripe tomatoes
• 2 cloves garlic, thinly sliced
• 1 teaspoon oregano
• dash of salt
• 4 tablespoons extra-virgin olive oil
• 8 leaves fresh basil, torn

Wine: a dry rosé (Rosato del Salento)

Right:
Pizza napoletana

■ INGREDIENTS

BASE
- 1 quantity pizza dough (see recipe p. 344)

TOPPING
- 8 oz (250 g) tomatoes, canned, drained, and chopped
- 7 oz (200 g) Mozzarella cheese, diced
- 4 tablespoons Pecorino romano cheese, freshly grated
- 4–6 anchovy fillets, crumbled
- salt and freshly ground black pepper
- 4 tablespoons extra-virgin olive oil
- 6 leaves fresh basil, torn

Wine: a dry white (Sylvaner)

■ INGREDIENTS

BASE
- 1 quantity pizza dough (see recipe p. 344)

TOPPING
- 8 oz (250 g) tomatoes, canned, drained and chopped
- 8 oz (250 g) Mozzarella cheese, thinly sliced
- dash of salt
- 1 tablespoon Parmesan cheese, freshly grated (optional)
- 3 tablespoons extra-virgin olive oil
- 9 leaves fresh basil, torn

Wine: a dry rosé (Lacryma Christi)

Left: *Pizza Margherita*

Roman-style pizza
Pizza alla romana

Makes: 1 pizza, about 12 in (30 cm) in diameter; Preparation: 30 minutes; Rising time: about 1 hour; Cooking: 15-20 minutes; Level of difficulty: Medium

Prepare the dough as shown on pages 342–343. § When the rising time has elapsed, knead the dough for 1 minute on a lightly floured work surface. § Shape the pizza as explained on page 344 and transfer to an oiled baking sheet. § Spread the tomatoes evenly over the top and sprinkle with the Mozzarella, Pecorino romano, and anchovies. Season with salt and pepper and drizzle with 1 tablespoon of oil. § Bake in a preheated oven at 500°F/250°C/gas 8 for 15–20 minutes. § When cooked, sprinkle with the basil leaves, drizzle with the remaining oil, and serve hot.

Pizza Margherita
Pizza Margherita

According to legend, this pizza was created especially for Queen Margherita of Italy when she was staying in the royal palace of Capodimonte in Naples in 1889.

Makes: 1 pizza, about 12 in (30 cm) in diameter; Preparation: 30 minutes; Rising time: about 1 hour; Cooking: 15-20 minutes; Level of difficulty: Medium

Prepare the dough as shown on pages 342–343. § When the rising time has elapsed, knead the dough for 1 minute on a lightly floured work surface. § Shape the pizza as explained on page 344 and transfer to an oiled baking sheet. § Spread the tomatoes evenly over the top, cover with the Mozzarella and sprinkle with the salt and Parmesan, if using. Drizzle with 1 tablespoon of oil. § Bake in a preheated oven at 500°F/250°C/gas 8 for 15–20 minutes. § When cooked, sprinkle with the basil leaves, drizzle with the remaining oil, and serve hot.

VARIATION
– For a plain or White Margherita pizza, omit the tomatoes, and double the quantity of Parmesan. Add a generous grinding of black pepper just before serving.

Pizza with anchovies
Pizza alle acciughe

This delicious topping calls for fresh anchovies. If the thought of cleaning them seems daunting, ask your fish vendor to do it for you.

Makes: 1 pizza, about 12 in (30 cm) in diameter; Preparation: 30 minutes; Rising time: about 1 hour; Cooking: 12-15 minutes; Level of difficulty: Medium

Prepare the dough as shown on pages 342–343. § To clean the anchovies, remove the heads, slit the bodies open and discard the bones, then separate the two halves. If liked, leave them joined at the tail. Rinse well and pat dry with paper towels. § When the rising time has elapsed, knead the dough for 1 minute on a lightly floured work surface. § Shape the pizza as explained on page 344 and transfer to an oiled baking sheet. § Brush the dough with a little oil and arrange the anchovies on top. Sprinkle with the garlic, oregano, salt, and pepper. Drizzle with 1 tablespoon of oil. § Bake in a preheated oven at 500°F/250°C/gas 8 for 12–15 minutes. § When cooked, drizzle with the remaining oil, and serve hot.

■ INGREDIENTS

BASE
• 1 quantity pizza dough (see recipe p. 344)

TOPPING
• 12 oz (350 g) fresh anchovies
• 3 tablespoons extra-virgin olive oil
• 2 cloves garlic, thinly sliced
• 1 teaspoon oregano
• salt and freshly ground black pepper

Wine: a dry white (Pomino)

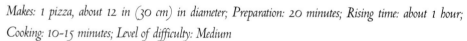

Tomato pizza
Pizza al pomodoro

Makes: 1 pizza, about 12 in (30 cm) in diameter; Preparation: 20 minutes; Rising time: about 1 hour; Cooking: 10-15 minutes; Level of difficulty: Medium

Prepare the dough as shown on pages 342–343. § To peel the tomatoes, plunge them into a pot of boiling water for 30 seconds and then into cold. Slip off the skins, cut in half and squeeze to remove some of the seeds. Chop coarsely and set aside in a colander to drain for 10 minutes. § When the rising time has elapsed, knead the dough for 1 minute on a lightly floured work surface. § Shape the pizza as explained on page 344 and transfer to an oiled baking sheet. § Spread the tomatoes evenly over the top and sprinkle with the parsley, basil, salt, and pepper and drizzle with 1 tablespoon of oil. § Bake in a preheated oven at 500°F/250°C/gas 8 for 10–15 minutes. § When cooked, drizzle with the remaining oil, and serve hot.

■ INGREDIENTS

BASE
• 1 quantity pizza dough (see recipe p. 344)

TOPPING
• 12 oz (350 g) ripe tomatoes
• 2 teaspoons parsley, finely chopped
• 6 leaves fresh basil, torn
• 3 tablespoons extra-virgin olive oil
• salt and freshly ground black pepper

Wine: a young, dry red (Vino Novello)

VARIATION
– Sprinkle the pizza with 3 tablespoons of grated Parmesan or Pecorino cheese.

Right:
Pizza alle acciughe

Pizza with garlic and oil
Pizza aglio e olio

■ INGREDIENTS

BASE

• 1 quantity pizza dough
  (see recipe p. 344)

TOPPING

• 4 cloves garlic, thinly sliced

• 1-2 teaspoons oregano

• salt and freshly ground
  black pepper

• 4 tablespoons extra-virgin
  olive oil

*Wine: a dry white
(Orvieto Classico)*

Makes: 1 pizza, about 12 in (30 cm) in diameter; Preparation: 30 minutes; Rising time: about 1 hour; Cooking: 10 minutes; Level of difficulty: Medium

Prepare the dough as shown on pages 342–343. § When the rising time has elapsed, knead the dough for 1 minute on a lightly floured work surface. § Shape the pizza as explained on page 344 and transfer to an oiled baking sheet. § Sprinkle with the garlic, oregano, salt, and pepper and drizzle with 1 tablespoon of oil. § Bake in a preheated oven at 500°F/250°C/gas 8 for 10 minutes. § When cooked, drizzle with the remaining oil, and serve hot.

Ham pizza
Pizza al prosciutto

Makes: 1 pizza, about 12 in (30 cm) in diameter; Preparation: 30 minutes; Rising time: about 1 hour; Cooking: 15-20 minutes; Level of difficulty: Medium

Prepare the dough as shown on pages 342–343. § When the rising time has elapsed, knead the dough for 1 minute on a lightly floured work surface. § Shape the pizza as explained on page 344 and transfer to an oiled baking sheet. § Brush the dough with a little oil and arrange the ham on top. Sprinkle with the Mozzarella and the pepper (or chilies). Drizzle with 1 tablespoon of oil. § Bake in a preheated oven at 500°F/250°C/gas 8 for 15–20 minutes. § When cooked, drizzle with the remaining oil, and serve hot.

VARIATION
– Add 10 pitted black olives to the topping.

■ INGREDIENTS

BASE
• 1 quantity pizza dough (see recipe p. 344)

TOPPING
• 2 tablespoons extra-virgin olive oil
• 4 oz (125 g) ham, sliced, and each slice torn in 2–3 pieces
• 6 oz (180 g) Mozzarella cheese, diced
• freshly ground black pepper or ½ teaspoon crushed chilies (optional)

Wine: a dry red (Freisa d'Asti)

Olive pizza
Pizza alle olive

This pizza depends entirely on the quality of the olives. The small, dark, slightly bitter-tasting olives of Gaeta in southern Italy are perfect. If you can't get them, be sure to use high quality black olives packed in olive oil or brine imported from one of the Mediterranean countries rather than the tasteless pitted, canned varieties.

Makes: 1 pizza, about 12 in (30 cm) in diameter; Preparation: 30 minutes; Rising time: about 1 hour; Cooking: 15-20 minutes; Level of difficulty: Medium

Prepare the dough as shown on pages 342–343. § When the rising time has elapsed, knead the dough for 1 minute on a lightly floured work surface. § Shape the pizza as explained on page 344 and transfer to an oiled baking sheet. § Spread with the tomatoes and garnish with the olives, capers, and anchovies. Drizzle with 1 tablespoon of oil. § Bake in a preheated oven at 500°F/250°C/gas 8 for 15–20 minutes. § When cooked, drizzle with the remaining oil, and serve hot.

■ INGREDIENTS

BASE
• 1 quantity pizza dough (see recipe p. 344)

TOPPING
• 8 oz (250 g) tomatoes, canned, drained, and chopped
• 8–12 Gaeta olives
• 2–3 teaspoons capers
• 4–8 anchovy fillets, crumbled
• 3 tablespoons extra-virgin olive oil

Wine: a dry rosé (Salice Salentino)

Left: *Pizza al prosciutto*

Pizza with mixed topping
Pizza capricciosa

This is a modern recipe which has enjoyed great success. Capricciosa means "whimsical" and refers to the fact that there are no precise ingredients for the topping: choose whatever you like. These are the most commonly used ingredients.

Makes: 1 pizza, about 12 in (30 cm) in diameter; Preparation: 30 minutes; Rising time: about 1 hour; Cooking: 15-20 minutes; Level of difficulty: Medium

Prepare the dough as shown on pages 342–343. § When the rising time has elapsed, knead the dough for 1 minute on a lightly floured work surface. § Shape the pizza as explained on page 344 and transfer to an oiled baking sheet. § Spread the tomatoes evenly over the top, then add the ham, anchovies, Mozzarella, artichokes, mushrooms, olives and garlic. Sprinkle with oregano and drizzle with 1 tablespoon of oil. § Bake in a preheated oven at 500°F/250°C/gas 8 for 15–20 minutes. § When cooked, drizzle with the remaining oil, and serve hot.

■ INGREDIENTS

BASE
- 1 quantity pizza dough (see recipe p. 344)

TOPPING
- 7 oz (200 g) tomatoes, canned, drained and chopped
- 2 oz (60 g) ham, cut in strips
- 6 anchovy fillets, crumbled
- 4 oz (125 g) Mozzarella cheese, diced
- 2 oz (60 g) artichokes in oil, drained, and cut in half
- 2 oz (60 g) button mushrooms, cut in half
- 2 oz (60 g) green olives, pitted, and cut in thin rings
- 2 cloves garlic, sliced
- 1 teaspoon oregano
- 3 tablespoons extra-virgin olive oil

Tuna pizza
Pizza al tonno

Makes: 1 pizza, about 12 in (30 cm) in diameter; Preparation: 35 minutes; Rising time: about 1 hour; Cooking: 15-20 minutes; Level of difficulty: Medium

Prepare the dough as shown on pages 342–343. § To peel the tomatoes, plunge them into a pot of boiling water for 30 seconds and then into cold. Slip off the skins, cut in half, and squeeze to remove some of the seeds. Set aside in a colander for 10 minutes to drain. § Transfer the tomatoes to a sauté pan with 1-2 tablespoons of oil, the garlic, and salt. Sauté for 4–5 minutes then set aside. § When the rising time has elapsed, knead the dough for 1 minute on a lightly floured work surface. § Shape the pizza as explained on page 344 and transfer to an oiled baking sheet. § Spread the tomato mixture evenly on top, then add the tuna, anchovies, olives, and capers. § Bake in a preheated oven at 500°F/250°C/gas 8 for 15–20 minutes. § When cooked, drizzle with the remaining oil, and serve hot.

■ INGREDIENTS

BASE
- 1 quantity pizza dough (see recipe p. 344)

TOPPING
- 14 oz (450 g) fresh tomatoes
- 4 tablespoons extra-virgin olive oil
- 1 clove garlic, sliced
- dash of salt
- 7 oz (200 g) tuna packed in oil, drained and in chunks
- 8 anchovy fillets, crumbled
- 3 oz (90 g) black olives
- 1 tablespoon capers

Wine: a young, dry white (Trebbiano di Romagna)

VARIATION
– If you can't get fresh tomatoes, use 12 oz (350 g) of canned tomatoes, drained, and chopped.

Right: Pizza capricciosa

INGREDIENTS

BASE
- 1 quantity pizza dough
  (see recipe p. 344)

TOPPING
- 1 tablespoon lard
- 5 oz (150 g) fresh
  Pecorino cheese, sliced
- freshly ground black or
  white pepper
- 6 leaves fresh basil, torn

Wine: a dry white (Colli Albani)

Classic plain pizza
Pizza bianca

Makes: 1 pizza, about 12 in (30 cm) in diameter; Preparation: 30 minutes; Rising time: about 1 hour; Cooking: 10-15 minutes; Level of difficulty: Medium

Prepare the dough as shown on pages 342–343. § When the rising time has elapsed, knead the dough for 1 minute on a lightly floured work surface. § Shape the pizza as explained on page 344 and transfer to an oiled baking sheet. § Spread with the lard, arrange the Pecorino on top and sprinkle with pepper. § Bake in a preheated oven at 500°F/250°C/gas 8 for 10–15 minutes. § When cooked, sprinkle with the basil and serve hot.

Mushroom pizza
Pizza ai funghi

Makes: 1 pizza, about 12 in (30 cm) in diameter; Preparation: 30 minutes; Rising time: about 1 hour; Cooking: 15-20 minutes; Level of difficulty: Medium

Prepare the dough as shown on pages 342–343. § Clean the mushrooms and rinse carefully under cold running water. Pat dry and slice thinly. § Sauté the mushrooms in 1 tablespoon of oil over very high heat for 2–3 minutes. Drain off any excess liquid and stir in the parsley and garlic. Set aside. § When the rising time has elapsed, knead the dough for 1 minute on a lightly floured work surface. § Shape the pizza as explained on page 344 and transfer to an oiled baking sheet. § Spread the mushrooms over the top and sprinkle with salt and pepper. Drizzle with the remaining oil and bake in a preheated oven at 500°F/250°C/gas 8 for 10–20 minutes. § Serve hot.

■ INGREDIENTS

BASE
- 1 quantity pizza dough (see recipe p. 344)

TOPPING
- 8 oz (250 g) porcini mushrooms, or white mushrooms plus ¾ oz (25 g) dried porcini
- 3 tablespoons extra-virgin olive oil
- 1 tablespoon parsley, finely chopped
- 1 clove garlic, finely chopped
- salt and freshly ground black pepper

Wine: a dry red (Grignolino)

Four-seasons pizza
Pizza quattro stagioni

Makes: 1 pizza, about 12 in (30 cm) in diameter; Preparation: 40 minutes + 1 hour to soak mussels; Rising time: about 1 hour; Cooking: 15-20 minutes; Level of difficulty: Medium

Prepare the dough as shown on pages 342–343. § Soak the mussels in a large bowl of water for at least 1 hour to purge them of sand. Pull off their beards, scrub, and rinse well in cold water. § Rinse the mushrooms, slice, and sauté in 1 tablespoon of oil over medium heat for 3–4 minutes. Season with salt and set aside. § Place the mussels in a large skillet (frying pan) over high heat. Stir frequently until the shells are open. Discard the shells of all but 4 mussels. Strain the liquid produced and set aside with the mussels in a bowl. § When the rising time has elapsed, knead the dough for 1 minute on a lightly floured work surface. § Shape the pizza as explained on page 344 and transfer to an oiled baking sheet. § Spread the tomatoes on top and sprinkle with salt. § Now, imagine the pizza divided into 4 equal parts: garnish one quarter with mushrooms, one with artichokes, one with olives and anchovies, and one with garlic. § Bake in a preheated oven at 500°F/250°C/gas 8 for 15–20 minutes. § When cooked, arrange the mussels on the quarter with tomato and garlic. Drizzle with the remaining oil and serve.

■ INGREDIENTS

BASE
- 1 quantity pizza dough (see recipe p. 344)

TOPPING
- 5 oz (150 g) white mushrooms
- 3 tablespoons extra-virgin olive oil
- dash of salt
- 12 oz (350 g) mussels, in shell
- 7 oz (200 g) tomatoes, canned, drained, and chopped
- 3 oz (90 g) artichokes in oil, drained and halved
- 3 oz (90 g) black olives, pitted
- 2–3 anchovy fillets, crumbled
- 1 clove garlic, thinly sliced

Wine: a dry red (Chianti)

Right: Pizza ai funghi

Four-cheese pizza
Pizza ai quattro formaggi

Vary the cheeses according to what you like (and what you have in the refrigerator).
Aim for a balance between texture and intensity of taste.

Makes: 1 pizza, about 12 in (30 cm) in diameter; Preparation: 30 minutes; Rising time: about 1 hour;
Cooking: 15-20 minutes; Level of difficulty: Medium

Prepare the dough as shown on pages 342–343. § When the rising time has elapsed, knead the dough for 1 minute on a lightly floured work surface. § Shape the pizza as explained on page 344 and transfer to an oiled baking sheet. § Spread the surface with the cheeses and, if liked, sprinkle with crushed chilies. Drizzle with the oil. § Bake in a preheated oven at 500°F/250°C/gas 8 for 15–20 minutes. § Serve hot.

■ INGREDIENTS

BASE
- 1 quantity pizza dough (see recipe p. 344)

TOPPING
- 4 oz (125 g) Mozzarella cheese, diced
- 3 tablespoons Parmesan cheese, freshly grated
- 4 oz (125 g) Gorgonzola cheese, diced
- 3 oz (90 g) Emmental cheese, thinly sliced
- ½ teaspoon crushed chilies (optional)
- 1 tablespoon extra-virgin olive oil

Italian Riviera-style pizza
Pizza Sardenaira

This recipe comes from Liguria, on the Italian Riviera. A similar recipe exists
across the border in France, on the Côte d'Azur, where it is called the Pissaladière.
Debate rages about the nationality of this pizza.

Makes: 1 pizza, about 12 in (30 cm) in diameter; Preparation: 40 minutes; Rising time: about 1 hour;
Cooking: 20-25 minutes; Level of difficulty: Medium

Prepare the dough as shown on pages 342–343, adding the oil to the flour mixture. § Sauté the onions in oil for 15 minutes, stirring frequently, until they are soft and lightly browned. Season with salt and pepper and set aside to cool. § When the rising time has elapsed, knead the dough for 1 minute on a lightly floured work surface. § Shape the pizza as explained on page 344 and transfer to an oiled baking sheet. § Spread the onions over the pizza and sprinkle with the olives, anchovies, garlic, and oregano, if using. § Bake in a preheated oven at 500°F/250°C/gas 8 for 20–25 minutes. Serve hot.

■ INGREDIENTS

BASE
- 1 quantity pizza dough (see recipe p. 344)
- 2 tablespoons extra-virgin olive oil

TOPPING
- 10 oz (300 g) onions, thinly sliced
- 2 tablespoons extra-virgin olive oil
- salt and freshly ground black pepper
- 3 oz (90 g) black olives
- 12 anchovy fillets, crumbled
- 3 cloves garlic, finely chopped (optional)
- 1 teaspoon oregano (optional)

Wine: a dry white (Vermentino)

VARIATIONS
– Before adding the onions, spread the dough with 3–4 tablespoons of drained and chopped canned tomatoes.
– Add 1–2 tablespoons of capers to the topping.

Right: *Pizza Sardenaira*

INGREDIENTS

BASE
- 1 quantity pizza dough
  (see recipe p. 344)

TOPPING
- 12 oz (350 g) tomatoes,
  canned, drained, and
  chopped
- 6 leaves fresh basil, torn
- 3 oz (90 g) black olives
- 1 small onion, thinly sliced
- 2 oz (60 g) Pecorino
  cheese, freshly grated
- 1 teaspoon oregano
- 4–6 anchovy fillets,
  crumbled
- 3 tablespoons extra-virgin
  olive oil

Wine: a dry rosé (Etna Rosato)

Sicilian-style pizza
Pizza siciliana

Traditional Sicilian pizza has a thicker, softer base than pizza from northern Italy.
For this pizza, stretch the dough to a diameter of not more than 11 in (28 cm).

Makes: 1 pizza, about 11 in (28 cm) in diameter; Preparation: 30 minutes; Rising time: about 1½ hours;
Cooking: about 30 minutes; Level of difficulty: Medium

Prepare the dough as shown on pages 342–343. § When the rising time has elapsed, knead the dough for 1 minute on a lightly floured work surface. § Shape the pizza as explained on page 344 and transfer to an oiled baking sheet. § Spread the tomatoes evenly over the pizza, and sprinkle with the basil, olives, and onion, followed by the Pecorino and oregano. Finish with the anchovies and drizzle with 1 tablespoon of oil. § Bake in a preheated oven at 500°F/250°C/gas 8 for about 30 minutes. § When cooked, drizzle with the remaining oil, and serve hot.

VARIATION
– Add 4 oz (125 g) diced Mozzarella cheese to the topping.

INGREDIENTS

BASE
- 1 quantity pizza dough
  (see recipe p. 344)

TOPPING
- ⅔ cup (5 oz/150 g) fresh
  Ricotta cheese
- 6 oz (180 g) Gorgonzola
  cheese, diced
- 2 tablespoons chives,
  finely chopped
- 1 small clove garlic, finely
  chopped
- 1–2 tablespoons fresh
  cream
- 1 tablespoon extra-virgin
  olive oil

Wine: a dry red (Pignoletto)

Two-cheese pizza
Pizza ai due formaggi

Makes: 1 pizza, about 12 in (30 cm) in diameter; Preparation: 30 minutes; Rising time: about 1 hour;
Cooking: 10-15 minutes; Level of difficulty: Medium

Prepare the dough as shown on pages 342–343. § Combine the Ricotta, Gorgonzola, chives, garlic, cream, and oil in a bowl and mix thoroughly. § When the rising time has elapsed, knead the dough for 1 minute on a lightly floured work surface. § Shape the pizza as explained on page 344 and transfer to an oiled baking sheet. § Spread the topping evenly over the pizza and bake in a preheated oven at 500°F/250°C/gas 8 for 10–15 minutes. § Serve hot.

Left: *Pizza siciliana*

Eggplant pizza
Pizza alle melanzane

Makes: 1 pizza, about 12 in (30 cm) in diameter; Preparation: 40 minutes; Rising time: about 1 hour; Cooking: 15-20 minutes; Level of difficulty: Medium

Prepare the dough as shown on pages 342–343. § Cut the eggplant into slices ½ in (1 cm) thick and brush lightly with oil. § Grill for 3–4 minutes in a hot grill pan, turning them over only once. Sprinkle with salt, garlic, and parsley. Set aside. § When the rising time has elapsed, knead the dough for 1 minute on a lightly floured work surface. § Shape the pizza as explained on page 344 and transfer to an oiled baking sheet. § Spread the tomatoes evenly over the pizza and sprinkle with the Mozzarella. Drizzle with 1 tablespoon of oil. § Bake in a preheated oven at 500°F/250°C/gas 8 for 10–15 minutes. § Take the pizza out of the oven and cover with the slices of eggplant. Return to the oven for 5 minutes more. § When cooked, sprinkle with the basil, drizzle with the remaining oil, and serve hot.

■ INGREDIENTS

BASE
- 1 quantity pizza dough (see recipe p. 344)

TOPPING
- 10 oz (300 g) eggplant (aubergine)
- 3 tablespoons extra-virgin olive oil
- dash of salt
- 2 cloves garlic, finely chopped
- 1 tablespoon parsley, finely chopped
- 7 oz (200 g) tomatoes, canned, drained and chopped
- 5 oz (150 g) Mozzarella cheese, diced
- 6 leaves fresh basil, torn

Wine: a dry red (Chianti dei Colli Senesi)

Pizza with bell peppers
Pizza ai peperoni

Makes: 1 pizza, about 12 in (30 cm) in diameter; Preparation: 40 minutes; Rising time: about 1 hour; Cooking: 15-20 minutes; Level of difficulty: Medium

Prepare the dough as shown on pages 342–343. § Sauté the onion in 2 tablespoons of oil for 3 minutes over medium heat. Add the bell peppers and, after 1–2 minutes, the tomatoes and capers. Season with salt and cook, stirring continuously, for 5–7 minutes. § Add the basil leaves and turn off the heat. § When the rising time has elapsed, knead the dough for 1 minute on a lightly floured work surface. § Shape the pizza as explained on page 344 and transfer to an oiled baking sheet. § Spread the bell pepper mixture evenly over the pizza, sprinkle with the cheese, and drizzle with the remaining oil. § Bake in a preheated oven at 500°F/250°C/gas 8 for 15–20 minutes. § Serve hot.

■ INGREDIENTS

BASE
- 1 quantity pizza dough (see recipe p. 344)

TOPPING
- 1 small onion, sliced
- 3 tablespoons extra-virgin olive oil
- 12 oz (350 g) bell peppers (capsicums), cut in strips
- 7 cup (200 g) tomatoes, canned, chopped, not drained
- 1 tablespoon capers
- dash of salt
- 6 leaves fresh basil, torn
- 3 tablespoons Pecorino cheese, freshly grated

Wine: a dry sparkling red (Lambrusco)

Right: *Pizza ai peperoni*

Artichoke pizza
Pizza ai carciofi

■ INGREDIENTS

BASE
• 1 quantity pizza dough
  (see recipe p. 344)

TOPPING
• 4 globe artichokes
• juice of 1 lemon
• 4 tablespoons extra-virgin
  olive oil
• salt and freshly ground
  black pepper
• 4 oz (125 g) Fontina
  cheese, very thinly sliced

*Wine: a dry white
(Vernaccia di San Gimignano)*

Makes: 1 pizza, about 12 in (30 cm) in diameter; Preparation: 30 minutes; Rising time: about 1 hour; Cooking: 15-20 minutes; Level of difficulty: Medium

Prepare the dough as shown on pages 342–343. § Clean the artichokes by removing the stalks and tough outer leaves. Trim off and discard the tops. Cut in half and remove the fuzzy inner choke with a sharp knife. Place in a bowl of cold water with the lemon juice for 10 minutes. § Drain the artichokes, pat dry with paper towels, and slice thinly. § Transfer to a sauté pan with 1 tablespoon of oil and cook over medium heat for 3 minutes, stirring frequently. Season with salt. § When the rising time has elapsed, knead the dough for 1 minute on a lightly floured work surface. § Shape the pizza as explained on page 344 and transfer to an oiled baking sheet. § Brush the pizza with ½ tablespoon of oil and spread with the slices of artichoke. Season with salt and pepper and arrange the Fontina slices on top. Drizzle with 1 tablespoon of oil. § Bake in a preheated oven at 500°F/250°C/gas 8 for 15–20 minutes. § When cooked, drizzle with the remaining oil, and serve hot.

Leek pizza
Pizza ai porri

■ INGREDIENTS

BASE
• 1 quantity pizza dough
  (see recipe p. 344)

TOPPING
• 2 tablespoons butter
• 14 oz (450 g) leeks, sliced
• 3 oz (90 g) pancetta, diced
• salt and freshly ground
  black pepper
• 1 egg
• 1½ tablespoons fresh cream
• 4 tablespoons Parmesan
  cheese, freshly grated
• 2 oz (60 g) Gruyère
  cheese, very thinly sliced

Makes: 1 pizza, about 12 in (30 cm) in diameter; Preparation: 45 minutes; Rising time: about 1 hour; Cooking: 15-20 minutes; Level of difficulty: Medium

Prepare the dough as shown on pages 342–343. § Melt the butter in a sauté pan and add the leeks and pancetta. Sauté over medium-low heat for 10 minutes, stirring frequently. Season with salt and pepper and set aside to cool. § When the rising time has elapsed, knead the dough for 1 minute on a lightly floured work surface. § Shape the pizza as explained on page 344 and transfer to an oiled baking sheet. § Beat the egg with the cream in a bowl. Add the leek and pancetta mixture and the two cheeses. Mix well. § Spread the mixture evenly over the pizza and bake in a preheated oven at 450°F/230°C/gas 7 for 15–20 minutes. § Serve hot.

Left: Pizza ai carciofi

Pizza with arugula and mozzarella cheese
Pizza alla rucola in bianco

This is a modern classic. It has become extremely popular in pizzerias throughout Italy.

Makes: 1 pizza, about 12 in (30 cm) in diameter; Preparation: 30 minutes; Rising time: about 1 hour; Cooking: 12-16 minutes; Level of difficulty: Medium

Prepare the dough as shown on pages 342–343. § When the rising time has elapsed, knead the dough for 1 minute on a lightly floured work surface. § Shape the pizza as explained on page 344 and transfer to an oiled baking sheet. § Brush the surface with 1 tablespoon of oil and sprinkle with a little salt. § Bake in a preheated oven at 450°F/230°C/gas 7 for 6–8 minutes. § Take the pizza out of the oven and sprinkle with the Mozzarella. Return to the oven and cook for 6–8 minutes more. § When cooked, garnish with the prosciutto and arugula, drizzle with the remaining oil, and serve hot.

VARIATIONS
– Replace the prosciutto with the same amount of ham.
– Break the prosciutto, or ham, into pieces before garnishing the pizza.

■ INGREDIENTS

BASE
• 1 quantity pizza dough (see recipe p. 344)

TOPPING
• 2 tablespoons extra-virgin olive oil
• dash of salt
• 5 oz (150 g) Mozzarella cheese, sliced or diced
• 3 oz (90 g) prosciutto, thinly sliced
• ½ oz (15 g) arugula (rocket), washed, dried, and coarsely chopped

Wine: a dry white (Bianco di Pitigliano)

Pizza with arugula, tomato, and mozzarella cheese
Pizza alla rucola in rosso

Makes: 1 pizza, about 12 in (30 cm) in diameter; Preparation: 30 minutes; Rising time: about 1 hour; Cooking: 15-20 minutes; Level of difficulty: Medium

Prepare the dough as shown on pages 342–343. § When the rising time has elapsed, knead the dough for 1 minute on a lightly floured work surface. § Shape the pizza as explained on page 344 and transfer to an oiled baking sheet. § Spread the tomatoes evenly over the pizza and bake in a preheated oven at 500°F/250°C/gas 8 for about 10 minutes. § Remove the pizza from the oven, cover with the Mozzarella and drizzle with 1 tablespoon of oil. Return to the oven and cook for 6–8 minutes more. § When cooked, garnish with the arugula and a generous grinding of black pepper, if liked. Drizzle with the remaining oil and serve hot.

■ INGREDIENTS

BASE
• 1 quantity pizza dough (see recipe p. 344)
TOPPING
• 7 oz (200 g) tomatoes, canned, drained, and chopped
• 5 oz (150 g) Mozzarella cheese, sliced
• 2 tablespoons extra-virgin olive oil
• ½ oz (15 g) arugula (rocket), washed, dried, and coarsely chopped
• freshly ground black pepper (optional)

Wine: a young, dry red (Chianti)

Right: *Pizza alla rucola in bianco*

Pizza with cheese and smoked pancetta
Pizza affumicata

Makes: 1 pizza, about 12 in (30 cm) in diameter; Preparation: 30 minutes; Rising time: about 1 hour; Cooking: 15 minutes; Level of difficulty: Medium

Prepare the dough as shown on pages 342–343. § Cook the smoked pancetta for 2–3 minutes in a skillet (frying pan) over low heat, without adding any fat. Drain and cut into strips the width of a finger. § When the rising time has elapsed, knead the dough for 1 minute on a lightly floured work surface. § Shape the pizza as explained on page 344 and transfer to an oiled baking sheet. § Spread the pizza with the Robiola (or Crescenza), and sprinkle with the pancetta, followed by the cubes of Provolone. § Bake in a preheated oven at 500°F/250°C/gas 8 for 15 minutes and serve.

VARIATION
– For extra zest, sprinkle the cooked pizza with 1 oz (30 g) of chopped smoked herring fillet.

■ INGREDIENTS

BASE
• 1 quantity pizza dough (see recipe p. 344)

TOPPING
• 4 oz (125 g) smoked pancetta, or bacon, sliced
• ½ cup (125 g) Robiola, Crescenza, or similar soft, fresh cheese
• 5 oz (150 g) smoked Provolone cheese, diced

Wine: a dry red (Cirò)

Mussel pizza
Pizza alle cozze

Makes: 1 pizza, about 12 in (30 cm) in diameter; Preparation: 40 minutes; Rising time: about 1 hour; Cooking: 10-12 minutes; Level of difficulty: Medium

Prepare the dough as shown on pages 342–343. § Soak the mussels in a large bowl of water for 1 hour. Pull off their beards, scrub, and rinse in abundant cold water. § Place the mussels in a large skillet (frying pan) over high heat. Stir frequently. They will open after a couple of minutes. Discard the shells of all but 4 or 5 mussels. Strain the liquid the mussels have produced and set aside with the mussels in a bowl. § When the rising time has elapsed, knead the dough for 1 minute on a lightly floured work surface. § Shape the pizza as explained on page 344 and transfer to an oiled baking sheet. § Drizzle with 1 tablespoon of oil and bake in a preheated oven at 500°F/250°C/gas 8 for 8–10 minutes. § Drain the mussels. § Take the pizza out of the oven and arrange the mussels and remaining shells on top. Sprinkle with the parsley, garlic, oregano, salt, and pepper, and drizzle with the remaining oil. § Bake for 1–2 minutes more. § Serve hot.

VARIATION
– Mix 7 oz (200 g) of chopped tomatoes with the garlic, and drizzle all the oil over the base before baking.

■ INGREDIENTS

BASE
• 1 quantity pizza dough (see recipe p. 344)

TOPPING
• 2 lb (1 kg) mussels, in shell
• 3 tablespoons extra-virgin olive oil
• 1 tablespoon parsley, finely chopped
• 2 cloves garlic, finely chopped
• 1 teaspoon oregano
• salt and freshly ground black pepper

Wine: a dry white (Cinqueterre)

Right: *Pizze rapidissime*

Quick pizzas
Pizze rapidissime

These "pizzas" are delicious and quick to prepare. Vary the toppings according to taste.

Makes: 4 "pizzas"; Preparation: 10 minutes; Cooking: 8-10 minutes; Level of difficulty: Simple

Brush both sides of the slices of bread with half the oil. § Spread the tomatoes on top, followed by the Mozzarella, anchovies, capers, and oregano. § Drizzle with the remaining oil and place on a baking sheet. § Bake in a preheated oven at 450°F/230°C/gas 7 for 8–10 minutes, or until the Mozzarella melts and turns pale gold. The bread should be crisp and lightly browned.

■ INGREDIENTS

• 4 thick slices bread

• 4 tablespoons extra-virgin olive oil

• 8 oz (250 g) tomatoes, chopped

• 7 oz (200 g) Mozzarella cheese, sliced

• 4–8 anchovy fillets

• 1 tablespoon capers

• 1 teaspoon oregano

*Wine: a dry red
(Merlot del Trentino)*

Calzoni

To make calzoni, just fold the pizza dough over the filling in a half-moon shape and bake in a hot oven.

Neapolitan calzone
Calzone alla napoletana

Makes: 4 calzoni; Preparation: 35 minutes; Rising time: about 1 hour; Cooking: 20-25 minutes; Level of difficulty: Medium

Prepare the dough as shown on pages 342–343. § Mix the Ricotta, Pecorino (or Parmesan), and eggs in a bowl. Add the Mozzarella, salami, and salt. Mix well and set aside. § When the rising time has elapsed, knead the dough for 1 minute on a lightly floured work surface, then divide into 4 equal portions. § Stretch the dough into circular shapes, about 9 in (23 cm) in diameter, as explained on page 344. § Spread the filling on one half of each calzone, leaving a ¾-in (2-cm) border around the edge for sealing. Fold the other half of the dough over the top, pressing down firmly on the edges to seal. § Arrange the calzoni on two lightly oiled baking sheets. Mix the tomatoes with 3 tablespoons of oil and the salt, and spread over the calzoni. § Bake in a preheated oven at 450°F/230°C/gas 7 for 20–25 minutes. The calzoni should be puffed and golden brown. § Serve hot.

■ INGREDIENTS

BASE
- 3 quantities pizza dough (see recipe p. 344)

FILLING
- 1 cup (250 g) fresh Ricotta cheese
- 4 tablespoons Pecorino romano, or Parmesan cheese, freshly grated
- 2 eggs
- 8 oz (250 g) Mozzarella cheese, diced
- 4 oz (125 g) Neapolitan salami, diced
- dash of salt
- 4 tablespoons extra-virgin olive oil
- 3 oz (90 g) tomatoes, canned, drained and chopped

Wine: a dry red (Ischia)

Apulian-style calzone with ham
Calzone alla pugliese con prosciutto

Makes: 4 calzoni; Preparation: 35 minutes; Rising time: about 1 hour; Cooking: 20-25 minutes; Level of difficulty: Medium

Prepare the dough as shown on pages 342–343. § When the rising time has elapsed, knead the dough for 1 minute on a lightly floured work surface, then divide into 4 equal portions. § Stretch the dough into circular shapes, about 9 in (23 cm) in diameter, as explained on page 344. § Spread half of each calzone with the Ricotta, then sprinkle with the Mozzarella and ham, leaving a ¾-in (2-cm) border around the edge for sealing. Fold the other half of the dough over the top, pressing down firmly on the edges to seal. § Arrange the calzoni on two lightly oiled baking sheets. Mix the tomatoes with 2 tablespoons of oil and the salt, and spread over the calzoni. § Bake in a preheated oven at 450°F/230°C/gas 7 for 20–25 minutes. The calzoni should be puffed and golden brown. § Serve hot.

■ INGREDIENTS

BASE
- 3 quantities pizza dough (see recipe p. 344)

FILLING
- 8 oz (250 g) soft Ricotta cheese
- 8 oz (250 g) Mozzarella cheese, diced
- 8 oz (250 g) ham, thinly sliced
- 3 tablespoons extra-virgin olive oil
- 3 oz (90 g) tomatoes, canned, drained and chopped
- dash of salt

Wine: a dry white (Orvieto Classico)

Right: *Calzone alla napoletana*

Eggplant calzone
Calzone alle melanzane

Makes: 4 calzoni; Preparation: 40 minutes; Rising time: about 1 hour; Cooking: 20-25 minutes; Level of difficulty: Medium

Prepare the dough as shown on pages 342–343. § Fry the eggplant in the oil in a large, heavy-bottomed pan over medium-high heat, stirring frequently. After 8–10 minutes, add the marjoram, garlic, salt, and, if necessary, a little more oil. Cook for 2–3 minutes more, until the eggplant is lightly browned. § Add the tomatoes, parsley, basil, and Pecorino. Stir for 1 minute then remove from heat. § When the rising time has elapsed, knead the dough for 1 minute on a lightly floured work surface, then divide into 4 equal portions. § Stretch the dough into circular shapes, about 9 in (23 cm) in diameter, as explained on page 344. § Spread the filling on one half of each calzone, leaving a ¾-in (2-cm) border around the edge for sealing. Fold the other half of the dough over the top, pressing down firmly on the edges to seal. § Brush the calzoni with the remaining oil and arrange them on two lightly oiled baking sheets. § Bake in a preheated oven at 450°F/230°C/gas 7 for 20–25 minutes. § Serve hot.

> VARIATIONS
> – Replace the marjoram with 1 teaspoon of oregano.
> – Omit the Pecorino and use the same quantity of Mozzarella cheese combined with 1 tablespoon of freshly grated Parmesan.

■ INGREDIENTS

BASE
• 3 quantities pizza dough (see recipe p. 344)

FILLING
• 1 lb (500 g) eggplant (aubergine), diced
• ½ cup (125 ml) extra-virgin olive oil
• 3 tablespoons fresh marjoram, finely chopped
• 1 clove garlic, finely chopped
• dash of salt
• 7 oz (200 g) tomatoes, canned, drained and chopped
• 2 teaspoons parsley, finely chopped
• 6 leaves fresh basil, torn
• 5 oz (150 g) Pecorino cheese, diced

Wine: a dry white (Corvo di Salaparuta)

Swiss chard calzone
Calzone alle bietole

This is recipe comes from Basilicata, in the south. The region is known for its austere cuisine, which is livened up by the liberal use of hot chilies.

Makes: 4 calzoni; Preparation: 40 minutes; Rising time: about 1 hour; Cooking: 20-25 minutes; Level of difficulty: Medium

Prepare the dough as shown on pages 342–343. § Clean the Swiss chard, rinse thoroughly, drain well, and cut into strips. Place in a heavy-bottomed saucepan with 2–3 tablespoons of oil, the garlic, chilies, and salt to taste. Cook over medium-low heat, initially with the lid on, for 10 minutes, stirring from time to time. The Swiss chard should be tender but not watery. Add the olives and cook for 2–4 minutes more. Set aside to cool. § When the rising

■ INGREDIENTS

BASE
• 3 quantities pizza dough (see recipe p. 344)

FILLING
• 1¾ lb (800 g) fresh Swiss chard (silver beet)
• 4 tablespoons extra-virgin olive oil
• 2 cloves garlic, sliced

Right: *Calzone alle melanzane*

- 1 teaspoon crushed chilies
- dash of salt
- 7 oz (200 g) black olives, pitted

Wine: a dry white
(Bianco di Custoza)

time has elapsed, knead the dough for 1 minute on a lightly floured work surface, then divide into 4 equal portions. § Stretch the dough into circular shapes, about 9 in (23 cm) in diameter, as explained on page 344. § Spread the filling on one half of each calzone, leaving a ¾-in (2-cm) border around the edge for sealing. Fold the other half of the dough over the top, pressing down firmly on the edges to seal. § Brush the calzoni with the remaining oil, and arrange them on two lightly oiled baking sheets. § Bake in a preheated oven at 450°F/230°C/gas 7 for 20–25 minutes. § Serve hot.

VARIATION
– Add a few slices of Pecorino cheese or 2–3 tablespoons of freshly grated Parmesan to the filling.

Apulian-style calzone
Calzone alla pugliese

Makes: 4 calzoni; Preparation: 35 minutes; Rising time: about 1 hour; Cooking: 20-25 minutes; Level of difficulty: Medium

Prepare the dough as shown on pages 342–343. § Cook the onions with 2–3 tablespoons of oil in a large sauté pan for 5 minutes. Add the tomatoes, olives, anchovies, capers, basil, and salt. Mix and cook over medium heat for 3–4 minutes more. Remove from heat. § When the mixture is cool, add the Pecorino. § When the rising time has elapsed, knead the dough on a lightly floured work surface, then divide into 4 equal portions. § Stretch the dough into circular shapes, about 9 in (23 cm) in diameter, as explained on page 344. § Spread the filling on one half of each calzone, leaving a ¾-in (2-cm) border around the edge for sealing. Fold the other half of the dough over the top, pressing down firmly on the edges to seal. § Brush the calzoni with the remaining oil, and arrange them on two lightly oiled baking sheets. § Bake in a preheated oven at 450°F/230°C/gas 7 for 20–25 minutes. § Serve hot.

■ INGREDIENTS

BASE
• 3 quantities pizza dough (see recipe p. 344)

FILLING
• 1¼ lb (600 g) onions, sliced
• 4 tablespoons extra-virgin olive oil
• 8 oz (250 g) tomatoes, canned, drained, and chopped
• 7 oz (200 g) black olives, pitted and halved
• 8 anchovy fillets, crumbled
• 2 tablespoons capers
• 8 leaves fresh basil, torn
• dash of salt
• 4 oz (125 g) Pecorino cheese, diced

Wine: a dry rosé (Castel del Monte)

Calzone with prosciutto and cheese
Calzone al prosciutto e formaggi

Makes: 4 calzoni; Preparation: 35 minutes; Rising time: about 1 hour; Cooking: 20-25 minutes; Level of difficulty: Medium

Prepare the dough as shown on pages 342–343. § Combine the prosciutto, cheeses, and parsley in a bowl. Set aside. § When the rising time has elapsed, knead the dough for 1 minute on a lightly floured work surface, then divide into 4 equal portions. § Stretch the dough into circular shapes, about 9 in (23 cm) in diameter, as explained on page 344. § Spread the filling on one half of each calzone, leaving a ¾-in (2-cm) border around the edge. Fold the other half of the dough over the top, pressing down firmly on the edges to seal. § Brush the calzoni with the oil, and arrange them on two lightly oiled baking sheets. § Bake in a preheated oven at 450°F/230°C/gas 7 for 20–25 minutes. § Serve hot.

■ INGREDIENTS

BASE
• 3 quantities pizza dough (see recipe p. 344)

FILLING
• 3½ oz (100 g) prosciutto, coarsely chopped
• 5 oz (150 g) Provolone, or Caciocavallo cheese, diced
• 5 oz (150 g) salted Ricotta cheese, freshly grated
• 5 oz (150 g) Mozzarella cheese, diced
• 1 tablespoon parsley, finely chopped
• 2 tablespoons extra-virgin olive oil

Wine: a dry white (Bianco di Cervèteri)

Right: *Calzone alla pugliese*

Bread

The variety of breads available in Italy is enormous. Each region has developed its own special array of loaves and rolls. The recipes in this chapter are a selection of some of the classics.

White bread
Pane bianco

Basic breads like this one, made with flour, water, yeast, and salt, are best eaten the day
they are made. If you make more than you can eat or give away, remember that this bread
freezes very well. Wrap the bread tightly in plastic wrap, and place it
in the freezer. Breads made with milk, olive oil, or butter will keep longer.
Store them in a paper bag (not plastic) in a cool, dark place.

Makes: about 2 lb (1 kg) of bread; Preparation: 30 minutes; Rising time: about 2¼ hours; Cooking: 20–
40 minutes; Level of difficulty: Medium

Prepare the yeast as explained on page 342. § Combine the flour in a
large bowl with the yeast mixture, salt, and remaining water, and proceed
as shown on pages 342–343. § When the rising time has elapsed (about
1½ hours), use a spatula to transfer the dough to a lightly floured work
surface. Knead for several minutes. § Place the dough on an oiled baking
sheet and shape it into an oval or elongated loaf. § Sprinkle the surface
with flour and, using a serrated knife, make 5 or 6 diagonal slashes about
½ in (1 cm) deep along the top of the loaf. § For a large, ring-shaped
loaf, about 12 in (30 cm) in diameter, gently flatten the dough and make
a hole in the middle with your fingers. Carefully enlarge the hole,
shaping the dough into a ring. § To make rolls, divide the dough into
8–10 equal portions and shape them into long rolls. Remember that the
volume of the dough will double during rising, so position the rolls at
least 1½ in (4 cm) apart. § Cover with a cloth and set aside to rise for
40–50 minutes. § Bake in a preheated oven at 450°F/230°C/gas 7. Large
loaves will need about 40 minutes, the ring-shaped loaf about
30 minutes and the rolls about 25 minutes.

■ INGREDIENTS

• ¾ oz (25 g) fresh yeast or
  1½ packages active dry
  yeast
• 1 teaspoon sugar
• about 1⅓ cups (350 ml)
  lukewarm water
• 5 cups (750 g) unbleached
  white flour
• 2–4 teaspoons salt

VARIATIONS
— For loaves or rolls with golden crusts, instead of sprinkling the
dough with flour, brush the surface with a lightly beaten egg (or 2
tablespoons of milk) before baking.
— For crispy rolls, sprinkle the dough with coarse-grain cornmeal
before setting it aside to rise the second time.
— Shape the dough into long thin loaves, the thickness of your
wrist. Sprinkle the surface with flour and, using a serrated knife,
make an incision along the length of each loaf, or make several
diagonal slashes. The loaves will take 20–25 minutes to cook.
— Add 2 tablespoons of fennel seeds to the dough for extra taste.
Fresh, home-baked fennel bread should be served with a mixed
platter of ham, prosciutto, mortadella, salami, and cheeses.

Right:
Pane bianco e pane all'olio

Olive oil bread
Pane all'olio

■ INGREDIENTS

- ¾ oz (25 g) fresh yeast or 1½ packages active dry yeast
- 1 teaspoon sugar
- about 1¼ cups (300 ml) lukewarm water
- 5 cups (750 g) unbleached white flour
- 2–4 teaspoons salt
- 4 tablespoons extra-virgin olive oil

Makes: about 2 lb (1 kg) of bread; Preparation: 30 minutes; Rising time: about 2 hours; Cooking: 35 minutes; Level of difficulty: Medium

Proceed as for white bread (see previous page), adding the oil to the yeast mixture at the beginning. Instead of kneading, mix the soft, sticky dough in the bowl with a wooden spoon. § When the rising time has elapsed (about 1½ hours), mix the dough again for a few minutes. § Use a spatula to transfer it to an oiled baking pan about 12 in (30 cm) in diameter. Cover with a cloth and set aside to rise for 30 minutes. § Bake in a preheated oven at 450°F/230°C/gas 7.

Bread made with lard
Pane allo strutto

Makes: about 2 lb (1 kg) of bread; Preparation: 30 minutes; Rising time: about 2 hours; Cooking: 30-35 minutes; Level of difficulty: Medium

Melt the lard in a small saucepan over low heat. Remove from heat and set aside. § Prepare the yeast as explained on page 342. § Combine the flour in a large bowl with the lard, yeast mixture, salt, and remaining water, and proceed as shown on pages 342–343. § When the rising time has elapsed (about 1½ hours), use a spatula to transfer the dough to a lightly floured work surface and knead for several minutes. § Divide the dough into 6 equal portions and shape them into thin loaves about 12 in (30 cm) long. Pick each loaf up and twist it slightly, making sure it does not become too long. The loaves should have a very slight spiral shape. § As you finish twisting the loaves, place them on two oiled baking sheets, keeping them well spaced (their volume will double as they rise). § Cover with a cloth and set aside to rise for 30–40 minutes. § Bake in a preheated oven at 400°F/200°C/gas 6 for about 30–35 minutes.

INGREDIENTS

- 3 oz (90 g) lard
- 1 oz (30 g) fresh yeast or 2 packages active dry yeast
- 1 teaspoon sugar
- about 1¼ cups (300 ml) lukewarm water
- 5 cups (750 g) unbleached white flour
- 2–4 teaspoons salt

Oregano bread
Pane all'origano

Makes: about 2 lb (1 kg) of bread; Preparation: 30 minutes; Rising time: about 2 hours; Cooking: 35 minutes; Level of difficulty: Medium

Prepare the yeast as explained on page 342. § Combine the flour in a large bowl with the oregano, yeast mixture, salt and remaining water, and proceed as shown on pages 342–343. § When the rising time has elapsed (about 1½ hours), use a spatula to transfer the dough to a lightly floured work surface. Knead for several minutes. § Divide the dough into 4–6 equal portions and shape each into a loaf about 14 in (35 cm) long. § Place the loaves on two oiled baking sheets. Pull the ends of each loaf round and join them to make circular loaves, or leave them straight, as preferred. § Use a serrated knife to make a ½-in (1-cm) deep incision along the top of each loaf. § Cover with a cloth and set aside to rise for 30–40 minutes. § Bake in a preheated oven at 400°F/200°C/gas 6 for about 30 minutes.

INGREDIENTS

- ¾ oz (25 g) fresh yeast or 1½ packages active dry yeast
- 1 teaspoon sugar
- about 1¼ cups (300 ml) lukewarm water
- 5 cups (750 g) unbleached white flour
- 2 teaspoons finely chopped oregano
- 2–4 teaspoons salt
- ⅓ cup (90 ml) extra-virgin olive oil

Left: *Pane all'origano*

Whole-wheat bread
Pane integrale

Makes: about 2 lb (1 kg) of bread; Preparation: 30 minutes; Rising time: 3-4 hours; Cooking: 40 minutes; Level of difficulty: Medium

Prepare the yeast as explained on page 342. § Combine both flours in a large bowl with the yeast mixture, salt, and remaining water, and proceed as shown on pages 342–343. § When the rising time has elapsed (about 2 hours), use a spatula to transfer the dough to a lightly floured work surface and knead for 5 minutes. § Divide the dough into two equal portions and shape each into a long loaf. Sprinkle with flour and use a serrated knife to make diagonal slashes about ¼ in (6 mm) deep along the top of each loaf. Repeat, making slashes in the other direction to create a grid pattern. § Cover with a cloth and set aside to rise for about 1½ hours. § Bake in a preheated oven at 400°F/200°C/gas 6 for 40 minutes.

■ INGREDIENTS

- 1 oz (30 g) fresh yeast or 2 packages active dry yeast
- 1 teaspoon sugar
- about 1¼ cups (300 ml) lukewarm water
- 2¼ cups (350 g) whole-wheat (wholemeal) flour
- 2 cups (300 g) unbleached white flour
- 2–3 teaspoons salt

VARIATIONS
– For a darker bread, increase the quantity of whole wheat flour, reducing the white flour proportionally.
– Add 3–4 tablespoons of extra-virgin olive oil to the dough.

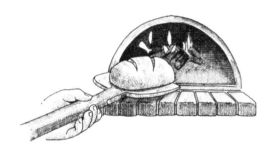

Sesame seed bread
Pane al sesamo

Sesame seed bread is made in Sicily in the south, where white loaves are sprinkled with the seeds before baking, and in Trento and Bolzano in the north. This recipe comes from the north.

Makes: about 2 lb (1 kg) of bread; Preparation: 30 minutes; Rising time: about 2 hours; Cooking: 30-40 minutes; Level of difficulty: Medium

Prepare the yeast as explained on page 342. § Combine both flours in a large bowl with half the sesame seeds. Mix carefully and sprinkle with salt. Add the yeast mixture and remaining water, and proceed as shown on pages 342–343. § When the rising time has elapsed (about 1 hour),

■ INGREDIENTS

- 1 oz (30 g) fresh yeast or 2 packages active dry yeast
- 1 teaspoon sugar
- about 1¼ cups (300 ml) lukewarm water
- 3 cups (450 g) unbleached white flour

Right: *Pane al sesamo*

- 2 cups (300 g) whole-wheat (wholemeal) flour
- 4 tablespoons sesame seeds
- 4 teaspoons salt
- 1 egg white

use a spatula to transfer the dough to a lightly floured work surface and knead for 2–3 minutes. § Divide the dough into two equal portions to make soft loaves, or in 8–10 equal portions for crusty rolls. § Arrange the loaves or rolls on one or two oiled baking sheets, keeping them well spaced (their volume will double as they rise). § Lightly beat the egg white with 1 teaspoon of water and brush the surface of the loaves or rolls with the mixture. Sprinkle with the remaining sesame seeds. § Cover with a cloth and set aside to rise for 1 hour. § Bake in a preheated oven at 400°F/200°C/gas 6 for 35–40 minutes for loaves and 30 minutes for rolls.

Rye bread
Pane di segale

This tasty, fragrant bread comes from Alto Adige and Trentino in northeastern Italy.

■ INGREDIENTS

- 1 oz (30 g) fresh yeast or 2 packages active dry yeast
- 1 teaspoon sugar
- about 1¼ cups (300 ml) lukewarm water
- 3 cups (450 g) rye flour
- 2 cups (300 g) unbleached white flour
- 1 tablespoon fennel seeds
- 2 teaspoons salt
- 2 tablespoons extra-virgin olive oil or lard, at room temperature

Makes: about 2 lb (1 kg) of bread; Preparation: 30 minutes; Rising time: 2–3 hours; Cooking: 30 minutes; Level of difficulty: Medium

Prepare the yeast as explained on page 342. § Combine both flours in a large bowl with the fennel seeds, salt, yeast mixture, oil (or lard), and the remaining water, and proceed as shown on pages 342–343. § When the rising time has elapsed (about 2 hours), use a spatula to transfer the dough to a lightly floured work surface and knead for 2–3 minutes. The dough should be quite soft. § Divide the dough into 4–6 equal portions and shape into round loaves. Transfer to two oiled baking sheets. Cover with a cloth and set aside to rise for about 1 hour. § Bake in a preheated oven at 400°F/200°C/gas 6 for about 30 minutes.

Garbanzo bean rolls
Pane con ceci

■ INGREDIENTS

- ¾ oz (25 g) fresh yeast or 1½ packages active dry yeast
- 1 teaspoon sugar
- about 1 cup (250 ml) lukewarm water
- 8 oz (250 g) garbanzo beans (chick peas), soaked and precooked, or canned
- 4 cups (600 g) unbleached white flour
- 4 teaspoons salt
- 5 tablespoons extra-virgin olive oil

Makes: about 16-20 rolls; Preparation: 30 minutes; Rising time: about 3 hours; Cooking: 18-20 minutes; Level of difficulty: Medium

Prepare the yeast as explained on page 342. § Drain the garbanzo beans and purée in a food processor with the remaining water. § Combine the flour in a large bowl with the salt, yeast mixture, garbanzo bean purée, and 4 tablespoons of oil, and proceed as shown on pages 342–343. § When the rising time has elapsed (at least 1½ hours), use a spatula to transfer the dough to a lightly floured work surface and knead for 2 minutes. § Divide the dough into 4 equal portions and shape into thin loaves about 14 in (35 cm) long. Divide each into 4–5 rolls. § Pour a few drops of the remaining oil onto each and spread it with your fingers while shaping the dough into round rolls. § Use a serrated knife to make a ¼-in (6-mm) deep cross in the surface of each roll. § Transfer to two oiled baking sheets, keeping the rolls well spaced (their volume will double as they rise). Cover with a cloth and set aside to rise for at least 1 hour. § Bake in a preheated oven at 400°F/200°C/gas 6 for 18–20 minutes.

Left: Pane di segale

Corn bread
Pane di mais

Makes: about 1½ lb (750 g) bread; Preparation: 30 minutes; Rising time: 1½ hours; Cooking: 30 minutes; Level of difficulty: Medium

Prepare the yeast as explained on page 342, using half the milk instead of water. § Combine both flours in a large bowl with the salt, egg, yeast mixture, and remaining milk, and proceed as shown on pages 342–343. § When the rising time has elapsed (about 1 hour), transfer the dough to a lightly floured work surface and knead for 2–3 minutes. § Divide the dough in half and shape into two round loaves. Sprinkle with flour and transfer to an oiled baking sheet. § Cover with a cloth and set aside to rise for about 30 minutes. § Bake in a preheated oven at 400°F/200°C/gas 6 for about 30 minutes.

■ INGREDIENTS

- 1½ oz (45 g) fresh yeast or 3 packages active dry yeast
- 1 teaspoon sugar
- about 1 cup (250 ml) lukewarm milk
- 2 cups (300 g) unbleached white flour
- 2 cups (300 g) finely ground cornmeal
- 4 teaspoons salt
- 1 egg, lightly beaten

Buckwheat bread
Pane di grano saraceno

Buckwheat flour is used only in a few parts of northern Italy. It produces a delicious coarse-grain bread, with a pronounced taste.

Makes: about 2 lb (1 kg) of bread; Preparation: 30 minutes; Rising time: 2 hours; Cooking: 30-35 minutes; Level of difficulty: Medium

Prepare the yeast as explained on page 342. § Combine both flours in a large bowl with the salt, yeast mixture, oil and remaining water, and proceed as shown on pages 342–343. § When the rising time has elapsed (about 1 hour), use a spatula to transfer the dough to a lightly floured work surface and knead for 2–3 minutes. § Divide the dough in 4 equal portions and shape into small round loaves. Sprinkle with flour and use a serrated knife to cut a ½-in (1-cm) deep cross in the surface of each loaf. § Transfer to one or two oiled baking sheets. Cover with a cloth and set aside to rise for 1 hour. § Bake in a preheated oven at 400°F/200°C/gas 6 for 30–35 minutes. § The loaves can also be cooked in two oiled and lightly floured rectangular loaf pans.

■ INGREDIENTS

- 1¼ oz (40 g) fresh yeast or 2½ packages active dry yeast
- 1 teaspoon sugar
- about 1⅓ cups (350 ml) lukewarm water
- 3⅓ cups (500 g) buckwheat flour
- 2 cups (300 g) unbleached white flour
- 3 teaspoons salt
- 4 tablespoons extra-virgin olive oil

Right:
Pane di mais

Walnut bread
Pane alle noci

This is a salted and not strictly traditional version of Pannociato from the Marches region in central Italy. It is excellent for snacks and goes well with soft, fresh cheeses, such as Mascarpone and Robiola.

Makes: about 2½ lb (1.2 kg) of bread; Preparation: 40 minutes; Rising time: 2 hours; Cooking: 25–30 minutes; Level of difficulty: Medium

Prepare the yeast as explained on page 342. § Combine the flour, Pecorino, walnuts, salt, and pepper in a large bowl. Mix well and add the lard (or oil), yeast mixture, and remaining water, and proceed as shown on pages 342–343. § When the rising time has elapsed (about 1 hour), transfer the dough to a lightly floured work surface and knead for 2–3 minutes. § Divide into 8–10 equal portions and shape into long rolls. § Place on two oiled baking sheets, keeping them well spaced (their volume will double as they rise). § Cover with a cloth and set aside to rise for about 1 hour. § Bake in a preheated oven at 400°F/200°C/gas 6 for 25–30 minutes.

■ INGREDIENTS

- 1 oz (30 g) fresh yeast or 2 packages active dry yeast
- 1 teaspoon sugar
- about 1¼ cups (300 ml) lukewarm water
- 3⅓ cups (500 g) unbleached white flour
- 5 oz (150 g) Pecorino cheese, diced
- 1¼ cups (150 g) walnuts, shelled and coarsely chopped
- 3 teaspoons salt
- freshly ground black pepper
- 2 tablespoons lard, at room temperature, or 3 tablespoons extra-virgin olive oil

Whole-wheat bread with hazelnuts
Pane integrale con nocciole

The distinctive nutty taste of this bread goes very well with fresh, creamy cheeses.

Makes: about 2 lb (1 kg) of bread; Preparation: 30 minutes; Rising time: 2 hours; Cooking: 30 minutes; Level of difficulty: Medium

Prepare the yeast as explained on page 342. § Combine both flours in a large bowl with the hazelnuts, mix well and sprinkle with salt. Add the yeast mixture, 3 tablespoons of oil, and the remaining water, and proceed as shown on pages 342–343. § When the rising time has elapsed (about 1 hour), use a spatula to transfer the dough (which will be very soft) to a lightly floured work surface and knead for 2–3 minutes. § Grease a nonstick baking pan 12 in (30 cm) in diameter with the remaining oil and place the dough in it. Cover with a cloth and set aside to rise for 1 hour. § Bake in a preheated oven at 400°F/200°C/gas 6 for about 30 minutes.

■ INGREDIENTS

- 1 oz (30 g) fresh yeast or 2 packages active dry yeast
- 1 teaspoon sugar
- about 1¼ cups (300 ml) lukewarm water
- 3⅓ cups (500 g) whole-wheat (wholemeal) flour
- 2 cups (300 g) unbleached white flour
- ¾ cup (90 g) roasted hazelnuts, shelled and coarsely chopped
- 3 teaspoons salt
- 4 tablespoons extra-virgin olive oil

VARIATIONS
– For softer bread, increase the quantity of water by 3 tablespoons and use a wooden spoon to mix the dough in the bowl instead of kneading it.
– For darker, drier bread, replace the white flour with whole-wheat (wholemeal) flour.

Right: *Pane alle noci*

Potato rolls
Pane con patate

■ INGREDIENTS

• ¾ oz (25 g) fresh yeast or 1½ packages active dry yeast
• 1 teaspoon sugar
• about ¾ cup (200 ml) lukewarm water
• 5 oz (150 g) boiled potatoes, still warm
• 2 tablespoons extra-virgin olive oil
• 3⅓ cups (500 g) unbleached white flour
• 3 teaspoons salt

Makes: about 2 lb (1 kg) of bread; Preparation: 30 minutes; Rising time: 2 hours; Cooking: 25-30 minutes; Level of difficulty: Medium

Prepare the yeast as explained on page 342. § Mash the potatoes in a large bowl and stir in the oil, flour, salt, yeast mixture, and remaining water. Proceed as shown on pages 342–343. § When the rising time has elapsed, transfer the dough to a floured work surface and knead for 1 minute. § Divide into 4–6 equal portions and shape into rolls. § Place on oiled baking sheets, keeping well spaced. Cover with a cloth and set aside to rise for 45 minutes. § Bake in a preheated oven at 400°F/200°C/gas 6 for 25–30 minutes.

Rosemary and raisin rolls
Pan di ramerino

This recipe comes from Tuscany, where rosemary is often called ramerino. Traditionally served during Lent, these delicious rolls are ideal for snacks and picnics all year round.

Makes: about 1¼ lb (600 g) bread; Preparation: 30 minutes; Rising time: 1½ hours; Cooking: 20 minutes; Level of difficulty: Medium

Combine 1½ tablespoons of rosemary with 4 tablespoons of oil in a small pan and cook over low heat for about 10 minutes. Remove from heat, discard the rosemary, and set the oil aside to cool. § Prepare the yeast as explained on page 342. § Combine the flour in a large bowl with the salt, rosemary oil, yeast mixture, sugar, and remaining water, and proceed as shown on pages 342–343. § When the rising time has elapsed (about 1 hour), transfer the dough to a lightly floured work surface and knead for 2–3 minutes. Incorporate the raisins and remaining rosemary into the dough as you knead. § Divide in 6–8 equal portions, drizzle with the remaining oil and shape into oval rolls. § Place on an oiled baking sheet, keeping them well spaced. Use a serrated knife to make a ½-in (1-cm) deep cross in the surface of each roll. § Cover with a cloth and set aside to rise for 30 minutes. § Bake in a preheated oven at 400°F/200°C/gas 6 for 20 minutes.

■ INGREDIENTS

- 2 tablespoons fresh rosemary leaves
- 5 tablespoons extra-virgin olive oil
- ½ oz (15 g) fresh yeast or 1 package active dry yeast
- 2 teaspoons sugar
- about ⅔ cup (150 ml) lukewarm water
- 3 cups (450 g) unbleached white flour
- 2 teaspoons salt
- ⅔ cup (2½ oz/75 g) raisins, rinsed, drained, and dried

Raisin bread
Pane con l'uva

This is a very old recipe, common to many parts of Italy. The raisins and sugar make it slightly sweet. Serve with Mascarpone or another mild, creamy cheese.

Makes: about 1¾ lb (800 g) of bread; Preparation: 30 minutes; Rising time: 1½ hours; Cooking: 20 minutes; Level of difficulty: Medium

Prepare the yeast as explained on page 342. § Combine the flour in a large bowl with the remaining sugar and water, the salt and yeast mixture, and proceed as shown on pages 342–343. § Soak the raisins in 2 cups of lukewarm water for 15–20 minutes. Drain, dry, and lightly sprinkle with flour. § When the rising time has elapsed (about 1 hour), transfer the dough to a lightly floured work surface and knead. Incorporate the raisins and butter into the dough as you knead. § Divide in 7–8 equal portions, sprinkle with flour and shape into long rolls. § Place on an oiled baking sheet, keeping them well spaced. Cover with a cloth and set aside to rise for about 30 minutes. § Bake in a preheated oven at 400°F/200°C/gas 6 for about 20 minutes.

■ INGREDIENTS

- ¾ oz (25 g) fresh yeast or 1½ packages active dry yeast
- 2 tablespoons sugar
- about ⅔ cup (150 ml) lukewarm water
- 3 cups (450 g) unbleached white flour
- 2½ tablespoons butter, at room temperature, chopped into small pieces
- 1½ cups (180 g) Malaga (or Corinth) raisins
- 2 teaspoons salt

Right:

Pan di ramerino

Breadrings
Tarallucci

Taralluci are a speciality of southern Italy. This version comes from Apulia, the so-called "heel" of the Italian peninsula. These small breadrings can be seasoned with fennel seeds, chilies, or lard. They make perfect appetizers and snacks.

Makes: about 65 breadrings; Preparation: 1½ hours; Cooking: 35 minutes; Level of difficulty: Medium

Combine the flour in a large bowl with the salt, oil, and wine. Mix well with a fork until all the flour has been absorbed. § Use a spatula to transfer the dough to a lightly floured work surface. Knead as shown on page 343 until the dough is soft, smooth, and elastic. § Return to the bowl and set aside for 20 minutes. § Divide the dough into 8–10 equal portions and shape each one into a long roll about the thickness of your little finger. The dough will be very elastic and tend to contract; wet your hands so that you can work more easily. § Divide each roll into segments about 3 in (8 cm) long. Using your fingers and thumb, pinch the ends of each segment together to form a ring. Place the breadrings on paper towels. § Bring a large pan containing about 3 quarts (3 liters) of salted water to a boil. Add the tarallucci (not more than 20 at a time), and boil until they rise to the surface. Scoop them out with a slotted spoon and place them on three or four oiled baking sheets. § Cover with lightly oiled foil and set aside to dry for about 30 minutes. § Bake in a preheated oven at 400°F/200°C/gas 6 for 20–25 minutes.

> VARIATIONS
> – Replace the oil with the same quantity of melted and slightly cooled lard.
> – Add 3 teaspoons of freshly ground black pepper, or a heaped tablespoon of fennel seeds, or 3 teaspoons of crushed chilies to the flour.

■ INGREDIENTS
- 3⅓ cups (500 g) unbleached white flour
- 4 tablespoons extra-virgin olive oil
- about 1 cup (250 ml) dry white wine
- 2 teaspoons salt

Breadsticks
Grissini

Makes: about 16 oz (500 g) breadsticks; Preparation: 30 minutes; Rising time: 2 hours; Cooking: 4-5 minutes; Level of difficulty: Medium

Prepare the yeast as explained on page 342. § Combine the flour in a large bowl with the salt, yeast mixture, and remaining water, and proceed as shown on pages 342–343. § When the rising time has elapsed (about 1 hour), transfer the dough to a lightly floured work surface and knead for 2–3 minutes. § Divide the dough into portions about the size of an egg, then shape them

■ INGREDIENTS
- ¾ oz (25 g) fresh yeast or 1½ packages active dry yeast
- 1 teaspoon sugar
- about ¾ cup (200 ml) lukewarm water
- 3 cups (450 g) unbleached white flour
- 1 teaspoon salt

into sticks about the thickness of your little finger. § Sprinkle with flour and transfer to three oiled baking sheets, keeping them a finger's width apart. § Cover with a cloth and set aside to rise for 1 hour. § Bake in a preheated oven at 450°F/230°C/gas 7 for 5 minutes. When cooked, the breadsticks should be well-browned. Leave to cool before removing from the sheets.

VARIATIONS
– Use whole-wheat flour instead of white, or a mixture of the two.
– Add 3 tablespoons of extra-virgin olive oil to the dough. Reduce the amount of water proportionally.
– Increase the amount of yeast to 1 oz (30 g) fresh yeast, or 2 packages of active dry yeast.
– Replace the water partly or entirely with milk.

Above:

Tarallucci and Grissini

Parmesan bread
Pane al formaggio

Makes: about 2 lb (1 kg) of bread; Preparation: 30 minutes; Rising time: 2 hours; Cooking: 30 minutes; Level of difficulty: Medium

Prepare the yeast as explained on page 342. § Combine the flour in a large bowl with the cheese and pepper, if liked. Mix well, sprinkle with salt, and add the yeast mixture and remaining water. Proceed as shown on pages 342–343. § When the rising time has elapsed (about 1 hour), transfer the dough to a lightly floured work surface and knead for 2 minutes. § Divide the dough into 4 equal portions and shape each into a roll about 16 in (40 cm) long. Brush each roll with the egg. Sprinkle two rolls with poppy seeds and two with sesame seeds. § Fold each roll in two, twisting the two parts of each carefully, to make a false braid. § Transfer to two oiled baking sheets. § Cover with a cloth and set aside to rise for 1 hour. § Bake in a preheated oven at 400°F/200°C/gas 6 for 30 minutes.

VARIATIONS
– Replace the water partly or entirely with milk.
– Replace the Parmesan with the same quantity of another tasty cheese.
– Add 3 tablespoons of extra-virgin olive oil to the dough, reducing the amount of water proportionally.

■ INGREDIENTS

- ¾ oz (25 g) fresh yeast or 1½ packages active dry yeast
- 1 teaspoon sugar
- about 1¼ cups (300 ml) lukewarm water
- 4 cups (600 g) unbleached white flour
- 2 cups (250 g) freshly grated Parmesan cheese
- freshly ground white pepper (optional)
- 2 teaspoons salt
- 1 egg, lightly beaten
- 2 tablespoons poppy seeds
- 2 tablespoons sesame seeds

Unleavened bread, Emilia-Romagna-style
Piadine

This small, thin focaccia is traditionally charcoal-grilled on a red hot testo, a slab of heatproof clay.

Makes: about 10 piadine; Preparation: 1 hour; Cooking: 30 minutes; Level of difficulty: Medium

Combine the flour in a large bowl with the salt. Make a hollow in the flour and add the lard and water. Mix well, then transfer to a lightly floured work surface. § Knead until the dough is smooth and elastic. Return to the bowl. Cover with a cloth and set aside for about 30 minutes. § Knead again for 1 minute. § Divide into pieces about the size of an egg. Sprinkle with flour and roll into ⅛-in (3-mm) thick round shapes about 6 in (15 cm) in diameter. Prick well with a fork. § Cook one at a time in a very hot iron or cast-iron pan, without adding any fat. After 2–3 minutes, turn the piadine and cook for 2–3 minutes more. § Stack the piadine up on a plate and serve hot with cured meats and fresh, soft cheeses.

■ INGREDIENTS

- 3 cups (450 g) unbleached white flour
- ⅓ cup (900 g) lard, at room temperature, thinly sliced
- about ½ cup (125 ml) lukewarm water
- 1 teaspoon salt

Right: *Piadine*

Focacce

Salty or sweet, leavened or unleavened, focaccia is as old as bread itself. It is made in a huge variety of ways, depending on local ingredients and traditions.

Focaccia with oil
Focaccia all'olio

Liguria is famous for the quality of its many focacce. This is the basic recipe; several variations follow. Focacce can be served hot, warm, or cold; they are always delicious.

Makes: 1 focaccia, about 12 in (30 cm) in diameter; Preparation: 20 minutes; Rising time: 1½ hours; Cooking: 20 minutes; Level of difficulty: Medium

Prepare the yeast as explained on page 342. § Combine the flour in a large bowl with the fine salt, yeast mixture, 3 tablespoons of oil, and the remaining water, and proceed as shown in the sequence on pages 342–343. § When the rising time has elapsed (about 1½ hours), transfer the dough to a lightly floured work surface and knead for 2–3 minutes. § Place the dough on an oiled baking sheet and, using your hands, spread it into a circular shape about 12 in (30 cm) in diameter and ½ in (1 cm) thick. Dimple the surface with your fingertips, drizzle with the remaining oil, and sprinkle with the coarse salt. § Bake in a preheated oven at 450°F/230°C/gas 7 for about 20 minutes. The focaccia should be well-browned but soft. The bottoms of the dimples in the surface should be light gold.

■ INGREDIENTS

• ½ oz (15 g) fresh yeast or 1 package active dry yeast
• 1 teaspoon sugar
• about ¾ cup (200 ml) lukewarm water
• 3 cups (450 g) unbleached white flour
• 1 teaspoon salt
• ½ cup (125 ml) extra-virgin olive oil
• 1 teaspoon coarse salt

Wine: a light, dry white (Soave)

VARIATIONS
– Use a rolling pin to flatten and spread the dough at first, then complete the process by hand.
– Spread the dough in an oiled, rectangular nonstick pan. The crisp corner pieces are especially good.
– After spreading the dough into a circular shape, sprinkle the surface evenly with a little flour.

Rosemary focaccia
Focaccia al rosmarino

Makes 1 focaccia, about 12 in (30 cm) in diameter; Preparation: 20 minutes; Rising time: 1½ hours; Cooking: 20 minutes; Level of difficulty: Medium

Prepare the focaccia as explained in the recipe above. § Incorporate the rosemary into the dough as you knead after the second rising. § Alternatively, instead of chopping the rosemary leaves, sprinkle them whole over the surface of the dough when spread.

■ INGREDIENTS

• 1 quantity dough for *Focaccia all'olio* (see recipe above)
• 1 tablespoon finely chopped rosemary

Wine: a dry white (Frascati)

Right: *Focaccia al rosmarino*

Sage focaccia
Focaccia alla salvia

Makes 1 focaccia, about 12 in (30 cm) in diameter; Preparation: 20 minutes; Rising time: 1½ hours; Cooking: 20 minutes; Level of difficulty: Medium

Prepare the focaccia as described in the recipe on page 400. § Incorporate the sage into the dough as you knead after the second rising. § Alternatively, sauté the sage in 1 tablespoon of olive oil over medium heat for 1 minute before adding. In this case, reduce the amount of oil added to the flour by 1 tablespoon.

■ INGREDIENTS

- 1 quantity dough for *Focaccia all'olio* (see recipe page 400)
- 1 heaped tablespoon fresh sage leaves, coarsely chopped

Wine: a dry white (Pigato)

Focaccia with black olives
Focaccia con olive nere

Makes 1 focaccia, about 12 in (30 cm) in diameter; Preparation: 20 minutes; Rising time: 1½ hours; Cooking: 20 minutes; Level of difficulty: Medium

Prepare the focaccia as described in the recipe on page 400. § Incorporate the olives into the dough as you knead after the second rising.

■ INGREDIENTS

- 1 quantity dough for *Focaccia all'olio* (see recipe page 400)
- 1½ cups (200 g) black olives, pitted and coarsely chopped

Wine: a light, dry red (Lambrusco)

Focaccia with green olives
Focaccia con olive verdi

Makes: 1 focaccia, about 12 in (30 cm) in diameter; Preparation: 20 minutes; Rising time: 1½ hours; Cooking: 20 minutes; Level of difficulty: Medium

Prepare the focaccia as described in the recipe on page 400. § When the focaccia is ready, arrange the olives face down on the dough. Press them down with your fingers to make them sink into the dough a little.

■ INGREDIENTS

- 1 quantity dough for *Focaccia all'olio* (see recipe page 400)
- 1 cup (125 g) green olives, pitted, and cut in half

Wine: a dry white (Pinot Bianco)

Cheese focaccia
Focaccia al formaggio

Makes: 1 focaccia, about 12 in (30 cm) in diameter; Preparation: 20 minutes; Rising time: 1½ hours; Cooking: 20 minutes; Level of difficulty: Medium

Prepare the focaccia as described in the recipe for on page 400. § When the focaccia is ready, arrange the slices of cheese on top and bake.

■ INGREDIENTS

- 1 quantity dough for *Focaccia all'olio* (see recipe page 400)
- 7 oz (200 g) Fontina cheese, or similar, cut in thin slices

Right: *Focaccia con olive verdi, Focaccia alla salvia, Focaccia al formaggio*

Focaccia con cipolla

Onion focaccia

Makes 1 focaccia, about 12 in (30 cm) in diameter; Preparation: 20 minutes; Rising time: 1½ hours; Cooking: 20 minutes; Level of difficulty: Medium

Prepare the focaccia as described in the recipe on page 400. § Cook the onion in a pot of boiling, salted water for 3–4 minutes. Drain well, cut into fairly thick slices, and spread over the surface of the focaccia before sprinkling with the salt and drizzling with the oil.

■ INGREDIENTS

• 1 quantity dough for
  Focaccia all'olio
  (see recipe page 400)
• 1 large white onion

Wine: a dry white
(Corvo)

Whole-wheat focaccia
Focaccia integrale

Makes: 1 focaccia, about 12 in (30 cm) in diameter; Preparation: 30 minutes; Rising time: about 1½ hours; Cooking: 25 minutes; Level of difficulty: Medium

Prepare the yeast as explained on page 342. § Combine both flours in a large bowl with the salt, yeast mixture, 3 tablespoons of oil and the remaining water, and proceed as shown in the sequence on pages 342–343. § When the rising time has elapsed (about 1½ hours), transfer the dough to a lightly floured work surface and knead for 2-3 minutes. § Place the dough on an oiled baking sheet and, using your hands, spread it into a circular shape about 12 in (30 cm) in diameter and ½ in (1 cm) thick. Sprinkle with the olives and chilies, pressing them lightly into the dough with your fingertips. Drizzle with the remaining oil. § Bake in a preheated oven at 400°F/200°C/gas 6 for 25 minutes.

Focaccia filled with creamy cheese
Focaccia di Recco

This wonderful focaccia comes from Recco, near the city of Genoa in the northwest.

Makes: 1 focaccia about 13 in (32 cm) in diameter; Preparation: 30 minutes; Rising time: about 1½ hours; Cooking: 15 minutes; Level of difficulty: Medium

Prepare the yeast as explained on page 342. § Combine the flour in a large bowl with the salt, yeast mixture, 2 tablespoons of oil and the remaining water, and proceed as shown in the sequence on pages 342–343. § When the rising time has elapsed (about 1½ hours), transfer the dough to a lightly floured work surface and knead for 2–3 minutes. § Divide into two portions, one slightly larger than the other, and roll them out. The larger portion should be about 14 in (35 cm) in diameter, the smaller about 13 in (32 cm). § Transfer the larger one to an oiled baking sheet. Spread with the cheese, leaving a ¾-in (2-cm) border around the edge. § Cover with the smaller piece of dough. Fold back the edges of the larger sheet and press with your fingers to seal thoroughly. Prick several holes in the surface with a fork and brush with the remaining oil. § Bake in a preheated oven at 500°F/250°C/gas 8 for 15 minutes.

Left: *Focaccia integrale*

Focaccia with onions
Fitascetta

This is a regional recipe from the city of Como, in Lombardy, where it is made with the same dough as the renowned local bread.

Makes: 1 round focaccia, about 12 in (30 cm) in diameter; Preparation: 30 minutes; Rising time: 1½ hours; Cooking: 30 minutes; Level of difficulty: Medium

Prepare the yeast as explained on page 342. § Combine the flour in a large bowl with the salt, yeast mixture and remaining water, and proceed as shown in the sequence on pages 342–343. The dough should be rather soft; if it is difficult to knead, leave it in the bowl and mix for several minutes with a wooden spoon. § While the dough is rising, peel and slice the onions. Cook over medium-low heat with the butter and 2 tablespoons of water for 30 minutes. Remove from heat and leave to cool. § When the rising time has elapsed (about 1 hour), transfer the dough to a lightly floured work surface and knead for 2–3 minutes. § Shape into a loaf about 3 ft (1 m) long. § Transfer the loaf to an oiled baking sheet, and shape it into a ring, joining the two ends together, and leaving a large hole in the middle. § Cover with a cloth and set aside to rise for about 30 minutes. § When the second rising time has elapsed, flatten the dough a little with your hands and spread the onions on top. Sprinkle with salt. § Bake in a preheated oven at 400°F/200°C/gas 6 for about 30 minutes. § Serve hot.

■ INGREDIENTS
- ¾ oz (25 g) fresh yeast or 1½ packages active dried yeast
- 1 teaspoon sugar
- about ¾ cup (200 ml) lukewarm water
- 3 cups (450 g) unbleached white flour
- 2 teaspoons salt
- 1 lb (500 g) red onions
- 2 tablespoons butter

Wine: a dry red (Oltrepò Pavese)

VARIATIONS
– If you are short of time, omit the second rising time and put the fitasecca directly into the oven as soon as you switch it on. Lengthen cooking time by 10 minutes.
– For a sweet focaccia, omit the salt and sprinkle the onions with 1 tablespoon of sugar.
– Purists disapprove, but there is an excellent variation in which 7 oz (200 g) of thinly sliced fresh cheese is placed on top of the onions. Because the cheese will melt during cooking and will probably drip, spread the dough into a 1-in (2.5-cm) thick circular shape, rather than a ring. Leave a narrow border around the edge without topping. Cooking time will be shortened by several minutes.

Right: *Fitascetta*

Focaccia with tomato and garlic
Puddica

A fragrant focaccia from the Apulia region, in the south.

Makes: 1 focaccia, 12 in (30 cm) in diameter; Preparation: 30 minutes; Rising time: about 1½ hours; Cooking: 20-25 minutes; Level of difficulty: Medium

Prepare the yeast as explained on page 342. § Combine the flour in a large bowl with the salt, yeast mixture, 2 tablespoons of oil and the remaining water, and proceed as shown in the sequence on pages 342–343. § To peel the tomatoes, plunge them into a pot of boiling water for 30 seconds and then into cold. Slip off the skins, cut in half, and squeeze to remove some of the seeds. § When the rising time has elapsed (about 1½ hours), transfer the dough to a lightly floured work surface and knead for 1 minute. § Place on an oiled baking sheet, or in an oiled, nonstick rectangular baking pan and spread with your hands. § Dimple the surface with your fingertips and fill the dimples with pieces of garlic and tomato. § Drizzle the surface with the remaining oil and sprinkle with oregano and pepper. § Bake in a preheated oven at 450°F/230°C/gas 7 for 20–25 minutes. § Serve hot, warm or at room temperature.

■ INGREDIENTS

- ½ oz (15 g) fresh yeast or 1 package active dry yeast
- 1 teaspoon sugar
- ¾ cup (200 ml) lukewarm water
- 3 cups (450 g) unbleached white flour
- 1 teaspoon salt
- 4 tablespoons extra-virgin olive oil
- 6 small ripe tomatoes
- 3 cloves garlic, cut vertically in 4
- 2 teaspoons oregano
- freshly ground black pepper

Wine: a dry white (Locorotondo)

Focaccia with potatoes
Focaccia con patate

This soft, delicious focaccia is always a great success.
It will keep for at least 3 days.

Makes: 1 focaccia, about 12 in (30 cm) in diameter; Preparation: 30 minutes; Rising time: 1½ hours; Cooking: 20-25 minutes; Level of difficulty: Medium

Prepare the yeast as explained on page 342. Use all the water to dissolve the yeast. § Mash the boiled potatoes while still hot. § Combine the potatoes in a large bowl with the flour, fine salt, yeast mixture and 1 tablespoon of oil, and proceed as shown in the sequence on pages 342–343. The dough will be too soft to knead by hand; leave it in the bowl and mix vigorously with a

■ INGREDIENTS

- ½ oz (15 g) fresh yeast or 1 package active dry yeast
- 1 teaspoon sugar
- about 4 tablespoons lukewarm water
- 8 oz (250 g) boiled potatoes, still warm
- 2 cups (300 g) unbleached white flour

Right: Puddica

- 2 teaspoons fine salt
- 4 tablespoons extra-virgin olive oil
- 1 teaspoon coarse salt

Wine: a dry white
(Roero Arneis)

wooden spoon for 2–3 minutes. Set aside to rise. § When the rising time has elapsed (about 1 hour), mix again for 1 minute. § Transfer to an oiled nonstick baking pan 12 in (30 cm) in diameter. Spread the dough with your hands. Cover with a cloth and set aside to rise for 30 minutes. § Sprinkle with the coarse salt. Dimple the surface with your fingertips and drizzle with the remaining oil. § Bake in a preheated oven at 400°F/200°C/gas 6 for 20–25 minutes. § Serve hot or at room temperature.

VARIATION
– Shape the dough into small focacce (*focaccette*) about 6 in (15 cm) in diameter and ¾ in (2 cm) thick. They will take 15–20 minutes to cook. Serve hot, or reheat briefly in the oven before serving.

Filled Breads
and Pies

Many of the recipes in this chapter are from southern Italian cuisine. Hearty and rustic, they make wonderful light lunches or picnic dishes.

Calabrian-style filled bread
Pitta alla calabrese

Makes: 1 filled bread, about 9 in (23 cm) in diameter; Preparation: 40 minutes; Rising time: about 2 hours; Cooking: 30 minutes; Level of difficulty: Medium

Prepare the dough as explained on pages 342–343, using the first 5 ingredients listed for the dough. § For the filling, combine the tomatoes, garlic, and half the oil in a saucepan. Cook over medium-low heat for 8–10 minutes, stirring frequently. Remove from heat and leave to cool. § Add the tuna, olives, anchovies, and capers. Mix well and taste before seasoning with salt and pepper. § When the rising time has elapsed (about 1½ hours), knead the dough on a lightly floured work surface for half a minute. Flatten the dough and spread with the lard. Add the egg yolk and knead again. § Break off about a third of the dough and set aside. § Roll the rest into a disk about 12 in (30 cm) in diameter. § Oil a 9-in (23-cm) springform pan and line the bottom and sides with the dough. § Spread with the filling. § Roll the remaining dough into a disk as large as the springform pan and cover the filling. Seal the dish by folding the edges of the first sheet of dough over the top sheet to make a border. § Brush the surface with oil, cover with a cloth, and set aside to rise for 30 minutes. § Bake in a preheated oven at 400°F/200°C/gas 6 for 30 minutes. Serve hot.

■ INGREDIENTS

DOUGH
- ½ oz (15 g) fresh yeast or 1 package active dry yeast
- 1 teaspoon sugar
- about ¾ cup (200 ml) lukewarm water
- 2⅓ cups (350 g) unbleached white flour
- 2 teaspoons salt
- ¼ cup (60 g) lard (or butter), at room temperature
- 1 egg yolk

FILLING
- 10 oz (300 g) tomatoes, peeled and chopped
- 1 clove garlic, finely chopped
- 4 tablespoons extra-virgin olive oil
- 1¼ cups (250 g) tuna in oil, drained, and chopped
- ¾ cup (90 g) black olives, pitted (stoned), cut in quarters
- 8 anchovy fillets, crumbled
- 1 tablespoon capers
- salt and freshly ground black pepper

Wine: a dry red (Savuto)

Filled bread with ricotta and sausage
Pitta alla reggina

Makes: 1 filled bread, about 9 in (23 cm) in diameter; Preparation: 40 minutes; Rising time: about 2 hours; Cooking: 30 minutes; Level of difficulty: Medium

Prepare the dough as explained on pages 342–343, adding the oil to the flour. § Mix the Ricotta, sausage, Pecorino, parsley, salt, and pepper in a bowl. § When the rising time has elapsed (about 1¾ hours), knead the dough on a lightly floured work surface for half a minute. § Break off about a third of the dough and set aside. § Roll the rest into a disk about 12 in (30 cm) in diameter. Grease a 9-in (23-cm) springform pan with a little of the lard and line the base and sides with the dough. § Spread with half the filling, followed by a layer of egg. Cover with the rest of the

■ INGREDIENTS

DOUGH
- ½ oz (15 g) fresh yeast or 1 package active dry yeast
- 1 teaspoon sugar
- about ¾ cup (200 ml) lukewarm water
- 2⅓ cups (350 g) unbleached white flour
- 3 tablespoons extra-virgin olive oil
- 2 teaspoons salt

Right: *Pitta alla Reggina*

FILLING

- 1 cup (250 g) soft Ricotta cheese
- 4 oz (125 g) Italian sausage, crumbled
- 4 tablespoons freshly grated Pecorino cheese
- 1 tablespoon finely chopped parsley
- salt and freshly ground black pepper
- 2 hard-cooked (hard-boiled) eggs, sliced
- 1 tablespoon lard

filling. § Roll the remaining dough into a disk as large as the springform pan and cover the filling. Seal the dish by folding the edges of the first sheet of dough over the second to make a border. Prick the surface with a fork and dot with the remaining lard. Cover with a cloth and set aside in a warm place for 30 minutes. § Bake in a preheated oven at 400°F/200°C/gas 6 for 30 minutes. § Serve hot or at room temperature.

VARIATION
– Replace the sausage with the same quantity of prosciutto cut in a single, thick slice, and diced into cubes.

INGREDIENTS

DOUGH

- ½ oz (15 g) fresh yeast or 1 package active dry yeast
- 1 teaspoon sugar
- ¾ cup (200 ml) lukewarm water
- 2⅓ cups (350 g) unbleached white flour
- 2 teaspoons salt
- 1 tablespoon lard, thinly sliced

FILLING

- 10 oz (300 g) Pecorino cheese, sliced
- 10 oz (300 g) ripe tomatoes
- salt and freshly ground black pepper
- 8 anchovy fillets, crumbled
- 2 tablespoons finely chopped onion
- 1 tablespoon lard, chopped
- 1 tablespoon extra-virgin olive oil

Wine: a dry red (Cirò Rosso)

INGREDIENTS

- ¾ oz (25 g) fresh yeast, or 1½ packages active dry yeast
- 3½ tablespoons warm water
- 1 teaspoon sugar
- 3 eggs + 1 yolk, beaten
- ⅓ cup (90 ml) extra-virgin olive oil
- 2 cups (300 g) unbleached white flour
- 2 cups (250 g) freshly grated Parmesan cheese
- 2 teaspoons salt
- ½ teaspoon white pepper

Wine: a dry rosé (Brindisi Rosato)

Filled bread with pecorino, tomato, and anchovies
Scacciata

Makes: 1 filled bread, about 9 in (23 cm) in diameter; Preparation: 35 minutes; Rising time: about 2 hours; Cooking: 30 minutes; Level of difficulty: Medium

Prepare the dough as explained on pages 342–343, incorporating the lard while kneading. § Place the tomatoes in boiling water for 1 minute, then peel. Cut them in two, remove the seeds and cut in half again. § When the rising time has elapsed (about 1½ hours), knead the dough for 1 minute on a lightly floured work surface. § Break off about a third of the dough and set aside. § Roll the rest into a disk about 12 in (30 cm) in diameter. § Oil a 9-in (23-cm) springform pan and line the base and sides with the dough. § Cover with the cheese, then the tomatoes. Sprinkle with salt and pepper. Add the anchovies, onion, and lard. § Roll the remaining dough into a disk as large as the springform pan and cover the filling. Seal the dish by folding the edges of the first sheet of dough over the second to make a border. Prick the surface with a fork and brush with the oil. Cover with a cloth and set aside to rise for about 30 minutes. § Bake in a preheated oven at 400°F/ 200°C/gas 6 for 30 minutes.

Cheese flat bread
Torta al formaggio

An Easter speciality from Umbria, this cheese flat bread is traditionally served piping hot with sliced ham, prosciutto, salami, mortadella and other preserved meats.

Makes: 1 flat bread, about 10 in (25 cm) in diameter; Preparation: 40 minutes; Rising time: about 4 hours; Cooking: 40 minutes; Level of difficulty: Simple

Mix the yeast with the water, add the sugar and set aside for 10 minutes. § Combine the eggs with the oil in a bowl. § Combine the flour in a bowl with the salt. Stir in the yeast mixture and the eggs until the flour absorbs all the ingredients. The dough will be soft and sticky. § Mix for 6–8 minutes with a wooden spoon. Cover with a cloth and set aside to rise for 2 hours. § When the rising time has elapsed, add the cheese and pepper and mix again for 3–4 minutes. § Oil and flour a 10-in (25-cm) springform pan. Fill with the dough, cover with a cloth and set aside to rise for 2 hours. § Bake in a preheated oven at 375°F/190°C/gas 5 for 40 minutes. § Serve hot.

Left: *Torta al formaggio*

Swiss chard pie
Torta di bietole

Makes: 1 filled bread, about 10 in (25 cm) in diameter; Preparation: 45 minutes + 30 minutes standing; Cooking: 25-30 minutes; Level of difficulty: Medium

Put the flour in a mixing bowl and add the salt, water, and oil. Stir well the knead as explained on page 343 until the dough is soft and elastic. Cover and set aside for 30 minutes. § For the filling, heat 3 tablespoons of oil in a sauté pan, add the onion and, after 2–3 minutes, the Swiss chard, marjoram, and borage. Sauté over medium-low heat for 5–7 minutes. § Transfer to a mixing bowl and leave to cool. § Add the egg, cheese, salt, and pepper, and mix well. § Break off about a third of the dough and set aside. § Roll the rest into a disk about 12 in (30 cm) in diameter. Use as little additional flour as possible when rolling the dough; it should be very elastic. § Oil a 10-in (25-cm) springform pan and line the base and sides with the dough. § Spread with the filling. § Roll the remaining dough into a disk as large as the springform pan and cover the filling. Seal the dish by folding the edges of the first sheet of dough over the second to make a border. § Brush the surface with the remaining oil, and bake in a preheated oven at 400°F/200°C/gas 6 for 25–30 minutes. § Serve hot.

■ INGREDIENTS

DOUGH
- 2 cups (300 g) unbleached white flour
- 1 teaspoon salt
- ½ cup (125 ml) cold water
- 3 tablespoons extra-virgin olive oil

FILLING
- 4 tablespoons extra-virgin olive oil
- 2 tablespoons finely chopped onion
- 1¼ lb (600 g) Swiss chard (silver beet), boiled squeezed, and chopped
- 1 tablespoon marjoram
- 4 leaves borage, chopped
- 1 egg
- ¾ cup (90 g) freshly grated Parmesan cheese
- salt and freshly ground black pepper

Wine: a dry white (Tocai)

Cheese, cream, and speck pie
Crostata al formaggio

Makes: 1 pie, about 9 in (23 cm) in diameter; Preparation: 10 minutes + 40 minutes for the pastry; Cooking: 30-35 minutes; Level of difficulty: Medium

Prepare the pastry base. § Combine the eggs in a bowl with salt and pepper to taste. Add the Emmental and cream. § Remove the pastry base from the refrigerator and discard the plastic wrap. Sprinkle the speck over the base, then pour the egg, cheese, and cream mixture over the top. § Bake in a preheated oven at 350°F/180°C/gas 4 for 30–35 minutes. Raise the oven temperature a little for the last 5 minutes, so that the pie crust will turn golden brown. § Serve hot.

■ INGREDIENTS

DOUGH
- 1 quantity *Ricotta pastry* (see recipe p. 58)
- 3 eggs, lightly beaten
- salt and freshly ground black pepper
- 1 cup (125 g) freshly grated Emmenthal cheese
- ⅔ cup (150 ml) light (single) cream
- ¾ cup (100 g) speck, coarsely chopped

Right: Crostata di ricotta

DOUGH
- 1 quantity *Special* or *Plain pastry* (see recipes p. 58)

TOPPING
- 1¼ cups (300 g) fresh Ricotta cheese
- 2 eggs, beaten
- ¼ cup (60 g) ham + ⅓ cup (90 g) mortadella, chopped
- ½ cup (60 g) freshly grated spicy Provolone cheese
- 2 tablespoons light cream
- salt and freshly ground black pepper

Ricotta pie
Crostata di ricotta

Makes: 1 pie, about 9 in (23 cm) in diameter; Preparation: 30 minutes + 40 minutes for the pastry; Cooking: 40 minutes; Level of difficulty: Medium

Prepare the pastry base. § Combine the Ricotta, eggs, ham, mortadella, Provolone, cream, salt, and pepper in a mixing bowl. § Remove the pastry base from the refrigerator and discard the plastic wrap. § Spread the base evenly with the filling and bake in a preheated oven at 375°F/190°C/gas 5 for about 40 minutes, or until the top is golden brown. § Leave to cool and serve at room temperature. This pie can be prepared ahead of time.

Filled bread with Belgian endive or escarole

Pizza di scarola

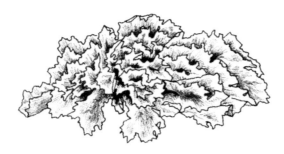

This is a traditional recipe for a Christmas Eve dish from Campania, the region around Naples, in the south. Use either endives or escarole, whichever is easier to find.

Makes: 1 filled bread, 9 in (23 cm) in diameter; Preparation: 45 minutes; Rising time: about 2 hours; Cooking: 30 minutes; Level of difficulty: Medium

Prepare the dough as shown on pages 342–343. § Blanch the Belgian endive or escarole in 5 pints (2 liters) of boiling water for 2–3 minutes. Drain, squeeze out excess moisture, and coarsely chop. § Sauté the garlic in two-thirds of the oil until it turns light gold. Discard the garlic. § Add the endive (or escarole), capers, and olives and sauté over medium heat for 7–8 minutes. § Turn off the heat and add the anchovies. Stir well and set aside to cool. § When the rising time has elapsed (about 1½ hours), knead the dough for half a minute on a lightly floured work surface. § Break off about a third of the dough and set aside. § Roll the rest into a disk about 12 in (30 cm) in diameter. § Grease a 9-in (23-cm) springform pan with the lard and line the base and sides with the dough. § Taste the filling and season with salt if necessary. Spread the base with the filling and, if liked, sprinkle with the raisins. § Roll the remaining dough into a disk as large as the springform pan and cover the filling. Seal the dish by folding the edges of the first sheet of dough over the second to make a border. Brush the surface with the remaining oil, cover, and set aside to rise for 30 minutes. § Bake in a preheated oven at 400°F/200°C/gas 6 for 30 minutes. § This dish is usually served hot, but it is also delicious at room temperature.

INGREDIENTS

DOUGH
- ½ oz (15 g) fresh yeast or package active dry yeast
- 1 teaspoon sugar
- about ¾ cup (200 ml) lukewarm water
- 2⅓ cups (350 g) unbleached white flour
- 2 teaspoons salt

FILLING
- 2½ lb (1.25 kg) Belgian endives or escarole, cleaned and washed
- 1 clove garlic, cut in half
- ½ cup (125 ml) extra-virgin olive oil
- 2 tablespoons capers
- 1 cup (100 g) black olives, pitted
- 8 anchovy fillets, chopped
- 1 tablespoon lard
- salt
- 1 tablespoon raisins, rinsed in warm water (optional)

Wine: a dry white (Greco di Tufo)

VARIATIONS
– Add a generous grinding of fresh black pepper to the dough.
– Sprinkle the filling with pine nuts in place of, or together with, the raisins.

Right:
Pizza di scarola

Asparagus pie
Torta di asparagi

Makes: 1 pie, about 10 in (25 cm) in diameter; Preparation: 40 minutes + 30 minutes standing; Cooking: 35-40 minutes; Level of difficulty: Medium

Asparagus pie is prepared in the same way as the Onion pie on page 430. § Steam the asparagus, drain, and discard all but the green tips. Divide the tips into 2–3 strips and sauté for a few minutes in the butter. § Mix with the egg, cheese, and other ingredients and proceed as with the Onion pie. § In the same way it is possible to use French beans (about 1¾ lb/800 g), boiled and sautéed briefly in butter, or porcini mushrooms (about 1¾ lb/800 g) sautéed for 7–8 minutes over a high heat with 4 tablespoons extra-virgin olive oil, 2 cloves finely chopped garlic, and 2 tablespoons finely chopped parsley.

■ INGREDIENTS

DOUGH
• 1 quantity *Plain pastry* (see recipe p. 58)

FILLING
• 3 lb (1.5 kg) fresh asparagus
• 4 eggs
• ½ cup (60 g) freshly grated Parmesan cheese
• 1 cup (250 g) soft Ricotta cheese
• 3 tablespoons butter
• 3 tablespoons oil
• salt and freshly ground black pepper

Wine: a dry white (Galestro)

Filled bread with cheese, ham, and salami
Torta rustica

Makes: 1 filled bread, about 9 in (23 cm) in diameter; Preparation: 35 minutes; Rising time: about 2 hours; Cooking: 25-30 minutes; Level of difficulty: Medium

Prepare the dough as shown on pages 342–343, setting the lard aside. § Combine all the filling ingredients, except the oil, in a bowl, and mix. § When the rising time has elapsed (about 1½ hours), knead the dough for half a minute on a lightly floured work surface. § Flatten the dough, sprinkle with the lard and knead again. § Break off about a third of the dough and set aside. § Roll the rest into a disk about 12 in (30 cm) in diameter. § Oil a 9-in (23-cm) springform pan and line the base and sides with the dough. § Spread with the filling. § Roll the remaining dough into a disk as large as the springform pan and cover the filling. Seal the dish by folding the edges of the first sheet of dough over the second to make a border. Brush the surface with the oil, cover with a cloth and set aside to rise for 30 minutes. § Bake in a preheated oven at 400°F/200°C/gas 6 for about 25–30 minutes. § Serve warm or cold.

■ INGREDIENTS

DOUGH
• ½ oz (15 g) fresh yeast or 1 package active dry yeast
• 1 teaspoon sugar
• about ¾ cup (200 ml) lukewarm water
• 2⅓ cups (350 g) unbleached white flour
• 2 teaspoons salt
• ⅓ cup (90 g) lard

FILLING
• ¾ cup (225 g) Ricotta cheese
• 1¾ cups (225 g) Pecorino cheese, grated
• ⅔ cup (75 g) prosciutto, diced
• ½ cup (60 g) salami, diced
• 1 egg
• salt and pepper
• 2 tablespoons extra-virgin olive oil

Right: Torta di asparagi

■ INGREDIENTS

DOUGH

- ½ oz (15 g) fresh yeast or 1 package active dry yeast
- 2 teaspoons sugar
- 3–4 tablespoons lukewarm milk (or water)
- 2 cups (350 g) unbleached white flour
- 1 heaped teaspoon salt
- ⅔ cup (150 g) butter, at room temperature, in thin slices
- 4 eggs, lightly beaten

FILLING

- 14 oz (450 g) ripe tomatoes
- 2 tablespoons extra-virgin olive oil
- 10 oz (300 g) Mozzarella cheese, sliced
- salt and freshly ground black pepper
- 8–10 leaves fresh basil, torn
- 5 oz (150 g) prosciutto, sliced and cut in strips
- 4 tablespoons freshly grated Parmesan cheese
- 1 egg, beaten
- 2 tablespoons butter

Wine: a dry white (Pinot Grigio)

Neapolitan filled bread
Pizza alla Campofranco

Makes: 1 filled bread, about 9 in (23 cm) in diameter; Preparation: 45 minutes; Rising time: about 3 hours; Cooking: 25-30 minutes; Level of difficulty: Medium

Crumble the yeast into a bowl and add the sugar. Mix with the milk (or water) and set aside for 5 minutes. § Put the flour in a mixing bowl, sprinkle with salt and make a hollow in the center. Fill with the yeast mixture, butter, and eggs. Mix with a wooden spoon until the flour absorbs most of the ingredients. § Transfer to a lightly floured work surface. Use a spatula to remove all the mixture from the bowl. § Knead for several minutes until the dough becomes soft and elastic. § Place in a bowl, cover with a cloth, and set aside to rise for 2 hours. § Place the tomatoes in boiling water for 1 minute, then peel, cut in half, and remove the seeds. § Sauté the tomatoes in the oil over high heat for 3–4 minutes. Shake the pan from time to time to move and turn the tomatoes, rather than stirring them. § Butter and flour a 9-in (23-cm) springform pan. § When the rising time has elapsed (about 2 hours), transfer the dough to a lightly floured work surface and tap lightly with your fingers so that it contracts a little. § Break off about a third of the dough and set aside. § Place the rest in the springform pan and spread by hand to line the base and sides of the pan. § Cover with half the Mozzarella, followed by the tomatoes. Sprinkle with salt and pepper, scatter with the basil, and cover with the prosciutto and remaining Mozzarella. Sprinkle with the Parmesan and, if liked, more pepper. § Roll the remaining dough into a disk as large as the springform pan. Brush the edges of the dough with half the beaten egg. Cover the filling with the dough and seal the edges by pressing them together lightly with your fingers. § Cover with a cloth and set aside to rise for about 1 hour. § Brush the surface of the dish with the remaining egg and bake in a preheated oven at 400°F/200°C/gas 6 for 25–30 minutes. § Serve hot.

Left: Pizza alla Campofranco

Spinach pie
Crostata di spinaci

Makes: 1 pie, about 9 in (23 cm) in diameter; Preparation: 10 minutes + time for the pastry; Cooking: 40 minutes; Level of difficulty: Medium

Prepare the pastry base. § Mix the spinach and Ricotta in a bowl. Add the Parmesan, eggs, cream, salt, pepper, and, if liked, nutmeg. Mix well. § Remove the pastry base from the refrigerator and discard the plastic wrap. § Spread evenly with the topping and sprinkle with the bread crumbs. § Sprinkle with the butter and bake in a preheated oven at 350°F/180°C/gas 4 for about 40 minutes. § This pie can be served hot or at room temperature.

■ INGREDIENTS

DOUGH
- 1 quantity *Plain pastry* (see recipe p. 58)

TOPPING
- 1½ lb (750 g) spinach, cooked, squeezed dry, and chopped
- 1 cup (250 g) Ricotta cheese
- ½ cup (60 g) freshly grated Parmesan cheese
- 2 eggs, beaten
- ⅔ cup (150 ml) cream
- salt and freshly ground black pepper
- nutmeg
- 2 tablespoons bread crumbs
- 2 tablespoons butter, chopped

Filled bread with tomatoes, olives, and onion
Pizza alla barese

Makes: 1 filled bread, about 9 in (23 cm) in diameter; Preparation: 40 minutes; Rising time: about 2 hours; Cooking: 30 minutes; Level of difficulty: Medium

Prepare the dough as explained on pages 342–343. § Plunge the tomatoes into boiling water for 1–2 minutes, then into cold. Peel and cut into segments, removing the seeds. § Heat 3 tablespoons of oil in a sauté pan. Add the onion and, after 1 minute, the tomatoes. Cook over high heat for 3–4 minutes, stirring as little as possible to avoid crushing the tomatoes. Remove from heat. § Add the olives to the tomato mixture. Season with salt and pepper. § When the rising time has elapsed (about 1½ hours), knead the dough on a lightly floured work surface for half a minute. § Break off a third of the dough and set aside. Roll the rest into a disk about 12 in (30 cm) in diameter. § Oil a 9-in (23-cm) springform pan and line the base and sides with the dough. § Spread with the tomato mixture and sprinkle with the Ricotta. § Roll the remaining dough into a disk as large as the springform pan and cover the filling. Seal the dish by folding the edges of the first sheet of dough over the second to make a border. Brush the surface with the oil, cover with a cloth and set aside to rise for 30 minutes. § Bake in a preheated oven at 400°F/ 200°C/gas 6 for about 30 minutes. § Serve hot.

■ INGREDIENTS

DOUGH
- ½ oz (15 g) fresh yeast or 1 package active dry yeast
- 1 teaspoon sugar
- about ¾ cup (200 ml) lukewarm water
- 2⅓ cups (350 g) unbleached white flour
- 2 teaspoons salt

FILLING
- 1 lb (500 g) ripe tomatoes
- ⅓ cup (90 ml) extra-virgin olive oil
- 1 medium onion, sliced
- ¾ cup (90 g) black olives, pitted (stoned), and cut in 4 lengthwise
- salt and freshly ground black pepper
- 2 cups (250 g) Ricotta salata cheese, flaked

Wine: a dry red (Bardolino)

Right: Crostata di spinaci

Easter pie
Torta pasqualina

This extraordinary dish comes from Liguria, the region around the city of Genoa. It is not quick or easy to make but, if you persevere, it is well worth the effort. According to tradition, the pie should be made with 33 sheets of pastry - Christ's age when he died. Nowadays, the number is usually reduced, as in the following version.

Makes: 1 pie, about 10 in (25 cm) in diameter; Preparation: 1½ hours + 40 minutes standing; Cooking: 50 minutes; Level of difficulty: Complicated

Put the flour in a mixing bowl, sprinkle with salt, and make a hollow in the center. Fill with the oil and water. Mix with a wooden spoon until most of the flour has been absorbed. § Transfer the mixture to a lightly floured work surface and knead until the dough is smooth and elastic. § Divide into 15 portions, 14 the same size and one slightly larger. Cover with a damp cloth and set aside for 30 minutes. § Remove the white part from the stalks of the Swiss chard, rinse well, and cook for 5–7 minutes in a little salted, boiling water. Drain, squeeze, and coarsely chop. § Sauté the onion, garlic, and parsley in 3 tablespoons of oil for 2 minutes over medium-low heat. § Add the Swiss chard and cook, stirring frequently, for about 5 minutes. Turn off the heat, add the marjoram, stir well and set aside to cool. § Combine the Ricotta, cream, flour, and 2 eggs in a bowl, season with salt and pepper, and mix well. § Roll out the larger piece of dough to obtain a very thin disk large enough to cover the base of the springform pan. § Oil the springform pan and line with the dough. Stretch the dough carefully so that it covers the sides and overlaps a little. The dough should be very thin, almost transparent. Brush with oil. § Prepare another 6 sheets of dough, large enough to cover the base and three-quarters of the sides of the springform pan. Place them in the pan one by one, brushing their surfaces with oil, except for the last one. § Spread the Swiss chard evenly over the top sheet and sprinkle with half the Parmesan. Drizzle with 2 tablespoons of the oil and cover with the Ricotta mixture. § Use the back of a spoon to make 6 fairly deep hollows evenly spaced in the filling. Place a little butter in each hollow, then break an egg into each, taking care to keep the yolks intact. Season with salt and pepper, drizzle each egg with a few drops of olive oil, and sprinkle with the remaining Parmesan. § Use the remaining dough to make another 6 sheets about the same size as the springform pan. Place them over the filling one by one, brushing their surfaces with oil. § Fold back the edges of the first sheet, sealing

■ INGREDIENTS

DOUGH
- 3⅓ cups (500 g) unbleached white flour
- 2 teaspoons salt
- 2 tablespoons extra-virgin olive oil
- 1 cup (250 ml) water

FILLING
- 2 lb (1 kg) fresh Swiss chard (silver beet)
- 2 heaped tablespoons finely chopped onion
- 1 clove garlic, finely chopped (optional)
- 1 tablespoon finely chopped parsley
- ⅓ cup (90 ml) extra-virgin olive oil
- 1 heaped teaspoon fresh marjoram
- ¾ cup (200 g) soft Ricotta cheese
- ⅓ cup (90 ml) fresh cream
- 1 tablespoon all-purpose (plain) flour
- 8 eggs
- salt and freshly ground black pepper
- ½ cup (60 g) freshly grated Parmesan cheese
- 2 tablespoons butter

Wine: a dry white (Colli di Luni)

Right: *Torta pasqualina*

the edges of the sheets inside, and forming a border around the pie. Brush the surface with oil and prick with a fork, taking care not to break the egg yolks inside. § Bake in a preheated oven at 375°F/190°C/gas 5 for 50 minutes. § Serve lukewarm or at room temperature.

VARIATION
– Replace the Swiss chard with 8 globe artichokes, previously cleaned, sliced, and cooked with the onion, garlic, and parsley as above, but using 2½ tablespoons of butter instead of the oil.

■ INGREDIENTS

DOUGH
- 2⅓ cups (350 g) unbleached white flour
- 1 teaspoon salt
- ⅓ cup (90 g) lard (or butter), thinly sliced and at room temperature
- about ⅔ cup (150 ml) cold water

FILLING
- 2½ tablespoons lard (or butter)
- 1 cup (120 g) pancetta, chopped
- 1 tablespoon onion, chopped
- 1 clove garlic, finely chopped
- 1 tablespoon finely chopped parsley
- 1 lb (500 g) spinach
- 1¼ cups (125 g) freshly grated Parmesan cheese
- 2 eggs
- salt and freshly ground black pepper
- dash of nutmeg (optional)
- 1 tablespoon light (single) cream (or milk)

Wine: a dry red (Sangiovese di Romagna)

Filled bread with spinach, pancetta, and parmesan cheese
Scarpazzone

This traditional bread comes from the Emilia-Romagna region, in central Italy.

Makes: 1 pie, about 9 in (23 cm) in diameter; Preparation: 40 minutes + 30 minutes standing; Cooking: 30 minutes; Level of difficulty: Medium

Combine the flour in a bowl with the salt. Make a hollow in the flour and fill with the lard and water. Mix with a fork until the ingredients are roughly amalgamated. § Transfer to a lightly floured work surface and knead until the dough is smooth and soft. Cover with a cloth and set aside for at least 30 minutes. § Clean the spinach, rinse well, and cook for 5–7 minutes in a little salted, boiling water. Drain, squeeze, and coarsely chop. § Place 2 tablespoons of lard in a large sauté pan with the pancetta, onion, garlic, and parsley. Sauté over medium-low heat for a few minutes. Add the spinach and cook, stirring frequently, for 8–10 minutes. § Transfer the mixture to a bowl and set aside to cool. § Add the Parmesan, eggs, salt, and pepper, and, if liked, a little nutmeg. § Break off about a third of the dough and set aside. § Roll the rest into a disk about 11 in (28 cm) in diameter. § Grease a springform pan with the remaining lard and line the base and sides with the dough. § Spread evenly with the filling. § Roll the remaining dough into a disk slightly larger than the springform pan and cover the filling. Seal the dish by folding the edges of the first sheet of dough over the second to make a border. Prick the surface with a fork and brush with the cream. § Bake in a preheated oven at 375°F/190°C/gas 5 for about 30 minutes. § Serve hot or at room temperature.

VARIATION
– Replace the spinach with the same quantity of Swiss chard (silver beet), or use equal quantities of each.

Left: Scarpazzone

Onion pie

Crostata di cipolle

Makes: 1 pie, about 9 in (23 cm) in diameter; Preparation: 40 minutes + 40 minutes for the pastry; Cooking: 40 minutes; Level of difficulty: Medium

Prepare the pastry. § Sauté the onions in the butter over low heat for 25-30 minutes, stirring frequently. When cooked, the onions should be soft and golden brown. § Lightly beat the egg in a bowl, then add the milk and the flour, mixing well so that no lumps form. Season with salt and pepper. § Remove the pastry base from the refrigerator and discard the plastic wrap. § Cover the base with a sheet of foil, pressing it down carefully so that it adheres to the pastry. § Bake in a preheated oven at 350°F/180°C/gas 4 for 15 minutes. § Take the pie plate or springform pan out of the oven and, using the palm of a gloved hand, carefully press the base down so that it contracts a little. § Discard the foil and return the pie to the oven for 5 minutes more. § Take the base out again, spread evenly with the onion mixture and pour the egg and milk mixture over the top. § Bake for 20 minutes more. § Serve hot.

■ INGREDIENTS

DOUGH
• 1 quantity *Plain pastry* (see recipe p. 58)

TOPPING
• 2 lb (1 kg) onions, sliced
• 3 oz (90 g) butter
• 1 egg
• ¾ cup (180 ml) milk
• 1 tablespoon flour
• salt and freshly ground black pepper

Wine: a dry white (Pinot Bianco)

Pea pie

Crostata di piselli

Makes: 1 pie, about 9 in (23 cm) in diameter; Preparation: 40 minutes + 40 minutes for the pastry; Cooking: 40 minutes; Level of difficulty: Medium

Prepare the pastry base. § Parboil the peas in a pot of salted, boiling water for 5–10 minutes. Drain and place in a small, heavy-bottomed saucepan with 2 tablespoons of melted butter. Sauté over medium-low heat, stirring frequently, for about 5 minutes, or until the peas are tender. Season with salt. § Remove the pastry base from the refrigerator and discard the plastic wrap. Cover the base with a sheet of foil, pressing it down carefully so that it adheres to the pastry. § Bake in a preheated oven at 350°F/180°C/gas 4 for 15 minutes. § Take the pie plate or springform pan out of the oven and, using the palm of a gloved hand, carefully press the base down so that it contracts a little. § Discard the foil and return the base to the oven for 5 minutes more. § In the meantime, melt the remaining butter in a small saucepan. Add the

■ INGREDIENTS

DOUGH
• 1 quantity *Plain* or *Ricotta pastry* (see recipes p. 58)

TOPPING
• 1 cup (180 g) fresh or frozen peas
• 3 tablespoons butter
• salt and freshly ground black pepper
• 1 tablespoon flour
• about ¾ cup (180 ml) hot milk
• 1 egg white

Right:
Crostata di cipolle

- ⅔ cup (90 g) coarsely chopped ham
- 4 tablespoons freshly grated Parmesan cheese

Wine: a dry white (Chardonnay di Franciacorta)

flour and cook over low heat for 2 minutes, stirring constantly. Add the milk, a little at a time, stirring continuously. In about 5 minutes you will obtain a smooth béchamel; it should be rather dense, so do not use too much milk. § Beat the egg white until stiff and combine with the peas, béchamel, ham, Parmesan, salt, and pepper. § Mix well and pour into the pastry base. § Bake in a preheated oven at 350°F/180°C/gas 4 for about 30 minutes or until the surface is light gold. § Serve hot.

Zucchini pie
Crostata di zucchine

Makes: 1 pie, about 9 in (23 cm) in diameter; Preparation: 40 minutes + 40 minutes for the pastry; Cooking: 35-40 minutes; Level of difficulty: Medium

Prepare the pastry base. § Soak the mushrooms in a little warm water for about 15 minutes. Drain and coarsely chop. § Remove the rind from the pancetta and sauté over medium-high heat for 3–4 minutes. Set aside, discarding the fat that the pancetta produces. § Heat the oil in the same sauté pan and cook the zucchini and mushrooms over medium heat for 10–15 minutes, stirring frequently. Season with salt and pepper and set aside to cool. § Lightly beat the eggs in a mixing bowl, add the two cheeses, marjoram, zucchini, and pancetta. § Remove the pastry base from the refrigerator and discard the plastic wrap. § Spread the topping over the base and sprinkle with the bread crumbs. § Bake in a preheated oven at 350°F/180°C/gas 4 for 35–40 minutes. § Serve hot or warm.

■ INGREDIENTS

DOUGH
- 1 quantity *Plain pastry* (see recipe p. 58)

TOPPING
- 1 oz (30 g) dried mushrooms
- 4 oz (125 g) smoked pancetta (or bacon), sliced
- 3 tablespoons extra-virgin olive oil
- 6 medium zucchini (courgettes), sliced
- salt and freshly ground black pepper
- ¾ cup (90 g) Pecorino cheese, flaked
- 3 tablespoons freshly grated Parmesan cheese
- 2 eggs
- 1 tablespoon marjoram
- 1 tablespoon bread crumbs

Wine: a dry white (Pinot Grigio)

Leek pie
Crostata di porri

Makes: 1 pie, about 9 in (23 cm) in diameter; Preparation: 40 minutes; Cooking: 40 minutes + 40 minutes for the pastry; Level of difficulty: Medium

Prepare the pastry. § Clean the leeks and slice thinly, using the white part only. § Sauté the leeks in 3 tablespoons of butter over medium-low heat for 15–20 minutes. Season with salt and pepper and set aside to cool. § In the meantime, melt the remaining butter in a small saucepan. Add the flour and cook over low heat for 2 minutes, stirring constantly. Add the milk, a little at a time, stirring continuously. In 4–5 minutes you will obtain a smooth béchamel; it should be rather dense, so do not use too much milk. § Beat the egg white until stiff and combine with the leeks, béchamel, Gruyère, salt, and pepper. Mix well. § Remove the pastry base from the refrigerator and discard the plastic wrap. § Pour the leek mixture over the top and sprinkle with the Parmesan. Bake in a preheated oven at 350°F/180°C/gas 4 for 40 minutes. § Serve hot.

■ INGREDIENTS

DOUGH
- 1 quantity *Special pastry* (see recipe, p. 58)

TOPPING
- 2 lb (1 kg) leeks
- 4 tablespoons butter
- salt and black pepper
- 1 tablespoon flour
- ¾ cup (200 ml) hot milk
- 1 egg white
- 4 tablespoons freshly grated Gruyère (or Emmenthal) cheese
- 2 tablespoons freshly grated Parmesan cheese

Right: Crostata di porri

Fried Dishes

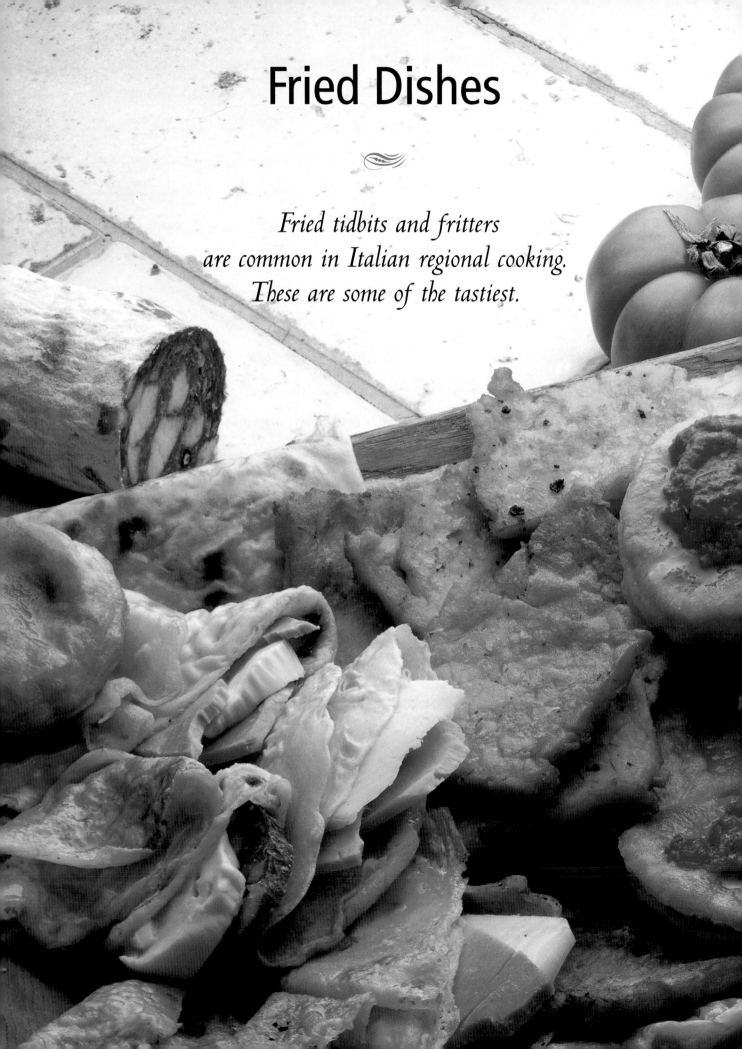

*Fried tidbits and fritters
are common in Italian regional cooking.
These are some of the tastiest.*

Lard fritters
Borlenghi

This classic recipe comes from Emilia, the area around Bologna. In the richer modern version, the water is replaced by milk and an egg is added.

Makes: about 10 fritters; Preparation: 2 minutes; Cooking: 15 minutes; Level of difficulty: Simple

Mix the flour, water, and salt together in a bowl. The mixture should be fairly liquid. § Place a cast-iron or iron pan not larger than 8 in (20 cm) in diameter over high heat. Lightly grease with a thin slice of lard. § When the lard is hot, add 2 tablespoons of the mixture and tip the pan this way and that so that the mixture spreads evenly, forming a thin layer that will set almost immediately. § After 30–40 seconds turn the fritter over with the aid of a wooden spatula and cook on the other side. § Repeat the process until all the mixture is used up. § Traditionally, these fritters are served hot, lightly spread with a mixture of lard, fresh rosemary, and finely chopped garlic, sprinkled with grated Pecorino or Parmesan cheese, and folded in four.

VARIATION
– Use extra-virgin olive oil to grease the pan instead of lard.

■ INGREDIENTS

• 1 cup (150 g) unbleached white flour
• 1¼ cups (300 ml) water
• 1 teaspoon salt
• 1 tablespoon lard

Wine: a dry red (Gutturnio)

Emilian fritters
Crescente

Emilian regional cookery has many fried dishes. They are usually served with a mixed platter of ham, prosciutto, mortadella, and other deli meats, and cheeses.

Serves: 4; Preparation: 30 minutes + 30 minutes standing; Cooking: 15 minutes; Level of difficulty: Medium

Put the flour in a bowl with the salt, and mix. Make a hollow in the center and fill with the olive oil and milk. § Mix well and transfer to a lightly floured work surface. Knead until the dough is soft and smooth. § Cover with a cloth and set aside for 30 minutes. § Roll the dough out to about ½ in (1 cm) thickness. Cut in strips four fingers wide and roll each strip to about ⅛ in (3 mm) thick. § Cut the strips into diamond-shapes with sides 3 in (7.5 cm) long and place on clean paper towels. § Fry the fritters 3 or 4 at a time in 1¼ in (3 cm) of very hot oil. They will swell and often turn over by themselves. Cook for about 1 minute, or until they are golden brown. § Drain well and place on paper towels to absorb excess oil. § Serve hot.

■ INGREDIENTS

• 2½ cups (375 g) unbleached white flour
• 1 teaspoon salt
• ½ cup (125 ml) extra-virgin olive oil
• about ⅔ cup (150 ml) warm milk
• 2 cups (500 ml) oil, for frying

Wine: a dry red (Colli Piacentini Barbera)

Right:
Crescente

Fried gnocchi
Torta fritta

Also known as gnocco fritto, this recipe also comes from Emilia, in central Italy.

Serves: 4; Preparation: 30 minutes; Rising time: about 1½ hours; Cooking: 15-20 minutes; Level of difficulty: Medium

Prepare the yeast as explained on page 342. § Put the flour in a bowl and sprinkle with salt. Make a hollow in the center and fill with the lard (or butter). § Pour in the yeast mixture and the remaining water and mix the ingredients with a fork. § Transfer the dough to a lightly floured work surface. Knead until the dough is soft and smooth. § Shape the dough into a ball, cover with a cloth and set aside to rise for 1½ hours, or until it doubles in volume. § When the rising time has elapsed, roll the dough out to a thickness of about ½ in (1 cm). § Cut into diamond-shapes with sides 2 in (4–5 cm) long and place on clean paper towels. § Fry a few shapes at a time in about 1½ in (3 cm) of very hot oil. § Drain when golden brown on both sides and drain on paper towels. § Sprinkle with salt and serve hot.

■ INGREDIENTS

- ½ oz (15 g) fresh yeast or 1 package active dry yeast
- about ½ cup (125 ml) lukewarm water
- 2 cups (300 g) unbleached white flour
- 2 tablespoons lard (or butter), thinly sliced
- 1 teaspoon salt
- 2 cups (500 ml) oil, for frying

Wine: a dry red
(Colli di Parma Rosso)

Chestnut flour fritters
Ciacci

This is another delicious recipe from Emilia. Something very similar, called necci, though cooked in a waffle-iron, is made near Pistoia, in Tuscany. Both are served with soft, fresh cheeses, such as Ricotta.

Serves: 4; Preparation: 3-4 minutes; Cooking: 15-20 minutes; Level of difficulty: Simple

Mix the flour with the water and salt using a food processor or hand blender to prevent lumps from forming. The mixture should be fairly liquid. § Grease the bottom of a cast-iron or iron pan no larger than 8 in (20 cm) in diameter with a little olive oil. Place over high heat. § When the oil is very hot, add 2–3 tablespoons of the mixture to cover the bottom of the pan in a thin layer. Turn over after about 1 minute, or when the mixture is well set, and cook on the other side. § Repeat the process until all the mixture is used up. Stack the fritters on a plate resting on a pot of boiling water to keep them warm. § Serve immediately.

■ INGREDIENTS

- 1⅓ cups (200 g) chestnut flour
- 1⅓ cups (350 ml) water
- 1 teaspoon salt
- 4 tablespoons extra-virgin olive oil

Wine: a dry, sparkling red
(Lambrusco di Sorbara)

Left: *Ciacci*

Filled fritters
Panzerotti

I have suggested two simple fillings. Mix the ingredients in a bowl until smooth

and fill the panzerotti as directed.

Serves: 4; Preparation: 25-30 minutes; Rising time: 1 hour; Cooking: 15 minutes; Level of difficulty: Simple

Prepare the dough as explained on pages 342–343. § When the rising time has elapsed (about 1 hour), transfer the dough to a lightly floured work surface and knead for 1 minute. § Shape into a long thin loaf and divide into 10–12 portions. § Flatten the dough with your hands into small disks about 3 in (8 cm) in diameter. § Place a heaped teaspoon of filling on one half of each and spread a little. Fold the dough over the top to form crescent shapes. Moisten the edges with 2–3 drops of water and seal by pressing down with your fingertips. § Fry the panzerotti 5 or 6 at a time in about 1¼ in (3 cm) of very hot oil. § When browned, drain well, and transfer to paper towels to absorb excess oil. § Serve hot.

■ INGREDIENTS

- ½ oz (15 g) fresh yeast or 1 package active dry yeast
- 1 teaspoon sugar
- ⅔ cup (150 ml) lukewarm water
- 2⅓ cups (350 g) unbleached white flour
- 1–2 teaspoons salt
- oil for frying

FILLINGS:

- **Mixed cheese:** 3 oz (90 g) Ricotta cheese; 2 oz (60 g) Provolone freshly grated cheese; 2 oz (60 g) Mozzarella cheese, diced; 2 oz (60 g) smoked Provola cheese, diced; 1 tablespoon milk, 1 teaspoon finely chopped parsley
- **Ham and Ricotta:** 1 cup (150 g) ham, coarsely chopped; 1 cup (250 g) Ricotta cheese; black pepper

Parmesan fritters
Chizze

Serves: 4; Preparation: 30 minutes; Cooking: 15-20 minutes; Level of difficulty: Medium

Put the flour in a bowl, add the salt, lard, and butter and mix well with a fork. Add the water gradually, and when nearly all the flour has been absorbed, transfer the mixture to a lightly floured work surface. § Knead until the dough is smooth and elastic. § Roll out to about ⅛ in (3 mm) thick and cut into 3-in (8-cm) squares. Place a slice of Parmesan on one half of each square and fold the dough over the top to form a triangle. Moisten the edges with 2–3 drops of water and seal by pressing down with your fingertips. § Fry the fritters 3 or 4 at a time in about 1¼ in (3 cm) of very hot oil. § When browned, drain well and transfer to paper towels to absorb excess oil. § Serve hot or at room temperature.

■ INGREDIENTS

- 2 cups (300 g) unbleached white flour
- 1 teaspoon salt
- 2 tablespoons lard
- 2 tablespoons butter
- about ½ cup (125 ml) lukewarm water
- 5 oz (150 g) Parmesan cheese, thinly sliced
- 2 cups (500 ml) oil, for frying

Wine: a dry red (Gutturnio)

VARIATION
– Replace the Parmesan with Emmental or Fontina cheese.

Right: *Chizze*

Garbanzo bean fritters
Panelle

Serves: 4; Preparation: 10 minutes; Cooking: 40 minutes; Level of difficulty: Simple

Mix the flour, water and salt using a food processor or hand blender. The mixture will be fairly thick. § Transfer to a heavy-bottomed saucepan and cook over low heat for 30 minutes, stirring constantly. § Add the parsley. § Transfer the dough to a lightly oiled work surface and spread with a spatula until it is about ¼ in (½ cm) thick. § Leave to cool, then cut into diamond shapes or squares. Fry 2–3 at a time in very hot oil. § When browned, drain well, and place on paper towels. § Serve hot.

■ INGREDIENTS

- 2 cups (300 g) garbanzo bean (chickpea) flour
- 2 quarts (1 liter) water
- 1 teaspoon salt
- 1 tablespoon finely chopped parsley
- 2 cups (500 ml) oil, for frying

Wine: a dry white (Greco di Tufo)

Fritters filled with tomato and mozzarella cheese
Panzerotti con pomodoro e mozzarella

Serves: 4; Preparation: 25-30 minutes; Rising time: about 1 hour; Cooking: 25 minutes; Level of difficulty: Simple

Prepare the dough and set aside to rise. § Place the tomatoes in a small saucepan over medium heat with no added seasoning. Cook for 8–10 minutes until they reduce a little. § When the rising time has elapsed, shape the dough into panzerotti as explained on p. 118. § Place a teaspoonful of tomato filling on each, cover with a slice of Mozzarella and sprinkle with salt and pepper. Moisten the edges with 2–3 drops of water and seal by pressing down with your fingertips. § Fry the panzerotti 5 or 6 at a time in about 1¼ in (3 cm) of very hot oil. § When brown, drain well, and place on paper towels to absorb excess oil. § Serve hot.

■ INGREDIENTS

DOUGH
• 1 quantity panzerotti dough (see recipe p. 440)
• 2 cups (500 ml) oil, for frying

FILLING
• 1¼ cups (300 g) diced tomatoes
• 10 oz (300 g) Mozzarella cheese, sliced
• salt and freshly ground black pepper

Wine: a dry red (Chianti Classico)

Anchovy fritters
Crispeddi

Serves: 4; Preparation: 30 minutes; Rising time: 1½ hours; Cooking: 10 minutes; Level of difficulty: Simple

Prepare the yeast as explained on page 342. § Combine the flour in a bowl with the salt. Make a hollow in the flour and fill with the lard, yeast mixture and remaining water. Proceed as shown on pages 342–343. § Wash the anchovies thoroughly under cold running water and pat dry with paper towels. § When the rising time has elapsed (about 1 hour), place the dough on a lightly floured work surface and knead for 1 minute. Divide into egg-sized portions and shape into long rolls. § Cut them open lengthwise and place an anchovy fillet and a sprinkling of oregano in each. Close up the dough and place the rolls on a clean cloth. § Cover with another cloth and leave to rise for 30 minutes. § Fry the rolls 2 or 3 at a time in about 1¼ in (3 cm) of very hot oil. When browned, drain well, and place on paper towels to absorb excess oil. § Serve hot.

■ INGREDIENTS

• ½ oz (15 g) fresh yeast or 1 package active dry yeast
• ½ cup (125 ml) lukewarm water
• 2 cups (300 g) unbleached white flour
• 1 tablespoon lard, chopped
• 5 oz (150 g) salted anchovy fillets
• oregano
• 1 teaspoon salt
• 2 cups (500 ml) oil, for frying

Wine: a dry white (Corvo)

Right: *Panzerotti con pomodoro e mozzarella*

Neapolitan fritters in tomato sauce
Pizzelle

These wonderful fritters are from Naples. The only drawback is that you can never make enough of them!

Serves: 4; Preparation: 30 minutes; Rising time: 2 hours; Cooking: 20 minutes; Level of difficulty: Simple

Prepare the yeast as explained on page 16. § Combine the flour in a large bowl with the salt, yeast mixture, and remaining water, and proceed as shown in the sequence on pages 342–343. § When the rising time has elapsed (about 1 hour), knead the dough on a floured work surface for 2–3 minutes. Divide in 8–10 portions. Shape into balls, cover with a cloth and set aside to rise for about 1 hour. § Put the tomatoes in a small saucepan, add the garlic, oregano, and oil, and cook over low heat for 15 minutes, or until they reduce. § When the second rising time has elapsed, use your hands to flatten the dough into round shapes 3 in (8 cm) in diameter. § Fry the rolls 2–3 at a time in 1¼ in (3 cm) of very hot oil. Turn the fritters halfway through cooking. They will be ready in about 1½ minutes. The fritters should be light golden brown. § Drain well and place on paper towels to absorb excess oil. § Arrange the fritters on a heated serving dish and cover each one with a tablespoon of the hot tomato sauce. § Serve hot.

- INGREDIENTS

- ½ oz (15 g) fresh yeast or 1 package active dry yeast
- ⅔ cup (150 ml) lukewarm water
- 2⅓ cups (350 g) unbleached white flour
- 12 oz (350 g) tomatoes, peeled and chopped
- 1 clove garlic, finely chopped
- 1 teaspoon oregano
- 1 tablespoon extra-virgin olive oil
- 1 teaspoon salt
- 2 cups (500 ml) oil, for frying

Wine: a dry red (Vesuvio)

Fried mozzarella sandwiches
Mozzarella in carrozza

Serves: 4; Preparation: 15 minutes; Cooking: 8-10 minutes; Level of difficulty: Simple

Cover four slices of bread with the Mozzarella, making sure the cheese doesn't overlap the edges of the bread. Season with salt and pepper and cover with the remaining slices of bread. Transfer to a plate and cut the sandwiches in half diagonally. § Beat the eggs and milk with salt to taste. Pour over the sandwiches and leave to stand for 2 minutes. Turn the sandwiches over so that they absorb all the egg mixture. § If liked, roll in the bread crumbs. Make sure that the edges are well soaked with the egg mixture so that they will set on contact with the hot oil, sealing the Mozzarella inside. § Fry the sandwiches 4 at a time in about 1¼ in (3 cm) of very hot oil. Turn after about 1 minute. § When browned on both sides, drain well and place on paper towels to absorb excess oil. § Serve hot.

- INGREDIENTS

- 8 slices day-old sandwich bread, with crusts removed
- 8 oz (250 g) Mozzarella cheese, sliced
- 2 eggs
- 3 tablespoons milk
- 10 tablespoons bread crumbs (optional)
- salt and freshly ground black pepper
- 2 cups (500 ml) oil, for frying

Wine: a dry red (Ischia)

Right: *Mozzarella in carrozza*

Turkey and Chicken

Turkey and chicken are widely available in Italy. Both meats are reasonably cheap and are used in a wide variety of dishes.

Braised chicken with tomato sauce and green olives
Pollo alla cacciatora

Serves: 4-6; Preparation: 15 minutes + 4 hours marinating; Cooking: 1 hour; Level of difficulty: Simple

Wash the chicken pieces under cold running water and pat dry with paper towels. § Place the chicken in a bowl and cover with 3 tablespoons of oil, the lemon juice, salt, and a generous grinding of pepper. Set aside to marinate for at least 4 hours. § Sauté the onion, carrot, and celery in the remaining oil over medium-high heat until the onion is soft. § Add the chicken pieces and sauté until golden. § Pour in the wine and cook until it evaporates, stirring frequently. § Add the tomatoes and water. Cover the sauté pan, lower the heat to medium, and continue to cook, stirring frequently. § After 15 minutes add the olives. Simmer gently over low heat for another 20 minutes, or until the chicken is tender. § Serve hot with green beans braised in tomatoes, or cooked spinach or Swiss chard sautéed briefly in garlic and oil.

> VARIATIONS
> – Replace the green olives with the same quantity of black olives.
> – Replace the chicken with the same quantity of rabbit and cook as above.

■ INGREDIENTS

- 1 chicken, about 3 lb (1.5 kg) cut in 6–8 pieces
- 4 tablespoons extra-virgin olive oil
- juice of 1 lemon
- salt and freshly ground black pepper
- 1 onion, coarsely chopped
- 1 carrot, coarsely chopped
- 1 stalk celery, coarsely chopped
- ½ cup (125 ml) dry white wine
- 1 lb (500 g) tomatoes, peeled and chopped
- ½ cup (125 ml) cold water
- 1¼ cups (150 g) green olives

Wine: a dry red
(Piave Merlot or Corvo Rosso)

Turkey loaf wrapped in savoy cabbage
Polpettone avvolto nella verza

Serves: 4-6; Preparation: 20 minutes; Cooking: 1¼ hours; Level of difficulty: Medium

Combine the turkey, sausage, pancetta, Parmesan, eggs, bread, nutmeg, salt, and pepper in a large bowl and mix thoroughly. Set aside. § Parboil the cabbage leaves in plenty of salted water for 4–5 minutes. Drain well and carefully pat dry with paper towels. § Arrange the cabbage leaves on a work surface to form a rectangle; they should be overlapping so that there is no space between the leaves. § Place the turkey mixture in the middle of the rectangle and shape into a meat loaf. § Wrap the cabbage leaves around the turkey loaf, taking care not to tear the leaves. Tie with a few twists of kitchen string. § Transfer the turkey loaf to an ovenproof dish with the shallots, tomatoes, and oil. § Bake in a

■ INGREDIENTS

- 1 lb (500 g) ground turkey breast
- 5 oz (150 g) Italian pork sausage, peeled and crumbled
- ½ cup (60 g) pancetta, finely chopped
- ½ cup (60 g) freshly grated Parmesan cheese
- 1 egg + 1 yolk
- 2 tablespoons crustless bread, soaked in hot milk and well squeezed
- dash of nutmeg
- salt and freshly ground

Right: *Pollo alla cacciatora*

black pepper
- 8–10 leaves Savoy cabbage
- 2 shallots, sliced
- 10 oz (300 g) tomatoes, peeled and chopped
- ⅓ cup (90 ml) extra-virgin olive oil
- ½ cup (125 ml) dry white wine
- ½ cup (125 ml) *Beef stock* (see recipe p. 48)

Wine: a dry rosé
(Rosato dei Colli Piacentini)

preheated oven at 400°F/200°C/gas 6 for 1¼ hours, basting frequently with the wine. When all the wine has been added, continue basting with the stock. § Slice the turkey loaf when lukewarm and serve.

VARIATION
– The turkey loaf can be cooked on the stove top over medium heat for 1½ hours instead of in the oven.

Turkey breast wrapped in pancetta
Fesa di tacchino bardata alla pancetta

■ INGREDIENTS

- 2½ lb (1.2 kg) turkey breast
- 1 tablespoon mixed, chopped sage, rosemary, and garlic
- salt and freshly ground black pepper
- 10 oz (300 g) pancetta, sliced
- 4 tablespoons extra-virgin olive oil
- 1 lb (500 g) white baby onions, peeled
- 10 oz (300 g) carrots, peeled and sliced
- 1 lb (500 g) new potatoes, scraped
- ¾ cups (200 ml) dry white wine
- 2 cups (500 ml) *Beef stock* (see recipe p. 48)

Wine: a dry red (Rosso di Gallura)

Serves: 4-6; Preparation: 30 minutes; Cooking: 1 hour; Level of difficulty: Medium

Use a sharp knife to open the turkey breast out to a rectangular shape. Beat lightly with a meat pounder, taking care not to tear the meat. § Sprinkle with the herb mixture, salt, and pepper. § Roll the meat up and sprinkle with a little more salt and pepper. § Wrap the rolled turkey in the slices of pancetta so that it is completely covered and tie with kitchen string. § Transfer to a heavy-bottomed saucepan and add the oil. Sauté over high heat, turning all the time, until the meat is evenly browned. § After about 10 minutes, add the onions, carrots, and potatoes. § Add the wine, reduce the heat, cover, and cook for about 50 minutes more, stirring from time to time. Add stock as required during cooking to keep the meat moist – the bottom of the pan should always be covered with liquid. § When cooked, untie the turkey, slice (not too thinly), and arrange on a serving dish with the vegetables. § Serve hot with the cooking juices passed separately.

Marengo chicken
Pollo alla Marengo

■ INGREDIENTS

- 1 chicken, about 3 lb (1.5 kg) cut into 6–8 pieces
- 2 tablespoons butter
- 2 tablespoons extra-virgin olive oil
- salt and freshly ground black pepper
- dash of nutmeg
- ½ cup (125 ml) dry white wine
- 1 tablespoon flour
- ¾ cup (200 ml) *Beef stock* (see recipe p. 48)
- juice of ½ lemon

Wine: a dry white (Vespaiolo di Breganze)

Napoleon Bonaparte's cook is said to have improvised this dish on the eve of the Battle of Marengo. The French General won a narrow victory over the Austrians on the Marengo Plain in northern Italy on June 4, 1800. Napoleon remained fond of the dish to the end of his days.

Serves: 4-6; Preparation: 15 minutes; Cooking: 1 hour; Level of difficulty: Simple

Wash the chicken under cold running water and pat dry with paper towels. § Transfer to a heavy-bottomed pan with the butter and oil and sauté until lightly browned. Season with salt, pepper, and nutmeg. § Discard most of the liquid that may have formed in the pan, add the wine, and stir in the flour. § Cook over medium-low heat for about 50 minutes, or until the chicken is tender. Add the stock as required during cooking to keep the chicken moist. § Arrange the chicken on a serving dish and drizzle with the lemon juice. § Serve hot with globe artichokes slowly braised in oil, garlic, and parsley.

Left:

Fesa di tacchino bardata alla pancetta

Italian-style roast chicken
Pollo arrosto

Serves: 4; Preparation: 10 minutes; Cooking: 1 hour; Level of difficulty: Simple

Wash the chicken under cold running water and pat dry with paper towels. § Combine the sage, rosemary, garlic, salt, and pepper in a bowl. Mix well, then use to season the chicken inside and out. § Wash the lemon thoroughly, prick well with a fork and insert in the abdominal cavity of the chicken. This will make the meat tastier and absorb fat. § Place the chicken in a roasting pan greased with the oil. Bake in a preheated oven at 400°F/200°C/gas 6 for about 1 hour. § Turn the chicken every 15 minutes and baste with the oil and cooking juices. When cooked, the chicken should be very tender and the meat should come off the bone easily. The skin should be crisp. § Transfer to a heated serving dish. § Serve with roast or fried potatoes and a green salad.

■ INGREDIENTS

- 1 chicken, about 2½ lb (1.2 kg)
- 1 tablespoon fresh sage, finely chopped
- 1 tablespoon fresh rosemary, finely chopped
- 2 cloves garlic, finely chopped
- salt and freshly ground black pepper
- 1 lemon
- 4 tablespoons extra-virgin olive oil

Wine: a dry red (Chianti Classico)

Spring chicken cooked in coarse salt
Pollo novello al sale grosso

Cooking meat or fish in salt enhances its taste. A crisp, salty crust forms on the outside, which can be nibbled on or discarded, as preferred, while the inside stays moist and tender. Surprisingly, in view of the cooking method, the meat is not at all salty.

Serves: 4; Preparation: 5 minutes; Cooking: 1½ hours; Level of difficulty: Simple

Spread 3 lb (1.5 kg) of coarse salt on the bottom of a high-sided baking dish. § Tie the herbs together and insert in the abdominal cavity of the chicken with the garlic. § Place the chicken in the baking dish and cover with the rest of the salt. No parts of the chicken should be visible. § Bake in a preheated oven at 375°F/190°C/gas 5 for 1½ hours. § Take out of the oven and remove the salt and herbs. Transfer to a heated serving dish. § Serve hot with baked potatoes and a green salad.

■ INGREDIENTS

- 9 lb (4½ kg) coarse salt
- 3 sprigs fresh sage
- 3 sprigs fresh rosemary
- 1 clove garlic, whole
- 1 chicken, about 2½ lb (1.2 kg)

Wine: a dry red (Rosso Conero)

Right:
Pollo novello al sale grosso

Chicken galantine
(cold stuffed chicken)
Galantina di pollo

This delicate dish is often served at Christmas time. It can be prepared well in advance and will keep for up to a week in the refrigerator. Serve thinly sliced as an appetizer or with a green or mixed salad as a light lunch or main course.

Serves: 8; Preparation: 40 minutes + 12 hours in refrigerator; Cooking: 1½ hours; Level of difficulty: Medium

Combine the beef, pork, turkey, veal, and mortadella in a large bowl. Mix well and add the pistachios, egg, and truffle. Sprinkle with salt and pepper and mix thoroughly. § Stuff the chicken with the mixture and sew up the neck and stomach cavity openings with a trussing needle and string. § Use your hands to give it a rectangular shape. Wrap in a piece of cheesecloth (muslin) and tie with kitchen string. § Place a large saucepan of salted water over medium heat. Add the onion, carrot, celery, parsley, peppercorns, and stock cube. § When the water is boiling, carefully add the stuffed chicken and simmer over low heat for 1½ hours. § Remove from the heat and drain the stock (which makes an excellent, light soup). § Remove the cheesecloth and place the chicken between two trays, with a weight (for example, a brick) on top. This will help to eliminate any liquid absorbed by the meat during cooking and will give it a rectangular shape. § When cool transfer to the refrigerator, with the weight still on top, and leave for at least 12 hours. § In the meantime prepare the gelatin, following the directions on the package. Be sure to add the lemon juice while the gelatin is still liquid. § Serve the galantine thinly sliced on a serving dish, topped with the diced gelatin.

■ INGREDIENTS

- 11 oz (325 g) lean ground beef
- 5 oz (150 g) lean ground pork
- 5 oz (150 g) ground turkey breast
- 5 oz (150 g) ground suckling veal
- 2 oz (60 g) ground mortadella
- ½ cup (75 g) pistachios, shelled
- 1 egg
- 1 oz (30 g) black truffle, finely sliced (optional)
- salt and freshly ground black pepper
- 1 chicken, boneless, about 4 lb (2 kg)
- 1 onion, cut in half
- 1 carrot, cut in 3
- 1 stalk celery, cut in 3
- 2 sprigs parsley
- 7–8 peppercorns
- 1 chicken stock cube
- 2 gelatin cubes
- juice of ½ lemon

Wine: a light, dry white (Soave Classico)

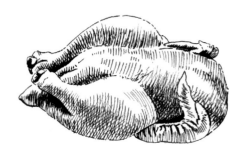

VARIATION
– Make the chicken galantine without the truffle. It will certainly be cheaper to make, though with the truffle it is another dish entirely!

Right:
Galantina di pollo

Chicken breast with cheese sauce
Filetti di pollo alla crema di formaggio

- 1 lb (500 g) chicken breast, sliced in fillets
- 4 tablespoons extra-virgin olive oil
- salt and black pepper
- 4 oz (125 g) Fontina cheese, sliced
- ¼ cup (60 g) chopped ham (optional)
- ¾ cup (200 ml) milk

Wine: a dry white (Cirò Bianco)

Serves: 4; Preparation: 10 minutes; Cooking: 20 minutes; Level of difficulty: Simple

Place the fillets of chicken in a large sauté pan with the oil over medium heat and sauté until golden brown on both sides. Season with salt and pepper. § Cover each fillet with slices of cheese and a sprinkling of ham, if using. Carefully pour the milk over the top. § Continue cooking until the cheese has melted and the milk has reduced to a creamy sauce. § Serve hot with a side dish of baked fennel (lightly boiled fennel in béchamel sauce sprinkled with Parmesan cheese and baked in a hot oven).

Chicken and bell pepper salad

Insalata di pollo e peperoni sott'olio

This delicious salad is easy to prepare.
It makes an ideal appetizer or light lunch.

Serves: 4; Preparation: 20 minutes + 1 hour for the chicken; Cooking: 1 hour; Level of difficulty: Simple

Boil the chicken in a large pot of water with the carrot, onion, celery, parsley, and salt for about 1 hour. When cooked, drain and set aside to cool. § Remove the skin and bones and cut the chicken into small pieces. Transfer to a salad bowl. § Drain the bell peppers from the oil and coarsely chop. Add to the chicken together with the pine nuts and arugula. § Season with salt, pepper, oil, and vinegar just before serving. Toss well.

■ INGREDIENTS

• 1 chicken, about 2 lb (1 kg)
• 1 carrot, 1 onion, 1 stalk celery, cut in half
• small bunch parsley
• salt and freshly ground black pepper
• 4 oz (125 g) red bell peppers (capsicums) in oil
• ½ cup (100 g) pine nuts
• 2 bunches arugula (rocket), coarsely chopped
• 4 tablespoons extra-virgin olive oil
• 2 tablespoons white vinegar

Wine: a dry, sparkling white (Prosecco di Valdobbiadene)

Turkey breast pie

Fesa di tacchino in crosta

Serves: 4-6; Preparation: 45 minutes; Cooking: 1¼ hours; Level of difficulty: Medium

Use a sharp knife to open the turkey breast out to a rectangular shape. Beat lightly with a meat pounder, taking care not to tear the meat. § Sauté the zucchini, carrot, and onion in 2 tablespoons of butter until the onion is soft. Season with salt and pepper and set aside to cool for a few minutes. § Sprinkle the turkey with salt and pepper, cover with the ham, and scatter with the vegetables. § Roll the meat up and wrap with slices of pancetta. Truss with kitchen string, making two twists lengthwise as well, to fix the pancetta firmly to the turkey. § Place the meat in an ovenproof dish with the garlic, sage, and oil. Cook in a preheated oven at 400°F/200°C/gas 6 for 50 minutes, turning the meat over during cooking and basting with the wine from time to time. § Set the meat aside to cool. Discard the kitchen string; the meat will keep its shape when cool. § On a lightly floured work surface, roll the pastry out to a thin sheet. Wrap it round the meat, brush with the egg and decorate with pieces of leftover pastry. § Butter and flour a baking sheet and bake in a preheated oven at 400°F/200°C/gas 6 for 20 minutes. § Serve hot with a green or mixed salad.

■ INGREDIENTS

• 2½ lb (1.2 kg) turkey breast
• 1 zucchini (courgette) and 1 carrot, sliced in julienne strips
• 1 onion, thinly sliced
• 2½ tablespoons butter
• salt and freshly ground black pepper
• 1 cup (125 g) ham, sliced
• 1¾ cups (200 g) pancetta, thinly sliced
• 1 clove garlic, cut in half
• 4 leaves sage
• ⅓ cup (90 ml) extra-virgin olive oil
• ½ cup (125 ml) dry white wine
• 10 oz (300 g) frozen puff pastry, thawed
• 1 egg, beaten

Wine: a dry white (Pinot Grigio)

Right: *Fesa di tacchino in crosta*

Chicken balls with bell peppers and black olives

Polpettine di pollo ai peperoni e olive nere

Serves: 6; Preparation: 40 minutes; Cooking: about 40 minutes; Level of difficulty: Medium

Cut the eggplant in thick slices, sprinkle with salt and place in a colander for about 20 minutes. Cut into cubes. § Heat 4 tablespoons of the oil in a large sauté pan over medium heat and sauté the garlic and onion until soft. § Add the peppers, eggplant, zucchini, tomatoes, and olives. Season with salt and pepper. Stir and cook for about 20 minutes, adding a little water if the pan becomes too dry. § In the meantime, combine the chicken, bread, Parmesan, egg, parsley, and a little salt in a bowl and mix thoroughly. § Shape the mixture (which should be quite firm) into small round balls, then coat with flour. § Heat the remaining oil in a large sauté pan over a medium heat and fry the balls until golden brown all over. § Add the vegetable mixture, season with salt and pepper, and cook for 15 minutes more, stirring carefully. If the dish dries out too much, add stock as required. § Transfer to a heated serving dish, sprinkle with the basil and serve hot.

■ INGREDIENTS

- 1 eggplant (aubergine)
- salt and freshly ground black pepper
- ½ cup (125 ml) extra-virgin olive oil
- 1 clove garlic
- 1 large onion, thickly sliced
- 2 bell peppers (capsicums), red, yellow, or green, diced
- 1 zucchini (courgette), diced
- 10 cherry tomatoes, cut in half
- ½ cup (50 g) black olives
- 1¼ lb (600 g) ground chicken breast
- 2 tablespoons crustless bread, soaked in milk and squeezed
- ½ cup (60 g) freshly grated Parmesan cheese
- 1 egg
- 1 tablespoon parsley, finely chopped
- ½ cup (75 g) flour
- ½ cup (125 ml) *Beef stock* (see recipe p. 48)
- 10 leaves basil, torn

Wine: a dry white (Verdicchio)

Chicken with porcini mushrooms

Pollo ai funghi porcini

If you can't get porcini mushrooms, use the same quantity of white mushrooms mixed with 1½ tablespoons of dried porcini (soaked in warm water for 20 minutes, squeezed dry, and chopped).

Serves: 4-6; Preparation: 30 minutes; Cooking: about 1 hour; Level of difficulty: Medium

Wash and dry the chicken and cut into 8–10 pieces. § Clean the mushrooms, rinse and pat dry carefully with paper towels. Cut the stems into chunks, and the caps into fairly large strips. § Melt 1 tablespoon of butter in a heavy-bottomed pan over medium heat. Add 1 tablespoon of oil and sauté the garlic briefly. § Add the mushrooms and mint. Season

■ INGREDIENTS

- 1 chicken, about 2½ lb (1.2 kg)
- 1 lb (500 g) porcini mushrooms
- 2 tablespoons butter
- 3 tablespoons extra-virgin olive oil
- 1 clove garlic, finely chopped

Right: *Polpettine di pollo ai peperoni e olive nere*

- 2 sprigs mint
- salt and freshly ground black pepper
- 1 tablespoon parsley, finely chopped
- ½ cup (125 ml) dry white wine
- 1 white onion, coarsely chopped
- ¾ cup (200 ml) milk

Wine: a dry white
(Riesling Renano dei Colli Berici)

with salt, and pepper and cook for a few minutes. Scatter with the parsley, remove from heat and set aside. § Place the remaining butter and oil in a sauté pan over medium heat. Add the chicken, salt, and pepper, and brown on all sides. § Pour in the wine and cook over high heat until it evaporates. § Add the onion and cook until soft. § Pour in the milk and reduce the heat. Add salt and pepper to taste, cover the pan and cook for 30 minutes more, stirring frequently. § Remove the lid; if the sauce is too liquid, raise the heat until it reduces a little. § Add the mushrooms, stir well, and cook over medium-low heat for 5 minutes more. § Transfer to a heated serving dish and serve hot.

Chicken pieces with curry
Bocconcini di pollo al curry

Serves: 4; Preparation: 15 minutes; Cooking: 25 minutes; Level of difficulty: Simple

Chop the chicken into bite-sized pieces, rinse under cold running water, and pat dry with paper towels. § Place the flour in a bowl and dredge the chicken pieces, shaking off excess flour. § Melt the butter in a skillet (frying pan) and sauté the onion over medium heat until soft. § Add the chicken, season with salt and pepper, and sauté for 2–3 minutes. § Pour in the cognac. When it has evaporated, add the cream and curry. § Continue cooking over low heat, partially covered, and stirring frequently for about 20 minutes, or until the sauce reduces. § Transfer to a heated serving dish. Serve hot with boiled spring carrots and new potatoes, or spring peas with parsley.

VARIATION
– Serve the chicken and vegetables on a bed of boiled white or brown rice for a nourishing one-course meal.

■ INGREDIENTS

• 2 lb (1 kg) chicken, boned
• 4 tablespoons flour
• 4 tablespoons butter
• 1 white onion, thinly sliced
• salt and freshly ground black pepper
• ½ cup (125 ml) cognac (or brandy)
• ½ cup (125 ml) fresh cream
• 1 teaspoon curry powder

Wine: a dry rosé (Cerveteri Rosato or Bardolino Chiaretto)

Chicken breast in cream of onion sauce
Fesa di tacchino alla crema di cipolle

Serves: 6; Preparation: 15 minutes; Cooking: 1¼ hours; Level of difficulty: Simple

Roll the turkey breast and tie with kitchen string. Season with salt and pepper and roll in the flour. § Transfer to a heavy-bottomed pan with the oil and butter and sauté over high heat for 5–7 minutes. § Add the onions, stirring carefully and making sure the turkey is always touching the bottom of the pan (rather than on the onions). Sauté for 5 minutes more. § Pour in enough stock to almost cover the meat. Partially cover the pan and lower the heat to medium. Add more stock during cooking, as required. § When cooked, the turkey will be light brown and the onions will have melted to form a delicious, creamy sauce. § Serve hot cut in ½-in (1-cm) thick slices or cold in thin slices. Arrange the slices on a serving dish and smother with the onion sauce. If serving cold, reheat the onion sauce just before serving. § Serve with hot potato purée.

VARIATION
– Replace the onions with 6–8 medium carrots cut in slices. Equally delicious, the sauce will be sweeter with a more delicate taste.

■ INGREDIENTS

• 2½ lb (1.2 kg) turkey breast
• salt and freshly ground black pepper
• 3 tablespoons flour
• ½ cup (125 ml) extra-virgin olive oil
• 1 tablespoon butter
• 4 large white onions, coarsely sliced
• 4 cups (1 liter) *Beef stock* (see recipe p. 48)

Wine: a dry red (Donnaz)

Right: *Fesa di tacchino alla crema di cipolle*

Veal and Beef

Many of the most popular Italian meat dishes are made with veal or beef. These range from classics like Florentine steak, or Beef braised in red wine, to more refined dishes, such as Carpaccio and arugula, or Veal scaloppine in white wine.

Tuscan-style braised beef
Stracotto toscano

In this traditional Tuscan recipe, the beef is braised slowly in red wine and stock. After 3 hours the meat is extremely tender. If there is any braised beef leftover, chop the meat finely, mix with the sauce and serve the next day with fresh pasta, such as tagliatelle or tortelloni.

Serves: 4-6; Preparation: 25 minutes; Cooking: 3 hours; Level of difficulty: Medium

Mix the garlic and rosemary with a generous quantity of salt and pepper. Using a sharp knife, make several incisions in the meat and fill with the herb mixture. § Tie the meat loosely with kitchen string. § Heat the oil in a heavy-bottomed pan over medium-high heat and brown the meat well on all sides. § Add the onions, carrots, celery, parsley, sage, and bay leaves and sauté for a few minutes. § Season with salt and pepper, then pour in the wine. When the wine has evaporated, add the tomatoes, partially cover and simmer over medium-low heat for about 2½ hours. § Turn the meat from time to time, adding the stock gradually so that the sauce doesn't dry out. § When the meat is cooked, transfer to a heated serving dish and cut in slices. Spoon the sauce and cooking juices over the top, and serve hot.

VARIATION
– For an even tastier dish, wrap the meat in 3½ oz (100 g) of sliced pancetta (tied firmly with kitchen string) before cooking.

■ INGREDIENTS

• 1 clove garlic, finely chopped
• 1 tablespoon rosemary, finely chopped
• salt and freshly ground black pepper
• 2 lb (1 kg) beef (rump or sirloin)
• ⅓ cup (90 ml) extra-virgin olive oil
• 2 onions, coarsely chopped
• 2 carrots, coarsely chopped
• 1 stalk celery, coarsely chopped
• 1 tablespoon parsley, finely chopped
• 3 leaves sage, torn
• 2 bay leaves
• ¾ cup (200 ml) dry red wine
• 14 oz (450 g) tomatoes, peeled and chopped
• 2 cups (500 ml) *Beef stock* (see recipe p. 48)

Wine: a dry red (Chianti Classico)

Kidneys with oil, garlic, parsley, and sage
Rognoncini trifolati alla salvia

This tasty peasant dish is now served in top restaurants, where it passes for haute cuisine.

Serves: 4; Preparation: 15 minutes + 1 hour for the meat; Cooking: 8 minutes; Level of difficulty: Simple

Slice the kidneys in two lengthways, and remove the fatty parts and sinews. Cut into thin slices and set aside in a bowl of cold water and vinegar for about 1 hour. § Heat the oil and butter in a heavy-bottomed pan over medium-high heat. Add the garlic, parsley, and sage and sauté for 2–3 minutes. § Add the kidneys. Season with salt and pepper and pour in the wine. § Cook for 5 minutes only, or the kidneys will become tough. § Serve hot with potato purée and the cooking juices from the pan.

■ INGREDIENTS

• 1 lb (500 g) calf's kidneys
• ¾ cup (200 ml) vinegar
• 4 tablespoons extra-virgin olive oil
• 1 tablespoon butter
• 2 cloves garlic, finely chopped
• 1 tablespoon parsley, finely chopped
• 5 sage leaves
• salt and black pepper
• ½ cup (125 ml) red wine

Right: Stracotto toscano

Aosta Valley-style veal slices
Fetta di vitello alla valdostana

■ INGREDIENTS

- 1 lb (500 g) veal, cut from the rump, in a single slice
- salt and freshly ground black pepper
- 4 oz (125 g) sliced speck
- 4 oz (125 g) Fontina cheese, sliced
- 1 scant tablespoon oregano
- ⅓ cup (90 ml) extra-virgin olive oil
- ½ cup (125 ml) dry white wine
- 1 cup (250 ml) *Beef stock* (see recipe p. 48)

Wine: a dry red (Grignolino)

Serves: 4; Preparation: 15 minutes; Cooking: 1¼ hours; Level of difficulty: Simple

Remove any pieces of fat from the meat. Cover with foil and beat lightly with a meat pounder (the foil prevents the meat from breaking). § Sprinkle with salt and pepper. Cover with the speck and top with the Fontina. § Sprinkle with the oregano and roll up the meat. Tie with kitchen string and transfer to a heavy-bottomed pan. § Pour in the oil and place over a medium-high heat. Cook until brown on both sides. § Pour in the wine and reduce the heat. § When the wine has evaporated, partially cover and cook for about 1 hour, adding stock as the pan dries out, and turning the meat from time to time. § Transfer to a heated serving dish and smother with the cooking juices. § Serve with boiled broccoli sautéed in garlic, crushed chilies, and olive oil.

Thinly sliced sirloin with arugula
Straccetti alla rucola

This light and healthy dish is always delicious, especially in summer.

■ INGREDIENTS

- 10 oz (300 g) sirloin, thinly sliced
- 2 bunches arugula (rocket)
- salt and freshly ground black pepper
- juice of ½ lemon
- 4 tablespoons extra-virgin olive oil

Wine: a dry, aromatic white (Müller Thurgau)

Serves: 4; Preparation: 10 minutes; Cooking: 20 minutes; Level of difficulty: Simple

Wash and dry the arugula, cut finely, and set aside. § Heat a large nonstick sauté pan over medium-high heat. Cook the slices of beef, 2–3 at a time, by dropping them into the pan and turning them immediately. They will only take a minute or two to cook. § When all the beef is cooked, arrange the slices on a heated serving dish, sprinkle with salt and pepper, and cover with the arugula. Sprinkle lightly with salt and pepper again and drizzle with the oil and lemon juice. § Toss the arugula and serve immediately.

Left: Straccetti alla rucola

Veal slices with prosciutto and sage
Saltimbocca alla romana

■ INGREDIENTS

- 14 oz (450 g) veal, preferably rump, cut in 8 slices
- 4 oz (125 g) prosciutto
- 8 leaves sage
- 4 tablespoons all-purpose (plain) flour
- 2 tablespoons butter
- 3 tablespoons extra-virgin olive oil
- salt and freshly ground black pepper
- ½ cup (125 ml) dry white wine

Wine: a dry red (Chianti Classico)

Serves: 4; Preparation: 15 minutes; Cooking: 12 minutes; Level of difficulty: Simple

Pound the slices of meat and lightly flour. § Place ½ slice of prosciutto on each and top with a sage leaf. § Use a toothpick to fix the prosciutto and sage to the slice of veal. § Melt the butter and oil in a large sauté pan. Add the veal slices, with the prosciutto facing downward. Brown on both sides over high heat. § Season with salt and pepper (taste first, the prosciutto is already salty and you may not need much more). § Pour in the wine and cook for 5–6 minutes more. § Serve hot with a side dish of spinach or Swiss chard sautéed in butter.

Grilled T-bone steak, Florentine-style
Bistecca alla fiorentina

■ INGREDIENTS

- 2 lb (1 kg) T-bone steak
- salt and freshly ground black pepper

Wine: a dry red (Brunello di Montalcino)

For steak-lovers, a grilled Florentine T-bone steak is the ultimate treat. In Italy, the steak is cut from Chianina beef (a breed native to Tuscany) and hung for at least 6 days before cooking. For best results, the steak should be cooked over the embers of a charcoal or wood-burning grill. Florentines eat their steaks very rare; some claim that the meat inside, near the bone, should only just be warm! This is a matter of taste and you can increase the cooking time accordingly.

Serves: 2; Preparation: 3 minutes; Cooking: 10 minutes; Level of difficulty: Simple

Remove any sinews and excess fat from the meat. Season with a generous grinding of black pepper. § Place on a grill over very hot embers. After 5–6 minutes turn the steak using a wooden spatula (do not use a fork since the steak must not be pierced), and cook for another 5–6 minutes. The secret of this dish lies in the speed of cooking: the meat must be well roasted outside, but rare inside so that when it is cut the juices ooze out onto the plate. § Sprinkle with salt and serve straight from the grill. § Serve with grilled mushroom caps (preferably porcini) seasoned with thyme, sliced garlic, salt, and pepper.

Right:
Saltimbocca alla romana

Florentine-style tripe
Trippa alla fiorentina

*Tripe vendors can still be seen in the streets of Florence selling their tripe
sandwiches or containers with hot tripe (plastic nowadays, and served with plastic forks).
The mouth-watering aroma of tomato and tripe wafts through the streets and few real
Florentines can resist stopping off now and then for a bite to eat.*

Serves: 4-6; Preparation: 20 minutes; Cooking: 1 hour; Level of difficulty: Simple

Rinse the tripe, drain well, and cut into strips about ½ in (1 cm) wide and 3 in (7.5 cm) long. § Sauté the onion, carrot, celery, and garlic in the oil and butter in a heavy-bottomed pan, preferably made of earthenware. § When the vegetable mixture is pale gold, pour in the wine and cook until it evaporates. § Add the tripe. The tripe will release water as it cooks; cook until this has reduced and then add the tomatoes. § Season with salt and pepper, stir well and add a ladleful of stock. § Cover and continue cooking over low heat for about 1 hour. Stir frequently, adding more stock if the tripe becomes too dry. § If the sauce is too liquid, uncover the pan and increase the heat until the sauce reduces. § Serve hot with the Parmesan and with a side dish of boiled white or red kidney beans seasoned with oil, salt, and pepper.

■ INGREDIENTS

- 2 lb (1 kg) ready-to-cook honeycomb tripe, thawed, if frozen
- 1 medium onion, 1 carrot, 1 stalk celery, 1 clove garlic, all finely chopped
- 4 tablespoons extra-virgin olive oil
- 3 tablespoons butter
- ½ cup (125 ml) dry white wine
- 12 oz (350 g) tomatoes, peeled and chopped
- 2 cups (500 ml) *Beef stock* (see recipe p. 48)
- salt and freshly ground black pepper
- 1 cup (125 g) freshly grated Parmesan cheese

*Wine: a dry red
(Rosso di Montalcino)*

Milanese-style tripe
Trippa alla milanese

Serves: 4; Preparation: 25 minutes; Cooking: 1 hour; Level of difficulty: Simple

Sauté the leek, carrot, and celery in the oil in a heavy-bottomed pan, preferably made of earthenware. § When the vegetables are pale gold, add the tripe and season with salt and pepper. § Stir again and add the shin bone. § Partially cover and cook gently for about 1 hour in the liquid produced by the tripe. Stir frequently, adding a little hot water if the tripe dries out too much. § Sprinkle with the Parmesan and serve hot.

■ INGREDIENTS

- 1 leek, 1 carrot, 1 stalk celery, finely chopped
- 4 tablespoons extra-virgin olive oil
- 1¾ lb (800 g) ready-to-cook honeycomb tripe, thawed, if frozen
- salt and freshly ground black pepper
- 1 shin bone
- 1 cup (125 g) freshly grated Parmesan cheese

Wine: a dry white (Riesling)

Right: Trippa alla fiorentina

Sautéed calf's liver, Venetian-style
Fegato alla veneziana

■ INGREDIENTS

- 2 medium onions, sliced
- 4 tablespoons extra-virgin olive oil
- 1¼ lb (600 g) calf's liver, cut in short, thin strips
- ½ cup (125 ml) dry white wine
- ½ cup (125 ml) white vinegar
- salt and freshly ground black pepper

Wine: a dry red (Raboso Veronese)

Serves: 4; Preparation: 15 minutes; Cooking: 20-25 minutes; Level of difficulty: Simple

Sauté the onions in the oil over medium-low heat for about 10 minutes. § Add the liver, turn up the heat and stir rapidly. § Pour in the wine and vinegar and season with salt and pepper. Cook until the liquids have evaporated. § When the sauce is well-reduced, turn off the heat. § Serve hot with a side dish of potato purée.

VARIATION
– For a stronger tasting dish, use the darker liver of a full-grown animal.

Boiled beef in leek and tomato sauce
Francesina ai porri

This recipe provides a good way to use up the leftover beef when you have made beef stock. The boiled beef will keep in the refrigerator for 2 days, so you can make these the day after making stock.

Serves: 4; Preparation: 15 minutes; Cooking: 30 minutes; Level of difficulty: Simple

Cut the boiled beef into bite-sized pieces. § Heat the oil in a heavy-bottomed pan and sauté the leeks for a few minutes. § Pour in the stock and partially cover. Cook until the liquid has almost completely reduced. § Add the meat and tomatoes, season with salt and pepper, and continue cooking for about 20 minutes, or until the meat is literally falling apart. § Transfer to a serving dish and serve hot with potatoes or rice.

VARIATION
– The classic version of this recipe calls for the same quantity of thickly sliced white or red onions in place of the leeks. Scallions (spring onions) can also be used.

■ INGREDIENTS
- 1 lb (500 g) boiled beef (neck, shoulder, short ribs, brisket, various cuts of lean beef)
- 4 tablespoons extra-virgin olive oil
- 4 leeks, sliced
- ¾ cup (200 ml) *Beef stock* (see recipe p. 48)
- 12 oz (350 g) tomatoes, peeled and chopped
- salt and freshly ground black pepper

Wine: a dry red (Barbera)

Braised beef in a red wine sauce
Brasato al barolo

Serves: 6; Preparation: 15 minutes + 24 hours to marinate; Cooking: 2¼ hours; Level of difficulty: Simple

Place the meat in a bowl with the onion, carrot, celery, bay leaves, and peppercorns. Cover with the wine and set aside to marinate for 24 hours. § Remove the meat from the marinade and pat dry with paper towels. Tie firmly with kitchen string. § Heat the oil and butter over medium heat in a heavy-bottomed saucepan just large enough to contain the meat. Add the meat, sprinkle with salt, and brown on all sides. § In the meantime, strain the wine from the marinade. Pour about half the wine over the meat, cover the pan and simmer gently for 2 hours, turning the meat from time to time. § The sauce should be quite thick when the meat is cooked. § Slice the meat and transfer to a heated serving dish. Pour the sauce over the top and serve hot with a side dish of potato purée.

■ INGREDIENTS
- 2½ lb (1.2 kg) boneless beef roast, preferably chuck
- 1 onion, sliced
- 1 carrot, sliced
- 1 stalk celery, sliced
- 2 bay leaves
- 1 teaspoon peppercorns
- 4 cups (1 liter) Barolo wine (or another good, robust red wine)
- ⅓ cup (90 ml) extra-virgin olive oil
- 1 tablespoon butter
- salt

Wine: a dry red (Barolo)

Right: *Francesina ai porri*

Veal roll with cheese and prosciutto filling
Vitello al latte farcito

This versatile dish can be served with most boiled or braised vegetables, and salads.

Serves: 6; Preparation: 20 minutes; Cooking: about 1 hour; Level of difficulty: Medium

Remove any small pieces of fat from the meat. Cover with foil (to prevent the meat from breaking) and lightly pound. § Season with salt and pepper, cover with slices of prosciutto and Fontina, and sprinkle with Parmesan. § Roll the veal up tightly (with the grain of the meat running parallel to the length of the roll, so that it will be easier to slice) and tie firmly with kitchen string. § Heat the oil over medium-low heat in a heavy-bottomed saucepan just large enough to contain the roll. § Brown the roll on all sides and sprinkle with salt and pepper. § Pour in the milk (which should cover the roll), partially cover the saucepan, and continue cooking over medium heat until the milk reduces. This will take about 1 hour. Turn the meat from time to time during cooking. § Transfer to a serving dish, slice and serve hot or at room temperature. If serving cold, reheat the sauce, and pour over the sliced roll.

■ INGREDIENTS

- 1½ lb (750 g) slice of veal, preferably rump
- salt and freshly ground black pepper
- 4 oz (125 g) prosciutto
- 4 oz (125 g) Fontina cheese, sliced
- 4 oz (125 g) Parmesan cheese, in flakes
- 4 tablespoons extra-virgin olive oil
- 2 cups (500 ml) milk

Wine: a dry white (Müller Thurgau)

Loin of veal with leeks
Carré di vitello ai porri

Serves: 6; Preparation: 20 minutes; Cooking: 1¼ hours; Level of difficulty: Medium

Tie the veal firmly with kitchen string. Season with salt and pepper. § Sauté the meat with the oil and butter in a heavy-bottomed saucepan just large enough to contain the veal. § When the meat is brown, add the leeks and cook for 5 minutes, stirring frequently. Season with salt and pepper. § Pour in the milk so that it covers the meat and cook for about 1 hour, or until the milk evaporates. § Remove the meat, slice and transfer to a heated serving dish. § Chop the sauce in a food processor or food mill and spoon it over the meat. § Serve hot with boiled peas and parsley.

■ INGREDIENTS

- 2½ lb (1.2 kg) veal loin
- salt and freshly ground black pepper
- ⅓ cup (90 ml) extra-virgin olive oil
- 2 tablespoons butter
- 3 leeks, sliced
- 4 cups (1 liter) milk

Wine: a dry red (Chianti dei Colli Fiorentini)

VARIATION
– Replace the leeks with 2 large white onions.

Right:
Vitello al latte farcito

INGREDIENTS

- 1 onion, finely chopped
- 4 tablespoons extra-virgin olive oil
- 4 hamburgers made from 1 lb (500 g) lean beef
- salt and black pepper
- ½ cup (125 ml) dry white wine
- ½ cup (125 ml) *Beef stock* (see recipe p. 48)
- 4 teaspoons mustard

Wine: a dry red (Dolcetto d'Alba)

Hamburgers in white wine and mustard sauce
Hamburger alla salsa di senape

Serves: 4; Preparation: 10 minutes; Cooking: 20 minutes; Level of difficulty: Simple

Sauté the onion in the oil in a heavy-bottomed pan over medium heat until soft. § Add the hamburgers and season with salt and pepper. Pour in the wine and cook until it evaporates, turning the hamburgers frequently. § Gradually add the stock and cook for 10–15 minutes. § Transfer the meat to a heated serving dish. § Stir the mustard into the sauce left in the pan. Mix well. § Spoon the mustard sauce over the hamburgers and serve hot with potato purée and a green salad.

Veal scaloppine with pizza topping
Scaloppine alla pizzaiola

Serves: 4; Preparation: 25 minutes; Cooking: 15 minutes; Level of difficulty: Simple

Remove any small pieces of fat from the scaloppine. § Pound the meat lightly, dredge in the flour, then shake thoroughly. § Heat the oil in a large sauté pan and brown the scaloppine on both sides. § Season with salt and pepper and sprinkle with the garlic and the capers. Cover each slice with a little tomato sauce and cook for 10–12 minutes (no longer, as the meat will become tough). § Sprinkle with the parsley and serve hot with boiled spinach or Swiss chard briefly sautéed in finely chopped garlic and extra-virgin olive oil.

VARIATION
– During the last 3–4 minutes of cooking, place a thin slice of Mozzarella cheese on top of each scaloppine.

■ INGREDIENTS

- 1¼ lb (600 g) small, thinly sliced veal scaloppine (cut from rump)
- 1 cup (150 g) all-purpose (plain) flour
- ⅓ cup (90 ml) extra-virgin olive oil
- salt and freshly ground black pepper
- 2 cloves garlic, finely chopped
- 1 tablespoon capers, coarsely chopped
- 2 tablespoons finely chopped parsley
- 1¼ cups (300 g) *Simple tomato sauce* (see recipe p. 28)

Wine: a dry red (Sangiovese)

Cold veal with tuna sauce
Vitello tonnato

This wonderful dish requires careful preparation, but the end result is well worth the effort. Firstly, the veal needs to cool in its cooking water (to stop it from becoming tough). Furthermore, the sauce should be spooned over the cool meat and left for several hours before serving. Prepare it a day ahead, so that the veal and tuna sauce are fully blended.

Serves: 4; Preparation: 25 minutes + 6 hours to macerate; Cooking: 2 hours; Level of difficulty: Medium

Remove any fat from the meat and tie firmly with kitchen string. § Put the meat, carrot, celery, bay leaf, and onion stuck with the cloves in a pot with just enough boiling water to cover the meat. Season with salt, cover, and simmer for 2 hours. Leave the veal to cool in its cooking water. § Prepare the mayonnaise. § Drain the oil from the tuna and place the fish in a food processor with the mayonnaise, capers, lemon juice, oil, salt, and pepper. Mix until smooth. § Slice the veal thinly, transfer to a serving dish, and spoon the sauce over the top. Garnish with capers and slices of lemon. § Set aside for at least 6 hours. § Serve by itself as an appetizer or with boiled vegetables as a light lunch or main course.

VARIATION
– Add 4 anchovy fillets and 6 pickled gherkins when making the sauce.

■ INGREDIENTS

- 2 lb (1 kg) lean veal roast, preferably rump
- 1 carrot
- 1 stalk celery
- 1 bay leaf
- 1 onion
- 2 cloves
- salt and black pepper
- 1 quantity *Mayonnaise* (see recipe p. 42)
- ¾ cup (150 g) tuna, packed in oil
- 2 tablespoons capers, plus some to garnish
- juice of 1 lemon, plus ½ lemon to garnish
- 4 tablespoons extra-virgin olive oil

Wine: a dry, sparkling white (Prosecco di Conegliano)

Right: *Scaloppine alla pizzaiola*

Beef rolls with artichokes
Involtini ai carciofi

Serves: 6; Preparation: 25 minutes; Cooking: 20 minutes; Level of difficulty: Medium

Remove any small pieces of fat from the beef and pound lightly. § Beat the eggs in a small bowl with the parsley, garlic, and salt. § Heat 2 tablespoons of oil in a small sauté pan, pour in the egg mixture and cook until firm on both sides. Set aside to cool. § To clean the artichokes, remove the tough outer leaves and trim the tops and stalks. Wash well in cold water and lemon juice. Cut each artichoke into 6 segments. § Heat 2 tablespoons of oil in a sauté pan over medium heat and cook the artichokes for 5 minutes. Season with salt and pepper and set aside. § To prepare the rolls, lay the slices of meat on a work surface and place a piece of mortadella on each. § Cut the cooked egg into 18 pieces. Place a piece of egg and a segment of artichoke on the mortadella. § Roll the meat into filled rolls and close with a toothpick. § Dredge in the flour and place in a sauté pan with the remaining oil. Sprinkle with salt and pepper, and brown on all sides. § Pour in the wine and cook for 20 minutes, adding stock if the pan becomes too dry. § Serve hot with potato purée or braised lentils.

> VARIATIONS
> – Replace the egg mixture with thin slices of Fontina cheese.
> – Use a single, large slice of meat, fill with the same ingredients to make a roll. Cooking time will increase by 30 minutes.

■ INGREDIENTS

- 1¼ lb (600 g) beef rump sliced extra thin (18 slices)
- 4 eggs
- 1 tablespoon parsley and garlic, finely chopped
- salt and freshly ground black pepper
- ½ cup (125 ml) extra-virgin olive oil
- 3 globe artichokes
- juice of ½ lemon
- 5 oz (150 g) mortadella slices, cut in half (18 pieces)
- 3 tablespoons all-purpose (plain) flour
- ½ cup (125 ml) dry white wine
- ½ cup (125 ml) *Beef stock* (see recipe p. 48)

Wine: a dry red (Chianti Classico)

Slices of tenderloin with balsamic vinegar
Medaglione di filetto profumate all'aceto balsamico

This quick and simple dish always makes a good impression, even for elegant dinner parties.

Serves: 4; Preparation: 10 minutes; Cooking: 10 minutes; Level of difficulty: Simple

Melt the butter in a heavy-bottomed pan over high heat. When it is foaming, add the shallot and then the meat. Cook for about 4 minutes each side. § Pour in the balsamic vinegar and season with salt and pepper. Cook for 1–2 minutes more. § Set the meat aside in a warm oven. § Return the cooking juices to the heat until they foam, then stir in the cornstarch. § Pour the sauce over the meat and serve hot with a green salad.

■ INGREDIENTS

- 2 tablespoons butter
- ½ shallot, finely chopped
- 4 slices of tenderloin beef, weighing about 5 oz (150 g) each
- ½ cup (125 ml) balsamic vinegar
- salt and freshly ground black pepper
- 1 tablespoon cornstarch (corn flour)

Wine: a dry, fruity red (Teroldego Rotaliano)

Right: *Involtini ai carciofi*

Veal scaloppine with Parmesan and fresh tomatoes
Scaloppine al parmigiano e pomodoro fresco

Serves: 4; Preparation: 25 minutes; Cooking: 25 minutes; Level of difficulty: Simple

Remove any little pieces of fat from the meat. § Cover with foil and pound lightly. § Dredge in the flour, then shake to eliminate any excess. § Heat the oil and butter in a large sauté pan over medium heat. Add the scaloppine and season with salt and pepper. Brown on both sides. § Pour in the wine and cook until it evaporates. § Remove the slices of meat and set aside in a warm oven. § Add the shallots to the pan and lightly brown. § Add the tomatoes, salt, and pepper to taste, and cook until the tomatoes reduce. § Add the scaloppine and sprinkle with the Parmesan, parsley, and basil. § Turn off the heat, cover, and leave to stand for a few minutes. § Serve hot or at room temperature with a green salad.

■ INGREDIENTS

- 8 veal scaloppine, about 12 oz (350 g)
- ½ cup (75 g) all-purpose (plain) flour
- 4 tablespoons extra-virgin olive oil
- 2 tablespoons butter
- salt and freshly ground black pepper
- ½ cup (125 ml) dry white wine
- 2 shallots, coarsely chopped
- 10 oz (300 g) tomatoes, peeled and diced
- 4 oz (125 g) Parmesan cheese, flaked
- 1½ tablespoons each finely chopped parsley and basil

Wine: a dry white (Pinot Bianco)

Mixed boiled meats with three sauces
Bollito misto alle tre salse

I have suggested three sauces that go particularly well with mixed boiled meats. Try the Onion sauce (see p. 34), Hot tomato sauce (see p. 40) and the Tartare sauce (see p. 44) too.

Serves: 12; Preparation: 25 minutes; Cooking: 1½ hours; Level of difficulty: Simple

Fill a large saucepan with cold water and add the onion, carrot, celery, parsley, half the peppercorns, and a scant teaspoon of salt (use less to be on the safe side; you can always add more, if necessary). § When the water is boiling, add the beef. Simmer for 1½ hours. § After 30 minutes, add the chicken and veal to the saucepan with the beef. § In another saucepan, cover the tongue with cold water and add the wine, bay leaves, and remaining peppercorns. Bring to a boil and then simmer for 1 hour. § When the meats are cooked, break into pieces (except for the tongue, which should be sliced) and arrange on a large heated serving dish. Moisten with a ladleful of boiling stock. § While the meat is

■ INGREDIENTS

- 1 large onion, cut in 4
- 1 carrot, cut in 4
- 1 stalk celery, cut in 2
- 2 sprigs parsley
- 2 teaspoons black peppercorns
- salt
- 2 lb (1 kg) boneless beef brisket or chuck
- 1 chicken, about 2 lb (1 kg)
- 2 lb (1 kg) veal breast with short ribs
- 1 beef tongue, about 2 lb (1 kg)

Right: *Scaloppine al parmigiano e pomodoro fresco*

- ½ cup (125 ml) dry white
  wine
- 2 bay leaves
- 1 quantity *Mustard sauce*
  (see recipe p. 46)
- 1 quantity *Garlic mayonnaise*
  (see recipe p. 42)
- 1 quantity *Parsley sauce with
  capers, anchovies, garlic, and oil*
  (see recipe p. 44)

*Wine: a dry red
(Chianti Classico)*

cooking, prepare (or reheat) the three sauces. Put them in separate serving bowls. § Serve the meats with a platter of mixed boiled vegetables, such as potatoes, carrots, zucchini (courgettes), fennel, and globe artichokes.

VARIATION
— Sieve the beef and chicken stock and use it to make soups, *stracciatella* (stock with egg and cheese), or tortellini in stock. If there is any left over, pour into glass bottles and keep in the refrigerator. It will keep for 3 or 4 days.

Milanese-style stewed veal shanks
Ossibuchi alla milanese

Ossobuco means "bone with a hole" which perfectly describes the calf's hind shank used in this classic Milanese dish. For those who like it, the bone marrow is considered a special delicacy. Gremolada, a mixture of lemon peel, garlic, and parsley, is traditionally added just before removing from the heat. It is optional.

Serves: 4-6; Preparation: 25 minutes; Cooking: 1¾ hours; Level of difficulty: Medium

Make 4–5 incisions around the edge of each shank to stop them curling up during cooking. § Dredge the shanks in the flour and sprinkle with salt and pepper. § Heat the oil in a large, heavy-bottomed saucepan over medium-high heat and cook the shanks briefly on both sides. Remove and set aside. § Melt the butter in the pan and add the carrot, onion, celery, and sage. § When the vegetables are soft, add the meat and cook for a few minutes. § Pour in the wine. When the wine has evaporated, add the stock and tomatoes, and season with salt and pepper to taste. § Cover and simmer over low heat for 1½ hours, adding extra stock if necessary. § When cooked, stir in the lemon peel, garlic, and parsley, if liked. § Transfer to a heated serving dish and serve hot with classic Milanese-style risotto.

■ INGREDIENTS

- 6 veal hind shanks, cut in 1½-in (4-cm) thick slices
- ½ cup (75 g) all-purpose (plain) flour
- salt and freshly ground black pepper
- 4 tablespoons extra-virgin olive oil
- 3 tablespoons butter
- 1 carrot, 1 onion, 1 stalk celery, all finely chopped
- 4 sage leaves, torn
- ¾ cup (200 ml) dry white wine
- 1 cup (250 ml) *Beef stock* (see recipe p. 48)
- 3 tablespoons tomatoes, peeled and diced, or *Simple tomato sauce* (see recipe p. 28)

For the *gremolada* (optional)
- peel of 1 lemon, 1 clove garlic, 1 tablespoon parsley, all finely chopped

Wine: a dry red (Chianti Classico Ruffino)

Roast beef in mustard sauce
Roast-beef alla senape

Serves: 6; Preparation: 5 minutes; Cooking: 25 minutes; Level of difficulty: Simple

Heat the oil in a large, heavy-bottomed pan. § Sprinkle the beef with a generous coating of pepper and add to the pan. § Brown the meat evenly on all sides over high heat. § After about 10 minutes, lower heat and smother the beef with the mustard and brandy. Cook for 15 minutes more. § Sprinkle the meat with salt only after it is cooked; if added before, the meat will be less tender. § Slice thinly, arrange on a heat serving dish and serve hot. § For the perfect side dish: boil enough asparagus for six in salted water until almost cooked. Transfer to a baking dish, cover with thinly sliced Fontina cheese and bake in a hot oven for 5 minutes.

■ INGREDIENTS

- ½ cup (125 ml) extra-virgin olive oil
- boneless beef roast, about 2½ lb (1.2 kg)
- salt and freshly ground black pepper
- 7½ oz (225 g) mustard
- ½ cup (125 ml) brandy

Wine: a dry red (Pinot Nero dei Colli Piacentini)

Right:
Ossibuchi alla milanese

Glazed topside with mushrooms sautéed in garlic and parsley

Magatello glassato con champignons

Serves: 6; Preparation: 25 minutes; Cooking: 1½ hours; Level of difficulty: Medium

Sprinkle the meat with salt and pepper. Transfer to a roasting pan and drizzle with 5 tablespoons of the oil. Add the whole clove of garlic and the sage and rosemary. § Cook in a preheated oven at 400°F/200°C/gas 6. After about 15 minutes, when the meat is brown all over, pour half the wine over the top and continue cooking for about 1 hour, basting from time to time. If the meat becomes too dry, add more wine or a little stock. § In the meantime, wash the mushrooms under cold running water. Cut off and discard the stems. Peel the mushroom caps and cut into large strips. If the mushrooms are small, leave them whole. § Heat the remaining oil in a sauté pan over medium heat and sauté the chopped garlic and parsley for 2–3 minutes. § Add the mushrooms and sprinkle with salt and pepper. Stir well and cook for 5–7 minutes. § Pour in the remaining wine and cook until it evaporates. Add the stock and cook over medium heat for about 20–25 minutes, or until the liquid reduces, stirring frequently. The mushrooms should be tender, but not mushy. § When the meat is cooked, transfer to a heated serving dish and set aside in a warm place. § Discard the garlic, rosemary, and sage from the cooking juices. Place the sauce over high heat, and stir in the flour. Stir constantly as it thickens, then pour over the meat (the sauce will give it a glazed appearance). § Arrange the mushrooms around the meat and serve hot.

■ INGREDIENTS

- 2½ lb (1.2 kg) slice of veal or beef, preferably rump, rolled and tied with kitchen string
- salt and freshly ground black pepper
- ½ cup (125 ml) extra-virgin olive oil
- 3 cloves garlic (1 whole, 2 finely chopped)
- 1 twig sage
- 1 twig rosemary
- 1 cup (250 ml) dry white wine
- 1 cup (250 ml) *Beef stock* (see recipe p. 48)
- 1½ lb (750 g) white mushrooms
- 1 tablespoon finely chopped parsley
- 2 tablespoons flour

Wine: a dry red
(Chianti dei Colli Fiorentini)

Veal roll stuffed with smoked provola cheese

Tasca di vitello farcita alla provola affumicata

Serves: 6; Preparation: 20 minutes; Cooking: 1 hour; Level of difficulty: Simple

Make a deep incision in the veal with a sharp knife and open a "pocket" in the meat. § Fill with the cubes of Provola and ham. § Close the meat around the cheese and ham and sew up with a needle and kitchen thread. § Transfer to an ovenproof dish with the oil, rosemary, and garlic. § Sprinkle with salt and pepper, and place in a preheated oven at 400°F/200°C/gas 6. § After 5 minutes, pour the

■ INGREDIENTS

- 1 lb (500 g) piece of veal, preferably rump
- 5 oz (150 g) smoked Provola cheese, cubed
- 5 oz (150 g) ham, cubed
- ½ cup (125 ml) dry white wine
- ¾ cup (200 ml) *Beef stock* (see recipe p. 48)

Right:
Magatello glassato con champignons

- ⅓ cup (90 ml) extra-virgin olive oil
- salt and freshly ground black pepper
- 1 sprig rosemary
- 1 clove garlic

Wine: a dry red (Merlot)

wine over the meat and cook for another 55 minutes, basting from time to time. If the meat becomes too dry, add a little stock. § When cooked, discard the kitchen thread and cut the meat into rather thick slices. The Provola should be almost completely melted. § Arrange the slices on a heated serving dish and spoon the sauce over the top. Serve hot with lightly boiled artichokes sautéed briefly in garlic, oil, and parsley.

Beef stew with porcini mushrooms

Stufato di manzo ai funghi porcini

If you can't get fresh porcini, use the same quantity of white mushrooms mixed with 2 tablespoons of dried porcini soaked in warm water for 15–20 minutes.

Serves: 4; Preparation: 25 minutes; Cooking: 1¼ hours; Level of difficulty: Simple

Remove any small pieces of fat from the meat. § Sauté the garlic and onion in the oil in a heavy-bottomed pan (preferably earthenware) over medium heat. § Add the meat when the onion is soft. Season with salt and pepper and simmer in the liquid produced by the meat. § When this liquid has reduced, pour in the wine and cook until it has evaporated. § Add the tomato sauce, stir well and simmer gently over medium-low heat. § In the meantime, clean and wash the mushrooms. Cut the caps into thick strips and the stems into chunks. § Add the mushrooms and mint to the stew after about 40 minutes. Partially cover the pan and simmer until cooked, stirring frequently. Add a little stock if the sauce dries out too much. § Serve hot with potato purée and a mixed salad.

■ INGREDIENTS

- 1¾ lb (800 g) boneless beef chuck, cut into bite-sized pieces
- 1 clove garlic, finely chopped
- 1 onion, finely chopped
- 4 tablespoons extra-virgin olive oil
- salt and freshly ground black pepper
- ½ cup (125 ml) dry white wine
- ½ quantity *Simple tomato sauce* (see recipe p. 28)
- 1½ lb (750 g) porcini mushrooms
- 2 sprigs mint
- 1 cup (250 ml) *Beef stock* (see recipe p. 48)

Wine: a dry red (Barbera d'Asti)

Veal scaloppine in lemon sauce

Scaloppine di vitello al limone

Serves: 4; Preparation: 15 minutes; Cooking: 12–15 minutes; Level of difficulty: Simple

Remove any small pieces of fat from the meat. § Cover with foil (to prevent the veal from breaking), and pound lightly. § Dredge the scaloppine in the flour, shaking off any excess. § Sauté the veal in the butter and oil in a heavy-bottomed pan over high heat, turning often until both sides are evenly browned. Season with salt and pepper. § Lower the heat to medium and continue cooking, adding a little stock to moisten. § After about 12 minutes, when the veal is cooked, turn off the heat and pour the lemon juice over the top. § Sprinkle with the parsley and serve hot with glazed carrots (carrots cooked whole in butter, beef stock, salt, parsley, and a teaspoon of sugar).

■ INGREDIENTS

- 8 veal scaloppine, about 1 lb (500 g)
- ½ cup (75 g) all-purpose (plain) flour
- 2½ tablespoons butter
- 2 tablespoons extra virgin olive oil
- salt and freshly ground black pepper
- ½ cup (125 ml) *Beef stock* (see recipe p. 48)
- juice of 1 lemon
- 1 tablespoon finely chopped parsley

Wine: a dry white (Orvieto Classico)

VARIATION
– Transfer the cooked scaloppine to a heated serving dish. Add ½ cup (125 ml) of Marsala wine to the juices left in the pan, and reduce over medium-high heat. Pour the Marsala sauce over the veal and serve immediately.

Right:
Scaloppine di vitello al limone

Meat loaf with tomato sauce
Polpettone al pomodoro

■ INGREDIENTS

- 1 lb (500 g) lean ground veal
- 1 egg
- 1 thick slice mortadella, finely chopped
- dash of nutmeg (optional)
- 2 tablespoons bread, soaked in milk and squeezed thoroughly
- 1 clove garlic, finely chopped
- 2 tablespoons finely chopped parsley
- salt and freshly ground black pepper
- 4 tablespoons all-purpose (plain) flour
- ½ cup (125 ml) extra-virgin olive oil
- 1 tablespoon butter
- ½ onion, finely chopped
- 1 small carrot, finely chopped
- 1 small stalk celery, finely chopped
- 10 oz (300 g) tomatoes, peeled and chopped, or 1 quantity *Simple tomato sauce* (see recipe p. 28)
- 1 cup (250 ml) *Beef stock* (see recipe p. 48)

Wine: a dry red
(Brusco dei Barbi)

Serves: 6; Preparation: 30 minutes; Cooking: 1¼ hours; Level of difficulty: Medium

Mix the veal with the egg, mortadella, nutmeg, bread, garlic, and parsley in a bowl. Season with salt and pepper. § Shape the mixture into a meat loaf. § Put the flour in a large dish and carefully roll the meat loaf in it. § Heat 4 tablespoons of oil in a large, heavy-bottomed pan over medium heat and brown the meat loaf on all sides. Use a fork (but don't prick or pierce the surface) and a wooden spatula when turning. This is the most delicate moment; when the meat loaf is most likely to crumble or break. § The meat will take about 10 minutes to brown. § Drain the meat loaf of the cooking oil and set aside. § In the meantime, heat the butter and the remaining oil in a sauté pan. Add the onion, carrot, celery, and parsley and sauté for 4–5 minutes. § Add the tomatoes (or tomato sauce) and cook for 5 minutes. § Place the meat loaf in the pan and season with salt and pepper. § Partially cover the pan and simmer over low heat for just under 1 hour. Stir frequently, so that the meat loaf does not stick to the bottom. § If the sauce becomes too dense, add a few ladlefuls of stock. § When cooked, set aside to cool. The meat loaf should only be sliced when almost cold, otherwise the slices may break. § Arrange the sliced meat loaf on a serving dish. Heat the sauce just before serving and pour over the slices. Serve with potato purée or mixed stir-fried vegetables.

VARIATIONS
– Omit the tomatoes or tomato sauce and serve the meat loaf with the juice of half a lemon.
– For a Piemontese-style meat loaf, omit the tomatoes or tomato sauce. Place two shelled hard-cooked (hard-boiled) eggs inside the loaf when shaping it. It will be much more attractive when sliced.

Left: *Polpettone al pomodoro*

Elda's meatballs
Polpettine Elda

This recipe was given to me by my mother-in-law, Elda.
Simple and hearty, these meatballs make a wonderful family meal.

Serves: 4; Preparation: 20 minutes; Cooking: 25 minutes; Level of difficulty: Simple

Combine the meat, egg, bread soaked in milk, salt, and pepper in a bowl. Mix well until the mixture is firm. § Take egg-sized pieces of the mixture and shape them into oval meatballs. Coat them in bread crumbs and then flatten slightly. § Heat the oil in a large, heavy-bottomed pan over medium heat. § Add the meatballs when the oil is very hot (but not smoking) and fry until they are brown on both sides. § Moisten with the stock and cook until it evaporates. § Taste for salt and pepper. § Add the milk and cook until it reduces, forming a dense cream. § Serve hot with boiled peas, dotted with butter and sprinkled with parsley.

VARIATION
– The meatballs can be prepared ahead of time. When they are coated in bread crumbs, transfer to a plate, cover with plastic wrap and place in the refrigerator. They will keep for 1–2 days.

■ INGREDIENTS

- 12 oz (350 g) lean ground veal
- 1 egg
- 1 heaped tablespoon bread, soaked in milk and thoroughly squeezed
- salt and freshly ground black pepper
- 1 cup (125 g) bread crumbs
- 4 tablespoons extra-virgin olive oil
- ½ cup (125 ml) *Beef stock (see recipe p. 48)*
- ½ cup (125 ml) milk

Wine: a dry white (Bianco di Franciacorta)

Sirloin with capers and anchovies
Scannello ai capperi e acciughe

Serves: 6; Preparation: 20 minutes; Cooking: 35-40 minutes; Level of difficulty: Medium

Place the meat in a large, heavy-bottomed pan with the oil over high heat. Brown on both sides. § Add the onion, carrot, and celery, and sprinkle with a little salt and pepper (be sure not to add too much salt —

■ INGREDIENTS

- 2½ lb (1.2 kg) sirloin
- ⅓ cup (90 ml) extra-virgin olive oil
- 1 onion, coarsely chopped
- 1 carrot, coarsely chopped
- 1 stick celery, coarsely chopped
- salt and freshly ground black pepper

Right:
Scannello ai capperi e acciughe

- 1 heaped tablespoon capers
- 2 anchovy fillets, well cleaned and washed
- ½ cup (125 ml) dry white wine
- ½ cup (125 ml) *Beef stock* (see recipe p. 48)

Wine: a dry red
(Aprilia Merlot)

the anchovies to be added later can be quite salty). Stir well and cook for 4–5 minutes. § Pour in the wine, partially cover, and cook for about 30 minutes, turning the meat often. § When the meat is tender, set aside on a chopping board, ready to be sliced. § Turn off the heat and add the capers and anchovies to the vegetables. Mix well and purée in a food processor or food mill, to make a thick vegetable cream. § Slice the sirloin and arrange on a heated serving dish. Spoon the sauce over the top and serve hot. Serve with potato purée.

VARIATION
– For a simpler dish, or if you don't like capers and anchovies, omit them. In this case, season the mashed vegetables with a little freshly ground nutmeg.

Boiled meat and potato meatballs
Polpettine di lesso e patate

■ INGREDIENTS

- 2 large potatoes, boiled
- 13 oz (400 g) boiled brisket or chuck
- 2 eggs
- 1 tablespoon finely chopped parsley
- 1 clove garlic, finely chopped
- salt and freshly ground black pepper
- 1 cup (125 g) bread crumbs
- ½ cup (125 ml) oil, for frying

Wine: a dry rosé (Rosé Antinori)

Serves: 4; Preparation: 25 minutes; Cooking: 20-25 minutes; Level of difficulty: Medium

Mash the potatoes in a food mill or with a potato masher. Do not use a food processor because the mixture will become too sticky and the meatballs will be difficult to fry. Transfer the mixture to a bowl. § In the meantime, grind the boiled meat in a food processor. § Add to the bowl with the potatoes. § Stir in one egg, the parsley, and garlic. Season with salt and pepper, and mix well. The mixture should be quite dense, but if it is too dry, add the other egg. § Shape the mixture into oblong meatballs (like croquettes), and roll them in bread crumbs. § Heat the oil in a heavy-bottomed pan until hot (but not smoking) and fry the meatballs until they are golden brown. § Drain on paper towels. Sprinkle with salt and serve hot with a fresh, green salad.

Fried Milanese-style chops with anchovy sauce
Costolette fritte alla milanese con acciugata

■ INGREDIENTS

- 8 veal loin chops, about 1 lb (500 g)
- 2 eggs
- salt
- ⅓ cup (50 g) all-purpose (plain) flour
- 1 cup (125 g) bread crumbs
- ½ cup (125 ml) oil for frying
- ½ cup (125 g) butter
- 1 tablespoon anchovy paste

Wine: red (Trentino Marzemino)

Serves: 4; Preparation: 20 minutes; Cooking: 10 minutes; Level of difficulty: Simple

Rinse the chops under cold running water and pat dry with paper towels. Make little cuts around the edges to stop them from curling up during cooking. §. Lightly coat the chops with flour, shaking off any excess. § Beat the eggs in a bowl with the salt. Dip the chops in the beaten egg, then coat with bread crumbs, making sure that they stick to the chops. § Heat the oil in a heavy-bottomed pan until very hot and fry the chops. Fry over medium heat, so that the meat is well-cooked right through and not burnt on the outside. The bread crumbs should be golden brown and crispy. § Drain the chops on paper towels. § Prepare the anchovy sauce by melting the butter in a small, heavy-bottomed saucepan over low heat. Stir in the anchovy paste. When smooth, spoon over the chops. § Serve hot, with French fries and a green or mixed salad.

Left: *Polpettine di lesso e patate*

Farmhouse stew with potatoes
Spezzatino con patate alla contadina

Serves: 6; Preparation: 25 minutes; Cooking: 1 hour and 10 minutes; Level of difficulty: Simple

Heat the oil in a large, heavy-bottomed pan and add the chopped vegetables and herbs. Sauté briefly. § Remove any little pieces of fat from the meat. Add the meat to the pan, season with salt and pepper, and cook until brown. § Pour in the wine and cook until it evaporates. § Cover the pan and simmer for about 1 hour, gradually adding the stock. Stir frequently, to stop the meat from sticking to the pan. § Add the potatoes about 30 minutes before the meat is cooked. § Serve hot.

VARIATION
– Double the quantity of garlic, onion, carrot, and celery, and chop coarsely (instead of finely). Halve the quantity of potatoes or omit them entirely.

■ INGREDIENTS

- ⅓ cup (90 ml) extra-virgin olive oil
- 1 clove garlic, 1 onion, 1 carrot, 1 stalk celery, all finely chopped
- 2 medium tomatoes, peeled and chopped
- 1 tablespoon mixed herbs (sage, parsley, oregano, rosemary, thyme), chopped
- 1½ lb (750 g) beef chuck with muscle, cut into bite-sized pieces
- salt and freshly ground black pepper
- ¾ cup (200 ml) red wine
- 2 cups (500 ml) *Beef stock* (see recipe p. 48)
- 1¼ lb (600 g) potatoes, peeled and cut in bite-sized chunks

Wine: a dry red (Trentino Rosso)

Beef fillets with green pepper
Filetti al pepe verde

Serves: 4; Preparation: 10 minutes; Cooking: 10 minutes; Level of difficulty: Simple

Mash the green peppercorns with a fork. Use your hands to press the crushed peppercorns so that they stick to both sides of the fillets. § Heat the butter and oil in a heavy-bottomed pan. § Season the fillets with salt and add to the pan. § Pour in the cognac and cook until it evaporates. § Add the cream and cook for about 5 minutes more, turning the meat over at least once. If the sauce is too liquid, remove the fillets and set them aside in a warm oven. Turn up the heat and cook the sauce until it reduces sufficiently. § Arrange the fillets on a heated serving dish and spoon the sauce over the top. § Serve hot with green beans cooked in butter or fennel *au gratin*.

■ INGREDIENTS

- 2 tablespoons soft green peppercorns (in liquid)
- 4 beef fillets, cut 1-in (2.5-cm) thick slices
- 2 tablespoons butter
- 4 tablespoons extra-virgin olive oil
- salt
- ½ cup (125 ml) cognac (or brandy)
- 2 tablespoons fresh cream

Wine: a dry white (Vernaccia di San Gimignano)

Right: *Filetti al pepe verde*

■ INGREDIENTS

- 2 lb (1 kg) lean suckling veal, in bite-sized pieces
- 4 tablespoons extra-virgin olive oil
- 2 cloves garlic, finely chopped
- 2 tablespoons finely chopped parsley
- ¾ cup (200 ml) milk
- ½ cup (125 ml) *Beef stock* (see recipe p. 48)
- salt and freshly ground black pepper

Wine: a dry white
(Tocai Friulano)

Veal stew with parsley
Spezzatino in bianco al prezzemolo

Serves: 6; Preparation: 15 minutes; Cooking: about 1 hour; Level of difficulty: Simple

Remove any pieces of fat from the veal. § Heat the oil in a large, heavy-bottomed pan over medium heat and sauté the garlic and parsley for 2–3 minutes. § Add the meat and cook in its juices until it reduces. Season with salt and pepper. § Pour in the milk and stock. The meat should be almost, but not completely, covered. Reduce the heat and partially cover the pan, so that the liquid evaporates. Cook very slowly, stirring frequently since the milk tends to stick, until the liquid reduces, forming a dense sauce. § Transfer to a heated serving dish and serve hot with a side dish of lightly boiled peas briefly sautéed in olive oil, garlic, and parsley.

VARIATION
– This stew can be prepared in advance (even the day before), and reheated just before serving.

■ INGREDIENTS

- 1¼ lb (600 g) calf's liver, sliced
- 2 heaped tablespoons all-purpose (plain) flour
- 2 tablespoons extra-virgin olive oil
- 2 cloves garlic, finely chopped
- 10 leaves fresh sage
- salt and freshly ground black pepper

Wine: a dry red
(Chianti dei Colli Fiorentini)

Sautéed calf's liver with fresh sage
Fegato alla salvia

This simple, elegant dish is also known as Fegato alla fiorentina (Sautéed calf's liver, Florentine-style). It originally comes from the Tuscan capital, although it is becoming more and more difficult to find in the city's trattorias and restaurants.

Serves: 4; Preparation: 5 minutes; Cooking: 7-10 minutes; Level of difficulty: Simple

Ask your butcher to slice the liver ready for cooking. § Lightly flour the liver and set aside on a plate. § Heat the oil in a large, heavy-bottomed pan and add the garlic and sage. Sauté over medium-high heat for 2 minutes, then add the liver. § Cook until well-browned on both sides. § Serve hot with potato purée and a green salad.

VARIATION
– Replace the oil with the same amount of butter.

Left:
Spezzatino in bianco al prezzemolo

Black pepper stew
Peposo

■ INGREDIENTS

- 3½ lb (1.7 kg) muscle from veal shanks, cut in bite-sized pieces
- 4 cloves garlic, finely chopped
- 1¼ lb (600 g) tomatoes, peeled and chopped
- salt
- 3 tablespoons freshly ground black pepper
- 4 cups (1 liter) cold water
- 1½ cups (350 ml) robust, dry red wine

Wine: a dry red (Carmignano)

Serves: 8; Preparation: 10 minutes; Cooking: 3 hours; Level of difficulty: Simple

Place the meat in a large, heavy-bottomed saucepan (preferably earthenware) with the garlic, tomatoes, salt, and pepper. Pour in just enough of the water to cover the meat. § Cook over medium heat for 2 hours, adding extra water if the sauce becomes too dry. Stir from time to time. § After 2 hours, pour in the wine and cook for 1 hour more, or until the meat is very tender. § Serve hot with mixed boiled vegetables.

Mixed meat and vegetable skewers
Piccoli spiedini misti di carne e verdure

■ INGREDIENTS

- 3 fresh Italian pork sausages
- 10 oz (300 g) of pork
- 12 oz (350 g) boned veal, shoulder, or shank
- 1 lb (500 g) chicken breast
- 1 yellow and 1 red bell pepper (capsicum)
- 10 oz (300 g) baby onions
- 20 cherry tomatoes
- 5 slices crusty bread
- 10 leaves fresh sage
- salt and freshly ground black pepper
- ¼ cup (60 ml) extra-virgin olive oil

Wine: a dry red (Santa Cristina)

There are many variations on the traditional recipe for mixed meat and vegetable skewers. The basic dish calls for bite-sized chunks of two or three different meats alternated with cherry tomatoes, baby onions, bell peppers, and bread. Always place the bread next to the meat, so that it absorbs the cooking juices. The crisp, mouthwatering pieces of roasted bread are one of the best parts of this dish. These skewers are also very good when cooked over a barbecue.

Serves: 6; Preparation: 1 hour; Cooking: 30 minutes; Level of difficulty: Medium

Remove any fat from the meat. § Chop the meat, vegetables, and bread into large cubes or squares. Slice the sausages thickly. § Thread the cubes onto wooden skewers, alternating pieces of meat, sausage, vegetables, bread, and sage leaves. § Arrange the skewers in a roasting dish and season with salt and pepper. Drizzle with the oil. § Bake in a preheated oven at 400°F/200°C/gas 6 for 30 minutes, turning occasionally and adding beef stock to moisten, if required. § When the meat is well browned, remove from the oven and serve hot. These skewers are particularly good when served with a dish of hot polenta.

Right: *Peposo*

Pork

*Succulent pork is always good as
a simple roast, but it also combines
well with a wide range of
vegetables and fruit.*

Fillet of pork with apple
Filetto di maiale alle mele

Pork is always good in sweet-and-sour dishes with fruit like apples or prunes. This dish, hearty and easy-to-prepare, is perfect for cold winter evenings.

Serves: 4; Preparation: 5 minutes + 2 hours marinating; Cooking: 1 hour; Level of difficulty: Simple

Cut the apples in half and remove the cores. Place in a bowl, cover with the wine, and set aside to marinate for at least 2 hours (you may leave them even longer if you have the time). § Season the pork with salt and pepper and transfer to a baking pan with the oil. § Bake in a preheated oven at 400°F/200°C/gas 6. After 10 minutes, pour about half the wine used to marinate the apples over the pork. Turn the pork and cook for another 20 minutes. § Arrange the apples around the pork in the baking pan and add more wine if the pan is dry. Cook for 30 minutes more. § Slice the pork and transfer to a serving dish. Arrange the apples around the pork and serve hot with a bowl of steaming potato purée.

■ INGREDIENTS

- 6 Golden Delicious apples
- 2 cups (500 ml) dry white wine
- 2 pork fillets, about 1 lb (500 g)
- salt and freshly ground black pepper
- 4 tablespoons extra-virgin olive oil

Wine: a dry red (Freisa)

Pan-roasted pork with potatoes
Arista arrosto

In Tuscany pork loin with ribs is known as "arista." This dish is normally eaten cold and can be cooked the day before.

Serves: 6; Preparation: 20 minutes; Cooking: 1½ hours; Level of difficulty: Simple

Detach the loin from the ribs. Use a sharp knife to make fairly deep incisions in the loin and fill with the garlic, rosemary, and sage mixed with salt and pepper. § Tie the ribs to the loin with 2 or 3 twists of kitchen string. The ribs will make the dish tastier. § Heat the butter and oil in a heavy-bottomed pan over medium heat. § Add the meat and brown all over. § Pour a ladle of stock over the top, cover, and continue cooking, adding the stock gradually to keep the pan moist. § Peel the potatoes and cut them into bite-sized pieces. § When the pork has been cooking for 30 minutes, add the potatoes and unpeeled cloves of garlic. § When cooked, untie the ribs and arrange the meat and potatoes in a heated serving dish. The cooking juices can be spooned over the top or served separately.

■ INGREDIENTS

- 2 lb (1 kg) pork loin rib roast
- 2 cloves garlic, finely chopped
- 1 tablespoon finely chopped rosemary
- 1 tablespoon finely chopped sage,
- salt and freshly ground black pepper
- 1 tablespoon butter
- ½ cup (125 ml) extra-virgin olive oil
- 4 cups (1 liter) *Beef stock* (see recipe p. 48)
- 2 lb (1 kg) potatoes
- 2 cloves garlic, unpeeled

Right: *Filetto di maiale alle mele*

INGREDIENTS

- 4 tablespoons extra-virgin olive oil
- 2 cloves garlic, chopped
- 4 leaves sage
- 1 lb (500 g) white kidney beans, precooked
- 1 lb (500 g) tomatoes, peeled and diced
- 8 Italian pork sausages
- salt and freshly ground black pepper

Wine: a dry red (Chianti Classico)

Pork sausages and beans with garlic, sage, and tomato sauce

Salsicce e fagioli all'uccelletto

This traditional Tuscan dish is a meal in itself. For best results, use fresh or dried beans (the latter should be soaked for 12 hours) cooked in salted water until tender. Otherwise use high quality canned beans.

Serves: 4; Preparation: 5 minutes; Cooking: 30 minutes; Level of difficulty: Simple

Heat the oil in a heavy-bottomed pan, preferably earthenware, and sauté the garlic and sage. § Add the beans and cook for a few minutes so that they absorb the seasoning. § Add the tomatoes and season with salt and pepper. § Prick the sausages with a fork and add to the beans. Cover and cook over medium-low heat for about 25 minutes, stirring frequently. § Serve hot.

Stewed large sausage with lentils
Zampone con lenticchie stufate

Zampone and cotechino are regional dishes from the city of Modena in Emilia-Romagna. They are large sausages made with a mixture of pork, salt, pepper, nutmeg, cloves, and other seasonings wrapped in pig's trotter for zampone and in rind from pig snout and jowl for cotechino. The large sausage must be soaked in cold water for at least 4 hours before cooking to soften the rind. In Italy this dish is traditionally served on New Year's day.

Serves: 6; Preparation: 15 minutes + at least 4 hours soaking; Cooking: 3 hours; Level of difficulty: Simple

Soak the sausage in abundant cold water for at least 4 hours. § Drain the sausage and transfer to a pot with enough lightly salted cold water to cover it completely. Cover and simmer gently for 3 hours. Be careful not to puncture the skin during cooking. § In the meantime, prepare the lentils. Sauté the carrot, celery, and onion with the oil in a sauté pan over medium-high heat. § When the vegetables are soft, add the lentils and sauté for 2–3 minutes more. Season with salt and pepper and add the tomatoes. § Cook for a few minutes more, then pour in the stock. Cover and cook for 40 minutes. § Spoon the lentils onto a heated serving dish. Slice the sausage thickly and arrange the slices on the lentils. § Serve hot with a side dish of mashed potatoes.

> VARIATION
> – Some excellent precooked *zamponi* and *cotechini* are now available. These do not need to be soaked and they only take about 20–30 minutes to cook.

■ INGREDIENTS

- 1 *zampone* (large sausage wrapped in pig's trotter), about 2 lb (1 kg), or 1¼ lb (600 g) *cotechino* (pork sausage) about 3 in (7.5 cm) in diameter and 8 in (20 cm) long
- salt and freshly ground black pepper
- 5 cups (500 g) lentils, precooked
- 1 carrot, finely chopped
- 1 stalk celery, finely chopped
- 1 small onion, finely chopped
- 4 tablespoons extra-virgin olive oil
- 8 oz (250 g) tomatoes, canned
- 2 cups (500 ml) *Beef stock* (see recipe p. 48)

Wine: a dry red (Gutturnio)

Ham with Calvados
Prosciutto di maiale al Calvados

Serves: 6; Preparation: 2 minutes for the ham + 15 minutes for the mash; Cooking: 1¼ hours; Level of difficulty: Medium

Clean the ham of any small pieces of fat or skin. Season with salt and pepper and bake with the oil in a preheated oven at 400°F/200°C/gas 6. § After 15 minutes, dilute the honey in the orange juice and brush the meat with this mixture. Return to the oven, this time at 375°F/190°C/gas 5. § After 15 minutes turn the ham over, brush with the honey mixture again, and return to the oven. § Repeat this process twice more, before you finish cooking. This will take about 1 hour. § In the meantime, halfway

■ INGREDIENTS

- 1 ham, 2¼ lb (1.2 kg)
- salt and freshly ground black pepper
- ⅓ cup (90 ml) extra-virgin olive oil
- 3 tablespoons honey
- juice of 1 orange

Right:
Zampone con lenticchie stufate

- 6 apples, peeled and in segments
- ½ cup (125 ml) Calvados liqueur (made with distilled apples)
- 2 lb (1 kg) potatoes
- 2 tablespoons butter

Wine: a dry red (Chianti Classico)

through cooking, add the apples to the ham and pour half the Calvados over them. § Wash the potatoes and boil them in their skins in a large pan of salted water. § When the ham is cooked, transfer to a heavy-bottomed pan with its juice and the apples. Place over high heat, pour in the remaining Calvados, and cook until the liqueur has evaporated. § When the potatoes are cooked, drain, peel, and mash. § Mash the apples cooked with the ham, season with salt and butter, and combine with the potatoes. If the mixture is too liquid, add a little flour. Place over low heat, stirring frequently, until thick. § Slice the ham and transfer to a heated serving dish. § Serve hot with the potato and apple purée.

Pork loin with prunes
Carré di maiale farcito alle prugne

Serves: 6; Preparation: 20 minutes + 30 minutes to marinate the prunes; Cooking: 1¼ hours; Level of difficulty: Simple

Place 10 prunes in a bowl with the cognac, diluted with enough water to cover the fruit. Set aside to marinate. § After 30 minutes drain well so that all the marinade has been removed. § Use a sharp knife to make incisions in the pork. Fill with a little salt and pepper and the prunes. § Place the rosemary on the meat and tie with kitchen string. Sprinkle with salt and pepper to taste. § Heat the butter and oil in an ovenproof pan over medium heat. As soon as the butter foams, add the pork and brown all over. § Transfer to a preheated oven at 350°F/180°C/gas 4. § Halfway through cooking, pour the wine over the meat and add the remaining prunes. Continue cooking, adding stock if the pan dries out. § Serve hot or at room temperature with the sauce (heated, if the meat is lukewarm), and prunes. § This dish is delicious served with a side dish of potatoes lightly fried with a finely chopped onion. When the onion and potatoes are golden brown, cover with stock and cook until the stock reduces.

■ INGREDIENTS

- 20–25 dried prunes, pitted
- ½ cup (125 ml) cognac
- 2 lb (1 kg) boneless pork loin
- salt and freshly ground black pepper
- 4 sprigs rosemary
- 2 tablespoons butter
- 4 tablespoon extra-virgin olive oil
- ¾ cup (200 ml) dry white wine
- 1 cup (250 ml) *Beef stock* (see recipe p. 48)

Wine: a dry red (Cabernet di Breganze)

Pork loin with juniper berries
Lonza di maiale al ginepro

Serves: 6; Preparation: 25 minutes + 2 hours to marinate; Cooking: 1½ hours; Level of difficulty: Medium

Marinate the loin for 2 hours, covered with the coarsely sliced shallot, the onion, juniper berries, bay leaves, salt, pepper, 3 tablespoons of oil, and the wine. § After marinating, drain the meat thoroughly and wrap in the pancetta. Tie with a few twists of kitchen string. Transfer to an ovenproof dish. § Strain the vegetables and herbs used in the marinade and add to the meat. § Add the remaining oil and place in a preheated oven at 375°F/190°C/gas 5. § Cook for 1½ hours, basting from time to time with wine from the marinade and turning the meat over every so often. § Slice and serve hot. Strain the cooking juices and spoon over the meat. Serve with baked fennel (lightly boiled fennel baked with béchamel and Parmesan).

■ INGREDIENTS

- 2½ lb (1.2 kg) pork loin (part of loin without bone and without fillet)
- 1 shallot
- 1 onion, chopped
- 10–15 juniper berries
- 2 bay leaves
- salt and freshly ground black pepper
- ⅓ cup (90 ml) extra-virgin olive oil
- ½ cup (125 ml) dry white wine
- 4 oz (125 g) pancetta, sliced

Wine: a dry red (Chianti)

Right: *Carré di maiale farcito alle prugne*

Pork loin with milk and vinegar
Arista all'aceto e latte

Serves: 6; Preparation: 10 minutes; Cooking: 1¼ hours; Level of difficulty: Simple

Season the pork with salt and pepper, and roll and tie with a few twists of kitchen string. § Heat the butter and oil in a heavy-bottomed pan with the rosemary. When the butter foams, add the onion and cook until soft. § Add the pork and lightly brown all over. § Pour the vinegar over the pork and cook until it has evaporated. § Add the milk and the crumbled meat stock cube. Partially cover and cook for 1 hour, turning the meat from time to time. When cooked, the sauce in the pan should be well-reduced and thick. § Slice the pork, transfer to a heated serving dish and spoon the sauce over the top. § Serve hot with boiled new potatoes and green beans.

■ INGREDIENTS

- 2¼ lb (1.2 kg) pork loin, boneless
- salt and freshly ground black pepper
- 2 tablespoons butter
- 4 tablespoons extra-virgin olive oil
- 1 sprig rosemary
- 1 onion, finely chopped
- ¾ cup (200 ml) white vinegar
- 1¾ cups (450 ml) milk
- 1 beef stock cube

Wine: a young, dry red (Sangiovese di Romagna)

Mixed pork stewed in red wine
Misto di maiale stufato al vino rosso

To make this dish even tastier, replace the canned tomatoes with the same quantity of Simple tomato sauce (see recipe on p. 28).

Serves: 6; Preparation: 25 minutes; Cooking: 1½ hours; Level of difficulty: Medium

Ask your butcher to chop each sparerib into 3 pieces. Cut the neck, shanks, and sausages into bite-sized pieces. § Heat the oil in a heavy-bottomed saucepan over medium-high heat. Add the onion, carrot, celery, parsley, and bay leaves and sauté for 3–4 minutes. § Add the pork, season with salt and pepper, and brown all over. § Pour in the wine and cook until it is partially evaporated. § Stir in the tomatoes. § Cover and simmer gently over low heat for about 1¼ hours. Add the stock gradually as the sauce dries out. Turn the meat from time to time. § Serve hot. This dish is traditionally served with polenta.

■ INGREDIENTS

- 3 lb (1.5 kg) mixed cuts of pork (spareribs, boned neck, boneless shanks)
- 3 Italian pork sausages
- ⅓ cup (90 ml) extra-virgin olive oil
- 1 onion, 1 carrot, 1 stalk celery, coarsely chopped
- 1 clove garlic, finely chopped
- 1 tablespoon finely chopped parsley
- 2 bay leaves
- salt and freshly ground black pepper
- ¾ cup (200 ml) robust red wine
- 12 oz (350 g) canned tomatoes
- 1 cup (250 ml) *Beef stock* (see recipe p. 48)

Wine: a dry red (Barolo)

Right: *Misto di maiale stufato al vino rosso*

Roast suckling pig with mixed vegetables
Lattonzolo al forno

Serves: 6; Preparation: 10 minutes; Cooking: 1¾ hours; Level of difficulty: Medium

Sauté the vegetables in a large, heavy-bottomed pan with 2 tablespoons of oil over high heat for 5–6 minutes. § Sprinkle with salt and stir thoroughly. Remove from heat and set aside. § Add the remaining oil to the same pan used for the vegetables and brown the pork. § Transfer the meat and any liquid it has produced to a roasting pan. Sprinkle with a little more salt and the peppercorns. Add the bay leaves and turn the meat in its juices. § Cook in a preheated oven at 400°F/200°C/gas 6 for 1½ hours, basting frequently and gradually adding the wine. § When the pork has been in the oven for about 1 hour, add the vegetables and sprinkle with the garlic and parsley. § When the meat is cooked, it will have a dark, crisp layer of crackling. § Arrange on a heated serving dish with the vegetables and serve hot.

■ INGREDIENTS

- 2 onions, 2 carrots, 2 stalks celery, 2 zucchini (courgettes), 3 potatoes, diced
- 1 leek, sliced
- ⅓ cup (90 ml) extra-virgin olive oil
- salt
- ½ suckling pig, about 4 lb (2 kg)
- 10 peppercorns
- 2 bay leaves
- ¾ cup (200 ml) dry white wine
- 1 tablespoon finely chopped garlic and parsley

Wine: a dry red (Grignolino)

Pork cutlets with black cabbage
Bistecchine di maiale al cavolo nero

Black cabbage is a special Tuscan vegetable with a strong, slightly bitter taste. It is difficult to find outside Tuscany. However, this dish is just as good when prepared with the same amount of Swiss chard (silver beet). The Swiss chard does not need to be boiled for 30 minutes before chopping; 8–10 minutes will be enough.

Serves: 4; Preparation: 15 minutes; Cooking: 1 hour; Level of difficulty: Simple

Wash the black cabbage, remove the tough stalks, and cook in a pot of salted, boiling water for about 30 minutes. § Drain, and when lukewarm, chop finely. § Sauté the onion and garlic in the oil in a large, heavy-bottomed pan until soft. § Add the cutlets, sprinkle with salt and pepper, and brown on both sides. § Pour in the wine and cook for 15–20 minutes, or until the cutlets are tender. § When the meat is cooked set it aside and add the black cabbage to the cooking juices in the pan. Cook over medium for 10 minutes, stirring frequently. § Return the cutlets to the pan and reheat. § Serve hot.

■ INGREDIENTS

- 1¾ lb (800 g) leaf cabbage
- salt and freshly ground black pepper
- 1 onion, finely chopped
- 1 clove garlic, finely chopped
- 4 tablespoons extra-virgin olive oil
- 4 pork cutlets, about 1¼ lb (600 g)
- ¾ cup (200 ml) red wine

Wine: a dry red (Velletri Rosso)

Right: *Bistecchine di maiale al cavolo nero*

Roast pork shanks with mixed vegetables
Stinchetti di maiale al forno con verdure miste

■ INGREDIENTS

- 3 pork shanks, weighing about 3 lb (1.5 kg)
- 4 tablespoons flour
- ⅓ cup (90 ml) extra-virgin olive oil
- salt and freshly ground black pepper
- ¾ cup (200 ml) dry white wine
- 2½ cups (400 g) carrots, 2 cups (300 g) celery, 2 cups (300 g) onions, 2½ cups (400 g) potatoes, 2 cups (300 g) zucchini (courgettes), all peeled and chopped in large dice
- 2 cups (500 ml) *Beef stock* (see recipe p. 48)

Wine: a dry red
(Nobile di Montepulciano)

Serves: 6; Preparation: 50 minutes; Cooking: 2 hours; Level of difficulty: Medium

Remove any remaining hairs from the shanks. Rinse under cold running water and pat dry with paper towels. § Roll in the flour and sprinkle with salt and pepper. § Heat 4 tablespoons of the oil in a large, heavy-bottomed pan, add the shanks and cook over high heat until they are golden brown. § Transfer the shanks and their cooking juices to a roasting pan. Place in a preheated oven at 400°F/200°C/gas 6. § Cook for 20 minutes. Add the wine and cook for 40 minutes more, adding a little stock if the pan becomes too dry. § Meanwhile, heat the remaining oil in a heavy-bottomed pan and sauté the vegetables over high heat for 5–7 minutes. § When the shanks have been in the oven for about 1 hour, add the vegetables and their cooking juices. § Return to the oven and cook for 1 hour more, basting with stock as required to stop the pan from drying out. § When cooked, arrange the meat and vegetables on a heated serving dish and serve hot.

Left: *Stinchetti di maiale al forno con verdure miste*

VARIATION
– If you have the time, lower the oven temperature to 300°F/150°C/gas 2 and extend the second cooking to two hours. Turn the heat up again to 400°F/200°C/gas 6 for 10 minutes just before serving. The pork and vegetables will be even more tender and delicious.

Lamb

*Lamb is eaten throughout Italy, but it is more typical
of the south and the islands of Sicily and Sardinia.*

Lamb stew with eggplant
Agnello con dadolata di melanzane

Serves: 4; Preparation: 20 minutes + 2 hours for the eggplants; Cooking: 1¼ hours; Level of difficulty: Medium

Rinse the eggplants under cold running water and, without peeling them, cut into bite-sized cubes. Place in a colander, sprinkle with coarse sea salt, and leave to degorge for about 2 hours. § Heat the oil in a heavy-bottomed pan and sauté the lamb over medium-high heat until golden brown. Season with salt and pepper. § Add the onion and cook for 10 minutes, stirring continually so that it doesn't stick. § Add the eggplant, marjoram, and thyme and cook for 5 minutes. § Pour in the tomato sauce and mix well. § Cover the pan partially and cook over medium-low heat for about 1 hour, adding the stock gradually as the sauce dries out. § Serve hot with new boiled potatoes and a green salad.

■ INGREDIENTS

- 2 eggplants (aubergines)
- 2 tablespoons coarse salt
- 4 tablespoons extra-virgin olive oil
- 2 lb (1 kg) lamb shoulder, cut in 2-in (5-cm) pieces with bone
- salt and freshly ground black pepper
- 1 onion, coarsely chopped
- 1 teaspoon each finely chopped marjoram and thyme
- 1 quantity *Simple tomato sauce* (see recipe p. 28)
- 1¼ cups (300 ml) *Beef stock* (see recipe p. 48)

Wine: a dry red (Barbaresco)

Roman-style, pan-roasted lamb
Abbacchio alla romana

Pan-roasted, very young lamb is one of the Eternal City's classic dishes. In Rome, the lamb used is never more than a month old. Ideally, it should not have fed on anything stronger than its mother's milk. You will probably not be able to obtain such young lamb; but you can still count on excellent results with slightly older spring lamb.

Serves: 4; Preparation: 25 minutes; Cooking: 1 hour; Level of difficulty: Simple

Cut the lamb into 2-in (5-cm) pieces. § Heat the oil in a heavy-bottomed pan large enough to contain the meat. Add the 2 whole cloves of garlic and the lamb and sauté over medium-high heat until the lamb is golden all over. § Sprinkle with 1 tablespoon of the rosemary and sage and season with salt and pepper. § After about 10 minutes pour in the wine. When it has evaporated, lower the heat, partially cover the pan and continue cooking for about 40 minutes, turning from time to time. § In the meantime, place the anchovies and finely chopped garlic in a bowl with the remaining rosemary and sage and the vinegar. § When the lamb is cooked, raise the heat, pour the vinegar mixture over the top and cook for another 5 minutes. § Serve hot with roast potatoes.

■ INGREDIENTS

- 2 lb (1 kg) lamb shoulder, with some loin attached
- ⅓ cup (90 ml) extra-virgin olive oil
- 3 cloves garlic (2 whole, 1 finely chopped)
- 2 tablespoons rosemary and sage, finely chopped
- salt and freshly ground black pepper
- ¾ cup (200 ml) dry white wine
- 4 anchovy fillets, crumbled
- ½ cup (125 ml) white vinegar

Wine: a dry red (Merlot di Aprilia)

Right: *Abbacchio alla romana*

Lamb stew with fresh rosemary, garlic, and peas
Agnello con i piselli

Serves: 6; Preparation: 10 minutes; Cooking: 1½ hours; Level of difficulty: Medium

Sauté the garlic, rosemary, and pancetta in a large sauté pan in the oil over medium heat for 4–5 minutes. § Add the lamb and season with salt and pepper. § Pour in the wine and cook until it has evaporated. § Stir in the tomatoes, lower heat, and partially cover the pan. Cook for about 50 minutes, stirring from time to time. § Remove the lamb from the pan, and set aside in a warm oven. Add the peas to the pan and sauté briefly in the sauce. § Add the lamb again and cook for 30 minutes more. § Serve hot with boiled rice and a mixed salad.

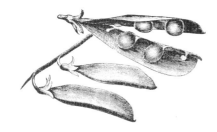

■ INGREDIENTS

- 2 cloves garlic, finely chopped
- 1 tablespoon rosemary, finely chopped
- ½ cup (60 g) diced pancetta
- ⅓ cup (90 ml) extra-virgin olive oil
- 2½ lb (1.2 kg) lamb shoulder, cut into pieces, with bone
- salt and freshly ground black pepper
- ½ cup (125 ml) dry white wine
- 3 tomatoes, peeled and chopped
- 3½ cups (500 g) fresh or frozen shelled peas

Wine: a dry red (Barolo)

Roast leg of lamb with aromatic herbs
Cosciotto d'agnello alle erbe aromatiche

Serves: 4; Preparation: 10 minutes; Cooking: 1¾ hours; Level of difficulty: Simple

Cut the crusts off the bread and chop in a food processor with the garlic and aromatic herbs (leaves only). Season with salt and a generous grinding of pepper. § Put the butter in a roasting pan and place in a preheated oven at 375°F/190°C/gas 5 for a few minutes, until the butter melts. § Place the lamb in the roasting pan, drizzle with the oil, and scatter with the chopped herbs and bread. § Return to the oven and cook for 1½ hours, basting from time to time with the wine. § Transfer to a heated serving dish and serve hot. Carve the meat at the table. § Serve with roast, baked, or boiled potatoes and a mixed salad.

VARIATION
– Use the same ingredients and method to prepare a roast leg of turkey. Turkey has a less distinctive aroma than lamb which the herbs will enhance (whereas they tend to mellow and blend with the stronger taste of the lamb).

■ INGREDIENTS

- 3 slices sandwich bread
- 2 cloves garlic
- mixture of aromatic herbs: 4 leaves sage, 1 twig rosemary, 1 twig thyme, 1 twig marjoram, 1 large bunch parsley
- salt and freshly ground black pepper
- 2 tablespoons butter
- 2 lb (1 kg) leg of lamb
- 4 tablespoons extra-virgin olive oil
- ⅔ cup (150 ml) dry white wine

Wine: a dry red (Rosso di Franciacorta)

Right: *Cosciotto d'agnello alle erbe aromatiche*

Lamb stewed in butter, brandy, rosemary, and milk

Agnello al latte

Serves: 6; Preparation: 15 minutes; Cooking: 1¼ hours; Level of difficulty: Medium

Dredge the lamb in the flour and then shake off any excess. § Melt the butter in a large, heavy-bottomed pan and sauté the pancetta for 2–3 minutes over medium heat. § Add the lamb, rosemary, salt, and pepper. § Sauté for 4–5 minutes, then pour in the brandy. Stir continuously until the brandy has evaporated. § Add the milk, partially cover the pan, and cook over medium-low heat, stirring often, for about 1 hour, or until the milk has reduced to a dense sauce. § Serve hot with a side dish of lightly boiled peas sautéed briefly in garlic, parsley, and oil.

■ INGREDIENTS

- 2½ lb (1.2 kg) lamb shoulder and leg, cut in pieces
- 1 cup (125 g) all-purpose (plain) flour
- 2½ tablespoons butter
- 1 cup (125 g) diced pancetta
- 1 tablespoon finely chopped rosemary
- salt and freshly ground black pepper
- ½ cup (125 ml) brandy
- 2 cups (500 ml) milk

Wine: a dry red (Bardolino Rosso)

Hot and spicy tomato and lamb stew

Agnello al pomodoro

Serves: 4-6; Preparation: 15 minutes; Cooking: 1¼ hours; Level of difficulty: Simple

Sauté the onion, carrot, celery, garlic, parsley, chilies, and pancetta over medium-high heat with the oil in a large, heavy-bottomed pan, preferably earthenware. § When the pancetta and onion are golden brown, add the lamb and cook with the vegetable mixture, stirring continuously, for 7–8 minutes more. § Season with salt and pepper and pour in the wine. Cook until the wine has evaporated. § Add the tomatoes, lower the heat to medium and partially cover. Cook for about 1 hour, adding a little hot water if the sauce reduces too much. § Serve hot with boiled rice, or boiled or baked potatoes, and a fresh green salad.

■ INGREDIENTS

- 1 onion, 1 carrot, 1 stalk celery, 2 cloves garlic, all finely chopped
- 2 tablespoons finely chopped parsley
- 1 teaspoon chilies, crushed
- ½ cup (60 g) diced pancetta
- 4 tablespoons extra-virgin olive oil
- 2¼ lb (1.2 kg) lamb, shoulder or leg, cut in pieces
- salt and freshly ground black pepper
- ⅔ cup (150 ml) dry white wine
- 1 lb (500 g) peeled and chopped ripe tomatoes

Wine: a dry rosé (Cirò)

Right: *Costolette d'agnello fritte*

Breaded and fried lamb chops
Costolette d'agnello fritte

■ INGREDIENTS

• 8 lamb chops

• salt

• ½ cup (75 g) all-purpose (plain) flour

• 1 egg

• 1 cup (125 g) bread crumbs

• ¾ cup (200 ml) oil, for frying

Wine: a dry red (Carmignano)

Serves: 4; Preparation: 10 minutes; Cooking: 5-10 minutes; Level of difficulty: Simple

Pound the chops lightly to spread the meat as much as possible. § Sprinkle with salt, roll in the flour, and shake to remove excess. § Dip in the egg and coat well with the bread crumbs. § Heat the oil in a heavy-bottomed pan and fry the chops, turning them so that they are golden brown on both sides. § Drain on paper towels and serve very hot with a mixed platter of fried zucchini (courgettes), artichokes, and potatoes and a green salad.

INGREDIENTS

- 1¼ lb (600 g) lamb (boneless leg and shoulder), cut in pieces
- salt and freshly ground black pepper
- ½ cup (125 ml) extra-virgin olive oil
- juice of 1½ lemons
- 3 globe artichokes
- 1½ cloves garlic, finely chopped
- ¾ cup (200 ml) dry white wine
- ¾ cup (200 ml) *Beef stock* (see recipe p. 48)
- 1 egg
- 1 tablespoon finely chopped parsley

Wine: a dry white (Malvasia Secca del Carso)

Lamb and artichoke fricassee
Spezzatino d'agnello e carciofi in fricassea

Serves: 4; Preparation: 25 minutes + 2 hours to marinate the lamb; Cooking: 1¼ hours; Level of difficulty: Simple

Place the lamb in a bowl with salt, pepper, 4 tablespoons of oil, and the juice of half a lemon. Marinate for 2 hours. § Remove the tough outer leaves from the artichokes and trim the stalks and tops. Slice the tender inner hearts into segments. Wash in cold water and the juice of a lemon. § Heat 2 tablespoons of oil in a sauté pan over medium heat. Add the garlic and artichokes, sauté for 5–6 minutes, then set aside. § Drain the lamb thoroughly, and sauté in a separate heavy-bottomed pan with the remaining oil. § When the lamb is well browned, pour in the wine and cook until it evaporates. § Transfer the lamb to the sauté pan with the artichokes and season with salt to taste. § Partially cover the pan and cook over a medium heat for 1 hour, adding stock from time to time as the sauce reduces, and stirring frequently. § When the lamb is cooked, beat the egg with a little salt and the juice of half a lemon. Pour the egg mixture over the stew and turn off the heat. Toss carefully so that the egg cooks and sets. § Sprinkle with the parsley and serve hot.

INGREDIENTS

- 2½ lb (1.2 kg) lamb, leg or shoulder, cut in pieces
- 2 tablespoons butter
- 2 tablespoons extra-virgin olive oil
- salt and freshly ground black pepper
- ½ cup (125 ml) dry white wine
- juice of 2 lemons

Wine: a robust, dry white (Donnafugata)

Lamb stewed in butter, oil, and white wine
Agnello all'agro

Serves: 6; Preparation: 10 minutes; Cooking: 1¾ hours; Level of difficulty: Simple

Sauté the lamb in the butter and oil over high heat in a large, heavy-bottomed pan. § Season with salt and pepper, mix well, and pour in half the wine and lemon juice. § Reduce heat to medium-low, partially cover the pan, and cook for about 1½ hours. Gradually stir in the remaining wine and lemon juice as the sauce reduces. § Serve hot with a side dish of lightly boiled Swiss chard sautéed briefly in extra-virgin olive oil with garlic, salt, pepper, and a little lemon juice.

Left: *Spezzatino d'agnello e carciofi in fricassea*

Game

Many regional dishes are based on more unusual meats, such as rabbit, hare, wild boar, goat, and venison. The recipes in this chapter are a selection of the most popular ones.

Rabbit fricassee
Coniglio in fricassea

Serves: 4; Preparation: 15 minutes; Cooking: 1 hour; Level of difficulty: Simple

Rinse the rabbit under cold running water and pat dry with paper towels. § Cut into small pieces, roll in the flour and shake off any excess. § Sauté the onion in the butter and oil over medium-high heat in a large, heavy-bottomed pan until soft. § Add the rabbit and cook until the meat is white (not brown). § Pour in the wine and cook until it evaporates. Season with salt and pepper. § Reduce the heat, partially cover and cook for about 40 minutes, adding the stock gradually as the sauce reduces. § When the rabbit is cooked, beat the egg yolks in a bowl with the lemon juice and parsley. Pour the mixture over the rabbit and turn off the heat. Toss carefully so that the egg cooks and sets. § Serve hot with lightly boiled globe artichokes briefly sautéed in garlic, olive oil, and parsley.

> VARIATIONS
> – For a tastier dish, replace the butter with the same quantity of lard.
> – For a different but equally delicious dish, replace the rabbit with the same quantity of chicken.

■ INGREDIENTS

- 1 rabbit, about 2½ lb (1.2 kg)
- 2 tablespoons all-purpose (plain) flour
- 1 onion, thinly sliced
- 2 tablespoons butter
- 4 tablespoons extra-virgin olive oil
- ½ cup (125 ml) dry white wine
- salt and freshly ground black pepper
- 1 cup (250 ml) *Beef stock* (see recipe p. 48)
- 1 tablespoon finely chopped parsley
- 2 egg yolks, very fresh
- juice of 1 lemon

Wine: a dry white (Galestro)

Crispy, rolled roast rabbit
Rotolo di coniglio in porchetta

Serves: 6; Preparation: 15 minutes; Cooking: 1 hour; Level of difficulty: Simple

Open the rabbit out into a single flat slice and lightly beat with a meat pounder. § Season with salt and pepper and sprinkle with the herbs, garlic, and fennel seeds. § Roll the rabbit up and tie with kitchen string. § Place in an ovenproof dish with the oil and bake in a preheated oven at 400°F/200°C/gas 6 for 1 hour. Turn the rabbit from time to time during cooking and baste with the wine so that the meat does not become too dry. If the wine is insufficient, add a little more (or, alternatively, add a little beef stock). § Slice the roast rabbit and serve hot with a green salad. Serve the cooking juices separately.

■ INGREDIENTS

- 2½ lb (1.2 kg) boneless rabbit
- salt and freshly ground black pepper
- 2 tablespoons finely chopped aromatic herbs (thyme, sage, rosemary)
- 2 cloves garlic, finely chopped
- 1 teaspoon fennel seeds
- 4 tablespoons extra-virgin olive oil
- ½ cup (125 ml) dry white wine

Wine: a dry white (Rosso di Gallura)

Right: *Rotolo di coniglio in porchetta*

Rabbit stew with pine nuts and green olives
Spezzatino di coniglio ai pinoli e olive verdi

■ INGREDIENTS

- 1 rabbit, about 2½ lb (1.2 kg), cut in pieces
- 4 tablespoons extra-virgin olive oil
- 1 clove garlic, finely chopped
- salt and freshly ground black pepper
- ½ cup (125 ml) dry white wine
- ¾ cup (200 ml) *Beef stock* (see recipe p. 48)
- 1 cup (100 g) green olives
- ⅓ cup (60 g) pine nuts

Wine: a dry white
(Trebbiano d'Abruzzo)

Serves: 6; Preparation: 10 minutes; Cooking: 1 hour; Level of difficulty: Simple

Rinse the rabbit under cold running water and pat dry with paper towels. § Heat the oil in a large, heavy-bottomed pan over medium heat and sauté the garlic for 1–2 minutes. § Add the rabbit, sprinkle with salt and pepper, and brown all over. § Pour in the wine and cook until it has evaporated. § Reduce the heat to medium-low, partially cover and cook for 40 minutes, adding the stock gradually as the meat dries out. You may not need to add it all. § Add the olives and pine nuts and cook for 15 minutes more. The rabbit should be very tender. § Serve hot with boiled potatoes or rice.

Old-fashioned boned rabbit
Coniglio dissosato all'antica

■ INGREDIENTS

- 1 boned rabbit, about 2 lb (1 kg)
- 1 tablespoon each finely chopped sage and rosemary,
- 1 clove garlic, finely chopped
- salt and freshly ground black pepper
- 4 tablespoons extra-virgin olive oil
- 2 eggs
- 1 rabbit liver, coarsely chopped
- 1 chicken liver, coarsely chopped
- ½ cup (125 ml) dry white wine

Wine: a dry red
(San Severo Rosso)

Serves: 4-6; Preparation: 25 minutes; Cooking: 1 hour; Level of difficulty: Medium

Open the rabbit out into a single flat slice and lightly beat with a meat pounder. § Sprinkle with the sage, rosemary, garlic, salt, and pepper. § Beat the eggs in a bowl with a little salt. § Heat 1 tablespoon of oil in a sauté pan and cook the eggs until firm. § Place the cooked eggs over the rabbit. Sprinkle with the livers and salt to taste. § Roll the rabbit up and tie with kitchen string. Place in a roasting pan with the remaining oil and bake in a preheated oven at 400°F/200°C/gas 6 for 1 hour. Turn from time to time, basting with the wine so that the meat does not dry out. If the wine is insufficient, add a little more (or, alternatively, use a little beef stock). § Cut the rabbit into thick slices and transfer to a heated serving dish. Serve hot, with the cooking juices served separately. Serve with lightly boiled broccoli or chopped cabbage, sautéed briefly in extra-virgin olive oil with garlic and crushed chilies.

Left: *Spezzatino di coniglio ai pinoli e olive verdi*

Braised hare in red wine sauce
Lepre brasata al vino rosso

Serves: 8; Preparation: 40 minutes + 8 hours marinating; Cooking: 2 hours; Level of difficulty: Medium

Place the hare in a large bowl with the red wine, celery, carrot, onion, rosemary, sage, bay leaves, garlic, and juniper berries. Set aside to marinate for at least 8 hours. § Drain the marinade from the hare. Set the liquid aside for cooking and finely chop the celery, carrot, onion, and garlic. Set the bunch of herbs aside. § Heat the oil and butter over medium heat in a heavy-bottomed pan, add the vegetables, and sauté for 5–7 minutes. § Lightly flour the pieces of hare and add them to the vegetables. Add the bunch of herbs and sauté for 5–10 minutes. § Pour in the wine and cook until it has evaporated. Season with salt and pepper to taste. § Add the tomato paste, tomatoes, and hot water. Partially cover and cook for 1¾ hours, or until the hare is very tender. Stir from time to time. § Discard the bunch of herbs. § Serve on a bed of potato purée.

■ INGREDIENTS

• 1 hare, about 4 lb (2 kg), cut in pieces
• 2 cups (500 ml) red wine
• 1 stalk celery, 1 carrot, 1 onion, all coarsely chopped
• 1 twig rosemary, 1 twig sage, 3 bay leaves, all tied together in a bunch
• 2 cloves garlic, whole
• 1 teaspoon juniper berries
• ⅓ cup (90 ml) extra-virgin olive oil
• 2 tablespoons butter
• 2 tablespoons all-purpose (plain) flour
• salt and freshly ground black pepper
• 3 tablespoons tomato paste
• 12 oz (350 g) tomatoes, peeled and chopped
• ½ cup (125 ml) hot water

Wine: a dry red
(Aglianico di Vulcano)

Roast pigeon stuffed with sausage and liver
Piccione ripieno ai fegatini

Serves: 4; Preparation: 25 minutes; Cooking: 45 minutes; Level of difficulty: Simple

Clean the pigeons, discarding all internal organs except the livers. Wash the pigeons under cold running water and pat dry with paper towels. § Chop the pigeon livers with the chicken livers and sausages on a cutting board using a heavy, well-sharpened knife. § Transfer the sausage and liver mixture to a bowl. Season with salt and pepper and mix well. § Fill each pigeon with the stuffing and close them up with toothpicks, or by sewing with a needle and kitchen thread. § Fix 2 leaves of sage to each pigeon with a toothpick. § Sprinkle the birds with salt and pepper and place in a roasting pan. Drizzle with the oil and roast in a preheated oven at 375°F/190°C/gas 5 for 45 minutes. § Serve hot with a side dish of lightly boiled zucchini (courgettes) or Brussels sprouts briefly sautéed in garlic, parsley, and olive oil.

■ INGREDIENTS

• 4 squab pigeons, with their livers
• 2 chicken livers
• 2 Italian pork sausages
• salt and freshly ground black pepper
• 8 leaves sage
• ⅓ cup (90 ml) extra-virgin olive oil

Wine: a dry red
(Colli Piacentini Bonarda)

Right: *Lepre brasata al vino rosso*

Wild boar and leek stew
Cinghiale in bianco ai porri

Serves: 6; Preparation: 15 minutes + 24 hours marinating; Cooking: 2¾ hours; Level of difficulty: Medium
Place the wild boar in a large bowl with the wine, cloves, and bay leaves. Sprinkle with salt and pepper and set aside to marinate for at least 24 hours. § Drain the marinade from the wild boar. Set the liquid aside for cooking and discard the cloves and bay leaves. § Heat the oil in a large, heavy-bottomed pan over medium heat and sauté the prosciutto for 1–2 minutes. § Add the leeks and a ladleful of stock and cook until the leeks begin to soften. § Add the meat and gently brown all over. § Pour in the liquid from the marinade, partially cover the pan, and cook for about 2½ hours, adding stock so that the meat doesn't dry out. § When the meat is tender, add the vinegar and pine nuts and stir well. Dissolve the flour in 2 tablespoons of cold water and stir into the sauce until it thickens. § Serve the stew hot on polenta or with baked or boiled potatoes.

■ INGREDIENTS

- 2 lb (1 kg) wild boar, in pieces
- 4 cups (1 liter) dry white wine
- 3 cloves
- 2 bay leaves
- salt and freshly ground black pepper
- ⅓ cup (90 ml) extra-virgin olive oil
- 1 cup (125 g) chopped prosciutto
- 3 leeks, in thin slices
- 2 cups (500 ml) *Beef stock* (see recipe p. 48)
- 4 tablespoons white vinegar
- 1 teaspoon pine nuts
- 1 tablespoon all-purpose (plain) flour

Wine: a dry red (Morellino)

Wild boar in red wine and tomato sauce
Cinghiale stufato

Wild boar has a very strong and distinctive taste. To enjoy it at its best, it should be marinated for at least 12 hours before cooking. I prefer to leave it for a full day before use. This delicious stew is traditionally served with hot polenta.

Serves: 6; Preparation: 30 minutes; Cooking: 2¼ hours + 24 hours marinating; Level of difficulty: Medium
Place the wild boar in a large bowl with the onion, carrot, celery, garlic, cloves, bay leaves, salt, and pepper. Cover with the wine and set aside to marinate for 12–24 hours. § Drain the marinade from the wild boar. Set the liquid aside for cooking, discard the cloves and bay leaves, and coarsely chop the vegetables. § Heat the oil in a large, heavy-bottomed pan over medium heat and sauté the vegetables for 5–7 minutes. § Add the meat and sauté until brown all over. § Add the tomato sauce, stir well and pour in the liquid from the marinade. Partially cover the pan and cook over medium-low heat for 2 hours, stirring from time to time. When cooked, the wild boar should be tender and the sauce quite thick. § Serve hot on freshly-made polenta.

■ INGREDIENTS

- 2¾ lb (1.3 kg) wild boar, cut in pieces
- 1 onion, sliced
- 1 carrot, thickly sliced
- 1 stalk celery, thickly sliced
- 1 clove garlic, cut in half
- 2 cloves
- 2 bay leaves
- 1 cup (250 ml) robust red wine
- ⅓ cup (90 ml) extra virgin olive oil
- ½ quantity *Simple tomato sauce* (see recipe p. 28)
- salt and freshly ground black pepper

Wine: a dry red (Barbaresco)

VARIATION
– For a milder stew, do not reuse the vegetables from the marinade; replace with equal quantities of fresh chopped vegetables.

Right: *Cinghiale in bianco ai porri*

Duck with celery balls

Nana con polpettine di sedano alla figlinese

Serves: 4; Preparation: 40 minutes; Cooking: 1½ hours; Level of difficulty: Medium

Sear the duck and cut into pieces. § Sauté the chopped vegetables with the oil in a heavy-bottomed pan over medium heat. § After about 5 minutes, add the duck. Season with salt and pepper and continue cooking until the duck is brown. § Pour in the wine and cook until it evaporates. § Stir in the tomatoes, partially cover the pan, and simmer for about 1½ hours. Stir frequently, gradually adding the stock as the sauce reduces. § In the meantime, wash the celery stalks and cut into large pieces. Boil in a little salted water for 25–30 minutes. Drain well, squeeze out excess moisture and chop (not too finely). § Shape the celery into small balls, dip in the flour, then the egg. § Fry the celery balls in the oil in a heavy-bottomed pan over medium heat. Drain and set aside on paper towels. § Add the celery balls to the duck during the last 15 minutes of cooking. Take care when stirring or the balls may come apart. § Serve hot.

■ INGREDIENTS

- 1 duck, cleaned, about 2 lb (1 kg)
- 1 clove garlic, 1 onion, 1 stalk celery, 1 carrot, all finely chopped
- 1 lb (500 g) tomatoes, peeled and chopped
- ½ cup (125 ml) robust dry red wine
- 2 cups (500 ml) *Beef stock (see recipe p. 48)*
- ⅓ cup (90 ml) extra-virgin olive oil
- salt and freshly ground black pepper
- 2 large stalks celery
- ¾ cup (100 g) all-purpose (plain) flour
- 1 egg, beaten
- ¾ cup (200 ml) olive oil, for frying

Wine: a dry red (Chianti Classico Santa Cristina)

Duck breast with orange sauce

Petto d'anatra all'arancia

Serves: 4; Preparation: 20 minutes; Cooking: 25 minutes; Level of difficulty: Simple

Wash the duck under cold running water and pat dry with paper towels. § Place in a roasting dish with the oil. Sprinkle with salt and pepper and bake in a preheated oven at 400°F/200°C/gas 6 for 20–30 minutes. § When cooked, set the duck aside in a warm oven. § Peel the orange and cut the peel in thin strips. § Put the peel in a pot of boiling water for 1 minute then drain. Remove the peel with a slotted spoon, wait for the water to boil again, and repeat the process. This will take the bitter taste out of the peel. § Squeeze the orange and strain the juice. § Skim the fat from the juices in the roasting pan. Place the pan over medium heat and add the cognac and orange juice. After a few minutes add the sugar and salt to taste. Boil for 3–4 minutes then add the orange peel. § Slice the duck thinly and arrange on a heated serving dish. Spoon the sauce over the top. § Serve hot with potato purée.

■ INGREDIENTS

- 1¼ lb (600 g) duck breast
- 4 tablespoons extra-virgin olive oil
- salt and freshly ground black pepper
- 1 orange
- ½ cup (125 ml) dry red wine
- 2 teaspoons castor sugar

Wine: a dry white (Bianco di Custoza)

Right:
Petto d'anatra all'arancia

Quails wrapped with pancetta
Quagliette bardate alla pancetta

Serves: 6; Preparation: 30 minutes; Cooking: 45 minutes; Level of difficulty: Simple

Remove the heads from the quails, and sear to eliminate any remaining plumage. § Sprinkle the quail with salt and pepper. Wrap each bird with 2 slices of pancetta and tie with kitchen string. § Place in a baking dish with the oil, carrot, celery, and prosciutto. Add the bay leaf and juniper berries and scatter the scallion over the top. § Bake in a preheated oven at 400°F/200°C/gas 6 for about 45 minutes. § Pour the wine over the quails during cooking. When the wine is finished, continue with the stock. § Serve the quails hot with their sauce spooned over the top. § Serve with zucchini (courgettes), cut thinly lengthways, and sautéed for a few minutes in olive oil, finely chopped garlic, and parsley.

Roast duck with herbs
Anatra agli aromi

Serves: 4; Preparation: 10 minutes; Cooking: about 1 hour; Level of difficulty: Simple

Peel and wash the onion, leaving it whole. Stick with the bay leaf and the other sprigs of herbs so that they will not come out during cooking. § Clean and sear the duck to eliminate any remaining plumage. § Place in a roasting pan and sprinkle with the salt and oil. § Add the onion, crumbled stock cube, and pink pepper. § Bake in a preheated oven at 400°F/200°C/gas 6. § After about 10 minutes, pour the wine and vinegar over the top. Cook for about 50 minutes more, basting from time to time. § Cut the duck into small pieces and arrange them on a heated serving dish with the chopped onion and herbs. § Serve hot with Swiss chard (silver beet) lightly boiled in salted water and briefly sautéed in olive oil and finely chopped garlic.

■ INGREDIENTS

- 6 quails
- salt and freshly ground black pepper
- 12 slices pancetta
- 1 carrot, 1 stalk celery, finely chopped
- 2 oz (60 g) prosciutto, finely chopped
- 1 scallion (shallot), coarsely chopped
- 1 bay leaf
- 2 juniper berries
- ½ cup (125 ml) dry white wine
- 1 cup (250 ml) *Beef stock* (see recipe p. 48)
- salt and freshly ground black pepper
- 4 tablespoons extra-virgin olive oil

Wine: a dry red (Brunello di Montalcino)

■ INGREDIENTS

- 1 large onion
- 1 duck, about 2 lb (1 kg)
- 1 bay leaf
- mixed sprigs fresh herbs: sage, rosemary, thyme, marjoram
- salt
- 4 tablespoons extra-virgin olive oil
- 1 tablespoon pink pepper
- ½ cup (125 ml) dry white wine
- ½ cup (125 ml) white vinegar
- 1 chicken stock cube

Wine: a dry white (Sauvignon di Parma)

Left: *Quagliette bardate alla pancetta*

Venison marinated with vinegar
Capriolo marinato all'aceto

Serves: 6; Preparation: 30 minutes + 24 hours marinating; Cooking: 2½ hours; Level of difficulty: Medium

Sauté the garlic, onion, carrot, celery, parsley, thyme, and pepper corns in the oil over medium-high heat. § Sprinkle with salt and pour in the wine and vinegar. Cook for 20 minutes. § Chop the sautéed mixture in a food processor. § Combine the puréed mixture in a bowl with the venison. If the mixture is too thick, add a little more white wine and 1 tablespoon of extra-virgin olive oil. § Stir well and set aside to marinate for 24 hours. § Drain the venison from the marinade. Set the marinade aside in a bowl. § Sauté the pancetta in the lard (or butter) in a large, heavy-bottomed pan for a few minutes. § Add the venison, season with salt and pepper, partially cover, and cook over low heat for about 2½ hours. Stir frequently, gradually adding the marinade and the the stock. § Serve hot with freshly-made polenta.

■ INGREDIENTS

- 1 clove garlic, 1 onion, finely chopped
- 1 carrot, cut in wheels
- 1 stalk celery, sliced
- 1 tablespoon finely chopped parsley
- 1 tablespoon finely chopped thyme
- 6–8 pepper corns
- ⅓ cup (90 ml) extra-virgin olive oil
- salt and freshly ground black pepper
- ¾ cup (200 ml) dry white wine
- ½ cup (125 ml) white vinegar
- 2 lb (1 kg) venison
- ½ cup (150 g) diced pancetta
- 4 tablespoons lard or butter
- 2 cups (500 ml) *Beef stock* (see recipe p. 48)

Wine: a dry red (Chianti Classico)

Pheasant with black olives
Fagiano alle olive nere

Serves: 4; Preparation: 15 minutes; Cooking: 1¼ hours; Level of difficulty: Simple

Clean and sear the pheasant to eliminate any remaining plumage. § Season with salt and pepper inside and out. Sprinkle with flour and shake to remove any excess. § Sauté the onion in the oil in a large, heavy-bottomed pan. § Add the pheasant and sauté for a few minutes. § Pour in the wine and cook until it evaporates. § Stir in the tomatoes and season with salt. Partially cover and cook over medium heat for about 45 minutes. Gradually add the stock as the sauce reduces. § Add the olives, stir well and cook for 15 minutes more. § Remove the pheasant from the pan and cut into pieces. Return to the sauce to reheat over medium heat. § Arrange on a heated serving dish. Serve hot with lightly boiled spinach briefly sautéed in olive oil and finely chopped garlic.

■ INGREDIENTS

- 1 pheasant, 2 lb (1 kg)
- 1 large white onion, sliced
- 1 cup (100 g) black olives
- 4 tablespoons all-purpose (plain) flour
- 14 oz (450 g) tomatoes, peeled and chopped
- ⅓ cup (90 ml) extra-virgin olive oil
- ¾ cup (200 ml) dry white wine
- ¾ cup (200 ml) *Beef stock* (see recipe p. 48)
- salt and freshly ground black pepper

Wine: a dry red (Barolo)

Right: *Fagiano alle olive nere*

Fish and Seafood

Fresh fish is plentiful in Italy. In bustling markets, from beneath the Rialto Bridge in Venice to the Vuccirìa market in Palermo, fish vendors ply their trade.

Fillets of sole with artichoke sauce
Sogliole ai carciofi

■ INGREDIENTS

• 3 artichokes
• juice of ½ lemon
• 2 cloves garlic
• 1 small onion
• 1 bunch parsley
• ⅓ cup (90 ml) milk
  (if you prefer a richer
  dish, use cream)
• salt and freshly ground
  black pepper
• 4 medium sole fillets,
  about 1–1¼ lb
  (500–600 g)
• ¼ cup (30 g) all-purpose
  (plain) flour
• 4 tablespoons butter
• 2 tablespoons extra-virgin
  olive oil

Wine: a dry white
(Cervaro della Sala)

Serves: 4; Preparation: 15 minutes: Cooking: about 25 minutes; Level of difficulty: Medium

Clean the artichokes, discarding the tougher leaves and the tips. Place in a large bowl with 4 cups (1 liter) of water and the lemon juice (this will prevent the artichokes from turning black) for 10 minutes. § Drain the artichokes and bring to a boil in a pan of lightly salted water, calculating the cooking time at 10 minutes after boiling point has been reached. Drain, reserving 3 tablespoons of the cooking water. § Put the artichokes in a food processor and add the garlic, onion, parsley, and the reserved cooking liquid. Process to a smooth cream and add the milk (or cream) salt, and pepper. § Rinse the sole fillets and dry carefully with paper towels. Dust well with the flour. § Melt the butter with the oil in a large skillet (frying pan) and fry the fillets for about 6 minutes, turning them carefully twice. Season lightly with salt. Lower the heat to very low and pour the artichoke cream over the top. Cook for 10 more minutes. § Arrange the fillets in the artichoke sauce on a preheated serving platter and serve.

Sole meunière
Sogliole alla mugnaia

■ INGREDIENTS

• 4 soles, about 8 oz
  (250 g) each, cleaned
• 1 cup (150 g) all-purpose
  (plain) flour
• 4 tablespoons butter
• 3 tablespoons extra-virgin
  olive oil
• salt and freshly ground
  white pepper
• juice of 2 lemons
• ½ cup (125 ml) white wine
• 1 tablespoon finely
  chopped parsley

Wine: a dry white
(Alghero Bianco)

*The delicate flavor of sole makes it one of the most highly prized of all fish.
It is especially suitable for children, because the bones are so easy to remove.*

Serves: 4; Preparation: 25 minutes; Cooking: 12 minutes; Level of difficulty: Medium

Lightly flour the sole just before cooking (otherwise they will absorb too much). § Melt the butter with the oil in a large skillet (frying pan) and fry the sole for 3–4 minutes each side, turning them carefully twice. § Season lightly with salt and pepper. § Moisten with the lemon juice and wine and cook for another 4 minutes. § Turn the sole in the sauce and sprinkle with the parsley. § Place on a preheated serving platter. Pour the pan juices over the top and serve with boiled peas sautéed in garlic and parsley.

Left: *Sogliole alla mugnaia*

Sole roulades with peas
Involtini di sogliola con i piselli

■ INGREDIENTS

Serves: 4; Preparation: 25 minutes: Cooking: 40 minutes; Level of difficulty: Medium

Wash the sole fillets and dry with paper towels. § Heat the oil and 2 tablespoons of the butter in a large skillet (frying pan) and sauté the onion, garlic, basil, celery, and bay leaf. After about 5 minutes add the tomatoes and season with salt and pepper. Cover and cook for 5 minutes. § Add the peas to the sauce in the pan and cook for 15 minutes. § While the peas are cooking, roll up the sole fillets, securing them with wooden toothpicks. Roll lightly in the flour. § Melt the remaining butter in a skillet (frying pan) with the sage. Add the rolled-up sole fillets and brown them gently for 5 minutes. § Remove from heat and transfer to the pan with the peas. Add a little water if necessary. Check the seasoning, adding more salt if necessary, and cook for 10 more minutes. § Serve hot.

VARIATION
– Use fresh peas in season. The cooking times will remain the same but the flavor will be something special!

- 4 sole fillets, about 8 oz (250 g) each
- 2 tablespoons extra-virgin olive oil
- 3 tablespoons butter
- 1 onion, finely chopped
- 2 cloves garlic, finely chopped
- 4 basil leaves, torn
- ½ celery stalk, finely chopped
- 1 bay leaf, chopped
- 2 plum tomatoes, peeled and mashed with a fork
- salt and freshly ground black pepper
- 14 oz (450 g) frozen peas
- 2 tablespoons all-purpose (plain) flour
- 4 sage leaves, chopped

Wine: a dry white
(San Vito di Luzzi Bianco)

Island porgy
Orata all'isolana

This dish is very delicate. In this recipe, the tomato adds a particularly light touch to the flavor.

■ INGREDIENTS

Serves: 4; Preparation: 25 minutes; Cooking: 30 minutes; Level of difficulty: Medium

Clean the fish as described on page 26. § Stuff the cavity with the garlic, rosemary, salt, and pepper. § Pour 4 tablespoons of the oil into an ovenproof dish and cover with alternate layers of potato slices and tomatoes. § Season with salt and pepper, and lay the fish over the vegetables. Drizzle with the remaining oil. Bake in a preheated oven at 375°F/190°C/gas 5 for 30 minutes. § Serve hot.

- 2 porgy (bream), about 2 lb (1 kg)
- 2 cloves garlic, finely chopped
- 1 tablespoon finely chopped rosemary
- salt and freshly ground black pepper
- ⅓ cup (90 ml) extra-virgin olive oil
- 3 potatoes, very thinly sliced
- 4 firm tomatoes, sliced

Wine: a dry white (Galestro)

Right: *Orata all'Isola*

Baked stuffed scorpionfish
Pesce scorfano rosa

Serves: 4; Preparation: 20 minutes: Cooking: 30 minutes; Level of difficulty: Medium

Rinse the cleaned fish carefully and dry with paper towels. § Stuff the cavity of the fish with the rosemary, sage, chilies, and garlic. Season with salt. Secure with a needle and kitchen thread. § Pour the oil into an ovenproof dish and lay the fish in it. Bake in a preheated oven at 400°F/200°C/gas 6 for 30 minutes. § Serve hot with roast potatoes.

■ INGREDIENTS

- 1¼ lb (600 g) scorpionfish, scaled and gutted (see p. 26)
- 1 sprig rosemary
- a few sage leaves
- 2 fresh or dried hot red chilies
- 2 cloves garlic, whole
- salt
- 4 tablespoons extra-virgin olive oil

Wine: a dry white (Langhe Bianco)

Porgy baked in a salt crust
Orata al sale grosso

From a culinary point of view, porgy is among the most prized of all fish because of its delicate white flesh. Cooking in a salt crust is a special method: it is very simple because it requires no ingredients other than coarse salt. It is delicious because an outer crust forms, keeping the fish moist, flavorful, and not at all salty inside.

Serves: 4; Preparation: scant 10 minutes; cooking: 30 minutes; Level of difficulty: Simple

Rinse the cleaned fish carefully and dry with paper towels. § Choose a roasting pan or casserole (with a lid) just large enough to hold the fish. Cover the bottom with a layer of salt. Put the fish on top and cover completely with salt. Bake in a preheated oven at 375°F/190°C/gas 5 for 30 minutes. § Take the roasting pan or casserole out of the oven and break the salt crust. Lift out the fish, cleaning them by discarding the skin and scales. It does not matter if a few grains of salt remain on the fish, as it will add to the flavor. § Serve hot with a tomato salad.

■ INGREDIENTS

- 2 porgy (bream), about 2 lb (1.kg) each, gutted (see p. 26)
- 8 lb (3.5 kg) coarse sea salt (the amount will vary according to the size of the dish; the fish must be completely covered)

Wine: a dry white (Collio Traminer)

VARIATION
— Replace the porgy with sea bass. If liked, slip a clove of garlic and a sprig of rosemary under the fish before cooking.

Right:
Pesce scorfano rosa

Stockfish in milk
Baccala mantecato

■ INGREDIENTS

- 2 lb (1 kg) stockfish, presoaked
- 1¼ cups (300 ml) extra-virgin olive oil
- 2 cloves garlic, finely chopped
- 1 tablespoon finely chopped parsley
- salt and freshly ground black pepper
- 1¼ cups (300 ml) milk

Wine: a dry white (Orvieto Classico)

Serves: 4; Preparation: 15 minutes; Cooking: 1 hour 40 minutes: Level of difficulty: Simple

Cut the stockfish into 2–3-in (5–8-cm) pieces and place in a heavy-bottomed pan with the oil. Add the garlic and parsley and season with salt and pepper. Place over medium heat for 10 minutes. § Add the milk, then cover and cook over low heat for 1½ hours. If the liquid is too thick, add a little more milk. § Serve hot.

Stockfish Vicenza-style
Baccala alla vicentina

■ INGREDIENTS

- 2 lb (1 kg) stockfish
- 3 yellow onions, finely chopped
- 1 scallion (spring onion), finely chopped
- 3 cloves garlic, finely chopped
- 3 cups (750 ml) oil, for frying
- 2 oz (60 g) anchovy fillets, chopped
- 1 tablespoon finely chopped parsley
- ¾ cup (110 g) all-purpose (plain) flour
- 1 cup (125 g) freshly grated Parmesan cheese
- salt and freshly ground black pepper
- 2 cups (500 ml) milk

Wine: a dry white (Bolgheri Sauvignon)

Stockfish is air-dried Norwegian cod. Unlike salt cod, it is not cured in salt. It takes its name from the Dutch word "stokvisch," which refers to the way it is dried on wooden sticks. This recipe is time-consuming, but definitely worth the effort. Buy presoaked stockfish to save time.

Serves: 4; Preparation: 30 minutes + 3 days to soak the fish; Cooking: 4 hours; Level of difficulty: Medium

Soak the stockfish for 12 hours in several changes of water. § Drain the fish and remove the skin. Open it out lengthwise to remove the backbone. Place the stockfish on a clean work surface. § Heat ½ cup (125 ml) of oil in a skillet (frying pan) and sauté the onion, scallion, and garlic over medium heat for about 5 minutes, or until pale gold. § Add the anchovies and parsley. Mix well and spoon half of this mixture over the opened-out stockfish. § Combine half the flour with half the Parmesan cheese. Sprinkle this over the fish and season lightly with salt and pepper. Don't add too much salt; the anchovies are already quite salty. § Close up the stockfish and cut into 1½–2-in (4–5-cm) pieces. Roll these in the remaining flour and Parmesan cheese and arrange them in a single layer in a flameproof dish (preferably earthenware). Pour the milk over the top. § Cover the dish tightly and cook for 4 hours over very low heat. Do not stir, but shake the dish gently from time to time. § Serve hot with boiled potatoes.

Left:
Baccala alla Vicentina

Salt cod Leghorn-style
Baccala alla livornese

Serves: 4; Preparation: 25 minutes; Cooking: 25 minutes; Level of difficulty: Medium

Cut the salt cod into 1½-in (4-cm) pieces. § Sprinkle the flour onto a plate and roll the salt cod pieces in it, shaking off any excess. § Heat 6 tablespoons of the oil in a large skillet (frying pan) over medium heat and fry the salt cod on all sides until golden (about 3 minutes each side). Remove the fish pieces, draining off the oil, and set aside. § Heat the remaining oil in a skillet. Sauté the garlic and parsley for 3 minutes, then add the tomatoes. § Add the salt cod and season lightly with salt and pepper. § Cook for 15 minutes, turning the salt cod pieces carefully so as not to break them. § Serve hot with spinach or Swiss chard (silver beet) sautéed in oil with a clove of finely chopped garlic.

VARIATION
– Fresh cod can be cooked in the same way. Do not roll it in flour, but cook with the garlic, chopped tomatoes, and fresh basil.

■ INGREDIENTS

- 2 lb (1 kg) salt cod, presoaked
- 1 cup (150 g) all-purpose (plain) flour
- ⅔ cup (150 ml) extra-virgin olive oil
- 2 cloves garlic, finely chopped
- 2 tablespoons finely chopped parsley
- 14 oz (450 g) plum tomatoes, peeled and chopped
- salt and freshly ground black pepper

*Wine: a dry white
(Vernaccia di San Gimignano)*

Cod with capers
Merluzzo ai capperi

Serves: 4; Preparation: 25 minutes; Cooking: 30 minutes; Level of difficulty: Medium

Heat the oil in a skillet (frying pan) and sauté the onion and garlic for 10 minutes over medium heat. Add the tomatoes and cook for 5 minutes. Add the capers and cook for 5 more minutes. § Rinse the cod fillets carefully and pat dry with paper towels. Cut in 3-in (8-cm) pieces. § Season with salt and place in the tomato sauce. Reduce heat and cook for 10 minutes more. § Remove from heat. Transfer the cod in its sauce to a heated serving dish, sprinkle with the parsley, and serve.

VARIATION
– Cod cooked in this way makes an excellent main course, but it can also be used as a pasta sauce. Allow about 10 oz (300 g) of cod per person and flake with a fork before combining with the cooked pasta.

■ INGREDIENTS

- 4 tablespoons extra-virgin olive oil
- 1 onion, finely chopped
- 3 cloves garlic, finely chopped
- 4 plum tomatoes, peeled and chopped
- 2 tablespoons capers, chopped
- 1¾ lb (800 g) fresh cod fillets
- 1 tablespoon finely chopped parsley
- salt

*Wine: a dry white
(Pinot Grigio)*

Right:
Baccala alla Livornese

Stuffed baby cuttlefish with tomatoes

Seppioline ripiene al pomodoro

Serves: 4; Preparation: 30 minutes; Cooking: 30 minutes: Level of difficulty: Medium

Clean the cuttlefish (or squid) as described on page 26. Rinse well and dry on paper towels. § Soften the bread in the milk then drain, squeezing out excess moisture. § Chop 1 cuttlefish finely with a heavy knife. Place in a bowl, combine the bread, two-thirds of the parsley, two-thirds of the garlic, the anchovies, the Parmesan, and egg. Mix well with a fork. § Stuff the cuttlefish with the mixture and secure the openings with a wooden toothpick. § Arrange carefully in a single layer in an ovenproof dish. Sprinkle with the sage, rosemary, bay leaf, remaining parsley and garlic, lemon juice, oil, and a little salt. Let stand for 1 hour. § Place in a preheated oven at 400°F/200°C/gas 6. § After about 10 minutes, when lightly colored on all sides, moisten with the wine. § Check the seasoning and add more salt and pepper if necessary. Add the tomatoes and hot water and continue cooking in the oven (at 300°F/150°C/gas 2) for 20 minutes. § Serve hot on a heated serving platter with steamed spinach.

Squid stuffed with Ricotta cheese and spinach

Seppie ripiene con ricotta e spinaci

Serves: 4; Preparation: 30 minutes; Cooking: 45 minutes; Level of difficulty: Medium

Clean the squid as described on page 26. Rinse well and dry on paper towels. § Put the spinach in a pan of cold water, bring to a boil, and cook for 8–10 minutes. Drain, squeeze out excess moisture, and chop finely. § Place in a bowl and add the Ricotta and Parmesan. Season with salt and pepper. Mix with a fork until evenly blended. § Fill the squid with this mixture and close them by securing with a wooden toothpick. § Arrange the stuffed squid in a large skillet (frying pan) with the oil and fry on all sides over high heat for 10 minutes. § Season lightly with

■ INGREDIENTS

- 1 lb (500 g) baby cuttlefish (or squid), tentacles removed
- 2¾ oz (75 g) soft white bread, crusts removed
- 1 cup (250 ml) milk
- 3 tablespoons parsley, chopped
- 3 cloves garlic, finely chopped
- 2 anchovy fillets packed in oil, finely chopped
- 3 tablespoons freshly grated Parmesan cheese
- 1 egg, beaten
- 2 sage leaves, chopped
- 1 small sprig rosemary
- 1 bay leaf, chopped
- 1 tablespoon lemon juice
- ½ cup (125 ml) extra-virgin olive oil
- salt and freshly ground black pepper
- ½ cup (125 ml) dry white wine
- 3 plum tomatoes, peeled and chopped
- ½ cup (125 ml) hot water

Wine: a dry white (Pomino Bianco)

■ INGREDIENTS

- 1½ lb (750 g) squid, tentacles removed
- 5 oz (150 g) spinach
- 1 cup (250 g) Ricotta cheese
- 3 tablespoons freshly grated Parmesan cheese
- salt and freshly ground black pepper
- 4 tablespoons extra-virgin olive oil

- 2 tablespoons cognac
- 4 tablespoons tomatoes, skinned and finely chopped

Wine: a dry white
(Trebbiano di Romagna)

salt. Drizzle with the cognac and cook until it evaporates. Lower the heat and cook, covered, for 10 more minutes. Remove the squid and set aside. § Add the tomatoes and more salt, if required. Then add ½ cup (125 ml) water. § Cook the tomato sauce for about 10 minutes then return the stuffed squid to the pan. Cook for 5 minutes. § Place on a heated serving platter and serve.

VARIATION
— Use frozen spinach instead of fresh.

Above:
Seppie ripiene con ricotta e spinaci

Stuffed squid
Totani ripieni

Serves: 4; Preparation: 50 minutes; Cooking: about 1 hour; Level of difficulty: Medium

Clean the squid as described on page 26, reserving the tentacles. § Pour 3 tablespoons of the oil into a flameproof (preferably earthenware) pan and sauté half the garlic and parsley over medium heat for 1–2 minutes. Chop the tentacles coarsely and add to the pan with the beef and pork. Cook for 5 minutes over medium heat, stirring frequently. Season with salt and pepper. Pour in half the wine and cook until it evaporates. § Remove from heat. Add the eggs, Parmesan, Pecorino, and bread crumbs to the pan and mix well. § Stuff the squid with this mixture, securing with wooden toothpicks. § Heat the remaining oil in the same pan and sauté the remaining parsley and garlic with the stuffed squid, turning to brown on all sides, for about 5 minutes. Add the remaining wine and cook until it evaporates. § Finally, add the tomatoes, season lightly with salt, and bake in a preheated oven at 375°F/190°C/gas 5 for about 30 minutes. § Serve hot with sautéed spinach.

■ INGREDIENTS
- 2 lb (1 kg) medium squid
- 4 tablespoons extra-virgin olive oil
- 3 cloves garlic, finely chopped
- 1 tablespoon finely chopped parsley
- 2 oz (60 g) ground beef
- 2 oz (60 g) ground pork
- salt and freshly ground black pepper
- 1 cup (250 ml) dry white wine
- 2 eggs, beaten
- ¼ cup (30 g) freshly grated Parmesan cheese
- ½ cup (60 g) freshly grated Pecorino cheese
- 2 tablespoons bread crumbs
- 10 oz (300 g) firm, ripe tomatoes, peeled, seeded, and chopped

Wine: a dry white (Isonzo Traminer Aromatico)

Baby cuttlefish and artichoke stew
Stufato di seppioline e carciofi

Serves: 4; Preparation: 20 minutes; Cooking: 35 minutes: Level of difficulty: Medium

Clean the artichokes by trimming the stalks and tops and removing all the tough outer leaves. Cut in half and remove the fuzzy choke with a knife. Cut in wedges and place in a bowl of water with the lemon juice for 10 minutes. § Clean the baby cuttlefish as described on page 26. Rinse well and dry on paper towels. § Cut the cuttlefish in two. (If they are very small, leave them whole.) § Heat the oil in a large skillet (frying pan) and sauté the parsley, garlic, and chile for 4–5 minutes. Add the cuttlefish and season with salt and pepper. Stir well, then pour in the wine. Stir again and cook, partially covered, over medium heat for 30 minutes. If the cooking liquid dries out too much, gradually add the stock. § Serve hot on a heated serving platter.

■ INGREDIENTS
- 4 globe artichokes
- ½ lemon
- 1¾ lb (800 g lb) baby cuttlefish (or squid)
- 4 tablespoons extra-virgin olive oil
- 2 tablespoons finely chopped parsley
- 2 cloves garlic, finely chopped
- 1 fresh red chile, sliced
- salt and pepper
- ½ cup (125 ml) dry white wine
- 1 cup (250 ml) stock made with a stock cube

Wine: a dry white (Pinot Bianco)

Left: *Stufato di seppioline e carciofi*

Sea bass with diced tomatoes
Branzino al cartoccio con dadolata di pomodoro

■ INGREDIENTS

- 1 sea bass, about 2½ lb (1.2 kg)
- 2 cloves garlic, finely chopped
- 1 tablespoon finely chopped parsley
- 1 tablespoon finely chopped rosemary
- salt and freshly ground black pepper
- 4 tablespoons extra-virgin olive oil
- 3 firm tomatoes, peeled and chopped
- 4 potatoes, thinly sliced

Wine: a dry white (Greco di Tufo)

Serves: 4; Preparation: 25 minutes; Cooking: 40 minutes; Level of difficulty: Medium

Clean the sea bass as described on page 26. Lay the fish on a sheet of baking parchment (paper) or foil. § Combine the garlic, parsley, and rosemary in a bowl and season with salt and pepper. Use this mixture to stuff the cavity of the fish. Reserve a little to sprinkle over the top of the fish. Drizzle with 3 tablespoons of the oil. Spoon the tomatoes over the top. Close the baking parchment or foil around the fish. § Arrange the potatoes in a fairly large ovenproof dish. Season with salt and drizzle with the remaining oil. Cook in a preheated oven at 375°F/ 190°C/gas 5 for 10 minutes. § Take the potatoes out of the oven and place the fish packet on top of them. Return the dish to the oven for 30 minutes. § Take the dish out of the oven and open the packet. Drain any liquid that may have formed and transfer the sea bass to a platter in the packet. § Serve the fish with the potatoes, or divide it into portions and arrange a little fish, a tablespoonful of tomatoes, and a few potatoes on individual serving plates. While slicing the fish, return the potatoes to the oven for 5 minutes if they are not quite done.

Foil-wrapped sea bass
Branzino al cartoccio

■ INGREDIENTS

- 1 sea bass, about 3 lb (1.5 kg)
- 1 tablespoon finely chopped rosemary
- 1 tablespoon finely chopped parsley
- 2 cloves garlic, finely chopped
- ½ lemon
- salt and freshly ground black pepper
- 4 tablespoons extra-virgin olive oil

Left:
Branzino al cartoccio

Serves: 4; Preparation: 15 minutes; Cooking: 25 minutes; Level of difficulty: Simple

Clean the sea bass as described on page 26. Rinse well and pat dry with paper towels. § Combine the rosemary, parsley, and garlic in a bowl and mix well. Season with the salt and pepper. Stuff the fish with this mixture, filling the belly and gill cavities. § Wash the lemon, slice thinly, and place in the belly, leaving some slices slightly exposed to add a touch of color. Sprinkle the outside of the fish with salt and pepper. Place on a sheet of foil on a baking sheet. § Sprinkle with oil, and fold the foil to seal. Cook in a preheated oven at 400°F/ 200°C/gas 6 for 25 minutes. § Serve hot with boiled potatoes and a mixed salad.

Baked stuffed trout
Trota del musichiere

Only a few Italian rivers and lakes now contain edible wild trout.
However, there are many trout farms that raise delicious rainbow trout for the markets.

Serves:4; Preparation: 15 minutes; Cooking: 45 minutes; Level of difficulty: Medium

Clean the trout as explained on page 26. Rinse well and dry with paper towels. § Cut along the backbone, without removing it, to make an opening. Insert four anchovy fillets into this opening and the rest into the cavity. § Mix the Parmesan with the nutmeg and salt in a bowl, and stuff the cavity of the trout with this mixture, pressing it in firmly so that it does not ooze out during cooking. § Place the trout in an ovenproof dish and drizzle with the oil. Bake in a preheated oven at 300°F/150°C/gas 2 for 35 minutes, then increase the heat to 350°F/180°C/gas 4 and cook for 10 more minutes. § Serve hot with roast potatoes.

■ INGREDIENTS

• 2 lb (1 kg) trout
• 8 anchovy fillets, packed in oil
• 1 cup (125 g) freshly grated Parmesan cheese,
• 1 teaspoon freshly grated nutmeg
• salt
• 5 tablespoons extra-virgin olive oil

*Wine: a dry white
(Parrina Bianco)*

Salmon steaks with dried porcini mushrooms
Salmone ai funghi porcini

Serves: 4; Preparation: 20 minutes: Cooking: 35 minutes; Level of difficulty: Medium

Clean the mushrooms, removing all traces of soil. Rinse carefully under cold running water. Drain and pat dry with paper towels. § Slice thinly and place in a heavy-bottomed pan with the butter and oil. Cook over high heat for about 2 minutes, then lower heat and cook for 20 minutes, stirring occasionally with a wooden spoon. If the pan is too dry, add 1–2 tablespoons of water. § When done, season with salt and pepper and sprinkle with the chopped chives and parsley. Set aside. § Meanwhile, cook the salmon steaks for 5 minutes each side in an electric grill pan — if you do not have one, cook in a little oil in an ordinary skillet (frying pan) over medium heat. § Arrange the salmon steaks on a plate and remove the skin and bones, then transfer to a serving plate. Top with the reheated mushroom sauce and serve immediately.

■ INGREDIENTS

• 4 medium porcini mushrooms, dried
• 2 tablespoons butter
• 1 tablespoon extra-virgin olive oil
• salt and freshly ground black pepper
• 4 tablespoons chives, coarsely chopped
• 4 tablespoons finely chopped parsley
• 4 salmon steaks ½ in (1 cm) thick, about 5 oz (150 g) each

*Wine: a dry white
(Castel San Lorenzo Bianco)*

VARIATION
– This makes an excellent meal in itself served with rice.

Right:
Trota del musichiere

Marinated raw salmon
Carpaccio di salmone

■ INGREDIENTS

- 12 oz (350 g) very fresh salmon, thinly sliced
- juice of 3 lemons
- salt and freshly ground black pepper
- 4 tablespoons scallions (spring onions), chopped
- 1 bunch arugula (rocket), coarsely chopped

Wine: a dry white
(Valcalepio Bianco)

Serves: 4; Preparation: 10 minutes + 3 hours marinating; Level of difficulty; Simple

Lay the salmon slices on a serving platter and drizzle the lemon juice over the top as evenly as possible. § Season with salt and pepper, then sprinkle with the chopped scallions and arugula. § Leave to marinate for about 3 hours (the salmon is ready when it turns pale pink), then serve.

VARIATION
– This dish can be prepared a day before serving.

Poached salmon with a selection of cold sauces
Salmone bollito alla salse

Serves: 4; Preparation: 10 minutes; Cooking: 55 minutes; Level of difficulty: Simple

Select a pan large enough to hold the salmon. Fill with cold water and add the onion, carrot, celery, parsley, peppercorns, and coarse sea salt. Simmer gently for about 30 minutes. (Precooking the stock in this way will make the salmon more flavorful, but it is not strictly necessary. You can also just place the fish in the water and cook it immediately.) § Carefully add the salmon to the pan. Partially cover and cook over medium heat for about 25 minutes. § As soon as the fish is done, lift it out of the stock using two fish slices, taking care not to break it. Place on a large heated plate. Remove the head, skin, and backbone. § Place on a heated serving platter. Serve with boiled potatoes and the mayonnaise, cocktail, and tartare sauces.

■ INGREDIENTS
- 1 salmon (2½ lb/1.2 kg)
- 1 white onion (or leek), thickly sliced
- 1 carrot, thickly sliced
- 1 stalk celery, thickly sliced
- 1 bunch parsley
- 6–8 peppercorns
- coarse sea salt
- ½ quantity *Mayonnaise* (see recipe p. 42)
- ⅓ quantity *Cocktail sauce* (see recipe p. 42)
- ⅓ quantity *Tartare sauce* (see recipe p. 44)

Wine: a dry white
(Friuli Latisana Tocai)

Trout with mixed herbs
Trota farcita al pesto di erbe aromatiche

Serves: 4; Preparation: 20 minutes; Cooking: 20 minutes; Level of difficulty: Simple

Put half the oil, the garlic, rosemary, mint, thyme, and olives in a large bowl. Season with salt and pepper and mix well. § Lay half the trout fillets on a clean work surface and sprinkle with the mixture. Lay another fillet on top of each one. § Pour the remaining oil into an ovenproof dish and carefully place the pairs of fillets in it. Season with salt and cover with the lettuce leaves. Bake in a preheated oven at 350°F/180°C/gas 4 for 20 minutes. § Take out of the oven and serve hot with boiled potatoes.

■ INGREDIENTS
- ½ cup (125 ml) extra-virgin olive oil
- 6 cloves garlic, finely chopped
- 1 tablespoon very finely chopped rosemary
- 10 mint leaves, finely chopped
- 2 tablespoons fresh or dried thyme
- 10 green or black olives, pitted
- salt and freshly ground black pepper
- 2 lb (1 kg) fillets of trout
- 6 lettuce leaves, washed and dried

Wine: a dry white (Colli Orientali del Friuli Ribolla)

Right: *Trota farcita al pesto di erbe aromatiche*

Swordfish steaks with marjoram
Trancio di pesce spada alla maggiorana

Serves: 4; Preparation: 15 minutes; Cooking: about 30 minutes: Level of difficulty: Medium

Rinse the swordfish steaks in cold running water. Dry carefully with paper towels. § Pour 6 tablespoons of the oil into a large skillet (frying pan) and place over high heat. § Flour the fish steaks and, when the oil is hot, fry them until golden brown (about 15 minutes). Remove from the skillet and drain on paper towels. Place on a serving platter in a warm oven. § Make the sauce by mixing the remaining oil, garlic, parsley, marjoram, and chile in a small pan. Season with salt and pepper and cook over medium heat for 15 minutes. § Pour over the fish and serve hot.

■ INGREDIENTS
- 4 swordfish steaks, about 1¼ lb (600 g)
- ⅔ CUP (150ml) extra-virgin olive oil
- 4 tablespoons all-purpose (plain) flour
- 2 cloves garlic, finely chopped
- 3 tablespoons finely chopped parsley
- 1 tablespoon finely chopped marjoram
- 1 red hot chiei, finely chopped
- salt and freshly ground black pepper

Wine: a dry white (Lamezia Bianco)

Pan-fried hake with mixed vegetables
Nasello in teglia con verdure miste

Serves: 4; Preparation; 20 minutes; Cooking: 55 minutes; Level of difficulty: Medium

Wash and peel the potatoes, slice them lengthwise, and boil in salted water for about 20 minutes. Drain while still quite firm. § Meanwhile, place the oil, onion, scallions, leek, and carrots in a large skillet (frying pan) over medium heat. Season with salt. Cook for about 15 minutes, adding a little water if necessary, and stirring frequently. § Add the hake and cook for 5 minutes, stirring occasionally. § Pour in the wine and cook until it evaporates. Add the potatoes and cook for 5 more minutes. § Sprinkle with the parsley, thyme, and chives, adding a little water if necessary. Cover and cook over medium heat for 5 more minutes. § Serve hot.

VARIATION
– This recipe can also be made with monkfish.

■ INGREDIENTS
- 2 potatoes
- 4 tablespoons extra-virgin olive oil
- 1 onion, finely chopped
- 3 scallions (spring onions), finely chopped
- 1 leek, chopped
- 3 medium carrot, scraped and sliced into wheels about ¼ in (5 mm) thick
- salt
- 1¼ lb (600 g) hake, filleted
- ½ cup (125 ml) dry white wine
- 1 tablespoon each finely chopped parsley, thyme, and chives

Wine: a dry white (Trebbiano d'Abruzzo)

Right:
Nasello in teglia con verdure miste

Swordfish steaks with rice pilaf
Pesce spada con riso pilaf

Serves: 4; Preparation: 15 minutes; Cooking: 30 minutes; Level of difficulty: Medium

In a large heavy-bottomed pan, sauté the onion in the butter over medium heat for 5 minutes. Add the rice, enough boiling water to cover it by three fingers, and the stock cube. Cover and cook for 15 minutes, stirring frequently. § Meanwhile, rinse the swordfish steaks under cold running water. Dry carefully with paper towels. § Cook in a grill pan or under a broiler at high heat for 10 minutes. For even tastier fish, grill on a barbecue. § Remove from heat and season with salt and pepper. Place on a heated serving platter. § Sprinkle with oregano and garnish with the capers. Set aside in a warm oven. § Remove the rice from heat and stir in the parsley and oil. Spoon the rice over the fish steaks on the platter. § Serve immediately with steamed cauliflower.

■ INGREDIENTS

- 2 tablespoons butter
- ½ onion, finely chopped
- 1½ cups (300 g) long-grain rice
- 1 stock cube
- 4 swordfish steaks (1¼ lb/600 g)
- salt and freshly ground black pepper
- 1 tablespoon oregano
- 1 tablespoon capers, whole
- 1 tablespoon finely chopped parsley
- 4 tablespoons extra-virgin olive oil

Wine: a dry white (Vernaccia di San Gimignano)

Swordfish steaks with arugula and basil sauce
Pesce spada in salsa di rucola e basilico

Serves: 4; Preparation: 20 minutes; Cooking: 15 minutes: Level of difficulty: Medium

Rinse the swordfish steaks under cold running water. Dry carefully with paper towels. Do not remove the skins. § Place the steaks on a plate and sprinkle with salt and pepper. Drizzle with the oil, coating on both sides, and set aside. § Heat a grill pan or broiler and, when hot, put the swordfish steaks in or under it and cook for 15 minutes, turning twice. § Combine the garlic, parsley, basil, arugula, and remaining oil in a bowl. Add a dash of salt, a generous grinding of pepper, and the lemon juice. Beat with a fork until well blended. § When the steaks are done, place them on a heated serving platter. Drizzle with the sauce and serve immediately.

■ INGREDIENTS

- 4 swordfish steaks ½ in (1 cm) thick
- salt and freshly ground black pepper
- ½ cup (125 ml) extra-virgin olive oil
- 2 cloves garlic, finely chopped
- 1 tablespoon finely chopped parsley
- 7 basil leaves, torn
- ½ bunch arugula (rocket), coarsely chopped
- juice of 1 lemon

Wine: a dry white (Alghero Sauvignon)

Right: *Pesce spada in salsa di rucola e basilico*

Smooth hound with pink peppercorns
Palombo al pepe rosa

Smooth hound belongs to the shark family. Cooking it in a foil package works particularly well, because all the moisture and flavor is retained. The pink peppercorns in this recipe are dried aromatic peppercorns from Mauritius. Pink peppercorns can replace black or white pepper; they are more delicate but just as spicy. They are good with both fish and meat dishes.

Serves: 4; Preparation: 15 minutes: Cooking: 25 minutes; Level of difficulty: Simple

Cover an ovenproof dish with a sheet of foil and lay the washed and dried smooth hound steaks in it. § Drizzle with the oil and sprinkle with the rosemary, chives, pink peppercorns, and salt. § Close the package and bake in a preheated oven at 300°F/150°C/gas 2 for 25 minutes. § Serve immediately, straight from the package. § This dish is good with celery braised in a fresh tomato sauce.

■ INGREDIENTS

- 4 smooth hound steaks (1¼ lb/600 g)
- 2 tablespoons extra-virgin olive oil
- 1 teaspoon finely chopped rosemary
- 1 teaspoon finely chopped chives
- 2 tablespoons pink peppercorns
- salt

*Wine: a dry white
(Sylvaner della Valle Isarco)*

White perch fillets with basil
Filetti di persico al basilico

Serves: 4; Preparation: 15 minutes: Cooking; 5–10 minutes; Level of difficulty: Medium

Rinse the white perch fillets under cold running water and dry with paper towels. § In a mixing bowl, combine the bread crumbs with the salt, pepper, rosemary, and sage, and mix well. § Beat the eggs with a fork in a small bowl. § Dip the fillets first in the beaten egg, then in the herbed bread crumbs. § Heat the oil in a large skillet (frying pan) and when very hot, fry the well-coated fillets for 2 minutes on each side. Remove from the skillet and drain on paper towels. § Place in a heated serving platter. Drizzle with the lemon juice and sprinkle with the basil. § Serve immediately with a mixed salad.

■ INGREDIENTS

- 6 white perch fillets
- 4 tablespoons bread crumbs
- salt and freshly ground black pepper
- 1 tablespoon finely chopped rosemary
- 1 tablespoon finely chopped sage
- 2 eggs
- 5 tablespoons extra-virgin olive oil
- juice of 1 lemon
- 3 tablespoons basil, finely chopped

*Wine: a dry white
(Collio Pinot Grigio)*

Right:
Palombo al pepe rosa

Tuna preserved in oil
Tonno sott'olio

Serves: 4; Preparation: 30 minutes + 12 hours to stand; Cooking: 1¾ hours; Level of difficulty: Medium

Bring a large pan of water to the boil over medium heat. Add the tuna and salt and cook for 1¾ hours. § Drain the tuna and dry carefully with paper towels. Let stand for 12 hours. § Remove the skin and bones from the tuna, then flake the fish into pieces with your hands. Divide the pieces evenly among 4 1-cup (250-ml) glass jars. Cover with oil and seal hermetically. § If the jars are to be kept for any length of time, they should be sterilized before being filled. To sterilize, boil them for 10 minutes in a wide pan full of water. § Serve the preserved tuna at room temperature with a salad of boiled white beans with extra-virgin olive oil, salt, pepper, and a little coarsely chopped red onion or scallion.

■ INGREDIENTS

- 1½ lb (750 g) fresh tuna, sliced
- ⅔ cup (125 g) fine salt
- 4 cups (1 liter) extra-virgin olive oil

Wine: a dry white (Piave Verduzzo)

Roast grouper
Cernia arrosto

Many fish, including sea bass, porgy, bream, monkfish, salmon, and turbot, can be roasted using this same method.

Serves: 4; Preparation: 1 hour; Cooking: 30 minutes; Level of difficulty: Medium

Clean and gut the fish as described on page 26. Rinse under cold running water and dry with paper towels. Stuff the cavity with the garlic, 1 sprig rosemary, 3 sage leaves, salt, pepper, and the lemon slices. § Pour 1 tablespoon of oil into an ovenproof dish and sprinkle with the remaining rosemary and sage. Lay the fish over this. Season with salt and pepper and drizzle with the remaining oil. Bake in a preheated oven at 400°F/200°C/gas 6 for 10 minutes. § Remove from the oven and pour in the wine. Return to the oven, lowering the heat to 325° F/160° C/gas 3, and cook for 20 more minutes. § Remove from the oven and serve immediately, dividing it into portions at the table (skin and bones should be removed) or, as this can be a time-consuming operation, skin, bone, and slice it in the kitchen before bringing to the table. § Serve with roast potatoes.

■ INGREDIENTS

- 1 grouper, about 2 lb (1 kg), cleaned and gutted
- 2 cloves garlic, peeled and whole but lightly crushed
- 2 sprigs rosemary
- 6 sage leaves
- salt and freshly ground black pepper
- ½ lemon, sliced
- 4 tablespoons extra-virgin olive oil
- ½ cup (125 ml) dry white wine

Wine: a dry white (Torbato di Alghero)

Right:
Tonno sott'olio

Monkfish with onions
Pescatrice con cipolle

Serves: 4; Preparation: 15 minutes; Cooking: 25 minutes; Level of difficulty: Medium

Put the monkfish in a deep dish. Cover with the onion, lemon slices, bay leaf, half the parsley, and a few peppercorns, then drizzle with 4 tablespoons oil. Set aside to marinate for about 1 hour. § Drain the marinade from the fish. § Season the fish with salt and pepper. Lightly flour and fry in 4 tablespoons of oil in a flameproof oven pan over high heat, turning carefully. § Transfer the pan to a preheated oven and cook at 375°F/190°C/gas 5 for 20 minutes, moistening the fish occasionally with the wine and pan juices. Drain, reserving the cooking juices, and transfer to a serving platter. Keep warm in the oven. § Add the remaining parsley and the lemon juice to the pan juices and stir. Drizzle over the fish. Serve immediately, accompanied by a platter of steamed vegetables (potatoes, zucchini, courgettes, fennel).

■ INGREDIENTS

- 2 lb (1 kg) monkfish
- 3 baby onions, sliced
- 1 lemon, sliced
- 1 bay leaf
- 4 tablespoons parsley, chopped
- peppercorns and ground pepper
- ⅔ cup (150 ml) extra-virgin olive oil
- salt
- 3 tablespoons all-purpose (plain) flour
- ½ cup (125 ml) dry white wine

Wine: a dry white (Bianco dei Trulli)

Broiled stuffed fresh anchovies
Alici alla griglia ripiene

Serves: 4; Preparation: 30 minutes; Cooking: 10 minutes; Level of difficulty: Medium

Rinse the anchovies and clean as described on page 26. Dry well on paper towels and lay them out on a large plate, opened out. § Mix the garlic, chilies, sage, bread crumbs, lemon juice, oil, and salt in a large bowl. § Blend all the ingredients thoroughly and fill one half of each anchovy with the mixture. § Cover with the other half, pressing down gently with your hands. Broil under a very hot broiler (grill) for 10 minutes, turning at least once. § Serve immediately with a mixed salad.

VARIATION
– The anchovies in this recipe can also be cooked in a grill pan over high heat.

■ INGREDIENTS

- 1 lb (500 g) fresh anchovies
- 4 cloves garlic, finely chopped
- 2 hot red chilies, finely chopped
- 2 sage leaves, finely chopped
- ⅔ cup (40 g) bread crumbs
- juice of ½ lemon
- 2 tablespoons extra-virgin olive oil
- salt

Wine: a dry white (Vermentino)

Right:
Pescatrice con cipolle

Fried mackerel with a herb dressing
Sgombri fritti e marinati

Serves: 4; Preparation: 15 minutes; Cooking: 25 minutes; Level of difficulty: Simple

Clean and gut the mackerel as described on page 26. § Flour lightly, shaking off any excess. § Heat the oil in a large skillet (frying pan) until very hot, and fry the mackerel over high heat for 2 minutes on each side. Drain on paper towels, then place on a heated serving platter. § To make the dressing, put the garlic, parsley, and rosemary in a bowl, and pour in the vinegar, lemon juice, and oil. Season with salt and pepper and blend thoroughly. Serve separately with the mackerel and a dish of boiled cauliflower.

■ INGREDIENTS

- 1 lb (500 g) small mackerel
- 1 cup (150 g) all-purpose (plain) flour
- 2 cups (500 ml) oil, for frying

DRESSING:

- 5 cloves garlic, finely finely chopped
- 4 tablespoons finely chopped parsley
- 1 tablespoon finely chopped rosemary
- 4 tablespoons white wine vinegar
- juice of ½ lemon
- ½ cup (125 ml) extra-virgin olive oil
- salt and freshly ground black pepper

Wine: a dry white (Corvo Bianco)

Fresh anchovies with onion
Acciughe con cipolla

The anchovy, a tiny silver-colored fish, differs from the sardine in that it is rounder in shape and more delicate in flavor. This dish can be served as an appetizer or a main course. It is just as good served the next day.

Serves: 4; Preparation: 20 minutes + 2 hours to macerate; Level of difficulty: Simple

Lay the anchovy fillets out in a deep dish and cover with vinegar. Leave to macerate for about 2 hours (the time required will depend on the strength of the vinegar you use). The fillets will "cook" in the vinegar. When they are ready they will turn white. § Drain well and place in layers on a dish, alternating with the sliced onion and a little salt. § Drizzle with the oil and serve.

■ INGREDIENTS

- 1¼ lb (600 g) fresh anchovy fillets
- 1¾ cups (450 ml) white wine vinegar
- 2 red onions, thinly sliced
- salt
- 1 cup (250 ml) extra virgin olive oil

Wine: a dry white (Cervaro della Sala)

Right:
Sgombri fritti e marinati

Baked sardines
Sarde in forno

■ INGREDIENTS

• 1 lb (500 g) sardines, filleted
• ⅓ cup (90 ml) extra-virgin olive oil
• salt
• 4 tablespoons parsley, chopped
• 4 tablespoons bread crumbs
• juice of ½ lemon

Wine: a dry white
(Pinot bianco Aquileia del Friuli)

Serves: 4; Preparation: 14 minutes; Cooking: 15 minutes; Level of difficulty: Simple

Place the sardine fillets in a single layer in a wide ovenproof dish. Drizzle with the oil and season with salt. § Sprinkle with the parsley and bread crumbs, and drizzle with the lemon juice. Bake in a preheated oven at 350°F/180°C/gas 4 for 15 minutes. § Serve immediately with shredded celery root (celeriac).

Fish balls
Polpettine di pesce

Serves: 4; Preparation: 20 minutes; Cooking: 30 minutes; Level of difficulty: Medium

Clean and gut the fish as described on page 26. Rinse under cold running water. § Fill a large pan with water and bring to a boil over high heat. Add the salt and cook the fish for 10 minutes. Drain well and remove the heads, skin, and bones. § Put the fish in a large bowl and mash coarsely with a fork. Stir in the egg. Add the butter, Parmesan, garlic, parsley, nutmeg, and salt, and mix well. § Form tablespoonfuls of the mixture into balls. Roll in the bread crumbs and set aside on a plate. § Heat the oil in large skillet (frying pan) and fry the fish balls in batches until golden brown. § Drain on paper towels and place on a heated serving platter. Serve immediately with fried baby artichokes or a mixed salad.

■ INGREDIENTS

- 1¼ lb (600 g) cod, hake, or grouper
- 1 teaspoon salt
- 1 fresh egg
- 2 tablespoons butter, at room temperature
- 4 tablespoons freshly grated Parmesan cheese
- 2 cloves garlic, finely chopped
- 3 tablespoons finely chopped parsley
- 1 teaspoon nutmeg
- ½ cup (30 g) bread crumbs
- 2 cups (500 ml) oil, for frying

Wine: a dry white (Nuragus di Cagliari)

Tuna and Ricotta rissoles
Polpettine di tonno e ricotta

Serves: 4; Preparation: 15 minutes: Cooking: 15 minutes; Level of difficulty: Medium

Drain the Ricotta and place in a large bowl. § Mash it with a fork and add the drained and coarsely flaked tuna, the parsley, Parmesan, salt, and egg. Mix well until evenly blended. § Form tablespoonfuls of the mixture into rissoles and roll in the flour. § Heat the oil in large skillet (frying pan) until very hot and fry the rissoles in batches, turning constantly, until golden brown. Scoop out with a slotted spoon and drain on paper towels. § Serve hot with boiled potatoes.

■ INGREDIENTS

- 1½ cups (350 g) Ricotta cheese
- 1 cup (200 g) tuna, packed in oil
- 2 tablespoons finely chopped parsley
- 3 tablespoons freshly grated Parmesan cheese
- salt
- 1 egg
- ⅓ cup (50 g) all-purpose (plain) flour
- 2 cups (500 ml) oil, for frying

Wine: a dry white (Trentino Chardonnay)

VARIATION
– Make slightly smaller rissoles and poach them in fish stock.

Right: *Polpette di pesce*

Periwinkle salad

Chiocciole di mare in insalata

Serves: 4; Preparation: 30 minutes + 1 hour to purge the periwinkles; Cooking: 12 minutes; Level of difficulty: Medium

Place the periwinkles in a large bowl of water with the baking soda and soak for 1 hour. § Wash the periwinkles thoroughly under cold running water. § Cook in a pot of boiling water for about 12 minutes. Drain well. Extract the periwinkles from their shells and chop finely. § Place in a wide serving dish. Combine the parsley, garlic, lemon juice, salt, pepper, and oil and mix well. Drizzle over the periwinkles and serve with boiled new potatoes.

■ INGREDIENTS

• 2 lb (1 kg) periwinkles
• 3 tablespoons baking soda (bicarbonate of soda)
• ½ cup (30 g) finely chopped parsley
• 5 cloves garlic, finely chopped
• juice of ½ lemon
• salt and freshly ground black pepper
• ⅓ cup (90 ml) extra-virgin olive oil

Wine: a dry white (Ambra Bianco)

Salmon burgers

Hamburger di salmone

Serves: 4; Preparation: 30 minutes; Cooking: 35 minutes; Level of difficulty: Medium

Cook the potatoes in their skins in salted, boiling water for 25 minutes, or until tender. Drain, cool, and peel. § Rinse the salmon fillet under cold running water and dry with paper towels. Use a sharp knife to remove the skin. Bone carefully and chop finely. § Put the drained crabmeat in a large bowl and chop coarsely. Add the salmon, potatoes, egg, and salt, mixing well with a fork. § Using your hands, work the mixture into medium-sized balls, then flatten to form burgers. Alternatively, if you have the appropriate machine, make the hamburgers in this, following the manufacturer's directions. § Sprinkle the flour onto a plate and dredge the salmon burgers in it. § Heat the oil into a large skillet (frying pan) until very hot over high heat. Fry the burgers for 5 minutes on each side. § Drain on paper towels and serve hot with boiled turnip greens or spinach, pan-fried with oil, garlic, and chile.

■ INGREDIENTS

• 8 oz (250 g) boiling potatoes
• 8 oz (250 g) salmon fillet
• 8 oz (250 g) crabmeat, canned
• 1 egg
• salt
• ½ cup (75 g) all-purpose (plain) flour
• 3 tablespoons extra-virgin olive oil

Wine: a dry white (Terre di Franciacorta Bianco)

Right: *Hamburger di salmone*

Razor shells in white wine
Cannolicchi al vino bianco

■ INGREDIENTS

- 2 lb (1 kg) razor shell clams
- 4 tablespoons extra-virgin olive oil
- 5 cloves garlic, finely chopped
- ½ cup (30 g) finely chopped parsley
- 3 plum tomatoes, skinned and chopped
- salt
- ½ cup (125 ml) dry white wine

Wine: a dry white (Sangioveto di Coltibuono)

Serves: 4; Preparation: 20 minutes: Cooking: 25 minutes; Level of difficulty: Simple

Wash the razor shells carefully under cold running water (they can contain a lot of sand). Put them in a large nonstick skillet (frying pan) over high heat for 10 minutes until they open. Discard any that have not opened. § Lay a piece of cheesecloth (muslin) over a bowl and filter the cooking liquid through it. § Wash the skillet in which the razor shells were steamed. Add the oil and sauté the garlic and parsley for 5 minutes over medium heat. § Add the tomatoes and razor shells. Season with salt. Pour in the wine and cook for 10 minutes. § Serve immediately on a heated serving platter with roasted bell peppers.

Venus shells au gratin
Fasolari gratinati

■ INGREDIENTS

- 2 lb (1 kg) Venus shell clams
- ⅔ cup (40 g) bread crumbs
- juice of 1 lemon
- salt

Wine: a dry white (Valle Venosta Chardonnay)

Serves: 4; Preparation; 20 minutes: Cooking: 20 minutes; Level of difficulty: Medium

Put the Venus shells in a large skillet over high heat and cook for 10 minutes. § As they open, remove them from the pan and place on a serving plate. Turn off the heat. Take the mollusks out of the shells, taking care that no sand is left inside (if there is, rinse well under cold running water). Chop finely. § Discard half the shells and arrange those you have reserved in a large ovenproof dish. Fill with the chopped mollusks. § Sprinkle with the bread crumbs, drizzle with the lemon juice, and season with salt. Place in a preheated oven at 450°F/230°C/gas 7 for 10 minutes. § Serve hot, accompanied by baby onions cooked in vinegar, with a little sugar added.

Left:
Fasolari gratinati

Whelks with wild fennel
Lumache di mare al finocchio

Serves: 4; Preparation: 20 minutes + 10 minutes to purge the whelks; Cooking: 1¾ hours; Level of difficulty: Medium

Carefully wash the whelks and soak them in a bowl with the baking soda for 10 minutes to purge. Rinse under cold running water and drain well. § In a large skillet (frying pan), sauté the garlic, parsley, onion, and celery in the oil over medium heat for 2 minutes, then add the whelks. § Cook for 10 minutes. Moisten with the wine and cook until it evaporates — this will take about 3 minutes — then stir in the fennel with a wooden spoon. § Add the tomatoes and season with salt. Cover and cook over low heat for 1½ hours. § Transfer to a heated serving dish and serve immediately with steamed or boiled carrots.

Baked scallops
Capesante in forno

Scallops are always attractive when served in their shells. However, since most high quality scallops are sold already shucked, you may have to ask your fish vendor for shells.

Serves: 4; Preparation: 20 minutes; Cooking: 15 minutes; Level of difficulty: Simple

If not already shucked, use a sharp knife to open the scallops. Extract the white mollusk, leaving the red coral. § Rinse the scallops thoroughly under cold running water. § If you have scallop shells, place 16 half shells in a shallow ovenproof pan and place a scallop in each one. (If you don't have shells, place the scallops in an ovenproof dish.) Sprinkle with the mushrooms, garlic, and parsley. Top with the bread crumbs and puréed tomatoes, a few drops of lemon juice, and the oil. Season with salt. § Cook in a preheated oven at 350°F/180°C/gas 4 for 12 minutes. Moisten with the wine and cook for another 3 minutes. Serve hot.

■ INGREDIENTS

- 2 lb (1 kg) whelks (scungilli) or periwinkles
- 3–4 tablespoons baking soda (bicarbonate of soda)
- 4 cloves garlic, finely chopped
- ½ cup (30 g) finely chopped parsley
- ½ onion and ½ stalk celery, chopped
- ⅓ cup (90 ml) extra-virgin olive oil
- ½ cup (125 ml) dry white wine
- 3 tablespoons wild fennel, (or the tops from a bulb of fennel), chopped
- 10 oz (300 g) plum tomatoes, peeled and chopped
- salt

Wine: a dry white (Bianco d'Italia)

■ INGREDIENTS

- 16 sea scallops
- 16 cultivated mushrooms, finely chopped
- 4 cloves garlic, finely chopped
- 4 tablespoons finely chopped parsley
- 1½ cups (90 g) bread crumbs
- 4 tablespoons puréed tomatoes (passata)
- juice of 1 lemon
- 1 teaspoon extra-virgin olive oil
- salt
- ½ cup (125 ml) dry white wine

Wine: a dry white (Valle Venosta Chardonnay)

Right: *Capesante in forno*

Whitebait fritters
Frittelle di bianchetti

Serves: 4; Preparation: 20 minutes; Cooking: 20 minutes; Level of difficulty: Medium

Because they are so tiny, whitebait are never cleaned (gutted) but simply washed and dried and cooked whole. Put the whitebait in a bowl and add the garlic, parsley, Parmesan, egg, bread crumbs, and salt. Mix thoroughly and, using a spoon and your hands, shape the mixture into fritters. § Heat the oil in large skillet (frying pan) and fry the fritters in batches until golden brown. § Scoop them out with a slotted spoon and drain on paper towels. Place on a heated serving platter. Serve hot with French fries.

■ INGREDIENTS

- 1¼ lb (600 g) whitebait, washed and dried
- 4 cloves garlic, finely chopped
- 4 tablespoons finely chopped parsley
- 3 tablespoons freshly grated Parmesan cheese
- 2 eggs, beaten
- 1 tablespoon bread crumbs
- salt
- 2 cups (500 ml) oil, for frying

Wine: a dry white (Bianco Vergine Valdichiana)

Mixed deep-fried fish
Fritto misto

This dish is made using the most popular types of fish. If you prefer, you can add a few smaller fish to the selection such as anchovies, whitebait, thin strips of filleted sole, etc.

Serves: 4; Preparation: 20 minutes; Cooking: 20-25 minutes; Level of difficulty: Medium

Prepare the squid, cuttlefish (if using), and shrimp as described on page 26. Cut the squid into rings and leave the tentacles whole. Cut the cuttlefish in half and leave the tentacles whole. Leave the shells on the shrimp. § Sprinkle the flour on a large piece of foil and roll all the different kinds of fish in it, shaking off any excess (if there is too much flour, it will separate from the fish during cooking and burn, making the oil cloudy). Place the floured fish on a large platter. § Heat the oil in large skillet (frying pan) and fry the pieces of fish in batches until golden brown. Don't put too many pieces in the skillet at once. § Scoop

■ INGREDIENTS

- 14 oz (450 g) squid
- 10 oz (300 g) baby cuttlefish or, if unavailable, strips of filleted sole
- 14 oz (450 g) shrimp (prawns)
- 2 cups (300 g) all-purpose (plain) flour

Right:
Fritto misto

- 4 cups (1 liter) oil,
  for frying
- salt
- 1 lemon, cut into wedges

Wine: a dry white
(Bianco Vergine Valdichiana)

them out with a slotted spoon and drain on paper towels. Place on a heated serving platter and sprinkle with salt. Decorate with wedges of lemon. § Serve with fried vegetables using whatever is in season — onions, potatoes, artichokes, zucchini (courgettes).

Shrimp with white beans
Gamberetti e fagioli cannellini

Serves: 4; Preparation: 10 minutes; Cooking: 10 minutes; Level of difficulty: Medium

Cook the white beans in a pan of salted water with the garlic, sage, and tomato for about 30 minutes, or until tender. Drain and set aside. § Heat the oil in a large skillet (frying pan) and sauté the garlic and parsley for 2 minutes over medium heat. Add the shrimp and cook for 2 minutes, then add the beans. Season with salt and pepper. Stir well and cook for 6 more minutes. § Place in a heated serving dish and serve immediately.

VARIATIONS
– Use fresh shrimp or saltwater crayfish.
– Use dry beans. Soak them overnight and cook for 1 hour. If you are short of time, used canned beans and reduce the cooking time accordingly.

■ INGREDIENTS

• 10 oz (300 g) fresh white beans
• 1 clove garlic
• 2 sage leaves
• 1 small red tomato
• 4 tablespoons extra-virgin olive oil
• 4 cloves garlic, finely chopped
• 4 tablespoons finely chopped parsley
• 10 oz (300 g) frozen shrimp (prawns), thawed and coarsely chopped
• salt and freshly ground black pepper

Wine: a dry white (Sauvignon di Albarola)

Octopus in a mushroom and tomato sauce
Polpo in umido

Serves: 4; Preparation: 25 minutes; Cooking: 1¾ hours + 45 minutes to cook the octopus + 2 hours to soak the mushrooms; Level of difficulty: Medium.

Clean the octopus thoroughly and boil it (see recipe for *Marinated octopus* on page 587). Drain, reserving 1 cup (250 ml) of the cooking water. Cut the octopus into 1¼-in (3-cm) pieces and lay them on a large plate or dish. § Melt the butter with the oil in a flameproof, (preferably earthenware) pan about 11 in (28 cm) in diameter. § When the butter has melted, add the octopus pieces, the celery, carrot, soaked and drained porcini mushrooms, tomatoes, and the reserved octopus cooking water. Cover and bring to a boil, then lower the heat to minimum and cook, adding more water if necessary, for about 1 hour. § Season with salt and sprinkle with parsley. Stir well and serve.

■ INGREDIENTS

• 2 octopus, about 1 lb (500 g) each
• 2 tablespoons butter
• 3 tablespoons extra-virgin olive oil
• 1 stalk celery and 1 carrot, coarsely chopped
• 1 oz (30 g) dried porcini mushrooms, soaked in cold water for 2 hours
• 2 tablespoons puréed tomatoes (passata)
• 2 tablespoons finely chopped parsley
• salt

Wine: a dry white (Santa Lucia Bianco)

Right:
Gamberetti e fagioli cannellini

Marinated octopus
Polpo marinato

Serves: 4; Preparation: 30 minutes + 6 hours for the octopus to cool and 1–2 days to chill Level of difficulty: Medium

Clean the octopus as described on page 26. § Pour 6 cups (1½ liters) water into a large pan and add the salt, bay leaves, thyme, rosemary, lemon juice, and octopus. Place over medium heat and bring to a boil, then turn heat down to low and cook for 45 minutes. § Remove from heat and let cool in the water (this will take about 6 hours). It is important that the octopus cools in its liquid, because this will make it more tender. § Drain, reserving 1 cup (250 ml) of the cooking liquid. Remove the skin and chop into 2-in (5-cm) pieces. § Place in a bowl. Drizzle with the oil and sprinkle with the garlic, wine, chilies, and reserved cooking water. § Cover, and chill in the refrigerator for 1–2 days. § Drain the octopus from the marinade. Serve with boiled potatoes or cultivated mushrooms cooked with parsley and garlic.

VARIATION
– If you cannot find a single octopus of the weight specified, use 2 small octopus, but cook them for 25 rather than 45 minutes.

Pretend fish
Pesce finto

This dish reminds me of my childhood summers. My mother cooks it in a special way and, following the family tradition, I cook it very often too, mostly in the summer months. It is an appetizing recipe, easy to prepare, and economical. Children usually like it, and they will certainly enjoy helping to prepare it.

Serves: 4; Preparation: 20 minutes: Cooking: 30 minutes to boil the potatoes; Level of difficulty: Simple

Scrub the potatoes thoroughly and boil in a large pan of salted water for 25 minutes, or until tender. Drain and peel, then mash in a food processor or by hand. § Let the potatoes cool to lukewarm or cold, then add the tuna, garlic, and parsley. Season with salt and mix well. § Spoon the mixture onto a large serving platter and mold it into a fish shape. Spread with mayonnaise and garnish with capers. § Chill in the refrigerator until ready to serve, and slice as you would a meat loaf. § Serve with a salad of boiled green beans or shelled beans.

Left:
Pesce finto

Braised and Sautéed Vegetables

Almost all vegetables can be braised or sautéed. The idea is to exalt the flavors of the main ingredient without overwhelming it. The authentic recipes in this chapter are only a tiny portion of the full Italian repertoire. Once you have mastered these, use your imagination and personal tastes to invent others.

Stuffed zucchini

Zucchine intere ripiene

If there is any left-over filling, roll it into walnut-sized balls, flour lightly and fry until golden brown. Serve with the filled zucchini.

Serves: 4; Preparation: 30-40 minutes; Cooking: 40 minutes; Level of difficulty: Simple

Cut the zucchini in half, remove the pulp and set it aside. § Mix the pork, sausage, mortadella, Parmesan, parsley, garlic, eggs, salt, and pepper in a bowl. Use a fork to blend the mixture thoroughly. § Stuff the hollowed-out zucchini with the filling. § Heat the frying oil in a sauté pan and fry the stuffed zucchini halves for 2–3 minutes. Drain on paper towels. § To make the sauce, pour the olive oil and tomatoes into a large skillet (frying pan), add 4–5 tablespoons of zucchini pulp, basil, and salt and pepper to taste. Cook over medium heat for 5 minutes. § Place the stuffed zucchini in the skillet with the sauce and add 1 cup (8 fl oz/250 ml) of water. Cook for 20 minutes covered with a sheet of aluminum foil with a small hole in it for the steam to escape. Uncover, and cook for 10 minutes more or until the sauce has reduced. § Serve hot on a bed of Parmesan or saffron risotto.

VARIATION
– For a spicier filling, use Pecorino romano cheese instead of Parmesan, and finely chopped prosciutto instead of mortadella.

■ INGREDIENTS

- 8 large zucchini (courgettes)
- 7 oz (200 g) finely ground lean pork
- 1 Italian pork sausage, peeled and crumbled
- 3½ oz (100 g) mortadella (or ham), coarsely chopped
- ½ cup (60 g) freshly grated Parmesan cheese
- 2 tablespoons parsley, 3 cloves garlic, finely chopped
- 2 eggs, beaten
- salt and freshly ground black pepper
- ½ cup (125 ml) oil, for frying
- 4 tablespoons extra-virgin olive oil
- 1⅔ lb (800 g) tomatoes, peeled and chopped
- 6 basil leaves, torn

Wine: a dry red (Barbera d'Asti)

Braised zucchini

Zucchine trifolate

Serves: 4: Preparation: 10 minutes; Cooking: 10-15 minutes; Level of difficulty: Simple

Cut the cloves of garlic in two and place them in a skillet (frying pan) with the oil. Sauté over medium heat until the garlic turns light gold. § Remove the garlic, add the butter and zucchini, and cook over high heat for 5 minutes. § Reduce heat to medium-low, cover, and simmer for 5 more minutes. § Season with salt and pepper, uncover, and complete cooking. Don't let the zucchini turn mushy; the wheels should stay whole. § Remove from heat, add the parsley, toss well, and transfer to a heated serving dish.

VARIATIONS
– Replace the parsley with 1 tablespoon of finely chopped fresh mint or tarragon.
– Add a finely chopped onion and 4 chopped cherry tomatoes.

■ INGREDIENTS

- 2 cloves garlic
- 2 tablespoons extra-virgin olive oil
- 2 tablespoons butter
- 1¾ lb small zucchini (courgettes), cut into wheels
- salt and freshly ground black pepper
- 3 tablespoons finely chopped parsley

Wine: a dry red (Chianti)

Right:
Zucchine trifolate

Tuscan-style kid...

Fagioli all'uc...

This is an old Florentine favorite. It is delicious...
For a spicier dish, add ½ teasp...

Serves: 4; Preparation: 10 minutes; Cooking: 25 minu...

Sauté the garlic in the oil and as soo...
tomatoes, sage, salt, and pepper. § Sir...
minutes. § As the sauce starts to thick...
about 15 more minutes. § Serve hot direc...

■ INGREDIENTS

- 4 cloves garlic, minced
- ⅓ cup (90 ml) extra-virgin olive oil
- 14 oz (450 g) tomatoes, peeled and chopped
- 8 leaves fresh sage
- salt and pepper
- 2¼ cups (250 g) white kidney beans, canned, or soaked and pre-cooked

Wine: a dry red (Chianti Classico)

Stuffed bell peppers
Peperoni ripieni in tegame

Serves: 4; Preparation: 20 minutes; Cooking: 35 minutes; Level of difficulty: Simple

Trim the stalks of the bell peppers to about 1 inch. Cut their to
half an inch from the top and set aside. Remove the core and s
the bread in cold water for 10 minutes. Squeeze out excess moist
and place in a bowl. Season with salt and pepper. § Add the c
garlic, parsley, basil, anchovies, tomatoes, Parmesan, and Provol
the vinegar and half the oil and mix thoroughly. § Stuff the bell p
the filling, replace the tops, and stand them upright in a pan that
tall as they are. Add the remaining oil and ½ cup (125 ml) of wate
cover the pan and cook over medium-high heat. § Baste the bell p
liquid from the bottom of the pan from time to time. § Aft
minutes pierce a bell pepper with the point of a sharp knife; if i
easily, remove the lid and let some of the moisture evaporate. Whe
bell peppers will be soft and well-cooked. § Serve hot. The del
stock can be poured over the bell peppers or served separately. §
makes a perfect entrée, or the main course in a light lunch.

Potatoes and zucchini with zucchini flow
Fiori e zucchine all'olio

*An eyecatching and distinctly southern Italian dish, from the Campania region arou
The original recipe calls for fresh chilies; add 2 for a mild dish and 4 for a spicy a
can't get fresh chilies, use the crushed dried variety. Add the chilies together with th*

Serves: 4; Preparation: 15 minutes; Cooking: 25 minutes; Level of difficulty: Simple

Sauté the garlic with the oil in a skillet until light gold. § Add th
cover, and simmer for 15 minutes, stirring frequently. § Add the zu
season with salt, pepper, and mint. Simmer, partially covered, for
more. If the vegetables are too watery, remove the lid and let sor
moisture evaporate. § Trim the stems of the zucchini flowers just
bloom, wash carefully, and pat dry with paper towels. § Add 15 flow
zucchini and potatoes and cook for 5 minutes more, or until the
are soft but not mushy. § Transfer to a heated serving dish, garnish
remaining zucchini flowers, and serve hot.

Mixed bell peppers with garlic and capers
Peperoni vivaci

Serves: 4; Preparation: 15 minutes; Cooking: 20-25 minutes; Level of difficulty: Simple

Cut the bell peppers lengthwise into ½-in (1-cm) strips. § Sauté the garlic with the oil in a large skillet (frying pan). Add the bell peppers and press them down with the lid. Season with salt. § Cook over medium heat for about 15 minutes, or until the strips start to wilt. Stir from time to time with a wooden fork. § When the bell peppers are tender, turn the heat up to high and pour the vinegar and capers over the top. Mix rapidly, and cook for 2–3 minutes more to let the vinegar evaporate. § Serve hot or at room temperature.

■ INGREDIENTS

• 2 red, 1 yellow, 1 green medium bell peppers (capsicums)
• 3 cloves garlic, finely chopped
• 4 tablespoons extra-virgin olive oil
• salt
• ⅓ cup 9o ml) red wine vinegar
• 2 tablespoons capers

Wine: a young dry red
(Chianti Novello)

VARIATION
– Add 4 crumbled anchovy fillets with the vinegar and capers. In this case, use less salt.

Mixed bell peppers
Peperonata

One of the classic Italian vegetable dishes.
It is particularly tasty when cooked in an earthenware pot.

Serves: 4; Preparation: 20 minutes; Cooking: 30 minutes; Level of difficulty: Simple

Place the vegetables in a large, heavy-bottomed saucepan or earthenware pot. Add the oil, garlic, basil, salt, and pepper. Cover and cook over medium heat. § After 15 minutes turn the heat up to medium-high and partially uncover to let some of the liquid from the bell peppers evaporate. § As the dish cooks, the potatoes will soften, absorbing the flavors of the other vegetables. § Traditionally served as a side dish with boiled or roasted meats, *Peperonata* is also good on its own with rice, couscous, or baked potatoes.

■ INGREDIENTS

• 4 bell peppers (capsicums), mixed red, yellow and green, cut in ½-in (1-cm) strips
• 3 onions, thickly sliced
• 1 lb (500 g) tomatoes, peeled and chopped
• 3 medium potatoes, cut in 1-inch squares
• ⅓ cup (90 ml) extra-virgin olive oil
• 3 cloves garlic, finely chopped
• 8 fresh basil leaves, torn
• salt and freshly ground black pepper

Wine: a dry red
(Sangiovese di Romagna)

VARIATION
– For a stronger, more distinctive flavor, add 1 medium diced eggplant (aubergine), black olives, and a sprinkling of oregano.

Right: *Peperoni vivaci*

■ INGREDIENTS

- 2 medium onions, cut in medium-thick slices
- 2 large cloves garlic, finely chopped
- 4 medium carrots, cut in wheels and crescents
- 1 lb (500 g) tomatoes, peeled and chopped
- 8 leaves fresh basil
- 1¼ lb (750 g) green beans
- 4 tablespoons extra-virgin olive oil
- salt and freshly ground black pepper

Wine: a dry red
(Dolcetto d'Alba)

Green beans and carrots cooked with onions, garlic, and tomatoes
Fagiolini in umido con carote

Serves: 4; Preparation: 15 minutes; Cooking: 30 minutes; Level of difficulty: Simple

Put all the ingredients in a large, heavy-bottomed pan (or earthenware pot). Season with salt and pepper. § Cover and cook for 20 minutes over medium heat, stirring frequently. At first the beans will stay on top until the steam softens them and you can mix them in. § Uncover the pan and continue cooking until the sauce has reduced and the beans are crunchy but cooked. § Serve hot or at room temperature as a side dish for boiled or sautéed meats, or with rice, potatoes, or fresh bread as a light lunch.

VARIATION
– Add two large stalks of diced celery.

■ INGREDIENTS

- 1¾ lb (800 g) white baby onions, peeled
- 2 tablespoons extra-virgin olive oil
- 3 tablespoons butter
- salt and freshly ground black pepper
- 2 cups (500 ml) white wine
- 3 whole bay leaves

Wine: a dry white
(Galestro)

Baby onions braised in white wine
Cipolline brasate al vino

Serves: 4; Preparation: 10 minutes; Cooking: 30 minutes; Level of difficulty: Simple

Place the onions, oil, and butter in sautè pan. Sauté over high heat for about 10 minutes, stirring the onions with a wooden spoon until evenly browned. Season with salt and pepper. § Add the wine and bay leaves, partially cover, and cook for 15 more minutes. § Uncover and let the sauce thicken. § Serve hot or cold with any kind of roast meat or fish.

VARIATIONS
– Add 1 tablespoon of tomato paste with the wine, to make the onions pink.
– For a sweeter, more aromatic dish, soak 2 tablespoons of raisins in the wine. Add the raisins and a bouquet of herbs (thyme, marjoram, mint) together with the bay leaves.

Left:

Fagiolini in umido con carote

Eggplant cooked in tomato and garlic
Melanzane al funghetto

This dish also makes an excellent pasta sauce. For 4 people, add 3 extra tomatoes and another tablespoon of oil to the ingredients listed here. Serve with 1 lb (500 g) of any sort of dried short pasta (penne, conchiglie, fusilli, macaroni) cooked in salted, boiling water until al dente.

Serves: 4; Preparation: 15 minutes; Cooking: 30 minutes; Level of difficulty: Simple

Trim the ends off the eggplants and cut them in quarters lengthwise. Slice the quarters into pieces about 1 in (2.5 cm) long. § Sauté the garlic in the oil in a large skillet (frying pan) until it turns gold. § Add the eggplant, season with salt and pepper, stir well and cover. Cook over medium-low heat for 15 minutes. § Add the tomatoes, mix well, and cook for 10 more minutes over medium heat. § For the last 5 minutes, remove the lid and add the herbs. § Serve hot as a pasta sauce, or as a side dish with roast or fried meat or fish.

■ INGREDIENTS

- 6 long eggplants (aubergines)
- 4 cloves garlic, finely chopped
- 3 tablespoons extra-virgin olive oil
- salt and freshly ground black pepper
- 3 medium tomatoes, peeled and chopped
- 2 tablespoons finely chopped parsley

Wine: a dry red (Valpolicella)

Filled eggplant sandwiches
Melanzane a librino

Serves: 4; Preparation: 2¼ hours; Cooking: 30 minutes; Level of difficulty: Medium

Using a sharp knife, cut each eggplant in three crosswise. Slice each piece down the middle, leaving it attached on one side, and open it out like a book. § Place the eggplants in layers in a large dish, and sprinkle with salt. Cover with a plate with a heavy weight on top to press the bitter liquid out of the eggplants. Leave to degorge for 2 hours. § Beat the eggs in a bowl until foamy, add the pork, parsley, garlic, and Parmesan. Blend well with a fork for 2–3 minutes. § Put the eggplants in a colander and rinse well under cold running water to remove all the salt. Squeeze the moisture out gently with your hands and pat dry with paper towels. § Using a teaspoon, stuff the pieces of eggplant with the filling so that they look like plump little sandwiches. § Heat the frying oil in a skillet and dip the eggplant sandwiches in one by one, turning them with two forks to seal the edges so that the filling stays inside. § Drain on paper towels. § Heat the olive oil in a sauté pan and add the tomatoes and basil. Cook over medium heat for 15 minutes. Season with salt and pepper. § Add the eggplant sandwiches and cover with sauce. Simmer over low heat for 10 minutes, or until the sauce begins to reduce. § Serve hot with a green salad as a main course.

■ INGREDIENTS

- 8 long eggplants (aubergines)
- salt
- 4 eggs
- 1 lb (500 g) ground pork
- 2 tablespoons finely chopped parsley
- 3 cloves garlic, finely chopped
- ¾ cup (90 g) freshly grated Parmesan cheese
- oil for frying
- 1¼ lb (600 g) tomatoes, peeled and chopped
- 6 leaves fresh basil
- 4 tablespoons extra-virgin olive oil
- freshly ground black pepper

Wine: a dry red (Brindisi Riserva)

Right:
Melanzane al funghetto

Roman-style stuffed braised artichokes
Carciofi ritti

This dish is also known as "Carciofi alla Romana" because it come from Lazio, the region around Rome.

Serves: 4; Preparation: 30 minutes; Cooking: 25-30 minutes; Level of difficulty: Simple

Clean the artichokes by trimming the tops and removing the tough outer leaves. Cut the stems very short so that the artichokes can stand upright. Place in a bowl of cold water with the lemon juice. Set aside for 10 minutes. § Place the artichokes in a sauté pan just large enough to hold them. They should stand upright. Add 2 tablespoons of oil. § Open the leaves carefully and stuff with garlic and parsley (leave 2 spoonfuls for garnishing), pancetta, Pecorino, and Parmesan. Press the filling down and close the leaves. § Sprinkle the stuffed artichokes with the remaining garlic and parsley and pour the wine and remaining oil over the top. Season with salt (not too much–the pancetta and Pecorino are both salty) and pepper. § Cover with foil, leaving a small opening for the steam, and cook over medium heat. § Baste the artichokes with their sauce from time to time during cooking. When the sauce has reduced to about 1 inch in the bottom of the pan, the artichokes are ready. § Serve hot as a light lunch, or as a side dish with roast or grilled meat.

■ INGREDIENTS

- 8 large artichokes
- juice of 1 lemon
- ⅓ cup (90 ml) extra-virgin olive oil
- 4 cloves garlic, 4 tablespoons parsley, finely chopped together
- 2 cups (250 g) pancetta, diced
- 5 oz (150 g) Pecorino romano cheese, flaked
- ½ cup (60 g) freshly grated Parmesan cheese
- 1¼ cups (300 ml) dry white wine
- salt and freshly ground black pepper

Wine: a rosé
(Lagrein Rosato)

> VARIATION
> – The artichokes can also be filled as follows: crumble about 7 oz of Mozzarella cheese in a bowl with 2 tablespoons of finely chopped parsley, 3 tablespoons of bread crumbs, 3 tablespoons of freshly grated Parmesan cheese, and 2 beaten eggs. Season with salt and pepper, mix well, and stuff the artichokes. Cook with wine and oil as above. This recipe gives the artichokes a more delicate flavor.

Artichoke stew
Spezzatino di carciofi

Serves: 4; Preparation: 20 minutes; Cooking: 25 minutes; Level of difficulty: Simple

Clean the artichokes as described above. Remove all but the tender, white inner leaves. Peel the stems and cut them into wheels. § Put the artichokes and stems in a bowl of cold water with the lemon juice for 10 minutes. § Drain the artichokes and cut them into quarters. § Place the artichoke quarters and stems, garlic, oil, wine, salt, and pepper in a heavy-bottomed pan. Cook for 20 minutes covered, then uncover and

■ INGREDIENTS

- 8 medium artichokes
- juice of 1 lemon
- 3 cloves garlic, finely chopped
- 4 tablespoons extra-virgin olive oil
- 1 cup (250 ml) dry white wine

Right:
Spezzatino di carciofi

- salt and freshly ground black pepper
- 3 tablespoons finely chopped parsley

Wine: a dry white (Greco di Tufo)

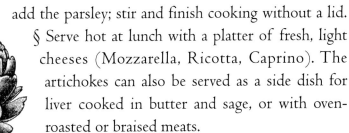

add the parsley; stir and finish cooking without a lid. § Serve hot at lunch with a platter of fresh, light cheeses (Mozzarella, Ricotta, Caprino). The artichokes can also be served as a side dish for liver cooked in butter and sage, or with oven-roasted or braised meats.

VARIATION
– Replace the parsley with mint or calamint and add 1½ tablespoons of tomato paste to the cooking liquid.

Stuffed artichokes
Mamme di carciofi ripiene

Serves: 4; Preparation: 20 minutes; Cooking: 1 hour; Level of difficulty: Medium

Clean the artichokes as described on page 600. Trim the stems short so that the artichokes will stand upright in the pot. Chop the stems coarsely and soak them with the artichokes in a bowl of cold water and lemon juice for 10 minutes. § Beat the eggs in a bowl until foamy. Season with salt and pepper. § Add the pork, sausage, prosciutto, Parmesan, garlic, parsley, salt, and pepper and blend well with a fork. § Using a teaspoon, fill the heart of each artichoke. § Heat the frying oil in a skillet (frying pan) and when it is hot enough hold each artichoke upside down in the oil for about 2 minutes, to seal in the filling. Roll the artichokes in the oil for 2 more minutes to cook the leaves. Using two forks, remove from the oil and set aside. § Place the olive oil, tomatoes, basil, artichoke stems, salt, and pepper in a sauté pan and simmer over medium heat for 10 minutes. § Add the stuffed artichokes and baste them with the sauce. Cover and simmer for 20 minutes. Uncover and cook for 10 more minutes, or until the sauce has reduced. § Serve hot.

■ INGREDIENTS

- 8 large artichokes
- juice of 1 lemon
- 4 eggs
- salt and freshly ground black pepper
- 5 oz (150 g) ground lean pork
- 1 Italian pork sausage, skinned and crumbled
- 1½ cups (350 g) chopped prosciutto
- 1½ cups (180 g) freshly grated Parmesan cheese
- 3 cloves garlic, 2 tablespoons parsley, finely chopped
- 1 cup (250 ml) oil, for frying
- ½ cup (125 ml) extra-virgin olive oil
- 1½ lb (750 g) tomatoes, peeled and chopped
- 10 fresh basil leaves

Wine: a dry red (Sassicaia)

Florentine artichoke omelet
Tortino di carciofi

A classic Florentine recipe, as old as the city itself. A real Florentine artichoke omelet should be slightly underdone; the eggs should be cooked underneath and moist on top.

Serves: 4; Preparation: 20 minutes; Cooking: 25-30 minutes; Level of difficulty: Simple

Clean the artichokes as described on page 600. Cut the stems short. Soak in a bowl of cold water and lemon juice for 10 minutes. § Cut the artichokes into ½-in slices and put them in a large skillet (frying pan) with the oil. Add the water and salt to taste, cover and cook for 7–8 minutes. § Uncover and continue cooking until the artichokes are tender and the water has evaporated. § Beat the eggs with salt and pepper until foamy and pour over the artichokes. Cover and cook for 5 minutes over medium heat. Uncover and continue cooking. As the egg begins to set, stir carefully so that it cooks evenly. § Serve hot with a green salad.

■ INGREDIENTS

- 5 large artichokes
- juice of 1 lemon
- 4 tablespoons extra-virgin olive oil
- 5 eggs
- ½ cup (125 ml) water
- salt and freshly ground black pepper

Wine: a dry red (Chianti)

Right:
Tortino di carciofi

Escarole with pine nuts, capers, olives, raisins, and anchovies
Indivia scarola dolce forte delicata

■ INGREDIENTS

• 3 large heads escarole
• 4 tablespoons extra-virgin olive oil
• ⅓ cup (60 g) pine nuts
• ⅓ cup (60 g) raisins, soaked for 30 minutes in water
• 12 pitted and chopped black olives
• salt and freshly ground black pepper
• ⅓ cup (50 g) capers
• 4 anchovy fillets, finely chopped, or 3 curls of anchovy paste

Wine: a dry white
(Pinot Grigio)

Serves: 4; Preparation: 10 minutes; Cooking: 25 minutes; Level of difficulty: Simple

Use the green leaves of the escarole and set the creamy white hearts aside to use in a salad. § Blanch the leaves in salted, boiling water, drain well, and spread in a colander to dry for about 10 minutes. § Heat the oil in a sauté pan and add the escarole, pine nuts, raisins, olives, salt, and pepper. Sauté over medium heat for 10 minutes. Toss the leaves from time to time as they cook. § Add the capers and anchovy, toss well and cook until any excess water has evaporated. § Serve hot as an entrée, or as a side dish with roast or barbecued meat – the earthy flavor is perfect with both white and red meats.

Celery hearts in cream sauce with pancetta and potato
Cuori di sedano delicati

■ INGREDIENTS

• 2 large heads celery
• juice of 1 lemon
• salt and freshly ground black pepper
• 4 tablespoons extra-virgin olive oil
• 1 large potato, diced
• ½ cup (60 g) pancetta, diced
• 1 cup (250 ml) fresh cream

Wine: a young dry red
(Vino Novello)

Serves: 4; Preparation: 5 minutes; Cooking: 30 minutes; Level of difficulty: Simple

Remove the tough outer stalks of celery and cut the ends off level with the hearts. Divide the inner stalks in half lengthwise. § Bring a pot of salted water with the lemon juice to a boil and cook the celery for 7–8 minutes. Drain well and place on a serving dish. § Heat the oil in a skillet (frying pan) and fry the potato until tender. § Remove most of the oil and cook the pancetta until crisp. § Heat the cream in a saucepan with salt and pepper to taste. Cook until it reduces. § Pour the cream over the celery hearts, and sprinkle the potatoes and pancetta on top. § Serve hot as an appetizer, or as side dish with braised white meats.

VARIATION
– For a tastier dish, add 2 tablespoons of sharp, grated cheese to the cream before heating it (Pecorino romano or Provolone) or Parmesan cheese with a tablespoon of *Simple tomato sauce* (see recipe p. 28).

Left:
Cuori di sedano delicati

Hot and spicy Brussels sprouts
Cavolini di Bruxelles alla diavola

Serves: 4-6; Preparation: 10 minutes; Cooking: 25 minutes; Level of difficulty: Simple

Cook the Brussels sprouts in salted, boiling water for 7–8 minutes, drain well, and set aside. § In a large skillet (frying pan), sauté the garlic in the oil until pale gold. § Add the pancetta and sausage. Sauté briefly and stir in the Brussels sprouts and crushed chilies. § Season with salt, cover, and cook for 10 minutes. § Uncover, sprinkle with the chives and cook for 5 more minutes. § Serve piping hot on a bed of rice as a main course, or as a side dish with barbecued pork chops or veal roast.

■ INGREDIENTS
- 2 lb (1 kg) Brussels sprouts
- 3 cloves garlic, finely chopped
- 3 tablespoons extra-virgin olive oil
- 1 cup (125 g) smoked pancetta (or bacon), diced
- 1 Italian sausage, skinned and crumbled
- ½ teaspoon crushed chilies
- salt
- 1 bunch chives, coarsely chopped

Wine: a dry red (Sangiovese)

Curried Brussels sprouts
Cavolini di Bruxelles al curry

Serves: 4-6; Preparation: 20 minutes; Cooking: 30 minutes; Level of difficulty: Simple

Sauté the onion in the butter in a large skillet until soft. § Add the flour and mix well, stirring rapidly with a wooden spoon. Add half the beef stock a little at a time, stirring constantly. § Add the apple and stir in the remaining stock a little at a time as the sauce simmers over low heat for about 20 minutes. The mixture should boil slowly as the apple disintegrates and blends in with the other ingredients. After 20 minutes the sauce should be thick and creamy. § Add the cream and curry powder, season with salt and pepper, and simmer for 5 more minutes, stirring constantly. § In the meantime, cook the Brussels sprouts for about 10 minutes in salted, boiling water. Drain well and arrange on a heated serving dish. § Pour the hot sauce over the top and serve immediately as a main course with saffron-flavored rice, or as a side dish with chicken cooked in a white wine sauce or veal scaloppini braised with onions.

■ INGREDIENTS
- 1 medium onion, finely chopped
- 2 tablespoons butter
- 1 tablespoon sifted all-purpose (plain) flour
- 2 cups (500 ml) *Beef stock* (see recipe p. 48)
- 1 Golden Delicious apple, peeled and thinly sliced
- 1 cup (8 fl oz/250 ml) fresh cream
- 1½ tablespoons curry powder
- salt and freshly ground black pepper
- 2 lb (1 kg) Brussels sprouts

Wine: a dry white (Sauvignon)

Right: *Cavolini di Bruxelles al curry*

Mixed mushrooms in egg sauce
Funghi misti in fricassea

Timing is important in this recipe. The egg sauce must be poured over the mushrooms the moment they are removed from the heat and tossed quickly so that the egg cooks evenly.

Serves: 4; Preparation: 15 minutes; Cooking: 25 minutes; Level of difficulty: Medium

Sauté the onion in a large skillet (frying pan) with the oil. § Chop the larger mushrooms in thick slices and leave the smaller varieties whole. § Add the mushrooms to the skillet. Season with salt and pepper, cover, and cook for 15–20 minutes over medium-low heat. Stir frequently. § When the mushrooms are cooked, remove from heat and transfer to a heated serving dish. § While the mushrooms are cooking, beat the egg yolks in a bowl with the lemon juice and parsley until foamy. § Pour the egg sauce over the mushrooms and toss quickly so that the egg cooks evenly. § Serve with a large green salad and fresh bread as a light lunch.

■ INGREDIENTS

- 1 medium onion, finely chopped
- 4 tablespoons extra-virgin olive oil
- 2 lb (1 kg) mixed fresh or frozen mushrooms (porcini, white, chanterelle, or Caesar's), washed and trimmed
- salt and freshly ground black pepper
- 4 egg yolks
- juice of 1 lemon
- 2 tablespoons finely chopped parsley

Wine: a young, dry red (Novello Falò)

Stewed porcini mushrooms
Funghi porcini trifolati

The traditional Italian recipe calls for fresh porcini mushrooms, which are hard to find outside Italy or France. If you can't get porcini mushrooms, replace them with the same quantity of fresh shiitake mushrooms, or with 1½ lb (750 g) of white mushrooms and ¼ cup of dried porcini mushrooms soaked in a bowl of warm water for 20 minutes.

Serves: 4-6; Preparation: 15 minutes; Cooking: 15 minutes; Level of difficulty: Simple

Trim the stalks of the mushrooms and separate the heads from the stems. § Cut the stems in half. Chop the stems and heads in thick slices. § Sauté the garlic in a large sauté pan until golden. Add the stems and sauté for 7–8 minutes. § Add the mushroom heads, salt, and pepper and stir carefully with a wooden spoon. § Add the calamint or thyme and finish cooking over low heat. § Serve hot as an appetizer on squares of toasted whole-wheat bread, or as a side dish with braised or stewed meat.

■ INGREDIENTS

- 2 lb (1 kg) fresh porcini mushrooms
- 3 large cloves garlic, finely chopped
- 4 tablespoons extra-virgin olive oil
- salt and freshly ground black pepper
- 1 tablespoon fresh, or ½ tablespoon dried, calamint or thyme

Wine: a dry red (Brunello di Montalcino)

VARIATION
– Replace the porcini with chanterelle mushrooms and add 3 cherry tomatoes (cut in half and squashed with a fork) halfway through cooking.

Right:
Funghi porcini trifolati

Mushrooms and potatoes with pine nuts
Funghetti e patatine ai pinoli

■ INGREDIENTS

- 2 lb (1 kg) white mushrooms
- 4 medium potatoes, diced
- ⅓ cup (90 ml) extra-virgin olive oil
- 3 cloves garlic, crushed
- salt and black pepper
- ⅔ cup (125 g) pine nuts
- ½ cup (2 oz/60 g) almond shavings
- 2 tablespoons finely chopped mint

Wine: a dry red (Teroldego)

Serves: 4; Preparation: 10 minutes; Cooking: 25 minutes; Level of difficulty: Simple

Chop any larger mushrooms in thick slices and leave the smaller ones whole. § Fry the potatoes with the oil and garlic in a large skillet. § Add the mushrooms and sauté. Season with salt and pepper, cover, and cook for 5 minutes. § Uncover and let some of the moisture evaporate. Stir in the pine nuts and almonds and cook for 10 more minutes. § Sprinkle with mint just before removing from heat. § Serve hot as a main course or light lunch with a large mixed salad.

Spring peas with prosciutto and parsley
Pisellini primavera al prezzemolo e prosciutto

Serves: 4; Preparation: 15 minutes; Cooking: 25 minutes; Level of difficulty: Simple

Sauté the prosciutto in the oil in a large skillet (frying pan) for 5 minutes. Remove from heat. § Let the oil cool, then add the peas, garlic, parsley, and water. Partially cover and simmer for about 15 minutes. § Season with salt and pepper. § Serve hot as a side dish with roast beef or oven-baked fish.

VARIATIONS
– Replace the garlic with 1 medium onion, finely chopped.
– Add a teaspoon of sugar to make the peas sweeter.

■ INGREDIENTS

• 1½ lb (750 g) fresh or frozen peas
• 4 tablespoons extra-virgin olive oil
• 1½ cups 350 g) prosciutto, diced
• 2 large cloves garlic, finely chopped
• 1 cup (250 ml) water
• 3 tablespoons finely chopped parsley
• salt and freshly ground black pepper

Wine: a dry red
(Chianti Classico)

Pea mousse
Mousse di piselli

Serves: 4; Preparation: 2½ hours; Cooking: 15 minutes; Level of difficulty: Simple

Bring 2 quarts (4 pints/2 liters) of salted water to a boil in a pan and cook the peas and onion for 10–15 minutes. § Drain well and set aside to cool. § Place the Ricotta, peas, onion, and oil in a food processor and chop until the mixture is creamy. Season with salt and pepper. § Line a 1-quart (1-liter) pudding mold with plastic wrap and pour the mixture in, pressing with a spoon to eliminate any air bubbles. Knock the mold against the work bench to eliminate air pockets. § Refrigerate for at least 2 hours. § Invert onto a round serving dish and garnish with the carrot wheels and sprigs of parsley. § Serve on slices of whole-wheat toast as an appetizer or as a side dish with braised or roast fish.

VARIATION
– For a sharper flavor, replace the Ricotta with Robiola or Caprino cheese and place 2 cups (1 lb/500 g) of finely chopped lean ham in layers at the center of the mousse.

■ INGREDIENTS

• 1 lb (500 g) shelled or frozen peas
• 1 medium onion, cut in half
• 1½ cups (450 g) Ricotta cheese
• 3 tablespoons extra-virgin olive oil
• salt and freshly ground black pepper
• 1 carrot, cut in very thin wheels
• 8 tiny sprigs parsley

Wine: a dry red
(Cabernet)

Right: *Pisellini primavera al prezzemolo e prosciutto*

Asparagus with brandy and cream sauce
Asparagi eleganti

Serves: 4; Preparation: 15 minutes; Cooking: 25 minutes; Level of difficulty: Simple

Choose a pan large enough to lay the asparagus flat, fill with cold water, and bring to a boil. Add 1 tablespoon of salt and cook the asparagus for 7–10 minutes (depending on the thickness of the stalks). § Drain well and cut off the tough white part at the bottoms of the stalks. § Melt the butter in a skillet and add the asparagus. Season with salt and pepper and cook for 3–4 minutes over medium heat. § Pour in the brandy and let it evaporate. Keep the asparagus moving by shaking the skillet gently by the handle. § Meanwhile, put the cream and bread crumbs in a saucepan, mix well and cook over medium heat for 10–15 minutes, or until the sauce is thick and creamy. Stir frequently. § Place the asparagus stalks on a heated serving dish and pour the sauce over the top. § Serve hot as an entrée.

■ INGREDIENTS

- 2 lb (1 kg) fresh asparagus
- salt and freshly ground black pepper
- 4 tablespoons butter
- ⅓ cup (90 ml) brandy
- 2⅓ cups (600 ml) heavy (double) cream
- 1 tablespoon bread crumbs

Wine: a dry white (Corvo Bianco)

Spicy chicory with garlic and anchovies
Cicoria catalogna in padella

Serves: 4; Preparation: 10 minutes; Cooking: 30 minutes; Level of difficulty: Simple

Trim the head of chicory, remove any yellow or wilted leaves and divide it in two. Wash in cold running water. § Cook in a pan of salted, boiling water for 10–15 minutes. § Drain thoroughly without squeezing and cut lengthwise into 1-in (2.5-cm) pieces. § Sauté the garlic in the oil in a large skillet until golden. § Add the chicory and chilies, and season with a dash of salt (not too much–remember the capers and anchovies to be added later). § Cook over medium heat for about 10 minutes, stirring frequently. § Stir the anchovies and capers in over high heat for 2–3 minutes. § Serve on a heated serving dish with beef sautéed in sage and garlic, broiled sausages, or mixed roast meats.

■ INGREDIENTS

- 1 large head chicory
- 5 cloves garlic, finely chopped
- ½ teaspoon crushed chilies
- ⅓ cup (100 ml) extra-virgin olive oil
- salt
- 8 anchovy fillets, crumbled
- ⅓ cup (50 g) capers

Wine: a dry red (Valpolicella)

Right:
Asparagi eleganti

Spinach sautéed with olive oil and garlic
Spinaci saltati

■ INGREDIENTS

- 2 lb (1 kg) fresh or frozen spinach
- 4 large cloves garlic, finely chopped
- 4 tablespoons extra-virgin olive oil
- salt

Wine: a dry white (Riesling Italico)

Serves: 6; Preparation: 10 minutes; Cooking: 30 minutes; Level of difficulty: Simple

Cook the spinach in a pot of salted, boiling water until tender (3–4 minutes if frozen, 8–10 minutes if fresh). Drain, cool under cold running water, squeeze out excess moisture, and chop coarsely. § Sauté the garlic in the oil until golden. § Add the spinach and cook over medium-high heat for 3–4 minutes, tossing continually, so that the spinach absorbs the flavors of the garlic and oil. § Serve hot with poached eggs and *Tomato and butter sauce* (see recipe page 28), or as a side dish with roast or braised meat.

Cardoons in meat sauce with Parmesan cheese
Cardi al sugo di carne e parmigiano

A cardoon looks a bit like a large white celery. It is closely related to the artichoke, although it has a much stronger taste. Cardoons are not always easy to find, even in Italy. For a completely different, but equally delicious dish, replace the cardoon with the same amount of celery. In this case, there is no need to soak the celery in lemon juice, and cooking time will be reduced to 15–20 minutes.

Serves: 4; Preparation: 15 minutes; Cooking: 35 minutes; Level of difficulty: Simple

Prepare the cardoon by removing any damaged outer stalks and tough filaments with a sharp knife. Separate the stalks from the heart and cut them into pieces about 3 in (8 cm) long. Wash well and soak in a bowl of cold water with the lemon juice for about 10 minutes. § Bring a pot of salted water to a boil. Add the flour and pieces of cardoon and cook for 20 minutes. Drain well. § Heat the meat sauce with the butter in a large sauté pan. Add the cardoon pieces a few at a time and mix well with the sauce. When they are all in the pan, season with salt and pepper. Partially cover, and cook over low heat for 10–15 minutes, or until the cardoons are tender. Stir frequently. § When cooked, sprinkle with Parmesan and let stand for a minute, covered. § Serve hot at lunch with fresh bread and a green or mixed salad.

■ INGREDIENTS

- 1 cardoon, about 2 lb (1 kg)
- juice of 2 lemons
- 1½ tablespoons all-purpose (plain) flour
- ¼ cup (60 g) butter
- ½ quantity *Bolognese meat sauce* (see recipe p. 30)
- salt and freshly ground black pepper
- 4 tablespoons freshly grated Parmesan cheese

Wine: a dry red (Rosso di Montepulciano)

Carrots in caramel sauce with parsley
Carote caramellate al prezzemolo

If the sauce reduces too much during cooking, sprinkle with white wine (before adding the parsley).

Serves: 6; Preparation: 10 minutes; Cooking: 25 minutes; Level of difficulty: Simple

Peel the carrots with a peeler or scrape them with a knife. Rinse well under cold running water. § Cut the carrots into sticks about 2 in (5 cm) long (if you are using baby carrots, leave them whole). § Place in a large sauté pan and almost cover with cold water. Add half the butter cut into cubes. § Cook over high heat until the water evaporates. § Season with salt and pepper, add the remaining butter, and sprinkle with the sugar. Sauté the carrots until they are all a bright orange color, shiny and caramel-coated. § Add the parsley, mix well, and serve hot with braised or roasted fish or meat.

■ INGREDIENTS

- 3 lb (1½ kg) carrots
- ½ cup (125 g) butter
- salt and freshly ground black pepper
- 2 tablespoons sugar
- 3 tablespoons finely chopped parsley

Wine: a dry white (Orvieto Classico)

Right:
Carote caramellate al prezzemolo

Fresh fava beans with pancetta
Fave fresche alla pancetta

Serves: 4; Preparation: 30 minutes; Cooking: 30 minutes; Level of difficulty: Simple

Pod the beans and set them aside in a bowl of cold water. § Put the pancetta and onion in a sauté pan with the oil and sauté over medium-low heat until the onion is light gold in color. § Drain the fava beans and add with the stock to the sauté pan. Season with salt and pepper. § Cover, and cook over medium-low heat for 20 minutes, or until the beans are tender and the stock has reduced. § Serve hot as an entrée.

■ INGREDIENTS

• 3 lb (1½ kg) fava beans (broad beans), in their pods
• ⅔ cup (90 g) pancetta, diced
• 2 tablespoons extra-virgin olive oil
• 1 medium onion, finely chopped
• 1 cup (250 ml) *Beef stock* (see recipe p. 48)
• salt and freshly ground black pepper

Wine: a dry white
(Vernaccia di San Gimignano)

Stewed lentils with Italian sausages
Lenticchie stufate con salsiccia

Serves: 4; Preparation: 10 minutes; Cooking: 1½ hours; Level of difficulty: Simple

Discard any lentils floating on top of the water. § Put the lentils in a pot with just enough cold water to cover them. Season with salt. Simmer for 30 minutes, then drain. § Put the onion, carrot, celery, and pancetta in a large sauté pan with the oil and sauté until golden brown. § Add the lentils and stir for 2–3 minutes to mix them in well. § Pour in the white wine and let it evaporate a little, then add the diluted tomato paste and the stock cube. Season with salt and pepper, and cover with hot water. Cook for 40 minutes over low heat. § In the meantime, brown the sausages in a skillet (frying pan) with 2 tablespoons of cold water. Drain the excess fat and add the sausages to the lentils when they have been cooking for about 20 minutes, so they add their flavor to the dish. § When cooked, the lentils should be tender and the stew slightly liquid. If it is too watery, stir over high heat until it reduces sufficiently. § Serve hot as a hearty and complete main course.

■ INGREDIENTS

• 1½ cups (180 g) lentils, soaked in cold water overnight
• 1 medium onion, 1 large carrot, 2 stalks celery, all finely chopped together
• ½ cup (125 ml) extra-virgin olive oil
• ½ cup (60 g) diced pancetta
• 1 cup (250 g) white wine
• 1½ tablespoons tomato paste, diluted in 2 tablespoons hot water
• 1 beef stock cube
• salt and freshly ground black pepper
• 5 Italian sausages, pricked with a fork so that excess fat is eliminated while frying

Wine: a dry red (Merlot)

VARIATION
– For a spicier dish, add 1 teaspoon crushed chilies with the tomato paste.

Left: *Lenticchie stufate con salsiccia*

Stuffed cabbage rolls
Involtini di verza

Serves: 4; Preparation: 50 minutes; Cooking: 45 minutes; Level of difficulty: Medium

Trim the cabbage, discarding the tough outer leaves. Choose 8 large cabbage leaves, make a small cut in the stem of each and blanch them in salted, boiling water for 4–5 minutes. Drain well, and lay them to dry on a clean dish towel. § Put the beef, pork, sausages, Parmesan, eggs, garlic, parsley, salt, and pepper in a bowl and mix well with a fork. § Distribute the filling evenly, placing a part on one half of each leaf. Fold the other half over the top, press down, and tuck in the two remaining open ends. Tie with kitchen string. § Sauté the onion in the butter and oil in a large skillet until light gold. § Add the stuffed cabbage leaves. Cook on both sides, turning them carefully with a fork or spoon. § Add the tomatoes, season with salt and pepper and cook over medium-low heat for about 40 minutes. If the sauce becomes too dry, add the beef stock. § Serve hot as a main course with saffron risotto or plain white rice.

■ INGREDIENTS
- 1 medium cabbage
- 5 oz (150 g) ground beef
- 5 oz (150 g) lean ground pork
- 5 oz (150 g) Italian sausage, crumbled
- ½ cup (60 g) freshly grated Parmesan cheese
- 2 eggs
- 2 cloves garlic, 2 tablespoons parsley, finely chopped
- salt and pepper
- 2 tablespoons butter
- 3 tablespoons extra-virgin olive oil
- 1 onion, finely chopped
- 1¼ lb (600 g) tomatoes, peeled and chopped
- 1 cup (250 ml) *Beef stock* (see recipe p. 48)

Wine: a dry red (Bonarda)

Stuffed lettuce-leaf rolls
Involtini di lattuga saporiti

Serves: 4; Preparation: 30 minutes; Cooking: 40 minutes; Level of difficulty: Medium

Wash the lettuce leaves, taking care not to tear them. § Bring a pot of salted water to a boil and blanch each leaf by dipping it into the water for about 20 seconds. Lay the leaves on a clean dish towel to dry. § Brown the sausages in a skillet (frying pan) without oil. Add the wine and let it evaporate. Remove from heat and set to cool on a plate, leaving any fat in the skillet. § Beat the eggs in a bowl, add the salt, pepper, Edam, Parmesan, bread crumbs, and sausage. Mix well to make a smooth filling. § Distribute the filling evenly among the lettuce leaves and roll them up, folding in the ends to make packages or rolls. Tie with kitchen string. § Put the onion in a skillet with the oil over medium heat and sauté until soft. § Place the stuffed lettuce leaves in the skillet with the onion, cover, and cook for 5 minutes. Turn the lettuce rolls with a fork, uncover and cook for 5 more minutes. § Serve hot as a main course with mushroom risotto.

■ INGREDIENTS
- 8 large lettuce leaves
- 8 oz (250 g) Italian sausage, skinned and crumbled
- ¾ cup (200 ml) white wine
- 2 eggs
- salt and black pepper
- 4 oz (125 g) freshly grated Edam cheese
- 1 cup (125 g) freshly grated Parmesan cheese
- 3 tablespoons bread crumbs
- 4 tablespoons extra-virgin olive oil
- 1 medium onion, finely chopped

Wine: a dry white (Chardonnay)

Right: *Involtini di verza*

Baked Vegetables

A wide variety of vegetables can be baked to create pies, crêpes, molds, filled, or gratin dishes. They can be served hot as entrées, main courses, or light lunches, or let cool and presented as healthy after school treats for hungry children or delicious snacks for the whole family.

Cauliflower mold with black olives
Sformato di cavolfiore con olive

Serves: 4; Preparation: 25 minutes; Cooking: 55 minutes; Level of difficulty: Simple

Divide the cauliflower into large florets and trim the stems. Cook in a pot of salted, boiling water for 5–7 minutes. Drain and set aside. § Prepare the béchamel sauce. § Chop the cauliflower with a heavy knife or in a food processor. § Combine the purée with the béchamel, Parmesan, olives, eggs, salt, pepper, and nutmeg. § Grease a ring mold about 10 in (25 cm) in diameter with a little butter and sprinkle with bread crumbs. Pour the mixture into the mold and place the mold in a larger container filled with water. § Cook in a preheated oven at 350°F/180°C/gas 4 for 45 minutes. § Invert the mold onto a platter while still hot. Serve hot or at room temperature.

■ INGREDIENTS

- 2 lb (1 kg) cauliflower head
- 1 quantity *Béchamel sauce* (see recipe p. 38)
- salt and freshly ground black pepper
- ¼ teaspoon nutmeg
- ½ cup (60 g) freshly grated Parmesan cheese
- 20 black olives, pitted and chopped
- 3 eggs, beaten until foamy
- butter to grease the mold and bread crumbs

Wine: a dry white (Melissa)

Spinach mold
Sformato di spinaci

Like all the molds in this chapter, Sformato di spinaci can be served as an entrée or main course, or as a side dish with meat or fish. Add a touch of color to this spinach mold by serving it with 1 quantity of Simple tomato sauce, well-reduced (see recipe p. 28).

Serves: 4; Preparation: 30 minutes; Cooking: 1 hour; Level of difficulty: Medium

Cook the spinach in a pot of salted, boiling water until tender (3–4 minutes if frozen, 8–10 minutes if fresh). Drain, cool under cold running water, and squeeze out excess moisture. Chop with a heavy knife or in a food processor. § Put the spinach in a saucepan with the cream and stir over medium heat until all the moisture has been absorbed. Remove from heat. § Prepare the béchamel sauce. Set aside to cool for 5 minutes. § Combine the béchamel with the spinach purée and add the Parmesan, nutmeg, and egg yolks. Season with salt and pepper. § Beat the egg whites until stiff and carefully fold them into the spinach mixture. § Grease a ring mold about 10 in (25 cm) in diameter with a little butter and dust with flour. Pour the mixture into the mold. § Place the mold in a larger container filled with water and cook in a preheated oven at 350°F/180°C/gas 4 for 45 minutes. § Invert onto a platter while still hot. Serve hot or at room temperature.

■ INGREDIENTS

- 1½ lb (750 g) fresh or frozen spinach
- salt and freshly ground black pepper
- 4 tablespoons heavy (double) cream
- 1 quantity *Béchamel sauce* (see recipe p. 38)
- ½ cup (60 g) freshly grated Parmesan cheese
- ¼ teaspoon nutmeg
- 2 eggs, separated
- butter and flour to grease and dust the mold

Wine: a dry white (Pinot Grigio)

Right: *Sformato di spinaci con salsa di pomodoro*

Zucchini and carrot mold
Sformato di zucchine con carote

Serves: 4-6; Preparation: 40 minutes; Cooking: 1½ hours; Level of difficulty: Medium

Put one-fifth of the zucchini in a skillet with 1 tablespoon of oil. Cook over medium heat for 5 minutes. Set aside. § Sauté the carrots and onions in the remaining oil for 5 minutes. § Add the remaining zucchini, partially cover, and cook for 10–15 minutes, or until the vegetables are tender. § Prepare the béchamel sauce. Let cool for 5–10 minutes. § Combine the béchamel with the Parmesan, eggs, vegetables, and mint. Season with salt and pepper. Mix well. § Grease a ring mold 10 in (25 cm) in diameter with the butter and sprinkle with bread crumbs. § Line the mold with the sliced zucchini by sticking them one by one to the butter and bread crumbs until the mold is covered. § Pour the mixture into the mold, taking care not to knock the zucchini off the sides of the mold. § Place the mold in a larger container filled with water and cook in a preheated oven at 400°F/200°C/gas 6 for 50 minutes. § Let stand for 10 minutes, then invert onto a serving dish.

■ INGREDIENTS

- 1¼ lb (600 g) zucchini (courgettes), thinly sliced
- 4 tablespoons extra-virgin olive oil
- 2 medium onions, 4 medium carrots, finely chopped together
- 1 quantity *Béchamel sauce* (see recipe p. 38)
- ½ cup (60 g) freshly grated Parmesan cheese
- 2 eggs, beaten until foamy
- 2 tablespoons finely chopped mint
- salt and freshly ground black pepper
- butter to grease the mold and bread crumbs

Wine: a dry white (Locorotondo)

Fluffy onion gratin
Gratin soffice di cipolle

Serves: 4-6; Preparation: 30 minutes; Cooking: 1½ hours; Level of difficulty: Simple

Boil the potatoes in their skins in a pot of salted water for about 25 minutes. Drain and cover to keep warm. § Place the onions, oil, half the butter, wine, water, stock cube, salt, and pepper in a saucepan, cover and simmer for 35 minutes, or until the onions are soft. § Peel the potatoes, chop coarsely, and mash. § Heat the milk in a saucepan and add the potatoes and the remaining butter (reserving 1 tablespoon) to make a smooth purée. Remove from heat and let cool for 10 minutes. § Combine the purée with the eggs, salt, and pepper. Stir in the Parmesan (reserving 2 tablespoons) and mix well. § Butter an ovenproof dish and spread with half the potato mixture in an even layer. § Drain the cooked onions of any liquid and spread over the potatoes. Sprinkle with the Gruyère and cover with the remaining potatoes. § Sprinkle with bread crumbs and Parmesan. § Bake in a preheated oven at 350°F/180°C/gas 4 for 25 minutes. § Serve hot as an entrée, light lunch, or side dish.

■ INGREDIENTS

- 3 lb (1.5 kg) potatoes
- 6 large onions, sliced
- 1 tablespoon extra-virgin olive oil
- ½ cup (125 g) butter
- 1 cup (250 ml) dry white wine
- ½ cup (125 ml) water
- 1 vegetable stock cube
- salt and black pepper
- 1¼ cups (300 ml) milk
- 3 eggs, beaten until foamy
- 1 cup (125 g) freshly grated Parmesan cheese
- 1 cup (125 g) freshly grated Gruyère cheese
- 2 tablespoons bread crumbs

Wine: a dry red (Refosco)

Right: Gratin soffice di cipolla

Cabbage, rice and tomato gratin
Gratin delicato di verza e riso

Serves: 4; Preparation: 25 minutes; Cooking: 55 minutes; Level of difficulty: Simple

■ INGREDIENTS

- 1 medium Savoy cabbage
- 2 onions, 2 cloves garlic, finely chopped
- 2½ tablespoons extra-virgin olive oil
- 1¼ cups (250 g) parboiled rice
- 1 lb (500 g) tomatoes, peeled and chopped
- 1 quantity *Béchamel sauce* (see recipe p. 38)
- 2 cups (250 g) Gruyère cheese, grated
- 1 tablespoon butter

Wine: a dry red (Chianti)

Cut the cabbage in half and then into strips. Blanch in salted, boiling water, drain well, and spread on a dishcloth to dry. § In a large skillet (frying pan), sauté the onion and garlic in the oil for 5 minutes. § Stir in the rice and season with salt and pepper. § Add the tomatoes and cook for 15 minutes, or until the rice is cooked. § Prepare the béchamel, adding half the Gruyère. § Grease an ovenproof dish and fill with alternate layers of cabbage and rice and tomatoes. § Cover with béchamel and sprinkle with the remaining cheese. Bake in a preheated oven at 350°F/180°C/gas 4 for 30 minutes.

Stuffed eggplants with provolone cheese
Melanzane farcite piccanti

Serves: 4; Preparation: 30 minutes + 1 hour to degorge the eggplants; Cooking: 40 minutes; Level of difficulty: Simple

Cut the eggplants in half lengthwise and make crosswise slits in the pulp without piercing the skin. Sprinkle with the coarse salt and place the halves face upward in a large flat dish. Cover with another dish facing upward and put a weight on top. Leave for at least 1 hour. § Drain and rinse under running water, squeeze gently and place face down on paper towels to dry. § Mix the garlic, pancetta, and two Provolone cheeses in a bowl. § Place the eggplants in an ovenproof earthenware dish with half the oil. Press the eggplants open and push the filling in the slits made earlier with the knife. § Cover with the tomatoes and sprinkle with Parmesan. Season with pepper (don't add salt, as the eggplants have already absorbed enough). § Drizzle with the remaining oil. § Pour in the stock and cook over medium-low heat for 10–15 minutes. § Bake in a preheated oven at 350°F/180°C/gas 4 for 25–30 minutes. Baste with the stock frequently. § Serve hot as a main course.

■ INGREDIENTS
- 6 long eggplants (aubergines)
- 2 tablespoons coarse salt
- 8 cloves garlic, chopped
- ½ cup (60 g) pancetta, diced
- 4 oz (125 g) each sharp and mild Provolone cheese, diced
- 1½ lb (750 g) tomatoes, peeled and chopped
- freshly ground black pepper
- ⅓ cup (50 g) freshly grated Parmesan cheese
- 4 tablespoons extra-virgin olive oil
- 1 cup *Beef* or *Vegetable stock* (see recipes p. 48)

Wine: a dry white (Lugana di Verona)

Eggplant in tomato sauce with parmesan and mozzarella cheese
Parmigiana di melanzane

A classic Italian recipe, originally from Sicily. It is a hearty dish and can be served as a complete main course. Try replacing the eggplant with 3 pounds of zucchini (courgettes) for a lighter dish.

Serves: 6-8; Preparation: 15 minutes + 1 hour to degorge the eggplants; Cooking: 50 minutes; Level of difficulty: Simple

Peel the eggplants and cut in ¼-in (6-mm) thick slices and sprinkle with coarse salt. Place in a flat dish. Cover with another dish with a weight on top. Leave for at least 1 hour. § Drain and rinse in cold water. Pat dry with paper towels. § Prepare the tomato sauce. § Dredge the eggplants in the flour. § Heat the oil in a large sauté pan, dip the eggplant slices in the egg mixture and fry until golden brown. § Drain on paper towels. § Place a layer of tomato sauce in the bottom of an ovenproof dish and cover with a layer of eggplant and a layer of Mozzarella and Parmesan. Repeat until you have several layers of each. Reserve a little tomato sauce and Parmesan for the top. § Dot with butter and bake in a preheated oven at 350°F/180°C/gas 4 for 35 minutes. § Serve hot.

■ INGREDIENTS
- 3 large round eggplants (aubergines)
- 2 tablespoons coarse salt
- 2 quantities *Simple tomato sauce* (see recipe p. 28)
- all-purpose (plain) flour to dredge
- 4 eggs, beaten with a dash of salt
- 3 cups (750 ml) oil, for frying
- 12 oz (350 g) Mozzarella cheese, thinly sliced
- 2 cups (300 g) freshly grated Parmesan cheese
- 2 tablespoons butter

Wine: a dry red (Merlot di Aprilia)

Right:
Parmigiana di melanzane

Belgian endives baked in béchamel sauce
Gratin di belga e prosciutto

■ INGREDIENTS

• 8 medium heads Belgian
  endives
• 3 tablespoons extra-virgin
  olive oil
• ½ cup (125 ml) water
• salt
• 1 quantity *Béchamel sauce*
  (see recipe p. 38)
• salt and freshly ground
  black pepper
• 1 tablespoon butter to
  grease the pan
• 8 thick slices ham
• 1 cup (125 g) freshly
  grated Gruyère cheese

Wine: a dry red
(Chianti Castelgreve)

Serves: 4; Preparation: 40 minutes; Cooking: 1 hour; Level of difficulty: Simple

Using a sharp knife, hollow out the base of the endives to remove the bitter part and ensure uniform cooking. § Place the heads in a large pan with the oil, water, and salt to taste. Cover and cook over medium heat for about 40 minutes. Drain well. § Prepare the béchamel sauce. § Wrap each endive in a slice of ham and arrange the heads in a greased ovenproof dish (place the part where the ham overlaps underneath). § Pour the béchamel over the rolls and sprinkle with the Gruyère. § Bake in a preheated oven at 350°F/180°C/gas 4 for 25 minutes, or until the topping is golden brown. § Serve hot as an entrée or main course.

Tomatoes baked with parmesan, parsley, and garlic
Pomodori in verde

■ INGREDIENTS

• 10 medium tomatoes
• 5 cloves garlic, finely
  chopped
• 1 cup (30 g) finely
  chopped parsley
• ½ cup (60 g) bread crumbs
• ½ cup (60 g) freshly
  grated Parmesan cheese
• ½ cup (125 ml) extra-virgin
  olive oil
• salt and freshly ground
  black pepper

Wine: a dry red (Bardolino)

Serves: 4-6; Preparation: 35 minutes; Cooking: 35 minutes; Level of difficulty: Simple

Cut the tomatoes in half, remove the seeds with your fingers, sprinkle with a little salt, and place upside down in a colander for 20 minutes. § Mix the garlic and parsley together in a bowl, add the bread crumbs and Parmesan, and, using a fork, work the oil in little by little. Season with salt and pepper. § Using a teaspoon, push the filling mixture into the tomato halves. Press it down with your fingers so that it sticks to the inside of the tomatoes (it will swell slightly in the oven and could overflow). § Place the filled tomatoes in a greased ovenproof dish and bake in a preheated oven at 350°F/180°C/gas 4 for 35 minutes. § Serve hot or warm as an appetizer, or as a side dish with roast beef. Perfect also with baked fish.

Left: *Pomodori in verde*

Crêpes stuffed with Swiss chard and goat's cheese

Crêpes farcite con bietolina e caprino

Serves: 6; Preparation: 60 minutes; Cooking: 30 minutes; Level of difficulty: Medium

Prepare the crêpes and set aside. § Cook the chard in a pot of salted water for 5 minutes. Drain, squeeze, and chop finely. § In a large skillet (frying pan), sauté the garlic in the butter until pale gold, then discard. § In the same skillet, sauté the chard with a dash of salt for 5 minutes. § Prepare the béchamel. § Spread the goat's cheese on the crêpes and grate a little nutmeg over the cheese. § Place 2 tablespoons of chard on half of each crêpe. § Fold the crêpes in half and then in half again to form triangles. § Grease an ovenproof dish and arrange the crêpes, overlapping, inside. § Pour the béchamel sauce over the top and sprinkle with the Gruyère. § Bake in a preheated oven at 350°F/180°C/gas 4 for 20–25 minutes. § Serve hot.

■ INGREDIENTS

- 1 quantity *Crêpes* (see recipe p. 62)
- 1½ lb (750 g) fresh Swiss chard (silver beet)
- salt and freshly ground black pepper
- 2 cloves garlic, cut in half
- 2 tablespoons butter
- 1 quantity *Béchamel sauce* (see recipe p. 38)
- 7 oz (200 g) fresh Caprino (goat's cheese)
- whole nutmeg, to grate
- ½ cup (60 g) freshly grated Gruyère cheese

Wine: a slightly sweet sparkling red (Brachetto d'Acqui)

Eggplant stuffed with chicken, mortadella, and ham

Fagottini di melanzane alla carne

Serves: 4; Preparation: 1½ hours; Cooking: 45 minutes; Level of difficulty: Simple

Cut the eggplants in ¼-in (6-mm) thick slices, sprinkle with the coarse salt and place in a flat dish. Cover with another dish facing upward with a weight on top. Leave for at least 1 hour. § Drain and rinse under cold running water. Pat dry with paper towels. § Chop the chicken, mortadella, and ham in a food processor. Place in a bowl with the Parmesan, eggs, garlic, pepper, and parsley and mix well. § Heat the frying oil in a large skillet (frying pan) and fry the eggplant, turning the slices until they are golden brown. Drain on paper towels. § Arrange the slices on a clean work bench in pairs, crosswise one over the other. Place a little filling in the middle of each pair and fold the inner slice first, followed by the outer slice. Fasten with a wooden toothpick. § Sauté the onion in the olive oil in a braiser for 5 minutes. Add the tomatoes, season with salt and pepper and cook for 5 more minutes. § Add the stuffed eggplant to the sauce and bake in a preheated oven at 350°F/180°C/gas 4 for 30 minutes. Baste with the sauce from time to time. § Serve hot with toast rubbed with garlic, or boiled potatoes with a little of the tomato sauce.

■ INGREDIENTS

- 4 medium eggplants (aubergines)
- ¼ cup (60 g) salt
- 10 oz (300 g) chicken breast
- 4 oz (125 g) mortadella
- 10 oz (300 g) ham
- 1 cup (125 g) freshly grated Parmesan cheese
- 1 egg + 1 yolk, beaten
- 2 tablespoons parsley, 3 cloves garlic, finely chopped
- freshly ground black pepper
- 2 cups (500 ml) oil, for frying
- 1 medium onion, finely chopped
- 4 tablespoons extra-virgin olive oil
- 1 15-oz (450-g) can tomatoes

Wine: a dry red (Barolo)

Right: *Crêpes farcite con bietolina e caprino*

Zucchini stuffed with almond macaroons
Zucchine farcite agli amaretti

Serves: 4; Preparation: 25 minutes; Cooking: 30 minutes; Level of difficulty: Simple

Cook the zucchini in a pot of salted, boiling water for 5 minutes. Drain and cool. § Cut in half lengthwise and, using a sharp knife, remove the pulp. § Crush the amaretti cookies and place in a bowl with the eggs, chopped zucchini pulp, Parmesan, finely chopped parsley, and salt. Blend well with a fork. § Fill the zucchini with the mixture and place in a buttered baking dish. § Sprinkle with the bread crumbs, drizzle with oil, and bake in a preheated oven at 350°F/180°C/gas 4 for 25 minutes. § Serve hot as an entrée.

■ INGREDIENTS

- 6 zucchini (courgettes)
- salt
- 1 egg + 1 yolk, beaten
- 4 tablespoons freshly grated Parmesan cheese
- 12 amaretti cookies
- 2 tablespoons parsley
- 1 tablespoon butter
- 2 tablespoons bread crumbs
- 3 tablespoons extra-virgin olive oil

Wine: a dry white (Riesling)

Zucchini and green bean pie
Plum-cake di zucchine e fagiolini

A savory, Italian version of the celebrated British fruitcake.

Serves: 6; Preparation: 30 minutes; Cooking: 1¼ hours; Level of difficulty: Medium

Cook the zucchini and beans in a pot of salted, boiling water for 10 minutes. Drain, and cut the zucchini into wheels and the beans into pieces. Dry on a clean cotton dish towel. § Melt the butter and place in a bowl with two whole eggs, two yolks, and the sugar. Beat vigorously for 2 minutes with a whisk or fork. Stir in the flour, zucchini, beans, pine nuts, and baking powder. § Beat the remaining egg whites to stiff peaks and carefully fold into the mixture. § Grease a large loaf pan with butter and pour in the mixture. § Bake in a preheated oven at 350°F/180°C/gas 4 for 1 hour. § Remove from the pan when cool and cut into thick slices. § Serve as an appetizer, or a side dish with braised meats.

■ INGREDIENTS

- 10 oz (300 g) zucchini (courgettes)
- 8 oz (250 g) green beans, cleaned
- 1 teaspoon salt
- ⅔ cup (150 g) butter
- 4 eggs
- ⅔ cup (125 g) sugar
- 1⅔ cups (250 g) all-purpose (plain) flour
- ⅔ cup (125 g) pine nuts
- 2 teaspoons baking powder
- butter to grease the cake pan

Wine: a dry red (Sangiovese di Romagna)

Baked fennel with parmesan cheese
Finocchi alla parmigiana

Serves: 4; Preparation: 15 minutes; Cooking: 25 minutes; Level of difficulty: Simple

Remove the outer leaves from each head of fennel, trim the tips and bottom, and cut in half. § Cook in salted, boiling water for 8–10 minutes, or until the fennel is cooked but still crunchy. § Drain, pat dry with paper towels, and cut into thick slices or wedges. § Melt three-quarters of the butter in a sauté pan over medium heat. Dredge the fennel slices lightly in the flour and fry in the butter until crisp and golden brown. § Place in a buttered baking dish. Sprinkle with salt, pepper, and Parmesan and dot with the remaining butter. § Bake in a preheated oven at 400°F/200°C/gas 6 for 15 minutes. § Serve hot as an entrée, or a side dish with oven-roasted fish or meat.

■ INGREDIENTS

- 5 large fennel bulbs
- salt and freshly ground black pepper
- ½ cup (125 g) butter
- ⅓ cup (50 g) all-purpose (plain) flour
- 1 cup (125 g) freshly grated Parmesan cheese

Wine: a dry white (Soave)

VARIATION
– For a richer dish: boil, slice and dry the fennel as above, then add 1 finely sliced small onion and brown with the fennel (add more butter if necessary). When brown, add 1½ cups (180 g) diced ham, 4 tablespoons fresh cream, and season with salt and pepper. Cover and reduce over low heat for about 15 minutes. Sprinkle with 1½ cups (180 g) freshly grated Parmesan and bake as above.

Right:
Porri gratinati al prosciutto

Baked leeks with béchamel and chopped ham
Porri gratinati al prosciutto

■ INGREDIENTS

• 2 lb (1 kg) fresh leeks
• salt and freshly ground
  black pepper
• 1 quantity *Béchamel sauce*
  (see recipe p. 38)
• 1 tablespoon butter
• 1 egg yolk
• 1 cup (125 g) ham, finely
  chopped
• ½ cup (60 g) freshly
  grated Gruyère cheese

Wine: a dry white (Tocai di Lison)

Serves: 4; Preparation: 15 minutes; Cooking: 45 minutes; Level of difficulty: Simple

Discard any withered leaves from the leeks and chop off the green tops. Cook in salted, boiling water for about 10 minutes, or until tender. § Prepare the béchamel and leave to cool. § Drain the leeks and sauté for 5 minutes in a skillet (frying pan) with the butter, salt, and pepper. Place in an ovenproof dish. § Combine the egg yolk and three-quarters of the ham with the béchamel, mix well, and pour over the leeks. Sprinkle with the Gruyère and remaining ham. § Bake in a preheated oven at 350°F/180°C/gas 4 for 20 minutes. § Serve hot as an entrée, or as a side dish with fish.

Baked potatoes with béchamel, ham, and walnuts

Patate gratinate con prosciutto e noci

Serves: 4-6; Preparation: 20 minutes; Cooking: 1 hour; Level of difficulty: Simple

Cook the potatoes in their skins in salted, boiling water for about 25 minutes. Drain and set aside to cool. § Prepare a rather thick béchamel sauce and stir in the Parmesan. § Peel the potatoes and cut in ½-in (1-cm) thick slices. Grease an ovenproof dish with half the butter and cover the bottom with a layer of potatoes. Fill in the gaps so that the bottom is sealed. § Cover with a layer of béchamel and sprinkle with the ham and chopped walnuts. Continue with another layer of potatoes and cover with the Mozzarella and a little béchamel sauce. Make a top layer of potatoes and cover with the remaining béchamel. Sprinkle with the bread crumbs and dot with the remaining butter. § Bake in a preheated oven at 350°F/180°C/gas 4 for 25 minutes. § Garnish with remaining walnut halves and serve hot as an entrée or main course.

- INGREDIENTS

- 2 lb (1 kg) boiling potatoes
- salt and freshly ground black pepper
- 1 quantity *Béchamel sauce* (see recipe p. 38)
- ½ cup (60 g) freshly grated Parmesan cheese
- 2 tablespoons butter
- 1¾ cups (200 g) finely chopped ham
- 1½ cups (180 g) shelled walnuts, almost all coarsely chopped
- 7 oz (200 g) Mozzarella cheese, thinly sliced
- 1 tablespoon bread crumbs

Wine: a dry red (Dolcetto d'Alba)

Potato and pumpkin pie

Torta di zucca e patate

Serves: 4; Preparation: 20 minutes; Cooking: 1¼ hours; Level of difficulty: Simple

Peel the pumpkin and cut it in slices. Cover with aluminum foil and bake in a preheated oven at 350°F/180°C/gas 4 for about 25 minutes, or until soft. § Boil the potatoes in their skins for about 25 minutes, drain, and peel. § Purée the potatoes and pumpkin together in a food processor. § Add half the butter, then the egg yolks and Parmesan. Mix rapidly, and season with salt and pepper. § Beat the egg whites to stiff peaks and fold them into the mixture. § Grease an ovenproof dish with butter and sprinkle with the bread crumbs. § Spread half the mixture evenly in the bottom of the dish and cover with the Mozzarella. Cover with the rest of the mixture. § Use a spoon to level, sprinkle with the Parmesan, and dot with the remaining butter. Bake in a preheated oven at 350°F/180°C/gas 4 for 50 minutes. § Serve hot with a green salad as a main course or light lunch, or as side dish with roast lamb or barbecued pork.

- INGREDIENTS

- 1 lb (500 g) pumpkin,
- 1 lb (500 g) boiling potatoes
- ⅓ cup (90 g) butter
- 4 eggs, separated
- 1 cup (125 g) freshly grated Parmesan cheese
- salt and freshly ground black pepper
- 2 tablespoons bread crumbs
- 12 oz (350 g) Mozzarella cheese, sliced

Wine: a dry red (Barbaresco)

Right: *Patate gratinate con prosciutto e noci*

Onions stuffed with brown rice and oregano
Cipolle farcite di riso integrale

Serves: 4; Preparation: 25 minutes; Cooking: 1½ hours; Level of difficulty: Medium

Cook the rice in a large pot of salted, boiling water and drain. § Peel the onions, trim the bottoms and slice off the tops. Cook for 7–8 minutes in a pot of salted, boiling water. Set aside to cool. § Hollow out the onions with a sharp knife leaving a ½-in (1-cm) thick shell. Set the pulp aside. § Beat the eggs in a bowl, and add the rice, half the oregano, Parmesan, Pecorino, chopped olives, salt, and pepper. Mix well. § Spoon the filling into the onions and sprinkle with the remaining oregano. § In a bowl, mix 4 tablespoons of onion pulp, the halved olives, 1 tablespoon of olive oil, salt, and pepper, and pour into an ovenproof dish. § Arrange the stuffed onions in the dish and pour the remaining oil, the wine, and stock over the top. Dot each onion with butter. § Bake in a preheated oven at 350°F/180°C/gas 4 for 40 minutes. § Serve hot as an entrée.

■ INGREDIENTS

- 1¼ cups (250 g) brown rice
- 8 large onions
- salt and pepper
- 3 eggs
- 2 tablespoons oregano
- ½ cup (60 g) freshly grated Parmesan cheese
- 1 cup (125 g) freshly grated Pecorino romano cheese
- 1½ cups (180 g) pitted black olives
- 4 tablespoons extra-virgin olive oil
- 1 cup (250 ml) dry white wine
- 1 cup (250 ml) *Vegetable stock (see recipe p. 48)*
- 2 tablespoons butter

Wine: a dry red (Freisa d'Asti)

Spinach and potato appetizers
Ciuffetti di patate e spinaci

Serves: 8; Preparation: 30 minutes; Cooking: 1 hour; Level of difficulty: Medium

Boil the potatoes in their skins for about 25 minutes. § Drain, peel, and mash. § Put the purée in a saucepan and add two-thirds of the butter, the salt, pepper, nutmeg, and milk. Place over low heat and, stirring constantly, dry out excess moisture. Set aside to cool. § Cook the spinach in a pot of salted, boiling water until tender (3–4 minutes if frozen, 8–10 minutes if fresh). Drain well and squeeze out excess moisture. Chop finely. § Beat the egg and one yolk together and mix well with the potato purée. § Divide the potato purée in two and mix the spinach and a dash of salt into one half. If the mixture is too moist, stir over low heat to dry. § Grease a baking sheet, spoon the potato mixture into a pastry bag, and squeeze out into walnut-sized rosettes. Repeat with the spinach mixture. § Beat the remaining egg yolk and brush the rosettes with it. § Bake in a preheated oven at 400°F/200°C/gas 6 for 20 minutes. § Scoop the rosettes off the sheet with a spatula and serve hot as appetizers.

■ INGREDIENTS

- 2 lb (1 kg) boiling potatoes
- ½ cup (125 g) butter
- salt and freshly ground black pepper
- dash of nutmeg
- 1 cup (250 ml) milk
- 1 lb (500 g) fresh or frozen spinach
- 1 egg + 2 yolks

Wine: a dry sparkling red (Lambrusco di Sorbara)

Right:
Cipolle farcite di riso integrale

■ INGREDIENTS

- 1 quantity *Puff pastry* (see recipe p. 56)
- 6 *large onions, thinly sliced*
- 4 tablespoons butter
- 2 cups (500 ml) dry white wine
- 1 cup (250 ml) *Vegetable stock* (see recipe p. 48) or water
- 1 beef stock cube
- 2½ cups (280 g) dried beans, such as garbanzo beans (chickpeas)
- ¾ cup (200 g) fresh creamy cheese, such as Robiola or Mascarpone
- 1 teaspoon fresh mint

Wine: a dry white (Tocai)

Onion pie
Crostata di cipolla

Serves: 6; Preparation: 20 minutes + 1½ hours for the pastry; Cooking: 1 hour; Level of difficulty: Simple

Prepare the pastry dough. § In a large skillet (frying pan), sauté the onions in the butter. Season with salt and pepper. When the onions are soft, add the wine, followed by the vegetable stock and beef stock cube. § Simmer over low heat for 30 minutes, or until the onions are creamy. If the liquid evaporates during cooking, add water or more stock. § On a clean, lightly floured work bench, roll out the pastry dough and use it to line a greased ovenproof 10-in (25-cm) pie plate. Prick the dough with a fork. § Cover the pie crust with a sheet of aluminum foil, weigh it down with the dried beans, and bake in a preheated oven at 375°F/190°C/gas 5 for 35 minutes. § Remove the foil and beans and bake for 10 minutes more. § Set aside to cool, then spread with creamy cheese. § Spread a layer of onion over the cheese and sprinkle with the mint. § Serve hot or at room temperature.

■ INGREDIENTS

- 1 quantity *Puff pastry* (see recipe p. 56)
- 2 red bell peppers
- 4 zucchini (courgettes)
- 4 large carrots
- salt and freshly ground black pepper
- 3 tablespoons extra-virgin olive oil
- 2 tablespoons butter
- ½ cup (125 g) white wine
- 2½ cups (280 g) dried beans, such as garbanzo beans (chickpeas)

Wine: a dry white (Est! Est!! Est!!! di Montefiascone)

Vegetable pie
Crostata di verdure miste

Serves: 6; Preparation: 20 minutes + 1½ hours for the pastry; Cooking: 1 hour; Level of difficulty: Simple

Prepare the pastry dough. § Cut the bell peppers in thin strips, the zucchini in wheels, and the carrots in ribbons. § Sauté the bell peppers, a dash of salt, and the oil in a skillet over high heat for 10 minutes, stirring frequently. Take the bell peppers out and set aside. § Use the same oil to sauté the zucchini with a dash of salt. Remove from the skillet and set aside. § Use a paper towel to eliminate the oil in the skillet. Put the butter, carrots, wine, and a pinch of salt in it and cook until the liquid has evaporated and the carrots are tender. Set the carrots aside. § On a clean, lightly floured work bench, roll out the pastry dough and use it to line a greased ovenproof pie plate 10 in (25 cm) in diameter. Prick the dough with a fork. § Cover the pie crust with a sheet of aluminum foil, weigh it down with the dried beans, and bake in a preheated oven at 375°F/190°C/gas 5 for 35 minutes. § Remove the foil and beans and bake for 10 minutes more. § Garnish with the vegetables and serve as an appetizer, or with a platter of fresh cheeses (Ricotta, Mozzarella, Stracchino, Robiola, Caprino, or Mascarpone) as a light lunch.

Left: *Crostata di verdure miste*

Broccoli and leek pie

Crostata di broccoli e porri

Both the broccoli and leek pie and the pea and artichoke pie
(see variation) freeze well. Prepare them ahead of time.
They make a delicious lunch for unexpected guests.

Serves: 6; Preparation: 1 hour + 1 hour for the pastry; Cooking: 1½ hours; Level of difficulty: Medium

Prepare the pastry dough and set it aside in the refrigerator. § Cut the root and the green tops off the leeks and chop the white parts into fairly thin wheels. § Put the leeks in a sauté pan with the oil, cover and cook for 15 minutes. Remove from heat and set aside. § Dry the oil in the pan with paper towels and sauté the pancetta until crispy and brown. Set aside. § Divide the broccoli into florets with ½-in (1-cm) stems and cook in a pot of salted, boiling water for 7–10 minutes, or until cooked. § Roll out the pastry dough and use it to line a greased 10-in (25-cm) pie plate. Press the dough into the bottom and sides so it sticks to the plate. Prick well with a fork. Cover the pie crust with a sheet of aluminum foil and weigh it down with the dried beans. § Bake in a preheated oven at 350°F/180°C/gas 4 for 15 minutes, remove the foil and garbanzo beans and bake for 5 minutes more. § In the meantime, beat the eggs in a bowl and add the milk, cream, Parmesan, salt, and pepper. Beat with a whisk until frothy. § Put the leeks and broccoli in the baked pie shell, sprinkle with the pancetta, and pour the eggs and cheese over the top. § Bake in a preheated oven at 350°F/180°C/gas 4, turning the plate from time to time to make sure the pie cooks evenly. After 35 minutes check if the cream is cooked by sticking a toothpick into it; if it comes out damp, cook for 5–10 minutes more. § Serve hot as an entrée or snack.

■ INGREDIENTS

- 1 quantity *Plain pastry* (see recipe p. 58)
- 2 medium leeks
- 1½ tablespoons extra-virgin olive oil
- 1¼ cups (150 g) diced pancetta
- 1 lb (500 g) broccoli
- 1 tablespoon butter
- salt and freshly ground black pepper
- 2½ cups (280 g) dried beans, such as garbanzo beans (chickpeas)
- 3 eggs + 2 yolks
- 1½ cups (375 ml) milk
- 1 cup (250 ml) heavy (double) cream
- ¾ cup (90 g) freshly grated Parmesan cheese

Wine: a dry white
(Isonzo Sauvignon)

VARIATION
– An alternative pie can be made by replacing the leeks and broccoli with peas and artichokes. Prepare the peas (8 oz/250 g) and 4 artichokes as indicated in the recipes *Piselli primavera al prezzemolo e prosciutto* (see p. 610) and *Spezzatino di carciofi* (see p. 600). The vegetables should be well drained of cooking juices before placing them in the pie shell. Cover with the eggs and cheese and bake and serve as above.

Right:
Crostata di broccoli e porri

Fried Vegetables

Even in tolerant Italy, serving crispy-fried golden
vegetables is considered rather sinful. But by following one
or two simple rules (see page 27 for instructions on how
to fry food), the damage can be kept to a minimum. Fried
vegetables need to be eaten hot, so prepare them ahead
of time and serve them as you cook.

Fried pumpkin marinated with mint and pine nuts
Zucca fritta alla menta e pinoli

Serves: 4; Preparation: 20 minutes + 3 hours marinating; Cooking: 30 minutes; Level of difficulty: Simple

Cut the pumpkin into bite-sized pieces and flour lightly. § Heat the frying oil to very hot and fry the pumpkin a few pieces at a time for 7–8 minutes. When the pieces are cooked, drain on paper towels. § Clean the oil, top up if necessary, and repeat until all the pumpkin is cooked. § Place on a serving dish and sprinkle with the garlic, half the mint, anchovy fillets, salt, and pepper. Dress with the olive oil and vinegar, and mix carefully. Set aside to marinate for at least 3 hours. § Add the pine nuts and remaining mint just before serving.

■ INGREDIENTS

- 2 lb (1 kg) pumpkin
- ¾ cup (110 g) all-purpose (plain) flour
- 2 cups (500 ml) oil, for frying
- 3 cloves garlic, sliced
- 30 fresh mint leaves
- 16 anchovy fillets, crumbled
- salt and freshly ground black pepper
- 3 tablespoons extra-virgin olive oil
- 2 tablespoons apple vinegar
- ⅓ cup (60 g) pine nuts, sautéed in a little oil for 2–3 minutes

Crispy-fried green tomatoes
Pomodori verdi fritti

This dish is comes from Tuscany, where it is served often throughout the summer months.

Serves: 4-6; Preparation: 15 minutes; Cooking: 40-50 minutes; Level of difficulty: Simple

Cut the tomatoes into ½-in (1-cm) thick slices. Discard the first and last slices which have skin on one side. § Place four bowls side by side and fill the first with the flour, the second with the beaten eggs and beer, and the last two with the bread crumbs. § Heat the frying oil in a large skillet (frying pan) until very hot. § Dip the tomato slices into the flour; make sure they are well-covered and shake off any excess. Flour all the slices and set them on paper towels. Don't lay the floured slices on top of each other. § Dip the slices in the egg, turn a couple of times, drain and pass to the first bowl of bread crumbs. Turn several times until they are well-coated. § Repeat with the second bowl of bread crumbs (which are drier). § Place a few slices in the hot oil and fry for about 10 minutes, or until they are golden brown. Turn them over carefully at least twice using tongs or two forks. § Clean the oil of any residue and top up if necessary. Continue to fry until all the tomatoes are cooked. § Drain the fried slices on paper towels and sprinkle with salt. § Serve hot on a heated serving dish as an appetizer, or side dish with mixed grilled meats.

■ INGREDIENTS

- 6 large green tomatoes
- 1 cup (150 g) all-purpose (plain) flour
- 4 eggs, beaten
- 5 cups (625 g) fine bread crumbs
- ⅓ cup (90 ml) beer
- 2 cups (500 ml) oil, for frying
- salt

Wine: a dry red (Chianti Classico)

Right:
Pomodori verdi fritti

Swiss chard and spinach fritters
Fagottini di bietola e spinaci

Serves: 6; Preparation: 30 minutes + 1 hour for the pastry; Cooking: 50 minutes; Level of difficulty: Simple

Prepare the pastry dough. § Cook the chard and spinach in a pot of salted, boiling water until tender (3–4 minutes if frozen, 8–10 minutes if fresh). Drain, cool under cold running water, squeeze out excess moisture, and chop finely. § Beat the 2 eggs in a bowl and add the Ricotta, Mozzarella, Parmesan, salt, and pepper, and mix well. § Add the chard and spinach and mix well. § Roll the pastry dough out on a clean, floured work surface until very thin. Cut into 4-in (10-cm) squares. § Place a little filling at the center of each and fold in half. Beat the remaining egg yolk and brush the edges of each square before pressing firmly to seal. § Heat the frying oil in a large skillet (frying pan) until very hot. § Fry the fritters in the oil for about 10 minutes, or until golden brown. Turn using tongs or two spoons. § Serve hot as an appetizer.

■ INGREDIENTS

• 1 quantity *Plain pastry* (see recipe p. 58)
• 12 oz (350 g) fresh or frozen Swiss chard (silver beet)
• 12 oz (350 g) fresh or frozen spinach
• salt and freshly ground black pepper
• 2 eggs + 1 yolk
• 1 cup (250 g) Ricotta cheese, crumbled
• ⅔ cup (150 g) Mozzarella cheese, diced
• 1 cup (125 g) freshly grated Parmesan cheese
• 2 cups (500 ml) oil, for frying

Wine: a young, dry red (Rosso di Montalcino)

Fried cauliflower florets with vinegar marinade
Cavolfiore fritto marinato

Serves: 4; Preparation: 15 minutes; Cooking: 40 minutes; Level of difficulty: Simple

Cook the cauliflower florets in a pot of salted, boiling water for 4–5 minutes, or until just tender. Drain well, and place on a cotton dishcloth to dry. § Combine the beaten eggs with the beer. § Heat the frying oil in a large skillet (frying pan) until very hot. § Place the flour in a bowl, dip the florets in, turn a few times and shake off excess. § When the oil is hot, dip about 10 florets in the egg mixture. Coat well and transfer to the pan. § Turn a couple of times with two forks or tongs. Fry for about 10 minutes, or until golden brown all over. § Remove from the skillet and drain on paper towels. § Repeat until all the florets are fried. Sprinkle with salt. § To prepare the marinade, place the vinegar in a small saucepan with the scallions. Boil for 5–6 minutes, then add the thyme, and remove from heat. Pour into a serving bowl. § Serve the marinade and cauliflower florets hot as an appetizer, or as a side dish with fried chicken or oven-roasted fish.

■ INGREDIENTS

• 1 small cauliflower (about 1 lb/500 g), divided in florets
• salt and freshly ground black pepper
• 3 eggs, beaten until foamy
• ¼ cup (60 ml) beer
• 2 cups (500 ml) oil, for frying
• 1 cup (150 g) all-purpose (plain) flour
• 1 cup (250 ml) white wine vinegar
• 2 scallions (spring onions), finely chopped
• 1 teaspoon fresh or ½ teaspoon dry thyme

Wine: a dry red (Pinot Nero)

Left: *Cavolfiore fritto marinato*

Tomato croquettes
Crocchette di pomodoro

■ INGREDIENTS

Serves: 4; Preparation: 20 minutes; Cooking: 40 minutes; Level of difficulty: Medium

Peel the tomatoes, squeeze out the seeds, chop coarsely, and set in a colander to drain. § Place the Ricotta and egg yolk in a bowl and mix to a smooth paste. § Add the tomatoes, parsley, nutmeg, salt, and pepper and mix well. § Prepare 3 separate bowls: one with the flour, one with the egg, and one with the bread crumbs. § Heat the frying oil in a large skillet (frying pan) until very hot. § Shape the mixture into croquettes about 2 in (5 cm) long and 1 in (2.5 cm) thick. If the mixture is not firm enough, add 1–2 tablespoons of dry bread crumbs or freshly grated Parmesan cheese. § Roll the croquettes in the flour, dip in the egg, and roll in the bread crumbs. Fry a few at a time for about 10 minutes, or until golden brown. Turn with tongs or a fork during cooking. § Use a slotted spoon to scoop them out and drain on paper towels. § Serve hot as appetizers, or a side dish with fried meat or fish.

- 10 oz (300 g) tomatoes
- ⅔ cup (150 g) Ricotta cheese, crumbled
- 1 egg (beaten until foamy) + 1 yolk
- 1½ tablespoons finely chopped parsley
- dash of nutmeg
- salt and freshly ground black pepper
- 1 cup (150 g) all-purpose (plain) flour
- 1 cup (125 g) bread crumbs
- 3 cups (750 ml) oil, for frying

Wine: a dry, fruity white (Vermentino)

Fried porcini mushrooms
Funghi porcini fritti

■ INGREDIENTS

This recipe calls for fresh, high-quality porcini mushrooms. If you can't get them, use fresh brown cremini or white mushrooms in their place. For a richer dish, coat the raw mushroom slices in batter (see recipe p. 54) and fry as below.

Serves: 4; Preparation: 15 minutes; Cooking: 25 minutes; Level of difficulty: Simple

Trim the roots from the mushrooms and carefully peel the bottom of the stem if discolored or dirty. § Detach the stems from the caps and rinse under cold running water, removing any dirt with your fingers. Set aside to dry on paper towels. § Cut the stems and caps in slices about ¼-in (6-mm) thick. § Dredge the slices in the flour, coating well, and shake to eliminate any excess. § Heat the frying oil in a large skillet (frying pan) until very hot. Fry the mushrooms a few pieces at a time until golden brown. Cook all the stems first, then the caps. § Drain on paper towels, sprinkle with salt, and serve immediately as an appetizer or side dish.

- 1¼ lb (600 g) fresh porcini mushrooms
- 1 cup (150 g) all-purpose (plain) flour
- 3 cups (750 ml) oil, for frying
- salt

Wine: a dry red (Collio di Pinot Nero)

Right: *Funghi porcini fritti*

Salvia fritta
Fried fresh sage leaves

Don't use an iron skillet to fry the leaves because it could react chemically with the sage.

Serves: 4; Preparation: 10 minutes; Cooking: 5 minutes; Level of difficulty: Simple

Wash the leaves, pat dry with paper towels, and dredge in the flour. § Dip in the egg and coat well with bread crumbs. § Heat the frying oil in a large skillet (frying pan) to very hot and add half the leaves. They will turn golden brown almost instantly. Turn once, then scoop out with a slotted spoon. Drain on paper towels. § Sprinkle with salt and serve as an appetizer or snack. For a sweeter version, add 1 teaspoon of sugar to the salt before sprinkling.

■ INGREDIENTS

- 40 large fresh sage leaves
- 2 tablespoons all-purpose (plain) flour
- 1 large egg, beaten until foamy with a pinch of salt
- 1½ cups (180 g) bread crumbs
- 2 cups (500 ml) oil, for frying

Wine: a dry (or sweet) sparkling white (Asti Spumante)

INGREDIENTS

- 3 lb (1.5 kg) boiling potatoes
- salt and freshly ground black pepper
- 1 lb (500 g) fresh or 12 oz (350 g) frozen spinach
- 1 egg + 1 yolk, beaten
- ½ cup (60 g) freshly grated Parmesan cheese
- 5 oz (150 g) Taleggio or Fontina cheese, cut in ¼-inch cubes
- 2 cups (250 g) bread crumbs
- 3 cups (750 ml) oil, for frying

*Wine: a dry white
(Pinot Grigio)*

Spinach croquettes
Crocchette di spinaci

Serves: 4-6; Preparation: 30 minutes; Cooking: 1 hour; Level of difficulty: Simple

Cook the potatoes in their skins in a pot of salted, boiling water for about 25 minutes. Drain, peel, and mash. § Cook the spinach in a pot of salted, boiling water until tender (3–4 minutes if frozen, 8–10 minutes if fresh). Drain, cool under cold running water, squeeze out excess moisture, and chop finely. § Combine with the potatoes and mix well. § Put the eggs in a bowl with the salt, pepper, potatoes, spinach, and Parmesan and blend with a fork until smooth. § Place a tablespoonful of the mixture in the palm of your hand. Press a cube of cheese into the center and close the mixture round to make an oblong croquette. The cheese must be completely covered. Roll in the bread crumbs. § Heat the frying oil in a large skillet (frying pan) until very hot. § Fry the croquettes a few at a time, turning them in the oil so that they are golden brown all over. Remove with a slotted spoon and drain on paper towels. Repeat until all the croquettes are cooked. § Serve hot as appetizers, or with a mixed salad as a main course.

> VARIATION
> – Replace the spinach with porcini mushrooms (see recipe *Funghi porcini trifolati* p. 608). In this case, either omit the cheese or use Mozzarella.

INGREDIENTS

- 1¼ lb (600 g) potatoes
- 2 eggs, beaten
- 2 tablespoons all-purpose (plain) flour
- salt and freshly ground black pepper
- 2 cups (500 ml) oil, for frying

*Wine: a dry rosé
(Lagrein Rosato)*

Potato patties
Frittelle di patate

Serves: 4; Preparation: 15 minutes; Cooking: 15-20 minutes; Level of difficulty: Simple

Peel the potatoes and grate into julienne strips with a grater. Rinse them in plenty of cold water, drain well, and spread on a cotton dishcloth to dry. § Place the eggs, flour, salt, and pepper in a bowl, add the potatoes and mix well. If the mixture is not firm enough, add a little more flour to thicken. § Heat the frying oil in a large skillet (frying pan) until very hot. Place 6–8 widely separated tablespoons of the mixture in the oil. Brown on one side then turn carefully and brown on the other. § Scoop the patties out with a slotted spoon and drain on paper towels. § Serve hot as appetizers, or as a side dish with fried meat or fish dishes.

Left: *Crocchette di spinaci*

Mixed fried summer vegetables
Fritto misto estivo

In winter, replace the summer vegetables with artichoke wedges, carrots and potatoes cut in sticks, sliced fennel, and florets of broccoli. The procedure is the same except that the fennel and broccoli must be cooked first in salted, boiling water until just tender and dried on paper towels before flouring.

Serves: 4-6; Preparation: 20 minutes; Cooking: 50 minutes; Level of difficulty: Simple

Cut the zucchini in half crosswise, and cut each half in quarters lengthwise. If you are using long eggplants, slice in ¼ in (6 mm) wheels. If you are using the larger, pear-shaped eggplants, cut in ¼-in (6-mm) thick slices and cut each slice in halves or quarters (depending on how big they are). § Trim the stems of the zucchini flowers and wash carefully. Place on paper towels to dry. § Put the flour in a large bowl next to another containing the eggs and beer. § Heat the frying oil in a large skillet (frying pan) until very hot. § Flour the vegetables, shake off any excess, and dip in the egg. Shake off excess egg. § Begin frying a few pieces at a time; if there are too many in the skillet at once they will stick together. § Turn the vegetables as they turn brown. When all the pieces are golden brown, scoop them up with a slotted spoon and drain on paper towels. Repeat until all the vegetables are cooked. § Sprinkle with salt and serve hot as an entrée, or as a side dish with fried or roast meat or fish dishes.

■ INGREDIENTS

- 4 zucchini (courgettes)
- 4 eggplants (aubergines)
- 12 large zucchini (courgette) flowers
- 2 cups (300 g) all-purpose (plain) flour
- 4 eggs, beaten
- ⅓ cup (90 ml) beer
- 3 cups (750 ml) oil, for frying
- salt

Wine: a dry white (Frascati)

Crispy-fried onion rings
Anelli di cipolla croccanti

Serves: 4; Preparation: 20 minutes + 1 hour for the batter; Cooking: 20 minutes; Level of difficulty: Simple

Prepare the batter. § Peel the onions and chop in ¼ in (6 mm) slices. Separate the rings and leave them to dry for a few minutes. § Heat the frying oil in a large skillet (frying pan) until very hot. § Beat the egg white to stiff peaks and fold into the batter. § Dip the rings in the batter one by one, let the excess batter drip off, and fry to golden brown, turning once or twice with tongs or a fork. Remember to keep the oil clean. § Drain on paper towels. § Serve hot as an appetizer.

■ INGREDIENTS

- 4 medium onions
- 1 quantity *Batter* (see recipe p. 54)
- 1 egg white
- 2 cups (500 ml) oil, for frying

Wine: a dry, sparkling white (Prosecco di Conegliano)

Right:

Fritto misto estivo

Grilled Vegetables

Cooking vegetables quickly under a broiler, in a grill pan, or over a barbecue enhances their natural flavors. Experiment with the dishes here, then try grilling a selection of different vegetables together and serve with oil, finely chopped parsley, and garlic as a light and healthy lunch, or as a second course after a hearty pasta dish.

Stuffed zucchini rolls
Involtini di zucchine grigliate

Serves: 4; Preparation: 15 minutes; Cooking: 10 minutes; Level of difficulty: Simple

Cut the tops off the zucchini and cut lengthwise in ⅛-in (3-mm) slices. § Heat the grill pan until hot and cook the slices over medium-high heat for about 3 minutes on each side. Transfer to a plate. § Put the Caprino in a bowl and mash with a fork. Add the tuna and mix well. Season with salt and pepper, add the parsley, and blend vigorously until the mixture is smooth. § Place 2–3 teaspoons of filling on each zucchini slice, add some basil and roll up, fastening with a wooden toothpick. § Place the rolls on a serving dish. Sprinkle with capers and basil leaves, and drizzle with oil. § Serve at room temperature as appetizers.

■ INGREDIENTS

- 4 large, long zucchini (courgettes)
- 1½ cups (350 g) Caprino (goat's) cheese
- 1 cup (200 g) tuna, packed in olive oil, crumbled
- salt and freshly ground black pepper
- 1 tablespoon parsley, finely chopped
- 1½ tablespoons capers
- 15 basil leaves, torn
- 3 tablespoons extra-virgin olive oil

Wine: a dry white (Verduzzo)

Grilled eggplants in oil and chile sauce
Melanzane alla griglia in olio piccante

Eggplants are now available throughout the year, but for successful grilling be sure to use them in their natural season—summer—when their full, flagrant flavor is at its peak. They can be served al naturale (sprinkled with a little finely chopped parsley and garlic and bathed in olive oil) or with the delicious spicy sauce given here. For an even richer flavor, sprinkle the grilled eggplants with 1 tablespoon of fresh oregano. Covered with oil, they will keep in the refrigerator for several days.

Serves: 4-6; Preparation: 15 minutes; Cooking: 20 minutes; Level of difficulty: Simple

Chop the ends off the eggplants and cut in ½-in (1-cm) thick slices. § Heat the grill pan to very hot and place the slices on it. Press them down with a fork so the eggplant adheres to the pan. Turn the slices after about 30 seconds (they will have black stripes on the cooked side). Eggplant cooks quickly so don't let the slices dry out. § As soon as the pulp is soft, remove from the grill pan and arrange on the serving dish. § Put the chilies, salt, and pepper in the oil and beat with a fork for a few minutes. Cover and set aside. § When the eggplants are all cooked, pour the spicy oil over the top and garnish with the basil leaves. § Serve warm or at room temperature as an appetizer, or side dish with mixed barbecued meats or fish.

■ INGREDIENTS

- 4 large round eggplants (aubergines)
- 2 hot chile peppers, finely chopped, or 1 teaspoon crushed chilies
- salt and freshly ground black pepper
- 1 cup (250 ml) extra-virgin olive oil
- 10 fresh basil leaves, torn

Wine: a dry red (Rossese di Dolceacqua)

Right: *Melanzane alla griglia in olio piccante*

- 8 medium ripe tomatoes
- salt and freshly ground black pepper
- 2 heaped tablespoons oregano
- 16 fresh basil leaves, torn
- 4 tablespoons extra-virgin olive oil to drizzle

Wine: a dry red (Refosco)

Grilled tomatoes
Pomodori rossi alla griglia

Serves: 4; Preparation: 10 minutes; Cooking: 15 minutes; Level of difficulty: Simple

Cut the tomatoes in half and squeeze out the seeds with your fingers. Place the halves upside down for 2–3 minutes. § Heat the grill pan to hot. § Sprinkle the tomatoes with salt, pepper, and oregano. § Place the tomatoes on the grill pan skin-side-down and cook over high heat without turning for about 15 minutes, or until they are cooked. § Remove from the pan, place a basil leaf in the center of each, and drizzle with the oil. § Serve hot on toasted whole-wheat or homemade bread as an appetizer, or as a side dish with grilled meat or fish.

■ INGREDIENTS

• 2 long zucchini
  (courgettes)
• 1 long eggplant
  (aubergine)
• 1 medium onion
• 1 small red, 1 small yellow,
  and 1 small green bell
  pepper (capsicum)
• 2½ tablespoons extra-
  virgin olive oil
• salt and freshly ground
  black pepper
• ½ teaspoon paprika
• juice of ½ lemon
• 1 teaspoon dried or
  1 tablespoon chopped
  fresh herbs (oregano,
  mint, or thyme)

*Wine: a dry, sparkling white
(Prosecco di Conegliano)*

Skewered mixed vegetables
Spiedini misti variopinti

Serves: 4; Preparation: 25 minutes + 2 hours marinating; Cooking: 20 minutes; Level of difficulty: Simple

Cut the zucchini in wheels. Chop the eggplant in thick slices, then divide them in 4. Divide the onion in 4 wedges, then cut each wedge in half. Cut the bell peppers in 1-in (2.5-cm) squares. § Thread the vegetable pieces onto wooden skewers. Set them on a plate. Prepare at least two skewers per person. § Place the oil, salt, pepper, paprika, lemon juice, and herbs in a small bowl and beat vigorously with a fork until the sauce is well mixed. § Pour over the skewers, cover with aluminum foil, and marinate in the refrigerator for 2 hours. § Heat a grill pan over high heat until very hot, drain the skewers, and place half of them in the pan. Cook for about 10 minutes, turning them so that they brown on all sides. Repeat with the remaining skewers. § Serve hot as a side dish with grilled meats or fish, or garnish with squares of grilled polenta and serve as an appetizer.

■ INGREDIENTS

• 4 heads fresh Belgian
  endives
• 4 heads red radicchio
• salt and freshly ground
  black pepper
• 4 tablespoons extra-
  virgin olive oil

*Wine: a dry white
(Soave Classico)*

Grilled Belgian endives and radicchio
Insalata belga e radicchio rosso alla griglia

Belgian endives and radicchio are both part of the chicory family. Radicchio can be very bitter; try to buy the long tapering variety with mottled red leaves called Radicchio di Treviso.

Serves: 4; Preparation: 10 minutes; Cooking: 15 minutes; Level of difficulty: Simple

Trim the bases of the Belgian endives and radicchio, remove any withered leaves, and cut the heads in half. § Heat a grill pan until very hot, then lower heat to medium, and place the Belgian endives and radicchio in it. § Cover with a lid or sheet of aluminum foil during the first 5 minutes of cooking, then uncover and turn often until cooked. § Arrange the endives and radicchio in alternate red and white strips in a preheated serving dish. Sprinkle with salt and pepper and drizzle with the oil. § For a delicious and healthy light lunch, serve hot on a bed of boiled brown rice and garnish with wedges of cherry tomatoes and freshly grated Pecorino romano cheese.

Left: *Spiedini misti variopinti*

Grilled wild mushrooms on toast with herb butter
Porcini alla griglia

The Italian recipe calls for fresh porcini, but you can use other wild mushrooms in their place. Experiment with shiitake, chanterelle, hedgehog, cremini, or portobello mushrooms (or a mixture).

Serves: 4; Preparation: 10 minutes; Cooking: 10-15 minutes; Level of difficulty: Simple

Remove any dirt from the mushrooms, trim the tough parts off the stems, and rinse carefully under cold running water. Dry with paper towels. § Detach the stems and slice them in half lengthwise. Make small slits with a sharp knife in the caps and stems and insert the garlic and thyme. Make at least 4 slits per cap and 2 per stem. § Mix the oil, salt, and pepper in a small bowl and drizzle it over the mushrooms. Set aside for a few minutes. § Place the butter, garlic, scallions, parsley, salt, and pepper in a small bowl and mix until smooth. Set aside. § Heat a grill pan to very hot and place the mushrooms in it, beginning with the stems (which may take a little longer to cook, depending on the type of mushroom). § Cook for 5–7 minutes, turning often so they don't stick. § Prepare slices of toast made with whole-wheat or homemade bread, spread with the herb butter, and distribute the mushrooms on top. § Serve immediately as an appetizer or snack.

■ INGREDIENTS

- 1½ lb (750 g) whole fresh wild mushrooms (shiitake, chanterelle, hedgehog, cremini, portobello)
- 4 cloves garlic, sliced
- 4 tablespoons fresh or 2 tablespoons dried thyme
- salt and freshly ground black pepper
- 4 tablespoons extra-virgin olive oil
- ½ cup (125 g) butter, softened
- 1 clove garlic, finely chopped
- 1 tablespoon scallions, finely chopped
- 2 tablespoons finely chopped parsley

Wine: a dry red (Chianti Classico Aziano)

Skewered grilled onions with bay leaves
Spiedini di cipolline e alloro

Serves: 4; Preparation: 10 minutes; Cooking: 20 minutes; Level of difficulty: Simple

Blanch the onions in a pot of salted, boiling water for 5 minutes. § Drain, dry, and thread onto 4 skewers (5 onions each, alternated with a half bay leaf). Skewer the onions horizontally so that they will lie flat in the grill pan during cooking. § Drizzle with oil and cook in a hot grill pan, turning often. Cook for about 15 minutes, or until the onions are golden brown. § Sprinkle with salt and pepper and serve as appetizers, or with sausages.

■ INGREDIENTS

- 20 small white onions, peeled
- 8 bay leaves, cut in half
- 1 tablespoon extra-virgin olive oil
- salt and freshly ground black pepper

Wine: a dry red (Pinot Nero)

Right: *Spiedini di cipolline e alloro*

Grilled bell peppers in garlic, parsley, and oil
Peperoni bruciati

Preparing this delicious dish takes a little time, but is definitely worth the effort.
The grilled bell peppers will keep in the refrigerator for about 6 days (cover well with oil),
so you can double or even triple the quantities given here.

Serves: 4; Preparation: 1 hour; Cooking: 30 minutes; Level of difficulty: Simple

Heat the grill pan to very hot. Place as many whole peppers in the pan as will fit and press down with a lid. The skins of the peppers must burn completely black. Turn them when one side is black. The peppers become soft as they cook; turn them often as they soften to avoid burning the pulp. § Wrap each cooked pepper in 2–3 layers of paper towels (they are easier to peel if kept warm). § When all the peppers are cooked, remove the blackened skins with your fingers and paper towels. § Remove the core, stem, seeds, and filaments. § Flatten the cleaned pieces and cut them into strips. § Place them on a serving dish and dress with the garlic, capers, basil, mint, salt, and plenty of oil. § Mix carefully and set aside for at least 1 hour before serving. § Serve as an appetizer with slices of toasted whole-wheat bread.

■ INGREDIENTS

- 5 large, fleshy, fresh bell peppers (capsicums) of different colors
- 5 cloves garlic, thinly sliced
- ½ cup (60 g) capers
- 20 fresh basil leaves, cut into strips
- 15 mint leaves, whole
- salt
- ½ cup (125 ml) extra-virgin olive oil

Wine: a dry red
(Recioto di Valpolicella)

Grilled onions filled with fresh creamy cheese
Cipolle grigliate con formaggio dolce fresco

If you have an open fire or barbecue, bury the onions in the hot coals or ashes for about 35
minutes. They will have an even more delicious, smoky flavor.

Serves: 4; Preparation: 10 minutes; Cooking: 45 minutes; Level of difficulty: Simple

Trim the onions top and bottom, taking a larger slice from the top. § Wrap each onion in a piece of aluminum foil. § Heat the grill pan over high heat until very hot. Place the onions in it and lower heat to medium so that the onions cook slowly. Turn from time to time. § After about 45 minutes, pierce an onion through the center with a wooden skewer. If it goes in easily, the onions are done; if the center still feels hard or moist continue cooking for 5–10 minutes. § Remove from the grill and cut in half, season with oil, salt, and pepper, and place half a tablespoon of cheese in each half. § Serve hot with barbecued pork chops or sausages.

■ INGREDIENTS

- 8 medium red or white onions
- 4 tablespoons extra-virgin olive oil
- salt and freshly ground black pepper
- ½ cup (125 g) creamy, slightly sweet cheese (Robiola, Mascarpone)

Wine: a dry red
(Leverano)

Right: *Cipolle grigliate*
con formaggio dolce fresco

Grilled salad
Insalata grigliata

■ INGREDIENTS

- 4 eggplants (aubergines)
- 4 bell peppers (capsicums)
- 6 ripe tomatoes
- 3 cloves garlic, finely chopped
- ½ cup (125 ml) extra-virgin olive oil
- salt and freshly ground black pepper
- 10 fresh basil leaves, torn

Wine: a dry white (Soave)

Serves: 6; Preparation: 10 minutes; Cooking: 45 minutes; Level of difficulty: Simple

Cut the eggplants in ½-in (1-cm) thick slices with their skins. § Heat the grill pan to very hot and cook the eggplants until tender. Set aside. § Cut the bell peppers in strips and cook in the grill pan, turning with a fork until they are cooked. Set aside. § Peel the tomatoes, cut them in half, and cook in the grill pan until they are pulpy. § Chop the eggplants and bell peppers in squares and place in a salad bowl with the tomatoes. § Sprinkle with salt, pepper, basil, garlic, and oil and toss.

Salads

Traditional Italian cuisine includes a plethora of delicious salads, from simple green and mixed dishes served after the main course to revive the palate, to more original regional salads, such as fava beans and Pecorino cheese in Tuscany, and green salads with oranges in the citrus-growing south.

Platter of raw vegetables with oil, salt, and pepper dip
Pinzimonio

Pinzimonio is a sort of do-it-yourself-salad. A platter of the season's raw vegetables, washed and cut into manageable pieces, is placed at the center of the table and each guest is given a tiny bowl of oil, salt, and pepper to dip the vegetables. Serve it as an appetizer with slices of toasted whole-wheat or homemade bread or as a refreshing course in itself after a hearty meat dish. These are the traditional pinzimonio vegetables, but use your imagination and whatever you have available in the pantry or garden. Raw zucchini sticks, sliced bell peppers, cherry tomatoes, or cubes of cucumber (with toothpicks for dipping) are just a few that spring to mind.
Serves: 4; Preparation: 20 minutes; Level of difficulty: Simple

Wash all the vegetables thoroughly under cold running water. § Artichokes: remove all but the pale inner leaves by pulling the outer ones down and snapping them off. Cut off the stem and the top third of the remaining leaves. Cut the artichokes in half lengthwise and scrape any fuzzy choke away with a knife. Cut each artichoke in wedges and soak in a bowl of cold water with the juice of 1 lemon for 15 minutes. § Carrots: scrub with a brush or peel and soak in a bowl of cold water with the remaining lemon juice for 10 minutes. § Celery: discard the stringy outer stalks and trim off the leafy tops. Keep the inner white stalks and the heart. § Fennel: slice off the base, trim away the leafy tops, and discard the blemished outer leaves. Divide into 4 or more wedges, depending on the size. § Scallions: remove the roots and the outer leaves and trim the tops. § Radishes: cut the roots off and trim the tops. § For the dip: blend the oil with salt and pepper to taste with a whisk or blender. Pour into 4 small bowls.

■ INGREDIENTS
- 4 artichokes
- juice of 2 lemons
- 4 carrots (or 8 baby spring carrots)
- 4 celery hearts
- 2 large fennel bulbs
- 12 scallions
- 12 radishes
- 1¾ cups (450 ml) extra-virgin olive oil
- salt and freshly ground black pepper
- 1 tablespoon oregano (optional)

Wine: a light, dry white (Verzemino)

Hot Piedmont-style dip for raw vegetables
Bagna cauda

Serves: 4-6; Preparation: 10 minutes; Cooking: 25 minutes; Level of difficulty: Simple
Place the garlic in a small pot with a pat of butter and a tablespoon of water. Simmer over very low heat, gradually adding all the butter; make sure the butter doesn't brown or the garlic fry. § Add the anchovy fillets and the oil, a little at a time. Mix well. § The dip is kept hot on the table in an earthenware pot over a warming apparatus (lacking all else, use a candle!). § Serve as a dip for raw vegetables. It is also good with cooked vegetables, roast bell peppers, and as a sauce for fresh pasta and potato gnocchi.

■ INGREDIENTS
- 6 cloves garlic, very finely chopped
- ¼ cup (60 g) butter
- ¾ cup (200 ml) extra-virgin olive oil
- 20 anchovy fillets (best if packed under salt), finely chopped

Right:
Insalata aranciata

■ INGREDIENTS

- 3 fresh oranges
- 5 oz (150 g) arugula (rocket)
- 5 oz (150 g) corn salad
- 2 medium red onions
- 1 cup (100 g) black olives, pitted and chopped
- ⅓ cup (90 ml) extra-virgin olive oil
- ⅓ cup (90 ml) red vinegar
- salt and black pepper

Arugula and oranges with olives and sweet red onions

Insalata aranciata

Serves: 6; Preparation: 20 minutes; Level of difficulty: Simple

Peel the oranges, discard any seeds and use a sharp knife to remove all the white part. Cut in thick slices and divide each slice in half. § Wash and dry the salad greens. § Cut the onions in thin slices. § Place the oranges, arugula, corn salad, onions, and olives in a salad bowl. § Mix the oil, vinegar, salt and pepper together in bowl and pour over the salad. Toss well. § Set aside for 20 minutes before serving. § Serve as an appetizer with toasted whole-wheat or homemade bread.

Raw spinach and parmesan salad
Insalata di spinaci e grana

Serves: 4; Preparation: 15 minutes; Level of difficulty: Simple

Trim the stems and discard any bruised spinach leaves, wash thoroughly, drain and dry on a clean cotton dish towel. § Grate the carrots in julienne strips. § Place the spinach in a large round dish or low, wide salad bowl and sprinkle with the carrots and corn. § Top with the flakes of Parmesan. § In a small bowl, dissolve the salt in the lemon juice, add the oil and pepper, and whisk to blend. § Dress the salad 5 minutes before serving. § This salad makes an eyecatching appetizer, but can also be served as a side dish with barbecued or braised meats.

> VARIATION
> – Add a small honeydew melon in balls (made with a melon baller) or cubes, and 5 ounces of lean prosciutto in strips.

■ INGREDIENTS

- 7 cups dwarf spinach, tender and very fresh
- 2 carrots, peeled
- 1 cup (125 g) canned corn kernels, or 8 baby corn cobs
- 1¼ cups (125 g) Parmesan cheese, in flakes
- ½ teaspoon salt
- juice of 1 lemon
- 4 tablespoons extra-virgin olive oil
- freshly ground black pepper

Wine: a dry white (Biondello del Metauro)

Asparagus salad
Asparagi in insalata

This tasty salad is also good with mayonnaise (see recipe p. 28)

Serves: 4; Preparation: 20 minutes; Cooking: 10 minutes; Level of difficulty: Simple

Trim the tough parts off the asparagus stalks and blanch for 7–10 minutes in a pot of salted, boiling water. Drain well and set aside to cool. § Wash and dry the radicchio and detach the leaves. § Arrange a bed of radicchio leaves on a serving dish and scatter with the mushrooms. Arrange the asparagus on top. § Dissolve the salt in the lemon juice and add the lemon peel and basil, oil, and pepper, and blend thoroughly. § Pour the dressing over the salad and serve as a light lunch with sliced hard-cooked eggs, tuna, and anchovy fillets.

■ INGREDIENTS

- 2 lb (1 kg) asparagus
- 6 heads red radicchio
- 3 cups (375 g) white mushrooms, thinly sliced
- ½ teaspoon salt
- peel of 2 lemons, finely chopped with 10 basil leaves
- ⅓ cup (90 ml) extra-virgin olive oil
- 3 tablespoons lemon juice
- freshly ground black pepper

Wine: a dry white (Gambellara)

Right: *Insalata di spinaci e grana*

Green bean salad with fried bread
Insalata di fagiolini con il pane fritto

Serves: 4; Preparation: 20 minutes; Cooking: 15 minutes; Level of difficulty: Simple

Cut the tips off the beans, cut in half, wash and cook in a pot of salted, boiling water for 7–8 minutes, or until tender. Drain, dry on paper towels, and place in a large salad bowl. § Sauté the bacon in a small skillet with 1 tablespoon of oil until crisp. Drain and set aside. § Fry the bread in a pan with 4 tablespoons of oil and the garlic, remove when golden brown, and drain on paper towels. § In a small bowl, dissolve the salt in the lemon juice, and add the pepper, oregano, parsley, scallions, and remaining oil. Dress the salad, sprinkle with the capers, and toss with the cubes of bread. § Serve as a light lunch, or as a side dish with barbecued meat.

> VARIATION
> – To make the salad more complete, add a simple omelet (4 eggs for 4 people). Beat the eggs with salt and pepper and cook in a large skillet so that it forms a thin layer. Cool and dice and toss with the salad.

■ INGREDIENTS

- 1 lb (500 g) green beans
- salt and black pepper
- 2 bunches chives, finely chopped
- 1¾ cups (210 g) bacon, diced
- ⅔ cup (150 ml) extra-virgin olive oil
- 5 1-in (2.5-cm)-thick slices firm-textured bread, cut in cubes
- 1 large clove garlic, cut in quarters
- juice of 2 lemons
- 1 tablespoon oregano
- 1 tablespoon finely chopped parsley
- 8 scallions (spring onions), chopped
- 2 tablespoons capers

Wine: a dry white (Riesling Italico)

Summer salad greens with strawberries and apples
Insalata allegra

Serves: 4; Preparation: 20 minutes; Level of difficulty: Simple

Blend the oil, chives, salt, and pepper with a whisk. Set aside for 20 minutes. § Wash and dry the salad greens. Arrange a bed of mixed salad leaves in four individual salad bowls. § Wash the apples thoroughly, divide in half, remove the core and cut in thin wedges, without peeling. § Arrange a ring of apple wedges over the salad in each bowl. § Scatter the sliced radishes over the apples. § Cut the strawberries in half and garnish each salad, placing a teaspoonful of Ricotta between each strawberry. § Pour the dressing over each plate. § Serve with crusty fresh bread or toast as an appetizer.

■ INGREDIENTS

- ¼ cup (60 ml) extra-virgin olive oil
- 2 tablespoons chives, chopped
- salt and freshly ground black pepper
- 13 oz (400 g) corn salad or green cutting lettuce
- 6 oz (200 g) red and green ryegrass or curly endive hearts
- 2 Red Delicious apples
- 10 red radishes, sliced
- 14 oz (350 g) firm ripe strawberries
- 1½ cups (350 g) Ricotta cheese

Wine: a dry white (Colli Albani)

Right: *Insalata allegra*

Woodland salad with raspberries and wild rice
Insalatina di bosco con riso selvatico

Serves: 4; Preparation: 20 minutes; Cooking: 40 minutes; Level of difficulty: Simple

Cook the rice in a pot of salted, boiling water for about 40 minutes, or until cooked. § Wash and dry the mixed salad greens. § Prepare the vinaigrette. Crush about 15 raspberries and add to the dressing. Blend well. § Place the salad greens in a large salad bowl (or 4 individual bowls), add the herbs, and toss well. § Sprinkle with the carrot and pour half the vinaigrette over the top. Garnish with 20 raspberries. § Drain the rice, shaking thoroughly to remove excess moisture. Transfer to a bowl and mix well with the oil. § Place in a large serving dish (or 4 individual bowls) and garnish with the remaining raspberries. Drizzle with the rest of the vinaigrette. § Serve the salad with the rice as an entrée or light lunch, or as a main course with grilled sole or bass, or with poached eggs.

■ INGREDIENTS

- ¾ cup (150 g) brown rice
- ⅔ cup (140 g) wild black or red rice
- 1 lb (500 g) mixed wild salad greens (dandelion, wild endives and green radicchio)
- 2 quantities *Vinagrette* (see recipe p. 46)
- 2 cups (500 g) fresh raspberries
- 1 bunch arugula, cut finely with scissors
- 1 bunch salad burnet
- 15 fresh mint leaves
- 1 bunch fresh chervil, in sprigs
- 2 bunches cress, coarsely chopped
- 4 carrots, finely grated
- 4 tablespoons extra-virgin olive oil

Wine: a dry red (Capri)

Lentil and herb salad
Insalata di lenticchie e odori

Serves: 4; Preparation: 20 minutes; Cooking: 45 minutes; Level of difficulty: Simple

Cook the lentils with the onion (with the cloves stuck in it), thyme, bay leaves, and carrots in a large pan of salted water for about 45 minutes. § Check the carrots during cooking and remove as soon as they are soft (which will be before the lentils are ready). § Drain the lentils, shaking well to remove excess moisture, and transfer a salad bowl. Discard the bay leaves, thyme, and cloves. § Cut the onion in thin slices and dice the carrots and add to the lentils. § While still hot, season with oil, salt, vinegar, and pepper, and mix well. § Add the chopped garlic and parsley and mix again. Set aside for 5 minutes. § Serve as an entrée, or as a side dish with broiled sausages.

■ INGREDIENTS

- 1 lb (500 g) lentils, soaked in water overnight
- 1 large onion
- 2 cloves
- 1 sprig fresh thyme
- 5 bay leaves
- 3 large carrots
- salt and black pepper
- ⅓ cup (90 ml) extra-virgin olive oil
- 2 tablespoons red wine vinegar
- 4 cloves garlic, 4 sprigs parsley, finely chopped

Wine: a dry red (Nebbiola d'Alba)

Right: *Insalatina di bosco con riso selvatico*

Tomatoes filled with tuna and mayonnaise
Pomodoro al tonno

Serves: 4; Preparation: 30 minutes; Level of difficulty: Simple

Wash the tomatoes and cut a ¼-in (6-mm) slice off the top of each. Hollow them out with a knife and teaspoon (be careful not to break the skin). Place them upside down on a plate to drain for 10 minutes. § Sprinkle the insides with salt and pepper. § Prepare the mayonnaise. § In a bowl, squash the egg yolks with a fork and mix with 2 tablespoons of mayonnaise. Add the olives, anchovies, capers, tuna, and parsley. Mix well, adding mayonnaise as you go. § Chop the egg whites and add them to the mixture. Keep mixing with the fork. Add pepper to taste. § Use a teaspoon to fill the tomatoes. Place a teaspoon of mayonnaise on the top of each and garnish with 2–3 capers and basil leaves. § Place the filled tomatoes in the bottom of the refrigerator for 20 minutes. § Serve as an entrée or light lunch with torn lettuce leaves dressed with oil and lemon and toasted whole-wheat or homemade bread.

■ INGREDIENTS

- 8 medium ripe tomatoes
- salt and freshly ground black pepper
- 4 hard-cooked eggs
- 2 quantities *Mayonnaise* (see recipe p. 42)
- 6 green olives, pitted and finely chopped
- 6 anchovy fillets, chopped
- ⅓ cup (40 g) capers (half finely chopped, rest whole to garnish)
- 2 cups (500 g) tuna in olive oil, chopped
- 1 tablespoon finely chopped parsley
- 16 fresh basil leaves

Wine: a dry white (Montescudaio)

Tuscan fava bean and pecorino cheese salad
Insalata di pecorino e baccelli

This salad is best in early spring when fava beans are just beginning to be appear in the shops. They should be fresh and tender from the earliest picking.

Serves: 4; Preparation: 20 minutes; Level of difficulty: Simple

Shell the fava beans and place in a large slightly concave dish. § Dice the Pecorino and mix with the beans. Add pepper, a sprinkling of salt, and the oil. § Mix well and serve the salad as an appetizer by itself or with a platter of cold meats such as prosciutto, ham, and salami.

■ INGREDIENTS

- 3 lb (1.5 kg) small, fresh fava (broad) beans in their pods
- 10 oz (300 g) fresh young Pecorino cheese
- salt and freshly ground black pepper
- 4 tablespoons extra-virgin olive oil

Wine: a dry red (Chianti dei Colli Senesi)

VARIATIONS
– Add the juice of ½ a lemon and 1½ cups of diced prosciutto.
– Add two peeled and diced sweet pears.

Right:
Insalata di pecorino e baccelli

Cabbage and onion salad
Insalata di verza e cipolla

■ INGREDIENTS

- half a medium white or red Savoy cabbage
- 2 sweet red onions
- 1 Golden Delicious apple
- 2 quantities *Vinaigrette* (see recipe p. 46)

Wine: a dry sparkling white (Trebbianino Val Trebbia)

Serves: 4; Preparation: 15 minutes; Level of difficulty: Simple

Cut the cabbage in thin strips and slice the onions thinly. Toss well together. § Peel and core the apples, dice and add to the cabbage. § Prepare the vinagrette and pour over the salad. § Toss well and set aside for 10–15 minutes before serving with barbecued pork chops or fried chicken.

VARIATION
– Replace the vinaigrette with 2 quantities of homemade mayonnaise (see recipe p. 42).

Shrimp and red bean salad
Insalata di gamberi e fagioli

Serves: 4; Preparation: 30 minutes; Cooking: 5 minutes; Level of difficulty: Simple

Wash and dry the salad vegetables. § Strip the red leaves from the radicchio and arrange in 4 small salad bowls. § Distribute the endive over the radicchio leaves. Chop the radicchio hearts and arrange over the endive. § Drain the beans and distribute in the 4 bowls over the salad. § Heat 2 tablespoons of oil in a skillet and sauté the shrimp with a little salt over high heat for 2 minutes. § Add the wine vinegar with the lemon peel and cook for 3–4 minutes more. § Place the remaining oil, with salt, pepper, scallions, and celery in a bowl and beat vigorously with a fork. § Divide the shrimp, 4 in each salad bowl, and pour the oil over the top. § Serve at once as an entrée (prepare grilled fish to follow), or as a second course preceded by a shellfish risotto.

■ INGREDIENTS

- 2 large heads red radicchio
- 2 hearts curly endive, chopped
- 1 14-oz (450 g) can red kidney beans
- 16 shrimp, shelled
- salt and freshly ground black pepper
- ½ cup (125 g) extra-virgin olive oil
- ⅓ cup (90 ml) white wine vinegar
- grated rind of ½ a lemon
- 4 scallions (spring onions), finely chopped
- 1 celery heart, finely chopped

Wine: a dry white (Falerio dei colli Ascolani)

VARIATION
– A simpler version can be made with white beans and shrimp cooked in salted, boiling water for 3 minutes and seasoned with extra-virgin olive oil, salt, freshly ground black pepper, and 2 tablespoons of finely chopped parsley.

Tomato and mozzarella cheese
Insalata caprese

Serves: 4; Preparation: 15 minutes; Level of difficulty: Simple

Cut the tomatoes in ¼-in (6-mm) thick slices and arrange on a flat serving dish. § Cut the Mozzarella in slices of the same width and alternate with the tomato. § Sprinkle with basil, salt, and pepper, and drizzle with the oil. § Serve as an entrée or light lunch (with lots of crusty fresh bread).

■ INGREDIENTS

- 7 large red tomatoes
- 1 lb (500 g) Mozzarella cheese
- 20 large basil leaves
- salt and freshly ground black pepper
- ⅓ cup (90 ml) extra-virgin olive oil

Wine: a dry white (Cinqueterre)

VARIATION
– For a tastier salad, sprinkle with 2 teaspoons of dried oregano.

Left: Insalata caprese

Spelt salad
Insalata di farro

Spelt has been grown in Italy for thousands of years. It is used in Italian cuisine for salads and soups. Look for it in specialty shops, or try replacing it with pearl barley. This delicious salad looks particularly appetizing when served in a wooden bowl. To give it even more color and flavor, add 4 raw diced courgettes and 8 crumbled anchovy fillets.

Serves: 4; Preparation: 15 minutes; Cooking: 40 minutes; Level of difficulty: Simple

Cook the spelt in a pot of salted, boiling water. The cooking time will depend on the freshness of the grain, so try a couple of grains after 40 minutes; it should be chewy but firm. § Drain and rinse under cold running water. Drain again and shake out excess moisture. § Transfer to a bowl. § Add the tomatoes, Mozzarella, scallions, basil, capers, salt, pepper, and oil, mix well and set aside for 5–10 minutes before serving. Put extra olive oil on the table with the salad because the spelt is very absorbent and may require more. § Serve as an entrée.

■ INGREDIENTS

- 3½ cups (500 g) spelt
- salt and freshly ground black pepper
- 16 cherry tomatoes, cut in half
- 2 cups (500 g) Mozzarella cheese, diced
- 6 scallions (spring onions), chopped
- 15 basil leaves, cut in strips with scissors
- ⅓ cup (40 g) capers
- ⅓ cup (90 ml) extra-virgin olive oil

Wine: a dry white (Vernaccia di San Gimignano)

Salad hearts with smoked salmon
Insalata di cuori con salmone

Serves: 4; Preparation: 20 minutes; Cooking: 7-8 minutes; Level of difficulty: Simple

Wash the salad greens and dry on a clean cotton dish towel. § Remove all but the pale inner leaves from the artichokes by pulling the outer ones down and snapping them off. Cut off the stem and the top third of the remaining leaves until only the tender heart remains. Cut the artichokes in half lengthwise and scrape any fuzzy choke away with a knife. Cut each heart in half and cook in a pot of salted, boiling water with the juice of 1 lemon for 7–8 minutes, or until they are white and tender. Drain and set aside to cool. § Dissolve ½ teaspoon of salt in the remaining lemon juice, add the oil and pepper, and mix well. § Place the lettuce, endive, celery, palm hearts, and scallions in a bowl and season with the dressing (leave a little for the artichoke hearts). § Mix well and arrange the salad in 4 plates. Place the artichoke hearts at the center of each and drizzle with the remaining dressing. § Garnish the 4 bowls with the salmon. § Serve as an entrée with toasted whole-wheat or homemade bread.

■ INGREDIENTS

- 2 heads lettuce, divided in leaves
- 4 large artichoke hearts
- salt and freshly ground black pepper
- juice of 2 lemons
- ¼ cup (60 ml) extra-virgin olive oil
- 1 large head Belgian endive, thinly sliced
- 2 celery hearts, chopped
- 4 palm hearts, sliced into thick wheels
- 4 scallions, chopped
- 12 oz (350 g) smoked salmon, thinly sliced

Wine: a dry, aromatic white (Pigato)

Right:
Insalata di farro

Green radicchio with crispy-fried pancetta
Radicchio verde alla pancetta croccante

Serves: 4; Preparation: 25 minutes; Cooking: 5 minutes; Level of difficulty: Simple

Discard any wilted leaves from the radicchio, trim the stems, wash thoroughly, drain and dry. § Sauté the pancetta in a skillet without oil (it produces enough of its own). Add the vinegar and cook until the pancetta is crisp. Remove from heat. § Season the radicchio with oil, salt, pepper, and vinegar and sprinkle the pancetta over the top. Toss well. § Serve with hard-cooked eggs and toasted homemade bread rubbed with garlic.

Artichoke salad
Insalata di carciofi

Serves: 4; Preparation: 25 minutes; Level of difficulty: Simple

Remove all but the pale inner leaves from the artichokes by pulling the outer ones down and snapping them off. Cut off the stem and the top third of the remaining leaves. Cut the artichokes in half lengthwise and scrape any fuzzy choke away with a knife. Cut each artichoke in wedges and soak in a bowl of cold water with the juice of 1 lemon for 10 minutes. § Dissolve the salt in the remaining lemon juice. Add the oil, pepper, parsley, and mint and beat vigorously to emulsify. § Cut the artichokes in thin slices, pour the dressing over the top, and toss well. § Serve as an appetizer, or as a side dish with barbecued meat or fish.

■ INGREDIENTS

- 5 large fresh artichokes
- juice of 2 lemons
- 2 dashes salt and freshly ground black pepper
- ⅓ cup (90 ml) extra-virgin olive oil
- 2 tablespoons finely chopped parsley
- 2 tablespoons finely chopped mint

Wine: a dry white (Trebbiano di Romagna)

Cooked mixed vegetable salad
Insalata cotta di verdura miste

A classic of Italian cookery, Insalata cotta is nearly always on the menu in any restaurant or trattoria, and is served in most homes at least once a week. The secret lies in the dressing, either homemade mayonnaise or extra-virgin oil and vinegar (or lemon juice). You can vary the vegetables according to the season or what you have on hand.

Serves: 4-6; Preparation: 25 minutes; Cooking: 25 minutes; Level of difficulty: Simple

Cook all the vegetables whole in abundant salted, boiling water until they are just tender. You can cook them all together if you wish, removing the different vegetables as they are ready. The beets will stain the other vegetables, so you might want to cook them apart. § Peel the potatoes and beets after cooking. To peel the beets, just press the skin with your fingers and it will slip off easily. § When all the vegetables are cooked, drain well and arrange (either sliced or whole) on a large tray, divided by types. § Serve warm with vinaigrette, mayonnaise, or a little lemon juice and olive oil. § In Italy this cooked salad is served as a side dish with roast meat or fish, or hard-cooked eggs and canned tuna.

■ INGREDIENTS

- 5 bulbs fennel
- 5 artichokes
- 6 medium carrots
- 6 long zucchini (courgettes)
- 6 medium potatoes
- 6 beets
- 1 lb (500 g) green beans
- 1 quantity *Mayonnaise* (see recipe p. 42) or 1 quantity *Vinaigrette* (see recipe p. 46)

Wine: a dry red (Chianti dei colli Aretini)

Right:
Insalata cotta di verdure miste

Cakes and Pies

Despite the wonderful cake shops all over Italy,
home-baked cakes and pies are as popular as ever.
This chapter has a selection of some classic recipes as
well as some personal favorites.

Sweet polenta pie
Amor polenta

This is another typical dish from Lombardy, in northern Italy.

Serves: 6-8; Preparation: 30 minutes; Cooking: 40 minutes; Level of difficulty: Medium

Melt the butter and set aside to cool. § Add all but 2 tablespoons of the confectioners' sugar and beat until creamy. § Add the whole eggs, one at a time, and then the yolks, beating continuously with a whisk. § Add the liqueur and almonds and sift in the cornmeal and flour. § Beat for some time, then mix in the baking powder and vanilla. § Pour the mixture into a buttered and floured soufflé dish or fluted mold 6 in (15 cm) in diameter and bake in a preheated oven at 350°F/180°C/gas 4 for about 40 minutes. § Serve sprinkled with the remaining confectioners' sugar.

■ INGREDIENTS

- 1 cup (250 g) butter
- 2⅔ cups (400 g) confectioners' (icing) sugar
- 3 whole eggs and 6 egg yolks
- 2 tablespoons Strega liqueur (or dark rum)
- 1⅓ cups (170 g) almonds, ground
- 1¾ cups (200 g) yellow cornmeal, coarsely ground
- 1 cup (150 g) all-purpose (plain) flour
- 2 teaspoons baking powder
- 1 teaspoon vanilla extract

Almond polenta cake
Torta sbrisolona

This simple but delicious cake is typical Lombardy peasant fare. As the Italian name implies, it crumbles easily; serve it in pieces broken into irregular shapes.

Serves: 4-6; Preparation: 20 minutes; Cooking: 40 minutes; Level of difficulty: Simple

Chop the almonds in a food processor with two-thirds of the sugar. § Transfer to a work surface and add the flour, cornmeal, lemon zest, remaining sugar, vanilla sugar, and salt. Shape into a mound and make a well in the center. § Combine the butter and lard with the egg yolks, and add to the flour mixture. Working quickly, use your fingertips to combine the mixture until it is smooth and crumbly. § Place the dough in a buttered and floured pie dish, 10 in (25 cm) in diameter, pressing down lightly with your fingertips to make an uneven surface. § Bake in a preheated oven at 375°F/190°C/gas 5 for 40 minutes. § If liked, sprinkle with confectioners' (icing) sugar before serving.

■ INGREDIENTS

- 1¾ cups (250 g) almonds, blanched
- ¾ cup (150 g) granulated sugar
- 1⅓ cups (200 g) all-purpose (plain) flour
- 2 cups (250 g) yellow cornmeal, finely ground
- grated zest of 1 lemon
- 1 teaspoon vanilla sugar
- dash of salt
- ½ cup (125 g) butter, cut in small pieces
- ⅓ cup (90 g) lard, cut in small pieces
- 2 egg yolks, beaten

VARIATIONS
– Replace the almonds with the same quantity of toasted hazelnuts.
– For a lighter cake, replace the lard with the same quantity of butter.

Right: *Torta sbrisolona*

Grandmother's pie
Torta della nonna

This is one of the most popular and delicious desserts in the Italian repertoire.

Serves: 6; Preparation: 30 minutes; Cooking: 40 minutes + time to make the cream; Level of difficulty: Medium

Cream the butter and granulated sugar and then beat in the eggs. Add the flour and baking powder and mix well. § Divide the dough in half and roll out into two rounds. § Place one in a buttered and floured pie dish 10 in (25 cm) in diameter, and cover with the pastry cream, piling it slightly higher in the center. § Cover with the other round and seal the edges together. § Bake in a preheated oven at 350°F/180°C/gas 4 for about 40 minutes. When the pie is cooked, decorate with the slivered almonds and sprinkle with the confectioners' sugar.

VARIATION
– Replace Vanilla cream with Chocolate pastry cream (see recipe p. 68).

■ INGREDIENTS

- ½ cup (125 g) butter
- ⅔ cup (125 g) granulated sugar
- 2 eggs
- 1⅔ cups (250 g) all-purpose (plain) flour, sifted
- 1 teaspoon baking powder
- dash of salt
- 1 quantity *Vanilla pastry cream* (see recipe p. 68)
- 2 tablespoons almonds, slivered (flaked)
- confectioners' (icing) sugar for sprinkling

Rice tart
Torta di riso

Serves: 6; Preparation: 10 minutes + time to make the pastry; Cooking: 1¼ hours; Level of difficulty: Medium

Prepare the pastry. § Cook the rice in the milk with a little salt for about 30 minutes. § When the milk has been completely absorbed, remove from heat, then add the sugar and mix well. Set aside to cool. § Add the egg yolks one at a time, then the raisins, lemon zest, and rum. § Beat the egg whites with a dash of salt until stiff, and fold them into the mixture. § Line a buttered and floured pie dish 10 in (25 cm) in diameter with the pastry, reserving some for decoration. Leave a raised edge about 1 in (2.5 cm) high, pinching the edges to make it look attractive. Prick the base with a fork to stop the pastry puffing up during baking. § Carefully pour in the rice mixture. § Cut the reserved pastry into strips or shapes and use to decorate the top. § Bake in a preheated oven at 350°F/180°C/gas 4 for about 40 minutes.

VARIATION
– Mix about half the rice mixture with 3 tablespoons of cocoa powder. Pour the chocolate rice into the pie dish over the pastry and cover with the white mixture for a two-tone pie.

■ INGREDIENTS

- 1 quantity *Sweet plain pastry* (see recipe p. 60)
- 1¼ cups (250 g) short-grain rice (preferably arborio)
- 4 cups (1 liter) milk
- dash of salt
- ½ cup (100 g) granulated sugar
- 4 eggs, separated
- ⅓ cup (60 g) raisins
- 1 tablespoon lemon zest, grated
- 1 tablespoon dark rum

Right:
Torta della nonna

Fresh Fruit cake
Torta Roberta

Serves: 6; Preparation: 10 minutes; Cooking: 30 minutes; Level of difficulty: Simple

Beat the eggs and sugar, then add the butter, salt, and sifted flour and, lastly, the baking powder and water. § Mix to a smooth cream. § Stir the fruit into the mixture. § Pour into a buttered and floured springform pan 8 in (20 cm) in diameter and bake in a preheated oven at 350°F/180°C/gas 4 for 30 minutes.

VARIATION
– This cake can be varied infinitely, depending on the fruit used. Try it with bananas, apricots, and pitted (stoned) cherries.

■ INGREDIENTS

- 2 eggs
- 4 tablespoons granulated sugar
- ½ cup (125 g) butter, melted
- dash of salt
- 4 tablespoons all-purpose (plain) flour
- 1 teaspoon baking powder
- 2 tablespoons water
- 1 pear, 1 apple, 1 peach, peeled, cored, and chopped into tiny pieces

Hazelnut cream pie
Torta alla crema gianduia

*Hazelnut and chocolate cream, known as Gianduia in Italian,
is typical of traditional Piedmontese baking.*

Serves: 6; Preparation: 20 minutes; Cooking: 45 minutes; Level of difficulty: Medium

Cream the first measure of butter and sugar and then beat in the eggs. § Stir in the first measure of flour, the baking powder, and cinnamon, and then add all but 2 tablespoons of the yogurt, and the lemon zest. Mix until smooth. § Pour half the mixture into a buttered and floured pie dish 10 in (25 cm) in diameter. § Spread the chocolate hazelnut paste over the base and cover with the remaining dough. § Combine the remaining flour, butter, and sugar with the nuts, until the mixture resembles coarse bread crumbs. § Sprinkle this over the pie and bake in a preheated oven at 350°F/180°C/gas 4 for about 45 minutes. § Whip the cream with the remaining yogurt and serve with the pie.

■ INGREDIENTS

- ¾ cup (200 g) butter
- ½ cup (100 g) granulated sugar
- 2 eggs
- 1⅔ cups (250 g) all-purpose (plain) flour
- 2 teaspoons baking powder
- dash of cinnamon, ground
- 1 cup (250 ml) yogurt
- grated zest of 1 lemon
- ¾ cup (200 g) chocolate hazelnut paste

TOPPING
- 2 tablespoons all-purpose (plain) flour
- 2 tablespoons butter
- 2½ tablespoons granulated sugar
- 1 cup (100 g) hazelnuts, toasted and coarsely chopped
- ⅓ cup (90 ml) heavy (double) cream

Mimosa cake
Torta mimosa

Serves: 6-8; Preparation: 10 minutes + time to make the sponge cake and pastry cream; Level of difficulty: Medium

Prepare the sponge cake and the pastry cream. § When the sponge has cooled, cut it crosswise into three layers, one slightly thinner than the others. § Carefully cut the outer crust off the thinnest layer and either crumble it into large crumbs or cut into tiny cubes. § Mix the Grand Marnier with the sugar and water and soak one of the thick layers in this. Spread with some of the pastry cream, mounding it up slightly in the center. § Cover with the remaining layer of sponge cake and spread the remaining pastry cream over the top and sides. § Finally, sprinkle the cake with the crumbs or tiny cubes to achieve the classic mimosa effect.

■ INGREDIENTS

- 1½ quantities *Italian sponge cake* (see recipe p. 62)
- 1 quantity *Vanilla pastry cream* (see recipe p. 68)
- ½ cup (125 ml) Grand Marnier
- ½ cup (100 g) granulated sugar
- ¾ cup (200 ml) water

Left:
Torta mimosa

VARIATION
– Replace the Grand Marnier with pineapple juice and mix finely-chopped pieces of canned pineapple into the pastry cream.

Hazelnut cake
Torta alle nocciole

*This cake is a gourmet's delight. The combination
of chocolate, nuts, and cream is irresistible.*

Serves: 6; Preparation: 40 minutes; Cooking: 50 minutes; Level of difficulty: Complicated

Cream the butter and brown sugar and then beat in the egg yolks one at a time. § Stir in the sifted flour and baking powder. § Add the nuts and chocolate. § Beat the egg whites with the salt until stiff and fold them into the mixture. § Pour the mixture into a buttered and floured springform pan 10 in (25 cm) in diameter, and bake in a preheated oven at 350°F/180°C/gas 4 for about 50 minutes. § Remove from the pan and place on a rack to cool. § Melt the chocolate in a double boiler. Use a wooden spoon to stir in the vanilla. § Whip the cream until stiff. § When the cake is cool, split it into two layers. § Sandwich the cake together with whipped cream and cover with the chocolate frosting. § Decorate with the hazelnuts.

VARIATION
– Stir a handful of chocolate chips into the cream for the filling.

■ INGREDIENTS
- ⅔ cup (150 g) butter, cut into pieces
- ¾ cup (150 g) brown sugar
- 4 eggs, separated
- ⅔ cup (100 g) all-purpose (plain) flour
- 1 teaspoon baking powder
- 1 cup (100 g) hazelnuts, toasted and chopped
- 7 squares (200 g) semi-sweet (dark) chocolate, chopped
- dash of salt

FROSTING:
- 5½ oz (165 g) semi-sweet (dark) chocolate
- 2–3 drops vanilla extract
- 2 tablespoons light (single) cream

FILLING:
- ½ cup (125 ml) heavy (double) cream

DECORATION:
- 2 tablespoons hazelnuts, chopped

Lemon cake
Torta con ghiaccia

Serves: 6; Preparation: 20 minutes; Cooking: 60 minutes; Level of difficulty: Simple

Beat the butter and lemon zest until fluffy, then beat in the granulated sugar and eggs alternately. § Stir in the two flours and the baking powder. § Pour the mixture into a buttered and floured loaf pan 8 x 3½ in (20 x 9 cm) in size, and bake in a preheated oven at 350°F/180°C/gas 4 for about 1 hour. § Beat the confectioners' sugar with enough lemon juice to make a stiff frosting. § Frost the cake while it is still hot.

■ INGREDIENTS
- ¾ cup (225 g) butter
- grated zest of 1 lemon
- 1¼ cups (250 g) granulated sugar
- 4 eggs
- 1 cup (150 g) potato starch (potato flour)
- 1 cup (150 g) all-purpose (plain) flour
- ½ teaspoon baking powder

FROSTING:
- 1 cup (150 g) confectioners' (icing) sugar
- 4 tablespoons lemon juice

Right: *Torta alle nocciole*

Mocha cream cake
Torta alla crema moka

This cream-filled cake is the classic combination of coffee and chocolate.

Serves: 6; Preparation: 30 minutes; Cooking: 45 minutes; Level of difficulty: Medium

Cream the egg yolks and sugar thoroughly using a whisk. § Stir in the milk, melted butter, cocoa, coffee, sifted flour, baking powder, and salt. § Beat the egg whites until stiff and fold them into the mixture. § Pour the mixture into a buttered and floured springform pan 10 in (25 cm) in diameter, and bake in a preheated oven at 350°F/180°C/gas 4 for about 30 minutes. § Remove from the pan and place on a rack to cool. § Prepare the pastry cream. § Dissolve the gelatin in the hot coffee and stir well. § Mix the coffee and gelatin into the pastry cream. § Slice the cooled cake crosswise in 2 rounds, and fill with the pastry cream. § Whip the cream with the cinnamon and spread it over the cake.

■ INGREDIENTS

- 4 eggs, separated
- ¾ cup (150 g) granulated sugar
- ⅓ cup (90 ml) milk
- 1 cup (250 g) butter, melted
- 2 tablespoons unsweetened cocoa powder
- 2 tablespoons instant coffee powder
- 1⅔ cups (250 g) all-purpose (plain) flour
- 1 teaspoon baking powder
- dash of salt
- 1 quantity *Vanilla pastry cream* (see recipe p. 68)
- ⅓ cup (90 ml) strong hot coffee
- 2 tablespoons gelatin
- ¾ cup (200 ml) heavy (double) cream
- dash of cinnamon

Caramel apple pie
Torta di mele caramellate

Serves: 6; Preparation: 45 minutes + resting time for the dough; Cooking: 40 minutes; Level of difficulty: Medium

Prepare the short crust pastry. § Peel and dice the apples. § Melt the butter, then add the apples and cook with the lemon juice and half the brown sugar until slightly softened. § Roll out the dough and use it to line a springform pan 10 in (25 cm) in diameter. § Prick the base with a fork and bake in a preheated oven at 350°F/180°C/gas 4 for 30 minutes. § Spread the pastry cream over the pastry and cover with the cooked apples. § Sprinkle with the remaining brown sugar and place the pie under the broiler (grill) until the sugar caramelizes over the apples.

■ INGREDIENTS

- 1 quantity *Plain sweet pastry* (see recipe p. 60)
- 2 lb (1 kg) Golden Delicious apples
- ⅓ cup (90 g) butter
- juice of ½ lemon
- ¾ cup (150 g) brown sugar
- ½ quantity *Vanilla pastry cream* (see recipe p. 68)

VARIATION
– This delicious pie is also very good when made with pears.

Right:
Torta di mele caramellate

Chocolate pound cake
Quattro quarti al cioccolato

Serves: 4-6; Preparation: 20 minutes; Cooking: 40 minutes; Level of difficulty: Simple

Beat the egg yolks and sugar until the mixture is creamy. § Add the melted butter, followed by the sifted flour, cocoa, vanilla extract, and baking powder. § Whisk the egg whites with the salt until very stiff and fold them into the dough. § Tip the mixture into a buttered and floured square pan 8 in (20 cm) in length, and bake in a preheated oven at 350°F/180°C/gas 4 for about 40 minutes. § When cool, cover the cake with the melted chocolate and decorate with chocolate shavings.

VARIATION
– The traditional recipe uses 1 cup (150 g) ground almonds instead of unsweetened cocoa.

■ INGREDIENTS

- 3 eggs, separated
- ¾ cup (150 g) granulated sugar
- ¾ cup (225 g) butter, melted
- 1⅓ cups (200 g) all-purpose (plain) flour
- 2 tablespoons unsweetened cocoa powder
- 2–3 drops vanilla extract (essence)
- 1 teaspoon baking powder
- dash of salt

FROSTING

- 7 oz (200 g) semi-sweet (dark) chocolate, melted
- chocolate shavings to decorate

Orange puff
Sfogliata di arance

The caramelized sugar contrasts perfectly with the tangy flavor of the oranges.

Serves: 6; Preparation: about 1 hour; Cooking: 30 minutes; Level of difficulty: Complicated

Cream the butter and brown sugar and spread it over the bottom of a 10 in (25 cm) pie dish lined with dampened baking parchment (paper). Chill in the refrigerator. § Remove the dish from the refrigerator, then cut the orange into very thin slices and arrange them on the butter-and-sugar base so that they overlap one another slightly. § Cover with a round of thinly rolled puff pastry. Prick the surface with a fork and bake in a preheated oven at 350°F/180°C/gas 4 for about 30 minutes. § When baked, turn out onto a serving dish. Remove the parchment carefully and serve. § If the surface is not well caramelized, place the pie under the grill (broiler) for a few minutes.

■ INGREDIENTS

- 4 tablespoons butter
- 4 tablespoons brown sugar
- 1 large orange
- ¼ quantity *Puff pastry* (see recipe p. 56)

VARIATION
– This pie is equally delicious made with apples.

Right: *Sfogliata di arance*

Buckwheat cake
Torta di grano saraceno

This cake comes from the Dolomite mountains, where buckwheat is cultivated in the deep valleys. Buckwheat flour is used in many regional dishes and country desserts.

Serves: 8; Preparation: 20 minutes; Cooking: 60 minutes; Level of difficulty: simple

Cream the butter and sugar and then add the egg yolks one at a time. § Add the flour, almonds, and vanilla extract and beat until smooth. § Beat the egg whites with the salt until stiff. Fold them into the mixture. § Pour into a buttered and floured pie dish 10 in (25 cm) in diameter, and bake in a preheated oven at 350°F/180°C/gas 4 for about 60 minutes. § Remove the cake from the oven and leave to cool on a rack. § Slice it crosswise into 2 rounds. Sandwich the rounds together with the redcurrant jelly and sprinkle the top with vanilla sugar.

■ INGREDIENTS

- 1 cup (250 g) butter
- 1¼ cups (250 g) granulated sugar
- 6 eggs, separated
- 1½ cups (250 g) buckwheat flour
- 2 cups (250 g) almonds, chopped
- 2–3 drops vanilla extract
- dash of salt
- 1¼ cups (400 g) redcurrant jelly (jam)
- 1 tablespoon vanilla sugar

VARIATION
– Serve with lightly whipped, unsweetened cream.

Potato cake
Torta di patate

This simple cake has a mild flavor,

which makes it particularly popular with children.

Serves: 6; Preparation: 40 minutes; Cooking: 40 minutes; Level of difficulty: Simple

Boil the potatoes in their skins until tender. Slip off the skins and mash while still warm. § Combine the sifted flour with the baking powder and lemon zest. § Mix the potatoes with the Ricotta, sugar, butter, and eggs. § Combine the flour and potato mixtures, and mix until smooth. Place in a buttered and floured springform pan 10 in (25 cm) in diameter. § Bake in a preheated oven at 350°F/180°C/gas 4 for about 40 minutes. Serve sprinkled with vanilla sugar.

■ INGREDIENTS

- 4 large potatoes
- 1⅓ cups (200 g) all-purpose (plain) flour
- 1 tablespoon baking powder
- 1 teaspoon grated lemon zest
- 1⅔ cups (400 g) Ricotta cheese
- 1½ cups (300 g) granulated sugar
- 4 tablespoons butter, melted
- 4 eggs
- 2 tablespoons vanilla sugar

VARIATION
– Flavor the cake with grated orange zest instead of lemon zest.

Right:
Torta di grano saraceno

■ INGREDIENTS

- 2 eggs
- 1 cup (200 g) granulated sugar
- 2½ cups (250 g) finely ground cornmeal
- 1⅔ cups (250 g) all-purpose (plain) flour
- 2 teaspoons baking powder
- ⅔ cup (150 ml) oil
- ½ cup (125 ml) white wine
- 1 apple
- juice of half a lemon
- 2 tablespoons granulated sugar

Cornmeal and apple cake
Torta di farina gialla e mele

Serves: 6. Preparation: 20 minutes; Cooking: about 50 minutes; Level of difficulty: Simple

Cream the eggs and sugar. § Stir in the sifted cornmeal and flour, then add the baking powder. § Pour in the oil in a thin stream, then add the wine. § When the dough is smooth and creamy, pour it into a buttered and floured springform pan 9 in (23 cm) in diameter. § Peel and core the apple and slice it thinly. Sprinkle it with the lemon juice. § Arrange the slices over the cake and sprinkle with the sugar. Bake in a preheated oven at 350°F/180°C/gas 4 for 50 minutes.

Country apple cake
Torta di mele rustica

■ INGREDIENTS

- ½ cup (125 g) butter
- ½ cup (100 g) granulated sugar
- grated zest of 1 lemon
- 2 eggs
- dash of salt
- 2⅔ cups (250 g) all-purpose (plain) flour
- ⅓ cup (90 ml) milk
- 2 teaspoons baking powder
- 4 medium cooking apples
- 2 tablespoons lemon juice
- 2 tablespoons apricot jelly (jam)

Serves: 6; Preparation time: 30 minutes; Cooking time: 45 minutes; Level of difficulty: Simple

Cream the butter and sugar together with the lemon zest. § Beat in the eggs, one at a time, followed by the salt and sifted flour, alternating them with the milk. Fold in the baking powder. § Place the dough in a buttered and floured pie dish 10 in (25 cm) in diameter. § Peel the apples, cut them in half, and core. Cut a grid pattern into the rounded sides, and sprinkle with lemon juice. § Place the apples, flat side down, in the top of the cake. § Bake in a preheated oven at 350°F/180°C/gas 4 for about 45 minutes. § When the cake is cooked, spread the top with a little of the warmed, strained apricot jelly and serve.

Praline savarin
Ciambella al caramello

■ INGREDIENTS

- 1¼ cups (250 g) granulated sugar
- 1¾ cups (250 g) almonds, toasted
- 3 eggs
- ⅓ cup (90 g) butter, melted
- dash of salt
- ¾ cup (110 g) all-purpose (plain) flour
- extra sugar for the pan

Serves: 6; Preparation: 35 minutes; Cooking: 35 minutes; Level of Difficulty: Medium

Place the sugar in a dry, nonstick, heavy-bottomed pan and cook lightly until it turns an amber color. Place on a sheet of baking parchment (paper) and leave to cool. § When the caramelized sugar is cold, grind it in a food processor with the toasted almonds. § Beat the eggs in a bowl. Gradually beat in the caramel and almond mixture. Slowly add the butter, salt, and sifted flour. § Turn the mixture into a buttered and sugared savarin or bundt pan 9½ in (24 cm) in diameter, and bake in a preheated oven at 350°/180°C/gas 4 for about 35 minutes.

VARIATION
– When making the caramel, a tablespoon of honey can be added to the sugar.

Left:
Torta di mele rustica

Lemon pie
Torta al limone

This delicately flavored, slightly sharp-tasting pie is perfect for teatime.

Serves: 6; Preparation: 45 minutes + time for the pastry to rest; Cooking: 40 minutes; Level of difficulty: Medium

Prepare the short crust pastry and use it to line a buttered and floured pie dish 10 in (25 cm) in diameter. Prick the base of the pie all over with a fork. § Beat the eggs and sugar in a bowl with the ground almonds, egg whites, melted butter, and the juice and zest of the lemons. § Spread this mixture over the dough and bake in a preheated oven at 350°F/180°C/gas 4 for about 40 minutes. § Decorate the pie with the candied peel and sprinkle with a little confectioners' sugar. Serve chilled.

> VARIATION
> – Cover with a layer of meringue, as in the recipe on page 710.

■ INGREDIENTS

- 1 quantity *Short crust pastry* (see recipe p. 60), made with sugar
- 2 eggs
- 1 cup (200 g) granulated sugar
- 1⅔ cups (200 g) finely ground almonds
- 2 egg whites
- ⅓ cup (90 g) butter, melted
- grated zest and juice of 2 lemons
- 10 pieces candied lemon peel
- confectioners' (icing) sugar for sprinkling

Apple strudel
Strudel di mele

This dessert is made throughout central Europe. In Italy, it is popular in the northeast – in Trentino, Alto Adige, and Venezia Giulia.

Serves: 4-6; Preparation: 30 minutes + 30 minutes for the dough to rest; Cooking: 60 minutes; Level of difficulty: Complicated

Heat the water and melt the butter in it. Leave to cool. § Sift the flour onto a work surface and shape into a mound. Make a well in the center and fill with salt, sugar, egg, and butter-and-water mixture. § Combine the ingredients well and knead vigorously for 20 minutes, until it forms a soft, elastic dough. Roll into a ball. Cover and leave in a warm place to rest for about 30 minutes. § Meanwhile, peel and core the apples and slice thinly. § Leave the raisins to soften in warm water for 10 minutes. § Mix the sugar with the cinnamon and lemon zest. § Toast the bread crumbs in half the butter. § At this point, place the dough on a large, floured cloth and roll it out partially with a rolling-pin. Then try to stretch it out as much as possible, placing your fists underneath the dough with your knuckles upward and pulling gently outward from the center. The dough should be almost as thin as a sheet of paper. § Brush it with melted butter. Sprinkle half the dough with the bread crumbs,

■ INGREDIENTS

- ⅓ cup (90 ml) water
- 4 tablespoons butter
- 1⅔ cups (250 g) all-purpose (plain) flour
- dash of salt
- 1 tablespoon sugar
- 1 egg

FILLING:
- 8 russet apples
- ⅔ cup (125 g) raisins
- ⅓ cup (80 g) granulated sugar
- ½ teaspoon cinnamon, ground
- grated zest of 1 lemon
- 1¼ cups (150 g) dry white bread crumbs
- ⅓ cup (90 g) butter

Right:

Strudel di mele

- ⅓ cup (90 g) apricot jelly
- confectioners' (icing) sugar for sprinkling

followed by the apples, raisins, and sugar mixture. Spread with the apricot jelly, which serves to bind the mixture. § Roll up the strudel carefully, sealing the edges well so that no filling will escape during cooking. Place on a baking sheet covered in baking parchment (paper). § Brush with melted butter and bake in a preheated oven at 350°F/180°C/gas 4 for about 1 hour. Serve sprinkled with confectioners' sugar.

VARIATION
– Try substituting 3½ cups (800 g) morello cherries and slivered (flaked) almonds for the apples and raisins. This is delicious served with lightly whipped cream.

Florentine cake

Schiacciata alla fiorentina

In Florence this dish is traditionally eaten on the Thursday before Lent.
It is delicious when filled with whipped cream.

Serves: 8; Preparation: 30 minutes + 3 hours to rise; Cooking: 30 minutes; Level of difficulty: Medium

Dissolve the yeast in a quarter of the warm water. Set aside for 10–15 minutes. § Place the flour in a large mixing bowl and pour in the yeast mixture. Stir until well mixed. Turn out onto a floured work surface and knead mixture vigorously until the dough is smooth and elastic. Roll into a ball. Cover and leave in a warm place to rise for about 1 hour. § Knead the dough again, then gradually work in the eggs, sugar, butter, orange zest, and salt. § Spread the dough in a buttered and floured 8 x 12 in (20 x 30 cm) baking dish, and leave to rise for 2 more hours. § Bake in a preheated oven at 350°F/180°C/gas 4 for about 30 minutes. When cool, sprinkle with confectioners' sugar and serve.

■ INGREDIENTS

- ½ oz (15 g) fresh yeast or 1 package active dry yeast (see p. 342)
- 1 cup (250 ml)
- 3⅓ cups (500 g) all-purpose (plain) flour
- 4 egg yolks
- ¾ cup (150 g) granulated sugar
- ⅓ cup (90 g) butter, melted
- grated zest of 1 orange
- dash of salt
- vanilla sugar
- confectioners' (icing) sugar for sprinkling

Ricotta cake with fruits of the forest

Torta di ricotta al frutti di bosco

Serves: 6; Preparation: 40 minutes + time to chill; Level of difficulty: Medium

Combine the Ricotta with just over half the sugar and the yogurt in a mixing bowl. § Whip the cream until stiff and fold it carefully into the mixture. § Lastly, stir in 3 tablespoons of berries. § Place a sponge cake round in the bottom of a cake pan 10 in (25 cm) in diameter and spread the Ricotta mixture over it. Cover with the other piece of sponge. § Cook the rest of the berries in the remaining sugar and lemon juice over a high heat until syrupy. § Spread the fruit over the the cake and refrigerate for at least 3 hours before serving.

VARIATION
– Buy the sponge cake ready-made to save time.

■ INGREDIENTS

- 2 cups (500 g) Ricotta cheese, strained
- 1¼ cups (250 g) granulated sugar
- 1 cup (250 ml) Greek yogurt
- 1¾ cups (450 ml) heavy (double) cream
- 2 cups (500 g) mixed berry fruits
- 2 quantities *Italian sponge cake* (see recipe p. 62), baked in two round pans 8 in (20 cm) in diameter
- juice of 1 lemon

Right:
Torta di ricotta ai frutti di bosco

Cherry cream pie
Crostata alla crema di amarene

■ INGREDIENTS

- 1 quantity *Sweet plain pastry* (see recipe p. 60)
- ½ quantity *Vanilla pastry cream* (see recipe p. 68), cooled
- 2 cups (500 g) wild cherries, pitted (stoned) and stewed
- ½ cup (75 g) confectioners' (icing) sugar for sprinkling

Serves: 6; Preparation: 20 minutes + time to make the pastry and pastry cream; Cooking: about 1 hour; Level of difficulty: Simple

Prepare the pastry. Use it to line a pie dish 9 in (23 cm) in diameter. Bake blind, following the method on page 60. § Let the pastry shell cool and then spread evenly with the pastry cream. § Arrange the cherries over the cream and place under a very hot broiler (grill) for about 10 minutes. § Sprinkle with confectioners' sugar and serve while still warm.

Grape bread
Schiacciata all'uva

■ INGREDIENTS

- 1 oz (30 g) fresh yeast or 2 packages active dry yeast
- ⅔ cup (150 ml) lukewarm water
- 3⅓ cups (500 g) all-purpose (plain) flour
- dash of salt
- 4 tablespoons granulated sugar

TOPPING

- 2 cups (500 g) black grapes, crushed
- ¾ cup (150 g) granulated sugar

This recipe for sweet focaccia comes from Tuscany, where it is made every year throughout the grape harvest using the small black grapes used to make the local Chianti wines.

Serves: 6-8; Preparation: 40 minutes + time for the dough to rise; Cooking: 45-50 minutes; Level of difficulty: Medium

Dissolve the yeast in a third of the warm water. Set aside for 10–15 minutes. § Sift the flour onto a work surface and add the sugar and salt. Shape into a mound and make a well in the center. Pour in the yeast mixture and work it into the flour. Knead vigorously, until the dough is soft and elastic. Roll into a ball. Cover and leave in a warm place to rise until it has doubled in size. § Divide the risen dough in two. Roll out two sheets about ¾ in (2 cm) thick. Place one of these on a buttered baking sheet and cover it with half the grapes and half the sugar. Place the other sheet on top and seal the edges thoroughly. § Spread the remainder of the grapes over the top, pressing them down into the dough. Sprinkle with the sugar and leave to rest for 1 hour. § Bake in a preheated oven at 350°F/180°C/gas 4 for 40–50 minutes.

VARIATION
– For extra flavor, fry a sprig of rosemary in 2 tablespoonfuls of extra-virgin olive oil. Strain the rosemary leaves from the oil then work it into the dough.

Left:
Crostata alla crema di amarene

Cherry jelly pie
La crostata della zia Ines

Serves: 6; Preparation: 45 minutes; Cooking: 30 minutes; Level of difficulty: Simple

Beat the whole egg and the yolks with the sugar until pale and creamy. Add the butter and mix well. § Sift the flour and stir it into the egg mixture together with the Maraschino, lemon zest, and baking powder. § When the dough is well mixed, cover the mixing bowl with a cloth and set aside to rest for 30 minutes. § Line a buttered and floured pie dish 10 in (25 cm) in diameter with two-thirds of the pastry, pressing it down with your fingertips. Prick the bottom of the pie with a fork. Spread the cherry jelly over the pastry. § Roll out the remaining pastry and cut into strips. Use them to make a lattice pattern on the top of the pie. § Bake in a preheated oven at 350°F/180°C/gas 4 for 30 minutes.

VARIATION
– Replace the cherry jelly with the same quantity of plum, blackberry, or apricot jelly.

■ INGREDIENTS

- 1 egg
- 2 egg yolks
- ⅓ cup (90 g) granulated sugar
- ⅔ cup (150 g) butter, melted
- 2 cups (300 g) all-purpose (plain) flour
- 1 tablespoon Maraschino liqueur (cherry liqueur)
- grated zest of 1 lemon
- ¾ cup (200 g)
- 1 teaspoon baking powder,
- 1 cup cherry jelly (jam)

Grape pie
Crostata di uva

Grapes, almonds, and sweet plain pastry – three simple ingredients to make a sophisticated dessert.

Serves: 6; Preparation: 30 minutes; Cooking: 30 minutes; Level of difficulty: Simple

Make the pastry, working half the ground almonds into the dough. Set aside to rest for 30 minutes. § Roll out the dough and use it to line a pie dish 10 in (25 cm) in diameter. § Sauté the grapes in the butter for 5 minutes. § Increase the heat to high and add the brown sugar and rum. Stir well and remove from heat. § Scatter the Amaretti cookies over the pastry shell, then add the grapes and all their juice. § Sprinkle with the remaining ground almonds and bake in a preheated oven at 350°F/180°C/gas 4 for about 30 minutes.

VARIATION
– Replace the grapes with an equal quantity of apples, pears, or plums.

■ INGREDIENTS

- 1 quantity *Sweet plain pastry* (see recipe p. 60)
- 1 cup (100 g) finely ground almonds
- 3 cups (750 g) white grapes, halved
- 1 tablespoon butter
- 1 tablespoon brown sugar
- 1 tablespoon dark rum
- 5 Amaretti cookies, crushed

Right:
La crostata della zia Ines

Neapolitan Ricotta pie
Pastiera Napoletana

The traditional recipe calls for lard in the pastry base. I usually replace this with the same quantity of butter. You may also replace the wheat with the same quantity of cooked rice.

Serves: 8; Preparation: 2 hours; Cooking: 1½ hours; Level of difficulty: Medium

Prepare the pastry and set aside to chill. § Cook the cracked wheat, milk, and butter for about 10 minutes, stirring constantly, then set aside to cool. § Beat the eggs and egg yolks into the Ricotta one at a time, then add the sugar, cinnamon, and orange flower water. § Stir in the wheat mixture. § Sprinkle the candied peel with flour and stir it into the filling. § Line a pan 12 in (30 cm) in diameter with two-thirds of the pastry so that it overlaps the edges a little. § Spread with the filling. Roll out the remaining pastry and cut into strips. Use them to make a lattice pattern on the top of the pie. § Bake in a preheated oven at 350°F/180°C/gas 4 for 1½ hours. § Cool for 10 minutes. Sprinkle with confectioners' (icing) sugar and serve.

■ INGREDIENTS

- 2 quantities *Sweet plain pastry* (see recipe p. 60), made with 2 extra whole eggs
- 4 tablespoons cracked wheat, cooked
- ¾ cup (200 ml) milk
- 4 tablespoons butter
- 7 whole eggs and 3 yolks
- ¾ cup (200 g) fresh Ricotta cheese
- 2¼ cups (500 g) granulated sugar
- dash of cinnamon
- 2 tablespoons orange flower water
- ¾ cup (90 g) candied lemon peel, chopped
- confectioners' (icing) sugar for sprinkling

Wild strawberry pie
Crostata di fragoline

The dough for this pie is simply Short crust pastry (see recipe page 60) in which the water is replaced by milk. The wild strawberries give it a slightly sharp taste plus an exquisite fragrance.

Serves: 6-8; Preparation: 30 minutes; Cooking: 1 hour; Level of difficulty: Simple

Use the first seven ingredients listed to prepare the short crust pastry, following the method on page 60. Use the pastry to line a cake pan 10 in (25 cm) in diameter. Bake blind in a preheated oven, following the method on page 60. § Beat the eggs with the sugar and add the cream, ground almonds, and flour. § Remove the pastry shell from the oven and cover with the wild strawberries. Pour the egg and cream mixture over the top. § Bake for another 35 minutes.

VARIATION
– Sprinkle the pie with vanilla sugar just before serving.

■ INGREDIENTS

- 1⅔ cups (250 g) all-purpose (plain) flour
- 4 tablespoons granulated sugar
- ½ cup (125 g) butter
- 3 tablespoons milk
- dash of salt

FILLING

- 2 eggs
- ⅓ cup (80 g) granulated sugar
- ⅓ cup (90 ml) light (single) cream
- 1 cup (100 g) almonds, ground
- 2 tablespoons all-purpose (plain) flour
- 1 cup (250 g) wild strawberries

Right: *Crostata di fragoline*

Meringue pie
Crostata meringata

Serves: 4-6; Preparation: 45 minutes; Cooking: 30 minutes; Level of difficulty: Simple

Prepare the pastry and bake it blind, following the instructions on page 60. § Prepare the pastry cream and pour it into the baked pastry shell. § Beat the egg whites with the salt until very stiff. Spread over the top of the pie, drawing it up into little peaks using the back of a tablespoon. § Return to the oven for about 10 minutes or until the meringue is golden brown.

VARIATION
– Add extra flavor to the vanilla pastry cream by boiling the zest of a lemon in the milk.

■ INGREDIENTS

- 1 quantity *Sweet plain pastry* (see recipe p. 60)
- 1 quantity *Vanilla pastry cream* (see recipe p. 68)
- 4 egg whites
- dash of salt

Meringue mille-feuilles
Millefoglie di meringa

This is a variation of the classic meringue dessert with cream, but with the addition of lemon-flavored custard.

Serves: 4-6; Preparation: 40 minutes; Cooking: 40 minutes; Level of difficulty: Complicated

Using an electric whisk, beat the egg whites with the salt until stiff, adding half of both sugars at the beginning and the rest bit by bit, gradually reducing the speed. § Spread the mixture on 2 large baking sheets in 3 disks about 8 in (20 cm) in diameter. § Bake in a preheated oven at 250°F/120°C/gas 1 for about 40 minutes. § To make the filling: beat the egg yolks and the sugar until the mixture falls in ribbons from the beater. § Add the potato starch and place over heat in the top of a double-boiler. § Whisk continuously, slowly adding the lemon juice. Stir over very low heat until the mixture thickens. § Leave to cool before folding in the whipped cream. § Spread half the mixture on top of two disks of meringue. Place one one on top of the other and cover with the third disk. § Serve sprinkled with confectioners' sugar, if liked.

VARIATION
– Subsitute the filling with 1 quantity of custard (see recipe on p. 66) and put flakes of semi-sweet chocolate between the layers.

■ INGREDIENTS

- 4 egg whites
- dash of salt
- ¾ cup (125 g) confectioners' (icing) sugar
- ½ cup (100 g) granulated sugar

FILLING:
- 3 egg yolks
- ½ cup (100 g) granulated sugar
- 1 tablespoon potato starch (potato flour)
- ⅓ cup (90 ml) lemon juice
- 1¼ cups (300 ml) heavy (double) cream, whipped

Right:
Crostata meringata

Chestnut ice cream with chocolate sauce
Mattonella meringata

Serves: 6; Preparation: 45 minutes + time to chill; Level of difficulty: Medium

Whip the heavy cream, then add the vanilla extract and the confectioners' sugar. § Fold in the meringues and marrons glacés, taking care not to let the mixture collapse. § Brush an oblong mold with rum. Pour in the mixture and place in the freezer for at least 3 hours. § To make the sauce: melt the chocolate in the top of a double-boiler with the butter and cream, mixing thoroughly with a spatula. § Pour over the ice cream and serve.

VARIATION
– Replace marrons glacés with berry fruit, toasted almonds, chocolate chips, or crushed nut brittle.

Raspberry mille-feuilles
Millefoglie ai lamponi

For best results, prepare the layers of pastry and the filling in advance, but do not make up the dessert until the last moment.

Serves: 6; Preparation: 40 minutes + time to make the puff pastry; Cooking: 45 minutes; Level of difficulty: Complicated

Prepare the pastry. § Prepare the zabaione. § Roll out the pastry very thinly, taking care not to tear it. Cut into four equal squares and prick with a fork. § Place on baking sheets and bake in a preheated oven at 400°F/200°C/gas 6 for 20 minutes. § When golden brown, sprinkle each piece with 1 tablespoon of confectioners' sugar and return to the oven for a few minutes to caramelize. § When the zabaione is completely cold, add the cream and crumbled meringues. § Just before serving, make up the dessert by alternating layers of the pastry, zabaione, raspberries, and almonds. § Sprinkle the top layer with raspberries, almonds, and the remaining confectioners' sugar.

Left:
Millefoglie ai lamponi

VARIATIONS
– Replace the raspberries with the same quantity of strawberries.
– If short of time, use store-bought puff pastry.

Grandma's chocolate cake
Torta al cioccolato della nonnina

This is an old family recipe that was probably invented as a way of using leftover egg whites.

Serves: 6; Preparation: 15 minutes; Cooking: 25 minutes; Level of difficulty: Simple;

Melt the chocolate and butter in the top of a double-boiler. § Remove from heat and beat in the sugar and then the flour. § Beat the egg whites with the salt until very stiff. Fold them into the cooled chocolate mixture. § Place in a buttered and floured springform pan 10 in (25 cm) in diameter and bake in a preheated oven at 300°F/150°C/gas 2 for 25 minutes. § The cake should have a slight crust, but still be soft inside.

■ INGREDIENTS

• 7 oz (200 g) semi-sweet (dark) chocolate
• ⅓ cup (90 g) butter
• 1 cup (200 g) granulated sugar
• 2 tablespoons all-purpose (plain) flour
• 4 egg whites
• dash of salt

VARIATION
– Serve with 1 cup (250 ml) heavy (double) cream whipped until stiff with 4 tablespoons confectioners' (icing) sugar.

Barley pie with plums
Crostata di orzo con le prugne

Serves: 4-6; Preparation: 1 hour; Cooking: 90 minutes; Level of difficulty: Medium; Equipment: 10 in (25 cm) pie dish, greased and floured

Prepare the pastry. § Boil the barley in salted water for about 40 minutes, then drain. § Add the milk and the vanilla bean, and continue to cook until all the liquid has been absorbed. Remove from the heat. § Add the sugar and then the yolks one by one, stirring until thoroughly combined. § Cook the plums with the sugar and lemon juice until soft but still intact, stirring occasionally. § Line a pie dish 10 in (25 cm) in diameter with the pastry, and fill with the barley, spreading it out evenly. § Top with the plums and bake in a preheated oven at 350°F/180°C/gas 4 for about 45 minutes.

■ INGREDIENTS

• 1 quantity *Sweet plain pastry* (see recipe p. 60)
• ½ cup (100 g) pearl barley
• dash of salt
• 1 cup (250 ml) milk
• 1 vanilla bean (pod)
• 4 tablespoons granulated sugar
• 4 egg yolks
• 1 lb (500 g) plums, pitted (stoned) and sliced
• ¾ cup (150 g) brown sugar
• juice of ½ lemon

VARIATION
– Make the pastry with whole-wheat (wholemeal) flour instead of white flour, adding 2 extra tablespoons of butter.

Right
Crostata di orzo con le prugne

Sicilian ricotta cake
Cassata Siciliana

Serves: 6; Preparation: 2¼ hours; Chilling: 2 hours; Level of difficulty: Complicated

Boil the sugar, water, and vanilla bean in a heavy-bottomed pan until the mixture turns to syrup. Set aside to cool. § Beat the Ricotta vigorously with a spatula, then add the syrup gradually, stirring until the mixture becomes soft and creamy. § Mix the chocolate and candied fruit (reserving some for decoration) with the Ricotta, then add the nuts and Maraschino. § Cut the sponge cake into thin slices and line a springform pan 10 in (25 cm) in diameter with them, adding a little apricot jelly to bind them together. § Fill with the Ricotta mixture, spreading it evenly. § Cover with the remaining sponge and chill in the refrigerator for at least 2 hours. § Prepare the glaze by heating the rest of the apricot jelly, vanilla sugar, and orange flower water, stirring until it becomes syrupy. § Remove the cake from the refrigerator, coat evenly with the glaze and decorate with the reserved pieces of candied fruit.

VARIATION
– This recipe is a simplified one as regards the glaze. The original recipe has fondant icing. To make this, beat 1⅔ cups (250 g) confectioners' (icing) sugar with two egg whites. Color with green food coloring and glaze the cake.

■ INGREDIENTS

- 1¼ cups (250 g) granulated sugar
- ½ cup (125 ml) water
- 1 vanilla bean (pod)
- 2 cups (500 g) fresh Ricotta cheese, strained
- 5 squares (150 g) semi-sweet (dark) chocolate, chopped in tiny pieces
- 3 cups (300 g) mixed candied fruit
- 1½ tablespoons pistachio nuts, shelled
- 2 tablespoons Maraschino or Kirsch liqueur
- 1 quantity *Italian sponge cake* (see recipe p. 62)
- 3 heaped tablespoons apricot jelly (jam)
- 1 tablespoon confectioners' (icing) sugar
- 2 tablespoons orange flower water

Chestnut cake
Castagnaccio

This Tuscan specialty is very easy to prepare.

Serves: 8; Preparation: 20 minutes; Cooking: 1 hour; Level of difficulty: Simple

Place the chestnut flour in a mixing bowl and gradually stir in the water, taking care that no lumps form. § Add the salt and 2½ tablespoons of the pine nuts. § Place the chestnut mixture in a layer about ½ in (1 cm) thick on an oiled baking sheet. Drizzle with the oil and scatter with the rosemary and remaining pine nuts. § Bake in a preheated oven at 400°F/200°/gas 6 for about 1 hour. § Serve immediately.

■ INGREDIENTS

- 3⅓ cups (500 g) chestnut flour, sifted
- 3¼ cups (800 ml) cold water
- dash of salt
- 2 tablespoons extra-virgin olive oil
- 1 tablespoon fresh rosemary
- 3 tablespoons pine nuts

VARIATION
– Add raisins or chopped walnuts to the mixture.

Right:
Cassata siciliana

■ INGREDIENTS

- ⅔ cup (200 g) butter, melted
- 8 eggs, separated
- 1 cup (200 g) granulated sugar
- dash of salt
- 1⅔ cups (250 g) all-purpose (plain) flour
- butter and flour for the cake pan
- 3½ cups (450 g) mixed berry fruit (wild strawberries, raspberries, blackberries, etc)
- ⅓ cup (50 g) confectioners' (icing) sugar

Mixed berry cake
Torta ai frutti di bosco

Serves: 6; Preparation: 30 minutes; Cooking: about 1 hour; Level of difficulty: Simple

Cream the butter and sugar, then add the egg yolks one by one. § Beat the egg whites with the salt until stiff and fold them into the mixture. Carefully add the flour and mix well. § Pour the mixture into a buttered and floured springform pan 10 in (25 cm) in diameter. Cover with the berries (some may sink into the batter), reserving a few for decorating. § Bake in a preheated oven at 375°F/190°C/gas 5 for about 1 hour. § Set aside to cool. Sprinkle with the confectioners' sugar and decorate with the reserved berries just before serving.

■ INGREDIENTS

- 1⅔ cups (200 g) almonds, toasted
- ⅔ cup (100 g) shelled walnuts
- 2 tablespoons candied lemon peel
- 1 cup (200 g) candied orange peel
- 1 cup (150 g) all-purpose (plain) flour
- ½ teaspoon each, coriander, mace, cloves, nutmeg
- ¾ cup (150 g) brown sugar
- ½ cup (150 g) honey

SPICE POWDER:
- 3 tablespoons cardamom
- 1 tablespoon cinnamon

Panforte
Panforte

A traditional cake from Siena dating from the Middle Ages.

Serves: 8; Preparation: 20 minutes; Cooking: 30 minutes; Level of difficulty: Medium

Chop the almonds and walnuts nuts coarsely. Cut the two candied peels into small diamonds. § Combine the peel in a mixing bowl with the flour and ground spices. § Heat the sugar and honey with 1 table-spoonful of cold water, preferably in a copper pan, and stir until dissolved. § When it starts to form small bubbles on the surface, remove a drop of the syrup with a wooden toothpick and place in cold water. Squeeze the drop between two fingers and if threads form when you open and close them, the syrup is ready. § Remove from heat and add the nut mixture. § Beat well until all the ingredients are well mixed. § Place the mixture on a baking sheet lined with rice paper. Shape the mixture into a disk about ½ in (1 cm) thick. § Sprinkle with the spice powder and bake in a preheated oven at 350°F/150°C/gas 4 for 3 minutes. § Before serving, cut the excess rice paper away from the edges.

Left:
Torta al frutti di bosco

Creamy Desserts

*From chocolate and liqueur-flavored molds
and mousses, to soft puddings and delectable desserts,
this chapter has a host of suggestions for
perfect ways to finish a family
meal or dinner party.*

Tiramisù
Tiramisù

This delicious dessert will never let you down — it is simple to prepare, never goes wrong, and always makes a wonderful impression. Make it the day before and chill in the refrigerator.

Serves: 6; Preparation: 20 minutes; Chilling: at least 3 hours; Level of difficulty: Simple

Whisk the egg yolks and sugar until pale and creamy. § Carefully fold in the Mascarpone. § Beat the egg whites with the salt until very stiff and fold them into the mixture. § Spread a thin layer over the bottom of a large oval serving dish. § Soak the ladyfingers briefly in the coffee and place a layer over the mixture on the bottom of the dish. § Cover with another layer of the mixture and sprinkle with a little chocolate. § Continue in this way until all the ingredients are in the dish. § Finish with a layer of cream and chocolate, and sprinkle with unsweetened cocoa.

VARIATION
— There are many variations. Try using Zabaione (see recipe p. 68) and crushed praline or nut brittle instead of the Mascarpone mixture.

■ INGREDIENTS

• 5 eggs, separated
• ¾ cup (150 g) granulated sugar
• 2 cups (500 g) Mascarpone cheese
• dash of salt
• about 30 ladyfingers (preferably *savoiardi*)
• 1 cup (250 ml) strong cool coffee
• 7 oz (200 g) semi-sweet (dark) chocolate, grated
• 1 tablespoon unsweetened cocoa (cocoa powder)

Bonet
Bonet

This dessert comes from Turin, the capital city of Piedmont and once home to the kings of Italy.

Serves: 6; Preparation: 30 minutes; Cooking: 1 hour; Level of difficulty: Medium

Whisk the eggs and sugar until pale and creamy. § Stir in the unsweetened cocoa and Amaretto di Saronno. § Pour in the milk gradually, stirring constantly, then add the crumbled Amaretti cookies. § Pour the mixture into a buttered pudding mold and place in a roasting pan half-filled with water. § Bake in a preheated oven at 350°F/180°C/gas 4 for about 1 hour. § Cool before unmolding onto a serving dish.

VARIATION
— Sprinkle the buttered mold with crumbled Amaretti cookies to make a delicious crust.

■ INGREDIENTS

• 6 eggs
• 1¼ cups (250 g) granulated sugar
• 2 tablespoons unsweetened cocoa (cocoa powder), sifted
• 2 tablespoons Amaretto di Saronno (almond) liqueur
• 2 cups (500 ml) milk, very hot
• 6 Amaretti cookies (macaroons), store-bought (or see recipe p. 743), crumbled

Right: *Tiramisù*

Custard with almond brittle
Crema al croccante di mandorle

- zest of 1 lemon, in one piece
- 1¼ cups (300 ml) milk
- 4 egg yolks
- ¾ cup (150 g) superfine (caster) sugar
- 4 teaspoons cornstarch (corn flour)
- ⅓ cup (100 g) almond brittle, crushed

Serves: 4; Preparation: 20 minutes; Cooking: 20 minutes; Level of difficulty: Simple

Bring the lemon zest and milk to a boil. § Place the egg yolks and sugar in a heavy-bottomed saucepan and whisk until pale and creamy. § Mix in the cornstarch and the hot milk and cook the mixture over very low heat until it comes to a boil. § Cook for another 3 minutes, stirring continuously. § Remove from heat and add the almond brittle, reserving some for decoration. § Serve the custard in small individual dishes decorated with the reserved almond brittle.

VARIATION
– Replace the almond brittle with Amaretti cookies (macaroons) and sprinkle the top with unsweetened cocoa.

Apple charlotte
Charlotte di mele

- 5 cooking apples, peeled and cored
- 4 tablespoons superfine (caster) sugar
- 2–3 drops vanilla extract (essence)
- 10 oz (300 g) sliced white bread, crusts removed
- ¾ cup (200 ml) butter, melted
- 1 egg white
- 4 tablespoons white rum
- confectioners' (icing) sugar, for sprinkling

Charlottes are molded desserts, made in a pan lined with bread,

cake, or ladyfingers and filled with fruit, pudding, or cream.

Serves: 8; Preparation: 50 minutes; Cooking: 40 minutes; Level of difficulty: Medium

Chop the apples into bite-sized pieces and cook in a small amount of water until soft and mushy. § Add 3 tablespoons of the sugar and a few drops of vanilla extract and continue cooking until the mixture thickens. § Butter a charlotte mold and line it with baking parchment (paper). § Cut the slices of bread in half and brush with some of the melted butter. Line the mold with them, overlapping slightly. § Beat the egg white with the remaining sugar and brush over the bread. § Finish with a light sprinkling of rum, then pour in the apple purée. § Cover with more bread slices spread with butter and sprinkled with rum. § Bake in a preheated oven at 350°F/180°C/gas 4 for 40 minutes. § Sprinkle with confectioners' sugar and serve.

VARIATION
– Repace the bread with the same weight of ladyfingers soaked in milk and brandy.

Right:
Crema al croccante di mandorle

Skull cap
Zuccotto

*This Florentine dessert takes its name (the Italian word zuccotto means "skullcap")
from the traditional head coverings worn by church dignitaries.*

Serves: 6-8; Preparation: 40 minutes; Chilling: at least 5 hours; Level of difficulty: Medium

Cut the sponge cake into small slices. § Prepare the syrup by boiling the
and water for a few minutes. Remove from heat, add the brandy and
rum, and leave to cool. § Moisten the edges of a domed mold with a
little syrup and line with half the sliced sponge cake. Brush with the
remaining syrup. § Mix the confectioners' sugar, nuts, candied fruit, and
chocolate into the whipped cream. Pour the mixture into the dish and
cover with the remaining sponge slices. § Chill the dessert for at least 5
hours. § To unmold, dip the dish briefly into cold water.

■ INGREDIENTS

- 1 quantity *Italian sponge cake* (see recipe page 62)
- ¾ cup (150 g) granulated sugar
- ¾ cup (200 ml) water
- 3 tablespoons brandy
- 3 tablespoons rum
- ⅓ cup (50 g) confectioners' (icing) sugar
- ⅓ cup (100 g) almonds, toasted and ground
- ⅓ cup (100 g) hazelnuts, toasted and ground
- 4 tablespoons candied fruit, chopped
- 5 oz (150 g) semi-sweet (dark) chocolate, flaked
- 4 cups (1 liter) whipped cream

VARIATION
– Mix 7 oz (200 g) of melted semi-sweet chocolate with half the
whipped cream to create two layers with two different flavors.

Raspberry charlotte
Charlotte al lamponi

Serves: 6-8 Preparation: 40 minutes; Chilling: overnight; Level of difficulty: Simple

Fold the confectioners' sugar, raspberries, and 1 crumbled meringue into
the whipped cream. § Stir in the raspberry syrup (reserving 2 tablespoons)
and liqueur. § Cut the sponge into slices and crumble the other
meringues. § Brush a charlotte mold with reserved raspberry syrup and
line it with slices of sponge cake. § Pour in half the filling and half the
crumbled meringues, then add the remaining filling and meringues. §
Cover with slices of soaked sponge cake, then chill in the refrigerator
overnight. § Unmold the charlotte by placing the mold in warm water for
a few minutes. § Serve decorated with raspberries and whipped cream.

■ INGREDIENTS

- 2 tablespoons confectioners' (icing) sugar
- 1 cup (250 g) raspberries, chopped
- ¼ quantity *Meringue* (see recipe p. 66)
- 2 cups (500 ml) whipped cream
- 1 cup (250 ml) raspberry syrup
- 2 tablespoons raspberry liqueur
- 2 tablespoons sugar syrup
- 1 quantity *Italian sponge cake* (see recipe p. 62)
- 20 whole raspberries
- 1 cup (250 ml) whipped cream

VARIATION
– Serve the charlotte with a sauce made by blending ⅓ cup (100 g)
raspberries with 4 tablespoons of sugar and a little lemon juice. Place
over low heat for a few minutes to thicken, then leave to cool.

Left: *Zuccotto*

Coppa di crema al mascarpone
Chocolate cream

Serves: 6; Preparation: 30 minutes; Chilling: about 2 hours; Level of difficulty: Medium

Beat the egg yolks and sugar until very pale and creamy. Mix in the Mascarpone gently and flavor with Marsala. § Melt the chocolate in the milk over very low heat. Set aside to cool. § Mix the chocolate and milk with one third of the Mascarpone mixture. § Crumble the meringues in the bottom of 6 ice-cream dishes and pour in the Mascarpone and chocolate mixtures. § Blend the surfaces of the two mixtures with a knife to give a marbled effect. § Leave in the refrigerator to chill for at least 2 hours, then serve.

■ INGREDIENTS

- 2 egg yolks
- ½ cup (100 g) granulated sugar
- 1⅓ cups (300 g) Mascarpone cheese
- 1 tablespoon Marsala wine
- 4 oz (125 g) semi-sweet (dark) chocolate, chopped
- 2 ½ tablespoons milk
- ⅓ quantity *Meringue* (see recipe, p 66)

Florentine trifle
Zuppa Inglese

■ INGREDIENTS

- ½ cup (125 ml) Alchermes liqueur
- ½ cup (125 ml) rum
- about 4 tablespoons water
- 2 tablespoons butter
- about 20 ladyfingers (preferably *savoiardi*)
- 1 quantity *Chocolate pastry cream* (see recipe page 68)
- 1 quantity *Vanilla pastry cream* (see recipe page 68)
- 1 cup (250 ml) whipped cream for decoration

The origins of this dessert date back to the splendid Florentine Renaissance court of the Medici family. Its present name (which translates literally as "English soup") probably dates to the 18th century, when it was apparently a favorite with the large expatriate English community in Florence.

Serves: 6; Preparation: 30 minutes; Chilling: about 12 hours; Level of difficulty: Medium

Mix the Alchermes, rum, and water in an earthenware bowl. § Butter a charlotte mold and line it with ladyfingers dipped in the water and liqueur mixture. § Pour the chocolate cream into the mold, then cover with a layer of dipped ladyfingers and spread the vanilla cream on top. § Finish with the remaining ladyfingers. Cover with foil and chill in the refrigerator for 12 hours. § To unmold, dip the dish briefly in warm water. § Serve decorated with whipped cream.

VARIATIONS
– Replace the ladyfingers with thin slices of Italian sponge cake.
– If Alchermes liqueur is unavailable, use another very sweet liqueur colored red with several drops of cochineal (red food coloring).

Cherry delight
Coppa delizia

■ INGREDIENTS

- 6 cups (1.3 kg) cherries, pitted (stoned)
- ½ cup (100 g) granulated sugar
- 2–3 drops vanilla extract (essence)
- dash of cinnamon
- 1 quantity *Italian sponge cake* (recipe p. 62)
- 4 tablespoons Maraschino or Kirsch
- 2 cups (500 ml) whipped cream

Serves: 6; Preparation: 30 minutes; Chilling: about 1 hour; Level of difficulty: Simple

Place the cherries in a heavy-bottomed saucepan with the sugar, vanilla extract, and cinnamon. § Cook over high heat for about 5 minutes, or until the cherries are lightly caramelized. § Reserve about 20 for decoration. § Slice the sponge thinly and use a part to line a deep serving bowl. Brush with liqueur, then cover with a layer of cherries followed by some whipped cream. Repeat this sequence until all the ingredients are in the bowl. § Decorate the top with the reserved cherries. Chill the dessert in the refrigerator for at least 1 hour before serving.

VARIATION
– Replace the cherries with other kinds of fruit, such as peaches. In this case, use rum instead of Maraschino or Kirsch.

Left:
Coppa di crema al mascarpone

Crème brùlée
Creme bruciata

*Made of baked custard, topped with caramelized sugar,
this dessert is a light yet satisfying way to finish a fairly heavy meal.*

Serves: 6; Preparation: 30 minutes; Cooking: 1 hour; Chilling: 2 hours; Level of difficulty: Simple
Whisk the eggs and egg yolks with the sugar until the mixture falls in ribbons. § Warm the cream slightly and beat it into the mixture. § Pour the mixture into individual ramekin dishes through a strainer. § Arrange the ramekins in a roasting pan lined with baking parchment (paper) to prevent them breaking. Pour water around the ramekins and bake them in a preheated oven at 350°F/180°C/gas 4 for about 1 hour. § Leave to cool then chill in the refrigerator for at least 2 hours. § Just before serving, sprinkle the ramekins with brown sugar and place under a hot broiler (grill) until the sugar is caramelized.

Variation
– If preferred, caramelize the brown sugar in a pan on the stove, then pour it over the cold crème brûlée, instead of using the broiler.

■ INGREDIENTS

• 2 eggs and 7 egg yolks
• 2½ cups (500 g) granulated sugar
• 2½ cups (500 ml) light (single) cream
• brown sugar for caramelizing

Limoncello cream
Crema al limoncello

Limoncello is a sweet lemon liqueur which is very much in vogue in Italy at the moment. Originally from the Amalfi coast, near Naples, it is now available throughout the peninsula (and abroad).

Serves: 4; Preparation 15 minutes; Cooking: 10 minutes; Chilling: 1 hour; Level of difficulty: Simple
Prepare the pastry cream. § Stir the Limoncello into the cream and leave to cool with a layer of plastic wrap (clingfilm) over the surface to prevent a skin forming. § Place in individual glass serving dishes and chill for at least 1 hour. § Before serving, decorate with the candied lemon peel and slivered almonds.

Variation
– Flavor the cream with other liqueurs, such as Kirsch or Marsala. If using Marsala, serve garnished with ladyfingers and ground pistachio nuts.

■ INGREDIENTS

• 1 cup (250 ml) Limoncello liqueur
• *Vanilla pastry cream* made with 4 egg yolks (see recipe p. 68)
• 4 slices candied lemon peel
• 4 tablespoons almonds, slivered (flaked)

Right:
Crema bruciata

Cooked cream with coffee
Panna cotta al caffé

■ INGREDIENTS

- 4 cups (1 liter) light (single) cream,
- ¾ cup (150 g) granulated sugar
- 2 tablespoons gelatin
- ⅔ cup (150 ml) strong, hot coffee
- whipped cream to decorate
- coffee beans to decorate

Serves: 6; Preparation: 15 minutes; Cooking: 10 minutes; Chilling: about 5 hours; Level of difficulty: Simple

Boil the cream with the sugar. § Dissolve the gelatin in the hot coffee and stir into the cream and sugar. § Pour the mixture into a domed or rectangular mold, and when it begins to set (not before, otherwise the gelatin and cream will separate) refrigerate for at least 5 hours. § Serve decorated with whipped cream and coffee beans.

Sweet rice with pears
Dolceriso

Serves: 6; Preparation: 1 hour; Cooking: 1 hour; Level of difficulty: Simple

Bring the milk to a boil. Add half the brown sugar and the salt and cook until the sugar has dissolved. Add the rice and continue to cook until all the milk has been absorbed. § Remove from heat, stir in the butter and leave to cool. § To make the filling, peel 3 of the pears. Dice them finely and cook with the lemon juice and all but 1 tablespoon of the remaining brown sugar until soft and syrupy. § Now add the eggs to the rice, one at a time. § Pour half the rice mixture into a springform pan 8 in (20 cm) in diameter, and sprinkle with the bread crumbs. § Cover with two-thirds of the pear mixture, then add another layer of rice, followed by the remaining pears. § Peel the reserved pear. Slice it thinly and arrange over the top. § Sprinkle with the remaining brown sugar and bake in a preheated oven at 350°F/180°C/gas 4 for about 1 hour.

■ INGREDIENTS

• 4 cups (1 liter) milk
• 1 cup (100 g) brown sugar
• dash of salt
• 1¼ cups (250 g) short-grain rice (preferably arborio)
• 4 tablespoons butter
• 4 pears
• juice of ½ lemon
• 2 whole eggs and 2 yolks
• 4 tablespoons dry bread crumbs

Rum baba
Babà al rhum

The word "baba" is of Polish origin, and so, it seems, is this dessert. But in Italy, the baba is just one more exquisite Neapolitan treat. There are many different versions of the rum baba. This is a home recipe, easy to make, and guaranteed to be successful.

Serves: 6; Preparation: 20 minutes; Cooking: 15 minutes; Level of difficulty: Medium

Dissolve the yeast in a little warm water and set aside until it foams. § Beat the eggs and sugar until pale and creamy. § Gradually add the oil, butter, and yeast mixture. § Lastly, stir in the sifted flour and salt. § Knead the mixture vigorously, until it forms a soft, elastic dough. § Fill baba molds just under half full, then cover and leave in a warm place to let the dough rise. § When the dough has risen to just below the rim of each mold, bake in a preheated oven at 350°F/180°C/gas 4 for about 15 minutes. § Meanwhile, prepare the rum syrup by boiling the sugar and water for about 10 minutes, until the mixture is syrupy. § Add the lemon and rum and leave to cool. § When the babas are cooked, leave to cool for a while, then soak in the rum syrup and leave on a wire rack to drain.

■ INGREDIENTS

• 1 oz (30 g) fresh yeast or 2 packages active dry yeast
• 4 tablespoons lukewarm water
• 5 eggs
• 2 tablespoons granulated sugar
• ½ cup (125 ml) extra-virgin olive oil
• 4 tablespoons butter, melted and cooled,
• 2⅓ cups (350 g) all-purpose (plain) flour
• dash of salt

RUM SYRUP
• 1½ cups (300 g) granulated sugar
• 2 cups (500 ml) water
• 1 lemon, sliced
• ½ cup (125 ml) rum

VARIATIONS
– In Naples, babas are often served with whipped cream.
– Some recipes suggest glazing the babas with apricot jelly (jam) dissolved in a little warm water.

Right:
Babà al rhum

Mont Blanc
Monte Bianco

■ INGREDIENTS

- 1 lb (500 g) chestnuts, shelled
- dash of salt
- 1 bay leaf
- ½ cup (60 g) unsweetened cocoa (cocoa powder)
- 1¼ cups (180 g) confectioners' (icing) sugar
- 2 tablespoons white rum
- 1¼ cups (300 ml) whipped cream

Serves: 4-6; Preparation: 40 minutes; Cooking: 40 minutes; Chilling: 1 hour; Level of difficulty: Medium

Cover the chestnuts with water, then add the salt and bay leaf and bring to a boil. § Cook for about 40 minutes, then peel the chestnuts, removing the inner skin. Mash them with a potato-masher while still hot, then place in a mixing bowl and stir in the unsweetened cocoa, confectioners' sugar, and rum. § Put the purée through a potato-ricer or strainer, letting it drop onto the serving dish in a little mound of vermicelli. § Chill for at least 1 hour. § Cover with whipped cream just before serving.

VARIATION
– Decorate the dessert with marrons glacés and candied violets.

Ricotta mousse with plum sauce
Mousse di ricotta con salsa di prugne

■ INGREDIENTS

- 1½ cups (350 g) Ricotta cheese
- ⅓ cup (90 g) vanilla sugar
- 3 egg yolks
- grated zest of 1 lemon
- 1 tablespoon rum
- ⅔ cup (150 ml) whipped cream
- 2 oz (60 g) semi-sweet (dark) chocolate, plus more for decoration
- 2 tablespoons candied orange peel, chopped
- 1 lb (500 g) plums, pitted (stoned)
- ½ cup (100 g) brown sugar
- juice of ½ lemon

The acidity of plums is a good counterbalance to the blandness of cream cheese in desserts.

Serves: 6; Preparation: 20 minutes; Cooking: 15 minutes; Chilling: 1 hour; Level of difficulty: Simple

Cream the Ricotta and vanilla sugar. § Add the yolks, lemon zest, and rum and beat until smooth. § Pour the mixture into a large mixing bowl and carefully fold in the cream, chocolate, and peel (reserve a few pieces for decoration). Chill in the refrigerator for at least 1 hour. § Meanwhile, cook the plums, brown sugar, and lemon juice over high heat until the mixture thickens and then whisk it until reduced to a sauce. § Place the mousse in individual bowls for serving, then pour the hot plum sauce over the top. Decorate with flaked chocolate and candied orange peel.

VARIATION
– If fresh plums are not available, use jelly (jam) heated with a few tablespoons of water.

Left:
Mousse di ricotta con salsa di prugne

Mascarpone mousse with strawberries

Mousse di mascarpone con fragole

Serves: 4; Preparation: 30 minutes; Chilling: 4 hours; Level of difficulty: Simple

Dissolve the gelatin in a little hot water, then add half to the liqueur and the other half to the wine. Stir both mixtures well, then set them aside to cool. § Beat the egg whites with the salt until stiff, then carefully fold in the confectioners' sugar. § Mix the Mascarpone with the jellied liqueur, then fold in the cream and lastly the egg white mixture. § Chill the mousse for about 4 hours. § Slice the strawberries thinly and place them in individual serving dishes. Pour over a little of the jellied wine and fill the dishes with the mousse. Sprinkle with confectioners' sugar and serve the rest of the jellied wine separately.

VARIATION
– Replace the strawberries with an equal quantity of raspberries.

■ INGREDIENTS

- 2 tablespoons gelatin
- 4 tablespoons strawberry liqueur
- 1¼ cups (300 ml) fruity white wine
- 2 egg whites
- dash of salt
- ½ cup (75 g) confectioners' (icing) sugar, plus extra for sprinkling
- 1 cup (250 g) Mascarpone cheese
- ¾ cup (200 ml) heavy (double) cream, whipped
- 1 cup (250 g) strawberries

Chestnut mousse with chocolate

Mousse di castagne al cioccolato

Serves: 6; Preparation: 20 minutes + 2 hours to chill; Level of difficulty: Simple

Place the chestnut purée (made by mashing boiled chestnuts; see recipe for Mont Blanc on page 735) in a mixing bowl . § Melt the chocolate in the top of a double-boiler and then add it to the purée with the cream. Mix thoroughly. § Beat the egg whites with the salt until stiff, then add the confectioners' sugar and mix carefully until the mixture becomes glossy. § Add the chestnut purée and use a spatula to mix the ingredients thoroughly. § Chill the mousse in the refrigerator for at least 2 hours. Serve in individual dishes, decorated with marrons glacés and sprinkled with chocolate shavings.

VARIATION
– Served with a bowl of stiffly whipped cream.

■ INGREDIENTS

- 1 cup (250 g) chestnut purée
- 3½ oz (100 g) semi-sweet (dark) chocolate
- ¾ cup (200 ml) light (single) cream
- 2 egg whites
- dash of salt
- ½ cup (75 g) confectioners' (icing) sugar
- 6 marrons glacés to decorate
- semi-sweet (dark) chocolate shavings for sprinkling

Right:
Mousse di castagne al cioccolato

Mousse al cioccolato
Chocolate mousse

■ INGREDIENTS

- 12 oz (350 g) semi-sweet (dark) chocolate
- 6 eggs, separated
- 4 tablespoons confectioners' (icing) sugar
- ¾ cup (200 ml) light (single) cream

Serves: 8; Preparation: 30 minutes; Chilling: about 12 hours; Level of difficulty: Simple

Melt the chocolate in the top of a double-boiler and leave until tepid. § Whisk the egg yolks and confectioners' sugar until very pale and creamy. Add the melted chocolate and return to heat for a few minutes, stirring all the time. Set aside to cool. § Whip the cream and the egg whites separately. § Carefully fold the egg whites and cream into the cooled egg-and-chocolate mixture, taking great care not to let the mixture collapse. § Chill the mousse for about 12 hours before serving.

Rice pudding Artusi-style
Budino di riso dell'Artusi

Food writer Pellegrino Artusi published L'Arte di mangiar bene (The Art of Eating Well) back in 1891, yet it remains the best-selling cook book in Italy. Artusi, who chose and classified 790 home recipes from Tuscany and Emilia Romagna, was the the first Italian food writer to write about everyday recipes and cooking. This is one of his classic desserts.

Serves: 8; Preparation: 15 minutes; Cooking: 35 minutes; Level of difficulty: Simple

Place the rice, milk, and vanilla bean over medium heat. Bring to a boil, add the superfine sugar, raisins, peel, salt, and butter, and simmer for 10 minutes. § When cooked, remove from heat. Remove the vanilla bean and set the mixture aside to cool. § Add the eggs one at a time, and then the rum. Pour this mixture into a buttered pudding basin coated with the bread crumbs. § Bake in a preheated oven at 350°F/180°C/gas 4 for about 35 minutes. Unmold and serve while still warm.

VARIATION
– Serve with 1 quantity *Vanilla pastry cream* (see recipe page 68).

■ INGREDIENTS

- 1 cup (150 g) short-grain rice (preferably arborio)
- 4 cups (1 liter) milk
- 1 vanilla bean (pod)
- ⅓ cup (90 g) granulated sugar
- ½ cup (100 g) golden raisins (sultanas),
- 1½ tablespoons mixed candied peel, chopped
- dash of salt
- 1 tablespoon butter
- 2 whole eggs and 2 yolks
- 1 cup (250 ml) rum or Cognac
- 2 tablespoons butter for greasing the pudding basin
- 4 tablespoons bread crumbs

Peach soufflé
Soffiato di pesche

Serves: 4; Preparation: 15 minutes; Cooking: about 1 hour; Level of difficulty: Simple

Cream the butter, superfine sugar, and salt. § Add the egg yolks one by one, then the Ricotta. Mix in the cornstarch, lemon juice and zest, and almonds. § Beat the egg whites until stiff, and fold gently into the mixture. Add the peaches and pour the mixture into 4 timbale molds coated with bread crumbs. § Bake in a preheated oven at 325°F/160°C/ gas 3 for about 1 hour. Serve warm, sprinkled with confectioners' sugar.

VARIATION
– Try this recipe with other kinds of fruit, such as apricots or nectarines.

■ INGREDIENTS

- 3½ tablespoons butter
- ½ cup (100 g) granulated sugar
- dash of salt
- 2 eggs, separated
- 1 cup (250 g) Ricotta cheese, strained
- ⅓ cup (50 g) cornstarch (corn flour),
- zest and juice of 1 lemon,
- 2 tablespoons almonds, toasted and ground
- 3 large yellow peaches, pitted (stoned) and sliced
- 4 tablespoons bread crumbs
- 2 tablespoons confectioners' (icing) sugar

Right:
Budino di riso dell'Artusi

Cookies

Every Italian region has its own special cookies.
There are many variations on the classic recipes.
In this chapter I have included our family favorites.

■ INGREDIENTS

- 3 cups (450 g) almonds, toasted
- 1¾ cups (350 g) granulated sugar
- 5 egg whites
- dash of cinnamon

Ugly but good
Brutti ma buoni

These cookies owe their name to the fact that they do not actually look particularly inviting. But their crispness and delicious almond flavor make them the perfect snack, or after-dinner treat, accompanied by dessert wine or coffee.

Serves: 6-8; Preparation: 40 minutes; Cooking: 30 minutes; Level of difficulty: Medium

Finely chop the almonds with 2 tablespoons of the sugar in a food processor. § Beat the egg whites until stiff and fold in the remaining sugar, almonds, and cinnamon. § Cook this mixture over very low heat, stirring continuously, until it comes away from the sides of the saucepan. Set aside for a few minutes. § Place heaped teaspoonfuls of the mixture on a baking sheet lined with baking parchment (paper). Allow room for spreading. § Bake in a preheated oven at 300°F/150°C/gas 2 for 30 minutes. § Serve cold.

VARIATION
– Try adding 2 tablespoons of unsweetened cocoa (cocoa powder) to the mixture. They are also delicious with toasted hazelnuts instead of almonds.

■ INGREDIENTS

- 1½ cups (180 g) sweet almonds, toasted
- 3 teaspoons bitter almonds, toasted
- 2 cups (300 g) confectioners' (icing) sugar
- 2 egg whites

Macaroons
Amaretti

Bitter almonds are an indispensable ingredient in these tasty cookies. Indeed, they owe their name to them ("amaro" meaning "bitter"). There are many recipes, but the one I have chosen is a classic version and sure to be a success. If you cannot get bitter almonds, add a few drops of almond extract (essence) to sweet almonds.

Makes about 30; Preparation: 20 minutes; Cooking: 30 minutes; Level of difficulty

Finely chop the sweet and bitter almonds with a little confectioners' sugar in a food processor. § Place in a mixing bowl and add half the confectioners' sugar, then one of the egg whites, followed by the remaining sugar, and the second egg white. § Mix by hand until smooth. Roll into cylinders 1–2 in (2.5–5 cm) in diameter. Cut into slices about ½ in (1 cm) thick, then form into balls, and squash them slightly. § Place on a buttered and floured baking sheet. Allow room for spreading. Sprinkle with confectioners' sugar, then bake in a preheated oven at 450°F/230°C/gas 7 for 30 minutes. Serve cold.

Left:
Brutti ma buoni and Amaretti

Ricciarelli
Ricciarelli

These traditional cookies from Siena are thought to be of Arab origin, imported during the Crusades.

Serves: 4; Preparation: 1 hour, + 5–6 hours to rest the dough; Cooking: 15 minutes; Level of difficulty: Complicated

Finely chop the sweet and bitter almonds (or extract) with the flour, ammonium bicarbonate, and orange peel in a food processor. § Put the granulated sugar and water in a saucepan and cook over a low heat until the mixture forms a thin syrup. Add to the almond paste and set aside for 5–6 hours. § Beat the egg white with the confectioners' sugar until stiff and then work it into the dough. § Sprinkle a work surface with flour. Roll the dough out to about ½ in (1 cm) thick. Cut into diamonds measuring about 2 in (5 cm) long. § Place on a baking sheet lined with rice paper, allowing room for spreading. Bake in a preheated oven at 300°F/150°C/gas 2 for about 15 minutes. They should not be brown, so take care not to overbake. § Sprinkle with confectioners' sugar and serve.

■ INGREDIENTS

- 2 cups (250 g) sweet almonds, toasted and ground
- 3 teaspoons bitter almonds, ground, or 3 drops almond extract
- 2 tablespoons all-purpose (plain) flour, plus some extra for the work surface
- dash of baking soda
- 3 teaspoons candied orange peel, chopped
- ⅔ cup (125 g) granulated sugar
- 3 tablespoons water
- 1 egg white
- 2 teaspoons confectioners' (icing) sugar, plus some extra to sprinkle on the cookies

Prato cookies
Biscottini di Prato

In Tuscany these are an almost obligatory ending to a meal.
They are dipped in Vin Santo while lingering at the table.

Makes: about 2 lb (1 kg) of cookies; Preparation: 30 minutes; Cooking: 30 minutes; Level of difficulty: Medium

Mix the orange zest with the sifted flour and baking powder. Place on a work surface, make a well in the center, and fill with the sugar, whole eggs and yolks, and salt. § Work the ingredients together briefly, then add the almonds, a few at a time. Knead the mixture vigorously, until it forms a soft, elastic dough. § Shape into cylinders about 1 in (2.5 cm) in diameter. Arrange on a buttered and floured baking sheet and brush with egg white. § Bake in a preheated oven at 325°F/160°C/gas 3 for about 15 minutes. § Slice the cylinders diagonally into pieces about 1 in (2.5 cm) long and return to the oven for 15 minutes, or until golden brown. § Serve when cold.

■ INGREDIENTS

- grated zest of 1 orange
- 3⅓ cups (500 g) all-purpose (plain) flour
- 1 teaspoon baking powder
- 1 cup (200 g) granulated sugar
- 2 whole eggs, 2 yolks, and 2 egg whites
- dash of salt
- 1¾ cups (250 g) almonds, whole

VARIATION
— Add a dash of saffron to the dough for extra color.

Right:
Ricciarelli and Biscottini di Prato

Cream crescents
Crestine alla crema

Serves: 6; Preparation: 30 minutes; Cooking: 20 minutes; Level of difficulty: Medium

Prepare the vanilla pastry cream and leave to cool. § Sift the flour onto a clean work surface, shape into a mound, and make a well in the center. Add the first measures of granulated and vanilla sugars, as well as the butter, lemon zest, egg yolks, and salt. § Work the ingredients together quickly, adding the baking powder last. § Roll the dough out to a thickness of ¼ in (6 mm) and use a cookie (pastry) cutter, or large glass, to cut out rounds. § Place a tablespoonful of the pastry cream on one side of each round, and fold the pastry in half to form a crescent-shaped cookies. Press down on the edges to seal the cream in. Continue until all the dough and cream are used up. § Place the cookies on a buttered and floured baking sheet, allowing room for spreading. Bake in a preheated oven at 350°F/180°C/gas 4 for about 20 minutes. Sprinkle with the remaining vanilla sugar and serve.

VARIATION
– You can also fill these crescents with thick jelly (jam) or fruit purée.

■ INGREDIENTS

- 1 quantity *Vanilla pastry cream* (see recipe p. 68)
- 3⅓ cups (500 g) all-purpose (plain) flour
- 1 cup (200 g) granulated sugar
- 1 tablespoon vanilla sugar
- 1 cup (250 g) butter, softened
- grated zest of 1 lemon
- 2 egg yolks
- dash of salt
- 3 teaspoons baking powder
- 2 tablespoons vanilla sugar for sprinkling

Grape delights
Delizie all'uva

These candies do not keep for long, so try and eat them all straight away.

Serves: 6; Preparation: 20 minutes + time to settle; Cooking: 5 minutes; Level of difficulty: Simple

Toss the grapes in 1 tablespoonful of rum. § Heat the water and sugar in a pan and stir until the sugar is completely dissolved. § Crumble the rusks to powder and sprinkle with the remaining rum, then stir the mixture into the sugar mixture, together with the almonds and 1 tablespoonful of unsweetened cocoa. § When cool, take a small piece of the mixture and place a grape in the center, then form into a small ball. Roll in the unsweetened cocoa and set aside. Coat all the grapes in this way and leave for a few hours before serving.

■ INGREDIENTS

- 15 large white seedless grapes
- 2 tablespoons rum
- ½ cup (125 ml) water
- 1¼ cups (250 g) granulated sugar
- 6 rusks (Zwieback)
- 2¼ cups (250 g) almonds, ground
- 1 cup (150 g) unsweetened cocoa (cocoa powder)

Right:
Crestine alla crema

Chocolate truffles
Tartufi al cioccolato

Quick and easy to make, these little homemade chocolates are perfect with coffee.

Serves: 6; Preparation: 30 minutes; Chilling: 2 hours; Level of difficulty: Simple

Cream the butter and confectioners' sugar, then beat in the egg yolks one at a time. § Bring the cream to the boil, then add the vanilla sugar and stir to dissolve. Pour the hot cream into the butter mixture and stir in the chocolate. Chill for at least 2 hours. § Using a tablespoon, form into balls and roll in the unsweetened cocoa. § Store in the refrigerator until it is time to serve.

VARIATION
– Roll the balls in granulated sugar or flavor the cream with a liqueur of your choice.

■ INGREDIENTS

- 3½ tablespoons butter
- ⅓ cup (50 g) confectioners' (icing) sugar
- 2 egg yolks
- ⅓ cup (90 ml) light (single) cream
- 2 tablespoons vanilla sugar
- 12 oz (350 g) semi-sweet (dark) chocolate, grated
- 4 tablespoons unsweetened cocoa (cocoa powder)

Chocolate pralines
Cioccolatini pralinati

Serves: 5; Preparation: 1 hour; Chilling: 2 hours; Cooking: 20 minutes; Level of difficulty: Complicated

Melt the chocolate in the top of a double-boiler. Stir in the coffee, butter, and 4 tablespoons of the sugar and leave to cool. § When lukewarm, stir in the egg yolks. Place this mixture in the refrigerator until solid. § Heat the remaining sugar in the water and when the sugar is dissolved, add the hazelnuts. Continue to stir over low heat until the mixture darkens. § Spread out on an oiled work surface, and leave to cool. Chop this praline mixture finely in a blender. § Shape the solid chocolate mixture into a roll. § Lightly whisk the egg whites. Dip the roll into them and then into the praline, making sure that the coating sticks. Chill for 2 hours. § Just before serving, cut into slices to make individual chocolates.

VARIATION
– Roll the chocolates in grated coconut instead of the praline.

■ INGREDIENTS

- 8 oz (250 g) semi-sweet (dark) chocolate
- 1 tablespoon strong hot coffee
- 4 tablespoons butter
- 1 cup (200 g) granulated sugar
- 1½ cups (180 g) hazelnuts, ground
- 2 eggs, separated
- ⅓ cup (90 ml) water
- oil for the work surface

Right:
*Cioccolatini pralinati and
Tartufi al cioccolato*

INGREDIENTS

- 1½ cups (300 g) brown sugar
- ⅔ cup (125 g) granulated sugar
- 1 cup (250 ml) light (single) cream
- ¾ cup (125 ml) milk
- 1⅓ cups (150 g) almonds, ground
- 10 drops vanilla extract

Croccantini
Croccantini

Makes about 20; Preparation: 15 minutes; Cooking: 15 minutes; Level of difficulty: Simple

Combine the 2 sugars with the cream and milk over medium heat and bring to a boil, then beat with an electric whisk until creamy. § Stir in the almonds and vanilla extract, then divide the mixture into small balls. § Place on a baking sheet lined with baking parchment (paper). Bake in a preheated oven at 350°F/180°C/gas 4 for about 15 minutes, or until golden brown. Serve cold.

Fritters and Crêpes

Many of the best regional sweets and treats in Italy are quickly fried in olive oil, sprinkled with granulated or confectioners' sugar, and served piping hot.

Sweet tortelli with ricotta cheese
Tortelli dolci di ricotta

*If you want the fritters to be crisp and golden brown, you must fry
them a few at a time to avoid reducing the temperature of the oil.*

*Serves: 6; Preparation: 15 minutes + time for the dough to rest; Cooking: 20 minutes; Level of
difficulty: Simple*

Strain the Ricotta and place in a mixing bowl. § Add the eggs,
granulated sugar, orange zest, salt, baking soda, and soaked raisins.
Lastly, stir in the sifted flour. Work the mixture into a smooth, well-
mixed dough and leave to rest for about 1 hour. § Heat the oil to very
hot in a large skillet (frying pan) and fry spoonfuls of the mixture until
golden brown. Drain on paper towels. Roll them in the confectioners'
sugar and serve hot.

■ INGREDIENTS

- 1½ cups (350 g) Ricotta
  cheese
- 3 eggs
- ⅓ cup (80 g) granulated
  sugar
- grated zest of 1 orange
- dash of salt
- dash of baking soda
  (bicarbonate of soda)
- 4 tablespoons raisins,
  soaked in rum overnight
- 1⅓ cups (200 g) all-
  purpose (plain) flour
- 2 cups (500 ml) olive oil,
  for frying
- 1 cup (150 g) confectioners'
  (icing) sugar

Carnival fritters
Sfrappole

*With minor variations, these fritters are made in all regions of Italy at Carnival time,
the period leading up to Lent. They are known under under different names depending
on the region. This recipe has come down through my husband's family,
who originally came from Emilia-Romagna.*

Serves: 8-10; Preparation: 20 minutes + time to rest; Cooking: 15 minutes; Level of difficulty: Simple

Sift the flour onto a clean work surface, add the granulated sugar and salt,
and shape into a mound. Make a well in the center and break the eggs into it,
then add the softened butter and cognac. Mix the ingredients together
carefully and leave the dough to rest in a warm place for 2–3 hours. § Roll
out a sheet of dough ⅛ in (3 mm) thick and cut it into strips about 1 in (2.5
cm) wide, using a ravioli wheel or knife. § Make the Sfrappole by tying a
knot in each strip. Heat the oil to very hot in a large skillet (frying pan) and
fry in small batches until light golden brown. § Sprinkle with confectioners'
sugar while still hot.

■ INGREDIENTS

- 3⅓ cups (500 g) all-
  purpose (plain) flour
- 2 tablespoons granulated
  sugar
- dash of salt
- 4 eggs
- 2 tablespoons butter
- ½ cup (125 ml) cognac
- 2 cups (500 ml) oil,
  for frying
- confectioners' (icing)
  sugar for sprinkling

VARIATION
— The original recipe uses lard for frying. This gives the Sfrappole
more flavor, but they will also be heavier. You can also use white
wine instead of cognac.

Right:
Sfrappole

St. Joseph's fritters
Frittelle di San Giuseppe

Rice fritters are popular in more or less all parts of northern Italy. They are given this name in Tuscany because they are usually made on St. Joseph's Day — March 19.

■ INGREDIENTS

- 2½ cups (500 g) short-grain rice (preferably arborio)
- 2 cups (500 ml) water
- 4 cups (1 liter) milk
- 1¼ cups (250 g) granulated sugar
- grated zest of 1 lemon
- dash of salt
- 3 egg yolks
- 2 tablespoons all-purpose (plain) flour
- 2–3 drops vanilla extract (essence)
- 1½ quarts (1½ liters) oil, for frying
- a little confectioners' sugar to sprinkle on the fritters

Makes: 50 fritters; Preparation: 20 minutes + time to rest; Cooking: 1 hour; Level of difficulty: Medium

Boil the rice in the water and milk, together with the granulated sugar and lemon zest (yellow part only) and salt until all the liquid is absorbed. Leave to settle overnight. § The next day, stir in the egg yolks one at a time, then add the flour and vanilla extract. § Form the mixture into roughly-shaped balls with aid of a teaspoon, taking care not to make them too small. Heat the oil to very hot in a large skillet (frying pan) and fry the fritters until golden brown. Drain on paper towels. § When cold, roll in the confectioners' sugar and serve.

VARIATION
– Flavor the dough with liqueur or add grated orange zest.

Jelly-filled fritters
Raviolini di marmellata

A typical dish from Emilia-Romagna, traditionally eaten at Carnival time.

■ INGREDIENTS

- 3⅓ cups (500 g) all-purpose (plain) flour,
- 1 cup (200 g) granulated sugar
- 1 tablespoon baking powder
- 3 eggs
- 4 tablespoons butter, melted
- 3 tablespoons Sassolino liqueur (or dark rum)
- 1½ cups (450 g) black cherry jelly (jam)
- 2 cups (500 ml) oil, for frying
- confectioners' (icing) sugar

Preparation 1 hour + time for the dough to rest; Cooking: 30 minutes; Level of difficulty: Medium

Mix the sifted flour with the granulated sugar and baking powder. Pour the mixture onto a work surface and make a well in the center. § Break the eggs into the well, add the melted butter a little at a time and the liqueur. Work the ingredients together until the dough is smooth and elastic, then leave to rest for at least 1 hour. § Roll the dough out to a thickness of ¼ in (6 mm) and cut out 2-in (5-cm) circles using a round cookie cutter. Place a little jelly on one half of each circle, then fold the other half over and seal the edges. § Heat the oil to very hot in a large skillet (frying pan) and fry the fritters a few at a time until golden brown. Drain on paper towels. § Serve hot, sprinkled with confectioners' sugar.

VARIATION
– You can use whatever jelly (jam) you like as long as the consistency is firm. In the traditional recipe, the Raviolini are fried in lard.

Left:

Frittele di San Giuseppe

Sicilian-style fritters with ricotta cheese
Cannoli alla siciliana

The basic ingredient in this well-known dessert is Ricotta cheese.
It should be made from ewe's milk and be extremely fresh.

Serves: 8-10; Preparation: 1 hour + time for the dough to rest; Cooking: 30 minutes; Level of difficulty: Complicated

Sift the flour onto a clean work surface, add the granulated sugar, salt, and unsweetened cocoa, and shape into a mound. Make a well in the center and break the egg into it. Add the softened butter, coffee, and lemon juice and zest. Mix well together, using as much wine as necessary to form a smooth, elastic dough. Leave to rest for 3 hours. § Roll the dough out into a thin sheet and cut into 4-in (10-cm) squares. Wrap each square round a Cannoli tube, sealing two opposite corners together. § Heat the oil to very hot in a large skillet (frying pan) and fry the cannoli until light golden brown. Drain and cool on paper towels, then remove them from the Cannoli tubes. § Strain the Ricotta, then add the granulated sugar, candied lemon peel, chocolate chips, and lemon zest. § Just before serving, fill the Cannoli with the Ricotta mixture, using a pastry (piping) bag, and sprinkle with confectioners' sugar.

■ INGREDIENTS

FOR THE PASTRY:
- 3⅓ cups (500 g) all-purpose (plain) flour
- 3 tablespoons granulated sugar
- dash of salt
- 2 teaspoons unsweetened cocoa (cocoa powder)
- 1 egg
- 3 tablespoons butter
- 2 tablespoons strong cool coffee
- sweet white wine, as required
- 2 cups (500 ml) oil, for frying

FILLING:
- 2 cups (500 g) ewe's milk Ricotta cheese
- 1½ cups (300 g) granulated sugar
- 2 cups (200 g) candied lemon peel
- 2 cups (200 g) chocolate chips
- grated zest of 1 lemon
- confectioners' (icing) sugar

Fried cinnamon custard
Crema fritta alla cannella

This recipes comes from traditional Venetian and Lombard cooking.

Serves: 4; Preparation: 30 minutes + time for the custard to cool; Cooking: 20 minutes; Level of difficulty: Simple

Prepare a thick pastry cream following the instructions on page 68, but first boiling the milk together with the cinnamon stick. Leave the custard to cool slightly. § Pour onto an oil-coated work surface and spread out to a thickness of 1 in (2.5 cm). When completely cold and firm, cut out shapes with a cookie cutter. Dip in the egg whites and coat with bread crumbs. Heat the oil to very hot in a large skillet (frying pan) and fry a few at a time until golden brown. Drain on paper towels and serve.

■ INGREDIENTS

- 1 quantity *Lemon custard cream* (see recipe p. 68)
- 1 stick cinnamon
- 2 egg whites, lightly beaten
- ¾ cup (100 g) dry bread crumbs
- 2 cups (500 ml) oil, for frying

VARIATION
– Make a thick *Vanilla pastry cream* (see recipe page 68) and fry as above.

Right:
Cannoli alla siciliana

Apple fritters with vanilla ice cream
Fritelle di mele con gelato di vaniglia

■ INGREDIENTS

• 1⅓ cups (200 g) all-purpose (plain) flour
• 2 eggs, separated
• 2 tablespoons oil
• 2 tablespoons grappa
• 2 dashes salt
• about 1 cup (250 ml) water
• 3 russet apples
• 4 tablespoons lemon juice
• 2 cups (500 ml) oil, for frying
• confectioners' (icing) sugar, for sprinkling
• 1⅓ cups (300 g) vanilla ice cream

Serves: 8; Preparation: 20 minutes + 1 hour for the batter to rest; Cooking: 20 minutes; Level of difficulty: Medium

Prepare the batter by beating the flour with the egg yolks, oil, grappa, and a dash of salt, then adding the water slowly, stirring all the time, until the mixture is smooth but not too liquid. Chill in the refrigerator for at least 1 hour. § Meanwhile, peel and core the apples. Cut them into rings approximately ½ in (1 cm) thick and sprinkle with lemon juice to prevent the flesh from browning. § Beat the egg whites with a dash of salt. Remove the batter from the refrigerator and gently fold in the egg whites. Dip the slices of apple in the batter. § Heat the oil to very hot in a large skillet (frying pan) and fry the apples a few at a time until golden brown. § Drain on paper towels, then sprinkle with confectioners' sugar. § Serve in individual dishes with a scoop of vanilla ice cream.

VARIATION
– Replace the water with the same quantity of milk.
– Sprinkle the fritters with brown sugar or moisten with honey.

Christmas fritters
Struffoli

■ INGREDIENTS

• 3⅓ cups (500 g) all-purpose (plain) flour
• 4 eggs
• 2 tablespoons granulated sugar
• ½ cup (125 ml) liqueur (Strega or anise)
• dash of salt
• 2 cups (500 ml) oil, for frying
• ⅔ cup (200 g) honey
• ¾ cup (90 g) each candied orange and lemon peel, diced
• 2 tablespoons sprinkles (hundreds-and-thousands)

This dessert is popular all over southern Italy, where it is often served at Christmas.

Serves: 10; Preparation: 1 hour; Cooking: 30 minutes; Level of difficulty: Medium

Pour the sifted flour onto a clean work surface and make a well in the center. Place the eggs, granulated sugar, liqueur, and salt in the well and work the ingredients together until they form a smooth elastic dough. § Leave to rest for a while, then divide into pieces and shape them by hand into sticks the thickness of a pencil. Cut each stick into sections no wider than ½ in (1 cm). § Heat the oil to very hot in a large skillet (frying pan) and fry a few at a time. Drain on paper towels. § Heat the honey until thoroughly melted. Add the Struffoli, and candied orange and lemon peels, and stir well to ensure that the honey is distributed evenly. § Tip the Struffoli out onto a serving dish and shape into a mound. Decorate with the sprinkles and serve.

Right:
Frittelle di mele con gelato di vaniglia

Fruit crêpes
Crespelle di frutta

These little pancakes are best eaten as soon as they are ready.

Serves: 6; Preparation: 20 minutes + 2 hours for the fruit; Cooking: 15 minutes; Cooling: 15 minutes; Level of difficulty: Simple

Prepare the batter for the crêpes and chill in the refrigerator for 30 minutes. § Meanwhile, peel the fruit and slice thinly. Leave to macerate for 2 hours in the granulated sugar and lemon juice. § When the batter is ready, drain the fruit thoroughly. Add the vanilla extract and fruit to the batter. § Cook the crêpes in the usual way and serve hot, sprinkled with confectioners' sugar.

VARIATION
– Replace the apple, pear, and banana with fruits of the forest.

■ INGREDIENTS

- ½ quantity *Crêpes* (see recipe p. 62)
- 1 apple
- 1 pear
- 1 banana
- 1 tablespoon granulated sugar
- juice of 1 lemon
- 2–3 drops vanilla extract
- butter for frying
- confectioners' (icing) sugar for sprinkling

Crêpes with cream and marrons glacés
Crespelle con panna e marrons glaces

Serves: 8; Preparation: 20 minutes + 2 hours to rest; Cooking: 20 minutes; Level of difficulty: Medium

Mix both flours with the eggs, granulated sugar, and melted butter. Add the milk gradually, beating the mixture with a whisk to prevent lumps from forming. § Brush a nonstick skillet (frying-pan) with oil and heat to very hot. Pour in a small ladleful of batter, rotating the skillet so that the mixture spreads evenly. Cook the crêpe on both sides without browning. Continue this process until all the batter is used. § Whip the cream with the confectioners' sugar and mix the chopped marrons glacés in gently. § Fill the crêpes with this mixture and serve sprinkled with confectioners' sugar.

VARIATION
– Add a handful of chocolate chips and sprinkle with unsweetened cocoa (cocoa powder).

■ INGREDIENTS

- ⅔ cup (100 g) chestnut flour, sifted
- 1 cup (150 g) all-purpose (plain) flour, sifted
- 3 eggs
- 1 tablespoon granulated sugar
- 3 tablespoons butter, melted
- 2 cups (500 ml) milk
- ¾ cup (200 ml) whipping (heavy) cream
- 2 tablespoons confectioners' (icing) sugar,
- 1 cup (250 g) marrons glacés, chopped

Right:
Crespelle con panna e marrons glacés

Crêpes with mascarpone cheese
Crespelle al mascarpone

■ INGREDIENTS

- 1 quantity *Crêpes*
  (see recipe p. 62)
- 1½ cups (350 g)
  Mascarpone cheese
- 2 egg yolks
- ¾ cup (150 g) granulated
  sugar
- 1 tablespoon rum
- grated zest of 1 lemon
- 2 tablespoons golden
  raisins (sultanas)
- butter for frying
- confectioners' (icing) sugar

Serves: 8; Preparation: 20 minutes + 2 hours to rest; Cooking: 20 minutes; Level of difficulty: Medium

Prepare the crêpes. § Place the Mascarpone in a mixing bowl with the egg yolks, granulated sugar, rum, and lemon zest and beat until soft and creamy. Incorporate the golden raisins (sultanas). § Fill the crêpes with this mixture and serve hot, sprinkled with confectioners' sugar.

VARIATION
– Instead of golden raisins, use grated semi-sweet (dark) chocolate and sprinkle the crêpes with unsweetened cocoa (cocoa powder).

Fig crêpes
Crespelle ai fichi

Serves: 8–10; Preparation: 20 minutes + 2 hours for the batter to rest; Cooking: 20 minutes; Level of difficulty: Medium

Prepare the crêpes. § Cut each fig into 4 segments. Place in a skillet (frying pan) and sprinkle with the grappa and a little confectioners' sugar. Cover and cook over low heat for 5–10 minutes. Leave to cool. § Whip the cream. § Fill the crêpes with the figs and serve sprinkled with confectioners' sugar. Serve the whipped cream separately.

VARIATIONS
– If fresh figs are not available, use fig jelly (jam).
– Add slivered (flaked) almonds to the filling.

Italian doughnuts
Bomboloni

An extremely popular recipe in Florence, these are a variation of the "krapfen" made in Alto Adige in the north. Children love them, and they are absolutely delicious served hot.

Makes: about 20 doughnuts; Preparation: 3½ hours; Cooking: 1 hour; Level of difficulty: Medium

Dissolve the yeast in the warm water and set aside for 10 minutes. § Mix the flour (reserving 3 tablespoons) with one-third of the granulated sugar, the salt, and lemon zest. Make a well in the center and add the butter and then the yeast mixture. § Combine all the ingredients, and when the dough is soft and elastic, cover it and leave it to rest in a warm place for about 2 hours. § On a floured work surface roll the dough out to a thickness of ½ in (1 cm) and use a large upturned glass to cut out as many 3-in (8-cm) rings as possible. § Cover and leave to rise for another hour. § Heat the oil to very hot in a large skillet (frying pan) and fry a few at a time until golden brown. Drain on paper towels, then roll in the remaining granulated sugar and serve hot.

VARIATION
– Make a hole in the center of each doughnut and use a piping-bag to fill them with custard or jelly (jam).

Left:

Bomboloni

Fruit and Ice Cream

*Italian ice cream, called gelato, is famous throughout the world.
It contains less sugar and fat then many other types,
and generally has a much stronger flavor.*

Chocolate fondue
Fonduta al cioccolato

This dessert is a delicious, eyecatching, and fun way to finish a dinner party!

Serves: 8; Preparation: 15 minutes; Cooking: 15 minutes; Level of difficulty: Medium

Wash the fruit and dry with care. Cut the larger pieces into bite-sized chunks. § If using apple, pear, or banana, immerse the chunks in water and lemon juice for a few seconds to prevent the flesh from browning, then dry carefully. § Arrange the fruit in an attractive bowl or serving dish. § Melt the chocolate in the top of a double-boiler over hot water. Dilute with the cream, then add the butter and sugar and mix thoroughly. § Pour the chocolate mixture into a fondue bowl and keep warm over the flame. § Place bowls filled with the almonds, hazelnuts, and coconut on the table, so that diners can dip their pieces of fruit into them, after having dipped them in the chocolate sauce.

VARIATION
– Flavor the chocolate sauce with a small glass of rum.

■ INGREDIENTS

- about 2 lb (1 kg) mixed fresh fruit (strawberries, grapes, bananas, apples, apricots, peaches, figs, plums, pears, etc)
- 2 cups (500 ml) water
- juice of 1 lemon
- 1 lb (500 g) semi-sweet (dark) chocolate, chopped
- 1 cup (250 ml) light (single) cream
- 4 tablespoons butter
- 4 tablespoons granulated sugar
- ⅓ cup (50 g) almonds, toasted and chopped
- ⅓ cup (50 g) hazelnuts, toasted and chopped
- ½ cup (50 g) shredded (desiccated) coconut

Glazed strawberries
Fragole glassate

Serves: 4-6; Preparation: 20 minutes + time to cool; Level of difficulty: Simple

Select the biggest and best strawberries. § Wash them in the white wine and dry carefully. § Melt the two chocolates in separate pans in the top of a double-boiler. Holding the strawberries by the stalks, dip some of them in the semi-sweet chocolate and some of them in the white chocolate. § Arrange on baking parchment (paper). Leave until the chocolate has solidified, then serve.

VARIATION
– Try dipping half of each strawberry first in the semi-sweet chocolate, then leave to dry before dipping the other half in the white chocolate. This way you will get two-tone strawberries.

■ INGREDIENTS

- 32 large strawberries, with stalks
- 1 cup (250 ml) white dessert wine
- 3½ oz (100 g) semi-sweet (dark) chocolate
- 3½ oz (100 g) white chocolate

Right:
Fonduta al cioccolato

Glazed pears with amaretti cream and chocolate
Pere glassate con crema di amaretti e cioccolato

- 6 large ripe yellow pears (Kaiser or Williams)
- 1½ cups (300 g) sugar
- dash of cinnamon
- 3½ oz (100 g) semi-sweet (dark) chocolate
- 1 quantity *Custard* using 3 eggs (see recipe p. 66)
- 6 Amaretti cookies, store-bought (or see recipe p. 743), crumbled
- 4 tablespoons light (single) cream

Serves: 6; Preparation: 30 minutes; Cooking: about 1 hour; Level of difficulty: Complicated

Peel the pears, and without removing the cores, place them whole, in a high-sided, narrow saucepan. § Cover with cold water and stir in the sugar and cinnamon. Cook over low heat until tender but still firm, then remove from the saucepan and leave to cool. § Prepare the custard, stirring in the crumbled Amaretti cookies at the last minute. § Melt the chocolate in the top of a double-boiler. § Meanwhile, bring the cream to a boil, then use it to dilute the liquid chocolate. § Serve the pears in individual dishes, covered with the melted chocolate and on a bed of the custard-and-macaroon mixture.

VARIATION
— These chocolate-covered glazed pears are also delicious with vanilla or chocolate ice cream.

Strawberries and melon with mint-flavored ice
Fragole e melone con ghiaccio alla menta

- 2 cantaloupes (rock melons)
- 1 cup (250 g) wild strawberries
- 24 strawberries
- 2 cups (500 ml) white port
- 3 cups (750 ml) sweet sparkling white wine
- juice of 1 lemon
- 4 tablespoons granulated sugar
- fresh mint leaves
- crushed ice

It is customary to eat melon with port and strawberries with champagne.
I have combined the two with interesting results.

Serves: 6; Preparation: 20 minutes + time to chill; Level of difficulty: Simple

Carve the cantaloupes into balls with the melon-baller, trying to waste as little as possible. § Place the melon balls in the bowl with the wild strawberries and the large strawberries sliced into segments. § Add the port, sparkling wine, lemon juice, sugar, and mint leaves. Chill in the refrigerator for at least 1 hour. § Add crushed ice immediately before serving.

VARIATION
— Prepare a mixture of raspberries, blackcurrants, and blueberries in the same way.

Left: *Pere glassate con crema di Amaretti e cioccolato*

Peach and fig bake
Teglia di pesche e fichi

Serves: 8; Preparation: 30 minutes; Cooking: about 40 minutes; Level of difficulty: Simple

Cut the figs and peaches into segments and arrange on a baking sheet lined with baking parchment (paper). § Sprinkle the peaches with a little of the sugar and place the fruit under the broiler (grill) for about 10 minutes. § Meanwhile, whisk the egg yolks, the remaining sugar, rusks, crumbled Amaretti cookies, and rum. Beat the egg whites with a dash of salt until stiff and fold them in. § Arrange the figs and peaches in a buttered ovenproof dish and pour the egg-and-rusk mixture over the top. Bake in a preheated oven at 350°F/180°C/gas 4 for about 30 minutes. § Serve the dessert while still warm.

VARIATION
– Serve with cream, lightly whipped with a dash of cinnamon.

■ INGREDIENTS

- 12 figs
- 6 peaches
- ½ cup (100 g) granulated sugar
- 6 egg yolks
- 10 rusks (Zwieback)
- 3 Amaretti cookies (macaroons), store-bought (or see recipe p. 743) and crumbled
- 4 tablespoons rum
- 3 egg whites
- dash of salt

Peaches and wine with zabaione
Pesche al vino con zabaione

Peaches, wine, and cinnamon are a classic combination.
The addition of zabaione gives the dish an extra elegant touch.

Serves: 6; Preparation: 40 minutes; Cooking: 30 minutes; Level of difficulty: Medium

Place the wine, sugar, cinnamon stick, and water in a large saucepan and bring to a boil. Boil for 5 minutes. § When the sugar has dissolved, immerse the peaches in this liquid and cook until tender but still firm. Remove from the saucepan and leave to cool. § Meanwhile, reduce the cooking juices over a high heat until they turn to syrup. § When this is cold, arrange it in individual dishes with the peaches and chill in the refrigerator. § Prepare the zabaione, then add to the peaches. Decorate each dish with ground pistachio nuts and serve.

VARIATION
– You will also get excellent results using pears instead of peaches.

■ INGREDIENTS

- 2 cups (500 ml) strong white wine
- ½ cup (125 g) granulated sugar
- 1 stick cinnamon
- ½ cup (125 ml) cold water
- 6 peaches, peeled
- 1 quantity *Zabaione* (see recipe p. 68)
- 4 tablespoons pistachio nuts, ground

Right:
Pesche al vino con zabaione

Oranges with ginger
Arance allo zenzero

Serves: 6; Preparation: 20 minutes + time to cool; Level of difficulty: Simple

Peel the oranges, removing the white parts, then cut into small thin slices. Divide each slice in two. § Arrange the oranges in a serving dish with the rum, confectioners' sugar, almonds, and ginger. § Chill for a few hours, then serve.

VARIATION
– If you don't like ginger, flavor the oranges with a few drops of vanilla extract (essence).

■ INGREDIENTS

- 6 oranges
- 4 tablespoons rum
- 4 tablespoons confectioners' (icing) sugar
- 4 tablespoons almonds, slivered (flaked)
- 1 teaspoon ginger, powdered

Pears with fruits of the forest sauce
Pere con salsa ai frutti di bosco

Of all fruits, the pear is definitely the most suitable for cooking purposes. Adding different flavors enhances the flavor of the pear. The combination of pear and fruits of the forest works particularly well.

Serves: 6; Preparation: 20 minutes; Cooking: 20 minutes; Level of difficulty: Medium

Peel the pears and cut in half. Remove the cores and sprinkle with lemon juice to prevent the flesh from darkening. § Place in a small saucepan with enough water to just cover them, plus 1 cup (200 g) of granulated sugar, the juice of half a lemon, and the cinnamon stick. Cook for about 15 minutes, or until they are tender but still firm. Remove from heat and leave to cool in their own syrup. § Meanwhile, take the fruits of the forest (reserving a few for decoration) and add the remaining granulated sugar, the water, the sweet white wine, and the juice of half a lemon. Place over low heat and cook until the mixture starts to thicken. § Purée the mixture in a food processor then push it through a fine-meshed strainer to remove the seeds. § Drain the pears, and place one pear half in each of six individual serving dishes. Cut into thin slices and place on top of a bed of fruits of the forest sauce. § Decorate with the reserved fruit, then sprinkle with confectioners' sugar, and serve.

■ INGREDIENTS

- 3 pears
- juice of 1½ lemons
- 1¾ cups (350 g) granulated sugar
- 1 stick cinnamon
- 1¼ cups (300 g) mixed fruits of the forest (raspberries, blackcurrants, blueberries, strawberries)
- 4 tablespoons water
- ½ cup (125 ml) sweet dessert wine
- confectioners' (icing) sugar

Right:
Arance allo zenzero

Summer fruit compôte
Composta di frutta estiva

Serves: 6; Preparation: 20 minutes; Cooking: 10 minutes; Level of difficulty: Simple

Dice the peaches and apricots. Halve the grapes, removing the seeds (pips). § Place the butter in a small saucepan and sauté the fruit. Add the sugar and a dash of wine and cook for about 10 minutes. § When the compote is cold, mix in the strawberries. Serve decorated with lightly whipped cream and a sprinkling of chopped, toasted hazelnuts.

> VARIATION
> – Use other varieties of fruit too, provided the colors go together. For example, plums, cherries, and raspberries.

■ INGREDIENTS

- 8 oz (250 g) peaches
- 8 oz (250 g) apricots
- ⅓ cup (100 g) white grapes
- 3 tablespoons butter
- ½ cup (100 g) granulated sugar
- 1 cup (250 ml) fruity white wine
- ¾ cup (100 g) strawberries
- ¾ cup (200 ml) whipping cream
- hazelnuts, toasted and chopped, for sprinkling

Maraschino cup
Coppa al maraschino

Serves: 6; Preparation: 20 minutes + time to chill; Level of difficulty: Simple

Mix the Maraschino with the water and sugar and leave for a few minutes to allow the sugar to dissolve. § Arrange the fruit in the bowl and pour the Maraschino mixture over it. Mix the ingredients together gently and chill for 1 hour before serving.

■ INGREDIENTS

- 1 cup (250 ml) Maraschino liqueur
- 1 cup (250 ml) water
- 4 tablespoons granulated sugar
- 1¾ cups (450 g) cherries
- 1¾ cups (450 g) raspberries
- 1¾ cups (450 g) wild strawberries

Citrus fruit with brown sugar
Agrumi allo zucchero di canna

Serves: 6; Preparation: 20 minutes; Cooking: about 10 minutes; Level of difficulty: Simple

Slice the bananas and leave to soak for a few minutes in the lemon juice and an equal quantity of water. § Peel the grapefruit down to the flesh and slice with the oranges and tangerines. § Dry the bananas thoroughly and mix with the rest of the fruit. § Divide the fruit among individual serving dishes. Cover with plenty of brown sugar and place under a hot broiler (grill) until the sugar is caramelized. Serve at once.

> VARIATION
> – Pour a layer of *Vanilla pastry cream* (see recipe page 68) into the dish before adding the fruit.

■ INGREDIENTS

- 3 bananas
- juice of 1 lemon
- 3 pink grapefruit
- 3 oranges
- 3 tangerines
- brown sugar, to sprinkle over the fruit

Right:
Composta di frutta estiva

Apricot pockets
Albicocche al cartoccio

An effective way to savor all the fragrance of baked fruit.

Serves: 6; Preparation: 30 minutes; Cooking: 30 minutes; Level of difficulty: Simple

Place the wine, brown sugar, honey, and cinnamon in a saucepan and cook over a high heat until the mixture becomes syrupy. § Cut out 6 pieces of baking parchment (paper) with which to make pockets. § Place 2 pitted (stoned), halved apricots in each pocket. Pour a little of the syrup over them, then sprinkle with the crumbled Amaretti cookies and decorate with the pine nuts and raisins. Tie up the pockets with kitchen string and bake in a preheated oven at 400°F/200°C/gas 6 for about 15 minutes. § Serve while still warm.

VARIATION
– Peaches are also delicious prepared in this way.

■ INGREDIENTS

- 1 cup (250 ml) white wine
- 4 tablespoons brown sugar
- 2 tablespoons honey
- ½ stick cinnamon
- 12 apricots
- 10 Amaretti cookies (macaroons), store-bought (or see recipe p. 743), crumbled
- 2 tablespoons pine nuts
- 2 tablespoons raisins

Plums au gratin
Gratin di prugne

Serves: 6; Preparation: 30 minutes; Cooking: 10 minutes; Level of difficulty: Medium

Prepare the custard. § Cut the plums in half and pit (stone) them. § Combine the crumbled Amaretti cookies with the almonds and sugar. § Place the plums in an ovenproof glass dish with the cut surfaces upward. Cover with the custard and sprinkle with the crumbled Amaretti mixture. § Place under a broiler (grill) and cook under high heat for about 10 minutes before serving.

VARIATION
– Replace the plums with the same quantity of peaches.

■ INGREDIENTS

- 1 quantity *Custard* (see recipe p. 66)
- 12 plums
- ⅔ cup (150 g) Amaretti cookies, store-bought (or see recipe p. 743), crumbled
- ⅔ cup (90 g) almonds, slivered (flaked) and toasted
- 3 tablespoons granulated sugar

Right:
Albicocche al cartoccio

Peaches with honey
Macedonia di pesche al miele

Desserts made with wine, honey, and fruit date back to ancient Roman times.

Serves: 6; Preparation: 20 minutes; Chilling: 2-3 hours; Level of difficulty: Simple

Peel the peaches. Slice them thinly and place in a large serving bowl. §
Dissolve the honey in the wine and pour over the peaches. Mix the
peaches and wine together carefully. Chill in the refrigerator for at least
2–3 hours before serving.

■ INGREDIENTS

• 8 peaches
• 3 tablespoons honey
• 1 cup (250 ml) medium
  or sweet red wine

VARIATION
– Add a dash of cinnamon to the wine and honey.

Melons with fruits of the forest
Meloncini al misto di bosco

■ INGREDIENTS

• 3 medium-sized melons (Persian, Crenshaw, Cantaloupe, or Charentais)
• 2 cups (500 g) mixed fruits of the forest (raspberries, blueberries, strawberries)
• juice of 1 lemon
• ½ cup (100 g) granulated sugar
• ⅔ cup (150 g) raspberries
• ⅓ cup (90 ml) heavy (double) cream
• 2–3 drops vanilla extract (essence)

Serves: 6; Preparation: 20 minutes; Level of difficulty: Simple

Cut the melons in half. Use a melon-baller to scoop out balls of melon and place them in a bowl. § Mix the melon balls carefully with the fruits of the forest, lemon juice, and half the sugar, then spoon them into the melon shells. § Beat the raspberries with the remaining sugar. Whip the cream with the vanilla extract. § Serve the fruit-filled melons with the whipped cream and raspberry sauce passed separately.

VARIATION
– Add a few tablespoonfuls of rum to the fruit.

Lemon sorbet with peaches and apricots
Sorbetto di limone con pesche e albicocche

■ INGREDIENTS

• 1 cup (200 g) granulated sugar
• 2 cups (500 ml) water
• juice of 4 lemons
• 2 egg whites
• dash of salt

DECORATION
• 3 large peaches, peeled and thinly sliced
• 3 apricots, thinly sliced
• 2 tablespoons confectioners' sugar
• juice of 1 lemon

The word "sorbet" is probably of Arabic origin. It describes an extremely simple preparation based on a combination of sugar syrup and fruit juice, fruit purée, or liqueur.

Serves: 6; Preparation: 20 minutes + 3 hours to freeze; Cooking: 5 minutes; Level of difficulty: Simple

Prepare a syrup base by boiling the granulated sugar and water for a few minutes. Set aside until completely cool, then add the lemon juice. § Whisk the egg whites with a dash of salt until extremely stiff. Gradually stir in the lemon syrup, then place the mixture in the freezer. § Stir every 30 minutes to ensure that it freezes evenly, then whisk after 3 hours. Serve in individual dishes with the thinly sliced fruit sprinkled with confectioners' sugar and lemon juice.

VARIATION
– The whisked egg whites are not essential – they simply make the sorbet creamier. You can make different flavored sorbets using the same process. All you have to do is add fruit pulp, wine, liqueurs, or other types of flavoring to the basic syrup.

Left:
Meloncini al misto di bosco

Ice cream with wild strawberries
Gelato alla crema con fragoline di bosco

This is a basic recipe for ice cream. I am including simple instructions for making ice cream without an ice-cream machine. The results are a bit different from what we are used to, a little less delicate and more crystalline. But precisely for this reason, the recipe is somewhat special, and very good to eat. Prepare it a day in advance and whisk one last time before serving.

Serves: 4-6; Preparation: 30 minutes; Cooking: 15 minutes; Freezing: without an ice-cream machine, about 9 hours; Level of difficulty: Medium

Whisk the egg yolks and granulated sugar in a bowl until pale and creamy. § Bring the milk and cream to a boil, then set aside to cool for 10 minutes. Stir the milk and cream into the egg mixture. § Cook in the top of a double-boiler until the mixture is thick enough to coat the back of a spoon, making sure it never comes to a boil. Remove from heat and leave until completely cold. § Pour the cooled mixture into an ice-cream machine, if you have one, and follow the instructions to finish. § If you don't have an ice-cream machine, transfer the mixture to a large bowl and place in the freezer. After 3 hours, whisk the mixture to make sure it is freezing evenly. Return to the freezer for 3 hours, then whisk again. Whisk one last time after 3 more hours. § Place the wild strawberries in 4 to 6 individual ice cream dishes. Put scoops of ice cream on top and sprinkle with confectioners' sugar.

> VARIATIONS
> – Flavor the milk and cream with cinnamon or vanilla.
> – Add ½ cup (100 g) crumbled Amaretti cookies to the beaten egg mixture to make Amaretti-flavored ice cream.

■ INGREDIENTS

BASIC MIXTURE
- 4 egg yolks
- 1 cup (200 g) granulated sugar
- 2 cups (500 ml) milk
- 1 cup (250 ml) light (single) cream

DECORATION
- 2 cups (500 g) strawberries
- confectioners' (icing) sugar for sprinkling

Chocolate ice cream with raspberries and mint
Gelato al cioccolato con lamponi e menta

Serves: 6; Preparation: 30 minutes; Cooking: 15 minutes; Freezing: without an ice-cream machine, about 9 hours; Level of difficulty: Medium

Prepare the ice cream according to the basic recipe above, dissolving the unsweetened cocoa in the hot milk and cream. § Place the raspberries in 6 individual ice cream dishes. Put scoops of ice cream on top and garnish with fresh mint.

■ INGREDIENTS
- 1 quantity ice cream mixture (see recipe above)
- 4 tablespoons unsweetened cocoa (cocoa powder)
- 2 cups (500 g) raspberries
- fresh mint leaves for decoration

> VARIATION
> – Top with whipped cream, or decorate with chocolate shavings.

Right:
Gelato di crema con fragoline di bosco and Gelato di fragola

■ INGREDIENTS

- 2 cups (500 ml) milk
- 1 cup (250 ml) light (single) cream
- 1 cup (200 g) granulated sugar
- 1⅓ cups (300 g) strawberries

Strawberry ice cream
Gelato alle fragole

Serves: 4-6; Preparation: 20 minutes; Cooking: 5 minutes; Level of difficulty: Simple

Boil the milk with the cream. Dissolve the sugar in this mixture and leave to cool. § Purée the strawberries, then mix them with the milk and follow the recipe on page 780. § Serve in the individual ice-cream dishes.

VARIATIONS
– Serve with sliced strawberries sweetened with a little sugar.
– Use different kinds of fruit to make ice cream – for example, peaches, apricots, berries, cherries, or bananas.

Index